Contending with Terrorism: Roots, Strategies, and Responses

International Security Readers

Strategy and Nu ir Deterrence (1984)
Military Strateg nd the Origins of the First World War (1985)
Conventional Fo and American Defense Policy (1986)
The Star Wars C troversy (1986)
Naval Strategy a National Security (1988)
Military Strateg nd the Origins of the First World War, revised and ex ded edition (1991)
—published by inceton University Press

Soviet Military cy (1989)
Conventional Fo and American Defense Policy, revised edition (1989)
Nuclear Diploma and Crisis Management (1990)
The Cold War a After: Prospects for Peace (1991)
America's Strate in a Changing World (1992)
The Cold War a After: Prospects for Peace, expanded edition (1993)
Global Dangers: anging Dimensions of International Security (1995)
The Perils of An hy: Contemporary Realism and International Security (1995)
Debating the De cratic Peace (1996)
East Asian Secu (1996)
Nationalism and hnic Conflict (1997)
America's Strate Choices (1997)
Theories of War Peace (1998)
America's Strate Choices, revised edition (2000)
Rational Choice Security Studies: Stephen Walt and His Critics (2000)
The Rise of Chin 2000)
Nationalism and hnic Conflict, revised edition (2001)
Offense, Defense d War (2004)
New Global Dan s: Changing Dimensions of International Security (2004)
Primacy and Its contents: American Power and International Stability (2009)
Going Nuclear: lear Proliferation and International Security in the 21st Century (2)
Contending with rrorism: Roots, Strategies, and Responses (2010)
—published by e MIT Press

Contending with Terrorism
Roots, Strategies, and Responses

AN *International Security* READER

EDITED BY
Michael E. Brown
Owen R. Coté Jr.
Sean M. Lynn-Jones
and Steven E. Miller

THE MIT PRESS
CAMBRIDGE, MASSACHUSETTS
LONDON, ENGLAND

The contents of this b were first published in *International Security* (ISSN 0162-2889), a publication of the MIT Press under t ponsorship of the Belfer Center for Science and International Affairs at Harvard University. Copyright ach of the following articles is owned jointly by the President and Fellows of Harvard College and ie Massachusetts Institute of Technology.

Michael Mousseau, "N et Civilization and Its Clash with Terror," 27:3 (Winter 2002/03); Audrey Kurth Cronin, "Behind the C e: Globalization and International Terrorism," 27:3 (Winter 2002/03); Assaf Moghadam, "Motives Martyrdom: Al-Qaida, Salafi Jihad, and the Spread of Suicide Attacks," 33:3 (Winter 2008/09); An H. Kydd and Barbara F. Walter, "The Strategies of Terrorism," 31:1 (Summer 2006); Max Abrahms, "Why orism Does Not Work," 31:2 (Fall 2006); William Rose, Rysia Murphy, and Max Abrahms, "Correspon e: Does Terrorism Ever Work? The 2004 Madrid Train Bombings," 32:1 (Summer 2007); Max Abrahms, iat Terrorists Really Want: Terrorist Motives and Counterterrorism Strategy," 32:4 (Spring 2008); Erica C oweth, Nicholas Miller, Elizabeth McClellan, Hillel Frisch, Paul Staniland, and Max Abrahms, "Correspon e: What Makes Terrorists Tick," 33:4 (Spring 2009); Robert F. Trager and Dessislava P. Zagorcheva, "Deter Terrorism: It Can Be Done," 30:3 (Winter 2005/06); Daniel L. Byman, "Friends Like These: Counterinsurg and the War on Terrorism," 31:2 (Fall 2006); Renée de Nevers, "NATO's International Security e in the Terrorist Era," 31:4 (Spring 2007); Mette Eilstrup-Sangiovanni and Calvert Jones, "Assessing the gers of Illicit Networks: Why al-Qaida May Be Less Threatening Than Many Think," 33:2 (Fall 200 udrey Kurth Cronin, "How al-Qaida Ends: The Decline and Demise of Terrorist Groups," 31:1 (Summ 006).

Library of Congress C oging-in-Publication Data

Contending with terr n : roots, strategies, and responses / edited by Michael E. Brown ... [et al.].
p. cm. — (Intern ial security readers)
Includes bibliograp references.
ISBN 978-0-262-514 (pbk. : alk. paper) 1. Terrorism. 2. Terrorism—Prevention. I. Brown, Michael E.
HV6431.C6546 2010
363.325—dc22

2009049186

Contents

vii
The Contributors

ix
Acknowledgments

xi
Preface — *Sean M. Lynn-Jones*

PART I: ROOTS OF CONTEMPORARY TERRORISM

3
Market Civilization and Its Clash with Terror — *Michael Mousseau*

28
Behind the Curve: Globalization and International Terrorism — *Audrey Kurth Cronin*

57
Motives for Martyrdom: Al-Qaida, Salafi Jihad, and the Spread of Suicide Attacks — *Assaf Moghadam*

PART II: TERRORIST STRATEGIES: WHY ARE THEY CHOSEN? DO THEY WORK?

93
The Strategies of Terrorism — *Andrew H. Kydd and Barbara F. Walter*

125
Why Terrorism Does Not Work — *Max Abrahms*

162
Correspondence: Does Terrorism Ever Work? The 2004 Madrid Train Bombings — *William Rose and Rysia Murphy*; *Max Abrahms*

171
What Terrorists Really Want: Terrorist Motives and Counterterrorism Strategy — *Max Abrahms*

199
Correspondence: What Makes Terrorists Tick — *Erica Chenoweth, Nicholas Miller, and Elizabeth McClellan; Hillel Frisch; and Paul Staniland*; *Max Abrahms*

PART III: COUNTERING TERRORISM

229
Deterring Terrorism: It Can Be Done — *Robert F. Trager and Dessislava P. Zagorcheva*

266
Friends Like These: Counterinsurgency and the War on Terrorism — *Daniel L. Byman*

303 NATO's Interna[illegible]al Security Role in the Terrorist Era	*Renée de Nevers*
336 Assessing the D[illegible]gers of Illicit Networks: Why al-Qaida May Be [illegible] Threatening Than Many Think	*Mette Eilstrup-Sangiovanni and Calvert Jones*
PART IV: THE [illegible]TURE OF TERRORISM	
377 How al-Qaida E[illegible]s: The Decline and Demise of Terrorist Group[illegible]	*Audrey Kurth Cronin*

The Contributors

MICHAEL E. BROWN is Dean of the Elliott School of International Affairs and Professor of International Affairs and Political Science at the George Washington University.

OWEN R. COTÉ JR. is Co-Editor of *International Security* and Associate Director of the Security Studies Program at the Massachusetts Institute of Technology.

SEAN M. LYNN-JONES is Co-Editor of *International Security* and a research associate at the Belfer Center for Science and International Affairs, John F. Kennedy School of Government, Harvard University.

STEVEN E. MILLER is Editor-in-Chief of *International Security,* Co–Principal Investigator with the Project on Managing the Atom, and Director of the International Security Program at the Belfer Center for Science and International Affairs, John F. Kennedy School of Government, Harvard University.

MAX ABRAHMS is a postdoctoral fellow at the Center for International Security and Cooperation at *Stanford University.*

DANIEL L. BYMAN is Professor at Georgetown University and Research Director at the Saban Center for Middle East Policy at the Brookings Institution.

ERICA CHENOWETH is Assistant Professor of Government at Wesleyan University and Director of Wesleyan's Program on Terrorism and Insurgency Research.

AUDREY KURTH CRONIN is Professor of Strategy at the U.S. National War College, National Defense University.

RENÉE DE NEVERS is Assistant Professor in Public Administration at the Maxwell School of Citizenship and Public Affairs at Syracuse University.

METTE EILSTRUP-SANGIOVANNI is University Lecturer in International Studies at the Centre of International Studies and is a fellow in International Relations at Sidney Sussex College.

HILLEL FRISCH is Senior Lecturer in the Department of Political Studies and a senior research fellow at the Begin-Sadat Center for Strategic Studies at Bar-Ilan University.

CALVERT JONES is a doctoral student in the Department of International Relations at Yale University.

ANDREW H. KYD ; Associate Professor of Political Science at the University of Wisconsin.

ELIZABETH MCC .LAN is a program associate at the Public Interest Research Group.

NICHOLAS MILL is a graduate student in the Security Studies Program at the Massachusetts titute of Technology.

ASSAF MOGHAD is Senior Lecturer at the Lauder School of Government, Diplomacy, and St egy and a senior researcher at the International Institute for Counterterroris at the Interdisciplinary Center (IDC) Herzliya.

MICHAEL MOUS U is Professor of Political Science at Koç University in Istanbul.

RYSIA MURPHY graduate of Connecticut College.

WILLIAM ROSE i rofessor in the Department of Government and International Relations at Co ecticut College.

PAUL STANILAN ; Assistant Professor of Political Science at the University of Chicago.

ROBERT F. TRAG s Assistant Professor of Political Science at the University of California, Los geles.

BARBARA F. WAI R is Professor of International Relations and Pacific Studies at the Universit of California, San Diego.

DESSISLAVA P. Z ORCHEVA is a doctoral candidate in Political Science at Columbia Univers .

Acknowledgments

The editors gratefully acknowledge the assistance that has made this book possible. A deep debt is owed to all those at the Belfer Center for Science and International Affairs, Harvard University, who have played an editorial role at *International Security*. Special thanks go to Diane McCree and Katherine Bartel for their invaluable help in preparing this volume for publication.

Preface

Sean M. Lynn-Jones

When American Airlines flight 11 flew into the north tower of the World Trade Center at 8:46 A.M. on September 11, 2001, the world entered a new era. Terrorism had long been a fact of international life, but previous attacks had not been as spectacularly murderous. Policymakers in the United States and elsewhere immediately began trying to figure out how to prevent future attacks of similar or greater magnitude. U.S. national security policy was soon dominated by counterterrorism strategy, and the United States found itself at war in Afghanistan and Iraq. As national leaders grappled with these dilemmas, the attacks and the U.S. responses also prompted scholars in the field of international security studies to devote increased attention to the problem of terrorism.

The essays in this volume represent some of the research that has been stimulated by the September 11 attacks and by the continuing terrorist threat from al-Qaida. They explore three central topics in terrorism studies. First, what are the sources of contemporary terrorism? Possible explanations offered in this volume include the transformative impact of globalization, the rise of various types of religious beliefs, and the increasing dissatisfaction of the world's powerless with perceived injustices and the slow pace of reform.

Second, what do terrorists want? How are they using violence to achieve their goals? Do their violent campaigns achieve their goals? This volume offers different perspectives on these questions. Some contributors regard terrorists as essentially rational strategic actors who use violence as a means to their ends. These authors generally agree that terrorists often succeed in attaining their political goals. Other essays in this volume dispute whether terrorists act strategically and argue that terrorism rarely succeeds. The debate between these perspectives illuminates what we know—and what we need to know—about what motivates individual terrorists and how terrorist organizations behave. The outcome of the debate will have implications for formulating policies to prevent and defeat terrorism.

Third, how can the United States and other countries that are targets of contemporary terrorism respond? What policies are most likely to prevent terrorism? The essays here are generally critical of U.S. policies. Contributors to this volume call for improved efforts to deter terrorists, more effective collaboration between the United States and its allies, and improved intelligence capabilities. Several essays offer contending views on the threat posed by al-Qaida. Some authors claim that al-Qaida is a uniquely threatening informal terrorist network, whereas others contend that its status as a network is a source of

weakness that t United States can exploit. Most contributors agree that public diplomacy is sential in the fight against terrorist organizations such as al-
Qaida.

The first secti of essays in this volume explores the roots of contemporary
terrorism.

In "Market C lization and Its Clash with Terror," Michael Mousseau argues that the U d States and its allies need to understand the motivations of
terrorists if the re to succeed in their campaign to prevent terrorism. Rejecting claims t authoritarianism and poverty are the main causes of terrorism, Mousseau tends that terrorism is often a response to the global spread
of market-base conomies and liberal-democratic values. When globalization
and market eco nies threaten those who benefit from clientalist economies in
much of the de oping world, terrorism is often the result.

Mousseau cri izes the claim that people turn to terrorism when political
systems—parti rly authoritarian systems—fail to provide opportunities for
addressing soci onomic grievances. He notes that violence and terrorism occur in democra such as India, so the lack of democracy is not a convincing
explanation of orism. If poverty were the cause of terrorism, there should
have been muc ore terrorism in previous decades, when virtually every society was poore Moreover, individual terrorists, including most of the hijackers involved in e September 11 attacks, are often educated and have good
economic prosp ts.

Mousseau als ejects the argument that Islamic religious beliefs provide the
cultural founda n for contemporary terrorism. He notes that the Muslim
world did not duce suicidal mass murderers in previous decades. Non-
Islamic societie Northern Ireland and elsewhere have provided social support for terror, onstrating that Muslim culture cannot explain all terrorism.

In Mousseau view, the most promising explanation of contemporary terrorism can be fo d by examining the impact of market-based globalization on
clientalist econ ies. Clientalist economies, which exist in many developing
countries, invol complex systems of reciprocal obligations, patronage, and
kinship and eth ties. Market economies, on the other hand, rely on contracts
between strang and respect for the common law. Clientalist economies tend
to be associate ith inward-looking, hierarchical social and political arrangements. Market nomies foster individualism, universalism, tolerance, equity,
and the prevale of science over faith-based forms of knowledge. Mousseau
argues that the e of market economies has spurred the growth of market

civilization—a set of stable, prosperous, economically and politically liberal countries that share values and are at peace with one another.

Clientalist societies are likely to resent and reject the norms of market economies. They will see participants in market economies as untrustworthy and self-interested. Clientalist societies that are making the transition to market economies may be particularly unstable, as social anarchy may emerge as clientalist norms decline. The populations of such societies may blame the United States or the West for the breakdown of social order.

Mousseau points out that the emergence of market economies based on contractual exchange caused major disruptions in Europe. Contractual exchange began in northwestern Europe in the 1450s and precipitated several centuries of upheaval, including the Protestant Reformation, both world wars, and the rise and fall of multiple antimarket movements, including fascism and communism. It took until the twentieth century for contractual exchange to spread throughout Europe. Similar patterns exist in countries that are now in the midst of a similar transition.

Mousseau argues that leaders of clientalist structures are most likely to lead resistance to Westernization and marketization, because their positions are threatened by the erosion of clientalist societies. They are the potential terrorist leaders who are willing to engage in or condone the mass murder of Westerners to assert their own power and tap into widespread antimarket fury. As globalization appears to undermine local societies and economies, the social approval of terrorist mass murder grows. Mousseau contends that a "sense of rage against market civilization and its shared liberal values and beliefs—a rage that can be inflamed with the addition of any immediate cause—lies just beneath the surface in many developing countries."

Mousseau asserts that the United States must abandon three myths about the right strategy to use against terrorism: the myth that the United States must increase its economic aid and explain its policies more clearly; the myth that the United States should promote democracy more vigorously; and the myth that people would not hate the United States if they had greater exposure to American values. All three myths fail to take into account the clientalist sources of anti-Americanism.

The United States, in Mousseau's view, should wage the war against terrorism by helping developing countries "out of the mire of social anarchy and into market development." U.S. policies should encourage developing countries "(1) to create and enforce bodies of common law that are vital to the functioning of a market economy, and (2) to equitably subsidize local private enterprises witl 1e goal of widespread employment." These policies should be pursued mu aterally so that the United States does not have to shoulder the entire burd(Mousseau concludes that "it is through the establishment of market econom that the United States and its allies can be made safe from terror."

In "Behind tl Curve: Globalization and International Terrorism," Audrey Kurth Cronin i(ıtifies the causes of the current wave of terrorism and criticizes the Unite States for its inadequate responses. She argues that recent terrorist attacks e a response to globalization.

After acknow lging that defining terrorism is complicated and controversial, Cronin ad ts the following "shorthand" definition of terrorism: "the threat or use of mingly random violence against innocents for political ends by a nonstate a r." Thus defined, terrorism has been around for a very long time. In the mo n era, terrorism has been directed against empires, colonial powers, and th J.S.-led international system characterized by globalization. Cronin traces tl history of terrorism in its various forms. Although contemporary terrorisr eems to have religious roots, Cronin regards it as "part of a larger phenom(n of antiglobalization and tension between the have and have-not natio1 as well as between the elite and underprivileged within those nations." rorism exploits the frustrations of the common people in an era when refor1 omes too slowly.

Cronin argue ıat the latest phase of terrorism has deep causes and is likely to last at least a neration. Terrorism is now rooted in widespread alienation and religious i(ıtity and doctrine. Globalization has had few benefits for much of the wc l. Countries with poor governance and widespread poverty create an envir(nent in which terrorists can win support from people who feel powerless i a globalizing world.

According to onin, there are four types of contemporary terrorist organizations: left-wi1 terrorists, right-wing terrorists, ethnonationalist/separatist terrorists, and ligious terrorists. Each type has different motivations and agendas. I -wing terrorists tend to prefer "revolutionary, antiauthoritarian, antimat alistic agendas." They often engage in kidnapping, murder, arson, and bom ıg directed against elite targets. Many such organizations— especially in Eu pe—have been brutal, but ephemeral. Right-wing terrorists have tended to oose their targets on the basis of race, ethnicity, religion, or immigrant statu Their organizations tend to be less cohesive, impetuous, and hard to track. E onationalist/separatist terrorists usually have clear political or territorial ai1 that are negotiable. They generally have some popular support and often e age in conventional insurgencies as well as terrorist attacks.

Religious terrorists have distinctive characteristics that make them especially dangerous, for five reasons. First, they believe that they are engaged in a struggle of good against evil that justifies indiscriminate attacks. Second, they believe that they are acting to please a deity, which makes their behavior unpredictable and insensitive to the reactions of others. Third, they do not feel a need to follow secular laws and values and may even be attacking law-based secular society. If they aspire to overturn the current state system, they are a much more fundamental threat than, for example, separatist terrorists who seek their own state. Fourth, their alienation from the existing system may incline religious terrorists to stage highly destructive and apocalyptic attacks, such as those of September 11, 2001. Fifth, religious terrorism has dispersed popular support and can spread globally. Attempts to fight religious terrorists also may alienate those who share their faith.

Cronin identifies four trends in modern terrorism that had emerged by the late 1990s. First, religious terrorism was increasing. Second, the overall number of attacks was falling. Third, the number of casualties per terrorist attack was increasing, partly because more attacks were religiously motivated. Fourth, Americans were increasingly targeted. These trends prompted fears that the next step in the evolution of terrorism would be attacks with chemical, biological, nuclear, or radiological weapons. At the same time, terrorist organizations, including al-Qaida, have become more capable of acting globally, drawing funds, recruits, and support from multiple countries and staging attacks far from where the organizations are based.

Cronin suggests that globalization, defined as "a gradually expanding process of interpenetration in the economic, political, social, and security realms, uncontrolled by (or apart from) traditional notions of state sovereignty,"[1] is an important influence on contemporary patterns of terrorism. It has contributed to changes in terrorist methods. Information technologies have expanded the global reach of terrorist organizations, including al-Qaida, which rely on the internet to communicate, recruit, and raise funds. The removal of barriers to the flow of goods and people has enabled terrorists to move freely and to establish cells in many countries. Formal and informal international financial networks make it easier for terrorist groups to collect, disburse, and hide their funds. Globalization has also changed the objectives of terrorist organizations. It can bring disruptive changes to conservative cultures, or it can anger those who feel that they are not receiving their share of its benefits. In either case,

1. Cronin attributes this definition to Victor D. Cha, "Globalization and the Study of International Security," *Journal of Peace Research*, Vol. 37, No. 3 (March 2000), pp. 391–393.

the United Stat is likely to be blamed. The political incentives to attack the United States h increased as some cultures feel threatened by the United States and the ular vision of modernization it embraces. Cronin points out that the disenfr hised areas of the Arab world increasingly resent the United States as they behind the West in their human and economic development. She recog es, however, that anti-American terrorism is also motivated by a desire to c nge U.S. policies in the Middle East and the Persian Gulf.

Cronin recom ends that the United States continue to improve its military capabilities wh recognizing that nonmilitary instruments—intelligence, public diploma cooperation with allies, international legal instruments, and economic assist e and sanctions—will be more effective in the long run. She calls for the Un d States to create an incentive structure that rewards countries with good vernance and intervenes to assist failed states. The United States also mus project a vision of sustainable development—of economic growth, equal a ess to basic social needs such as education and health, and good governan –for the developing world."

The final ess in this section explains the rise of one type of contemporary terrorism: icide attacks. From the World Trade Center to Iraq and Afghanistan, s de terrorist attacks have become more frequent in recent years. What ex ns the rise of this particular form of terrorism? In "Motives for Martyrdom l-Qaida, Salafi Jihad, and the Spread of Suicide Attacks," Assaf Moghada examines the causes and characteristics of suicide terrorism. He argues that o factors explain the proliferation of suicide terrorism: "the evolution of al- ida into a global terrorist actor and the growing appeal of Salafi jihad, the iding ideology of al-Qaida and its associated movements."

According to ghadam's data, suicide attacks have increased dramatically since 2000. The vere relatively few attacks in the 1980s and early 1990s, followed by a slig ncrease in the mid-1990s. Suicide attacks then rose from 54 in 2001 to 535 i 07. During the same period, greater numbers of terrorist organizations per rated suicide attacks. More than 20,000 people were killed in suicide attacks ween December 1981 and March 2008.

Moghadam sses existing explanations of suicide terrorism and finds them inadequa Studies that have focused on the motivations of individual suicide terrorist ave found multiple motivations, including a commitment to a cause, a desir r revenge, expectations of benefits after death, and personal crisis. These st es have not, however, explained why some individuals in these categorie come suicide terrorists and others do not. They also cannot explain the glo ization of suicide terrorism.

Other studies nphasize organizational-strategic explanations of suicide terrorism. Some analysts claim that suicide attacks enable a terrorist organization to achieve its political goals and strengthen itself. Moghadam suggests that these studies may exaggerate the strategic effectiveness of suicide terrorism. In addition, they do not explain why, if suicide terrorism is effective, so many terrorist groups do not employ it as a tactic, or why its use has increased greatly since 2000.

Another set of explanations argues that terrorists will resort to suicide attacks when there is social support for the tactic. The veneration of suicide terrorists as martyrs in, for example, Lebanon, is said to account for the rise in suicide attacks there. Moghadam points out, however, that suicide attacks are becoming more frequent in places such as Afghanistan, where there is no tradition of domestic support for such attacks.

One of the most prominent explanations of the rise of suicide terrorism has been offered by Robert Pape, who argues that suicide terrorists are often responding to foreign occupation.[2] Moghadam disagrees, however, and points out that attacks occur in countries where there is no occupation, such as Pakistan. He also notes that suicide attacks are directed against internal groups that are not foreign occupiers (e.g., Shiites in Iraq), and are perpetrated by citizens of countries that are not under occupation. Moghadam argues that al-Qaida encourages suicide attacks for religious and ideological reasons, not because it is reacting to foreign occupations.

Another prominent explanation of suicide terrorism has been advanced by Mia Bloom, who argues that terrorist groups launch suicide missions as part of a process of "outbidding" in which they compete with other groups for the support of the local population.[3] Moghadam acknowledges that this thesis may apply to some groups, such as the Popular Front for the Liberation of Palestine, the Fatah al-Aqsa Martyrs Brigades, and Amal in Lebanon. The outbidding explanation does not appear to apply in other cases, however. In Sri Lanka the Tamil Tigers adopted suicide terrorism only after they eliminated their main rival. Moreover, in Sri Lanka there is little evidence that the population supports suicide attacks and would be more likely to back a group that used this tactic.

Moghadam argues that the best explanation of the global rise of suicide terrorism rests on (1) al-Qaida's emergence as a global actor, and (2) the growing

---

2. Robert A. Pape, *Dying to Win: The Strategic Logic of Suicide Terrorism* (New York: Random House, 2005).
3. Mia Bloom, *Dying to Kill: The Allure of Suicide Terror* (New York: Columbia University Press, 2005).

appeal of its id ogy of Salafi jihad. Al-Qaida was initially intended to be a rapid reaction f e that would assist threatened Muslims anywhere. Its globalization accele ed when foreign fighters who joined the war against Soviet forces in Afgh stan returned to their home countries or headed to other countries. In th nid-1990s, al-Qaida also decided to focus its efforts on the "far enemy"— United States—instead of local Arab regimes. Al-Qaida made suicide at ks its primary tactic. Its leaders developed a "cult of martyrdom" based on e morality of self-sacrifice and the promise that those who gave their lives ould be rewarded in paradise. When the Egyptian terrorist group al-Jihad rged with al-Qaida, its emphasis on suicide attacks influenced Osama b Laden's decision to make this tactic central in al-Qaida's operations. Suicid nissions also were adopted because they offered a means of imposing heav osts on powerful adversaries.

The ideology Salafi jihad is a radical offshoot of Salafism, which upholds a strict interpreta n of Islam based on emulating the lifestyle of the Prophet Mohammed an is disciples. Unlike ordinary Salafis, Salafi jihadists advocate violent jihad, in ding suicide operations. They label some fellow Muslims as infidels (a pract known as *takfir*) and condone the killing of civilians. Salafi jihadist preach in mosques and on the internet have instilled a cult of martyrdom in their llowers. Their teachings have become increasingly popular in Africa, Centr Asia, the Middle East, and Southeast Asia.

Moghadam f s that Salafi jihadist groups carried out 37.7 percent of all suicide terroris tacks between December 1981 and March 2008—more than any other type group. He claims it is likely that many of the 57.6 percent of suicide attacks t were perpetrated by unknown groups also can be attributed to Salafi ji lists, because many of these attacks occurred in Iraq, where Salafi jihadists ducted numerous suicide attacks. Salafi jihadist groups also make up an inc sing proportion of the groups that conduct suicide attacks. They have plac special emphasis on global suicide attacks in which terrorists connected to tra national networks attack targets outside their own countries.

How can We rn countries respond to suicide terrorism? Moghadam recommends that derate Muslims must take the lead in arguing against Salafi jihad. He write Western states can underscore what most Muslims already know: the credi ity of Salafi jihad suffers from a fundamental contradiction. On the one han Salafi jihadists claim to act for the benefit of Muslins. On the other hand, M ms suffer the consequences of Salafi jihadist ideology and terrorism more n any other group."

The next section of essays in this volume examines the strategies that terrorists choose to achieve their goals, whether these strategies are likely to succeed, and how the targets of terrorist attacks should respond. There is a rich debate over the effectiveness of terrorism and the motivations of terrorists. Multiple perspectives on these questions are included in these pages.

In "The Strategies of Terrorism," Andrew Kydd and Barbara Walter argue that terrorism often works. Terrorism instills fear in target populations, forces governments to make concessions, and provokes governments to respond in ways that aid the terrorists' cause. Kydd and Walter seek to explain terrorists' choice of goals and strategies, the effectiveness of the strategies chosen, and how to respond to terrorism. Kydd and Walter argue that terrorism is a form of costly signaling that attempts to persuade audiences that the terrorists are committed to their cause. Terrorist strategies may include (1) attrition, (2) intimidation, (3) provocation, (4) spoiling, and (5) outbidding. Understanding these five distinct strategic logics is crucial for devising effective counterterrorism policies.

Kydd and Walter observe that terrorism is usually not senseless violence, but a set of actions intended to achieve one or more political goals. They identify five goals that terrorists often pursue: regime change, territorial change, policy change, social control, and status quo maintenance. A given group may have multiple goals. Of the forty-two groups on the U.S. State Department's list of Foreign Terrorist Organizations, thirty-one seek regime change, nineteen seek territorial change, four seek policy change, and one seeks to maintain the status quo.

In international politics, uncertainty about states' power, resolve, and trustworthiness means that states often must rely on costly signals to communicate. Verbal statements may not be credible. In a crisis, for example, states order military mobilizations, and sometimes war itself is necessary to communicate resolve. Kydd and Walter contend that a similar logic applies to terrorists, who "need to provide credible information to the audiences whose behavior they hope to influence." Those audiences include governments whose policies they wish to change, as well as the terrorists' supporters.

Kydd and Walter analyze each of the five potential terrorist strategies to determine when each strategy can succeed and how each can be countered. Attrition strategies attempt to demonstrate that terrorists are strong and resolute and will inflict serious costs to achieve their goals. For example, Palestinians during the second intifada attempted to impose high costs on Israel in an effort to persuade Isr to withdraw from the occupied territories. Suicide terrorism is often a key el ent of an attrition strategy. Kydd and Walter argue that attrition strategies more likely to be effective when the target state has a relatively low le of interest in the disputed issue, when the target state's ability to retali is constrained, and when the target state is highly sensitive to the costs of lence. They identify five counterstrategies as the best responses to terr t attrition strategies: (1) conceding inessential issues in exchange for pea (2) retaliating against terrorist leaders, their followers, their assets, and oth bjects of value; (3) hardening likely targets to minimize the costs of attacks) denying terrorists access to nuclear and biological weapons; and (5) mi nizing the psychological costs of terrorism by educating the public about th ow risk of being killed by terrorists.

Intimidation ategies aim to show that terrorists can punish those who disobey them a that the government is powerless to stop them. Such strategies may consis f killing those who support a regime opposed by the terrorists. Terrorists ght adopt an intimidation strategy in cases where the government ha efused to yield to their demands and it is easier to impose their policy dir y on the population. The Taliban has adopted such a strategy in Afghani n since the U.S.-backed government of Hamid Karzai came to power. Intim tion strategies are more likely to succeed against weak states and states with ge territories or rough terrain. The best response to an intimidation strateg for the government to retake and control territory. The "clear-and-hold trategy pursued by U.S. forces in Iraq is a prime example. Strengthening l enforcement can also deny terrorists the ability to exercise social control.

Provocation tegies are intended to incite governments into retaliating against terroris n a way that harms the population and thereby builds support for the ter ists and opposition to the regime. The strategy recognizes that the popula may not initially support the terrorists, but that it will rally to their cause if government becomes more repressive or murderous. Indiscriminate attac reveal that a government does not care about its citizens. Kydd and Walt uggest that provocation works against governments that are "capable of mi ing levels of brutality." Provoking a highly brutal government may prod a massive response that will annihilate the constituency the terrorists hope epresent. At the other end of the spectrum, provocation may fail against a go nment that is so committed to human rights and the rule of law that it will retaliate indiscriminately. The best response to provocation is a discrimina g strategy that kills terrorists without inflicting collateral damage. Such a strategy requires excellent intelligence, which is not always available.

Spoiling strategies aim to prevent governments from reaching peace agreements with moderate leaders who share some of the terrorists' goals. Terrorists oppose negotiated agreements that might undermine support for their more radical goals. Spoiler attacks are intended to persuade the enemy that "moderates on the terrorists' side cannot be trusted to abide by a peace deal." Such attacks have hampered negotiations between Arabs and Israelis and between Protestants and Catholics in Northern Ireland. Spoiling attacks work when the other side believes that moderates on the terrorists' side are strong and capable of controlling the terrorists. In such cases, the attacks are seen as evidence that the moderates do not want to control the terrorists. The best responses to spoiling are to build trust and reduce vulnerabilities.

Outbidding strategies are adopted when two groups seek the support of their population. Each group tries to present itself as a zealous guardian of the population's interests, so that it will not be accused of being willing to sell out to the enemy. One way to be seen as a zealot is to commit violent acts against the enemy. The competition between Hamas and Fatah for the allegiance of the Palestinian population is a classic case. Outbidding emerges when multiple groups are competing for the allegiance of the population. One of the best responses to outbidding is to encourage competing groups to consolidate. Another response is to make concessions to the moderate groups.

Kydd and Walter conclude by arguing that information is a vital part of counterterrorism strategy. "Costly signaling," they argue, "is pointless in the absence of uncertainty on the part of the recipient of the signal." States with accurate information will, for example, avoid indiscriminate retaliation for terrorist attacks, because they will have the information that enables them to discriminate. Kydd and Walter also emphasize the importance of regime type. Democracies seem more susceptible to attrition and provocation strategies. They may be more sensitive to the costs of terrorist attacks, but they also may face popular pressure to respond to such attacks. Finally, Kydd and Walter note that intelligence gathering and target defense make sense regardless of the strategy adopted by the terrorists, as do attempts to eradicate the root causes of terrorism. Understanding the strategic logic of terrorism is just one part of an effective counterterrorism strategy.

In "Why Terrorism Does Not Work," Max Abrahms argues that terrorist attacks on civilians rarely coerce governments into making policy concessions. In contrast to what he regards as the prevailing view, Abrahms contends that there is little ev ence to support the pessimistic claim that terrorists usually succeed. Abrah analyzes the record of twenty-eight terrorist organizations and finds that t y achieved their policy objectives only 7 percent of the time. He suggests tha he act of attacking civilians undermines the ability of terrorists to achieve t r aims. The targets of terrorist attacks conclude that the terrorists only wa o destroy them and their societies and thus refuse to make concessions.

Abrahms beli es that the conventional wisdom is that terrorism is an effective coercive st gy. He cites many authors who have concluded that terrorism often work Ie points out, however, that this conclusion rests on limited empirical supp from a few cases, including apparent victories by Hezbollah, the Tamil Tiger nd Palestinian groups. In his view, even some of those victories have been l ited. For example, the limited Israeli withdrawals from parts of the Gaza Stri nd West Bank in 1994 were not a victory for Palestinian terrorists, because rael also increased the number of settlers in the West Bank during the sam eriod.

According to rahms, terrorists can engage in strategic terrorism, which attempts to chan government policies, and redemptive terrorism, which is intended to obt resources such as prisoners or money. He attempts to measure the strateg effectiveness of terrorism—whether it achieves its policy objectives—by mining the record of the twenty-eight terrorist groups described by the . State Department as foreign terrorist organizations since 2001. After dete ining the objectives of each group by examining their official statements, Ab ms codes the outcomes of each terrorist campaign as a "total success," "parti success," "limited success," or "no success." He finds that the terrorist gr s had a total of forty-two objectives, but achieved only three of them, for a ercent total or partial success rate—lower than the success rate for econon sanctions, which are often seen as ineffective.

When and w does terrorism succeed? Abrahms considers two explanations: type of o tive and target selection. He argues that terrorist campaigns with limited te orial objectives (e.g., ending a foreign military occupation) succeed more o n than campaigns with maximal objectives (e.g., destruction of a state), but t y still fail most of the time. Target selection is a much better explanation of success or failure of terrorist campaigns. When terrorist groups attack c lians, they rarely achieve their objectives.

Abrahms arg that attacking civilians is an ineffective strategy for terrorists because it c vinces the targets of such attacks that the terrorists want to destroy their v s, society, or both. He suggests that this outcome is consistent with social psychology's correspondent inference theory. This theory suggests that targets of terrorist attacks infer that the terrorists have maximal objectives when such attacks target civilians. The targets of these attacks do not believe that limited concessions will prevent further attacks, and thus they refuse to concede to any terrorist demands. Abrahms examines three cases that support this argument: the Russian response to the September 1999 apartment bombings; the U.S. response to the September 11 attacks; and the Israeli response to the first Palestinian intifada. In each case, citizens of the target state concluded that terrorists who attacked and killed civilians had maximal objectives. All three countries refused to agree to terrorist demands, and the campaigns of the terrorist groups failed to achieve their objectives.

Abrahms concludes that terrorists who attack the U.S. homeland and otherwise kill American civilians are unlikely to achieve their goals. In 2005, surveys in Muslim countries revealed declining support for al Qaida, although support for guerrilla warfare against U.S. forces in Iraq remained high. He recommends further research on why terrorists attack civilians even though this strategy almost always fails.

In a response to "Why Terrorism Does Not Work," William Rose and Rysia Murphy agree that terrorists rarely achieve their political objectives, but they argue that the March 11, 2004, Madrid train bombings reveal that terrorists who attack civilians can sometimes achieve their political goals. The case shows that Abrahms's theory does not always apply. The Madrid bombings influenced the outcome of the subsequent Spanish elections and brought to power a new government that decided to withdraw Spain's troops from Iraq. The jihadist network that carried out the bombings was attempting to compel Spain to withdraw its troops from Iraq. After the attack, public opinion polls showed that the Spanish public believed that the attack was a response to Spain's involvement in the Iraq War and that withdrawing Spain's forces from Iraq would make future attacks less likely. Three days after the attack, Spain's citizens voted into power the Socialist Party, which had called for pulling out of Iraq. Polls suggested that the bombings influenced the outcome of the election. The government's attempts to blame the Basque separatist group ETA were seen as a refusal to acknowledge the connection between Spain's role in the Iraq War and the attacks. Rose and Murphy acknowledge that this case may be unusual, but it demonstrates that terrorists sometimes succeed. They argue that the Spanish case suggests that policies intended to prevent terrorist attacks should focus on countries that are most likely to be vulnerable to terrorist coercion. vernments also will need to retain the trust of their citizens by not engagin n partisan interpretations of terrorist attacks.

Abrahms rep that the Madrid bombings case does not prove that terrorist coercion succee d, for three reasons. First, the Socialist Party may have won the election eve f the attacks had not taken place. Polls showed the parties were virtually t before the attacks and many undecided voters were leaning toward the Soci sts. Second, the voters may have turned against the government for its ap ent attempt to mislead the public about the attacks, not because of its p ies on Iraq. Third, the Madrid case is unusual because terrorism again democracies usually shifts the electorate toward the right. Abrahms ackn edges, however, that the attacks in Spain did not induce the Spanish public conclude that the terrorists had maximalist objectives. The public already l eved that Spanish involvement in Iraq made Spain vulnerable to terrorism d therefore it was inclined to believe that the terrorists had the limited obj ve of persuading Spain to withdraw from Iraq.

Max Abrahm nalyzes what motivates terrorists and why people become terrorists in "W t Terrorists Really Want: Terrorist Motives and Counterterrorism Strategy. Ie argues that determining what terrorists want is the key to devising effecti counterterrorism strategies. In his view, the strategic model, which holds th terrorists are rational actors who attack civilians for political ends," has bee he standard explanation of what terrorists want. Abrahms tests the strateg model, finds it flawed, and contends that most terrorists are motivated by th social—not political—benefits of terrorism and that counterterrorism strate s should be reoriented accordingly.

The strategic odel, according to Abrahms, rests on three assumptions. First, "terrorist re motivated by relatively stable and consistent political goals." Second, rrorist groups weigh their political options and resort to terrorism only aft determining that alternative political avenues are blocked." Third, terrorists xpect to achieve their political objectives by attacking civilians and aband armed struggle when it fails or when better options arise.

Abrahms que ons whether the strategic model actually applies to terrorist groups. He ide ies seven empirical puzzles that seem to contradict the premises of the st gic model: (1) terrorist groups do not achieve their goals; (2) terrorist org zations do not use terrorism as a last resort and rarely become nonviole political parties; (3) terrorists reject compromise proposals with significant ncessions; (4) terrorist organizations have protean political platforms; (5) t orist groups attack anonymously, preventing their targets from making p ical concessions; (6) terrorist groups with identical political platforms often attack one another; and (7) terrorist organizations do not disband when their goals have been achieved or when they consistently fail to achieve them.

If the strategic model is flawed, what explains terrorist behavior? Why do people become terrorists? Abrahms suggests that "people participate in terrorist organizations for the social solidarity, not for their political return." He draws on organization theory for the natural systems model, which holds that individuals join organizations on the basis of personal inducements, which are often unconnected to the organization's stated goals.

Abrahms offers evidence that people join terrorist groups to develop strong affective ties with other terrorists. Socially alienated individuals are disproportionately represented in terrorist organizations. Terrorists from many groups, including the Irish Republican Army (IRA), ETA, the Red Brigades, and Turkish terrorist organizations, say they joined to develop or maintain social relations with other members. Studies also show that al-Qaida, Hamas, and Hezbollah members often joined because a friend or relative was already a member. Many members of terrorist organizations never develop an understanding of their group's political purpose. Even leaders of such groups often cannot explain their organization's goals. Terrorist groups recruit from the ranks of the socially alienated. Their tight-knit structures attract new recruits and boost morale.

Viewed in the light of natural systems theory, the puzzles for the strategic model become explicable. Abrahms argues that the puzzles demonstrate that terrorist groups are "regularly prioritizing the maintenance of the terrorist organization over the advancement of its political agenda," just as the natural systems model predicts. He concludes that counterterrorism policies need to be reoriented. Instead of attempting to prevent terrorists from achieving their goals, encouraging accommodation to remove grievances, or promoting democracy, countries that want to prevent terrorism should focus on identifying and monitoring socially alienated individuals and break the social bonds within terrorist organizations.

Abrahms's analysis of terrorist motivations has provoked a lively debate over "what makes terrorists tick." In their response, Erica Chenoweth, Nicholas Miller, and Elizabeth McClellan welcome Abrahms's critique of rational choice interpretations of terrorist behavior, but argue that he goes too far in rejecting the strategic model. Drawing on a 2008 RAND study, they contend that a strategic perspective can account for each of the seven puzzles identified by Abrahms. In their view, Abrahms does not adequately address the strategic calculations of e leaders of terrorist groups, although he does contribute to our underst ling of why terrorist "foot soldiers" become and remain terrorists.

Hillel Frisch fers a different critique. He argues that Abrahms errs by lumping all ter ist organizations together; some terrorist groups are dedicated to achiev their political goals, whereas others are not. Frisch also argues that terr t groups behave more rationally and strategically than Abrahms sugge . Groups that, for example, fight other groups with similar goals, may be ategically pursuing hegemony. Terrorist groups may alter their goals or a ot protean platforms, but so do nonviolent political parties. Many political ganizations modify their objectives as they change their assessment of wh can be achieved. Like Chenoweth, Miller, and McClellan, Frisch question hether the same analytical framework can be applied to individual terrori and the strategies of the organization as a whole and its leaders. He rec nends that further research explore why some terrorist organizations act m strategically than others.

Paul Stanilan reply to Abrahms includes three criticisms. First, he argues that there are r ltiple reasons why individuals join terrorist organizations. Second, he poir out that the motivations of the foot soldiers in a group may be different fro he political goals of the group, as defined by its leadership. Individuals ma in a group for many different reasons, but the leaders generally harness the motivations toward a common goal. Third, Staniland argues that terrorist gr ps do not behave in the way predicted by Abrahms. He offers evidence fr the cases of the IRA and the Tamil Tigers. Staniland concludes that the pirical record "does not mean that either militants or armed groups are pur strategic or rational actors, but it does suggest that they are not simplistic s larity maximizers."

Abrahms res nds to these criticisms. In reply to Chenoweth, Miller, and McClellan, he a ies that studies find that terrorist recruits are motivated by social factors ar that terrorist leaders act in ways to keep their groups intact, instead of focu g on their political objectives. He suggests that the RAND study cited by enoweth, Miller, and McClellan supports his conclusions. The study, for e nple, finds that only 4 percent of terrorist groups since 1968 have achieved ir objectives. He also argues that terrorist groups behave rationally, if ratio behavior is defined as taking steps to perpetuate their own existence. They not, however, act strategically in pursuit of their political objectives.

Abrahms rep to Frisch by arguing that Frisch shows only that terrorist groups do not always engage in all of the behavioral tendencies that Abrahms enumerated. In response to Frisch's suggestion that some terrorist groups are motivated by social benefits but others are motivated by political benefits, Abrahms argues that "the terrorist groups of greatest concern to the United States and its allies are not rational political actors."

Abrahms responds to Staniland by pointing out that he focused on terrorist organizations, whereas Staniland draws on evidence from other types of "militant groups." He also points out that he was not trying to offer a single answer to the question, "What do terrorists want?" Instead, he compared social and political explanations of terrorist behavior to see which was more powerful. Abrahms argues that Staniland's empirical critique is flawed methodologically and rests on a misinterpretation of the history of the IRA. He contends "that Irish republican terrorist groups did not even remotely behave as political maximizers, notwithstanding the widespread belief in the strategic model."

The essays in the following section assess various aspects of how to respond to the terrorist threat. The authors analyze whether terrorists can be deterred, discuss how the United States can work more effectively with its allies, and consider whether al-Qaida's networked structure is an asset or a liability.

Many analysts and observers doubt that terrorists can be deterred. Such claims rest on assumptions that terrorists are irrational, unafraid of punishment, and impossible to locate and target. In "Deterring Terrorism: It Can Be Done," Robert Trager and Dessislava Zagorcheva argue that terrorists can be deterred by strategies that hold their political goals at risk. In addition, even if terrorists are hard to find and deter, they rely on support systems that may be more vulnerable to traditional forms of deterrence.

Trager and Zagorcheva note that deterrence is only one strategy for countering terrorism. Other strategies include a focus on "winning hearts and minds," economic aid and democratization, appeasement, and military force. They define a deterrence strategy as one that has two elements: "(1) a threat or action designed to increase an adversary's perceived costs of engaging in particular behavior, and (2) an implicit or explicit offer of an alternative state of affairs if the adversary refrains from that behavior." Deterrence includes threats of punishment in response to an actual or a threatened terrorist attack, as well as denial involving "hardening" of targets to make them too costly to attack. For deterrence to work, the threatened party must understand the threat and calculate the costs and benefits of its actions. In addition, the deterrer must be able to hold at risk something that the adversary values;

the adversary n ,t place a higher value on what is held at risk than the value of taking actior nd both parties must be able to make credible promises.

Trager and Z orcheva assert that the three main arguments posited by other scholars a analysts for why terrorists cannot be deterred are unpersuasive. First, they ıim that the "problem of irrationality" does not make it impossible to det errorists. Recent studies suggest that terrorist groups often have a "set of h archically ordered goals and choose strategies that best advance them." I n if terrorists combine rational and nonrational behavior, they can be d red because they are sufficiently sensitive to cost-benefit calculations.

Second, Trag and Zagorcheva argue deterrence can work even when a state is threate by highly motivated terrorists—the sort of terrorists who would be label anatics by most observers. They note that terrorist networks often contain le notivated elements, such as financiers, who can be deterred. It also may be p ible to deter state sponsors of terrorism. In addition, they argue that deterr e can work against a terrorist group that has local goals but also may coope with transnational terrorist networks that have other objectives. Groups s as the IRA, ETA, and the Tamil Tigers, for example, might be less likely to operate with anti-American terrorists if they knew that the United States ld retaliate against them and make it harder for them to achieve their o tives. In some cases, states may be able to deter major attacks while tac accepting minor attacks. Regardless of the motivations of terrorist groups eterrence by denial (hardening targets and increasing security) can be a ccessful strategy. Deterring multiple terrorist groups may require focusin eterrent threats on the most dangerous group.

Third, Trager d Zagorcheva question whether the "return address problem" actually p vents deterrence of terrorists. They argue that members of terrorist groups sually can be found if states invest sufficient resources in intelligence. Ev when terrorists cannot be found, states can make it harder for terrorists to tain their political goals. Trager and Zagorcheva advocate "providing eco nic and military aid to governments targeted by insurgents, pressuring targ d states not to make concessions to terrorists, aiding other groups with go that are opposed to those of the terrorist group, and imposing travel and ndraising restrictions on terrorist group members." They point out that l motivated terrorists will be deterred, even if the chances of catching all of t m are low.

Trager and Z rcheva test their central argument with evidence from the cases of the Mo Islamic Liberation Front (MILF) and the Abu Sayyaf Group.

Both of these groups operate in the southern Philippines. Coercion was attempted against the MILF, and force was used against the Abu Sayyaf Group.

The MILF is a rebel group that seeks greater autonomy for the Moros in the Philippines. It has engaged in terrorism, although it denies such charges, and it has cooperated with al-Qaida and Jemaah Islamiah, a radical Islamist group in Southeast Asia. Western intelligence reports indicate that the MILF operated camps for foreign jihadists at al-Qaida's request. The MILF, however, condemned the attacks on the World Trade Center and rejected the Taliban's call for a jihad against the United States. Although the MILF is highly motivated in its battle for Moro autonomy, coercive threats may deter it from cooperating with al-Qaida.

After the September 11 attacks, the United States threatened to include the MILF on its list of Foreign Terrorist Organizations if it did not cease its violence against civilians. It also warned that it would cut aid earmarked for areas in the southern Philippines if the MILF did not cut its ties with Jemaah Islamiah. The MILF responded by promising to help Philippine authorities arrest al-Qaida and Jemaah Islamiah operatives and to assist the government in its fight against the Abu Sayyaf Group.

Military action against the Abu Sayyaf group had mixed results. A joint Filipino-U.S. operation in 2002 killed several hundred Abu Sayyaf members and evicted the group from its stronghold on Basilan Island. On the other hand, the group's leadership remained intact and the group moved to Jolo Island. One American hostage was rescued, but two were killed. The Abu Sayyaf Group then began a series of bombings, one of which killed a U.S. soldier. Trager and Zagorcheva speculate that members of the group who survive U.S. attacks may become more radicalized and may even join global terrorist groups when they cannot achieve their local objectives.

Trager and Zagorcheva conclude by offering five recommendations for U.S. counterterrorism policy. First, it is sometimes possible to deter critical elements of terrorist networks from participating in terrorist enterprises. The United States should pursue those elements vigorously after any attacks to increase the chances of deterring other terrorists. In particular, the United States should pursue terrorist financiers and their assets. Second, even highly motivated groups can be deterred. The United States may be able to deter groups that might collaborate with al-Qaida if it threatens to deny such groups the ability to achieve their local goals. Trager and Zagorcheva write, "By holding at risk the local agendas of local groups…the United States can often more effectively achieve its ends of preventing cooperation between groups and denying sanctuary to those inst which force will have to be used.” Third, the United States may be to deter many terrorist groups from cooperating with al-Qaida, because Qaida is an unusual terrorist group with fanatical members and sweeping ls. Other groups may want to differentiate themselves from al-Qaida so that ey are not prime U.S. targets in the war on terrorism. Fourth, the United Stat should concentrate its resources on al-Qaida, which represents the greate hreat to the United States. It should also try to deter groups from cooperati with al-Qaida. Fifth, the United States should harden soft terrorist targets d demonstrate its resolve not to back down in the face of terrorist threats. T e steps will decrease the coercive leverage of terrorism and reduce terrorist notivation to carry out attacks.

Since the Se mber 11 attacks, the United States has aligned itself with states that are f ting Islamist insurgents who often have ties to al-Qaida. In “Friends Like se: Counterinsurgency and the War on Terrorism,” Daniel Byman examin he reasons why it is so difficult for the United States to work with such allie Ie argues that governments fighting al-Qaida–linked insurgencies often h multiple problems that make it difficult to mount effective counterinsurge campaigns. Such governments are often illegitimate, rent by civil-militar nsion, economically backward, and prone to social discrimination. To overc ne these problems, the United States needs better intelligence on its allies and eir security forces. In addition, it should increase its leverage by acting mor ke a third party in local conflicts, instead of aligning too closely with go nment forces. The United States will need to pick its battles more carefully avoid unwinnable wars.

Byman point it that al-Qaida is a terrorist organization, but it also actively encourages Isla st insurgencies. Such insurgencies benefit al-Qaida in many ways, providin ecruits, building unity, and adding legitimacy. Defeating al-Qaida will requ defeating or inhibiting its ability to engage in and benefit from insurgen in countries such as Afghanistan, Algeria, India, Iraq, Somalia, and U ekistan.

Counterinsu ncy against groups linked to al-Qaida depends on the military forces of U allies. In many cases, local allies will have an advantage over U.S. forces, bec se they know the local culture and language and are less likely to provok nationalist backlash. Local allies, however, do not have the same interests he United States. Their armed forces and security agencies may have the n sion of propping up an undemocratic regime, and they may use brutal tacti o do so. Byman argues that classic principal-agent dynamics come into play, cause the United States depends on its local allies yet cannot control them.

Fighting counterinsurgency wars is always difficult, because the security forces involved must combine military skills and political savvy. The forces of U.S allies may be "garrison militaries" that have trouble fighting small-unit engagements, taking the initiative, gathering and analyzing adequate intelligence, and coordinating different services and units. They also tend to have poor leadership, motivation, and creativity. Their political weaknesses often include tensions between the civilian leadership and military, dishonesty and corruption, penetration by insurgents, and little support from the population.

Byman attributes many of the weaknesses of U.S. allies to a set of structural weaknesses: illegitimate and repressive regimes, civilian suspicions that the military will launch a coup, economic backwardness, and social exclusion. One or more of these weaknesses can be found in U.S. counterinsurgency allies such as Afghanistan, Algeria, Egypt, India, Indonesia, Pakistan, the Philippines, Saudi Arabia, and Uzbekistan.

Byman argues that the United States cannot easily improve its counterinsurgency allies. The United States tends to ally itself with governments that, through their mistakes and policy failures, have provoked insurgencies. Once the United States backs a government, its support enables the government to avoid reforms. The United States cannot abandon allies that are deemed to be vital in the war against terrorism, so it has little leverage over them. Moreover, reforming some U.S. allies would require an enormous effort that would entail a massive commitment of U.S. resources.

Byman recommends that the United States adopt three new policies to make its counterinsurgency alliances more effective. First, the United States should gather more intelligence on its allies and, in particular, on its allies' information and collection and dissemination activities. Because allies may use information they gather to portray local insurgents as al-Qaida affiliates or to exaggerate the effectiveness of their security services, the United States needs to know more about such information and its sources. Second, the United States needs to gather information from sources other than allied governments, including the international media and independent investigative groups such as the International Crisis Group. Third, the United States sometimes must distance itself from its allies and act as a third party, fighting the insurgents but also demanding that the government reform itself. Most important, the United States needs to adopt realistic expectations about its allies and the limits of U.S. efforts to change them.

Byman offers two concluding observations. First, it will be difficult for the government of Iraq to take over the counterinsurgency war waged by the United States in that country. Second, although assisting allies in their counterinsurgency war ill often be in the U.S. national interest, there will be cases in which it would ake more sense for the United States to invest its resources elsewhere.

In addition t cal allies in counterinsurgency wars, the United States may turn to its NAT llies in the struggle against terrorists. In "NATO's International Security le in the Terrorist Era," Renée de Nevers examines how NATO has cont uted to counterterrorism missions. She finds that NATO has played a limite ole in the fight against terrorism. The United States and its European allies e engaged in multiple counterterrorism operations, but almost all of ther re conducted outside NATO's alliance structures.

Shortly after September 11 terrorist attacks, NATO invoked article 5 of its charter and dec ed that the attacks on the United States represented an attack on all its memb . It subsequently agreed to assist the U.S.-led coalition in its war in Afghani n. NATO then adopted a new concept for responding to terrorism that stat hat the alliance's goal should be to "help deter, defend, disrupt, and prot against terrorist attacks." The United States, on the other hand, has emp ized more offensive measures that would attempt to confront terrorists erseas and to hunt down and kill terrorists outside the United States. cording to de Nevers, "NATO's deeply institutionalized, consensus-base nodel is not the United States' preferred approach for multilateral cooper n in the war on terror." The United States has thus sought looser "coalitio f the willing" to assist it in its response to terrorist threats.

De Nevers a ses four categories of NATO's contribution to the U.S. war on terror: (1) vention and defense, (2) denial, (3) counterterrorism, and (4) consequenc anagement. NATO's efforts at prevention and defense include intellige sharing and surveillance operations, such as Operation Active Endeav n the Mediterranean. Because much of NATO's intelligence is gathered by t United States, there are limits to how much NATO can contribute to the w on terror in this area. The most vital terrorist-related intelligence gathere n Europe comes from police and domestic intelligence agencies, so it i utside the scope of NATO.

Denial inclu preventing terrorists from acquiring weapons of mass destruction (WM sanctuaries, and state support. NATO has done little as an alliance to den rrorists access to WMD, although its members have been involved in other orts to secure the Russian nuclear arsenal and to prevent nuclear prolifera in general. The United States has opted to pursue its counterprolifer n initiatives through informal coalitions. The United States' attitude towar reventive and preemptive attacks differs from that of its

European allies, which makes it harder for NATO to play an active role in denial. NATO has contributed substantially to the goal of denying terrorists sanctuaries, most notably through its contribution of forces in Afghanistan. NATO members have not, however, contributed as many troops as desired, and there are limits on how some of the forces can be deployed.

NATO has played a limited offensive counterterrorism role, because the alliance has focused on defense. Only in Afghanistan has NATO taken on combat missions. Even there, NATO members have questioned whether their forces should be engaged in war fighting on such a large scale.

NATO has attempted to enhance its capabilities for consequence management so that it can respond to terrorist attacks after they occur and minimize their effects. It has, for example, developed capabilities to respond to chemical and biological terrorism, and it has a Euro-Atlantic Disaster Response Center. NATO's consequence management programs have two limitations, however. First, individual countries must request NATO assistance. Neither Spain nor Britain requested help after the 2004 and 2005 bombings in those countries. Second, there is disagreement over whether NATO or the European Union should play the leading role in emergency response.

According to de Nevers, three factors explain why the United States has not cooperated more closely with NATO in the war against terror. First, the emergence of U.S. hegemony and the development of a security community in Europe since the end of the Cold War have caused NATO's members to differ on threat perceptions and the role of military force. Second, U.S. military capabilities are much more advanced and sophisticated than those of other NATO countries, which makes it hard for the allies to coordinate military operations. Third, much of the war against terrorism is fought by nonmilitary means, such as law enforcement and intelligence gathering, in which NATO has a limited role.

NATO's future military role in the war on terrorism is in doubt, de Nevers concludes. Its ability to contribute to the war in Afghanistan may be a crucial test of its viability. De Nevers notes, however, that there are signs that the United States is beginning to adopt "European policies on terrorism, which stress intelligence, law enforcement, and quiet engagement with the Muslim world." This convergence may ease transatlantic tensions, but it would not necessarily revive NATO.

Many observers have claimed that al-Qaida is a uniquely threatening terrorist group because of its decentralized network structure. This perspective emphasizes the difficulty of fighting a network that is resilient, flexible, and able to recruit from ıny different sources and areas. In "Assessing the Dangers of Illicit Netw .s: Why al-Qaida May Be Less Threatening Than Many Think," Mette I trup-Sangiovanni and Calvert Jones argue against this conventional wisd . They contend that networks such as al-Qaida have significant disadvant s.

Eilstrup-Sang anni and Jones define a network as a collection of actors that pursue exc ıge relations with one another but lack an organization to resolve disputes t arise in the course of such exchanges.[4] Unlike traditional hierarchical orga ıtions, networks are flat and decentralized. Decisionmaking is dispersed, an ocal actors enjoy much autonomy and form lateral links with one another. Th links involve high levels of trust and reciprocity.

Networks ha several apparent advantages over traditional hierarchical and centralized ganizations. First, information can flow quickly from one part of the net rk to another. Actors can process and act on information quickly. The inf nation itself may be of higher quality, because the trust between network actors enables people to "share and collectively interpret information." Sec d, networks have "scalability," the ability to grow sideways by adding link new actors. The advent of the internet has facilitated this type of expansi Third, networks are adaptable. The absence of a centralized structure enabl hem to change their form quickly. They also can easily expand into new graphical areas. Fourth, networks are resilient. They cannot be destroyed q kly, because they have multiple nodes and can reconstitute easily if one no is destroyed. Fifth, networks have a high learning capacity, because they tr fer information quickly and encourage experimentation.

Eilstrup-Sang anni and Jones argue that the advantages of networks have been exaggerat at least partly because little research has been done on failed networks and earchers have tended to overlook earlier examples of networks. They po out that networks also suffer from multiple disadvantages.

Networks ma ıot be superior structures for gathering and processing information. Decent zation and compartmentalization can make it hard to locate and share info ıtion. Individual cells of terrorists with loose ties to their leadership may mmunicate poorly.

Loose netwo also may make poor decisions and take excessive risks. Instead of being hly flexible and adaptive, they may make decisions slowly and the absenc f centralized leadership may reduce respect for those deci-

---

4. This definition is ed on one in Joel M. Podolny and Karen L. Page, "Network Forms of Organization," *Research* *)rganizational Behavior,* Vol. 12 (1990), pp. 58–59.

sions. Too much local autonomy can mean too little strategic planning. Insular underground organizations also may fall victim to "groupthink" and take excessive risks.

Although networks are said to be scalable, in reality their reliance on trust and interpersonal relations may limit their growth. Criminal and terrorist networks often depend on preexisting bonds of family or friendship. When networks try to link with other networks, they often splinter into separate groups. This pattern has emerged with Egyptian militants, Palestinian terrorists, and the Aum Shinrikyo cult. When networks manage to grow, they often lose their sense of unity and shared purpose. If multiple centers of power emerge, they may issue conflicting messages and undermine the group's legitimacy and popular support. Networks also may be less adaptable than the conventional wisdom suggests, because networks built on personal ties and reciprocity are not always flexible.

Collective action problems often plague networks. With much local autonomy, networks are beset by infighting between competing centers of power. The Palestine Liberation Organization is a prime example of this pathology. As a loose federation of different factions, the PLO has a long history of internal rivalry. Centralized hierarchical organizations, such as Shining Path in Peru, have avoided this level of fractiousness. Networks also have trouble coordinating their actions across great distances. Even in the age of the internet, groups can miscommunicate when there are limited opportunities for face-to-face interaction. It becomes harder to instill loyalty and commitment in a dispersed network.

Networks may be more vulnerable to security breaches. Once one cell is uncovered and destroyed, the network may unravel as other participants blame one another. When recruitment is dispersed, it becomes harder to monitor and screen new recruits.

The conventional wisdom holds that networks learn efficiently, but in practice limits on information flows may inhibit learning. In some networks, "compartmentalization means individual cells often absorb only those lessons they have learned directly rather than benefit from the experience of others." Networks supposedly facilitate the exchange of tacit knowledge, but the absence of centralization and hierarchy may mean that members do not receive necessary training. Militants often try to address this problem by establishing training camps, but such camps can be detected and become a security liability. Unlike centralized organizations, networks also have minimal institutional memory and "r y not be able to translate lessons learned into solid improvements in organi tional practice."

Eilstrup-Sang vanni and Jones look at the record of al-Qaida to determine whether that o nization has benefited from its loose networked structure. Many observers e al-Qaida as a prime example of a network that has been resilient and adap le. Eilstrup-Sangiovanni and Jones, however, make three arguments that c doubt on claims that al-Qaida is an effective decentralized terrorist netwo

First, al-Qaid was a hierarchical organization when it carried out its most successful miss s—including the September 11 attacks. The central leadership of al-Qaida as very structured and hierarchical in the 1990s, with "a tidy organization of mmittees with well-defined positions and responsibilities." The most spect lar al-Qaida attackers were closely managed by al-Qaida's central leadersh Moreover, al-Qaida was not a dispersed network. It had a headquarters ir fghanistan under the Taliban.

Second, as al ida has evolved into a more loosely structured network, it has lost unity l cohesion. When al-Qaida became a diffuse transnational network, local filiates staged attacks in, for example, Bali, Madrid, and London, witho central direction. Rifts may be emerging within al-Qaida as the network ex ds.

Third, many Qaida attacks have been foiled in recent years, suggesting that an appare y effective network is vulnerable to counterterrorism measures. Many of -Qaida's local affiliates have adopted poor security procedures, making easy for domestic police and security services to monitor and ultimately est their members. The dispersed elements of the network seem to be slov earners when it comes to adapting to new law enforcement techniques.

Eilstrup-Sang vanni and Jones conclude that al-Qaida may have become a less significant eat since it evolved into a networked structure. The group has not been a to plan and execute complex attacks since September 11, 2001. Most of i ttacks have been initiated by local affiliates. Although the ideology of al-Q da can inspire continuing violence, this danger cannot be attributed to its rported strength as a network. Eilstrup-Sangiovanni and Jones recomme that law enforcement agencies exploit the vulnerabilities of al-Qaida and ot r terrorist networks by "targeting networks repeatedly, forcing actors to ch ge their practices abruptly, or sowing doubt and mistrust through infiltra n and manipulation of information."

Is the world entering an age of continuing massive terrorist attacks? Will al-Qaida remain a major terrorist threat? Why do terrorist groups decline and disband? The final essay in this volume explores these questions. In "How al-Qaida Ends: The Decline and Demise of Terrorist Groups," Audrey Kurth Cronin argues that particular terrorist groups and the campaigns against them do not last forever; even if terrorism, like war, is an enduring feature of the international system. Al-Qaida in many ways is similar to previous terrorist groups, even if it has evolved into a unique network. Cronin recommends that U.S. policies be changed to take into account the lessons of previous counterterrorism campaigns and research on the rise and demise of terrorist groups.

Previous research on how terrorism ends has included analyses of how the causes and motivations of terrorism affect the rise and fall of terrorist groups. Cronin notes that research on the organizational dynamics and ideological commitment of terrorist groups may be less relevant to groups that rely on decentralized cells and the internet. She also points out that terrorist groups motivated by religion may have greater staying power.

Other research on the rise and decline of terrorism attempts to identify waves or cycles of terrorist activity, as well as stages through which terrorist groups pass. Cronin points out that cyclical hypotheses are hard to prove and that the current wave of jihadist terrorism may not resemble previous terrorist campaigns. She also notes that comparative case studies of terrorist groups and counterterrorism campaigns are often flawed, because researchers do not have access to all the relevant data or they choose to focus only on some variables.

Cronin identifies seven explanations for why terrorist groups decline and cease operations. First, capturing or killing a leader may cripple a terrorist organization. Recent examples of groups that suffered this fate include the Shining Path in Peru, the Kurdistan Workers' Party, the Real IRA in Northern Ireland, and Aum Shinrikyo in Japan. Cronin suggests that killing a group's leader may backfire if he or she is then seen as a martyr and new members are inspired to become terrorists. Arresting a leader may be more effective, provided that the leader is not allowed to send encouraging messages to his or her followers while incarcerated.

Second, terrorist groups may decline if they fail to pass their cause to a new generation of members. In the 1970s, for example, left-wing and anarchist groups such as the Baader-Meinhof group and the Japanese Red Army failed to inspire successor generations to adopt their goals, ideologies, and violent tactics. Right-w ; groups may have suffered a similar fate, although their racist ideas someti s endure as their organizations go underground and become a network of d ntralized cells.

Third, terrori groups may cease to exist once they have achieved their goals. The Irgu which fought to establish the state of Israel, and the African National Congr , which fought to end apartheid in South Africa, are two examples. Cronin tes that terrorist groups rarely succeed in their campaigns, but achieving t r goals may lead them to disband.

Fourth, terro groups may end their terrorist activities when they enter into negotiatior ind become legitimate political actors. The Provisional IRA and the Palesti Liberation Organization are two prominent organizations that have follow this path. In other cases, a terrorist group's entry into negotiations may ca the group to splinter. Some of the emerging splinter groups may be more lical and more violent than their "mother" organization. Cronin observe iat territorially based terrorist groups may be more likely to enter into nego ions than ideological or religious groups.

Fifth, terroris roups may decline or disband when they lose popular support. Terrorists en need active or passive support from the population. They may lose that s port if governments are able to offer rewards and punishments that ind the population to end their support. Populations also may become uninte ed in a terrorist group's ideology or revolted by its indiscriminate viole . The Real IRA and ETA have alienated potential supporters by engaging in ital bombing campaigns.

Sixth, terroris roups may decline when they are repressed with military force. This app ch has contributed to the decline of Shining Path and the Kurdistan Worl s' Party. Cronin argues that the results of such repression may only be ter orary. In some cases, such as the Russian repression of rebels in Chechnya, m ary success in one region may export the problem to another area. Military r ession is also likely to be costly and may be a particularly difficult strateg or democracies that profess respect for human rights.

Seventh, terr t groups may abandon terrorism and become criminal enterprises or pu e conventional military operations. Terrorist organizations that have incre igly focused on profit-making activities instead of the pursuit of political ids may include Abu Sayyaf in the Philippines and some narco-terrorist ups in Colombia. Terrorists that have escalated to insurgency or conve nal war include groups in Kashmir and Maoists in Nepal.

Is al-Qaida a ique terrorist organization? Does it have some of the characteristics that ha caused previous terrorist groups to decline? Cronin argues that al-Qaida's fluid organization, recruitment methods, funding, and means of communication distinguish it from previous terrorist organizations.

Al-Qaida has made the transition from being a "visible" organization with training camps in Afghanistan and is now a much more fluid network of multiple affiliated groups in many countries. These entities share a commitment to Sunni jihad, but they are hard to track because they rely on internet communications and consist of clandestine cells. It is difficult to estimate the number of al-Qaida members who might engage in terrorist operations.

Al-Qaida's recruitment pattern is more like that of a social network. New members are not recruited, but instead volunteer and become part of a social network based on ties of kinship and friendship. As a result, there are often no direct connections between al-Qaida's leadership and its operatives. It is extremely difficult for intelligence agencies to trace the command and control relationships.

Funding for al-Qaida comes from money channeled through charitable organizations and the profits from businesses that Osama bin Laden owns. Al-Qaida provides grants for local terrorist groups that often are able to conduct attacks with limited funds. Although some of al Qaida's funds have been frozen, it is very difficult to control informal networks for financial transfers or to prevent the flow of funds through charities.

Al-Qaida communicates using the full range of technologies of globalization: mobile phones, text messaging, email, websites, blogs, and chat rooms. The internet has provided easy access to the media and potential recruits. Al-Qaida has little difficulty distributing its message and practical advice on how to conduct terrorist attacks. Cronin suggests that al-Qaida no longer needs to be an organization in the traditional sense, because individuals can participate "with the stroke of a few keys."

Despite al-Qaida's innovations, it follows patterns established by earlier terrorist groups, many of which also had international links, sophisticated public communications, and a taste for mass-casualty attacks. Cronin argues that some lessons from the ways in which previous terrorist groups have declined may apply to al-Qaida.

First, in Cronin's view, killing bin Laden is unlikely to end al-Qaida. Previous organizations that have been crippled by the death of their leader have been hierarchically structured and have lacked a successor. Al-Qaida is not in these categories. It is not driven by a "cult of personality." If bin Laden were captured or killed, a successor would emerge and al-Qaida might even be strengthened by his martyrdom.

Second, Cron argues that al-Qaida will not decline out of a failure to pass on its cause to econd generation. Indeed, it has already inspired a second, third, and fourt eneration through its ability to attract radicalized followers who are conne l to existing local networks.

Cronin conte that the third and fourth ways in which terrorist groups decline—achievin he group's goal or entering into negotiations—are not relevant to al-Qaid day. Al-Qaida's goals, including establishing a new Islamic caliphate, rem ng existing regimes in Muslim countries, and expelling infidels from t Muslim world—are so broad that they are unlikely to be achieved or ne iated. The United States may, however, be able to drive a wedge between e disparate groups that have joined al-Qaida's coalition, provided that it d not treat al-Qaida as a monolith.

The fifth ave to the decline of terrorist groups—the erosion of popular support—may tribute to the decline of al-Qaida. Cronin argues that the U.S. campaign pread democracy in the Muslim world is the wrong way to erode support f l-Qaida. Democratization will take decades, and there is little evidence to port claims that democratization reduces terrorism. Cronin advocates incre d efforts to control or interdict al-Qaida's use of the internet to send messag as well as a much more robust effort to publicize the human cost of al-Qaida murderous attacks. The United States should not focus public diplomacy attempts to promote its values and bolster its image, but should tap into growing international norm against killing innocent civilians" to increas evulsion directed at al-Qaida.

The sixth fac that has ended terrorist groups, military repression, will have limited ef iveness against al-Qaida. The movement has shown its ability to evolve in e face of such action.

Al-Qaida is ady following the seventh pathway to the end of terrorist groups, the tra ion to criminal activity and conventional military campaigns (at least in Iraq) ronin notes that this is not a welcome development, because criminal enterp s are being used to fund al-Qaida terrorist operations. They therefore supp terrorism instead of replacing it.

Cronin concl s that the United States must learn from experience with previous terror groups and devise a counterterrorist campaign to accelerate al-Qaida's dem She argues that "al-Qaida will end when the West removes itself from the rt of [a civil war within the Muslim world], shores up international norms ainst terrorism, undermines al-Qaida's ties with its followers, and begins exploit the movement's abundant missteps."

The essays in is volume address some of the most prominent questions in the analysis of contemporary terrorism. They do not cover every topic related to terrorism. There is little discussion, for example, of the danger that terrorists will acquire nuclear weapons and use them to launch catastrophic attacks.[5] It also would have been well beyond the scope of this volume to offer detailed assessments of the many different terrorist groups that are active on every continent except Antarctica. We hope, however, that this collection will stimulate further research and analysis of one of the most important security issues of the early twenty-first century.

5. For further discussion of nuclear terrorism, see Matthew Bunn, "Nuclear Terrorism: A Strategy for Prevention," in Michael E. Brown, Owen R. Coté Jr., Sean M. Lynn-Jones, and Steven E. Miller, eds., *Going Nuclear: Nuclear Proliferation and International Security in the 21st Century* (Cambridge, Mass.: MIT Press, 2010).

Part I:
Roots of Contemporary Terrorism

Market Civilization and Its Clash with Terror

Michael Mousseau

Clausewitz's dictum that war is politics by other means is a reminder that the primary goal of the war against terror is not to defeat and eliminate those who aim to attack the United States and its allies. Rather it is to enhance the security of the American people and their allies. These goals are the same only if terrorist organizations such as al-Qaeda are isolated groups of criminals that need only be found and dealt with swiftly. But if al-Qaeda and its associated groups represent the values and beliefs of substantial numbers of people, and all signs indicate that this is the case, then defeating these groups will not end the struggle against terror. Only by changing the values and beliefs of supporters of terrorist groups can the United States and its allies expect to achieve this objective.

To win the war against terror, the United States and its allies must have both a military strategy and a political strategy. Achieving political victory requires an understanding of the social basis of terror—that is, the values and beliefs that legitimate the use of extreme and indiscriminate violence against the civilian populations of out-groups. Such understanding will not reveal much about terror groups that seem to lack social support, such as the Basque terrorists in Spain, but it will help to reduce the influence of those groups that appear to enjoy widespread support, such as al-Qaeda. Seeking to understand the motivations of terrorists, however, should not be confused with empathizing with them or acquiescing on issues that terrorists and their supporters claim motivate them.

Some scholars have sought to link poverty with terror. Poverty, they argue, fosters terror because it creates a sense of hopelessness, restricts educational opportunity, and produces frustration over inequality.[1] The direct causal linkages between poverty and terror are more elusive than scholars suggest, how-

Michael Mousseau is Associate Professor of International Relations at Koç University in Istanbul, Turkey.

It is with profound gratitude that the author dedicates this article to the memory of Stuart A. Bremer (1944–2002), whose brilliance, affection, and scholarly leadership will be deeply missed by his many students and colleagues.

1. For a summary of these views, see Martha Crenshaw, "The Causes of Terrorism," in Charles W. Kegley Jr., ed., *International Terrorism: Characteristics, Causes, Controls* (New York: St. Martin's, 1990), pp. 113–126. For recent examples, see Samuel P. Huntington, "The Age of Muslim Wars," *Newsweek*, December 17, 2001, pp. 42–48; and James D. Wolfensohn, "Making the World a Better and Safer Place: The Time for Action Is Now," *Politics*, Vol. 22, No. 2 (May 2002), pp. 118–123.

International Security, Vol. 27, No. 3 (Winter 2002/03), pp. 5–29

ever. Indeed I a ınaware of any comprehensive explanation in print for how poverty causes rror. Nor has there been any demonstrated correlation between the two. evertheless, there has been a chorus of calls to increase foreign aid as a to in the fight against terror.[3] Absent an understanding of the social origins of is phenomenon, however, there is little reason to believe that greater foreign l will have any significant positive effect. It may even increase the terro threat.

In this article argue that the social origins of terror are rooted less in poverty—or in grov ıg discontent with U.S. foreign policy—and more in the values and beliefs sociated with the mixed economies of developing countries in a globalizing orld. I show how liberal-democratic values and beliefs are embedded in th conomic infrastructure that prevails in market democracies, and how collec e-autocratic values and beliefs are embedded in clientalist economies. As esult of globalization, these values and beliefs are increasingly clashing the mixed market–clientalist economies of the developing world, triggerir ntense antimarket resentment directed primarily against the epitome of mar civilization: the United States. This study builds on several generations of r earch in anthropology, economics, political science, and sociology; it explai much of the historical record of sectarian terror around the globe and, mos nportant, suggests how the United States and its allies can combat it.

The article is ganized as follows. After reviewing the literature on rational and cultural exp nations for terror, I show how market democracies constitute a global civiliza n based not on interstate trade but on common liberal values and beliefs that rive in market economies. I then discuss the clash of these liberal values a beliefs with the values and beliefs embraced in many parts of the developi world. I next demonstrate how clientalist values are a necessary condition f the resort to terrorist violence. I conclude with recommendations for develc ng a political strategy to win the war on terror.

Rational and (ltural Explanations for Terror

The academic li ature offers two explanations, one rational and the other cultural, for why s ıe societies support terrorism. The first view holds that ter-

---

2. Alan B. Krueger l Jitka Maleckova, "The Economics and the Education of Suicide Bombers: Does Poverty Caus errorism?" *New Republic,* June 24, 2002, pp. 27–33.
3. Many of these c are made in the media. In the academic literature, see Ivo H. Daalder and James M. Lindsay, ısty, Brutish, and Long: America's War on Terrorism," *Current History,* December 2001, pp. 4(408; and Wolfensohn, "Making the World a Better and Safer Place."

rorism is a rational strategy for dealing with particular socioeconomic grievances in societies where the "paths to legal expression of opposition are blocked."[4] "Governments that fail to meet the basic welfare and economic needs of their peoples and suppress their liberties," argues Samuel Huntington, "generate violent opposition to themselves and to Western governments that support them."[5] In the context of the current war on terror, the Arab world is said to need "a managed political opening . . . that introduces pluralism into . . . political life."[6]

Rational explanations of the origins and social support of terror accord well with mainstream views in academia. Realism, for instance, assumes that values and beliefs play no role in the origin or resolution of conflict,[7] and thus the resort to terror is a predictable strategy of the weak. Liberal institutionalists argue that democracies are more likely than other kinds of states to resolve their internal (and external) differences through peaceful means.[8] In addition, they predict that societies in autocracies are more likely to experience violence and to support terror as an acceptable political tool. Although many developing countries have not produced widespread support for terrorism, such support does seem to be more pervasive in the developing world, especially in those countries lacking stable democratic institutions (e.g., Egypt, Indonesia, and Pakistan).

Rational models for explaining the social support of terror have several major weaknesses. The historical record, for instance, does not accord with the proposition that democracies are less likely to condone terror. India, as some observers suggest, has been democratic for more than half a century, yet the threat of sectarian violence seems omnipresent. Nor does the evidence support the notion that poverty or illiteracy increases the threat of terror.[9] If economic deprivation were the culprit, then a century or two ago most societies around the world should have supported terrorist activity, because they were generally worse off (in terms of diet, health care, leisure time, and material wealth) than most societies are today. In addition, it is perhaps noteworthy that fifteen of the nineteen hijackers who struck at the World Trade Center and the Penta-

---

4. Crenshaw, "The Causes of Terrorism," p. 116.
5. Huntington, "The Age of Muslim Wars," p. 48.
6. Larry Diamond, as cited in Thomas L. Friedman, "The Free-Speech Bind," *New York Times*, Mach 27, 2002, p. A23.
7. Kenneth N. Waltz, *Theory of International Politics* (New York: McGraw-Hill, 1979).
8. Larry Diamond, "Introduction: In Search of Consolidation," in Diamond, Marc F. Plattner, Yun-han Chu, and Hung-mao Tien, eds., *Consolidating the Third Wave Democracies* (Baltimore, Md.: Johns Hopkins University Press, 1997), pp. xiii–xlvii.
9. Krueger and Maleckova, "The Economics and the Education of Suicide Bombers."

gon on Septem 11, 2001, were from Saudi Arabia, one of the richest countries in the wo Most of them were highly educated and appeared to have had ample opp unities for building materially rewarding lives.

These facts s ;est that rational explanations for the social origins and support of terroris ıre inadequate. The September 11 hijackers were motivated by something eper—something that fundamentally distinguished them from their victi Put simply, terrorists and their supporters do not think like their victims. F ı the cultural perspective, terrorists are not merely engaged in a rational st gy of the weak. Rather there is something about ingrained habits and hist cal traditions that renders terrorism a socially acceptable method for ad ssing grievances in some societies, but not others.[10] When such traditions combined with social, economic, or political grievances, individuals can b socialized into violence from early childhood," particularly when they exp nce violence in their formative years.[11]

From a cultu perspective, the creation of a political strategy to combat terror must begin ith an examination of terrorists' values and beliefs. What motivates them Vhat values do they claim justify their actions? Because all the September hijackers were from Islamic countries, and all seemed to express religious tivations, the cultural approach would suggest that there is something inhe t in Islamic beliefs and values that yields the social approval of terror. For in nce, some observers argue that because the Koran offers instructions "for n the minutiae of everyday life," Islamic culture has tremendous difficulty ling with change and lacks "a tradition of self-criticism." As a result, some lysts suggest that Muslims tend to be "defensive and insecure"; they also likely to blame bad news on "exterior, malevolent powers."[12]

Like rational ories, cultural theories that seek to explain terrorism's origins and base o ıpport have significant weaknesses. For instance, traditional cultural mores a constant, not a variable, and thus cultural explanations cannot sufficie account for variation in levels of social support for terror across time an ılace. More specifically, Islamic values and beliefs cannot explain why th Auslim world did not produce suicidal mass murderers in, for instance, th 950s, or why millions of Muslims around the world joined others in expre ıg shock and horror at the events of September 11. Further,

10. Crenshaw, "Th uses of Terrorism," p. 115.
11. Martha Crensh "Thoughts on Relating Terrorism to Historical Contexts," in Crenshaw, ed., *Terrorism in Context* niversity Park: Pennsylvania State University Press, 1992), p. 74.
12. Hume Horan, " se Young Arab Muslims and Us," *Middle East Quarterly*, Vol. 9, No. 4 (Fall 2002), pp. 53–54.

the social support of terror has a tradition in non-Islamic societies (e.g., Catholics and Protestants in Northern Ireland), demonstrating that Muslim culture alone does not sufficiently explain this phenomenon.

Rational approaches have an advantage over cultural approaches because they focus on observable circumstances—poverty, economic inequality, illiteracy, and lack of democracy—that allow scholars to predict when and where social support for terror is likely to emerge. Explanations linking poverty and its related conditions with terror, however, are nebulous. Cultural approaches have an advantage over rational approaches because they are based on the seemingly apparent fact that those who engage in or support suicidal mass murder do not think like people in out-groups (in this case, people in the United States and the rest of the Western world). None of these approaches, however, helps scholars to predict—and thus expose and eradicate—the kinds of values and beliefs that support terror.

To grasp the origins of socially approved terror, scholars need an approach that combines the rationalist identification of observable circumstances with the culturalist emphasis on learning why people think and act as they do. In short, scholars must be able to predict when and where the use of indiscriminate violence against out-groups is likely to be socially approved and when and where it is not. Only then can potential terrorist targets devise a political strategy for eliminating this growing menace.

The Rise of Market Civilization

Many scholars of politics have suggested that there is a growing need to be able to predict variation in peoples' values and beliefs,[13] a need illustrated most dramatically by the September 11 terrorist attacks. In this view, political scientists do not have to start from scratch: Anthropologists, economic historians, and sociologists have been at this task for years. Anthropologists have long sought to explain the relationship between economic conditions and values and beliefs;[14] economic historians have for years linked certain economic conditions with particular sets of values and beliefs, identifying at least two primary kinds of socioeconomic integration in history—clientalism and mar-

13. Robert O. Keohane, "Governance in a Partially Globalized World," *American Political Science Review*, Vol. 95, No. 1 (March 2001), pp. 1–15; and Alexander Wendt, *Social Theory of International Politics* (Cambridge: Cambridge University Press, 1999).

14. See Marvin Harris, *Cultural Materialism: The Struggle for a Science of Culture* (Walnut Creek, Calif.: AltaMira Press, 2001 [1979]); and Maxine L. Margolis, "Introduction to the Updated Edition," in Marvin Harris, *The Rise of Anthropological Theory: A History of Theories of Culture*, updated ed. (Walnut Creek, Calif.: AltaMira Press, 2001), pp. vii–xiii.

kets;[15] and soci gists have documented the social implications of clientalist exchange.[16]

In clientalist nomies, the obligations of cooperating parties are implied (rather than ma explicit) and take the form of reciprocity, or gift giving. Exchange occurs t ugh the giving of gifts, which reinforces a sense of trust and enduring obliga n among the parties. Enforcement of obligations comes with the threat of p ishment: Violations of trust lead to severed relationships. Clientalist eco nies can be complex;[17] and with specialization, patrons emerge who ha more to give than others, creating a surplus of obligations accompanied b ncreased influence. Because reciprocal obligations are only implied and are cially enforced, patrons rather than states regulate economic cooperation. Ex nples of clientalist socioeconomies include feudal Europe, and in the conte porary period, mafias and the complex systems of patronage that characteriz he politics of redistribution in most developing countries.[18]

Because econ ic relations are enduring, clientalist economies are based on explicit social li ges, such as kinship and ethnicity. These linkages render ingroups more im rtant than out-groups, making clientalist communities more inward looking an market communities in terms of identity, values, and beliefs. Clientalist mmunities are also organized hierarchically: Patrons, such as lords, dons, uncles, receive gifts from clients as expressions of loyalty in exchange for lif ong protection.[19]

In market eco mies, in contrast, the mutual obligations of cooperating parties are made ex icit in the form of contracts. The quid pro quo nature of the

---

15. A third mode of egration, sharing, is common among hunting and gathering societies, but is not discussed here use it has not been a prominent mode of exchange in any state. See Janet L. Abu-Lughod, *Befor ropean Hegemony: The World System, A.D. 1250–1350* (New York: Oxford University Press, 1989); rl Polanyi, *The Great Transformation: The Political and Economic Origins of Our Time* (Boston: Beac 1957 [1944]); Marshall D. Sahlins, *Stone Age Economics* (Hawthorne: Aldine de Gruyter, 1972); a David W. Tandy and Walter C. Neale, "Karl Polanyi's Distinctive Approach to Social Analysis a he Case of Ancient Greece: Ideas, Criticisms, Consequences," in Colin A.M. Duncan and Tandy, ., *From Political Economy to Anthropology: Situating Economic Life in Past Societies* (London: Blac se, 1994), pp. 19–20.
16. See, for instanc Marcel Mauss, *The Gift: The Form and Reason for Exchange in Archaic Societies* (New York: W.W. N on, 2000 [1924]).
17. Polanyi, *The G Transformation*, pp. 49–50.
18. See S.N. Eisen t and René Lemarchand, *Political Clientalism: Patronage and Development* (Thousand Oaks, C .: Sage, 1981); and Luis Roniger and Ayþe Güneþ-Ayata, eds., *Democracy, Clientelism, and Civ ciety* (Boulder, Colo.: Lynne Rienner, 1994).
19. For further dis ion of the rules and norms of gift exchange, see Christopher A. Gregory, *Gifts and Commoditi* an Diego, Calif.: Academic Press, 1983); and Monica Prasad, "The Morality of Market Exchang ove, Money, and Contractual Justice," *Sociological Perspectives*, Vol. 42, No. 2 (Summer 1999), pp 1–214.

cooperation implies no obligation among the parties beyond that expressed in the contract. Unlike in clientalist economies, therefore, in market economies, strangers and even enemies can cooperate in prescribed ways.[20] Because contracts cannot be negotiated without explicit assertions of self-interest, their extensive use renders such assertions socially approved. Moreover, a contract imposes an equitable relationship on the parties.[21] The implications of this are profound: The norm of cooperating with strangers on the basis of legal equality is the logical prerequisite for respecting the rule of common law. Because contractual obligations are explicit, a state can enforce them, and a market economy can emerge if a state is willing and able to enforce contracts with impartiality. In these ways, markets develop and the liberal values of individualism, universalism, tolerance, and equity emerge concurrently with the rule of common law and democratic governance.[22] Examples of market economies include classical Athens and, in the contemporary period, Sweden and the United States.[23]

The market economy and its liberal belief system also account for the rise of science over faith-based forms of knowledge. Science is anchored in the notion that (1) some facts are universal (universalism), (2) any person can challenge another's assertions of fact, including those of his or her leader (freedom and equity), and (3) truth is sought through the competition of ideas (tolerance). The opposite of science is truth determined by an authority sanctioned by loyalty and faith—the norm in clientalism.

All societies have some combination of clientalist and market exchange. For markets to prevail, however—for a majority of people to engage regularly in making contracts—a complex division of labor associated with economic development is necessary. At lower levels of development and thus incomes, individuals engage in fewer exchanges, and the few big-ticket exchanges that do

20. In this way, the initial emergence of market norms allows for increased specialization and thus greater economic production, which in turn can stimulate a mutually reinforcing cycle of market-integrated growth. See Michael Mousseau, "Market Prosperity, Democratic Consolidation, and Democratic Peace," *Journal of Conflict Resolution*, Vol. 44, No. 4 (August 2000), p. 478.
21. William J. Booth, "On the Idea of the Moral Economy," *American Political Science Review*, Vol. 88, No. 3 (September 1994), pp. 653–667; and Ronald Inglehart, *Culture Shift in Advanced Industrial Society* (Princeton, N.J.: Princeton University Press, 1990), p. 46.
22. For further discussion of this process, see Mousseau, "Market Prosperity, Democratic Consolidation, and Democratic Peace"; and Michael Mousseau, "Globalization, Markets, and Democracy: An Anthropological Linkage," in Mehdi Mozaffari, ed., *Globalization and Civilizations* (London: Routledge, 2002), pp. 97–124.
23. Rondo Cameron, *A Concise Economic History of the World: From Paleolithic Times to the Present*, 3d ed. (New York: Oxford University Press, 1997), pp. 32–35.

occur—such as tting a job, buying a home, or purchasing expensive consumer goods— less likely to be mediated by the market (with price determined by supp and demand): More often than not, these will be seen as exchanges of gi among members of an in-group (with price determined by privileged disc it). As a result, developing countries tend to have political cultures charac zed by intergroup conflict (deep in-group/out-group feelings), less resp for individual freedom, stronger religious beliefs, greater respect for loy and hierarchy than for the rule of law, and extensive informal patrona networks (known for, among other things, high levels of corruption).[24]

Sociologists economic historians have documented the association of gift giving and tracting norms with, respectively, collectivist and individualist value orie tions.[25] Anthropologists and archaeologists have long considered econon conditions to be a leading influence on cultural mores and institutional st tures.[26] Rational choice theorists and others acknowledge that values affe olitical behavior[27]; and most agree that, for stability, democracy requires a eral political culture.[28] The chain of causation is well established: The evi ce linking economic development with liberal values is so overwhelming t the proposition has no serious detractors,[29] nor does the

24. Mousseau, "M et Prosperity, Democratic Consolidation, and Democratic Peace"; and Mousseau, "Global ion, Markets, and Democracy."
25. Abu-Lughod, *B e European Hegemony;* Fernand Braudel, *Afterthoughts on Material Civilization and Capitalism,* tran tricia Ranum (Baltimore, Md.: Johns Hopkins University Press, 1979), p. 63; Emile Durkheim, *Division of Labour in Society* (Basingstoke, U.K.: Macmillan, 1984 [1893]); Polanyi, *The Great sformation;* and Tandy and Neale, "Karl Polanyi's Distinctive Approach."
26. Harris, *Cultural terialism;* and Margolis, "Introduction to the Updated Edition."
27. Keohane, "Gov nce in a Partially Globalized World"; Margaret Levi, *Consent, Dissent, and Patriotism* (Cambric Cambridge University Press, 1997); James D. Morrow, *Game Theory for Political Scientists* (Princ , N.J.: Princeton University Press, 1994); Elinor Ostrom, *Governing the Commons: The Evolutio Institutions for Collective Action* (New York: Cambridge University Press, 1990); and Tom R. T , *Why People Obey the Law* (New Haven, Conn.: Yale University Press, 1990).
28. Gabriel A. Alm and Sidney Verba, *The Civic Culture: Political Attitudes and Democracy in Five Nations* (Princeton, .: Princeton University Press, 1963); Robert Alan Dahl, *Democracy and Its Critics* (New Haver nn.: Yale University Press, 1989); Samuel P. Huntington, "Will More Countries Become Demo tic?" *Political Science Quarterly,* Vol. 99, No. 2 (Summer 1984), pp. 193–218; and Seymour Mart ipset, "Some Social Requisites of Democracy: Economic Development and Political Legitimacy merican Political Science Review,* Vol. 53, No. 1 (March 1959), pp. 69–105.
29. Braudel, *Aftert hts on Material Civilization and Capitalism;* Geert Hofstede, *Culture's Consequences: Comparing es, Behaviors, Institutions, and Organizations across Nations,* 2d ed. (Thousand Oaks, Calif.: Sage, [1980]); and Ronald Inglehart and Wayne E. Baker, "Modernization, Cultural Change, and t ersistence of Traditional Values," *American Sociological Review,* Vol. 65, No. 1 (February 2000), p –52.

stabilizing impact of development on democracy.[30] Indeed virtually every economically developed democracy in history has been a market democracy.

Although the disciplines of anthropology, economics, political science, and sociology have all addressed different aspects of the relationship between market economies and society, none has examined this relationship in its entirety. Anthropologists and archaeologists typically link cultural mores not to modes of exchange but to environmental conditions;[31] some economists have argued that the social implications of markets invalidate the core assumptions of neoclassical liberalism,[32] and others have addressed the role of social capital in economic growth;[33] political scientists have focused on how development, not the market economy, stabilizes democracy;[34] and sociologists have highlighted the social, but apparently not the political, consequences of gift exchange.[35]

Findings from these four disciplines help to explain the rise of market civilization and its supremacy in the contemporary era. Surveys and other works have established that the inhabitants of high-income countries—most of which have developed market economies—share common liberal values;[36] other studies confirm that elected leaders seek to promote domestic values in making foreign policy.[37] If median voters in market democracies have liberal values

---

30. Ross E. Burkhart and Michael S. Lewis-Beck, "Comparative Democracy: The Economic Development Thesis," *American Political Science Review*, Vol. 88, No. 4 (December 1994), pp. 111–131; and Adam Przeworski and Fernando Limongi, "Modernization: Theories and Facts," *World Politics*, Vol. 49, No. 2 (January 1997), pp. 155–183.
31. See, for example, R. Brian Ferguson, *Yanomami Warfare: A Political History* (Sante Fe, N.M.: School of American Research Press, 1995).
32. See Polanyi, *The Great Transformation*.
33. Stephen Knack and Philip Keefer, "Does Social Capital Have an Economic Payoff? A Cross-country Investigation," *Quarterly Journal of Economics*, Vol. 112, No. 4 (November 1997), pp. 1251–1288.
34. Lipset, "Some Social Requisites of Democracy"; and Dietrich Rueschemeyer, Evelyne Huber Stephens, and John D. Stephens, *Capitalist Development and Democracy* (Chicago: University of Chicago Press, 1992).
35. Mauss, *The Gift;* and Prasad, "The Morality of Market Exchange."
36. Braudel, *Afterthoughts on Material Civilization and Capitalism;* Yun-han Chu, Fu Hu, and Chung-in Moon, "South Korea and Taiwan: The International Context," in Diamond et al., *Consolidating the Third Wave of Democracies*, pp. 267–294; Hofstede, *Culture's Consequences;* and Inglehart and Baker, "Modernization, Cultural Change, and the Persistence of Traditional Values."
37. George C. Edwards III and B. Dan Wood, "Who Influences Whom? The President, Congress, and the Media," *American Political Science Review*, Vol. 93, No. 2 (June 1999), pp. 327–345; Ronald H. Hinckley, *Peoples, Polls, and Policymakers: American Public Opinion and National Security* (New York: Lexington, 1992); Jeffrey W. Knopf, "How Rational Is the 'Rational Public'? Evidence from U.S. Public Opinion on Military Spending," *Journal of Conflict Resolution*, Vol. 42, No. 5 (October 1998),

and median vo s in all other types of democracies do not, then only the elected leaders the market democracies are likely to have liberal values and a political incer e to pursue a liberal foreign policy course. In this way, the common liberal lues of their electorates constrain leaders of market democracies (but not l lers of other types of democracies) to pursue common aims in foreign affai for instance, to respect and promote international law, human rights, anc n equitable global order.

Proponents o ie democratic peace note the apparent dearth of militarized conflict among mocratic nations.[38] It now appears, however, that this peace is limited to th dvanced market democracies.[39] Democratic dyads where at least one state l ked a developed market economy and that have had a history of militari confrontation include India and Pakistan, Greece and Turkey, and Ecuad and Peru. Moreover, market democracies—but not other types of democ ies—tend to cooperate with each other against other states.[40] They also tend t xpress common positions in the United Nations General Assembly.[41] Of cou e, leaders of market democracies do not agree on everything, but they do agr on the fundamentals: how the world should be organized—politically, econ ically, and socially—and what constitutes proper governmental behavi both internally and externally. When differences surface among market mocracies, the discourse is bounded by mutual respect for state rights (equ) and the primacy of international law—just as the domestic political behav of the governments of these democracies is culturally

pp. 544–571; Timotl McKeown, "The Cuban Missile Crisis and Politics as Usual," *Journal of Politics*, Vol. 62, No. 1 (ruary 2000), pp. 70–87; Benjamin I. Page and Robert Y. Shapiro, *The Rational Public: Fifty Years o nds in Americans' Policy Preferences* (Chicago: University of Chicago Press, 1992); and Douglas Van Belle and Steven W. Hook, "Greasing the Squeaky Wheel: News Media Coverage and U.S. velopment Aid, 1977–1992," *International Interactions*, Vol. 26, No. 3 (July–September 2000), p 21–346.

38. Stuart A. Brem 'Dangerous Dyads: Conditions Affecting the Likelihood of Interstate War, 1816–1965," *Journal onflict Resolution*, Vol. 36, No. 2 (June 1992), pp. 309–341; Bruce M. Russett, *Grasping the Democ Peace: Principles for a Post–Cold War World* (Princeton, N.J.: Princeton University Press, 1993) d James Lee Ray, *Democracy and International Conflict: An Evaluation of the Democratic Peace Pr ition* (Columbia: University of South Carolina Press, 1995).

39. Mousseau, "M t Prosperity, Democratic Consolidation, and Democratic Peace"; and Michael Mousseau, H rd Hegre, and John R. Oneal, "How the Wealth of Nations Conditions the Liberal Peace," *Eur n Journal of International Relations*, Vol. 9, No. 4 (June 2003), in press.

40. Michael Mouss , "An Economic Limitation to the Zone of Democratic Peace and Cooperation" *International I actions*, Vol. 28, No. 2 (April–June 2002), pp. 137–164.

41. Michael Mous , "The Nexus of Market Society, Liberal Preferences, and Democratic Peace: Interdisciplinary T y and Evidence," *International Studies Quarterly*, Vol. 47, No. 3 (September 2003), in press.

bounded by respect for individual rights and the primacy of democratic law. There is, in short, a market civilization.

The Clash against Market Civilization

Few if any states have predominantly clientalist economies. Most economies are heavily integrated with the market (market democracies) or include some mixture of clientalism and markets (developing countries). Although in many developing countries contracts are officially enforced and regulated, in-group linkages can diminish impartiality. In addition, because clientalist exchange is informal, it lies beyond the regulatory capacity of the state. In this mixed economy, the clash of clientalist and market cultures can lead to illiberal and unstable democracy, military dictatorship, state failure, sectarian violence, or some combination thereof—and bitter anti-Americanism.

In clientalist societies, cooperation occurs with the exchange of gifts, and trust is based on life-long friendships within in-groups. In market societies, loyalty to the in-group is downgraded, as cooperation with strangers is encouraged; trust is based not on friendship but on the perceived universal principle of the sanctity of contractual exchange. Individuals from market cultures thus seek out cooperation universally. From the clientalist perspective, however, those with market values are from out-groups and thus are untrustworthy. Moreover, by expressing self-interest, individuals with market values are viewed as selfish; they appear to have no culture and are seemingly interested in little beyond the crude pursuit of material gain.

Cultures change slowly; so when endogenous factors cause a rise in contractual exchange, a clientalist society's economic norms diverge from prevailing cultural values and beliefs. When this happens, individuals with deeply embedded clientalist values have difficulty grasping new market norms; they perceive that those who are driven by self-interest not only lack strong social ties but have no values at all. This perception is partly true: A society that undergoes economic change may experience a period when there is no common culture, as clientalist linkages break down before market values emerge.

During this period of social anarchy, a zero-sum culture may emerge in which strangers pursue their interests without any regard for shared values—market or clientalist. This explains the circumstances in many developing-world societies today: that is, widespread disrespect for the rule of law (everyone wants the law to apply to someone else); social chaos, as many act without regard for othe (e.g., unwillingness to wait in line or obey rules); and the apparent lack o mpathy for anyone outside one's in-groups (family, friends, and coworkers) From the market perspective, these conditions seem uncivil and are often a med to be a consequence of local indigenous culture (i.e., a "supposed" fu on of Arab culture, Asian culture, and so on). Academics from market cu res have assumed that what people in these countries need is more education a democratic form of government,[44] or time to develop.[45] As I have sought t ow, however, this behavior may not be associated with any particular indig ous culture, form of government, or inherent backwardness. Rather, it may ect the breakdown of clientalist linkages in economies that, facing severe a persistent economic shocks, have not replaced their clientalist values wi market values.

Although gr differences remain across the developing world, traditional clientalist prote ns tend to be strongest in rural areas. Urban communities, on the other ha , are more likely to be in flux, with new patron-client networks (e.g., pol al parties, unions, and mafias) increasingly replacing traditional patron-c t networks (e.g., clans and villages). Strangers in these communities, l ng in both empathy and mutual respect, frequently interact on the basis of if any common values and beliefs. Meanwhile, in-groups compete over s resources in a zero-sum way—with winners taking all. This helps to explai 1) the high frequency of political violence in developing countries; (2) democratic institutions in such countries seem to do so poorly in prod g public goods, such as roads and security; and (3) why the absence of a str state often results in chronic instability, civil conflict, and in some cases stat ilure.

No economic nsition can erase a society's collective history or memory, nor can it elimi the role of external influences, ethnic diversity, and historical animosity a ng competing factions. Moreover, the breakdown of traditional clientalis kages is not the only source of social anarchy in developing countries: War state failure can also be factors, as witnessed in Afghanistan and Soma where both rural and urban areas remain in tremendous

42. As documente Hofstede, *Culture's Consequences.*
43. Daniel Lerner, *Passing of Traditional Society: Modernizing in the Middle East* (New York: Free Press, 1958); and A Inkeles and David Smith, *Becoming Modern: Individual Change in Six Developing Countries* (nbridge, Mass.: Harvard University Press, 1974).
44. Diamond, "Intr ction: In Search of Consolidation."
45. Talcott Parsons volutionary Universals in Society," *American Sociological Review*, Vol. 29, No. 3 (June 1964), 339–357.

flux. Likewise, mineral wealth in a developing economy with weak market norms probably works to reinforce the influence of traditional clientalist in-groups, as patrons spread their riches in return for pledges of loyalty. For the majority of countries without mineral wealth, however, the mire of underdevelopment and economic displacement has meant a rise in social anarchy and civil insecurity.

For many individuals living in this rough-and-tumble Hobbesian world, the new zero-sum culture has a thoroughly Western or American character, as seen on television, in movies, and in other forms of popular culture exported from Europe and the United States. Lacking market values and beliefs, millions of people in developing countries believe that the breakdown of traditional clientalist relationships and the emergence of zero-sum anarchy are results of a growing Westernization or Americanization of their societies, and they deeply resent it. Moreover, a society with clientalist values and beliefs but with fading protections from in-groups is extremely vulnerable to any in-group system that promises to put an end to its deep sense of insecurity. This explains the allure of alternative value systems in developing countries that support ethnic sectarianism, extreme nationalism, or various types of religious fundamentalism.

A brief examination of the impact of economic change in the contemporary period confirms this view. Contractual exchange in the modern period began in northwestern Europe in the 1450s,[46] precipitating for the next 200 years the social and institutional changes brought about during the Protestant Reformation. For three centuries after that, many states in Europe (e.g., England and Holland) began to develop market economies—by enforcing contracts, subsidizing private enterprise, and breaking up clientalist linkages.[47] Only in the twentieth century, however, did the majority of Europeans possess the resources to engage regularly in contractual exchange. The combination of nineteenth-century industrialization and mass migration to the United States greatly increased the demand for, and thus the wages of, labor in Europe. As a result, Europe's majority, once clients in a clientalist world, became buyers in a new market world.[48]

The political repercussions of this socioeconomic transition were vast: Euro-

---

46. Braudel, *Afterthoughts on Material Civilization and Capitalism*, p. 24.
47. As documented by Polanyi, *The Great Transformation*.
48. See Simona Piattoni, ed., *Clientelism, Interests, and Democratic Representation: The European Experience in Historical and Comparative Perspective* (Cambridge: Cambridge University Press, 2001).

pean peasants g e up their way of life—including traditional in-group protection—only to ve in cities in the midst of rapid economic change and seemingly devo of common values and beliefs. Like their counterparts in the nineteenth cent , today's migrants confront a bewildering array of zero-sum conditions and bbesian anarchy. In both cases, the refugees created by these socioeconomic ruptions sought economic and political protection by joining new forms of c talist in-groups; and in both cases, they seem to have perceived the rise narket exchange as lacking any redeeming social value. The consequences w the same in both cases: Just as many Europeans in the last century were d vn to clientalist in-groups that championed antimarket (i.e., socialist, comm ist, or fascist) values, many of today's refugees have been pulled toward timarket socialist, nationalist, or religious political organizations. I say nizations because these clientalist in-groups are not civic-oriented politic parties: They offer all-encompassing social, economic, and political progra in exchange for absolute loyalty.

In the midst industrial change, many Europeans joined ethnic sectarian groups, includi some that identified European Jewry as the cause of their social anarchy. Fr uently, European Jews were merchants and thus tended to behave accordi to market norms by, among other things, expressing self-interest through e use of contracts. Faced with the increasing destruction of their traditional entalist linkages and rising social anarchy, many other Europeans began to ate the proliferation of zero-sum values with Jewish values. Seeking suppo n socially collapsing societies, some political leaders unleashed antima t passions by encouraging pogroms against the seemingly "cultureless" (b really just liberal) Jews. One such leader, Adolf Hitler, was himself from a r migrant section of Vienna—as were many of his followers. While German as in the midst of a rapid transition toward a market economy in the 192 hyperinflation eliminated the savings of the nascent middle class. This caus a widespread loss of faith in contracts, a revival of clientalist values, and an timarket fury that legitimated the mass murder of out-groups. This ex ins why the Nazis replaced the failing market with a state-directed econo and why the Germans (and others) became Hitler's willing executioners."[49] fact, across Europe and across time, the strength of anti-Semitism seem correlate negatively, and the stability of democracy positively, with the ensity of the market economy. One indication of this is the

49. Daniel J. Goldl n, *Hitler's Willing Executioners: Ordinary Germans and the Holocaust* (New York: Alfred A. Kn 1996).

availability of jobs that offer a living wage. Significantly, just one generation after the U.S. imposition and subsidization of a market economy in West Germany following the end of World War II, West Germans were well on their way toward developing a liberal political culture.[50]

Europe's transition to a market economy in the nineteenth and early twentieth centuries led to the rise of antimarket socialist, communist, and fascist movements as well as sectarian terror. Similarly, the transition toward a market economy in many contemporary developing countries is associated with antimarket socialist, ethnofascist, hypernationalist, and religious fundamentalist movements—as well as sectarian terror. Examples include the Marxist guerrillas in Latin America, such as the FARC in Colombia and the Shining Path in Peru; increasing ethnic identification, and popularity of hypernationalist political parties, in parts of Russia and Turkey; and the rise of religious fundamentalism in India and much of the Islamic world. Although the character of these movements varies, the catalyst is the same: bitter opposition to market (liberal) values. Herein lays the source of today's widespread anti-Americanism and anti-Westernism: The liberal way of life in the United States and the rest of the West—its cold materialism, from the clientalist perspective is being broadcast to homes around the world, many of which are transitioning to market economies. In this way, just as the Jews symbolized emerging market norms in Europe a century ago, today, with modern technology, American and Western culture symbolizes the dreaded market norms linked with globalization.

The Resort to Terror

Those on the lowest rung of the economic ladder are the most vulnerable to the negative consequences associated with globalization. Those with the most to lose, however, are patrons and their lieutenants who hold privileged positions in the old clientalist hierarchies. This is why leaders of terrorist organizations frequently come from privileged backgrounds. To maintain the clientalist structure that carries with it higher social status, these leaders seek to rally their client base by appealing to some antimarket ideology. Because it is in a

50. See Ronald Inglehart, *Modernization and Postmodernization: Cultural, Economic, and Political Change in Forty-three Societies* (Princeton, N.J.: Princeton University Press, 1997), p. 175. Of course, the socioeconomic transition cannot explain the long history of anti-Semitism in Europe, much of which predates the rise of markets.

client's interest have a powerful patron, leaders attract and maintain followers by demonst ons of strength. In this way, the mass murder of Westerners serves two pur es: It reflects the leader's power, and it taps into widespread antimarket fury

Islam itself is t responsible for the social approval of terror. Patrons fearing the loss of eir privileged status—such as Osama bin Laden—find an antimarket ide gy useful to attract followers. They manipulate Islam to serve their own ds, just like their counterparts in Europe did a century ago by contorting istianity to justify terror and mass murder.[51] In fact, Islam emerged in Me , the center of sixth-century Mediterranean and South Asian trade, and the an stress the market values of universalism, equity, contractual exchange, d a degree of tolerance toward outsiders (non-Muslims).[52] The market eco ny in this region declined before market norms—and liberal culture—intens d and expanded throughout the Islamic world, but the liberal origins of I n demonstrate that religion can be interpreted, and manipulated, to suit a ne's purposes.

In societies s ed in market values, it is difficult to comprehend how anyone can engage the mass murder of out-groups, or how anyone can support it. Individuals n market values believe that each person is responsible only for his or her a ns. Just as those who are not parties to contracts cannot be made obligated them, individuals cannot be assumed to be responsible for any and all beh or of other members of their apparent in-group. It therefore seems absurd t ame individuals for the alleged bad behavior of others, and this is the socia rigin of the presumption of individual innocence in market societies. From clientalist perspective, in contrast, no one is innocent: Individuals share r onsibility for the actions of others within the in-group; if followers do not pport their leaders, then they are betraying the entire in-group. From th lientalist perspective, all in-group members are privileged and all out-gro members are enemies or, at best, outsiders unworthy of em-

51. Although Osan in Laden is from Saudi Arabia, I do not contend that Saudi Arabia has an emerging market e my. On the contrary, its oil wealth has served to reinforce its clientalist linkages, as patron shei pread their wealth in return for loyalty. With globalization and satellite television, however, p s have reason to feel threatened by the perceived omnipresence of zero-sum norms and ricanization, a fear that fuels resentment toward the West and, more specifically, the pre e of U.S. troops on Saudi soil. Support for al-Qaeda appears in tribal linkages in Saudi Arab d Yemen, as well as in poor Muslim countries facing the social anarchy of development, such Egypt, Indonesia, and Pakistan.

52. Ali A. Mazrui, *tural Forces in World Politics* (Portsmouth, N.H.: Heinemann, 1990).

pathy. A paucity of empathy is necessary for doing harm to, and tolerating the suffering of, all out-group members. This is why international human rights are a concern promoted mostly by market democracies. It is also why widespread social support for both terrorism and sectarian violence frequently arises in developing countries but not in countries with deeply integrated markets.[53]

Clientalist values also lie at the core of the social approval of suicidal mass murder. From the market perspective, all behavior should have some immediate utility for the parties to a contract. It is thus difficult to comprehend the efficacy of suicide. But in cultures where the individual is less important than the group and the absence of science increases devotion to insular beliefs, suicide—under conditions of extreme socioeconomic disruption—may emerge as a socially approved way of expressing ultimate loyalty to the in-group. In this way, cultural insularism, characterized by the absence of a market economy, is a necessary condition for the social approval of suicidal mass murder and sectarian violence.

Cultural insularism combined with a particular grievance—such as the negative consequences associated with globalization—can create a deadly mix for Americans and other Westerners. Although latent anti-Americanism and anti-Westernism exist throughout much of the developing world, these are most likely to rise to the surface during economic crises—when nascent middle classes lose their status and turn against emerging liberal values. This is what is happening, for example, in Indonesia where the recent collapse of the local currency has eliminated the savings of the middle class, just as hyperinflation devastated the savings of Germany's middle class seventy-five years ago. Recent terrorist acts against Indonesian Christians (as symbols of the West) and Westerners directly (the November 2002 bombing of a disco in Bali) are reminiscent of Germany's middle class turning against those it identified with market values, such as European Jews and the West. The West, in this sense, means market civilization.

---

53. The closest possible exceptions that I am aware of are the socially approved lynchings of African Americans by white Southerners in the 1920s and 1930s and the sectarian murders during the Troubles in Northern Ireland. In my view, however, the economies of neither the Southern states in the United States nor Northern Ireland were primarily integrated with contracts—and this helps to explain the sectarian terror. Of course, this is an empirical issue that could be explored in future research.

The Eradicati of Terror

Terrorism has h expressed and underlying causes. Expressed causes are
those that terr ts assert themselves. Emic analysis, in which subjects are
asked to explai why they behave as they do, identifies expressed causes. It
does not explai however, why some acts inflame passions while others go
unnoticed. For tance, hundreds have died in recent violence between Hin-
dus and Musli in India, including many Muslims. Yet these killings have
elicited "an em nally muted headline in the Arab media." When Israelis kill
Muslims, howe , as has occurred in the most recent round of Middle East violence, "it infla s the entire Muslim world."[54] To understand these different
responses, scho s must engage not only in emic but also in etic analysis: They
need to be able interpret the behavior of their subjects. Why do so many Indonesians, for i ance, empathize with the plight of the Palestinians but seem
to express little trage over the deaths of Indian Muslims? The reason is Israel's identifica n with the United States and emerging markets. Although
identification w Islam may be an expressed cause of this rage, the underlying cause is not am but rather a deeply embedded antimarket and thus anti-
American passi —a fury that extends beyond the Islamic world and whose
origins are not derstood even by those espousing hatred for the West.

This sense of ge against market civilization and its shared liberal values
and beliefs—a e that can be inflamed with the addition of any immediate
cause—lies just neath the surface in many developing countries. This is not
to say that all even the majority of people living in the developing world
share this wrath ut that the potential for a clash is ever-present. Once policymakers underst d this, they can begin to develop the kinds of political strategies needed to minate the terrorist threat.

Since the ter st attacks of September 11, three myths have emerged regarding the dir on that these strategies should take; all three threaten to derail efforts to er cate terror. The first myth is that to win the hearts and minds
of people arou the world in the struggle against terror, the United States
must do more t ignal its friendly intentions—for instance, by increasing economic aid and plaining U.S. policies more clearly.[55] This view is mistaken.

---

54. Thomas L. Fri an, "The Core of Muslim Rage," *New York Times*, March 6, 2002, p. A21.
55. Articles represe g influential American think tanks that take this view include Daalder and
Lindsay, "Nasty, Br h, and Long"; and Peter G. Peterson, "Diplomacy and the War on Terrorism," *Foreign Affair* ol. 81, No. 5 (September–October 2002), pp. 74–96.

The rage against the United States as the leading symbol of the West is so deeply embedded in some societies that many will interpret whatever the United States does with malign intent. If the United States offers to increase economic aid, it is seen as imperialist; if it does not, it is neglectful. If the United States intervenes to protect Muslims, as it did in the 1999 Kosovo conflict, critics will rail against U.S. "imperialism" (there must be oil there) or, at best, charge that the United States intentionally delayed the intervention because Americans really hate Muslims. Consider that in clientalist cultures the notion of science—universal truth—is incomprehensible.[56] For this reason, even many educated people in the developing world believe in such nonsense as the notion that 4,000 Jews were warned not to go to work at the World Trade Center on September 11:[57] These people believe what they want to believe, regardless of the evidence before them. In fact, for those enraged against the United States for its perceived zero-sum values, friendly acts will have no positive effect. The implication of this is liberating: In terms of underlying causes, the United States need not worry about how societies that produce or harbor terrorists perceive its actions in the war against terrorism. Given that whatever the United States (and other market democracies) do will be interpreted as malevolent, they may as well behave as they see fit.

The second myth associated with September 11 is that terror arises in the absence of democracy,[58] and therefore the United States should push harder for democratic change in developing countries. This view is also flawed. Stable democracies emerge when people want them to, when they share the liberal values and beliefs that prevail in market economies. It is understandable that scholars, policymakers, and pundits in market democracies value democracy and consider it a cure-all against evil: In market civilization, democratic institutions are a deeply embedded value. There is little evidence, however, that democracy causes liberal values. History shows that democracy without lib-

56. The notion of science should not be confused with the use of advanced technology or education. Science is a process of discovery that assumes that some facts are universal, anyone can challenge another's assertions of fact, and truth is sought through the free competition of ideas. One can be taught the discoveries of advanced physics but still have no concept of challenging assertions of fact scientifically. This is why communist and developing nations can import and modify advanced technology, but the market democracies will always be in the avant-garde of developing knowledge.
57. Thomas L. Friedman, "Global Village Idiocy," *New York Times*, May 12, 2002, sec. 4, p. 15; see also Horan, "Those Young Arab Muslims and Us," p. 54.
58. For example, Crenshaw, "The Causes of Terrorism"; Friedman, "The Free-Speech Bind"; Huntington, "The Age of Muslim Wars"; and Nicholas D. Kristof, "What Is Democracy Anyway?" *New York Times*, May 3, 2002, p. A23.

eral values resu in illiberal democracy and the rise to power of antidemocratic regimes t t frequently display antimarket and clientalist—and therefore terrorist—(ntation, such as the Bolsheviks in Russia and the Nazis in Germany.

The third my to emerge after September 11 is that if people who detest the United States (y had greater exposure to American values, their hatred would dissipat This view is premised on the assumption that because Americans kno they are nice people, others will feel the same way if only they get to kno\ hem better. This view is also inaccurate. Anti-American rage is the result of ple knowing Americans too well. The problem is that they just do not like at they see, because from the clientalist perspective, American values refl a degeneration of culture and the ascendance of zero-sum norms. Ironical the notion that modern culture means no culture is also a common assum on of many academic models of global politics.[60] As I have deduced from analysis of the market economy, however, modern culture does possess v es—the values of contractual exchange. The task for the United States in e struggle against terrorism then is not to expose more of itself but to coun act the ill effects of too much exposure by more subtly demonstrating the eeming aspects of market culture.

To win the w gainst terrorism, the United States and other market democracies must re ve the underlying cause of terror: the deeply embedded antimarket rag ought on by the forces of globalization. To do this, the market democracie ave only one option: to boost developing countries out of the mire of social a rchy and into market development. Most developing countries cannot ma this transition alone, because their leaders are likely to hold clientalist rathe han market values and beliefs. Furthermore, maintaining their grasp on ver typically involves redistributing state resources among winning coaliti of clientalist in-groups. In this way, current forms of foreign aid may actuall einforce values and beliefs that condone terror, as recipient governments u the aid to pay off supporters and reinforce clientalist linkages. In fact, st es report that much foreign aid pays the salaries of bureaucrats and those orking for aid agencies.[61] Because these jobs are frequently

59. See, for instanc riedman, "Global Village Idiocy."
60. See, for instanc Bruce Bueno de Mesquita, James D. Morrow, Randolph M. Siverson, and Alastair Smith, "A stitutional Explanation of the Democratic Peace," *American Political Science Review*, Vol. 93, No. December 1999), pp. 791–807; and Waltz, *Theory of International Politics.*
61. See "Dubious " *Canada and the World Backgrounder*, Vol. 65, No. 6 (May 2000), p. 27.

obtained through clientalist linkages, current forms of aid can actually promote the very clientalist values that can legitimate the resort to terror.

Because governments of developing countries are unlikely to get out of the mire of social anarchy and into market development themselves, an outside power is needed to act as a sort of Leviathan: to push the governments of target countries to establish the prerequisites of a market economy. These include impartial enforcement of contracts and common law; destruction of clientalist linkages (corruption); subsidization of private enterprises (with fair bidding practices); widespread equitable subsidization of small loans so people can purchase homes or start small businesses; and redistribution to widen the scope of opportunities for market engagement. In the 1980s, Ronald Reagan's administration encouraged cuts in the number of state-owned enterprises in a variety of countries. State ownership of enterprises is not the problem, however: The problem is when state ownership prevents an enterprise from competing fairly in the market. In recent years the International Monetary Fund has begun to enforce rules of equity in banking practices.[62] For the most part, however, policymakers have placed greater emphasis on balancing budgets, supporting democratization,[63] and reducing poverty.[64] It is not deregulated markets, democracy, or an absence of poverty that produces liberal values, however, but rather a market economy.[65] Thus, to reduce the social support of terror, market democracies should use economic aid as both a means and an incentive for governments in developing countries (1) to create and enforce bodies of common law that are vital to the functioning of a market economy, and (2) to equitably subsidize local private enterprises with the goal of widespread employment. The latter is critical during the transition period: The availability of living-wage jobs in the market alleviates insecurity and prevents antimarket rage.

Given the deep distrust of U.S. motives among the millions living in the social anarchy of underdevelopment, other market democracies must share the burden of pulling them out of this mire. One option would be to create an in-

62. Ajit Singh, "Aid, Conditionality, and Development," *Development and Change*, Vol. 33, No. 2 (2002), pp. 299–300.
63. James K. Boyce, "Unpacking Aid," *Development and Change*, Vol. 33, No. 2 (2002), p. 242.
64. Graham Bird, "A Suitable Case for Treatment? Understanding the Ongoing Debate about the IMF," *Third World Quarterly*, Vol. 22, No. 5 (October 2001), pp. 823–848.
65. A market economy is not a free market. A market economy is one in which the majority of people routinely engage in contractual exchange. Thus a market economy may be highly regulated (e.g., Sweden) and, in theory at least, be publicly owned. A free market, in contrast, refers to a deregulated or partially regulated economy that can coexist with underdevelpment (e.g., Kenya).

ternational orga zation with substantial powers to monitor compliance with aid conditions, by the donor states yet unconstrained by their independent interests. In thi vay, multilateralism could legitimate the indirect external control of the e nomies of recipient states during their transitions. Multilateral action wou also allow the United States to keep a lower profile and include its allies partners in the war against terror.

The historica ecord shows that market democracies easily cooperate and establish legal gimes among themselves.[66] The European Union and the North Atlantic aty Organization are just two of the many regimes that bind these countries gether. Although differences do occur, they are mostly at the level of tactics not over major goals. Sharing preferences and bounded by the logic of con ctual exchange, market democracies manage their relationships and reso their disputes with other market democracies through a combination of utual respect (equity), common law, and in the absence of law, negotiatio nd compromise. As German Chancellor Gerhard Schröder described his c ntry's recent rift with the United States, "Between friends, there can be fa al differences."[67] Like West Germany after World War II, developing cou ies whose market economies are subsidized are likely to one day have mark conomies, at which time their newly emerged liberal values will reinforce th market-democratic institutions, and there will be no further need of foreign sistance. The social basis of terror against the United States and its allies c l thus be eradicated.

Conclusion

Until now there ve been two general approaches to understanding the motivations behind rorism, one rational and the other cultural. Rational explanations focus on role of political and economic grievances and assume that certain observa factors associated with poverty such as economic inequality, illiteracy, and k of democracy cause terror. None of these approaches, however, has blished a direct causal link between any of these factors and terror. No oes there appear to be a correlation between poverty and terror.

Cultural expl tions, in contrast, focus not on political or economic conditions but on th otion that the values and beliefs of terrorists and their sup-

66. Mousseau, "A onomic Limitation to the Zone of Democratic Peace and Cooperation."
67. Quoted in Stev rlanger, "Moves by Germany to Mend Relations Rebuffed by Bush," *New York Times*, Septem 24, 2002, p. A1.

porters are vastly different from those of their targets. Typically, however, these explanations identify indigenous culture as the causal variable, which makes this approach unsuitable for predicting variation in social support for terror within cultures across both time and place. To grasp the origins of terror and why some support it, scholars need an approach that combines the rationalist identification of observable circumstances with the culturalist emphasis on the way people think.

In this article I drew on several generations of research in anthropology, economics, political science, and sociology to show how the values and beliefs that support terror—a lack of empathy for out-groups, an emphasis on community over the individual, and an incomprehension for objective truth and individual innocence—arise from the clientalist economic linkages that are commonplace in many developing countries. In contrast, values that work against terror—individualism, tolerance, equity, and the rule of common law—arise with a market economy. Because all market economies in the contemporary period have been developed economies, there appears to be a link between underdevelopment and terror. As I have argued, however, the real culprit is social anarchy produced by globalization and the difficulties attending the transition to a market economy. Just as millions in the last century turned to antimarket and sectarian values during the rise of market economies in Europe, today millions in the developing world support antimarket and sectarian values reflected in support for ethnofacism, sectarian murder, and fundamentalist religions—anything that offers psychic comfort in the face of volatile social anarchy.

It follows that there is a market civilization based on common liberal values and beliefs, and that this civilization is in conflict with much of the developing world. Direct and expressed causes bring this conflict to the surface at particular times and places. Beneath the surface, however, lies a deeply embedded clash of cultures: market civilization versus the rest. A number of scholars have noted signs of this conflict but have typically identified indigenous culture, not the market economy, as exogenous.[68] The problem with this view is that it

68. The most prominent argument for this view in recent years appears in Samuel P. Huntington, *The Clash of Civilizations and the Remaking of World Order* (New York: Simon and Schuster, 1996). For empirical challenges to this thesis, see Errol Anthony Henderson and Richard Tucker, "Clear and Present Strangers: The Clash of Civilizations and International Conflict," *International Studies Quarterly*, Vol. 45, No. 2 (June 2001), pp. 317–338; and Bruce M. Russett, John R. Oneal, and Michaelene Cox, "Clash of Civilizations, or Realism and Liberalism Déjà Vu? Some Evidence," *Journal of Peace Research*, Vol. 37, No. 5 (September 2000), pp. 583–609. For Huntington's response to Russett, Oneal, and Cox, see Samuel P. Huntington, "Try Again: A Reply to Russett, Oneal, and Cox," ibid., pp. 609–610.

assumes that l ral values emerge from Western indigenous culture. Although this vie\ ; pervasive,[69] it runs contrary to the historical record. For instance, a genera n after Max Weber wrote about the virtues of the Protestant
ethic,[70] millions f Protestants in the West conspired to murder millions of
Jews.[71] The Naz are just one prominent example of Western barbarism; white
Southern Prote: nts in the United States who participated in lynchings in the
early twentieth ntury are another. To many, it may seem as though liberal
values are inhe tly Western, but this notion rests on a biased selection of the
evidence. It ign s cases of Western barbarity. Empirical research across several disciplines nonstrates that it is market development that correlates with
liberal values.[72] though this conclusion may be unsettling for many scholars
of global politi it offers a better accounting of global history. More important, it carries a erating implication for progressive leaders in the developing
world: The ris f markets and liberal culture will not make a developing
country any m Western than the rise of a market economy in England made
the British any re Dutch.

Nevertheless, ere is nothing in this thesis that argues against other possible sources of a -Americanism and anti-Westernism. Realists and world systems theorists r ;ht focus on the projection of U.S. military power from the
core into the p hery as the source of anti-Americanism; liberal institutionalists may focu n what they consider the unilateralist turn that U.S. foreign
policy recently ms to have taken. These sources of anti-Americanism, however, exist prim ly on the surface and are present mostly in the West and at
universities. A ;lobalization protesters within market democracies, for instance, frequen express anti-American and antimarket sentiments. These
protesters, how r, call for greater global equality—a deeply embedded lib-

69. See, for examp rancis Fukuyama, "The Primacy of Culture," *Journal of Democracy*, Vol. 6,
No. 1 (January 1995 p. 7–14; and Ronald Inglehart, "The Renaissance of Political Culture," *Amer-*
ican Political Scienc view, Vol. 82, No. 4 (December 1988), pp. 1203–1230.
70. Max Weber, *Th otestant Ethic and the Spirit of Capitalism*, trans. Talcott Parsons (New York:
Charles Scribner's s, 1958 [1904–05]).
71. See Goldhagen, *tler's Willing Executioners.*
72. For the observa that a rise in markets liberalizes values, see Braudel, *Afterthoughts on Mate-*
rial Civilization and pitalism. There is extensive cross-national data linking economic development and liberal va ;, with the overwhelming majority of observed cases of development being
cases of market-ori ed development. See Hofstede, *Culture's Consequences;* and Inglehart and
Baker, "Moderniza , Cultural Change, and the Persistence of Traditional Values." For specific
empirical confirma that it is market development—and not other kinds of development—that
promotes liberal v s, see Michael Mousseau, "Market Culture and Peace among Nations: It's
the Market Democr s That Ally," paper presented at the annual meeting of the American Political Science Associa , Boston, Massachusetts, August 26–September 1, 2002.

eral preference. Although these protesters may also express resentment of the market, they do so for the same reason that many people in developing countries resent the market: They are typically young students with little direct experience in the marketplace. Regardless, such anti-Americanism appears only among a minority of the West, and few would suggest that antiglobalization protesters would support the mass murder of Americans and other Westerners—a preference that requires a radically different set of values than those associated with market democracies.

Once the rise of market civilization and its clash with the rest is understood, political strategies for winning the war against terror can be developed. Just as the United States imposed and subsidized the emergence of market economies in Germany and Japan after World War II—effectively liberalizing their cultures—market democracies today must subsidize the rise of markets in developing countries. This does not mean deregulating their economies, which would do little to inhibit clientalist linkages or encourage trust in contractual exchange. Nor is wealth the source of liberal values: Saudi Arabia is one of the world's wealthiest states, but it has a predominantly clientalist economy, which is why it produces terrorists. Rather, it is through the establishment of market economies that the United States and its allies can be made safe from terror.

ehind the Curve

Globalizati and International Terrorism

Audrey Kurth Cronin

The coincidence between the evo ng changes of globalization, the inherent weaknesses of the Arab region, a the inadequate American response to both ensures that terrorism will co ue to be the most serious threat to U.S. and Western interests in the twenty- t century. There has been little creative thinking, however, about how to front the growing terrorist backlash that has been unleashed. Terrorism is a mplicated, eclectic phenomenon, requiring a sophisticated strategy orient toward influencing its means and ends over the long term. Few members the U.S. policymaking and academic communities, however, have the polit capital, intellectual background, or inclination to work together to forge effective, sustained response. Instead, the tendency has been to fall back o tablished bureaucratic mind-sets and prevailing theoretical paradigms tha ave little relevance for the changes in international security that became o us after the terrorist attacks in New York and Washington on September 11, 01.

The current ve of international terrorism, characterized by unpredictable and unpreced d threats from nonstate actors, not only is a reaction to globalization but acilitated by it; the U.S. response to this reality has been reactive and a hronistic. The combined focus of the United States on state-centric threats d its attempt to cast twenty-first-century terrorism into familiar strategic t s avoids and often undermines effective responses to this nonstate phen enon. The increasing threat of globalized terrorism must be met with flexi , multifaceted responses that deliberately and effectively exploit avenues globalization in return; this, however, is not happening.

Audrey Kurth Cron s Specialist in International Terrorism at the Congressional Research Service at the Library of Congress e article was written when she was Visiting Associate Professor at the Edmund A. Walsh School of F n Service and a Research Fellow at the Center for Peace and Security Studies, Georgetown Univer .

I am grateful for pful comments and criticisms on previous drafts from Robert Art, Patrick Cronin, Timothy t, James Ludes, and an anonymous reviewer. I have been greatly influenced by conversations other communications with Martha Crenshaw, to whom I owe a huge debt. None of these pe necessarily agrees with everything here. Also beneficial was a research grant from the School reign Service at Georgetown University. My thanks to research assistants Christopher Conn William Josiger, and Sara Skahill and to the members of my graduate courses on political violen nd terrorism. Portions of this article will be published as "Transnational Terrorism and Securi The Terrorist Threat to Globalization," in Michael E. Brown, ed., *Grave New World: Global Dan in the Twenty-first Century* (Washington, D.C.: Georgetown University Press, forthcoming).

International Security . 27, No. 3 (Winter 2002/03), pp. 30–58

As the primary terrorist target, the United Sates should take the lead in fashioning a forward-looking strategy. As the world's predominant military, economic, and political power, it has been able to pursue its interests throughout the globe with unprecedented freedom since the breakup of the Soviet Union more than a decade ago. Even in the wake of the September 11 terrorist attacks on the World Trade Center and the Pentagon, and especially after the U.S. military action in Afghanistan, the threat of terrorism, mostly consisting of underfunded and ad hoc cells motivated by radical fringe ideas, has seemed unimportant by comparison. U.S. strategic culture has a long tradition of downplaying such atypical concerns in favor of a focus on more conventional state-based military power.[1] On the whole, this has been an effective approach: As was dramatically demonstrated in Afghanistan, the U.S. military knows how to destroy state governments and their armed forces, and the American political leadership and public have a natural bias toward using power to achieve the quickest results. Sometimes it is important to show resolve and respond forcefully.

The United States has been far less impressive, however, in its use of more subtle tools of domestic and international statecraft, such as intelligence, law enforcement, economic sanctions, educational training, financial controls, public diplomacy, coalition building, international law, and foreign aid. In an ironic twist, it is these tools that have become central to the security of the United States and its allies since September 11. In an era of globalized terrorism, the familiar state-centric threats have not disappeared; instead they have been joined by new (or newly threatening) competing political, ideological, economic, and cultural concerns that are only superficially understood, particularly in the West. An examination of the recent evolution of terrorism and a projection of future developments suggest that, in the age of globalized terrorism, old attitudes are not just anachronistic; they are dangerous.

Terrorism as a phenomenon is not new, but for reasons explained below, the threat it now poses is greater than ever before. The current terrorist backlash is manifested in the extremely violent asymmetrical response directed at the United States and other leading powers by terrorist groups associated with or inspired by al-Qaeda. This backlash has the potential to fundamentally threaten the international system. Thus it is not just an American problem. Unless the United States and its allies formulate a more comprehensive re-

1. The issue of U.S. strategic culture and its importance in the response to international terrorism is explored in more depth in Audrey Kurth Cronin, "Rethinking Sovereignty: American Strategy in the Age of Terror," *Survival*, Vol. 44, No. 2 (Summer 2002), pp. 119–139.

sponse to terror ı, better balanced across the range of policy instruments, the results will be i reasing international instability and long-term failure.

The article pr eeds in five main sections. First, it provides a discussion of the definition, h ory, causes, and types of terrorism, placing the events of September 11, 2001 their modern context. Second, it briefly describes key trends in modern terro m, explaining how the phenomenon appears to be evolving. Third, it analyz he implications of these trends for the stability and security of the internati l community generally, and the United States and its allies more specificall Fourth, the article outlines the prospects of these trends. It concludes with ange of policy recommendations suggested by the analysis.

Definition, O ins, Motivations, and Types of Modern Terrorism

The terrorist ph omenon has a long and varied history, punctuated by lively debates over tl meaning of the term. By ignoring this history, the United States runs the k of repeating the plethora of mistakes made by other major powers that fac similar threats in the past. This section begins with an explanation of the inition of terrorism, then proceeds to an examination of terrorism's orig , major motivations, and predominant types.

DEFINITION OF RORISM

Terrorism is n riously difficult to define, in part because the term has evolved and in t because it is associated with an activity that is designed to be subjective. G erally speaking, the targets of a terrorist episode are not the victims who ar illed or maimed in the attack, but rather the governments, publics, or con uents among whom the terrorists hope to engender a reaction—such as r, repulsion, intimidation, overreaction, or radicalization. Specialists in th rea of terrorism studies have devoted hundreds of pages toward trying to velop an unassailable definition of the term, only to realize the fruitlessnes their efforts: Terrorism is intended to be a matter of perception and is thu en differently by different observers.[2]

Although inc duals can disagree over whether particular actions constitute terrorism, re are certain aspects of the concept that are fundamental.

---

2. On the difficulty lefining terrorism, see, for example, Omar Malik, *Enough of the Definition of Terrorism!* Royal In te of International Affairs (London: RIIA, 2001); and Alex P. Schmid, *Political Terrorism: A Re h Guide* (New Brunswick, N.J.: Transaction Books, 1984). Schmid spends more than 100 page appling with the question of a definition, only to conclude that none is universally accepted.

First, terrorism always has a political nature. It involves the commission of outrageous acts designed to precipitate political change.[3] At its root, terrorism is about justice, or at least someone's perception of it, whether man-made or divine. Second, although many other uses of violence are inherently political, including conventional war among states, terrorism is distinguished by its nonstate character—even when terrorists receive military, political, economic, and other means of support from state sources. States obviously employ force for political ends: When state force is used internationally, it is considered an act of war; when it is used domestically, it is called various things, including law enforcement, state terror, oppression, or civil war. Although states can terrorize, they cannot by definition be terrorists. Third, terrorism deliberately targets the innocent, which also distinguishes it from state uses of force that inadvertently kill innocent bystanders. In any given example, the latter may or may not be seen as justified; but again, this use of force is different from terrorism. Hence the fact that precision-guided missiles sometimes go astray and kill innocent civilians is a tragic use of force, but it is not terrorism. Finally, state use of force is subject to international norms and conventions that may be invoked or at least consulted; terrorists do not abide by international laws or norms and, to maximize the psychological effect of an attack, their activities have a deliberately unpredictable quality.[4]

Thus, at a minimum, terrorism has the following characteristics: a fundamentally political nature, the surprise use of violence against seemingly random targets, and the targeting of the innocent by nonstate actors.[5] All of these attributes are illustrated by recent examples of terrorism—from the April 2000 kidnapping of tourists by the Abu Sayyaf group of the Philippines to the various incidents allegedly committed by al-Qaeda, including the 1998 bombings of the U.S. embassies in Kenya and Tanzania and the September 11 attacks. For the purposes of this discussion, the shorthand (and admittedly imperfect) definition of terrorism is the threat or use of seemingly random violence against innocents for political ends by a nonstate actor.

---

3. Saying that terrorism is a political act is not the same as arguing that the political ends toward which it is directed are necessarily negotiable. If violent acts do not have a political aim, then they are by definition criminal acts.
4. The diabolical nature of terrorism has given resonance to Robert Kaplan's view that the world is a "grim landscape" littered with "evildoers" and requiring Western leaders to adopt a "pagan ethos." But such conclusions deserve more scrutiny than space allows here. See Steven Mufson, "The Way Bush Sees the World," *Washington Post*, Outlook section, February 17, 2002, p. B1.
5. R.G. Frey and Christopher W. Morris, "Violence, Terrorism, and Justice," in Frey and Morris, eds., *Violence, Terrorism, and Justice* (Cambridge: Cambridge University Press, 1991), p. 3.

ORIGINS OF TER RISM

Terrorism is as l as human history. One of the first reliably documented instances of terro n, however, occurred in the first century B.C.E. The Zealots-Sicarri, Jewish rorists dedicated to inciting a revolt against Roman rule in Judea, murdere heir victims with daggers in broad daylight in the heart of Jerusalem, ever lly creating such anxiety among the population that they generated a ma nsurrection.[6] Other early terrorists include the Hindu Thugs and the Muslin ssassins. Modern terrorism, however, is generally considered to have or nated with the French Revolution.[7]

The term "te " was first employed in 1795, when it was coined to refer to a policy system lly used to protect the fledgling French republic government against counter olutionaries. Robespierre's practice of using revolutionary tribunals as a n ns of publicizing a prisoner's fate for broader effect within the population art from questions of legal guilt or innocence) can be seen as a nascent exam of the much more highly developed, blatant manipulation of media attent by terrorist groups in the mid- to late twentieth century.[8] Modern terrori is a dynamic concept, from the outset dependent to some degree on the litical and historical context within which it has been employed.

DECOLONIZATIO ND ANTIGLOBALIZATION: DRIVERS OF TERRORISM?

Although indiv al terrorist groups have unique characteristics and arise in specific local c exts, an examination of broad historical patterns reveals that the intern nal system within which such groups are spawned does influence their ure and motivations. A distinguishing feature of modern terrorism has bee e connection between sweeping political or ideological concepts and incr ing levels of terrorist activity internationally. The broad political aim ha een against (1) empires, (2) colonial powers, and (3) the U.S.-led internation ystem marked by globalization. Thus it is important to understand the ge al history of modern terrorism and where the current threat fits within an i rnational context.

---

6. Walter Laqueur, *orism* (London: Weidenfeld and Nicolson, 1977, reprinted in 1978), pp. 7–8; and David C. Rapo t, "Fear and Trembling: Terrorism in Three Religious Traditions," *American Political Science Re* Vol. 78, No. 3 (September 1984), pp. 658–677.
7. David C. Rapop "The Fourth Wave: September 11 in the History of Terrorism," *Current History*, December 200 p. 419–424; and David C. Rapoport, "Terrorism," *Encyclopedia of Violence, Peace, and Conflict* (York: Academic Press, 1999).
8. Ironically, Robes re's tactics during the Reign of Terror would not be included in this article's definition of terrori because it was state terror.

David Rapoport has described modern terrorism such as that perpetuated by al-Qaeda as part of a religiously inspired "fourth wave." This wave follows three earlier historical phases in which terrorism was tied to the breakup of empires, decolonization, and leftist anti-Westernism.[9] Rapoport argues that terrorism occurs in consecutive if somewhat overlapping waves. The argument here, however, is that modern terrorism has been a power struggle along a continuum: central power versus local power, big power versus small power, modern power versus traditional power. The key variable is a widespread perception of opportunity, combined with a shift in a particular political or ideological paradigm. Thus, even though the newest international terrorist threat, emanating largely from Muslim countries, has more than a modicum of religious inspiration, it is more accurate to see it as part of a larger phenomenon of antiglobalization and tension between the have and have-not nations, as well as between the elite and underprivileged within those nations. In an era where reforms occur at a pace much slower than is desired, terrorists today, like those before them, aim to exploit the frustrations of the common people (especially in the Arab world).

In the nineteenth century, the unleashing of concepts such as universal suffrage and popular empowerment raised the hopes of people throughout the western world, indirectly resulting in the first phase of modern terrorism. Originating in Russia, as Rapoport argues, it was stimulated not by state repression but by the efforts of the czars to placate demands for economic and political reforms, and the inevitable disappointment of popular expectations that were raised as a result. The goal of terrorists was to engage in attacks on symbolic targets to get the attention of the common people and thus provoke a popular response that would ultimately overturn the prevailing political order. This type of modern terrorism was reflected in the activities of groups such as the Russian Narodnaya Volya (People's Will) and later in the development of a series of movements in the United States and Europe, especially in territories of the former Ottoman Empire.

The dissolution of empires and the search for a new distribution of political power provided an opportunity for terrorism in the nineteenth and twentieth centuries. It climaxed in the assassination of Archduke Franz Ferdinand on June 28, 1914, an event that catalyzed the major powers into taking violent action, not because of the significance of the man himself but because of the sus-

9. Rapoport, "The Fourth Wave."

picion of rival s ↄ involvement in the sponsorship of the killing. World War I, the convulsive : temic cataclysm that resulted, ended the first era of modern terrorism, acco ıg to Rapoport.[10] But terrorism tied to popular movements seeking greater ·mocratic representation and political power from coercive empires has no ·ased. Consider, for example, the Balkans after the downfall of the former st : of Yugoslavia. The struggle for power among various Balkan ethnic grou can be seen as the final devolution of power from the former Ottoman Empi This postimperial scramble is also in evidence elsewhere— for example, in ceh, Chechnya, and Xinjiang, to mention just a few of the trouble spots w in vast (former) empires. The presentation of a target of opportunity, such a liberalizing state or regime, frequently evokes outrageous terrorist acts.

According to poport, a second, related phase of modern terrorism associated with the cc ept of national self-determination developed its greatest predominance aft Vorld War I. It also continues to the present day. These struggles for pc ·r are another facet of terrorism against larger political powers and are spe cally designed to win political independence or autonomy. The mid-twent h-century era of rapid decolonization spawned national movements in t ·itories as diverse as Algeria, Israel, South Africa, and Vietnam.[11] An imp ınt by-product was ambivalence toward the phenomenon in the internation :ommunity, with haggling over the definition of terrorism reaching a feve itch in the United Nations by the 1970s.

The question political motivation became important in determining international attitud toward terrorist attacks, as the post–World War II backlash against the col al powers and the attractiveness of national independence movements led the creation of a plethora of new states often born from violence. Argumen over the justice of international causes and the designation of terrorist stru ;les as "wars of national liberation" predominated, with consequentialis hilosophies excusing the killing of innocent people if the cause in the lo run was "just." Rapoport sees the U.S. intervention in Vietnam, and espec ly the subsequent American defeat by the Vietcong, as having catalyzed a hird wave" of modern terrorism; however, the relationship between the Vi am conflict and other decolonization movements might just as easily be con lered part of the same phase. In any case, the victory of the

10. Ibid., pp. 419–4
11. Ibid., p. 420.

Vietcong excited the imaginations of revolutionaries throughout the world and, according to Rapoport, helped lead to a resurgence in terrorist violence. The Soviet Union underwrote the nationalist and leftist terrorist agendas of some groups, depicting the United States as the new colonial power—an easy task following the Vietnam intervention—and furthering an ideological agenda oriented toward achieving a postcapitalist, international communist utopia. Other groups, especially in Western Europe, rejected both the Soviet and capitalist models and looked admiringly toward nationalist revolutionaries in the developing world.[12] Leftist groups no longer predominate, but the enduring search for national self-determination continues, not only in the areas mentioned above but also in other hot spots such as the Basque region, East Timor, Sri Lanka, and Sudan.

Terrorism achieved a firmly international character during the 1970s and 1980s,[13] evolving in part as a result of technological advances and partly in reaction to the dramatic explosion of international media influence. International links were not new, but their centrality was. Individual, scattered national causes began to develop into international organizations with links and activities increasingly across borders and among differing causes. This development was greatly facilitated by the covert sponsorship of states such as Iran, Libya, and North Korea, and of course the Soviet Union, which found the underwriting of terrorist organizations an attractive tool for accomplishing clandestine goals while avoiding potential retaliation for the terrorist attacks.

The 1970s and 1980s represented the height of state-sponsored terrorism. Sometimes the lowest common denominator among the groups was the concept against which they were reacting—for example, "Western imperialism"—rather than the specific goals they sought. The most important innovation, however, was the increasing commonality of international connections among the groups. After the 1972 Munich Olympics massacre of eleven Israeli athletes, for example, the Palestinian Liberation Organization (PLO) and its associated groups captured the imaginations of young radicals around the world. In Lebanon and elsewhere, the PLO also provided training in the pre-

12. Adrian Gulke, *The Age of Terrorism and the International Political System* (London: I.B. Tauris, 1995), pp. 56–63.

13. This is not to imply that terrorism lacked international links before the 1970s. There were important international ties between anarchist groups of the late nineteenth century, for example. See David C. Rapoport, "The Four Waves of Modern Terrorism," in Audrey Kurth Cronin and James Ludes, eds., *The Campaign against International Terrorism* (Washington, D.C.: Georgetown University Press, forthcoming).

ferred techniqu of twentieth-century terrorism such as airline hijacking, hostage taking, an ombing.

Since the Sep nber 11 attacks, the world has witnessed the maturation of a new phase of t orist activity, the jihad era, spawned by the Iranian Revolution of 1979 as ll as the Soviet defeat in Afghanistan shortly thereafter. The powerful attrac n of religious and spiritual movements has overshadowed the nationalist eftist revolutionary ethos of earlier terrorist phases (though many of those ggles continue), and it has become the central characteristic of a growing i rnational trend. It is perhaps ironic that, as Rapoport observes, the forc f history seem to be driving international terrorism back to a much earlier ti with echoes of the behavior of "sacred" terrorists such as the Zealots-Sic clearly apparent in the terrorist activities of organizations such as al-Qae and its associated groups. Religious terrorism is not new; rather it is a con uation of an ongoing modern power struggle between those with power an ose without it. Internationally, the main targets of these terrorists are the ted States and the U.S.-led global system.

Like other er of modern terrorism, this latest phase has deep roots. And given the histo al patterns, it is likely to last at least a generation, if not longer. The jiha ra is animated by widespread alienation combined with elements of religi identity and doctrine—a dangerous mix of forces that resonate deep in th uman psyche.

What is diffe t about this phase is the urgent requirement for solutions that deal both h the religious fanatics who are the terrorists and the far more politicall notivated states, entities, and people who would support them because t feel powerless and left behind in a globalizing world. Thus if there is a tre in terrorism, it is the existence of a two-level challenge: the hyperreligious tivation of small groups of terrorists and the much broader enabling enviro ent of bad governance, nonexistent social services, and poverty that punct es much of the developing world. Al-Qaeda, a band driven by religious ext nism, is able to do so much harm because of the secondary support and sa uary it receives in vast areas that have not experienced the political and ec mic benefits of globalization. Therefore, the prescription for dealing with O a bin Laden and his followers is not just eradicating a relatively small nu er of terrorists, but also changing the conditions that allow them to acquir much power. Leaving aside for the moment the enabling environment, i useful to focus on the chief motivations of the terrorists themselves, es ially the contrasting secular and spiritual motivations of terrorism.

LEFTIST, RIGHTIST, ETHNONATIONALIST/SEPARATIST, AND "SACRED" TERRORISM

There are four types of terrorist organizations currently operating aound the world, categorized mainly by their source of motivation: left-wing terrorists, right-wing terrorists, ethnonationalist/separatist terrorists, and religious or "sacred" terrorists. All four types have enjoyed periods of relative prominence in the modern era, with left-wing terrorism intertwined with the Communist movement,[14] right-wing terrorism drawing its inspiration from Fascism,[15] and the bulk of ethnonationalist/separatist terrorism accompanying the wave of decolonization especially in the immediate post–World War II years. Currently, "sacred" terrorism is becoming more significant.[16] Although groups in all categories continue to exist today, left-wing and right-wing terrorist groups were more numerous in earlier decades. Of course, these categories are not perfect, as many groups have a mix of motivating ideologies—some ethnonationalist groups, for example, have religious characteristics or agendas[17]—but usually one ideology or motivation dominates.

Categories are useful not simply because classifying the groups gives scholars a more orderly field to study (admittedly an advantage), but also because different motivations have sometimes led to differing styles and modes of behavior. Understanding the type of terrorist group involved can provide insight into the likeliest manifestations of its violence and the most typical patterns of its development. At the risk of generalizing, left-wing terrorist organizations, driven by liberal or idealist political concepts, tend to prefer revolutionary, antiauthoritarian, antimaterialistic agendas. (Here it is useful to distinguish between the idealism of individual terrorists and the frequently contradictory motivations of their sponsors.) In line with these preferences, left-wing organizations often engage in brutal criminal-type behavior such as kidnapping, murder, bombing, and arson, often directed at elite targets that symbolize authority. They have difficulty, however, agreeing on their long-term

14. Groups such as the Second of June Movement, the Baader-Meinhof Gang, the Red Brigades, the Weathermen, and the Symbionese Liberation Army belong in this category.
15. Among right-wing groups would be other neo-Nazi organizations (in the United States and Europe) and some members of American militia movements such as the Christian Patriots and the Ku Klux Klan.
16. The list here would be extremely long, including groups as different as the Tamil Tigers of Sri Lanka, the Basque separatist party, the PLO, and the Irish Republican Army (IRA) and its various splinter groups.
17. Bruce Hoffman notes that secular terrorist groups that have a strong religious element include the Provisional IRA, Armenian factions, and perhaps the PLO; however, the political/separatist aspect is the predominant characteristic of these groups. Hoffman, "Terrorist Targeting: Tactics, Trends, and Potentialities," *Technology and Terrorism* (London: Frank Cass, 1993), p. 25.

objectives.[18] M left-wing organizations in twentieth-century Western Europe, for examp were brutal but relatively ephemeral. Of course, right-wing terrorists can b uthless, but in their most recent manifestations they have tended to be le cohesive and more impetuous in their violence than leftist terrorist groups heir targets are often chosen according to race but also ethnicity, religion, immigrant status, and in recent decades at least, have been more opportun c than calculated.[19] This makes them potentially explosive but difficult to k.[20] Ethnonationalist/separatist terrorists are the most conventional, usua having a clear political or territorial aim that is rational and potentially neg ble, if not always justifiable in any given case. They can be astoundingly vi nt, over lengthy periods. At the same time, it can be difficult to distinguish b veen goals based on ethnic identity and those rooted in the control of a pie of land. With their focus on gains to be made in the traditional state-orie d international system, ethnonationalist/separatist terrorists often trans n in and out of more traditional paramilitary structures, depending on h the cause is going. In addition, they typically have sources of support amo the local populace of the same ethnicity with whom their separatist goals appeals to blood links) may resonate. That broader popular support is usua the key to the greater average longevity of ethnonationalist/separatist grou n the modern era.[21]

---

18. An interesting nple is France's Action Directe, which revised its raison d'être several times, often altering it to ct domestic issues in France—anarchism and Maoism, dissatisfaction with NATO and the A canization of Europe, and general anticapitalism. See Michael Dartnell, "France's Action D e: Terrorists in Search of a Revolution," *Terrorism and Political Violence*, Vol. 2, No. 4 (Winter 19 pp. 457–488.

19. For example, i 1990s Germany and several other European countries experienced a rash of random arson a ks against guest houses and offices that provided services to immigrants, many of whom w Middle Eastern in origin. Other examples include the violence associated with groups such a rope's "football hooligans." A possible American example of the opportunistic nature of rig ving terrorism may be the anthrax letter campaign conducted in October 2001. See Susan Sch lt, "Anthrax Letter Suspect Profiled: FBI Says Author Likely Is Male Loner; Ties to Bin Laden Doubted," *Washington Post*, November 11, 2001, p. A1; and Steve Fainaru, "Officials Continue Doubt Hijackers' Link to Anthrax: Fla. Doctor Says He Treated One for Skin Form of Disease," *hington Post*, March 24, 2002, p. A23.

20. It is interesting note that, according to Christopher C. Harmon, in Germany, 1991 was the first year that the n er of indigenous rightist radicals exceeded that of leftists. Harmon, *Terrorism Today* (London: nk Cass, 2000), p. 3.

21. For example, i scussing the longevity of terrorist groups, Martha Crenshaw notes only three significant te st groups with ethnonationalist ideologies that ceased to exist within ten years of their form n (one of these, EOKA, disbanded because its goal—the liberation of Cyprus—was attained y contrast, a majority of the terrorist groups she lists as having existed for ten years or longer e recognizable ethnonationalist ideologies, including the IRA (in its many

All four types of terrorist organizations are capable of egregious acts of barbarism. But religious terrorists may be especially dangerous to international security for at least five reasons.

First, religious terrorists often feel engaged in a Manichaean struggle of good against evil, implying an open-ended set of human targets: Anyone who is not a member of their religion or religious sect may be "evil" and thus fair game. Although indiscriminate attacks are not unique to religious terrorists, the exclusivity of their faith may lead them to dehumanize their victims even more than most terrorist groups do, because they consider nonmembers to be infidels or apostates—as perhaps, for instance, al-Qaeda operatives may have viewed Muslims killed in the World Trade Center.

Second, religious terrorists engage in violent behavior directly or indirectly to please the perceived commands of a deity. This has a number of worrisome implications: The whims of the deity may be less than obvious to those who are not members of the religion, so the actions of violent religious organizations can be especially unpredictable. Moreover, religious terrorists may not be as constrained in their behavior by concerns about the reactions of their human constituents. (Their audience lies elsewhere.)

Third, religious terrorists consider themselves to be unconstrained by secular values or laws. Indeed the very target of the attacks may be the law-based secular society that is embodied in most modern states. The driving motivation, therefore, is to overturn the current post-Westphalian state system—a much more fundamental threat than is, say, ethnonationalist terrorism purporting to carve out a new secular state or autonomous territory.

Fourth, and related, religious terrorists often display a complete sense of alienation from the existing social system. They are not trying to correct the system, making it more just, more perfect, and more egalitarian. Rather they are trying to replace it. In some groups, apocalyptic images of destruction are seen as a necessity—even a purifying regimen—and this makes them uniquely dangerous, as was painfully learned on September 11.[22]

---

forms), Sikh separatist groups, Euskadi Ta Askatasuna, the various Palestinian nationalist groups, and the Corsican National Liberation Front. See Crenshaw, "How Terrorism Declines," *Terrorism and Political Violence*, Vol. 3, No. 1 (Spring 1991), pp. 69–87.

22. On the characteristics of modern religious terrorist groups, see Bruce Hoffman, *Inside Terrorism* (New York: Columbia University Press, 1998), especially pp. 94–95; and Bruce Hoffman, "Terrorism Trends and Prospects," in Ian O. Lesser, Bruce Hoffman, John Arguilla, Michelle Zanini, and David Ronfeldt, eds., *Countering the New Terrorism* (Santa Monica, Calif.: RAND, 1999), especially pp. 19–20. On the peculiar twists of one apocalyptic vision, see Robert Jay Lifton, *Destroying the*

Fifth, religioı errorism is especially worrisome because of its dispersed popular suppor ı civil society. On the one hand, for example, groups such as al-Qaeda are ab to find support from some Muslim nongovernmental foundations througl t the world,[23] making it truly a global network. On the other hand, in the ı cess of trying to distinguish between the relatively few providers of se us support from the majority of genuinely philanthropic groups, there is e real risk of igniting the very holy war that the terrorists may be seeking the first instance.

In sum, there e both enduring and new aspects to modern terrorism. The enduring featu center on the common political struggles that have characterized major a of international terrorism. The newest and perhaps most alarming aspect the increasingly religious nature of modern terrorist groups. Against this his ical background, the unique elements in the patterns of terrorist activity s ounding September 11 appear starkly.

Key Trends in lodern Terrorism

By the late 1990 our trends in modern terrorism were becoming apparent: an increase in the cidence of religiously motivated attacks, a decrease in the overall numbeı f attacks, an increase in the lethality per attack, and the growing targeti of Americans.

Statistics shov hat, even before the September 11 attacks, religiously motivated terrorist anizations were becoming more common. The acceleration of this trend has een dramatic: According to the RAND–St. Andrews University Chronolog f International Terrorism,[24] in 1968 none of the identified international terrı t organizations could be classified as "religious"; in 1980, in the aftermath o e Iranian Revolution, there were 2 (out of 64), and that number had expanc to 25 (out of 58) by 1995.[25]

World to Save It: Au ıinrikyo, Apocalyptic Violence, and the New Global Terrorism (New York: Henry Holt, 1999).

23. There is a lon t of people and organizations sanctioned under Executive Order 13224, signed on Septemb 3, 2001. Designated charitable organizations include the Benevolence International Foundati and the Global Relief Foundation. The list is available at http:// www.treas.gov/off /enforcement/ofac/sanctions/t11ter.pdf (accessed November 26, 2002).

24. The RAND–St. drews University Chronology of International Terrorism is a databank of terrorist incidents t begins in 1968 and has been maintained since 1972 at St. Andrews University, Scotland, and RAND Corporation, Santa Monica, California.

25. Hoffman, *Insid rorism*, pp. 90–91; and Nadine Gurr and Benjamin Cole, *The New Face of Terrorism: Threats from apons of Mass Destruction* (London: I.B. Tauris, 2000), pp. 28–29.

Careful analysis of terrorism data compiled by the U.S. Department of State reveals other important trends regarding the frequency and lethality of terrorist attacks. The good news was that there were fewer such attacks in the 1990s than in the 1980s: Internationally, the number of terrorist attacks in the 1990s averaged 382 per year, whereas in the 1980s the number per year averaged 543.[26] But even before September 11, the absolute number of casualties of international terrorism had increased, from a low of 344 in 1991 to a high of 6,693 in 1998.[27] The jump in deaths and injuries can be partly explained by a few high-profile incidents, including the bombing of the U.S. embassies in Nairobi and Dar-es-Salaam in 1998;[28] but it is significant that more people became victims of terrorism as the decade proceeded. More worrisome, the number of people killed per incident rose significantly, from 102 killed in 565 incidents in 1991 to 741 killed in 274 incidents in 1998.[29] Thus, even though the number of terrorist attacks declined in the 1990s, the number of people killed in each one increased.

Another important trend relates to terrorist attacks involving U.S. targets. The number of such attacks increased in the 1990s, from a low of 66 in 1994 to a high of 200 in the year 2000.[30] This is a long established problem: U.S. nationals consistently have been the most targeted since 1968.[31] But the percentage of international attacks against U.S. targets or U.S. citizens rose dramatically over the 1990s, from about 20 percent in 1993–95 to almost 50 percent in 2000.[32] This is perhaps a consequence of the increased role and profile of the United States in the world, but the degree of increase is nonetheless troubling.

The increasing lethality of terrorist attacks was already being noticed in the late 1990s, with many terrorism experts arguing that the tendency toward more casualties per incident had important implications. First it meant that, as had been feared, religious or "sacred" terrorism was apparently more dangerous than the types of terrorism that had predominated earlier in the twentieth

26. Statistics compiled from data in U.S. Department of State, *Patterns of Global Terrorism*, published annually by the Office of the Coordinator for Counterterrorism, U.S. Department of State.
27. Ibid. For a graphical depiction of this information, created on the basis of annual data from *Patterns of Global Terrorism*, see Cronin, "Rethinking Sovereignty," p. 126.
28. In the 1998 embassy bombings alone, for example, 224 people were killed (with 12 Americans among them), and 4,574 were injured (including 15 Americans). U.S. Department of State, *Patterns of Global Terrorism, 1998*.
29. Ibid. For a graphical depiction of deaths per incident, created on the basis of annual data from *Patterns of Global Terrorism*, see Cronin, "Rethinking Sovereignty," p. 128.
30. Ibid.
31. Hoffman, "Terrorist Targeting," p. 24.
32. U.S. Department of State, *Patterns of Global Terrorism*, various years.

century. The w(l was facing the resurgence of a far more malignant type of terrorism, whos ethality was borne out in the larger death toll from incidents that increasingl nvolved a religious motivation.[33] Second, with an apparent premium now a parently placed on causing more casualties per incident, the incentives for t(rist organizations to use chemical, biological, nuclear, or radiological (CBN weapons would multiply. The breakup of the Soviet Union and the resultir ncreased availability of Soviet chemical, biological, and nuclear weapons (sed experts to argue that terrorist groups, seeking more dramatic and dead results, would be more drawn to these weapons.[34] The 1995 sarin gas attack the Japanese cult Aum Shinrikyo in the Tokyo subway system seemed to firm that worry. More recently, an examination of evidence taken from Afg nistan and Pakistan reveals al-Qaeda's interest in chemical, biological, and clear weapons.[35]

In addition t he evolving motivation and character of terrorist attacks, there has been otable dispersal in the geography of terrorist acts—a trend that is likely to ntinue. Although the Middle East continues to be the locus of most terroris ctivity, Central and South Asia, the Balkans, and the Transcaucasus have b n growing in significance over the past decade. International connections the elves are not new: International terrorist organizations inspired by comn revolutionary principles date to the early nineteenth century; clandestir tate use of foreign terrorist organizations occurred as early as the 1920s (e.g he Mussolini government in Italy aided the Croat Ustasha); and complex m s of funding, arms, and other state support for international terrorist organi ions were in place especially in the 1970s and 1980s.[36] During the Cold V , terrorism was seen as a form of surrogate warfare and

33. Examples inclu(Bruce Hoffman, *"Holy Terror": The Implications of Terrorism Motivated by a Religious Imperative,* ND Paper P-7834 (Santa Monica, Calif.: RAND, 1993); and Mark Juergensmeyer, "Te Mandated by God," *Terrorism and Political Violence,* Vol. 9, No. 2 (Summer 1997), pp. 16–23.

34. See, for exampl teven Simon and Daniel Benjamin, "America and the New Terrorism," *Survival,* Vol. 42, No. pring 2000), pp. 59–75, as well as the responses in the subsequent issue, "America and the N Terrorism: An Exchange," *Survival,* Vol. 42, No. 2 (Summer 2000), pp. 156–172; and Hoffman, rrorism Trends and Prospects," pp. 7–38.

35. See Peter Finn Sarah Delaney, "Al-Qaeda's Tracks Deepen in Europe," *Washington Post,* October 22, 2001, p ; Kamran Khan and Molly Moore, "2 Nuclear Experts Briefed Bin Laden, Pakistanis Say," *Wa gton Post,* December, 12, 2001, p. A1; James Risen and Judith Miller, "A Nation Challenged: Cl ical Weapons—Al Qaeda Sites Point to Tests of Chemicals," *New York Times,* November 11, 2001 B1; Douglas Frantz and David Rohde, "A Nation Challenged: Biological Terror—2 Pakistani nked to Papers on Anthrax Weapons," *New York Times,* November 28, 2001; and David Rohde, Nation Challenged: The Evidence—Germ Weapons Plans Found at a Scientist's House in Kab *New York Times,* December 1, 2001.

36. Laqueur, *Terror,* pp. 112–116.

seemed almost palatable to some, at least compared to the potential prospect of major war or nuclear cataclysm.[37] What has changed is the self-generating nature of international terrorism, with its diverse economic means of support allowing terrorists to carry out attacks sometimes far from the organization's base. As a result, there is an important and growing distinction between where a terrorist organization is spawned and where an attack is launched, making the attacks difficult to trace to their source.

Reflecting all of these trends, al-Qaeda and its associated groups[38] (and individuals) are harbingers of a new type of terrorist organization. Even if al-Qaeda ceases to exist (which is unlikely), the dramatic attacks of September 2001, and their political and economic effects, will continue to inspire similarly motivated groups—particularly if the United States and its allies fail to develop broad-based, effective counterterrorist policies over the long term. Moreover, there is significant evidence that the global links and activities that al-Qaeda and its associated groups perpetuated are not short term or anomalous. Indeed they are changing the nature of the terrorist threat as we move further into the twenty-first century. The resulting intersection between the United States, globalization, and international terrorism will define the major challenges to international security.

The United States, Globalization, and International Terrorism

Whether deliberately intending to or not, the United States is projecting uncoordinated economic, social, and political power even more sweepingly than it is in military terms. Globalization,[39] in forms including Westernization, secularization, democratization, consumerism, and the growth of market capitalism, represents an onslaught to less privileged people in conservative cultures repelled by the fundamental changes that these forces are bringing—or angered by the distortions and uneven distributions of benefits that result.[40] This

---

37. Ibid., pp. 115–116.
38. Groups with known or alleged connections to al-Qaeda include Jemaah Islamiyah (Indonesia, Malaysia, and Singapore), the Abu Sayyaf group (Philippines), al-Gama'a al-Islamiyya (Egypt), Harakat ul-Mujahidin (Pakistan), the Islamic Movement of Uzbekistan (Central Asia), Jaish-e-Mohammed (India and Pakistan), and al-Jihad (Egypt).
39. For the purposes of this article, globalization is a gradually expanding process of interpenetration in the economic, political, social, and security realms, uncontrolled by (or apart from) traditional notions of state sovereignty. Victor D. Cha, "Globalization and the Study of International Security," *Journal of Peace Research*, Vol. 37, No. 3 (March 2000), pp. 391–393.
40. With respect to the Islamic world, there are numerous books and articles that point to the phenomenon of antipathy with the Western world, either because of broad cultural incompatibility or

is especially tru f the Arab world. Yet the current U.S. approach to this growing repulsion is lored by a kind of cultural naïveté, an unwillingness to recognize—let alo appreciate or take responsibility for—the influence of U.S. power except i s military dimension. Even doing nothing in the economic, social, and poli l policy realms is still doing something, because the United States is blame y disadvantaged and alienated populations for the powerful Western-led for of globalization that are proceeding apace, despite the absence of a focus coordinated U.S. policy. And those penetrating mechanisms of globalization uch as the internet, the media, and the increasing flows of goods and peo , are exploited in return. Both the means and ends of terrorism are being r rmulated in the current environment.

THE MEANS

Important chan in terrorist methods are apparent in the use of new technologies, the mov ent of terrorist groups across international boundaries, and changes in sou of support. Like globalization itself, these phenomena are all intertwined d overlapping but, for ease of argument, they are dealt with consecutively h .

First, the us f information technologies such as the internet, mobile phones, and ins t messaging has extended the global reach of many terrorist groups. Increas access to these technologies has so far not resulted in their widely feared in a major cyberterrorist attack: In Dorothy Denning's words, terrorist still prefer bombs to bytes."[41] Activists and terrorist groups have increasing turned to "hacktivism"—attacks on internet sites, including

---

a specific conflict b een Western consumerism and religious fundamentalism. Among the earliest and most notab re Samuel P. Huntington, "The Clash of Civilizations?" *Foreign Affairs,* Vol. 72, No. 3 (Summer 3); Benjamin R. Barber, *Jihad vs. McWorld: Terrorism's Challenge to Democracy* (New York: Rando ouse, 1995); and Samuel P. Huntington, *The Clash of Civilizations and the Remaking of World Or* New York: Simon and Schuster, 1996).

41. For more on rterrorism, see Dorothy Denning, "Activism, Hacktivism, and Cyberterrorism: The Inte as a Tool for Influencing Foreign Policy," paper presented at Internet and International Syste Information Technology and American Foreign Policy Decision-making Workshop at Geor wn University, http://www.nautilus.org/info-policy/workshop/papers/denning.html (acce l January 5, 2003); Dorothy Denning, "Cyberterrorism," testimony before the U.S. House C mittee on Armed Services, Special Oversight Panel on Terrorism, 107th Cong., 1st sess., M 23, 2001, available on the Terrorism Research Center website, http://www.cs.georgetow u/?denning/infosec/cyberterror.html (accessed January 5, 2003); Jerold Post, Kevin Ruby, a Eric Shaw, "From Car Bombs to Logic Bombs: The Growing Threat of Information Terrorism," *orism and Political Violence,* Vol. 12, No. 2 (Summer 2000), pp. 97–122; and Tom Regan, "Wher rorists Turn to the Internet," *Christian Science Monitor,* July 1, 1999, http://www.csmonitor.co ccessed January 5, 2003).

web defacements, hijackings of websites, web sit-ins, denial-of-service attacks, and automated email "bombings"—attacks that may not kill anyone but do attract media attention, provide a means of operating anonymously, and are easy to coordinate internationally.[42] So far, however, these types of attacks are more an expense and a nuisance than an existential threat.

Instead the tools of the global information age have led to enhanced efficiency in many terrorist-related activities, including administrative tasks, coordination of operations, recruitment of potential members, communication among adherents, and attraction of sympathizers.[43] Before the September 11 attacks, for example, members of al-Qaeda communicated through Yahoo email; Mohammed Atta, the presumed leader of the attacks, made his reservations online; and cell members went online to do research on subjects such as the chemical-dispersing powers of crop dusters. Although not as dramatic as shutting down a power grid or taking over an air traffic control system, this practical use of technology has significantly contributed to the effectiveness of terrorist groups and the expansion of their range.[44] Consider, for example, the lethal impact of the synchronized attacks on the U.S. embassies in 1998 and on New York and Washington in 2001, neither of which would have been possible without the revolution in information technology. When he was arrested in 1995, Ramzi Yousef, mastermind of the 1993 World Trade Center attack, was planning the simultaneous destruction of eleven airliners.[45]

The internet has become an important tool for perpetuating terrorist groups, both openly and clandestinely. Many of them employ elaborate list serves, collect money from witting or unwitting donors, and distribute savvy political messages to a broad audience online.[46] Groups as diverse as Aum Shinrikyo, Israel's Kahane Chai, the Popular Front for the Liberation of Palestine, the Kurdistan Worker's Party, and Peru's Shining Path maintain user-friendly

42. Ibid. Dorothy Denning cites numerous examples, among them: In 1989, hackers released a computer worm into the NASA Space Physics Analysis Network in an attempt to stop a shuttle launch; during Palestinian riots in October 2000, pro-Israeli hackers defaced the Hezbollah website; and in 1999, following the mistaken U.S. bombing of the Chinese embassy in Belgrade during the war in Kosovo, Chinese hackers attacked the websites of the U.S. Department of the Interior, showing images of the three journalists killed during the bombing.
43. Paul R. Pillar, *Terrorism and U.S. Foreign Policy* (Washington, D.C.: Brookings, 2001), p. 47.
44. Ibid.
45. Simon Reeve, *The New Jackals: Ramzi Yousef, Osama bin Laden, and the Future of Terrorism* (Boston: Northeastern University Press, 1999), p. 260.
46. Dorothy Denning, "Cyberwarriors: Activists and Terrorists Turn to Cyberspace," *Harvard International Review*, Vol. 23, No. 2 (Summer 2001), pp. 70–75. See also Brian J. Miller, "Terror.org: An Assessment of Terrorist Internet Sites," Georgetown University, December 6, 2000.

official or unoff al websites, and almost all are accessible in English.[47] Clandestine methoc include passing encrypted messages, embedding invisible graphic codes ng steganography,[48] employing the internet to send death threats, and hir ; hackers to collect intelligence such as the names and addresses of law orcement officers from online databases.[49] All of these measures help to ex d and perpetuate trends in terrorism that have already been observed: For mple, higher casualties are brought about by simultaneous attacks, a diffus in terrorist locations is made possible by internet communications, and ex mist religious ideologies are spread through websites and videotapes acce ble throughout the world.

More omino globalization makes CBNR weapons increasingly available to terrorist gro .[50] Information needed to build these weapons has become ubiquitous, esp lly through the internet. Among the groups interested in acquiring CBNR esides al-Qaeda) are the PLO, the Red Army Faction, Hezbollah, the urdistan Workers' Party, German neo-Nazis, and the Chechens.[51]

Second, glob ation has enabled terrorist organizations to reach across international bor s, in the same way (and often through the same channels) that commerce d business interests are linked. The dropping of barriers through the No American Free Trade Area and the European Union, for instance, has faci ted the smooth flow of many things, good and bad, among countries. This allowed terrorist organizations as diverse as Hezbollah, al-Qaeda, and the gyptian al-Gama'at al-Islamiyya to move about freely and establish cells a nd the world.[52] Movement across borders can obviously en-

47. Miller, "Terror " pp. 9, 12.
48. Steganography he embedding of messages usually in pictures, where the messages are disguised so that they not be seen with the naked eye. See Denning, "Cyberwarriors."
49. I am indebted orothy Denning for all of this information. The Provisional IRA hired contract hackers to fin e addresses of British intelligence and law enforcement officers. See Denning, "Cyberterrori "; and Denning, "Cyberwarriors."
50. There are many ent sources on CBNR. Among the best are Jonathan B. Tucker, ed., *Toxic Terror: Assessing Terror Use of Chemical and Biological Weapons* (Cambridge, Mass.: MIT Press, 2000); Joshua Lederberg, *ogical Weapons: Limiting the Threat* (Cambridge, Mass.: MIT Press, 1999); Richard A. Falkenra Robert D. Newman, and Bradley A. Thayer, *America's Achilles' Heel: Nuclear, Biological, and Chem Terrorism and Covert Attack* (Cambridge, Mass.: MIT Press, 1998); Gurr and Cole, *The New Face errorism;* Jessica Stern, *The Ultimate Terrorists* (Cambridge, Mass.: Harvard University Press, 1 ; and Brad Roberts, ed., *Terrorism with Chemical and Biological Weapons: Calibrating Risks and Re ses* (Alexandria, Va.: Chemical and Biological Arms Control Institute, 1997).
51. See Falkenrath, wman, and Thayer, *America's Achilles' Heel*, pp. 31–46.
52. A clear exampl this phenomenon was the uncovering in December 2001 of a multinational plot in Singapore b international terrorist group Jemaah Islamiyah to blow up several Western targets, including t .S. embassy. A videotape of the intended targets (including a description of

able terrorists to carry out attacks and potentially evade capture, but it also complicates prosecution if they are apprehended, with a complex maze of extradition laws varying greatly from state to state. The increased permeability of the international system has also enhanced the ability of nonstate terrorist organizations to collect intelligence (not to mention evade it); states are not the only actors interested in collecting, disseminating, and/or acting on such information. In a sense, then, terrorism is in many ways becoming like any other international enterprise—an ominous development indeed.

Third, terrorist organizations are broadening their reach in gathering financial resources to fund their operations. This is not just an al-Qaeda phenomenon, although bin Laden's organization—especially its numerous business interests—figures prominently among the most innovative and wealthy pseudocorporations in the international terrorist network. The list of groups with global financing networks is long and includes most of the groups identified by the U.S. government as foreign terrorist organizations, notably Aum Shinrikyo, Hamas, Hezbollah, and the Tamil Tigers. Sources of financing include legal enterprises such as nonprofit organizations and charities (whose illicit activities may be a small or large proportion of overall finances, known or unknown to donors); legitimate companies that divert profits to illegal activities (such as bin Laden's large network of construction companies); and illegal enterprises such as drug smuggling and production (e.g., the Revolutionary Armed Forces of Colombia—FARC), bank robbery, fraud, extortion, and kidnapping (e.g., the Abu Sayyaf group, Colombia's National Liberation Army, and FARC).[53] Websites are also important vehicles for raising funds. Although no comprehensive data are publicly available on how lucrative this avenue is, the proliferation of terrorist websites with links or addresses for contributions is at least circumstantial evidence of their usefulness.

The fluid movement of terrorists' financial resources demonstrates the growing informal connections that are countering the local fragmentation caused elsewhere by globalization. The transit of bars of gold and bundles of dollars

---

the plans in Arabic) was discovered in Afghanistan after al-Qaeda members fled. Thus there are clear connections between these organizations, as well as evidence of cooperation and coordination of attacks. See, for example, Dan Murphy, "'Activated' Asian Terror Web Busted," *Christian Science Monitor*, January 23, 2002, http://www.csmonitor.com (accessed January 23, 2002); and Rajiv Changrasekaran, "Al Qaeda's Southeast Asian Reach," *Washington Post*, February 3, 2002, p. A1.

53. Rensselaer Lee and Raphael Perl, "Terrorism, the Future, and U.S. Foreign Policy," issue brief for Congress, received through the Congressional Research Service website, order code IB95112, Congressional Research Service, Library of Congress, July 10, 2002, p. CRS-6.

across the bord between Afghanistan and Pakistan as U.S. and allied forces were closing in the Taliban's major strongholds is a perfect example. Collected by shopk ers and small businessmen, the money was moved by operatives across th order to Karachi, where it was transferred in the millions of dollars through e informal *hawala* or *hundi* banking system to the United Arab Emirates. here it was converted into gold bullion and scattered around the world befo ny government could intervene. In this way, al-Qaeda preserved and dis sed a proportion of its financial resources.[55] In addition to gold, money w transferred into other commodities—such as diamonds in Sierra Leone an he Democratic Republic of Congo, and tanzanite from Tanzania—all whil iding the assets and often making a profit,[56] and all without interference fro he sovereign governments that at the time were at war with al-Qaeda and t Taliban.[57]

As this exam illustrates, globalization does not necessarily require the use of high technol : It often takes the form of traditional practices used in innovative ways ac increasingly permeable physical and commercial borders. Terrorist group hose assets comparatively represent only a small fraction of the amount of ney that is moved by organized crime groups and are thus much more diff lt to track, use everything from direct currency transport (by couriers) to reli e on traditional banks, Islamic banks, money changers (using accounts at gitimate institutions), and informal exchange (the *hawala* or *hundi* system).

This is by no ans a comprehensive presentation of global interpenetration of terrorist mea , and some of the connections described above have existed for some time a in other contexts. The broad strategic picture, however, is of

---

54. Roger G. Wein The Financing of International Terrorism," Terrorism and Violence Crime Section, Criminal D ion, U.S. Department of Justice, October 2001, p. 3. According to Weiner, the *hawala* (or *hundi*) sy m "relies entirely on trust that currency left with a particular service provider or merchant be paid from bank accounts he controls overseas to the recipient specified by the party origina the transfer." Ibid. See also Douglas Frantz, "Ancient Secret System Moves Money Globally," *York Times*, October 3, 2001, http://www.nytimes.com (accessed October 3, 2001).
55. International ef s to freeze bank accounts and block transactions between suspected terrorists have hindered, east to some degree, al-Qaeda's ability to finance attacks; however, a proportion remains u ounted for. "Cash Moves a Sign Al-Qaeda Is Regrouping," *Straits Times*, March 18, 2002, htt www.straitstimes.asia1.com.sg (accessed March 18, 2002).
56. U.S. Departme State, *Patterns of Global Terrorism, 2001*. According to the U.S. Department of State, Hezbollah may have transferred resources by selling millions of dollars' worth of Congolese diamon finance operations in the Middle East.
57. Douglas Farah, Qaeda's Road Paved with Gold," *Washington Post*, February 17, 2002, pp. A1, A32.

an increasing ability of terrorist organizations to exploit the same avenues of communication, coordination, and cooperation as other international actors, including states, multinational corporations, nongovernmental organizations, and even individuals. It would be naïve to assume that what is good for international commerce and international communication is not also good for international terrorists[58]—who are increasingly becoming opportunistic entrepreneurs whose "product" (often quite consciously "sold") is violence against innocent targets for a political end.

THE ENDS

The objectives of international terrorism have also changed as a result of globalization. Foreign intrusions and growing awareness of shrinking global space have created incentives to use the ideal asymmetrical weapon, terrorism, for more ambitious purposes.

The political incentives to attack major targets such as the United States with powerful weapons have greatly increased. The perceived corruption of indigenous customs, religions, languages, economies, and so on are blamed on an international system often unconsciously molded by American behavior. The accompanying distortions in local communities as a result of exposure to the global marketplace of goods and ideas are increasingly blamed on U.S.-sponsored modernization and those who support it. The advancement of technology, however, is not the driving force behind the terrorist threat to the United States and its allies, despite what some have assumed.[59] Instead, at the heart of this threat are frustrated populations and international movements that are increasingly inclined to lash out against U.S.-led globalization.

As Christopher Coker observes, globalization is reducing tendencies toward instrumental violence (i.e., violence between states and even between communities), but it is enhancing incentives for expressive violence (or violence that is ritualistic, symbolic, and communicative).[60] The new international terrorism is

58. Pillar, *Terrorism and U.S. Foreign Policy,* p. 48.

59. Many in the United States focus on the technologies of terrorism, with a much less developed interest in the motivations of terrorists. Brian M. Jenkins, "Understanding the Link between Motives and Methods," in Roberts, *Terrorism with Chemical and Biological Weapons,* pp. 43–51. An example of a study that focuses on weapons and not motives is Sidney D. Drell, Abraham D. Sofaer, and George W. Wilson, eds., *The New Terror: Facing the Threat of Biological and Chemical Weapons* (Stanford, Calif.: Hoover Institution, 1999).

60. Christopher Coker, *Globalisation and Insecurity in the Twenty-first Century: NATO and the Management of Risk,* Adelphi Paper 345 (London: International Institute for Strategic Studies, June 2002), p. 40.

increasingly en; ıdered by a need to assert identity or meaning against forces of homogeneity ;pecially on the part of cultures that are threatened by, or left behind by, the ; ular future that Western-led globalization brings.

According to report recently published by the United Nations Development Programn the region of greatest deficit in measures of human development—the Aral vorld—is also the heart of the most threatening religiously inspired terrori .[61] Much more work needs to be done on the significance of this correlation, t increasingly sources of political discontent are arising from disenfranchised eas in the Arab world that feel left behind by the promise of globalization ar its assurances of broader freedom, prosperity, and access to knowledge. The ·sults are dashed expectations, heightened resentment of the perceived U.S.- hegemonic system, and a shift of focus away from more proximate targe within the region.

Of course, th ıotivations behind this threat should not be oversimplified: Anti-American rorism is spurred in part by a desire to change U.S. policy in the Middle Eas ıd Persian Gulf regions as well as by growing antipathy in the developing ›rld vis-à-vis the forces of globalization. It is also crucial to distinguish bet ·n the motivations of leaders such as Osama bin Laden and their followers. ıe former seem to be more driven by calculated strategic decisions to shift locus of attack away from repressive indigenous governments to the m attractive and media-rich target of the United States. The latter appear tc e more driven by religious concepts cleverly distorted to arouse anger ar passion in societies full of pent-up frustration. To some degree, terrorism lirected against the United States because of its engagement and policies ir 'arious regions.[62] Anti-Americanism is closely related to antiglobalizatio ɔecause (intentionally or not) the primary driver of the powerful forces resı ng in globalization is the United States.

Analyzing te ·ism as something separate from globalization is misleading and potentially ıngerous. Indeed globalization and terrorism are intricately intertwined for characterizing international security in the twenty-first century. The main ıestion is whether terrorism will succeed in disrupting the

61. The indicators ied included respect for human rights and human freedoms, the empowerment of women, ar road access to and utilization of knowledge. See United Nations Development Programme, b Fund for Economic and Social Development, *Arab Human Development Report, 2002: Creati ›pportunities for Future Generations* (New York: United Nations Development Programme, 2002).

62. Martha Crensh "Why America? The Globalization of Civil War," *Current History*, December 2001, pp. 425–432.

promise of improved livelihoods for millions of people on Earth. Globalization is not an inevitable, linear development, and it can be disrupted by such unconventional means as international terrorism. Conversely, modern international terrorism is especially dangerous because of the power that it potentially derives from globalization—whether through access to CBNR weapons, global media outreach, or a diverse network of financial and information resources.

Prospects for the Future

Long after the focus on Osama bin Laden has receded and U.S. troops have quit their mission in Afghanistan, terrorism will be a serious threat to the world community and especially to the United States. The relative preponderance of U.S. military power virtually guarantees an impulse to respond asymmetrically. The lagging of the Arab region behind the rest of the world is impelling a violent redirection of antiglobalization and antimodernization forces toward available targets, particularly the United States, whose scope and policies are engendering rage. Al-Qaeda will eventually be replaced or redefined, but its successors' reach may continue to grow via the same globalized channels and to direct their attacks against U.S. and Western targets. The current trajectory is discouraging, because as things currently stand, the wellspring of terrorism's means and ends is likely to be renewed: Arab governments will probably not reform peacefully, and existing Western governments and their supporting academic and professional institutions are disinclined to understand or analyze in depth the sources, patterns, and history of terrorism.

Terrorism is a by-product of broader historical shifts in the international distribution of power in all of its forms—political, economic, military, ideological, and cultural. These are the same forms of power that characterize the forces of Western-led globalization. At times of dramatic international change, human beings (especially those not benefiting from the change—or not benefiting as much or as rapidly from the change) grasp for alternative means to control and understand their environments. If current trends continue, widening global disparities, coupled with burgeoning information and connectivity, are likely to accelerate—unless the terrorist backlash, which is increasingly taking its inspiration from misoneistic religious or pseudoreligious concepts, successfully counters these trends. Because of globalization, terrorists have access to more powerful technologies, more targets, more territory, more means of recruitment, and more exploitable sources of rage than ever before. The West's twentieth-centu approach to terrorism is highly unlikely to mitigate any of these long-term ends.

From a Mani ean perspective, the ad hoc and purportedly benign intentions of the pre nderant, secular West do not seem benign at all to those ill served by glob ation. To frustrated people in the Arab and Muslim world, adherence to ra al religious philosophies and practices may seem a rational response to the rceived assault, especially when no feasible alternative for progress is offe by their own governments. This is not to suggest that terrorists should b xcused because of environmental factors or conditions. Instead, Western vernments must recognize that the tiny proportion of the population that ds up in terrorist cells cannot exist without the availability of broader sou s of active or passive sympathy, resources, and support. Those avenues ustenance are where the center of gravity for an effective response to the te rist threat must reside. The response to transnational terrorism must deal n the question of whether the broader enabling environment will increase or crease over time, and the answer will be strongly influenced by the policy c ices that the United States and its allies make in the near future.

Conclusions a Policy Prescriptions

The characteris and causes of the current threat can only be analyzed within the cont of the deadly collision occurring between U.S. power, globalization, and tl evolution of international terrorism. The U.S. government is still thinking in tdated terms, little changed since the end of the Cold War. It continues to loc t terrorism as a peripheral threat, with the focus remaining on states that in ny cases are not the greatest threat. The means and the ends of terrorism are anging in fundamental, important ways; but the means and the ends of the ategy being crafted in response are not.

Terrorism th hreatens international stability, and particularly U.S. global leadership, is c ered on power-based political causes that are enduring: the weak against t strong, the disenfranchised against the establishment, and the revolutiona against the status quo. Oversimplified generalizations about poverty and ter ism, or any other single variable, are caricatures of a serious argument.[63] Th se in political and material expectations as a result of the in-

63. A number of r t arguments have been put forth about the relationship between poverty and terrorism. See, xample, Anatol Lieven, "The Roots of Terrorism, and a Strategy against It,"

formation revolution is not necessarily helpful to stability, in the same way that rising expectations led terrorists to take up arms against the czar in Russia a century ago. Indeed the fact that so many people in so many nations are being left behind has given new ammunition to terrorist groups; produced more sympathy for those willing to take on the United States; and spurred Islamic radical movements to recruit, propagandize, and support terrorism throughout many parts of the Muslim world. The al-Qaeda network is an extremist religious terrorist organization, its Taliban puppet regime was filled with religious zealots, and its suicide recruits were convinced that they were waging a just holy war. But the driving forces of twenty-first-century terrorism are power and frustration, not the pursuit of religious principle. To dismiss the broad enabling environment would be to focus more on the symptoms than the causes of modern terrorism.

The prescriptions for countering and preventing terrorism should be twofold: First, the United States and other members of the international community concerned about this threat need to use a balanced assortment of instruments to address the immediate challenges of the terrorists themselves. Terrorism is a complex phenomenon; it must be met with short-term military action, informed by in-depth, long-term, sophisticated analysis. Thus far, the response has been virtually all the former and little of the latter. Second, the United States and its counterterrorist allies must employ a much broader array of longer-term policy tools to reshape the international environment, which enables terrorist networks to breed and become robust. The mechanisms of globalization need to be exploited to thwart the globalization of terrorism.

In the short term, the United States must continue to rely on capable military forces that can sustain punishing air strikes against terrorists and those who harbor them with an even greater capacity for special operations on the ground. This requires not only improved stealthy, long-range power projection capabilities but also agile, highly trained, and lethal ground forces, backed up

Prospect (London), October 2001, http://www.ceip.org/files/Publications/lieventerrorism.asp?from=pubdate (accessed November 17, 2002); and Daniel Pipes, "God and Mammon: Does Poverty Cause Militant Islam?" *National Interest*, No. 66 (Winter 2001/02), pp. 14–21. This is an extremely complex question, however, and much work remains to be done. On the origins of the new religious terrorism, see Hoffman, *Inside Terrorism;* and Mark Juergensmeyer, *Terror in the Mind of God: The Global Rise of Religious Violence* (Berkeley: University of California Press, 2000). Important earlier studies on the sources of terrorism include Martha Crenshaw, "The Causes of Terrorism," *Comparative Politics*, July 1981, pp. 379–399; Martha Crenshaw, *Terrorism in Context* (University Park: Pennsylvania State University Press, 1995); and Walter Reich, ed., *Origins of Terrorism: Psychologies, Ideologies, Theologies, States of Mind*, 2d ed. (Washington, D.C.: Woodrow Wilson Center for International Scholars, 1998).

with greater elligence, including human intelligence supported by individuals witl ınguage skills and cultural training. The use of military force continues to bo nportant as one means of responding to terrorist violence against the Wes ınd there is no question that it effectively preempts and disrupts some inte ıtional terrorist activity, especially in the short term.[64]

Over time, ho ever, the more effective instruments of policy are likely to remain the nonn ary ones. Indeed the United States needs to expand and deepen its nonn tary instruments of power such as intelligence, public diplomacy, cooperat with allies, international legal instruments, and economic assistance and ıctions. George Kennan, in his 1947 description of containment, put forth e same fundamental argument, albeit against an extremely different enemy The strongest response that the United States can muster to a serious threat s to include political, economic, and military capabilities—in that order; yet, U.S. government consistently structures its policies and devotes its resour in the reverse sequence.

The economi ıd political roots of terrorism are complex, increasingly worrisome, and de nding of as much breadth and subtlety in response as they display in their nesis. The United States must therefore be strategic in its response: An eff ive grand strategy against terrorism involves planning a global campaig vith the most effective means available, not just the most measurable, ob us, or gratifying. It must also include plans for shaping the global environn ıt after the so-called war on terrorism has ended—or after the current poli al momentum has subsided.

The United S es, working with other major donor nations, needs to create an effective inc ive structure that rewards "good performers"—those countries with good overnance, inclusive education programs, and adequate social programs– d works around "bad performers" and intervenes to assist so-called failed tes. Also for the longer term, the United States and its allies need to project vision of sustainable development—of economic growth, equal access to ic social needs such as education and health, and good governance—for th eveloping world. This is particularly true in mostly Muslim countries whos opulations are angry with the United States over a perceived double standar egarding its long-standing support for Israel at the expense

64. For more discu n on the traditional elements of U.S. grand strategy, especially military strategy, see Barry Posen, "The Struggle against Terrorism: Grand Strategy, Strategy, and Tactics," *International S rity*, Vol. 26, No. 3 (Winter 2001/02), pp. 39–55.

65. George F. Kenn "The Sources of Soviet Conduct," *Foreign Affairs*, Vol. 25, No. 4 (July 1947), pp. 575–576.

of Palestinians, policies against the regime of Saddam Hussein at the expense of some Iraqi people, and a general abundance of American power, including the U.S. military presence throughout the Middle East. Whether these policies are right or wrong is irrelevant here; the point is that just as the definition of terrorism can be subjective and value laden, so too can the response to terrorism take into account perceptions of reality. In an attempt to craft an immediate military response, the U.S. government is failing to put into place an effective long-term grand strategy.

This is not just a problem for the U.S. government. The inability to develop a strategy with a deep-rooted, intellectually grounded understanding of the history, patterns, motivations, and types of terrorism is reflective of the paucity of understanding of the terrorist phenomenon in the academic community. Terrorism is considered too policy-oriented an area of research in political science,[66] and it operates in an uncomfortable intersection between disciplines unaccustomed to working together, including psychology, sociology, theology, economics, anthropology, history, law, political science, and international relations. In political science, terrorism does not fit neatly into either the realist or liberal paradigms, so it has been largely ignored.[67] There are a few outstanding, well-established senior scholars in the terrorism studies community—people such as Martha Crenshaw, David Rapoport, and Paul Wilkinson—but in the United States, most of the publicly available work is being done in policy-oriented research institutes or think tanks that are sometimes limited by the narrow interests and short time frames of the government contracts on which they depend. Some of that research is quite good,[68] but it is not widely known within the academy. The situation for graduate students who wish to study terrorism is worse: A principal interest in terrorism virtually guarantees exclusion from consideration for most academic positions. This would not necessarily be a problem if the bureaucracy were more flexible and creative than the academy is, but as we know from the analysis of the behavior of U.S. agencies shortly before September 11, it is not. In the United States, academe is no more strategic in its understanding of terrorism than is the U.S. government.

66. See the extremely insightful article by Bruce W. Jentleson, "The Need for Praxis: Bringing Policy Relevance Back In," *International Security*, Vol. 26, No. 4 (Spring 2002), pp. 169–183.
67. I am indebted to Fiona Adamson for this observation.
68. Important terrorism scholars in the think tank community include Walter Laqueur (Center for Strategic and International Studies), Brian Jenkins (RAND), Bruce Hoffman (RAND) and, from the intelligence community, Paul Pillar. This list is illustrative, not comprehensive.

The globaliza n of terrorism is perhaps the leading threat to long-term stability in the tw y-first century. But the benefit of globalization is that the international res se to terrorist networks has also begun to be increasingly global, with in national cooperation on law enforcement, intelligence, and especially finan controls being areas of notable recent innovation.[69] If globalization is to c inue—and there is nothing foreordained that it will—then the tools of glo zation, including especially international norms, the rule of law, and intern onal economic power, must be fully employed against the terrorist backla There must be a deliberate effort to move beyond the current episodic in est in this phenomenon: Superficial arguments and short attention spans continue to result in event-driven policies and ultimately more attacks. T orism is an unprecedented, powerful nonstate threat to the international sy m that no single state, regardless of how powerful it may be in traditional t s, can defeat alone, especially in the absence of long-term, serious scholar engaged in by its most creative minds.

69. On these issues e Cronin and Ludes, *The Campaign against International Terrorism.*

Motives for Martyrdom

Al-Qaida, Salafi Jihad, and the Spread of Suicide Attacks

Assaf Moghadam

Suicide missions—or attacks whose success is dependent on the death of their perpetrator/s—are one of the most lethal tactics employed by terrorist and insurgent groups today. Moreover, they have demonstrated great potential to create turbulence in international affairs.[1] The four suicide attacks of September 11, 2001, and the war in Iraq—where suicide operations have become the signature mode of attack—have highlighted how this tactic can lead to considerable losses of human life and physical infrastructure while influencing the course of global events in their wake.

During the 1980s and 1990s, suicide missions wreaked considerable havoc on their targets; yet these targets were relatively few in number. The vast majority of attacks took place in only a handful of countries, namely, Israel, Lebanon, Sri Lanka, and Turkey.

More than thirty-five countries on every continent save for Antarctica and Australia have experienced the wanton violence brought on by suicide attacks. In the past decade, suicide bombings have not only occurred in a growing number of countries, but these attacks have been planned and executed by an even greater number of organizations and have killed larger numbers of people every year. The targets of these attacks have also undergone some shifts. More suicide bombings have occurred in Iraq since 2003 than in all other countries in the twenty-five years preceding the U.S.-led invasion of Iraq. Suicide missions have increasingly targeted Muslims and have been adopted as part of

Assaf Moghadam is Assistant Professor and Senior Associate at the Combating Terrorism Center at West Point, and Research Fellow at the Initiative on Religion in International Affairs at Harvard University's Belfer Center for Science and International Affairs. This article is drawn from his book The Globalization of Martyrdom: Al Qaeda, Salafi Jihad, and the Diffusion of Suicide Attacks *(Baltimore, Md.: Johns Hopkins University Press, 2008), but it analyzes a larger, more up-to-date set of data.*

The author would like to thank participants at Ph.D. colloquia and research seminars at the Fletcher School at Tufts University, the John M. Olin Institute for Strategic Studies, and the Belfer Center for Science and International Affairs, both at Harvard University. He is especially grateful to the anonymous reviewers for their valuable insights.

1. I use the terms "suicide missions," "suicide attacks," and "suicide operations" interchangeably. The term "suicide missions" is drawn from Diego Gambetta, ed., *Making Sense of Suicide Missions* (Oxford: Oxford University Press, 2005).

International Security, Vol. 33, No. 3 (Winter 2008/09), pp. 46–78

a strategy not o to gain a national homeland, but also to depose regimes regarded as un-Is nic. In recent years, suicide missions have been launched in countries with e or no prior history of such attacks, including Afghanistan, Pakistan, Soma Uzbekistan, and Yemen.[2] Perhaps most important for the West, suicide at ks are no longer a distant threat, having targeted cities such as London, Ma d, and New York.[3]

This article e nines the causes and characteristics of the phenomenon of the "globalizati of martyrdom."[4] Two interrelated factors explain the proliferation of suici missions: the evolution of al-Qaida into a global terrorist actor and the gro ng appeal of Salafi jihad, the guiding ideology of al-Qaida and its associat movements. Discussion of these factors is largely missing from scholarly rk on suicide attacks.[5] Although a few scholars have claimed that most conte porary suicide attacks can be attributed to jihadist groups,[6] this article is th irst to test this argument empirically.

In the first se n, I present my data set on suicide missions from December

---

2. Only a small nu r of suicide attacks occurred in some of these countries before the turn of the millennium. In kistan there were just three such attacks. On November 19, 1995, a truck bomb rocked the E tian embassy in Islamabad. On December 21, 1995, a car bomb exploded in a crowded street i shawar in northwestern Pakistan, killing at least 30 and wounding more than 100; and on A 29, 1996, a suicide bomber blew himself up inside a passenger-filled bus returning from a reli s festival in Punjab, killing 52. A handful of attacks occurred in 2000 and 2002, but suicide a s in Pakistan were widely adopted only after 2003.

3. Although the M d train bombings of March 11, 2004, were not a suicide mission, seven of the suspects deton themselves weeks later in the Madrid suburb of Leganes, as Spanish special forces were a to storm their apartment. See Rogelio Alonso and Fernando Reinares, "Maghreb Immigra Becoming Suicide Terrorists: A Case Study on Religious Radicalization Processes in Spain," in y Pedahzur, ed., *Root Causes of Suicide Terrorism: The Globalization of Martyrdom* (New York: R dge, 2006), pp. 179–198.

4. See Assaf Mogh m, "The New Martyrs Go Global," *Boston Globe*, November 18, 2005.

5. Some exception ist. Yoram Schweitzer and Sari Goldstein Ferber highlight the role of al-Qaida in internatio zing suicide attacks, but they do not emphasize the role of Salafi jihadist ideology. Schweitz d Goldstein Ferber, "Al-Qaida and the Internationalization of Suicide Terrorism," Jaffee Cen Memorandum, No. 78 (Tel Aviv: Jaffee Center for Strategic Studies, Tel Aviv University, Novem 2005). Mohammed M. Hafez discusses the appeal of Salafi jihadist ideology, but he limits his an is to the case of Iraq. Hafez, *Suicide Bombers in Iraq: The Strategy and Ideology of Martyrdom* (Wasl ton, D.C.: United States Institute of Peace Press, 2007).

6. Bruce Hoffman, g data from the RAND Terrorism Incident Database, said that 78 percent of all suicide attacks s 1968 occurred after September 11, 2001, adding that 31 out of the 35 groups employing this tact vere Islamic. He did not, however, specifically refer to jihadist groups, nor did he argue that th groups were ideologically motivated. Hoffman, email correspondence with author, December 2 005. Scott Atran points out that "most suicide terrorists today are inspired by a global Jihadis but he does not provide empirical support for his claim. See Atran, "The Moral Logic and G th of Suicide Terrorism," *Washington Quarterly*, Vol. 29, No. 2 (Spring 2006), p. 139. In an earlier dy, I, too, suggested that contemporary patterns of suicide attacks are dominated by Salafi jiha s without offering any empirical data. See Assaf Moghadam, "Suicide Terrorism, Occupation d the Globalization of Martyrdom: A Critique of 'Dying to Win,'" *Studies in Conflict and Terroris* Vol. 29, No. 8 (December 2006), pp. 707–729.

1981 through March 2008. In the second section, I review existing studies of suicide attacks and discuss their limitations. In the third section, I present the main argument of this study. In the fourth section, I discuss the theoretical implications of my findings. The conclusion offers practical implications of these findings for efforts to confront the challenges posed by suicide operations.

The Global Rise of Suicide Attacks

According to most indicators, suicide missions have been on the rise since 1981, but they have grown at an unprecedented pace since the turn of the millennium.[7] According to my data set, 1,857 suicide attacks were perpetrated from December 1981 through March 2008.[8] Throughout the 1980s and early 1990s, the number of suicide missions remained relatively small, not exceeding 7 attacks per year, with the exception of 1985, when 22 such attacks were carried out. Beginning in 1994, the number of suicide missions started to increase, peaking temporarily in 1995, when 27 attacks were launched. The number dropped slightly in the second half of the 1990s. The year 2000 witnessed 37 attacks—a record number. It also signaled the beginning of an upward trend in the number of suicide missions that would span most of the first decade of this century. Thus, between 2000 and 2007, the number of attacks rose steadily each year, from 54 in 2001 to 71 in 2002, 81 in 2003, 104 in 2004, 348 in 2005, 353 in 2006, and 535 in 2007 (see figure 1).[9]

The global proliferation of suicide missions is reflected in the rise in the number of organizations that employed them. From 1981 to 1990, an average of 1.6 organizations perpetrated suicide attacks every year. From 1991 to 2000,

7. Suicide attacks and their precursors have existed since biblical times. Prior to 1981, however, these attacks were not generally considered acts of terrorism. The modern phenomenon of suicide terrorism began in Lebanon with the December 1981 bombing of the Iraqi embassy. For an overview of modern-day suicide attacks and their historical precursors, see "Introduction," in Assaf Moghadam, *The Globalization of Martyrdom: Al-Qaida, Salafi Jihad, and the Diffusion of Suicide Attacks* (Baltimore, Md.: Johns Hopkins University Press, 2008).

8. The data set relies heavily on two sources. The first is the Suicide Terrorism Database collected by the National Security Studies Center at the University of Haifa in Israel. For a version of the database that includes 1,165 suicide attacks conducted until April 17, 2006, see http://www.laits.utexas.edu/tiger/terrorism_data/suicide_attacks_worldwide/. For data since April 18, 2006, as well as for all data related to suicide attacks in Iraq and Afghanistan, I used the National Counterterrorism Center's (NCTC) Worldwide Incidents Tracking System. The NCTC database is available at www.nctc.gov. After combining these two databases, eliminating duplicates, and updating the resulting database with additional information, I arrived at a data set with a total of 1,857 suicide attacks recorded from December 1981 to March 2008. For a copy of the data set, please contact me at assafm@hotmail.com.

9. One hundred nine attacks were recorded in the first quarter of 2008.

Figure 1. Number Suicide Missions, 1981–2007

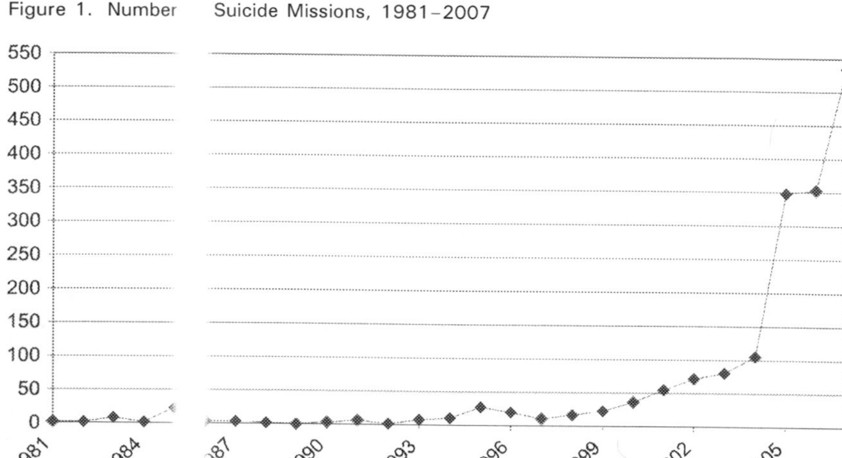

the average inc sed to 4.8. And from 2001 to 2007, it rose to an average of 14.3.

Suicide attacl have exacted an enormous human toll. The 1,857 suicide attacks recorded my data set claimed 20,603 lives and left at least 48,209 wounded. Of t e, more than 87 percent were killed and more than 80 percent injured in t decade alone (see figure 2). The overall trend in the number of injured in su le attacks is comparable to the numbers of people killed, although in two ars—1996 and 1998—the numbers of wounded (2,082 and 4,666) were par ularly high.[10] The sharp increase in dead and wounded beginning in 2003 emmed largely from the war in Iraq.

Based on my ta set, the average suicide mission in the period under review killed 11 ple and injured 26. These numbers should be approached with caution, h ever, because the range was exceedingly wide, and because information ab casualty rates (especially number of wounded) is often incomplete or mi ng altogether. The median of the numbers of people killed was 3, and that people wounded was 9.

From 1981 to 07, the number of countries in which suicide missions were

10. The 1996 figure ludes a suicide car bombing on January 31, 1996, by a member of the Liberation Tigers of Tam elam (LTTE), in which 19 people died and an estimated 1,400 people were wounded. The 199 ure includes the August 7, 1998, suicide bombing of the U.S. embassy in Nairobi, Kenya, wl killed 213 people and wounded an estimated 4,000.

Figure 2. Number of Casualties from Suicide Missions, 1981–2007

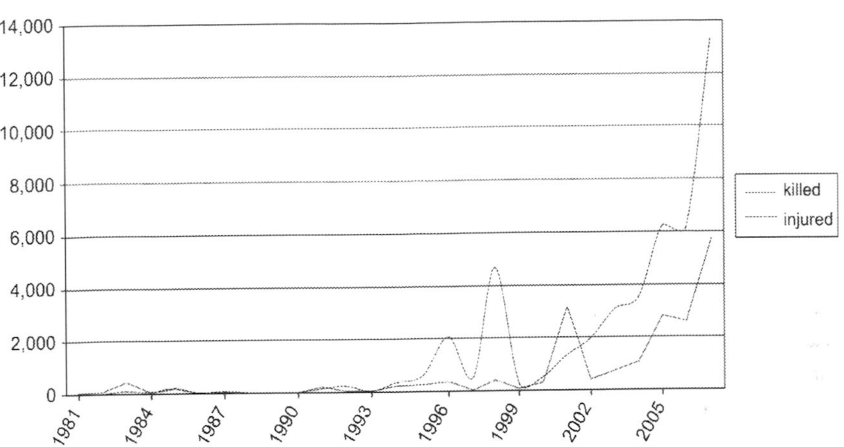

launched generally increased. The average number of countries that experienced a suicide attack from 1981 to 1994 was a relatively low 1.7 per year. Lebanon and Sri Lanka were the most frequently targeted countries. From 1995 to 2007, an average of 8.6 countries per year experienced a suicide attack. In both 2005 and 2006, suicide missions were executed in 15 countries—the highest number of countries recorded.

According to my data, 1,020 suicide missions took place in Iraq (54.9 percent of all suicide missions worldwide); 235 (12.7 percent) in Afghanistan; 188 (10.1 percent) in Israel (including the West Bank and Gaza Strip); 107 (5.8 percent) in Sri Lanka; 88 (4.7 percent) in Pakistan; 41 (2.2 percent) in Lebanon; 37 (2.0 percent) in Russia; and 141 (7.5 percent) in 29 other countries.[11]

Existing Theories on Suicide Attacks

Studies dedicated to explaining the causes of suicide attacks—rare until the terrorist attacks of September 11, 2001—can be divided into at least four gen-

11. These other countries are Algeria, Argentina, Bangladesh, China, Croatia, Egypt, Finland, India, Indonesia, Italy, Jordan, Kenya, Kuwait, Laos, Moldova, Morocco, Panama, Qatar, Saudi Arabia, Serbia, Somalia, Syria, Tanzania, Tunisia, Turkey, the United Kingdom, the United States, Uzbekistan, and Yemen.

eral categories: ›se that focus on the level of the individual bomber;[12] those stressing the ɡ up or organizational factors;[13] those emphasizing socio-structural cause ınd those suggesting the need to integrate multiple levels of analysis.[14]

At the indiv al level of analysis, scholars from a variety of disciplines have concluded ıat suicide bombers often believe that they are acting for altruistic reasons. Most analysts reject the notion that suicide bombers act irrationally, arguin ıat these "martyrs" believe that the benefits of perpetrating suicide attacks tweigh the costs.[16] In addition, they agree that profiling suicide bombers is irtually impossible given their diverse backgrounds. Moreover, they claim ıat suicide bombers—much like terrorists in general—do not suffer from a s ınt psychopathology,[17] and thus dismiss mental illness as a reason for their tions.[18]

Scholars focu l on individual motivations suggest the following: a strong commitment to group or cause,[19] a desire for revenge,[20] an expectation of

---

12. See, for exampl ›an Lachkar, "The Psychological Make-up of a Suicide Bomber," *Journal of Psychohistory*, Vol. No. 4 (Spring 2002), pp. 349–367; David Lester, Bijou Yang, and Mark Lindsay, "Suicide B bers: Are Psychological Profiles Possible?" *Studies in Conflict and Terrorism*, Vol. 27, No. 4 (July ıgust 2004), pp. 283–295; Eyad Sarraj and Linda Butler, "Suicide Bombers: Dignity, Despair, ar ıe Need of Hope," *Journal of Palestine Studies*, Vol. 31, No. 4 (Summer 2002), pp. 71–76; and Ana erko, *The Path to Paradise: The Inner World of Suicide Bombers and Their Dispatchers* (Westport, ın.: Praeger Security International, 2007).
13. Ehud Sprinzak, ıtional Fanatics," *Foreign Policy*, No. 120 (September/October 2000), pp. 67–73; Mia Bloom, *Dy to Kill: The Allure of Suicide Terror* (New York: Columbia University Press, 2005); Robert A. Pa *Dying to Win: The Strategic Logic of Suicide Terrorism* (New York: Random House, 2005); and ı Pedahzur, *Suicide Terrorism* (Cambridge: Polity, 2005).
14. Assaf Moghada "The Roots of Suicide Terrorism: A Multi-Causal Approach," in Pedahzur, *Root Causes of Suici errorism*, pp. 81–107; and Hafez, *Suicide Bombers in Iraq*.
15. See, for exampl ımi Pedahzur, Arie Perliger, and Leonard Weinberg, "Altruism and Fatalism: The Characte :s of Palestinian Suicide Terrorists," *Deviant Behavior*, Vol. 24, No. 4 (July 2003), pp. 405–423.
16. Sprinzak, "Rati l Fanatics"; Assaf Moghadam, "Palestinian Suicide Terrorism in the Second Intifada: Motivatio nd Organizational Aspects," *Studies in Conflict and Terrorism*, Vol. 26, No. 2 (March 2003), pp. 6 ; Bloom, *Dying to Kill*; Pedahzur, *Suicide Terrorism*; and Bruce Hoffman and Gordon H. McCorr , "Terrorism, Signaling, and Suicide Attack," *Studies in Conflict and Terrorism*, Vol. 27, No. 4 y 2004), pp. 243–281.
17. Clark R. McCa y and M.E. Segal, "Social Psychology of Terrorist Groups," in Clyde A. Hendrick, ed., *Gro rocesses and Intergroup Relations: Review of Personality and Social Psychology* (Newbury Park, Ca Sage, 1987).
18. Jeff Victoroff, e Mind of the Terrorist: A Review and Critique of Psychological Approaches," *Journal onflict Resolution*, Vol. 49, No. 1 (February 2005), pp. 3–42.
19. According to s researchers, suicide attackers tend to act out of a deep sense of commitment to a larger ca , to their social network, or to a terrorist organization. See, for example, Pedahzur, *Suicide T rism*, pp. 126–134.
20. A suicide attac may acquire a thirst for revenge after the death of a family member or friend, which can b inforced by a perceived sense of humiliation. For an application of humilia-

benefits after death,[21] and personal crisis.[22] No study, however, has identified either necessary or sufficient conditions for an individual's resort to suicide terrorism, that is, why some highly committed individuals become suicide bombers while others do not, or why revenge leads to suicide terrorism in some cases and not in others. Nor has any study explained the globalization of suicide terrorism.

A second category of studies focuses on the organizational-strategic level of analysis. Building on the theories advanced by Martha Crenshaw, who argues that terrorist organizations believe that violence is the best means to advance their political goals,[23] several scholars have suggested that terrorist organizations engage in suicide attacks to fulfill rational objectives, ranging from basic survival to sophisticated strategic and tactical plans for success. Suicide terrorism, the argument goes, can weaken an external opponent while strengthening the organization itself. Internally, suicide attacks can strengthen the group because they enhance its perceived need to survive.[24] They may also broaden support among the domestic population.[25] Externally, suicide attacks are a proven strategy to weaken the group's opponent. Robert Pape, for example, argues that their high degree of lethality makes suicide attacks a rational or "logical" choice for organizations and states under certain circumstances, asserting that "the main reason that suicide terrorism is growing is that terrorists have learned that it works."[26] Pape, however, appears to have exaggerated the success rate he ascribes to suicide terrorism.[27] Moreover, as Robert Brym and Bader Araj have noted, characterizing suicide missions as strategically ra-

tion-revenge theory, see Mark Juergensmeyer, *Terror in the Mind of God: The Global Rise of Religious Violence* (Berkeley: University of California Press, 2001).

21. Several authors have stressed the expectation of posthumous benefits as a motive for suicide attackers, particularly when the perpetrators of the attacks are Muslims. Such benefits can include the suicide attacker's elevated social status after death, rewards for the family, as well as the attainment of heavenly pleasures in the afterlife.

22. Personal crisis appears to be a particularly common motivation among women suicide bombers such as the Chechen Black Widows. Anat Berko and Edna Erez, "'Ordinary People' and 'Death Work': Palestinian Suicide Bombers as Victimizers and Victims," *Violence and Victims*, Vol. 20, No. 6 (December 2005), pp. 603–623.

23. Martha Crenshaw, "An Organizational Approach to the Analysis of Political Terrorism," *Orbis*, Vol. 29, No. 3 (Fall 1985), pp. 465–489; and Martha Crenshaw, "Theories of Terrorism: Instrumental and Organizational Approaches," in David C. Rapoport, ed., *Inside Terrorist Organizations* (London: Frank Cass, 1988).

24. On the organizational goals of survival and maintenance, see James Q. Wilson, *Political Organizations* (New York: Basic Books, 1973); and Crenshaw, "An Organizational Approach to the Analysis of Political Terrorism."

25. Mia M. Bloom, "Palestinian Suicide Bombing: Public Support, Market Share, and Outbidding," *Political Science Quarterly*, Vol. 119, No. 1 (Spring 2004), pp. 61–88; and Bloom, *Dying to Kill*.

26. Pape, *Dying to Win*, p. 61.

27. See Moghadam, "Suicide Terrorism, Occupation, and the Globalization of Martyrdom."

tional oversimp es the complexity of motivations at the organizational level. They find that cide bombings involve mixed rationales, including the urge for retaliation o he mere existence of opportunities to strike, which can prevail over purel rategic considerations.[28]

A consensus ong scholars does exist, however, with regard to the tactical utility of suicid nissions. Scholars agree that terrorist groups use suicide attacks because o ne disproportionate amount of fear they create in the target population;[29] t r ability to boost the groups' morale;[30] and operational benefits, such a heir cost efficiency and high precision, as well as the low security risks tl pose to the organization at large.[31]

Organization strategic explanations have several limitations. They do not explain why, if benefits of suicide missions are so numerous, many organizations avoid tl r use;[32] when a terrorist group is likely to engage in suicide attacks; or thei ramatic rise since the turn of the millennium.

The third ma category of studies of suicide attacks argues that individuals and organizatic will employ suicide terrorism if they are likely to enjoy social support for is tactic. This explanation appears to account for the widespread use of su de attacks in places such as Israel and Lebanon, where a cult of martyrdom h manifested itself in the veneration of suicide bombers; in the prominent use heroic and euphemistic labels for suicide attacks and their perpetrators; ai in the penetration of the suicide bomber into popular culture, including ovies, comics, and plays. Some researchers claim that sustained levels of cide terrorism depend entirely on strong support among the

---

28. Robert J. Brym Bader Araj, "Suicide Bombing as Strategy and Interaction: The Case of the Second Intifada," S *l Forces*, Vol. 84, No. 4 (June 2006), pp. 1969–1986.
29. Although this i key feature of all terrorist attacks, suicide attacks further demonstrate the inefficacy of the ta ed government, given in part the demoralization of the public and of law enforcement agenc In addition, the effect of a suicide attack can be particularly traumatizing and long-lasting. S for example, Keith B. Richburg, "Suicide Bomb Survivors Face Worlds Blown Apart," *Was ton Post*, January 31, 2004; and Amos Harel, "Suicide Attacks Frighten Israelis More Than S s," *Haaretz*, February 13, 2003.
30. Suicide attacks n lead to a sense of moral superiority of the groups' members over their adversaries, which m sult in a group's perception that it will eventually prevail over its enemies. See Adam Dolnik, and Let Die: Exploring Links between Suicide Terrorism and Terrorist Use of Chemical, Biolog , Radiological, and Nuclear Weapons," *Studies in Conflict and Terrorism*, Vol. 26, No. 1 (January 3), pp. 17–35.
31. See, for exampl prinzak, "Rational Fanatics"; and Boaz Ganor, "Suicide Attacks in Israel," in International P Institute for Counter-Terrorism (ICT), ed., *Countering Suicide Terrorism* (Herzliyya, Israel: 2001), pp. 140–154.
32. A notable exce n to these limitations is found in recent research conducted by Michael Horowitz, who em s adoption capacity theory to argue that groups with higher levels of organizational capital a ore likely to adopt suicide terrorism than groups with lower levels of capital. See Michael H witz, "Non-State Actors and the Diffusion of Innovations: The Case of Suicide Bombing," ublished manuscript, Harvard University, July 2008.

attacker's domestic population.[33] In recent years, however, an increasing number of suicide attacks have been carried out in countries where such domestic support appears to be lacking: examples include Afghanistan, Pakistan, and even Iraq.[34] A culture of martyrdom may influence the suicide bombers in these countries, but increasingly that culture seems to be found in cyberspace rather than in the streets.[35]

Another argument put forward by some scholars is that societies are more inclined to produce suicide bombers when they are subjected to foreign occupation. In the next section I examine the applicability of this "occupation thesis" as well as that of another explanation, the "outbidding thesis," to the globalization of suicide attacks.

OCCUPATION

In his book *Dying to Win*, Pape argues that the "bottom line is that suicide terrorism is mainly a response to foreign occupation."[36] He defines an occupation as "one in which a foreign power has the ability to control the local government independent of the wishes of the local community."[37] There are three reasons, however, why foreign occupation does not explain many contemporary suicide missions.[38] First, these attacks increasingly occur in countries where there is no discernible occupation, including Bangladesh, Indonesia, Jordan, Morocco, Pakistan, Saudi Arabia, the United Kingdom, the United States, Uzbekistan, and Yemen. Second, in foreign-occupied countries such as Iraq, the attacks are often not directed at the occupiers themselves who, according to the logic of the occupation thesis, should be the most obvious targets. Many suicide bombings in Iraq, for example, have targeted Kurds, Shiites, and Sufis, in an effort to stir ethnic tensions in the country and delegitimize the Iraqi government in the eyes of Iraqis. Third, even if they do target the occupation forces, many suicide attacks are not carried out by those individuals most directly affected by the occupation. In Iraq, for instance, most attacks against occupation forces are carried out by foreign jihadis from places

33. Bloom, *Dying to Kill.*
34. See Moghadam, "Suicide Terrorism, Occupation, and the Globalization of Martyrdom," pp. 707–729.
35. See, for example, Gabriel Weimann, *Terrorism on the Internet: The New Arena, The New Challenges* (Washington, D.C.: United States Institute of Peace Press, 2006), pp. 64–75; Marc Sageman, *Leaderless Jihad: Terror Networks in the Twenty-First Century* (Philadelphia: University of Pennsylvania Press, 2008), pp. 109–123; and Moghadam, *The Globalization of Martyrdom*, chap. 4.
36. Pape, *Dying to Win*, p. 23.
37. Ibid., p. 46.
38. For a more extensive critique of Pape's book *Dying to Win*, see Moghadam, "Suicide Terrorism, Occupation, and the Globalization of Martyrdom."

such as Kuwai Libya, Saudi Arabia, and Syria.[39] The perpetrators of the September 11 a cks were from Egypt, Saudi Arabia, and the United Arab Emirates.

Pape's focus occupation and his dismissal of religion or ideology as important variabl are most striking in his discussion of al-Qaida. "For al-Qaeda, religion atters," Pape writes, "but mainly in the context of national resistance to fo gn occupation."[40] The evidence, however, does not support Pape's argume A closer reading of statements issued by al-Qaida leaders suggests that re ion plays a more central role in the organization's ideology and mission th Pape would ascribe to it. Osama bin Laden and al-Qaida are engaged in a ensive jihad against what they portray as the "Crusader-Zionist alliance ecause they believe that the United States has made a "clear declaration of r on God, his messenger, and Muslims."[41] In a statement from Novembe 001, bin Laden declared, "This war is fundamentally religious. . . . Und no circumstances should we forget this enmity between us and the infidels or, the enmity is based on creed."[42] In another message, bin Laden went as as urging Americans to convert to Islam: "A message to the American peop Peace be upon those who follow the right path. . . . I urge you to become slims, for Islam calls for the principle of 'there is no God but Allah.'"[43]

Al-Qaida's u rstanding of occupation differs from that of Pape. Whereas Pape suggests foreign occupation consists of "boots on the ground"—or, as he puts it, th bility of a foreign power "to control the local government independent of th vishes of the local community"[44]—al-Qaida's understanding

39. In February 20 for example, Director of National Intelligence John Negroponte confirmed that "extreme Sunn adist elements, a subset of which are foreign fighters, constitute a small minority of the overa surgency, but their use of high-profile suicide attacks gives them a disproportionate impact." e Negroponte, "Statement by the Director of National Intelligence to the Senate Select Comm ee on Intelligence," 109th Cong., 2d sess., February 2, 2006. As recently as May 2007, for insta Gen. David Petraeus stated that "80 to 90 percent of the suicide bombers come from outside ." Quoted in Joshua Partlow, "An Uphill Battle to Stop Fighters at Border," *Washington Post*, M , 2007.

40. Pape, *Dying to* , p. 104.

41. Osama bin Lad "Text of Fatwa Urging Jihad against Americans," *Al-Quds al-Arabi* (London), February 23, , quoted in Christopher M. Blanchard, "Al-Qaida: Statements and Evolving Ideology," CRS Re for Congress (Washington, D.C.: Congressional Research Service, Library of Congress, Nove r 16, 2004), Order Code RS21973, p. 3.

42. Osama bin Lad speech broadcast on Al-Jazeera satellite channel television, November 3, 2001. Quoted in "B Laden Rails against Crusaders and UN," *BBC News*, November 3, 2001.

43. "Statement by ma bin Ladin," *Waqiaah*, October 26, 2002, quoted in Anonymous [Michael Scheuer], *Imperial ris: Why the West Is Losing the War on Terror* (Washington, D.C.: Brassey's, 2004), p. 154.

44. Pape, *Dying to* , p. 46.

of occupation is much broader. It includes a long history of injustices manifested today in the military, religious, political, economic, and cultural humiliation of the larger Muslim world by the "Crusader-Zionist alliance." It is this ideologically inspired definition of occupation that matters most for al-Qaida but that is absent from Pape's analysis.

Pape also does not explain why most suicide missions are perpetrated by groups claiming to act in the name of religion, while attacks by secular organizations have declined in recent years. Although he correctly notes that "modern suicide terrorism is not limited to Islamic fundamentalism,"[45] he does not acknowledge that most such attacks are perpetrated by radical Islamist groups. "Overall," Pape calculates, "Islamic fundamentalism is associated with about half of the suicide terrorist attacks that have occurred from 1980 to 2003."[46] Not included in Pape's count, however, is the high tally of suicide attacks that have occurred in Iraq since the 2003 U.S. invasion—a total of 1,020 such attacks by March 2008. According to my data set, Salafi-jihadist groups were the most dominant perpetrators of suicide missions in Iraq in the five years since the U.S.-led invasion.[47]

OUTBIDDING

Mia Bloom posits that terrorist groups may engage in suicide missions because they are trying to compete against other groups for the support of the local population. This tactic, known as "outbidding," is designed to increase the group's "market share" among that community. The thesis thus assumes that suicide bombing campaigns depend on the support of the local population. "In the war for public support," Bloom writes, "when the bombings resonate positively with the population that insurgent groups purport to represent, they help the organization mobilize support. If suicide bombing does not resonate among the larger population, the tactic will fail."[48]

The outbidding thesis appears plausible as an explanation for the adoption of suicide missions by several organizations, including the Popular Front for

---

45. Ibid., p. 16.
46. Ibid., p. 17.
47. Of the 1,020 suicide attacks in Iraq recorded in the data set, 208 were claimed by Salafi jihadist groups. The next most popular were nationalist-separatist groups, with 11 claimed attacks. Although the perpetrators of 794 attacks in Iraq are still unknown, anecdotal accounts suggest that the overwhelming number of all suicide attacks in Iraq are conducted by Salafi jihadist groups. See, for example, Hafez, *Suicide Bombers in Iraq;* and International Crisis Group, "In Their Own Words: Reading the Iraqi Insurgency," Middle East Report, No. 50 (Brussels: International Crisis Group, February 15, 2006).
48. Bloom, *Dying to Kill*, p. 78.

the Liberation c 'alestine (PFLP),[49] the Fatah al-Aqsa Martyrs Brigades,[50] and Amal in Lebanc [51] The outbidding thesis, however, falls short of providing a satisfactory exp ıation for the adoption of this tactic in many other cases, including some r :d by Bloom in *Dying to Kill.* For instance, it cannot explain why Sri Lanka' .iberation Tigers of Tamil Eelam (LTTE) adopted this tactic only in 1987, at ime when the internal rivalry between radical Tamil organizations had rea ed its pinnacle with the May 1986 massacre of the Tamil Eelam Liberatic Organization (TELO) and the killing of its leader.[52] By that time, the LTTE d eliminated not only the TELO but all of its other rivals as well.

Moreover, Bl n's own findings appear to contradict one of the central assumptions of th ›utbidding thesis, namely, that groups are vying for the support of the lo population. Her own survey data suggest that suicide missions in Sri ıka are not condoned among the Tamil population. Based on her interviews a l polls of "hundreds of Tamils all over Sri Lanka," she found that "there wa ⁄irtually no support for attacking civilians, regardless of whether they v e in Sinhalese territory or in the Tamil regions."[53] Despite this lack of sup rt, the LTTE continued its relentless suicide bombing campaign (includin ıttacks against civilians), apparently undeterred.

The outbiddi thesis fits within the traditional paradigm that sees suicide attacks as occu ng in the context of long-standing historical conflicts in which a large se ıent of the population supports the actions of suicide attackers as a legitima form of resistance designed to achieve self-determination, or at least some d ree of autonomy. That paradigm, however, is incompatible with the global ıad being waged by transnational groups such as al-Qaida that are seeking achieve less defined goals and that are unwilling to compromise. It is for th 'eason that the notion that suicide attackers are vying for domestic popular pport is most problematic with regard to al-Qaida and the global jihad mc ment.

The London nbers of July 2005, for example, targeted their own fellow citizens. Similaı a growing number of suicide missions being conducted in Iraq target Iraqi ather than the occupying forces. It is hard to argue that Iraqi

---

49. Bloom, "Palesti ı Suicide Bombing."
50. See assessment Ely Karmon, quoted in Christopher Dickey et al., "Inside Suicide, Inc.," *Newsweek,* April 15)2, p. 26.
51. Martin Kramer acrifice and Fratricide in Shiite Lebanon," *Terrorism and Political Violence,* Vol. 3, No. 3 (Autu 1991), pp. 30–47.
52. Bloom apparen 'ecognizes this problem and does not argue that outbidding has been a factor in the adoption suicide attacks by the LTTE. See Bloom, *Dying to Kill,* p. 71.
53. Ibid., p. 67.

suicide attackers are trying to gain the sympathy of the very people in whose midst they are blowing themselves up.

Al-Qaida, Salafi Jihad, and Suicide Attacks

The main reason for the global spread of suicide missions lies in two related and mutually reinforcing phenomena: al-Qaida's transition into a global terrorist actor and the growing appeal of its guiding ideology, Salafi jihad. This argument requires an explanation of two separate issues: first, why and how al-Qaida became a global entity in both outlook and practice; and second, al-Qaida's emphasis on suicide missions as the primary method of terrorist operations.

AL-QAIDA'S GLOBAL OUTLOOK

Three key factors influenced al-Qaida's decision to globalize its operations, the first being the group's core doctrine. As envisioned by Abdullah Azzam, bin Laden's mentor, al-Qaida was designed as the vanguard of an Islamic army similar to an international rapid reaction force that would come to the rescue of Muslims wherever and whenever they were in need. This Muslim legion would be self-perpetuating, generating new waves of Islamic warriors who would fight and defeat infidel and apostate countries the world over.

The second reason for the globalization of al-Qaida was the spread of the "Afghan Arabs," the foreign fighters who flocked to Afghanistan after the Soviet invasion, to other countries beginning in 1988. After the Red Army's withdrawal from Afghanistan, many Afghan Arabs returned to their home countries, where they participated in local jihads against entrenched regimes in countries such as Egypt, Jordan, and Saudi Arabia. Others moved to third countries, including some in Western Europe. Realizing Azzam's dream, many of these Afghan Arabs radicalized and mobilized Muslims in their countries. They regarded themselves as the vanguard that Azzam had foreseen, and many chose violence as their preferred tactic.[54]

Third, al-Qaida based its decision to globalize on a deliberate shift in strategy. Between 1995 and 1996, after heated internal discussions, al-Qaida decided not to attack the "near enemy" (i.e., the local Arab regimes it regarded as apostate), but the "far enemy" (i.e., Western "infidel" countries, above all the United States).[55] This shift in strategy was epitomized when, in 1996, al-Qaida

54. Jason Burke, *Al-Qaeda: The True Story of Radical Islam* (London: I.B. Tauris, 2004), p. 290.
55. Marc Sageman, "Global Salafi Jihad," statement to the National Commission on Terrorist At-

declared war o he United States, and again, two years later, when it announced the fo tion of a global alliance to defeat the "Crusader-Zionist" enemy. Al-Qaida' rst major suicide attack, the August 1998 bombings of the U.S. embassies Nairobi, Kenya, and Dar-es-Salaam, Tanzania, embodied that strategic sl .

AL-QAIDA AND E PRIMACY OF SUICIDE ATTACKS

In al-Qaida's ta al arsenal, suicide attacks play a pivotal role. No other tactic symbolizes al-(da's tenaciousness and ability to inspire a large number of Muslims world de as much as "martyrdom operations," to use the group's euphemistic lab ng. Al-Qaida has all but perfected this tactic and institutionalized it to an e nt not seen in other terrorist groups. It instilled the spirit of self-sacrifice in collective psyche of virtually all of its fighters, thus creating a cult of martyr n that far exceeds the Palestinian and Lebanese cult of death in both scope a depth.

Abdullah Az n was the first theoretician to succeed in turning martyrdom and self-sacrifi into a formative ethos of future al-Qaida members. It is largely becaus f him that self-sacrifice has become a moral code that al-Qaida has used justify suicide missions against its enemies.[56] More than any other individu Azzam persuaded jihadis in Afghanistan and beyond that those who die the sake of God *(fi sabil Allah)* will be rewarded in paradise. Ironically, Azz understood martyrdom not as involving suicide missions per se, but as t leath of any "true" Muslim waging jihad. Such martyrdom would wash a the jihadi's sins and bestow glory upon him.

Death-obsess Afghan Arabs were so deeply affected by Azzam's thinking that they beca a "curious sideshow to the real fighting in Afghanistan," Lawrence Wrig bserved. "When a fighter fell, his comrades would congratulate him and ep because they were not also slain in battle. These scenes struck other M ms as bizarre. The Afghans were fighting for their country, not for Paradis r an idealized Islamic community."[57]

Al-Qaida's d sion to engage in suicide attacks was also influenced by the Egyptian grou l-Jihad and its leader, Ayman al-Zawahiri. Years before Zawahiri and a had formally joined al-Qaida in 2001, the Egyptian organization had emplo l suicide missions as a terrorist tactic. In August 1993 a sui-

---

tacks upon the Uni States, July 9, 2003; and Fawaz A. Gerges, *The Far Enemy: Why Jihad Went Global* (Cambridge: mbridge University Press, 2005).

56. Reuven Paz, in iew by author, Washington, D.C., July 17, 2006.

57. Lawrence Wrig *The Looming Tower: Al-Qaeda and the Road to 9/11* (New York: Vintage, 2007), p. 125.

cide bomber smashed his explosives-laden motorcycle into the car of Egypt's interior minister, Hassan al-Alfi, who nevertheless survived the attack.[58] On November 19, 1995, al-Jihad staged another attack, this one at the Egyptian embassy in Islamabad, Pakistan, involving two assailants, including one suicide bomber. Sixteen people were killed.

In interviews with Fawaz Gerges, former jihadis confirmed that Zawahiri's advocacy of suicide bombings fundamentally influenced bin Laden's adoption of this tactic. The spectacular nature of al-Qaida's suicide attacks, they told him, were adopted from al-Jihad, which had always used extremely lethal and psychologically damaging attacks to differentiate itself from its jihadist rival in Egypt, the al-Gama'a al-Islamiyya.[59]

When pressed to explain the use of suicide bombers—a tactic still considered taboo, especially when used against fellow Muslims—Zawahiri stated that these martyrs represented a "generation of mujahideen that has decided to sacrifice itself and its property in the cause of God. That is because the way of death and martyrdom is a weapon that tyrants and their helpers, who worship their salaries instead of God, do not have."[60] Zawahiri made a claim that many other supporters of suicide attacks would repeat: the suicide attacker does not kill himself for personal reasons, but sacrifices himself for God. He is therefore not committing suicide, but achieving martyrdom. It was a game of words, but it provided justification for hundreds of future suicide bombers to emulate these early *shuhada*.

In August 1996, bin Laden formally declared war against the United States, imploring Muslim youths to sacrifice themselves. Seeking religious justification, bin Laden ties the longing for martyrdom to verses from the Quran, hadith, and poems. According to bin Laden, "Our youths believe in paradise after death. They believe that taking part in fighting will not bring their day nearer, and staying behind will not postpone their day either. Exalted be to Allah who said: 'And a soul will not die but with the permission of Allah, the term is fixed' (Aal Imraan: 3:145). . . . Our youths took note of the meaning of the poetic verse: 'If death is a predetermined must, then it is a shame to die cowardly.'" Bin Laden then highlights a number of sayings that together describe the rewards of the martyr in Paradise:

Allah, the Exalted, also said: "And do not speak of those who are slain in Allah's way as dead; nay, they are alive, but you do not perceive" (Bagarah;

58. The group al-Jihad is also known as Egyptian Islamic Jihad. Some authors dispute that al-Jihad was responsible for the attempt on al-Alfi's life and blame the al-Gama'a al-Islamiyya instead.
59. Gerges, *The Far Enemy*, pp. 142–143.
60. Quoted in Wright, *The Looming Tower*, pp. 248–249.

> 2:154). . . . An 'A martyr will not feel the pain of death except like how you feel when ou are pinched" (Saheeh Al-Jame' As-Sagheer). He also said: "A marty privileges are guaranteed by Allah; forgiveness with the first gush of hi ood, he will be shown his seat in paradise, he will be decorated with the els of belief (Imaan), married off to the beautiful ones, protected from th st in the grave, assured security in the day of judgement, crowned with crown of dignity, a ruby of which is better than this whole world (Duniah nd its entire content, wedded to seventy-two of the pure Houries (beauti ones of Paradise) and his intercession on the behalf of seventy of his rela s will be accepted."

Bin Laden goe to praise the courage of youths willing to sacrifice themselves, suggest that through death, young Muslims will prevail in the struggle agains e "Crusaders": "Those youths know that their rewards in fighting you, t JSA, is double than their rewards in fighting someone else not from the pe le of the book. They have no intention except to enter paradise by killing ."[61]

Al-Qaida's e hasis on suicide missions was on display in its Afghan training camps. A d ment found in an al-Qaida safe house in Afghanistan titled "Goals and Ob tives of Jihad," for example, ranked the goal of "attaining martyrdom in cause of God" second only to "establishing the rule of God on earth." Ano r document listed two "illegitimate excuses" for leaving jihad as "love of e world" and "hatred of death."[62]

Bin Laden so ht to spread the virtues of martyrdom through videotapes and statements the internet. In 2004, for instance, he urged his followers to "become dilige in carrying out martyrdom operations; these operations, praise be to Go ave become a great source of terror for the enemy. . . . These are the most in rtant operations."[63]

The use of s de attacks is also a logical outcome of al-Qaida's desire to maximize the p and suffering of its enemies in a protracted struggle. In his 2001 book, *Kni under the Prophet's Banner,* Zawahiri writes, "If our goal is comprehensive ange and if our path, as the Koran and our history have shown us, is a g road of jihad and sacrifices, we must not despair of repeated strikes a recurring calamities."[64] He adds that there is a need within

61. "Bin Laden's F a," *PBS Online Newshour,* August 8, 1996, http://www.pbs.org/newshour/terrorism/internati l/fatwa_1996.html.
62. C.J. Chivers an avid Rhode, "Turning Out Guerrillas and Terrorists to Wage a Holy War," *New York Times,* M 18, 2002.
63. Quoted in Blan rd, "Al-Qaida: Statements and Evolving Ideology," p. 10.
64. Ayman al-Zaw , *Knights under the Prophet's Banner* (London: Al-Sharq al-Awsat, 2001), part 11. The book was s ized in the London-based magazine *Al-Sharq al-Awsat* between December 2 and December 10, , and translated by the Foreign Broadcast Information Service (FBIS), FBIS-NES-2001-1202.

the jihadist movement to offset the power of the Muslims' enemies, whose numbers and capabilities have risen tremendously, as did "the quality of their weapons, their destructive powers, their disregard for all taboos, and disrespect for the customs of wars and conflict."[65] To address this asymmetry, Zawahiri suggests a number of steps, including "concentrat[ing] on the method of martyrdom operations as the most successful way of inflicting damage against the opponent and the least costly to the mujahidin in terms of casualties."[66]

SALAFI JIHAD AND SUICIDE ATTACKS

The Salafi jihad is a radical offshoot movement with roots in a broader Islamist trend known as Salafism, as well as in Wahhabism and Qutbist factions of the Muslim Brotherhood.[67] Salafis have adopted a strict interpretation of Islamic religious law, and their doctrine centers around a more literal understanding of the concept of *tawhid* (the unity of God) than does that of ordinary Muslims. For Salafis, the unity of God—a concept adhered to by all Muslims—extends to the belief that all man-made laws must be rejected because they interfere with the word and will of God. Salafis reject the division of religion and state and believe that only the *salaf*—the Prophet himself and his companions—led lives in accordance with God's will. Only by emulating that lifestyle can Muslims reverse the decline of Islam.

Whereas ordinary Salafis believe that God's word should be spread by *dawa* alone—the nonviolent call to Islam by proselytizing—Salafi jihadists advocate waging violent jihad. This advocacy of violence leads to four main points of contention between the two groups: unlike Salafis, Salafi jihadists elevate jihad to the same level as the five pillars of Islam; they engage in *takfir,* the process of labeling fellow Muslims as infidels *(kufr),* thus justifying violence against them; they condone the targeting of civilians; and they support the use of suicide operations.[68]

Salafi jihadists believe that suicide operations against "infidels" and "apostates" (i.e., non-Muslim heretics and nominally Muslim "traitors") represent the ultimate form of devotion to God and the optimal way to wage jihad. They present jihad and self-sacrifice as the antithesis to everything the West stands

---

65. Ibid.
66. Ibid.
67. Wahhabism is a puritanical strand of Islam closely related to Salafism, which is common in Saudi Arabia.
68. Quintan Wiktorowicz, "Anatomy of the Salafi Movement," *Studies in Conflict and Terrorism,* Vol. 29, No. 3 (May 2006), pp. 207–239.

for—hence the ntra, "The West loves life, while true Muslims love death." In the words of u Ayman al-Hilali, a key interpreter of bin Laden's ideas on Salafi jihadist w sites, "First we have to acknowledge a basic fact, proved by experience and lity, already acknowledged by the enemy, which is that the vital contradicti to the Zionist and American enemy is the doctrine of Jihad and Martyrdon stishhad)."[69]

In certain m ues, Salafi jihadist preachers such as Abu Hamza al-Mazri and Omar Bak Muhammed led thousands of Muslim youths to develop a cult-like fascina n with martyrdom. Other preachers are active mainly on the internet, provi legitimation for "martyrdom operations." Because Islam forbids the taki of one's own life, Salafi jihadists draw a conceptual distinction between su de and martyrdom, arguing that those committing ordinary suicide do so f ersonal reasons, such as distress or depression; in contrast, martyrs die pri rily for the sake of God, but also for the greater good of the Muslim comm y.

Although sta ical evidence for the growth of Salafi jihad is scant, there is ample anecdot vidence of its increasing popularity among both men and women[70] in ge ral,[71] and in Europe,[72] the Middle East,[73] Central Asia,[74] Southeast Asia, nd Africa[76] in particular.

In this study, rise of the Salafi jihad and its growing influence on suicide missions are ex ined through a coding of the fifty groups that employed them from Dec ber 1981 through March 2008 as part of their guiding ideol-

---

69. Cited in Reuve z, "Qa'idat Al-Jihad: A New Name on the Road to Palestine" (International Policy Institute fo ounter-Terrorism, May 7, 2002), http://www.global-report.co.il/prism/?l+en&a+4959.

70. On women, see example, Sebastian Rotella, "European Women Join Ranks of Jihadis," *Los Angeles Times*, Janu 10, 2006; and Katharina von Knop, "The Female Jihad: Al-Qaida's Women," *Studies in Conflict a errorism*, Vol. 30, No. 5 (May 2007), pp. 397–414.

71. See, for examp Gilles Kepel, *Jihad: The Trail of Political Islam* (Cambridge, Mass.: Harvard University Press, 2 ; and Olivier Roy, *Globalized Islam: The Search for a New Ummah* (New York: Columbia Universi ress, 2004).

72. Kathryn Haah merging Terrorist Trends in Spain's Moroccan Communities," *Terrorism Monitor*, Vol. 4, No (May 4, 2006), pp. 1–2; Pascale Combelles Siegel, "Radical Islam and the French Muslim Pri Population," *Terrorism Monitor*, Vol. 4, No. 15 (July 27, 2006), pp. 1–2; and Lorenzo Vidino, "T Danger of Homegrown Terrorism to Scandinavia," *Terrorism Monitor*, Vol. 4, No. 20 (October 19 06), pp. 5–6.

73. On the Middle t, see, for example, Marc Sageman, *Understanding Terror Networks* (Philadelphia: University of nsylvania Press, 2004).

74. See, for exampl nar Valiyev, "The Rise of Salafi Islam in Azerbaijan," *Terrorism Monitor*, Vol. 3, No. 13 (July 1, 2 , pp. 6–7.

75. See Internation risis Group, "Indonesia Backgrounder: Why Salafism and Terrorism Mostly Don't Mix," Asia R rt, No. 83 (Brussels: International Crisis Group, September 13, 2004).

76. Douglas Farah, lafists, China, and West Africa's Growing Anarchy" (Alexandria, Va.: International Assessme d Strategy Center, December 7, 2004).

ogy or doctrine (see table 1). In all, 1,857 such attacks took place. To be coded as Salafi jihadist, a group must be a Sunni Islamic group to which at least one of the following characteristics must also apply: (1) affiliation with and/or adherence to al-Qaida was reflected in the group's name;[77] (2) the group had "internalized the worldview of al-Qaida and global jihad";[78] (3) the group engaged in violence to overthrow an Islamic regime and create a transnational caliphate in its stead;[79] or (4) the group engaged in the labeling of some other Muslims as heretics.[80]

My analysis of the data yields the following findings: of the 788 suicide attacks from December 1981 to March 2008 in which the identity of the group could be identified, Salafi jihadist groups carried out 37.7 percent—more than any other group. They were followed by nationalist-separatist groups with 18.5 percent and hybrid groups with 17.8 percent. One thousand sixty-nine attacks (57.6 percent) were perpetrated by organizations whose identities remain unknown. Of these, however, 795 (74.4 percent) occurred in Iraq, where the vast majority of organizations conducting suicide bombings are known to be Salafi jihadist.[81] The bulk of suicide missions in the "unknown" category were therefore likely carried out by Salafi jihadist groups, too.

More important, according to the following criteria, Salafi jihadist groups have assumed the leadership among groups that employ this modus operandi: number of suicide attacks, number of organizations engaged in suicide attacks, total number of fatalities, and average number killed per attack. In 1997, for example, none of the groups that undertook suicide missions were Salafi jihadist. In 1998 a quarter of the groups that employed this tactic adhered to Salafi jihadist ideology. After 2004, at least half of all groups conducting suicide missions adhered to Salafi jihadist ideology in every given year.

The growing ascendancy of Salafi jihadist groups among groups employing suicide attacks is paralleled by the relative decline in the importance of groups

77. An example would be the group al-Qaida in Iraq.
78. This assessment is based on the best judgment of a group of eight terrorism experts at the RAND Corporation. See Angel Rabasa, Peter Chalk, Kim Cragin, Sara A. Daly, Heather Gregg, Theodore W. Krasik, Kevin A. O'Brien, and William Rosenau, *Beyond Al-Qaeda, Part 1: The Global Jihadist Movement*, and *Part 2: The Outer Rings of the Terrorist Universe* (Santa Monica, Calif.: RAND, 2006).
79. This excludes groups such as Hamas, which engages primarily in violence against Israel, a non-Muslim state, but has generally avoided systematic attacks against the Palestinian Authority (prior to Hamas's electoral victory in 2006) for fear of sparking a civil war.
80. *Takfir* is not generally practiced by mainstream Islamist groups and not even by all Salafi jihadists. Those groups and individuals who do practice this form of excommunication, however, are exclusively Salafi jihadist.
81. See International Crisis Group, "In Their Own Words"; and Hafez, *Suicide Bombers in Iraq*.

Table 1. Ideologic. \ffiliation of Groups Conducting Suicide Attacks, December 1981 through March 20

Organizations	Ideology	Organizations	Ideology
Al Dawa[1]	SH	Jemaah Islamiyya[24]	SJ
Al Jihad[2]	SJ	Jund al-Sham (Army of the Levant)[25]	SJ
Al-Gama'a al-Islan [3]	SJ	Kashmir Separatists[26]	H
Al-Qaida	SJ	Kurdistan Workers Party	M/NS
Al-Qaida in Iraq[4]	SJ	Lashkar-e-Jhangvi[27]	SJ
Al-Qaida in the Isl c Magreb[5]	SJ	Lashkar-e-Taibeh[28]	SJ
Amal	SH	Lebanese Liberation Organization[29]	U
Ansar al-Islam[6]	SJ	Liberation Tigers of Tamil Eelam	NS
Ansar Allah	SH	Mujahideen Army[30]	H
Ansar al-Sunnah[7]	SJ	Mujahideen Shura Council[31]	SJ
Armed Islamic Grc 3	SJ	Mujahideen Youth Movement[32]	SJ
As-Sirat al-Moustε m[9]	SJ	Palestinian Islamic Jihad	MI/NS
Chechen Separatis	H	Partisans of the Sunni	U
Chechen Separatis -Arbi Barayev[10]	H	Popular Front for the Liberation of Palestine	M/NS
Chechen Separatis -Karachaev Jamaat[11]	U	Popular Resistance Committees	MI/NS
Chechen Separatis -Ramzan Akhmadov[12]	H	Qari Zafar Group[33]	SJ
Fatah	NS	Revolutionary People's Liberation Party	M
Hamas[13]	MI/NS	Riyad us-Saliheyn Martyrs' Brigade[34]	H
Hezballah	SH	Saddam Loyalists	NS
Hizb-i-Islami[14]	SJ	Shields of Islam	U
Hizb-ul Mujahideer	SJ	Soldiers of the Prophet's Companion	SJ
Hizb-ut-Tahrir[16]	SJ	Syrian Baath Organization	NS
Islamic Army in Ir 7	MI/NS	Syrian Social Nationalist Party	M/NS
Islamic Courts Un 8	H	Taliban	H
Islamic Jihad of U kistan[19]	SJ	Tawhid wal Jihad[35]	SJ
Islamic Movement Uzbekistan[20]	SJ	Tehrik-i-Taliban[36]	H
Islamic State of Ir 1	SJ	Victory and Jihad in Greater Syria[37]	U
Jaish-e-Muhamma	SJ		
Jamatul Mujahedir Bangladesh[23]	SJ		

SOURCES: The follo ıg sources were used to ascertain the ideological or doctrinal orientation of groups that e loy suicide terrorism: The Terrorism Knowledge Base (TKB) of the Memorial Institute the Prevention of Terrorism (MIPT); the 2005 Country Reports on Terrorism, publishe by the U.S. Department of State's Office of the Coordinator for Counterterrorism ngel Rabasa, Peter Chalk, Kim Cragin, Sara A. Daly, Heather Gregg, Theodore W. Kr , Kevin A. O'Brien, and William Rosenau, *Beyond Al-Qaeda,* Part 1: *The Global Jihadist ement,* and Part 2: *The Outer Rings of the Terrorist Universe* (Santa Monica, Calif.: F D, 2006); and anecdotal information, when the first three sources did not provide suffi ıt information to establish ideological identity. The TKB integrates data from the RAND rorism Chronology and RAND-MIPT Terrorism Incident databases; the Terrorism Indict t database; and DFI International's research on terrorist organizations. On March 21, 2 3, the MIPT announced via email to subscribers of the TKB newsletter that the TKB wo "cease operations on March 31, 2008, and elements of the system will be merged with Global Terrorism Database, managed by the National Consortium for the Study of Te ism and Responses to Terrorism (START) at the University of Mary-

Table 1. (Continued)

land." The TKB website (http://www.tkb.org) is not longer accessible. The RAND studies detail information on the ideological affiliation of jihadist groups. The assessments made in the two RAND studies are based on the consensus agreement of eight RAND terrorism experts.

NOTE: Groups are coded as hybrid (H), Marxist (M), mainstream Islamist (MI), nationalist-separatist (NS), Shiite (SH), Salafi jihadist (SJ), unknown (U) groups, as well as in combinations (e.g., MI/NS or M/NS). Hybrid organizations comprise members who have adopted a Salafi jihadist ideology as well as those who seem to be motivated primarily by ethnonationalist and separatist concerns. Groups coded as mainstream Islamist groups, such as Hamas and Palestinian Islamic Jihad, differ from Salafi jihadist groups in that they participate in the political process—something that Salafi jihadist groups consider heretical, given that all power must derive from God, not from the electorate. In addition, mainstream Islamist groups do not engage in *takfir*—the labeling of other Muslims as *kufr,* or heretics. Salafi jihadists, all of whom are Sunnis, consider the Shiite stream of Islam to be heretical.

[1]Al-Dawa conducted at least three suicide attacks in Kuwait between 1983 and 1985. According to the Terrorism Knowledge Base (TKB), al-Dawa is a Shiite organization.

[2]Al-Jihad was led by Ayman al-Zawahiri. The group formally merged with al-Qaida in June 2001.

[3]Although the al-Gama'a al-Islamiyya has recently distanced itself from al-Qaida, it was one of the prominent Salafi jihadist groups during the 1990s and a major influence on al-Qaida.

[4]Al-Qaida in Iraq is a franchise of al-Qaida. The group was formerly known as Tawhid wal Jihad.

[5]Al-Qaida in the Islamic Maghreb is a franchise of al-Qaida. The group was formerly known as the Salafist Group for Call and Combat.

[6]Ansar al-Islam seeks the violent overthrow of Iraqi Kurdistan and conversion of the province into an Islamist state. A faction of Ansar al-Islam split off and established Tawhid wal Jihad. According to *GlobalSecurity.org,* Ansar al-Islam "has close links to and support from al-Qaida. Al-Qaida and Usama Bin Laden participated in the formation and funding of the group, which has provided safe haven to al-Qaida in northeastern Iraq." See "Ansar al Islam (Supporters of Islam)," *GlobalSecurity.org,* http://www.globalsecurity.org/military/world/para/ansar_al_islam.htm.

[7]According to the TKB, Ansar al-Sunnah (Followers of the Tradition) is an Iraqi jihadist group dedicated to the establishment of an Islamic state in Iraq based on sharia law. It seeks to achieve this objective by defeating coalition forces and the foreign occupation. Taken from "Group Profile: Ansar Al-Sunnah Army," *Terrorism Knowledge Base.* On Ansar al-Sunnah's Salafi roots, see also Mohammed M. Hafez, "Suicide Terrorism in Iraq: A Preliminary Assessment of the Quantitative Data and Documentary Evidence," *Studies in Conflict and Terrorism,* Vol. 29, No. 6 (September 2006), pp. 591–619; International Crisis Group, "In Their Own Words: Reading the Iraqi Insurgency," Middle East Report, No. 50 (Brussels: International Crisis Group, February 15, 2006); and Michael Eisenstadt and Jeffrey White, "Assessing Iraq's Sunni Arab Insurgency," *Policy Focus,* No. 50 (Washington, D.C.: Washington Institute for Near East Policy, December 2005), pp. 1–39.

[8]The Armed Islamic Group engages in *takfir.* See Rabasa et al., *Beyond Al-Qaeda,* Part 2, p. 28.

[9]As-Sirat al-Moustaquim is the cell responsible for the 2003 Casablanca bombings. It is sometimes referred to as Salafia Jihadiya. A panel of eight experts at the RAND Corporation concluded that Salafia Jihadiya has "internalized the Al-Qaida worldview of Global Jihad." See Rabasa et al., *Beyond Al-Qaeda,* Part 1, pp. xxii, 2, 79. Information also taken from "Group Profile: Salafia Jihadia," *Terrorism Knowledge Base.* There are persistent reports that As-Sirat al-Moustaquim/Salafia Jihadiya does not exist as a group, but is a term

Table 1. (Continue

invented by Mor :an authorities. There is little doubt, however, that the cell responsible for the bombings as driven by Salafi jihadist ideology. For a discussion of the controversy over the existe of Salafia Jihadiya, see Thomas Renard, "Moroccan Crackdown on Salafiya Jihadiya cruitment of Foreign Fighters for Iraq," *Terrorism Focus,* Vol. 5, No. 27 (July 23, 2008) 5.

[10]According to th aifa database, on June 7, 2000, a truck bomb driven by two Chechen suicide bombers ne male and one female) exploded in Alkhan Yurt, targeting an OMON (Special Forces ce) unit. Chechen separatists under the leadership of Arbi Barayev, who are also known he Special Purpose Islamic Regiment (SPIR), claimed responsibility. According to the T rism Knowledge Base, the primary objective of SPIR is the liberation of Chechnya and t ormation of an independent Chechen state. However, the Islamic fighters also promote more radical strain of Islam and a desire to install a fundamentalist Islamic republic g rned by Sharia law in Chechnya. Taken from "Group Profile: Special Purpose Islamic giment (SPIR)," *Terrorism Knowledge Base.*

[11]Chechen separa under the leadership of Karachaev sent three suicide bombers to detonate themselves coordinated attacks near the Russian border with Chechnya. They killed 20 and wounde bout 140. The purpose of the attacks remains unknown. No additional information was ailable about the group.

[12]The Chechen se tist group led by Ramzan Akhmadov was responsible for six suicide attacks in June a July 2000. Although information is to determine whether the group is Salafi jihadist in aracter is insufficient, Akhmadov was known as a radical Islamist and was likely influe d by Wahhabism. Like other Chechen terrorist groups, this group likely comprised both afi jihadists as well as more nationalist elements.

[13]Although Hamas rigins extend to the Muslim Brotherhood, its primary goal is the elimination of Israel. H s has resisted the adoption of al-Qaida's doctrine of global jihad, and it does not engag *takfir.* Its unwillingness to adopt al-Qaida's worldview of global jihad has elicited se l heated exchanges between al-Qaida's deputy leader, Ayman al-Zawahiri, and th lamas leadership. Zawahiri has appealed to Hamas—and to the Muslim Brotherhood at e—not to participate in the democratic process because he and other Salafi jihadists b ve that power derived from the electorate rather than from God is heretical. For addi al information, see Reuven Paz, "The Islamic Debate over Democracy: Jihadi-Salafi Res nses to Hamas' Victory in the Palestinian Elections," Project for the Research of Islami Movements (PRISM), Occasional Papers, Vol. 4, No. 1 (Herzliya, Israel: PRISM, January 06); and Stephen Ulph, "Al Zawahiri Takes Hamas to Task," *Terrorism Focus,* Vol. 3, 9 (March 7, 2006), p. 1.

[14]Hizb-i-Islami is by Gulbuddin Hekmatyar, who is believed to be allied with Osama bin Laden. Its goal i e end of occupation in Afghanistan and the establishment of an Islamist state there. See izb-i Islami Gulbuddin," *GlobalSecurity.org,* http://www.globalsecurity .org/security/pro s/hizb-i_islami_gulbuddin.htm/.

[15]Although Hizb-u Mujahideen has ties with Salafi jihadist groups, including Lashkar-e-Taibeh, its prim focus is the liberation of Kashmir and its accession to Pakistan. Taken from "Group Pro Hizbul Mujahideen (HM)," *Terrorism Knowledge Base.* It is also tied to Jamaat-i-Islami, mainstream Islamist party, and the equivalent of the Muslim Brotherhood in Pakista

[16]Hizb ut-Tahrir w esponsible for a suicide attack at the entrance to a children's clothing store in the loc market in Tashkent, Uzbekistan, on March, 29, 2004. According to *GlobalSecurity.o* Hizb ut-Tahrir al-Islami (Islamic Party of Liberation) is "a radical Islamic political movem that seeks 'implementation of pure Islamic doctrine' and the creation of an Islamic calip in Central Asia. . . . Its basic aim was struggle with infidels and the organization of iversal caliphate embracing all Islamic countries. . . . The political struggle is manifeste the struggle against the disbelieving imperialists, to deliver the Ummah from their domin on and to liberate her from their influence by uprooting their intellectual,

Table 1. (Continued)

cultural, political, economic and military roots from all of the Muslim countries." See "Hizb ut-Tahrir Al-Islami (Islamic Party of Liberation)," *GlobalSecurity.org,* http://www.globalsecurity.org/military/world/para/hizb-ut-tahrir.htm.

[17]The TKB does not provide sufficient information to determine whether the Islamic Army in Iraq is a Salafi jihadist organization. According to Mohammed Hafez, the Islamic Army in Iraq is both nationalist and Islamist. Hafez, *Suicide Bombers in Iraq: The Strategy and Ideology of Martyrdom* (Washington, D.C.: United States Institute of Peace Press, 2007).

[18]The Somali Islamic Courts Union consists of members with a mainstream Islamist orientation as well as Salafi jihadists with suspected ties to al-Qaida. "The Supreme Islamic Courts Union/al-Ittihad Mahakem al-Islamiya (ICU)," *GlobalSecurity.org,* http://www.globalsecurity.org/military/world/para/icu.htm/.

[19]The Islamic Jihad of Uzbekistan openly declared its participation in the "global jihad" and is a splinter group of the Salafi jihadist Islamic Movement of Uzbekistan. See "Islamic Jihad Group of Uzbekistan," *GlobalSecurity.org,* http://www.globalsecurity.org/security/profiles/islamic_jihad_group_of_uzbekistan.htm/.

[20]The Islamist Movement of Uzbekistan has "internalized the Al-Qaida worldview of Global Jihad." Rabasa et al., *Beyond Al-Qaeda,* Part 1, pp. xxii, 2, 79.

[21]The Islamic State of Iraq is the successor organization to the Salafi jihadist Mujahideen Shura Council and is dominated by al-Qaida in Iraq.

[22]Jaish-e-Muhammad has "internalized the al-Qaida worldview of Global Jihad." Rabasa et al., *Beyond Al-Qaeda,* Part 1, pp. xxii, 2, 79.

[23]According to the TKB, "Jamatul Mujahedin Bangladesh (JMB) is a terrorist group dedicated to removing the country's secular government and imposing a Taliban-inspired Islamic theocracy in its place. In addition to calling for an Islamic state based on Sharia law, JMB has denounced the U.S.-led invasion of Iraq, warning President [George W.] Bush and British Prime Minister [Tony] Blair to leave all Muslim countries." Taken from "Group Profile: Jamatul Mujahedin Bangladesh (JMB)," *Terrorism Knowledge Base.*

[24]Jemaah Islamiyya has "internalized the Al-Qaida worldview of Global Jihad." Rabasa et al., *Beyond Al-Qaeda,* Part 1, pp. xxii, 2, 79.

[25]A group named the Army of the Levant (Jund al-Sham) took responsibility for the March 19, 2005, bombing of a theater in Doha, Qatar, near a British school and popular among Westerners. The name has been claimed by several Sunni Islamic extremist entities, all or none of which may be linked. According to TKB, all of the Jund al-Sham entities desire to "achieve the unified purpose of replacing what they view as misguided forms of Islam and governmental rule with their vision of a traditional Islamic caliphate extending across the Levant. . . . Like many second- and third-tier Islamic extremist entities, the Jund al-Sham organizations are believed to be incorporated, however loosely, under the greater al-Qaeda umbrella." Taken from "Group Profile: Jund Al-Sham," *Terrorism Knowledge Base.*

[26]Lashkar-e-Taibeh, Jaish-e-Muhammad, and Harkat-ul-Mujahideen, the three major Kashmir separatist groups, have "internalized the Al-Qaida worldview of Global Jihad." Rabasa et al, *Beyond Al-Qaeda,* Part 1, pp. xxii, 2, 79.

[27]Lashkar-e-Jhangvi has "internalized the Al-Qaida worldview of Global Jihad." Ibid.

[28]Lashkar-e-Taibeh has "internalized the Al-Qaida worldview of Global Jihad." Ibid.

[29]On November 11, 1987, a female suicide bomber detonated 12 pounds of explosives packed in a briefcase at Beirut airport. On November 14, 1987, a female suicide bomber detonated 2 pounds of explosives connected to a nail-filled grenade concealed in a box of chocolates in the lobby of the American University Hospital in West Beirut. The Lebanese Liberation Army claimed responsibility, but no solid information on the ideology of this group is available. Given the use of female suicide bombers, however, it is unlikely that this was a Salafi jihadist group.

Table 1. (Continu

[30]The Mujahideen my, or Jaish-e Mujahideen, is "associated with Al-Qaida" but has recently distance self from al-Qaida's indiscriminatory killing. See "Jaysh al-Mujahideen Terrorist Lieute t and Propaganda Chief Captured," *GlobalSecurity.org,* http://www .globalsecurity.o military/library/news/2005/11/mil-051124-mnfi02.htm/. According to Evan F. Kohlma the Mujahideen Army has "wavered back and forth in its stated jihadist political platfor See Evan F. Kohlmann, "State of the Sunni Insurgency in Iraq: August 2007" (Washin , D.C.: NEFA Foundation, July 20, 2008), http://www.nefafoundation .org/miscellaneo raqreport0807.pdf/.

[31]The Mujahideen ura Council was the primary Salafi jihadist grouping in Iraq until it was renamed the Isla State of Iraq on October 15, 2006. Its stated goal was to manage "the struggle in the le of confrontation to ward off the invading infidels and their apostate stooges." Take om "Group Profile: Mujahideen Shura Council," *Terrorism Knowledge Base.*

[32]There is a high l ihood that the Mujahideen Youth Movement is directly influenced by al-Qaida. See Andr Black, "Somalia's Mujahideen Youth Movement," *Terrorism Focus,* Vol. 4, No. 19 (June , 2007), p. 2. The group's founder and leader, Adan Hashi Ayro, has close al-Qaida c ections. See Alisha Ryu, "Youth Mujahideen Group Leading Attacks in Somalia," *Glob curity.org,* June 19, 2007, http://www.globalsecurity.org/military/library/news/200 6/mil-070619-voa03.htm/.

[33]Qari Zafar is a s ter group of the Salafi jihadist Lashkar-e Jhangvi and affiliated with al-Qaida. See Abb Naqvi, "They Were Targeting Pakistan and Its Leaders," *Daily Times,* February 18, 2C

[34]According to the B, "The Riyad us-Saliheyn Martyrs' Brigade is a relatively young terrorist organization, dicated to the creation of an independent Islamic republic in Chechnya (and other prin ly Muslim parts of Russia such as Dagestan, Kabardino-Balkaria, Ingushetia, Osse and Tataria)." The group, whose name translates to "Requirements for Getting into Par se," espouses radical Islamic doctrine (Wahabbism) and is believed to have strong ties al-Qaida. Most experts, however, agree that the primary inspiration behind Riyad's act es is a desire for the independence of "Chechen lands," rather than religious zealotry. T n from "Group Profile: Riyad Us-Saliheyn Martyrs' Brigade," *Terrorism Knowledge Bas*

[35]Tawhid wal Jih s the forerunner of al-Qaida in Iraq.

[36]Led by Beitullah hsud, the Tehrik-i-Taliban, also known as the Pakistani Taliban, is dedicated to enforci haria law, fighting NATO, and conducting "defensive jihad" against the Pakistani gover nt. Its leader is said to have close ties to al-Qaida. See Hassan Abbas, "A Profile of Te -i Taliban," *CTC Sentinel,* Vol. 1, No. 2 (January 2008), pp. 1–4.

[37]This previously u nown group claimed responsibility for the killing of Lebanese Prime Minister Rafiq Harir February 14, 2005. At the time of this writing, no additional information about this g p was available. The investigation into the killing of Hariri was ongoing. For information he attack being most likely a suicide attack, see "UN Probe into Murder of Former Leba Leader Nears Sensitive Stage—Inquiry Chief," *United Nations News Centre,* Decemb 18, 2006.

Figure 3. Number of Attacks by Ideology, December 1981–March 2008

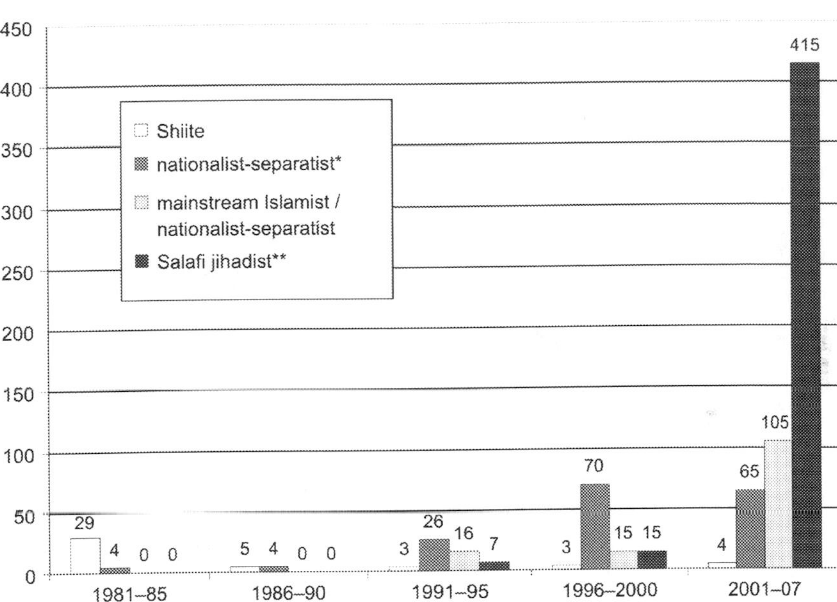

*Includes Marxist/nationalist-separatist groups.
**Includes hybrid groups.

adhering to other ideologies. Figure 3 illustrates the rise in the number of attacks by Salafi jihadist groups and the concomitant decline of attacks by groups guided by other ideologies.[82] During the 1980s, Shiite groups were the main perpetrators of suicide missions,[83] followed by groups with a nationalist-separatist agenda. During the 1990s, nationalist-separatist groups were the most frequent users of suicide attacks, followed by groups with a combination of a mainstream Islamist and nationalist-separatist agenda. Since the turn of the millennium, suicide attacks by Salafi jihadist groups have become more common than attacks by all other groups. The steep rise in this number is par-

82. Attacks by unknown groups, whose ideology could not be ascertained, are omitted from this table.
83. According to other databases, Shiite groups such as Hezbollah and Amal conducted fewer attacks in Lebanon than secular or Sunni groups. See, for example, Pape, *Dying to Win*. Indeed, the identity of many groups that conducted suicide attacks in Lebanon during the 1980s were not identified in the data set used here. It is therefore possible that Shiite groups may not have been the dominant perpetrators of suicide attacks during the 1980s.

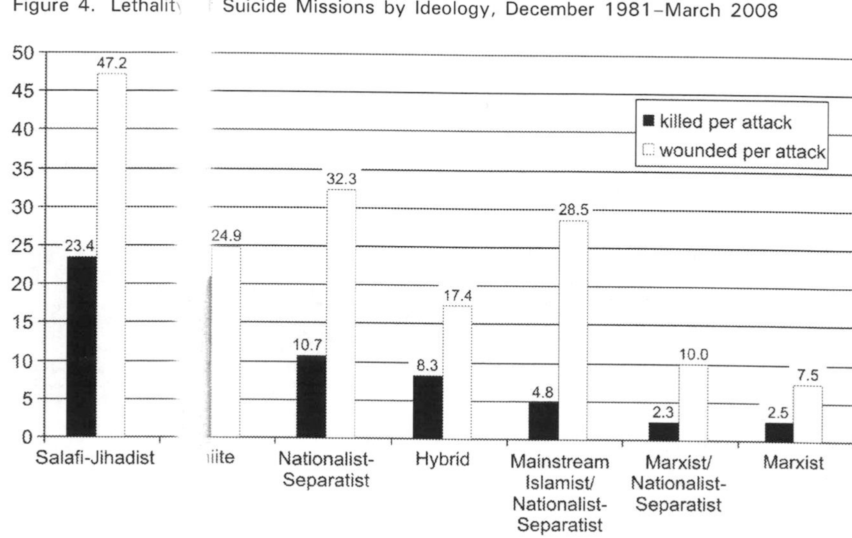

Figure 4. Lethalit Suicide Missions by Ideology, December 1981–March 2008

ticularly worris ie given that their attacks were much more lethal than those by non-Salafi ji list groups (see figure 4).

From Localize o Globalized Patterns of Suicide Attacks

Al-Qaida and it alafi jihadist ideology have produced an altogether new pattern of suicide acks, namely, "globalized suicide missions," which can be distinguished f n "localized" suicide missions, the more traditional pattern of suicide attac Localized and globalized patterns of suicide missions differ in five key area he types of conflicts in which these attacks are used; group ideology; the g raphic scope of these actors; their target definition; and their goals (see table

LOCALIZED SUIC E ATTACKS

The overwhelm majority of suicide missions during the 1980s and 1990s occurred in relati y localized settings.

CONFLICT TYI Suicide missions have traditionally occurred in the context of relatively lo ized conflicts between two belligerents. Examples include conflicts betwe srael and Hezbollah, Israel and the Palestinians, Tamils and Sinhalese, and rks and Kurds. These conflicts have generally endured for many years, an ften decades, between ethnic/religious groups.

Table 2. Patterns of Suicide Missions

	Localized	Globalized
Conflict	Identifiable; long-standing	Less identifiable; short-term
Ideology	Religious; ethno-nationalist; secular	Salafi jihadist
Actors	Subnational	Transnational
Target definition	Narrow	Broad
Goals	Limited	Unlimited
Examples	Hezbollah, Liberation Tigers of Tamil Eelam, Kurdistan Workers' Party, Hamas, Palestinian Islamic Jihad, Popular Front for the Liberation of Palestine, Fatah	Al-Qaida and associated movements

IDEOLOGY. Suicide attacks that fall into the traditional, localized pattern have been planned and executed by religious, secular, Marxist, ethnonationalist, and nationalist groups. Examples of religious groups include Hamas, Palestinian Islamic Jihad (PIJ), and Hezbollah. Secular or nationalist groups include the LTTE, the PFLP, Fatah's al-Aqsa Martyrs Brigades, the Kurdistan Workers' Party (PKK), and the Syrian Socialist Nationalist Party.

GEOGRAPHIC SCOPE OF ACTORS. Traditionally, suicide missions have been planned and executed by subnational terrorist or insurgent actors such as Hezbollah, the LTTE, Hamas, PIJ, and the PKK. Palestinian organizations employing suicide missions, for example, have largely conducted the operational planning of these missions locally, although they may have been receptive to the strategic message and direction of an exile leadership.[84] The subnational nature of these groups suggests that they recruited and trained suicide bombers mostly in or near the conflict area, and have rarely sought them from abroad. The majority of PKK recruits, for example, come from large, poor families residing in Turkey.[85] Among Palestinian organizations, more than 99 percent of the bombers between 1993 and 2008 were residents of the area of conflict—the West Bank, Gaza, and Israel proper. The only exceptions were two Britons involved in the attacks on the bar Mike's Place in Tel Aviv on April 30, 2003.[86] As for the LTTE, experts believe that it is unlikely to have drawn its recruits from outside Sri Lanka because they are chosen from within the ranks

84. Yoram Schweitzer, email communication with author, November 19, 2006.
85. Pedahzur, *Suicide Terrorism*, pp. 167–168.
86. They were Asif Mohammed Hanif, a 21-year-old student from West London who blew himself up at the Mike's Place bar in Tel Aviv on April 30, 2003; and 27-year-old Omar Khan Sharif, a married resident of Derby, England. Sharif also intended to perpetrate a suicide bombing at Mike's Place along with Hanif, but Sharif's explosive device failed to detonate. He fled the scene and later

of the regular I 'E army, where the motivation to serve is high.[87] According to Stephen Hop od, for example, "The emphasis on commitment to the cause both for regular dres and Black Tigers makes non-Sri Lankan or Indian Tamil recruits highly ikely. The LTTE seems to have no recruitment problems for Black Tigers, so oking outside would only be necessary if some ethnic or linguistic feature the operative's identity was necessary to accomplish the mission."[88]

TARGETS. Gr s that conducted localized suicide missions mostly targeted people and ass of the enemy state near or in the conflict area, while largely refraining from rgeting assets of their foes in other locations. The PKK, for instance, cond d all of its 16 suicide attacks in Turkey. Hamas and other Palestinian org zations did not execute a suicide mission against Israeli or Jewish targets side of Israel, the West Bank, and Gaza. Hezbollah's suicide operations aga t Israel were staged mostly against Israel Defense Forces troops inside L non—with the exception of two suicide attacks on Israeli and Jewish tar in Argentina, for which the group declined to assume responsibility.[89] T LTTE staged nearly all of its attacks in Sri Lanka proper—a notable excepti being the killing of Indian Prime Minister Rajiv Gandhi in the Indian city Madras in May 1991. Two experts on the LTTE whom I consulted were un are of additional suicide missions carried out by the LTTE outside of Sri L ka.[90] To quote Hopgood, "The LTTE is very careful to make it clear its tar is the Sri Lankan state and its collaborators, rather than all Sri Lankans. is conscious of its public image, and escalating to attack on foreign soil w d be counterproductive both to legitimacy and diaspora fundraising."[91]

GOALS. The national terrorist or insurgent movements that followed a localized patter f suicide attacks generally aim to advance limited and well-defined politic goals for the community they purport to represent. These political goals include an end to foreign occupation or military presence, increased regio autonomy, and self-determination. The struggle for an inde-

drowned in the M rranean. His body washed ashore on the Tel Aviv beach front on May 12, 2003.

87. Michael Rober email communication with author, November 20, 2006; and Stephen Hopgood, email co unication with author, November 24, 2006.

88. Hopgood, ema mmunication with author.

89. Hezbollah is be ed to have staged two attacks in Argentina: the March 17, 1992, suicide car bombing of the Isra mbassy in Buenos Aires, which killed 29 people and injured more than 250; and the July 18, 19 suicide car bombing of the Jewish Community Center building in Buenos Aires, which killed re than 80 people and wounded some 300.

90. Roberts, email munication with author; and Hopgood, email communication with author.

91. Hopgood, ema mmunication with author.

pendent homeland, whether it is Tamil Eelam, Kurdistan, or Palestine, lies at the center of the conflicts in which suicide missions have traditionally been employed.

GLOBALIZED SUICIDE ATTACKS

The localized pattern of suicide missions contrasts sharply with the new globalized pattern displayed by al-Qaida and its Salafi jihadist associated movements. Although the localized pattern continues to exist, the globalized pattern has become increasingly dominant since the millennium.

CONFLICT TYPE. Globalized suicide missions may occur in the context of clearly identifiable conflicts such as Iraq, but those conflicts need not have a long history. Suicide attacks in Iraq, for example, occurred less than a week after the start of the U.S.-led invasion in March 2003[92]—hardly long enough to produce the types of deep-seated grievances that influenced Palestinian, Tamil, or Kurdish suicide bombers in localized contexts. Nor are the targets of many globalized suicide bombers aware that they are involved in a conflict with a bitter enemy who seeks their death along with its own. Unlike traditional suicide attacks, globalized suicide operations frequently occur in areas that—by any objective standard—are not identified by all parties as zones of conflict. The September 11 attacks, for instance, did not take place in a region where a large ethnic group was vying for an independent state while battling an occupation army. The same is true for the U.S. embassy bombings in Kenya and Tanzania in August 1998 and the attack on the USS *Cole* in October 2000. Other examples include Djerba (April 2002), Bali (October 2002 and October 2005), Mombasa (November 2002), Casablanca (May 2003), Istanbul (November 2003), London (July 2005), and Amman (November 2005).

IDEOLOGY. Salafi jihadist groups have overwhelmingly planned and executed the new globalized suicide missions.

GEOGRAPHIC SCOPE OF ACTORS. Globalized suicide missions tend to be planned and executed by cells and groups that are connected to a transnational terrorist or insurgent network or movement. This transnational network suggests that the planning of suicide missions and their execution may occur in different places. Examples include the September 11 attacks and the July 2005 London bombings.

Additionally, organizations conducting globalized suicide missions no longer recruit and train suicide bombers exclusively in the country where the

92. Steven Lee Myers, "A Nation at War: Suicide Strike; With Bombing, Iraqis Escalate Guerrilla Tactics and Show New Danger on Front Lines," *New York Times*, March 30, 2003.

attacks are to ta place. This is true, again, in the case of the September 11 attacks and the 2 5 bombings in Amman, and it is especially evident in the preponderance foreigners who volunteer for suicide attacks in Iraq and Afghanistan.[93] November 2005 bombings in Amman, for example, were executed by thı Iraqis.[94]

TARGETS. Org izations and cells that stage globalized suicide missions do not limit their a cks to an identifiable zone of conflict. Due in large part to the expansive natu of Salafi jihad, many of today's suicide attackers regard much of the wo as a legitimate target. Hence, even though al-Qaida has declared the Unit States its main enemy, it does not limit its suicide attacks to the U.S. homel . Instead, it will strike U.S. interests wherever an opportunity may arise. addition, it may strike targets of real or perceived allies of the United Stat

GOALS. Suici missions that fall within the globalized category are generally perpetrate y organizations whose goals are more elusive than those in the localized ca ory. It is unclear, for instance, whether the suicide bombings in Amman in N ember 2005 were intended to punish the Hashemite monarchy for its pro- stern stance, including its relations with Israel; to target foreign diplomats; hurt Israeli and Jewish interests in the kingdom; to create instability and ark an anti-Hashemite backlash; or to extend the jihad in Iraq to the broa r Middle East. Similarly, Western analysts often argue over al-Qaida's goal nd motivations, although few would disagree that its demands are max alist.

IMPLICATIONS C INDINGS

Distinguishing tween localized and globalized patterns of suicide attacks has several the tical implications for the study of terrorism. It allows re-

93. According to a artment of Defense news briefing with Col. Sean MacFarland, commander of the First Brigad mbat Team, First Armored Division stationed in Ramadi, Iraq, "[Foreign fighters] are very f n number, although as far as we can tell, they constitute about 100 percent of the suicide bomb ." Quoted in Michael O'Hanlon and Nina Kamp, eds., "Iraq Index: Tracking Variables of Recons ction and Security in Post-Saddam Iraq" (Washington, D.C.: Brookings Institution, Novembe 3, 2006, updated October 1, 2007), p. 18. See also comments by Maj. Gen. Rick Lynch, who st on December 1, 2005, that "at least 96 percent of suicide bombers [in Iraq] are not Iraqis." Quo in Chris Tomlinson, "U.S. General: Suicide and Car Bomb Attacks Down in Iraq," Associated P , December 1, 2005. On Afghanistan, a recent report by the United Nations Assistance Mission fghanistan, for instance, suggests that there is little doubt that some perpetrators in Afghanis crossed the border from Pakistan, although at least some are Afghan refugees. United Nati Assistance Mission in Afghanistan (UNAMA), "Suicide Attacks in Afghanistan (2001– 7)" (New York: UNAMA, 2007).

94. Craig Whitlock mman Bombings Reflect Zarqawi's Growing Reach," *Washington Post*, November 13, 2005.

searchers to place existing explanations into their proper context, to recognize their limitations, and to define important new avenues for research. For instance, scholars can better assess the role of occupation, which appears to be a significant factor in countries whose suicide attacks have a more traditional, localized pattern. It plays a different role in the globalized pattern associated with Salafi jihadist ideology, which adopts an extremely loose definition of "occupation," rendering virtually any perceived offense an example of Western occupation.[95]

Conclusion

Most suicide attacks today are perpetrated by terrorist groups that adhere to a radical Salafi jihadist ideology. Although ideology thus plays an important role in explaining the global proliferation of suicide attacks, there is no evidence that it is the cause of suicide attacks per se. The causes of suicide attacks are complex: they can be found in the interplay of personal motivations, the strategic and tactical objectives of the sponsoring groups, societal and structural factors, as well as intergroup dynamics at the level of the terrorist cell.[96] In addition, individuals acquire ideology for reasons having to do with emotions and beliefs—a complex process whose examination exceeds the scope of this article. Ideology plays an important role, however, in helping reduce the suicide attacker's reservations to perpetrate the acts of killing and dying. It helps the suicide bomber justify his or her actions and to disengage morally from his act and his victims.

Because ideology is an important—and often neglected—factor in the genesis and spread of suicide attacks, challenging the appeal of this ideology is a crucial component of an overall counterterrorism strategy. The task for the United States in challenging the appeal of Salafi jihad will be particularly difficult because of widespread antipathies toward U.S. policies in parts of the Arab and Muslim world. According to a forty-seven-nation Pew Global Atti-

95. A theoretical division of suicide attacks into two patterns also helps contextualize the outbidding thesis. That explanation may account for the adoption of suicide attacks in some cases, but is less capable of accounting for cases of globalized suicide missions. The perpetrators of the London bombings of July 2005, for example, hardly vied for the sympathies of the domestic population—on the contrary, they detested the local population to such an extent that they blew themselves up in its midst. The outbidding thesis is therefore less relevant to our understanding of globalized suicide missions because the importance of killing "infidels" seems to supersede organizational rivalries.

96. On the importance of small group dynamics, see Sageman, *Understanding Terror Networks;* and Hafez, *Suicide Bombers in Iraq.*

tudes Survey re sed in the summer of 2007, for example, the "U.S. image remains abysmal most Muslim countries in the Middle East and Asia, and continues to de ne among the publics of many of America's oldest allies."[97] U.S. practices i etention centers such as Guantánamo Bay and Abu Ghraib and the rush to ar in Iraq have aggravated the negative views of the United States in Arab l Muslim countries and beyond. Partly because of the poor standing of the ited States, and more important, because of the grave danger Salafi jihad es to Muslims, nonviolent Salafists, Islamists, and moderate Muslims must gin to challenge this ideology.

The United S s and its allies can do little to influence what must primarily be an internal M slim debate over the future of the Muslim community. They can, however, d reetly convey to moderate Muslims and nonviolent Salafists why waging th nternal battle is so important, thus quietly supporting these communities w out running the risk of exposing them as "subservient" to the West. As M lims prepare for this debate, Western states can underscore what most Mus s already know: the credibility of Salafi jihad suffers from a fundamental co radiction. On the one hand, Salafi jihadists claim to act for the benefit of M lims. On the other hand, Muslims suffer the consequences of Salafi jihadist ic ology and terrorism more than any other group.

Moderate Mu ims can marshal the following three arguments to undermine Salafi jiha ts. First, Muslims are the primary victims of Salafi jihadist terrorism, inclu g suicide attacks. More Muslims than non-Muslims have died or been n med by Salafi jihadist terror in the last three decades. In Algeria alone, 1 000 or more Muslims have lost their lives to acts of violence largely commit by the Salafi jihadist Armed Islamic Group. In Iraq, where more than half all suicide attacks since 1981 have taken place, suicide missions have kille more Iraqi civilians than foreign military or foreign civilian personnel. In A anistan, civilians have been the prime victims of the growing number of cide attacks, even if these attacks were aimed at members of the Internation Security Assistance Force. In Pakistan, too, an increasing number of suic attacks have targeted the indigenous population.

Second, Sala hadists defend the killing of Muslims by claiming that the ends justify the eans. Innocent Muslims not only die as a by-product of war and insurgency aged by Salafi jihadists, but Salafi jihadists also seem to believe that Mu ms are expendable. As Abu Musab al-Zarqawi noted, "Admittedly, the k g of a number of Muslims whom it is forbidden to kill

97. Pew Global Att les Project, "Global Unease with Major World Powers: Rising Environmental Concern in 47-N on Survey" (Washington, D.C.: Pew Research Center, June 27, 2007), p. 3.

is undoubtedly a grave evil; however, it is permissible to commit this evil—indeed, it is even required—in order to ward off a greater evil, namely, the evil of suspending jihad."[98]

Third, the use of *takfir*—the labeling of some Muslims as infidels—is dividing the Islamic community and runs the risk of creating a Muslim civil war. The Algerian civil war of the 1990s offers a devastating example of this practice. The use of the *takfir* label has created serious tensions within the Islamic community, and it is used to justify scores of suicide bombings against Muslims in countries such as Afghanistan, Algeria, Iraq, Jordan, and Pakistan. Unless it is rejected by moderate Muslims, who form the majority of the Islamic community, such labeling will continue to lead the Islamic nation on a downward spiral of self-inflicted violence. Moderate Muslims should remind their coreligionists that wrongly accusing another Muslim of being an infidel is a major sin in Islam.

The battle against suicide attacks will not be won by exposing the inconsistencies of Salafi jihad alone. Like terrorism more generally, suicide missions are a tactic, and as such cannot be "defeated" entirely. Like war, there are countless reasons why terrorism occurs—and like war, it is unlikely that terrorism and suicide attacks will disappear. Governments struggling against terrorism should therefore conceive their battle not as a war whose goal is victory, but as a long-term effort that requires commitment, endurance, and ingenuity.

98. Quoted in Middle East Media Research Institute (MEMRI), "Abu Mus'ab Zarqawi: Collateral Killing of Muslims is Legitimate," Special Dispatch Series, No. 917 (Washington, D.C.: Jihad and Terrorism Project, MEMRI, June 7, 2005).

Part II: Terrorist Strategies: Why Are They Chosen? Do They Work?

The Strategies of Terrorism

Andrew H. Kydd and Barbara F. Walter

Terrorism often works. Extremist organizations such as al-Qaida, Hamas, and the Tamil Tigers engage in terrorism because it frequently delivers the desired response. The October 1983 suicide attack against the U.S. Marine barracks in Beirut, for example, convinced the United States to withdraw its soldiers from Lebanon.[1] The United States pulled its soldiers out of Saudi Arabia two years after the terrorist attacks of September 11, 2001, even though the U.S. military had been building up its forces in that country for more than a decade.[2] The Philippines recalled its troops from Iraq nearly a month early after a Filipino truck driver was kidnapped by Iraqi extremists.[3] In fact, terrorism has been so successful that between 1980 and 2003, half of all suicide terrorist campaigns were closely followed by substantial concessions by the target governments.[4] Hijacking planes, blowing up buses, and kidnapping individuals may seem irrational and incoherent to outside observers, but these tactics can be surprisingly effective in achieving a terrorist group's political aims.

Despite the salience of terrorism today, scholars and policymakers are only beginning to understand how and why it works. Much has been written on the origins of terror, the motivations of terrorists, and counterterror responses, but little has appeared on the strategies terrorist organizations employ and the conditions under which these strategies succeed or fail. Alan Krueger, David Laitin, Jitka Maleckova, and Alberto Abadie, for example, have traced the effects of poverty, education, and political freedom on terrorist recruitment.[5]

Andrew H. Kydd is Associate Professor of Political Science at the University of Pennsylvania. Barbara F. Walter is Associate Professor at the Graduate School of International Relations and Pacific Studies at the University of California, San Diego. This article is the second installment in a collaborative project, and the order of the authors' names was determined by alphabetical order.

The authors would like to thank the participants at the Project on International Affairs seminar at the University of California, San Diego, for helpful comments on an earlier draft.

1. Thomas L. Friedman, "Marines Complete Beirut Pullback: Moslems Move In," *New York Times*, February 27, 2004.
2. Don Van Natta Jr., "The Struggle for Iraq: Last American Combat Troops Quit Saudi Arabia," *New York Times*, September 22, 2003.
3. James Glanz, "Hostage Is Freed after Philippine Troops Are Withdrawn from Iraq," *New York Times*, July 21, 2004.
4. Robert A. Pape, *Dying to Win: The Strategic Logic of Suicide Terrorism* (New York: Random House, 2005), p. 65.
5. Alan B. Krueger and David D. Laitin, "Kto Kogo? A Cross-Country Study of the Origins and

International Security, Vol. 31, No. 1 (Summer 2006), pp. 49–80

Jessica Stern ha ·xamined the grievances that give rise to terrorism and the networks, mon(and operations that allow terrorist organizations to thrive.[6] What is lackin however, is a clear understanding of the larger strategic games terrorist: e playing and the ways in which state responses help or hinder them.

Effective cou rstrategies cannot be designed without first understanding the strategic lo; that drives terrorist violence. Terrorism works not simply because it instil ear in target populations, but because it causes governments and individual:) respond in ways that aid the terrorists' cause. The Irish Republican Arr (IRA) bombed pubs, parks, and shopping districts in London because its adership believed that such acts would convince Britain to relinquish Nort ·n Ireland. In targeting the World Trade Center and the Pentagon on Septe: er 11, al-Qaida hoped to raise the costs for the United States of supporting I: ·l, Saudi Arabia, and other Arab regimes, and to provoke the United States i: a military response designed to mobilize Muslims around the world. That many targeted governments respond in the way that terrorist organization ıtend underscores the need for understanding the reasoning behind this typ ·f violence.

In this article e seek answers to four questions. First, what types of goals do terrorists s(to achieve? Second, what strategies do they pursue to achieve these g(s? Third, why do these strategies work in some cases but not in others? And urth, given these strategies, what are the targeted governments' best res ıses to prevent terrorism and protect their countries from future attacks?

The core of o: argument is that terrorist violence is a form of costly signaling. Terrorists a :oo weak to impose their will directly by force of arms. They are sometimes : ·ng enough, however, to persuade audiences to do as they wish by alterin :he audience's beliefs about such matters as the terrorist's ability to impo: :osts and their degree of commitment to their cause. Given the conflict of i: ·est between terrorists and their targets, ordinary communication or "chea ılk" is insufficient to change minds or influence behavior. If al-Qaida had in med the United States on September 10, 2001, that it would

Targets of Terrorisr Princeton University and Stanford University, 2003; Alan B. Krueger and Jitka Maleckova, "] cation, Poverty, and Terrorism: Is There a Causal Connection?" *Journal of Economic Perspectiv* /ol. 17, No. 4 (November 2003), pp. 119–144; and Alberto Abadie, "Poverty, Political Freedom, : the Roots of Terrorism," Faculty Research Working Papers Series, RWP04-043 (Cambridge, M : John F. Kennedy School of Government, Harvard University, 2004).

6. Jessica Stern, *T r in the Name of God: Why Religious Militants Kill* (New York: Ecco-HarperCollins, 200

kill 3,000 Americans unless the United States withdrew from Saudi Arabia, the threat might have sparked concern, but it would not have had the same impact as the attacks that followed. Because it is hard for weak actors to make credible threats, terrorists are forced to display publicly just how far they are willing to go to obtain their desired results.

There are five principal strategic logics of costly signaling at work in terrorist campaigns: (1) attrition, (2) intimidation, (3) provocation, (4) spoiling, and (5) outbidding. In an attrition strategy, terrorists seek to persuade the enemy that the terrorists are strong enough to impose considerable costs if the enemy continues a particular policy. Terrorists using intimidation try to convince the population that the terrorists are strong enough to punish disobedience and that the government is too weak to stop them, so that people behave as the terrorists wish. A provocation strategy is an attempt to induce the enemy to respond to terrorism with indiscriminate violence, which radicalizes the population and moves them to support the terrorists. Spoilers attack in an effort to persuade the enemy that moderates on the terrorists' side are weak and untrustworthy, thus undermining attempts to reach a peace settlement. Groups engaged in outbidding use violence to convince the public that the terrorists have greater resolve to fight the enemy than rival groups, and therefore are worthy of support. Understanding these five distinct strategic logics is crucial not only for understanding terrorism but also for designing effective antiterror policies.[7]

The article is divided into two main sections. The first discusses the goals terrorists pursue and examines the forty-two groups currently on the U.S. State Department's list of foreign terrorist organizations (FTOs).[8] The second section develops the costly signaling approach to terrorism, analyzes the five strategies that terrorists use to achieve their goals, discusses the conditions in which each of these strategies is likely to be successful, and draws out the implications for the best counterterror responses.

The Goals of Terrorism

For years the press has portrayed terrorists as crazy extremists who commit indiscriminate acts of violence, without any larger goal beyond revenge or a de-

7. Of course, terrorists will also be seeking best responses to government responses. A pair of strategies that are best responses to each other constitutes a Nash equilibrium, the fundamental prediction tool of game theory.
8. Office of Counterterrorism, U.S. Department of State, "Foreign Terrorist Organizations," fact sheet, October 11, 2005, http://www.state.gov/s/ct/rls/fs/3719.htm.

sire to produce ear in an enemy population. This characterization derives some support f n statements made by terrorists themselves. For example, a young Hamas cide bomber whose bomb failed to detonate said, "I know that there are o r ways to do jihad. But this one is sweet—the sweetest. All martyrdom ope ions, if done for Allah's sake, hurt less than a gnat's bite!"[9] Volunteers for a icide mission may have a variety of motives—obtaining rewards in the af ife, avenging a family member killed by the enemy, or simply collecting f ncial rewards for their descendants. By contrast, the goals driving terroris rganizations are usually political objectives, and it is these goals that deter ne whether and how terrorist campaigns will be launched.

We define "te rrism" as the use of violence against civilians by nonstate actors to attain po cal goals.[10] These goals can be conceptualized in a variety of ways. Individu and groups often have hierarchies of objectives, where broader goals l l to more proximate objectives, which then become specific goals in more ta cal analyses.[11] For the sake of simplicity, we adopt the common distinction etween goals (or ultimate desires) and strategies (or plans of action to attain e goals).

Although the ltimate goals of terrorists have varied over time, five have had enduring in ortance: regime change, territorial change, policy change, social control, and atus quo maintenance. Regime change is the overthrow of a government an ts replacement with one led by the terrorists or at least one more to their ing.[12] Most Marxist groups, including the Shining Path (Sendero Lumi o) in Peru have sought this goal. Territorial change is taking territory away m a state either to establish a new state (as the Tamil Tigers seek to do in T il areas of Sri Lanka) or to join another state (as Lashkar-e Tayyiba would e to do by incorporating Indian Kashmir into Pakistan).

---

9. Quoted in Nasra ssan, "An Arsenal of Believers: Talking to the 'Human Bombs,'" *New Yorker*, November 19, 2001 37.

10. For discussion iffering definitions of terrorism, see Alex P. Schmid and Albert J. Jongman, *Political Terrorism: w Guide to Actors, Authors, Concepts, Data Bases, Theories, and Literature* (New Brunswick, N.J.: Tr action, 1988), pp. 1–38. We do not focus on state terrorism because states face very different ortunities and constraints in their use of violence, and we do not believe the two cases are simil nough to be profitably analyzed together.

11. For the distinct between goals and strategies, see David A. Lake and Robert Powell, eds., *Strategic Choice and rnational Relations* (Princeton, N.J.: Princeton University Press, 1999), especially chap. 1.

12. On revolutiona errorism, see Martha Crenshaw Hutchinson, "The Concept of Revolutionary Terrorism," *Jou of Conflict Resolution*, Vol. 16, No. 3 (September 1972), pp. 383–396; Martha Crenshaw Hutchin , *Revolutionary Terrorism: The FLN in Algeria, 1954–1962* (Stanford, Calif.: Hoover Institution s, 1978); and H. Edward Price Jr., "The Strategy and Tactics of Revolutionary Terrorism," *Con tive Studies in Society and History*, Vol. 19, No. 1 (January 1977), pp. 52–66.

Policy change is a broader category of lesser demands, such as al-Qaida's demand that the United States drop its support for Israel and corrupt Arab regimes such as Saudi Arabia. Social control constrains the behavior of individuals, rather than the state. In the United States, the Ku Klux Klan sought the continued oppression of African Americans after the Civil War. More recently, antiabortion groups have sought to kill doctors who perform abortions to deter other doctors from providing this service. Finally, status quo maintenance is the support of an existing regime or a territorial arrangement against political groups that seek to change it. Many right-wing paramilitary organizations in Latin America, such as the United Self-Defense Force of Colombia, have sought this goal.[13] Protestant paramilitary groups in Northern Ireland supported maintenance of the territorial status quo (Northern Ireland as British territory) against IRA demands that the territory be transferred to Ireland.[14]

Some organizations hold multiple goals and may view one as facilitating another. For instance, by seeking to weaken U.S. support for Arab regimes (which would represent a policy change by the United States), al-Qaida is working toward the overthrow of those regimes (or regime change). As another example, Hamas aims to drive Israel out of the occupied territories (territorial change) and then to overthrow it (regime change).

A cross section of terrorist organizations listed in Table 1 illustrates the range of goals and their relative frequency. Of the forty-two groups currently designated as FTOs by the U.S. State Department, thirty-one seek regime change, nineteen seek territorial change, four seek policy change, and one seeks to maintain the status quo.[15] The list is neither exhaustive nor representative of all terrorist groups, and it does not reflect the frequency of goals in the universe of cases. None of the FTOs appear to pursue social control, but some domestic groups, which are by definition not on the list, are more interested in

13. This group has recently surrendered its weapons.
14. Some analysts argue that many terrorist organizations have degenerated into little more than self-perpetuating businesses that primarily seek to enhance their own power and wealth, and only articulate political goals for rhetorical purposes. See, for example, Stern, *Terror in the Name of God*, pp. 235–236. This suggests that power and wealth should be considered goals in their own right. All organizations, however, seek power and wealth to further their political objectives, and these are better viewed as instrumental in nature.
15. A difficult coding issue arises in determining when a group is a nonstate actor engaged in status quo maintenance and when it is simply a covert agent of the state. Some death squads were linked to elements in the armed forces, yet were not necessarily responsive to the chief executive of the country. Others were tied to right-wing parties and are more clearly nonstate, unless that party is the party in power. See Bruce D. Campbell and Arthur D. Brenner, eds., *Death Squads in Global Perspective: Murder with Deniability* (New York: Palgrave Macmillan, 2002).

Table 1. Foreign Terrorist Organizations and Their Goals

Name	Ultimate Goals	RC	TC	PC	SC	SQM
Abu Nidal Organization	Destroy Israel; establish Palestinian state	X	X			
Abu Sayyaf Group	Secede from Philippines		X			
Al-Aqsa Martyrs' Brigade	Destroy Israel; establish Palestinian state	X	X			
[illegible]	[illegible]	X		X		
Armed Islamic Group	Establish Islamic state in Algeria	X				
Asbat al-Ansar	Establish Islamic state in Lebanon	X				
Aum Shinrikyo	Seize power in Japan; hasten the Apocalypse	X				
Basque Fatherland and Liberty (ETA)	Secede from Spain		X			
Communist Party of the Philippines/New People's Army	Establish Communist state in Philippines	X				
Continuity Irish Republican Army	Evict Britain from Northern Ireland; unite with Eire		X			
Al-Gama'a al-Islamiyya (Islamic Group)	Establish Islamic state in Egypt	X				
Hamas (Islamic Resistance Movement)	Destroy Israel; establish Palestinian Islamic state	X	X			
Harakat ul-Mujahidin	Evict India from Kashmir; unite with Pakistan		X			
Hezbollah (Party of God)	Originally: evict Israel from Lebanon; now: destroy Israel and establish Palestinian Islamic state	X	X			
Islamic Jihad Group	Establish Islamic state in Uzbekistan; reduce U.S. influence	X		X		
Islamic Movement of Uzbekistan	Establish Islamic state in Uzbekistan	X				
Jaish-e-Mohammed (Army of Mohammed)	Evict India from Kashmir; unite with Pakistan		X			
Jemaah Islamiya	Establish Islamic state in Indonesia	X				
Al-Jihad (Egyptian Islamic Jihad)	Establish Islamic state in Egypt	X				
Kahane Chai (Kach)	Expand Israel		X			
Kongra-Gel (formerly Kurdistan Workers' Party)	Secede from Turkey		X			
Lashkar-e Tayyiba (Army of the Righteous)	Evict India from Kashmir; unite with Pakistan		X			
Lashkar i Jhangvi	Establish Islamic state in Pakistan	X				
Liberation Tigers of Tamil Eelam	Secede from Sri Lanka		X			
Libyan Islamic Fighting Group	Establish Islamic state in Libya	X				
Moroccan Islamic Combatant Group	Establish Islamic state in Morocco	X				
Mujahedin-e Khalq Organization	Overthrow Iranian government	X				
National Liberation Army	Establish Marxist government in Colombia	X				
Palestine Liberation Front	Destroy Israel; establish Palestinian state	X	X			
Palestinian Islamic Jihad	Destroy Israel; establish Palestinian state	X	X			

Table 1. *continued*

Name	Ultimate Goals	RC	TC	PC	SC	SCM
Popular Front for the Liberation of Palestine	Destroy Israel; establish Palestinian state	X	X			
Popular Front for the Liberation of Palestine—General Command	Destroy Israel; establish Palestinian state	X	X			
Al-Qaida	Establish Islamic states in Middle East; destroy Israel; reduce U.S. influence	X	X	X		
Al-Qaida in Iraq (Zarqawi group)	Evict United States from Iraq; establish Islamic state	X		X		
Real Irish Republican Army	Evict Britain from Northern Ireland; unite with Eire		X			
Revolutionary Armed Forces of Colombia	Establish Marxist state in Colombia	X				
Revolutionary Nuclei (formerly Revolutionary People's Struggle)	Establish Marxist state in Greece	X				
Revolutionary Organization 7 November	Establish Marxist state in Greece	X				
Revolutionary People's Liberation Party/Front	Establish Marxist state in Turkey	X				
Salafist Group for Call and Combat	Establish Islamic state in Algeria	X				
Shining Path (Sendero Luminoso)	Establish Marxist state in Peru	X				
United Self-Defense Forces of Colombia	Preserve Colombian state					X
Total		31	19	4	0	1

SOURCE: Office of Counterterrorism, U.S. Department of State, "Foreign Terrorist Organizations," fact sheet, October 11, 2005.

NOTE: RC: regime change; TC: territorial change; PC: policy change; SC: social control; and SQM: status quo maintenance. Coding of goals is the authors'.

this goal.[16] Wha able 1 reveals, however, is the instrumental nature of terrorist violence anc me of the more popular political objectives being sought.

The Strategies Terrorist Violence

To achieve thei ng-term objectives, terrorists pursue a variety of strategies. Scholars have s gested a number of typologies of terrorist strategies and tactics over the y s. In a pathbreaking early analysis of terrorism, Thomas Thornton offere five proximate objectives: morale building, advertising, disorientation (of e target population), elimination of opposing forces, and provocation.[17] rtha Crenshaw also identifies advertising and provocation as proximate c ctives, along with weakening the government, enforcing obedience in tl population, and outbidding.[18] David Fromkin argues that provocation is strategy of terrorism.[19] Edward Price writes that terrorists must delegitim the regime and impose costs on occupying forces, and he identifies kidna ing, assassination, advertising, and provocation as tactics.[20] Although these alyses are helpful in identifying strategies of terrorism, they fail to derive tl from a coherent framework, spell out their logic in detail, and consider b responses to them.

A fruitful sta g point for a theory of terrorist strategies is the literature on uncertainty, co ct, and costly signaling. Uncertainty has long been understood to be a ca e of conflict. Geoffrey Blainey argued that wars begin when states disagree out their relative power, and they end when states agree again.[21] James ron and other theorists built upon this insight and showed

16. The Taliban, wl is not listed, does pursue social control; and the Israeli group Kach, which seeks to maintain subordinate status of Palestinians in Israel and eventually to expel them, may also be consid d to seek it. The Memorial Institute for the Prevention of Terrorism maintains a database of rist organizations that includes more than forty groups based in the United States. Some of the n be considered to seek social control, such as the Army of God, which targets doctors who p ide abortions. See http://www.tkb.org.

17. Thomas Perry rnton, "Terror as a Weapon of Political Agitation," in Harry Eckstein, ed., *Internal War: Proble nd Approaches* (London: Free Press of Glencoe, 1964), p. 87.

18. Martha Crensh "The Causes of Terrorism," *Comparative Politics*, Vol. 13, No. 4 (July 1981), pp. 379–399.

19. David Fromkin he Strategy of Terrorism," *Foreign Affairs*, Vol. 53, No. 4 (July 1975), pp. 683–698.

20. Price, "The Stra y and Tactics of Revolutionary Terrorism," pp. 54–58. Other related discussions include Paul lkinson, "The Strategic Implications of Terrorism," in M.L. Sondhi, ed., *Terrorism and Polit Violence: A Sourcebook* (New Delhi: Har-anand Publications, 2000); Paul Wilkinson, *Terroris d the Liberal State* (New York: New York University Press, 1986), pp. 110–118; and Schmid a ongman, *Political Terrorism*, pp. 50–59.

21. Geoffrey Blain *he Causes of War*, 3d ed. (New York: Free Press, 1988), p. 122.

that uncertainty about a state's willingness to fight can cause conflict.[22] If states are unsure what other states will fight for, they may demand too much in negotiations and end up in conflict. This uncertainty could reflect a disagreement about power, as Blainey understood, or a disagreement over resolve, willpower, or the intensity of preferences over the issue. The United States and North Vietnam did not disagree over their relative power, but the United States fatally underestimated North Vietnamese determination to achieve victory.

Uncertainty about trustworthiness or moderation of preferences can also cause conflict. Thomas Hobbes argued that if individuals mistrust each other, they have an incentive to initiate an attack rather than risk being attacked by surprise.[23] John Herz, Robert Jervis, and others have developed this concept in the international relations context under the heading of the security dilemma and the spiral model.[24] States are often uncertain about each other's ultimate ambitions, intentions, and preferences. Because of this, anything that increases one side's belief that the other is deceitful, expansionist, risk acceptant, or hostile increases incentives to fight rather than cooperate.

If uncertainty about power, resolve, and trustworthiness can lead to violence, then communication on these topics is the key to preventing (or instigating) conflict. The problem is that simple verbal statements are often not credible, because actors frequently have incentives to lie and bluff. If by saying "We're resolved," the North Vietnamese could have persuaded the United States to abandon the South in 1965, then North Vietnam would have had every incentive to say so even if it was not that resolute. In reality, they had to fight a long and costly war to prove their point. Similarly, when Mikhail Gorbachev wanted to reassure the West and end the Cold War, verbal declarations of innocent intentions were insufficient, because previous Soviet leaders had made similar statements. Instead, real arms reductions, such as the 1987 Intermediate-Range Nuclear Forces Treaty, were necessary for Western opinion to change.

---

22. James D. Fearon, "Rationalist Explanations for War," *International Organization*, Vol. 49, No. 3 (Summer 1995), pp. 379–414; and Robert Powell, "Bargaining Theory and International Conflict," *Annual Review of Political Science*, Vol. 5 (June 2002), pp. 1–30.
23. Thomas Hobbes, *Leviathan* (New York: Penguin, [1651] 1968), pp. 184.
24. John H. Herz, "Idealist Internationalism and the Security Dilemma," *World Politics*, Vol. 2, No. 2 (January 1950), pp. 157–180; Robert Jervis, *Perception and Misperception in International Politics* (Princeton, N.J.: Princeton University Press, 1976); Robert Jervis, "Cooperation under the Security Dilemma," *World Politics*, Vol. 30, No. 2 (January 1978), pp. 167–214; and Charles L. Glaser, "The Security Dilemma Revisited," *World Politics*, Vol. 50, No. 1 (October 1997), pp. 171–202.

Because talk [illegible] heap, states and terrorists who wish to influence the behavior of an advers[illegible] must resort to costly signals.[25] Costly signals are actions so costly that bluf[illegible] and liars are unwilling to take them.[26] In international crises, mobilizing [illegible] ces or drawing a very public line in the sand are examples of strategies that l[illegible] resolved actors might find too costly to take.[27] War itself, or the willingness [illegible] endure it, can serve as a forceful signal of resolve and provide believable [illegible] ormation about power and capabilities.[28] Costly signals separate the whea[illegible] rom the chaff and allow honest communication, although sometimes at a [illegible] rible price.

To obtain the[illegible] olitical goals, terrorists need to provide credible information to the audience[illegible] hose behavior they hope to influence. Terrorists play to two key audiences: [illegible] vernments whose policies they wish to influence and individuals on the [illegible] rorists' own side whose support or obedience they seek to gain.[29] The tar[illegible] d governments are central because they can grant concessions over poli[illegible] r territory that the terrorists are seeking. The terrorists' domestic audienc[illegible] also important, because they can provide resources to the terrorist group [illegible] d must obey its edicts on social or political issues.

Figure 1 sho[illegible] how the three subjects of uncertainty (power, resolve, and trustworthiness [illegible] ombine with the two targets of persuasion (the enemy government an[illegible] he domestic population) to yield a family of five signaling strategies. The[illegible] trategies form a theoretically cohesive set that we believe represents mos[illegible] the commonly used strategies in important terrorist campaigns around [illegible] world today.[30] A terrorist organization can of course pursue

25. Andrew H. Ky[illegible] *Trust and Mistrust in International Relations* (Princeton, N.J.: Princeton University Press, 2005)[illegible]

26. John G. Riley, [illegible] er Signals: Twenty-five Years of Screening and Signaling," *Journal of Economic Literature*, Vo[illegible], No. 2 (June 2001), pp. 432–478.

27. James D. Fearo[illegible] Signaling Foreign Policy Interests: Tying Hands vs. Sunk Costs," *Journal of Conflict Resolution*, [illegible] 41, No. 1 (February 1977), pp. 68–90.

28. Dan Reiter, "E[illegible] ring the Bargaining Model of War," *Perspectives on Politics*, Vol. 1, No. 1 (March 2003), pp. 2[illegible]; and Robert Powell, "Bargaining and Learning While Fighting," *American Journal of Political S[illegible] ce*, Vol. 48, No. 2 (April 2004), pp. 344–361.

29. Rival terrorist [illegible] oderate groups are also important, but terrorism is not often used to signal such groups. Some[illegible] s rival groups are targeted in an effort to eliminate them, but this violence is usually thought [illegible] internecine warfare rather than terrorism. The targeted government may also be divided int[illegible] ltiple actors, but these divisions are not crucial for a broad understanding of terrorist strategi[illegible]

30. This list is not [illegible] ustive. In particular, it omits two strategies that have received attention in the literature: adve[illegible] ng and retaliation. Advertising may play a role in the beginning of some conflicts, but it doe[illegible] t sustain long-term campaigns of terrorist violence. Retaliation is a motivation for some terro[illegible], but terrorism would continue even if the state did not strike at terrorists, because terrorism i[illegible] signed to achieve some goal, not just avenge counterterrorist attacks.

Figure 1. Strategies of Terrorist Violence

		Target of Persuasion: Enemy	Target of Persuasion: Own Population
Subject of Uncertainty	Power	attrition	intimidation
	Resolve	attrition	outbidding
	Trustworthiness	spoiling	provocation

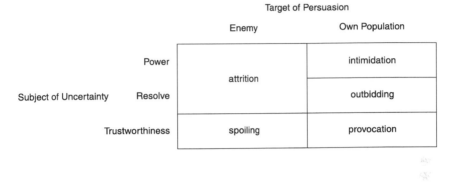

more than one strategy at a time. The September 11 terrorist attacks, for example, were probably part of both an attrition strategy and a provocation strategy. By targeting the heart of the United States' financial district, al-Qaida may have been attempting to increase the cost of the U.S. policy of stationing soldiers in Saudi Arabia. But by targeting prominent symbols of American economic and military power, al-Qaida may also have been trying to goad the United States into an extreme military response that would serve al-Qaida's larger goal of radicalizing the world's Muslim population. The challenge for policymakers in targeted countries is to calibrate their responses in ways that do not further any of the terrorists' goals.

Below we analyze the five terrorist strategies in greater detail, discuss the conditions under which each is likely to succeed, and relate these conditions to the appropriate counterterrorism strategies.

ATTRITION: A BATTLE OF WILLS

The most important task for any terrorist group is to persuade the enemy that the group is strong and resolute enough to inflict serious costs, so that the enemy yields to the terrorists' demands.[31] The attrition strategy is designed to accomplish this task.[32] In an attrition campaign, the greater the costs a terrorist

31. Per Baltzer Overgaard, "The Scale of Terrorist Attacks as a Signal of Resources," *Journal of Conflict Resolution*, Vol. 38, No. 3 (September 1994), pp. 452–478; and Harvey E. Lapan and Todd Sandler, "Terrorism and Signaling," *European Journal of Political Economy*, Vol. 9, No. 3 (August 1993), pp. 383–398.

32. J. Maynard Smith, "The Theory of Games and Evolution in Animal Conflicts," *Journal of Theoretical Biology*, Vol. 47 (1974), pp. 209–211; John J. Mearsheimer, *Conventional Deterrence* (Ithaca,

organization is e to inflict, the more credible its threat to inflict future costs, and the more li y the target is to grant concessions. During the last years of the British Emp , the Greeks in Cyprus, Jews in Palestine, and Arabs in Aden used a war of rition strategy against their colonizer. By targeting Britain with terrorist a :ks, they eventually convinced the political leadership that maintaining co ol over these territories would not be worth the cost in British lives.[33] acks by Hezbollah and Hamas against Israel, particularly during the seco intifada, also appear to be guided by this strategy. In a letter written in the e y 1990s to the leadership of Hamas, the organization's master bomb make Yahya Ayyash, said, "We paid a high price when we used only sling-shot id stones. We need to exert more pressure, make the cost of the occupation at much more expensive in human lives, that much more unbearable."[34]

Robert Pape sents the most thorough exposition of terrorism as a war of attrition in his a lysis of suicide bombing.[35] Based on a data set of all suicide attacks from 19 to 2003 (315 in total), Pape argues that suicide terrorism is employed by w k actors for whom peaceful tactics have failed and conventional military tics are infeasible because of the imbalance of power. The strategy is to in t costs on the enemy until it withdraws its occupying forces: the greater the ts inflicted, the more likely the enemy is to withdraw. Pape asserts that terr sts began to recognize the effectiveness of suicide terrorism with the 1983 I bollah attack against U.S. Marines in Beirut that killed 241 people. Since tl , suicide terrorism has been employed in nationalist struggles around the orld.

CONDITIONS 'ORABLE TO ATTRITION. A war of attrition strategy is more effective agains ome targets than others. Three variables are likely to figure in the outcome: e state's level of interest in the issue under dispute, the constraints on its a ity to retaliate, and its sensitivity to the costs of violence.

The first vari e, the state's degree of interest in the disputed issue, is fundamental. State with only peripheral interests at stake often capitulate to terrorist deman states with more important interests at stake rarely do. The

N.Y.: Cornell Univ y Press, 1983), pp. 33–35; and James D. Fearon, "Bargaining, Enforcement, and International C peration," *International Organization*, Vol. 52, No. 2 (Spring 1998), pp. 269–305.

33. Bernard Lewis, he Revolt of Islam," *New Yorker*, November 19, 2001, p. 61.

34. Quoted in Has "An Arsenal of Believers," p. 38.

35. Robert A. Pape he Strategic Logic of Suicide Terrorism," *American Political Science Review*, Vol. 97, No. 3 (Aug 2003), pp. 343–361; and Pape, *Dying to Win*.

United States withdrew from Lebanon following the bombing of the marine barracks because it had only a marginal interest in maintaining stability and preventing Syrian domination of that country. In that case, the costs of the attack clearly outweighed the U.S. interests at stake. Similarly, Israel withdrew from southern Lebanon in 2000 because the costs of the occupation outstripped Israel's desire to maintain a buffer zone in that region. In contrast, the United States responded to the September 11 attacks by launching offensive wars in Afghanistan and Iraq rather than withdrawing U.S. troops from the region, as al-Qaida demanded (though U.S. troops did ultimately leave Saudi Arabia for Iraq). Similarly, Israel is unlikely to withdraw from East Jerusalem, much less allow itself to become an Islamic state as Hamas has demanded.

The second variable, constraints on retaliation, affects the costs paid by the terrorists for pursuing a war of attrition. Terrorist organizations almost always are weaker than the governments they target and, as a result, are vulnerable to government retaliation. The more constrained the government is in its use of force, the less costly an attrition strategy is, and the longer the terrorists can hold out in the hopes of achieving their goal. For instance, the Israelis have the military means to commit genocide against the Palestinian people or to expel them to surrounding Arab countries. Israel, however, depends for its long-term survival on close ties with Europe and the United States. Western support for Israel would plummet in response to an Israeli strategy designed to inflict mass casualties, making such a strategy prohibitively costly. This constraint makes a war of attrition strategy less costly (and more attractive) for the Palestinians.

Democracies may be more constrained in their ability to retaliate than authoritarian regimes. Pape finds that suicide bombers target democracies exclusively and argues that this is in part because of constraints on their ability to strike back.[36] Capable authoritarian regimes are able to gather more information on their populations than democracies and can more easily round up suspected terrorists and target those sympathetic to them. They are also less constrained by human rights considerations in their interrogation and retaliation practices.[37]

The ease with which a terrorist organization can be targeted also influences

36. Pape, *Dying to Win,* p. 44. Krueger and Laitin also find that targets of terrorism tend to be democratic. See Krueger and Laitin, "Kto Kogo?"
37. The U.S. program of extraordinary rendition, for example, is an effort to evade the restrictions usually faced by democracies by outsourcing the dirty work.

a country's abi to retaliate forcefully. Terrorist organizations such as al-Qaida that are lely dispersed, difficult to identify, or otherwise hard to tar-get are at an ac ntage in a war of attrition because their enemies will have difficulty deliv ng punishment. Israel has, through superior intelligence gathering, been le to assassinate top members of Hamas's leadership at will, including its fo der and spiritual leader, Sheik Ahmed Yassin, as well as his successor, Abd ziz Rantisi. The United States, by contrast, has been unable to locate Osam in Laden and his top deputy, Ayman al-Zawahiri.

The third va le is a target's cost tolerance. Governments that are able to absorb heavier ts and hold out longer are less inviting targets for an attri-tion strategy. T orist organizations are likely to gauge a target's cost toler-ance based on a ast two factors: the target's regime type and the target's past behavior towar ther terrorists. Regime type is important because democra-cies may be le able to tolerate the painful effects of terrorism than non-democracies. C ens of democracies, their fears stoked by media reports and warnings of co ued vulnerability, are more likely to demand an end to the attacks. In mor thoritarian states, the government exerts more control over the media and disregard public opinion to a greater extent. The Russian government's h vy-handed response to hostage situations, for example, sug-gests a higher erance for casualties than a more fully democratic govern-ment would ha . Additionally, because terrorist organizations operate more freely in democ ies and politicians must interact with the public to maintain political suppo terrorists have an easier time targeting prominent indiv-iduals for assas ation. Of four leaders assassinated by terrorists in the past quarter centur Indira Gandhi, Rajiv Gandhi, Yitzak Rabin, and Anwar Sadat—three w leaders of democracies.

Among dem atic states, sensitivity to costs may vary with the party in power. When m dovish parties are in charge, the target may be perceived to have lower cost lerances than if a more hawkish party were at the helm. The dove-hawk dim sion may correlate with the left-right dimension in domestic politics, leading ft-wing parties to be more likely to grant terrorist demands. This traditional ivide between peace and security has characterized Israeli politics for yea Labor Party Prime Minister Ehud Barak was elected on a platform of wit rawing Israeli forces from Lebanon and making peace with the Palestinians n contrast, Likud Party Prime Minister Ariel Sharon was elected on a pl orm of meeting terrorists with military force. Hoping for greater concess s, terrorists may preferentially attack dovish parties.

The number prior concessions made to other terrorists is also likely to influence perceptions of the target's cost tolerance. Governments that have already yielded to terrorist demands are more likely to experience additional terrorist attacks. Evidence abounds that terrorists explicitly consider the prior behavior of states and are encouraged by signs of weakness. Israel's precipitous withdrawal from southern Lebanon in May 2000 convinced Hamas that the Israeli leadership's resolve was weakening and encouraged Hamas leaders to initiate the second intifada in September 2000.[38] Israelis fear the same inference will be drawn from their withdrawal from Gaza. A Hamas leader interviewed in October 2005 declared, "When we took up arms and launched [the second intifada], we succeeded in less than five years to force the Israelis to withdraw from the Gaza Strip. This fulfilled everyone's dream. I think we have to benefit from this experience by applying it accordingly to the West Bank and other occupied areas."[39] The past behavior of a targeted government, therefore, also provides important information to terrorist groups about its likely future behavior and the success of this particular strategy.

Perhaps the most important example of a terrorist group pursuing an attrition strategy is al-Qaida's war with the United States. In a November 2004 broadcast, bin Laden boasted, "We gained experience in guerilla and attritional warfare in our struggle against the great oppressive superpower, Russia, in which we and the mujahidin ground it down for ten years until it went bankrupt, and decided to withdraw in defeat. . . . We are continuing to make America bleed to the point of bankruptcy."[40] Al Qaida's goal—policy change—is well suited to an attrition strategy. Bin Laden has frequently argued that the United States lacks the resolve to fight a long attritional war, as in his February 1996 declaration of jihad:

> Where was this false courage of yours when the explosion in Beirut took place in 1983 A.D.? You were transformed into scattered bits and pieces; 241 soldiers were killed, most of them Marines. And where was this courage of yours when two explosions made you leave Aden in less than twenty-four hours!
>
> But your most disgraceful case was in Somalia; where, after vigorous propaganda about the power of the U.S. and its post–cold war leadership of the new world order, you moved tens of thousands of international forces, including twenty-eight thousand American soldiers, into Somalia. However, when tens of your soldiers were killed in minor battles and one American pilot was

38. Debate Goes On Over Lebanon Withdrawal, *Haaretz*, May 23, 2001; and Daoud Kuttab, "The Lebanon Lesson," *Jerusalem Post*, May 25, 2000.
39. Interview with Mahmoud Khalid al-Zahar, *Al Jazeera*, October 22, 2005.
40. Osama bin Laden, *Messages to the World: The Statements of Osama bin Laden*, trans. James Howarth, ed. Bruce Lawrence (London: Verso, 2005), pp. 241–242.

dragged in the eets of Mogadishu, you left the area in disappointment, humiliation, and eat, carrying your dead with you. Clinton appeared in front of the whole w l threatening and promising revenge, but these threats were merely a prepa ion for withdrawal. You had been disgraced by Allah and you withdrew; e extent of your impotence and weaknesses became very clear.[41]

Although dif ult to prove, it also appears that bin Laden believed that he and his organi on would be hard to target with counterattacks, making a war of attrition ategy even more appealing. In 2001 the Taliban was on the verge of elimin g armed resistance in northern Afghanistan; and, as a landlocked country fghanistan must have seemed relatively invulnerable to a U.S. invasion. United States had bombed al-Qaida camps before to no effect. Even if th nited States invaded, Afghanistan was both costly and difficult to conque s the Soviets discovered in the 1980s. In the end, of course, the Taliban wo have been well advised to insist that the September 11 attacks be delaye ntil the Northern Alliance was defeated, but the latter's dramatic success w U.S. help was perhaps difficult to anticipate.

BEST RESPONS TO ATTRITION. There are at least five counterstrategies available to a state e ged in a war of attrition. First, the targeted government can concede inesse l issues in exchange for peace, a strategy that we believe is frequently purs d though rarely admitted.[42] In some cases, the terrorists will genuinely care re about the disputed issue and be willing to outlast the target. In such cas concessions are likely to be the state's best response. Other potential challe rs, however, may perceive this response as a sign of weakness, which co lead them to launch their own attacks. To reduce the damage to its reput n, the target can vigorously fight other wars of attrition over issues it cares e deeply about, thus signaling a willingness to bear costs if the matter is o fficient consequence.

Second, whe he issue under dispute is important enough to the targeted state that it doe ot want to grant any concessions, the government may engage in targete taliation. Retaliation can target the leadership of the terrorist group, its follo rs, their assets, and other objects of value. Care must be taken, however at the retaliation is precisely targeted, because the terrorist

41. Osama bin La "Declaration of War against the Americans Occupying the Land of the Two Holy Places," -*Quds Al-Arabi*, August 1996, http://www.pbs.org/newshour/terrorism/international/fatw 96.html.
42. Peter C. Sederb , "Conciliation as Counter-terrorist Strategy," *Journal of Peace Research*, Vol. 32, No. 3 (August), pp. 295–312.

organization could simultaneously be pursuing a strategy of provocation. A harsh, indiscriminate response might make a war of attrition more costly for the terrorists, but it would also harm innocent civilians who might then serve as willing recruits for the terrorists. The Israeli policy of assassination of terrorist leaders is shaped by this concern.

Third, a state can harden likely targets to minimize the costs the terrorist organization can inflict. If targeted governments can prevent most attacks from being executed, a war of attrition strategy will not be able to inflict the costs necessary to convince the target to concede. The wall separating Israel from the West Bank and Gaza is a large-scale example of this counterstrategy. The United States has been less successful in hardening its own valuable targets, such as nuclear and chemical plants and the container shipping system, despite the creation of the Department of Homeland Security.[43] Protecting these types of targets is essential if one seeks to deter additional attacks and discourage the use of attrition.

Fourth, states should seek to deny terrorists access to the most destructive weapons, especially nuclear and biological ones. Any weapon that can inflict enormous costs will be particularly attractive to terrorists pursuing a war of attrition. The greater the destruction, the higher the likelihood that the target will concede increasingly consequential issues. Particular attention should be placed on securing Russian stockpiles of fissile material and on halting the spread of uranium enrichment technology to Iran and North Korea. No other country has as much material under so little government control as Russia, and Iran and North Korea are vital because of the links both countries have to terrorist organizations.[44]

Finally, states can strive to minimize the psychological costs of terrorism and the tendency people have to overreact. John Mueller has noted that the risks associated with terrorism are actually quite small; for the average U.S. citizen, the likelihood of being a victim of a terrorist attack is about the same as that of being struck by lighting.[45] Government public education programs should therefore be careful not to overstate the threat, for this plays into the hands of

---

43. Stephen Flynn, *America the Vulnerable: How Our Government Is Failing to Protect Us from Terrorism* (New York: HarperCollins, 2004).
44. Graham T. Allison, Owen R. Coté Jr., Richard A. Falkenrath, and Steven E. Miller, *Avoiding Nuclear Anarchy: Containing the Threat of Loose Russian Nuclear Weapons and Fissile Material* (Cambridge, Mass.: MIT Press, 1996); and Graham Allison, *Nuclear Terrorism: The Ultimate Preventable Catastrophe* (New York: Times Books, 2004).
45. John Mueller, "Six Rather Unusual Propositions about Terrorism," *Terrorism and Political Violence*, Vol. 17, No. 4 (Winter 2005), pp. 487–505.

the terrorists. I mericans become convinced that terrorism, while a deadly problem, is no re of a health risk than drunk driving, smoking, or obesity, then al-Qaida's trition strategy will be undercut. What the United States should seek to id are any unnecessary costs associated with wasteful and misguided cou rterror programs. The more costs the United States inflicts on itself in the ne of counterterrorism policies of dubious utility, the more likely a war of rition strategy is to succeed.

INTIMIDATION: E REIGN OF TERROR

Intimidation is n to the strategy of deterrence, preventing some undesired behavior by m s of threats and costly signals.[46] It is most frequently used when terrorist anizations wish to overthrow a government in power or gain social cont over a given population. It works by demonstrating that the terrorists have power to punish whoever disobeys them, and that the government is pow ess to stop them.

Terrorists are ten in competition with the government for the support of the population. rrorists who wish to bring down a government must somehow convince t government's defenders that continued backing of the government will b stly. One way to do this is to provide clear evidence that the terrorist organi on can kill those individuals who continue to sustain the regime. By target the government's more visible agents and supporters, such as mayors, poli prosecutors, and pro-regime citizens, terrorist organizations demonstrate th they have the ability to hurt their opponents and that the government is weak to punish the terrorists or protect future victims.

Terrorists can o use an intimidation strategy to gain greater social control over a populat . Terrorists may turn to this strategy in situations where a government ha onsistently refused to implement a policy a terrorist group favors and whe efforts to change the state's policy appear futile. In this case, terrorists use in idation to impose the desired policy directly on the population, gaining co liance through selective violence and the threat of future reprisals. In the ited States, antiabortion activists have bombed clinics to prevent indivi ls from performing or seeking abortions, and in the 1960s racist groups b ed churches to deter African Americans from claiming their

46. The literature o eterrence is vast. See, for example, Thomas C. Schelling, *Arms and Influence* (New Haven, Conn le University Press, 1966); and Christopher H. Achen and Duncan Snidal, "Rational Deterren heory and Comparative Case Studies," *World Politics*, Vol. 41, No. 2 (January 1989), pp. 143–

civil rights. In Afghanistan, the Taliban beheaded the principal of a girls school to deter others from providing education for girls.[47]

An intimidation strategy can encompass a range of actions—from assassinations of individuals in positions of power to car bombings of police recruits, such as those carried out by the Zarqawi group in Iraq. It can also include massacres of civilians who have cooperated with the government or rival groups, such as the 1957 massacre at Melouza by the National Liberation Front during the Algerian war for independence.[48] This strategy was taken to an extreme by the Armed Islamic Group in Algeria's civil war of the 1990s. In that war, Islamist guerrillas massacred thousands of people suspected of switching their allegiance to the government. Massacres were especially common in villages that had once been under firm rebel control but that the army was attempting to retake and clear of rebels. Stathis Kalyvas argues that these conditions pose extreme dilemmas for the local inhabitants, who usually wish to support whoever will provide security, but are often left exposed when the government begins to retake an area but has not established effective control.[49]

CONDITIONS FAVORABLE TO INTIMIDATION. When the goal is regime change, weak states and rough terrain are two factors that facilitate intimidation. James Fearon and David Laitin argue that civil wars are likely to erupt and continue where the government is weak and the territory is large and difficult to traverse. These conditions allow small insurgent groups to carve out portions of a country as a base for challenging the central government.[50] Intimidation is likely to be used against civilians on the fault lines between rebel and government control to deter individuals from supporting the government.

When the goal is social control, weak states again facilitate intimidation. When the justice system is too feeble to effectively prosecute crimes associated with intimidation, people will either live in fear or seek protection from nonstate actors such as local militias or gangs. Penetration of the justice system by sympathizers of a terrorist group also facilitates an intimidation strategy, because police and courts will be reluctant to prosecute crimes and may even be complicit in them.

---

47. Noor Khan, "Militants Behead Afghan Principal for Educating Girls," *Boston Globe,* January 5, 2006.
48. Crenshaw Hutchinson, "The Concept of Revolutionary Terrorism," p. 390.
49. Stathis N. Kalyvas, "Wanton and Senseless? The Logic of Massacres in Algeria," *Rationality and Society,* Vol. 11, No. 3 (August 1999), pp. 243–285.
50. James D. Fearon and David D. Laitin, "Ethnicity, Insurgency, and Civil War," *American Political Science Review,* Vol. 97, No. 1 (February 2003), pp. 75–90.

BEST RESPONS TO INTIMIDATION. When the terrorist goal is regime change, the best respon to intimidation is to retake territory from the rebels in discrete chunks a in a decisive fashion. Ambiguity about who is in charge should be mini zed, even if this means temporarily ceding some areas to the rebels to conce ite resources on selected sections of territory. This response is embodied in "clear-and-hold strategy" that U.S. forces are employing in Iraq. The 2005 N ional Strategy for Victory in Iraq specifically identifies intimidation as the " itegy of our enemies."[51] The proper response, as Secretary of State Condolee Rice stated in October 2005, "is to clear, hold, and build: clear areas fron nsurgent control, hold them securely, and build durable national Iraqi inst tions."[52] If rebels control their own zone and have no access to the governm zone, they will have no incentive to kill the civilians they control and no lity to kill the civilians the government controls. In this situation, there is uncertainty about who is in control; the information that would be provi d by intimidation is already known. The U.S. military developed the clear- l-hold strategy during the final years of U.S. involvement in Vietnam. A pri pal strategy of the Vietcong was intimidation—to prevent collaboration w the government and build up control in the countryside. In the early years the war, the United States responded with search and destroy missions, entially an attrition strategy. Given that the insurgents were not pursuing a trition strategy, and were not particularly vulnerable to one, this initial coun strategy was a mistake. Clear-and-hold was the more appropriate response cause it limited the Vietcong's access to potential targets and thus undercut i strategy.[53]

Clear-and-ho has its limitations. It is usually impossible to completely deny terrorists ry into the government-controlled zones. In 2002 Chechen terrorists were le to hold a theater audience of 912 people hostage in the heart of Mosco and 130 were killed in the operation to retake the building. The Shining Pa requently struck in Lima, far from its mountain strongholds. In such situatio a more effective counterstrategy would be to invest in protecting the targ of attacks. In most states, most of the time, the majority of state agents do need to worry about their physical security, because no one

51. United States N nal Security Council, *National Strategy for Victory in Iraq* (Washington, D.C.: White House, Nov er 2005), p. 7.
52. Secretary of St Condoleezza Rice, "Iraq and U.S. Policy," testimony before the U.S. Senate Committee on For Relations, October 19, 2005, 109th Cong., 1st sess., http://www.foreign .senate.gov/testim /2005/RiceTestimony051019.pdf.
53. See Lewis Sorl *Better War: The Unexamined Victories and the Final Tragedy of America's Last Years in Vietnam* (N York: Harcourt, 1999). This thesis is not without controversy. See Matt Steinglass, "Vietna nd Victory," *Boston Globe*, December 18, 2005.

wants to harm them. However, certain state agents, such as prosecutors of organized crime, are more accustomed to danger, and procedures have been developed to protect them. These procedures should be applied to election workers, rural officials and police, community activists, and any individual who plays a visible role in the support and functioning of the embattled government.

When the terrorist goal is social control, the best response is strengthening law enforcement. This may require more resources to enable the government to effectively investigate and prosecute crimes. More controversial, it may mean using national agencies such as the Federal Bureau of Investigation to bypass local officials who are sympathetic to the terrorist group and investigating law enforcement agencies to purge such sympathizers if they obstruct justice. The state can also offer additional protection to potential targets and increase penalties for violence against them. For instance, the 1994 federal Freedom of Access to Clinic Entrances Act, passed in the wake of the 1993 killing of a doctor at an abortion clinic in Florida, prohibits any violence designed to prevent people from entering such clinics.

PROVOCATION: LIGHTING THE FUSE

A provocation strategy is often used in pursuit of regime change and territorial change, the most popular goals of the FTOs listed by the State Department. It is designed to persuade the domestic audience that the target of attacks is evil and untrustworthy and must be vigorously resisted.

Terrorist organizations seeking to replace a regime face a significant challenge: they are usually much more hostile to the regime than a majority of the state's citizens. Al-Qaida may wish to topple the House of Saud, but if a majority of citizens do not support this goal, al-Qaida is unlikely to achieve it. Similarly, if most Tamils are satisfied living in a united Sri Lanka, the Tamil Tigers' drive for independence will fail. To succeed, therefore, a terrorist organization must first convince moderate citizens that their government needs to be replaced or that independence from the central government is the only acceptable outcome.

Provocation helps shift citizen support away from the incumbent regime. In a provocation strategy, terrorists seek to goad the target government into a military response that harms civilians within the terrorist organization's home territory.[54] The aim is to convince them that the government is so evil that the

54. Fromkin, "The Strategy of Terrorism."

radical goals of e terrorists are justified and support for their organization is warranted.[55] Th is what the Basque Fatherland and Liberty group (ETA) sought to do ir pain. For years, Madrid responded to ETA attacks with repressive measu against the Basque community, mobilizing many of its members again he government even if they did not condone those attacks. As one expert o his conflict writes, "Nothing radicalizes a people faster than the unleashing undisciplined security forces on its towns and villages."[56]

David Lake a ues that moderates are radicalized because government attacks provide i portant information about the type of leadership in power and its willingn to negotiate with more moderate elements.[57] Ethan Bueno de Mesquita an Eric Dickson develop this idea and show that if the government has the a ity to carry out a discriminating response to terrorism but chooses an und riminating one, it reveals itself to be unconcerned with the welfare of the c ntry's citizens. Provocation, therefore, is a way for terrorists to force an ene y government to reveal information about itself that then helps the organ tion recruit additional members.[58]

CONDITIONS I ORABLE TO PROVOCATION. Constraints on retaliation and regime type are gain important in determining when provocation is successful. For provoca n to work, the government must be capable of middling levels of brutality. government willing and able to commit genocide makes a bad target for p vocation, as the response will destroy the constituency the terrorists repre t. At the opposite pole, a government so committed to human rights and e rule of law that it is incapable of inflicting indiscriminate punishment als makes a bad target, because it cannot be provoked. Such a government mi t be an attractive target for an attrition strategy if it is not very good at st ping attacks, but provocation will be ineffective.

What explai why a government would choose a less discriminating counterstrategy er a more precise one? In some instances, a large-scale military response w enhance the security of a country rather than detract from it. If the target gov nment is able to eliminate the leadership of a terrorist orga-

---

55. Crenshaw, "Th uses of Terrorism," p. 387; and Price, "The Strategy and Tactics of Revolutionary Terrorism," 58.
56. Paddy Woodw , "Why Do They Kill? The Basque Conflict in Spain," *World Policy Journal*, Vol. 18, No. 1 (Spri 2001), p. 7.
57. David A. Lake, tional Extremism: Understanding Terrorism in the Twenty-first Century," *Dialog-IO*, Vol. 56, 2 (Spring 2002), pp. 15–29.
58. Ethan Bueno d Mesquita and Eric S. Dickson, "The Propaganda of the Deed: Terrorism, Counterterrorism, Mobilization," Washington University and New York University, 2005. Bueno de Mesquita l Dickson also argue that government violence lowers economic prosperity, which favors extrer s in their competition with moderates.

nization and its operatives, terrorism is likely to cease or be greatly reduced even if collateral damage radicalizes moderates to some extent. A large-scale military response may also enhance the security of a country, despite radicalizing some moderates, if it deters additional attacks from other terrorist groups that may be considering a war of attrition. Target governments may calculate that the negative consequences of a provocation strategy are acceptable under these conditions.

Domestic political considerations are also likely to influence the type of response that the leadership of a target state chooses. Democracies may be more susceptible to provocation than nondemocracies. Populations that have suffered from terrorist violence will naturally want their government to take action to stop terrorism. Unfortunately, many of the more discriminating tools of counterterrorism, such as infiltrating terrorist cells, sharing intelligence with other countries, and arresting individuals, are not visible to the publics these actions serve to protect. Bueno de Mesquita has argued that democratic leaders may have to employ the more public and less discriminating counterterror strategies to prove that their government is taking sufficient action against terrorists, even if these steps are provocative.[59] Pressure for a provocative counterresponse may also be particularly acute for more hard-line administrations whose constituents may demand greater action.[60] Counterstrategies, therefore, are influenced in part by the political system from which they emerge.

The United States in September 2001 was ripe for provocation, and al-Qaida appears to have understood this. The new administration of George W. Bush was known to be hawkish in its foreign policy and in its attitude toward the use of military power. In a November 2004 videotape, bin Laden bragged that al-Qaida found it "easy for us to provoke this administration."[61] The strategy appears to be working. A 2004 Pew survey found that international trust in the United States had declined significantly in response to the invasion of Iraq.[62] Similarly, a 2004 report by the International Institute for Strategic Studies found that al-Qaida's recruitment and fundraising efforts had been given a

59. Ethan Bueno de Mesquita, "Politics and the Suboptimal Provision of Counterterror," *International Organization* (forthcoming).
60. On the other hand, more dovish regimes might feel political pressure to take strong visible actions, whereas a regime with hawkish credentials could credibly claim that it was pursuing effective but nonvisible tactics. For a similar logic, see Kenneth A. Schultz, "The Politics of Risking Peace: Do Hawks or Doves Deliver the Olive Branch?" *International Organization*, Vol. 59, No. 1 (Winter 2005), pp. 1–38.
61. Bin Laden, *Messages to the World*, pp. 241–242.
62. Pew Research Center for the People and the Press, Pew Global Attitudes Project: Nine-Nation Survey, "A Year after the Iraq War: Mistrust of America in Europe Ever Higher, Muslim Anger Persists," March 16, 2004.

major boost by e U.S. invasion of Iraq.[63] In the words of Shibley Telhami, "What we're se g now is a disturbing sympathy with al-Qaida coupled with resentment tow l the United States."[64] The Bush administration's eagerness to overthrow S ldam Hussein, a desire that predated the September 11 attacks, has, in th vords of bin Laden, "contributed to these remarkable results for al-Qaida."[65]

BEST RESPONS TO PROVOCATION. The best response to provocation is a discriminating stra gy that inflicts as little collateral damage as possible. Countries should see ut and destroy the terrorists and their immediate backers to reduce the like ood of future terror attacks, but they must carefully isolate these targets fr the general population, which may or may not be sympathetic to the ter ists.[66] This type of discriminating response will require superior intelligence pabilities. In this regard, the United States' efforts to invest in information- hering abilities in response to September 11 have been underwhelming. I n the most basic steps, such as developing a deeper pool of expertise in the gional languages, have been slow in coming.[67] This stands in contrast to U.S havior during the Cold War, when the government sponsored research ters at top universities to analyze every aspect of the Soviet economic, milit , and political system. The weakness of the U.S. intelligence apparatus has l n most clearly revealed in the inability of the United States to eliminate bir aden and al-Zawahiri, and in the United States' decision to invade Iraq.[68] I lty U.S. intelligence has simultaneously protected al-Qaida leaders from th and led to the destruction of thousands of Muslim civilians—exact the response al-Qaida was likely seeking.

SPOILING: SABO ING THE PEACE

The goal of a sp ing strategy is to ensure that peace overtures between moderate leaders o he terrorists' side and the target government do not suc-

63. See Internation stitute for Strategic Studies, *Strategic Survey, 2003/4: An Evaluation and Forecast of World Affairs* ndon: Routledge, 2005).
64. Quoted in Dafr inzer, "Poll Shows Growing Arab Rancor at U.S.," *Washington Post*, July 23, 2004.
65. Bob Woodwar *lan of Attack* (New York: Simon and Schuster, 2004), pp. 21–23; and bin Laden, *Messages to World*, pp. 241–242.
66. A program of e omic and social assistance to these more moderate elements would provide counterevidence th e target is not malicious or evil as the terrorist organizations had claimed.
67. Farah Stockma Tomorrow's Homework: Reading, Writing, and Arabic," *Boston Globe*, January 6, 2006.
68. For an analysis obstacles to innovation in U.S. intelligence agencies, see Amy B. Zegart, "September 11 and Adaptation Failure of U.S. Intelligence Agencies," *International Security*, Vol. 29, No. 4 (Spri 2005), pp. 78–111.

ceed.[69] It works by playing on the mistrust between these two groups and succeeds when one or both parties fail to sign or implement a settlement. It is often employed when the ultimate objective is territorial change.

Terrorists resort to a spoiling strategy when relations between two enemies are improving and a peace agreement threatens the terrorists' more far-reaching goals. Peace agreements alarm terrorists because they understand that moderate citizens are less likely to support ongoing violence once a compromise agreement between more moderate groups has been reached. Thus, Iranian radicals kidnapped fifty-two Americans in Tehran in 1979 not because relations between the United States and Iran were becoming more belligerent, but because three days earlier Iran's relatively moderate prime minister, Mehdi Bazargan, met with the U.S. national security adviser, Zbigniew Brzezinski, and the two were photographed shaking hands. From the perspective of the radicals, a real danger of reconciliation existed between the two countries, and violence was used to prevent this.[70] A similar problem has hampered Arab-Israeli peace negotiations, as well as talks between Protestants and Catholics in Northern Ireland.

A spoiling strategy works by persuading the enemy that moderates on the terrorists' side cannot be trusted to abide by a peace deal. Whenever two sides negotiate a peace agreement, there is uncertainty about whether the deal is self-enforcing. Each side fears that even if it honors its commitments, the other side may not, catapulting it back to war on disadvantageous terms. Some Israelis, for example, feared that if Israel returned an additional 13 percent of the West Bank to the Palestinians, as mandated by the 1998 Wye accord, the Palestinian Authority would relaunch its struggle from an improved territorial base. Extremists understand that moderates look for signs that their former enemy will violate an agreement and that targeting these moderates with violence will heighten their fears that they will be exploited. Thus terrorist attacks are designed to persuade a targeted group that the seemingly moderate opposition with whom it negotiated an agreement will not or cannot stop terrorism, and hence cannot be trusted to honor an agreement.

Terrorist acts are particularly effective during peace negotiations because opposing parties are naturally distrustful of each other's motives and have limited sources of information about each other's intentions. Thus, even if moderate leaders are willing to aggressively suppress extremists on their side,

69. Stephen John Stedman, "Spoiler Problems in Peace Processes," *International Security*, Vol. 22, No. 2 (Fall 1997), pp. 5–53.
70. Lewis, "The Revolt of Islam," p. 54.

terrorists know at isolated violence might still convince the target to reject the deal. A reas for this is that the targeted group may not be able to readily observe the ext of the crackdown and must base its judgments primarily on whether terrori occurs or not. Even a sincere effort at self-policing, therefore, will not n ssarily convince the targeted group to proceed with a settlement if a terror attack occurs.

CONDITIONS ORABLE TO SPOILING. Terrorists pursuing a spoiling strategy are likely to be re successful when the enemy perceives moderates on their side to be stron nd therefore more capable of halting terrorism.[71] When an attack occurs, t target cannot be sure whether moderates on the other side can suppress th own extremists but choose not to, or are weak and lack the ability to stop em. Israelis, for example, frequently questioned whether Yasser Arafat w simply unable to stop terrorist attacks against Israel or was unwilling to do . The weaker the moderates are perceived to be, the less impact a terrorist ack will have on the other side's trust, and the less likely such an attack o convince them to abandon a peace agreement.

The Israeli-Pa tinian conflict, and in particular the Oslo peace process, has been plagued b poilers. On the Palestinian side, Hamas's violent attacks coincided with th atification and implementation of accords—occasions when increased mistr could thwart progress toward peace. Hamas also stepped up its attacks p to Israeli elections in 1996 and 2001, in which Labor was the incumbent part n an effort to persuade Israeli voters to cast their votes for the less cooper ve and less trusting hard-line Likud Party.[72] Terrorism was especially effec after Arafat's 1996 electoral victory, when it became clear to the Israelis that afat was, at the time, a popular and powerful leader within the Palestinian nmunity.[73] This in turn suggested to the Israelis that Arafat was capable of cking down aggressively on terrorist violence but was unwilling to do s sign that he could not be trusted to keep the peace.

BEST RESPON TO SPOILING. When mutual trust is high, a peace settlement can be implem ed despite ongoing terrorist acts and the potential vulnerabilities the agr nent can create. Trust, however, is rarely high after long conflicts, which why spoilers can strike with a reasonable chance that their

71. Andrew Kydd l Barbara F. Walter, "Sabotaging the Peace: The Politics of Extremist Violence," *Internationa ganization*, Vol. 56, No. 2 (Spring 2002), pp. 263–296.
72. Claude Berrebi l Esteban F. Klor, "On Terrorism and Electoral Outcomes: Theory and Evidence from the Isra Palestinian Conflict," Princeton University and Hebrew University of Jerusalem, 2004.
73. Kydd and Wal "Sabotaging the Peace," pp. 279–289.

attack will be successful. Strategies that build trust and reduce vulnerability are, therefore, the best response to spoiling.

Vulnerabilities emerge in peace processes in two ways. Symmetric vulnerabilities occur during the implementation of a deal because both sides must lower their guard. The Israelis, for example, have had to relax controls over the occupied territories, and the Palestinians were obligated to disarm militant groups. Such symmetric vulnerabilities can be eased by third-party monitoring and verification of the peace implementation process. Monitoring can help reduce uncertainty regarding the behavior of the parties. Even better, third-party enforcement of the deal can make reneging more costly, increasing confidence in the deal and its ultimate success.[74]

Vulnerabilities can also be longer term and asymmetric. In any peace deal between Israel and the Palestinians, the ability of the Palestinians to harm Israel will inevitably grow as Palestinians build their own state and acquire greater military capabilities. This change in the balance of power can make it difficult for the side that will see an increase in its power to credibly commit not to take advantage of this increase later on. This commitment problem can cause conflicts to be prolonged even though there are possible peace agreements that both sides would prefer to war.[75]

The problem of shifting power can be addressed in at least three ways. First, agreements themselves can be crafted in ways that limit the post-treaty shift in power. Power-sharing agreements such as that between the Liberals and Conservatives to create a single shared presidency in Colombia in 1957 are one example of this. Allowing the defeated side to retain some military capabilities, as Confederate officers were allowed to do after the surrender at Appomattox, is another example.[76] Second, peace settlements can require the side about to be advantaged to send a costly signal of its honorable intentions, such as providing constitutional protections of minority rights. An example is the Constitutional Law on National Minorities passed in Croatia in 2002,

74. Barbara F. Walter, *Committing to Peace: The Successful Settlement of Civil Wars* (Princeton, N.J.: Princeton University Press, 2002); and Holger Schmidt, "When (and Why) Do Brokers Have To Be Honest? Impartiality and Third-Party Support for Peace Implementation after Civil Wars, 1945–1999," Georgetown University, 2004.

75. Fearon, "Rationalist Explanations for War"; James D. Fearon, "Commitment Problems and the Spread of Ethnic Conflict," in David A. Lake and Donald Rothchild, eds., *The International Spread of Ethnic Conflict: Fear, Diffusion, and Escalation* (Princeton, N.J.: Princeton University Press, 1998); and Robert Powell, "The Inefficient Use of Power: Costly Conflict with Complete Information," *American Political Science Review*, Vol. 98, No. 2 (May 2004), pp. 231–241.

76. As part of the terms of surrender, Confederate officers were allowed to keep their sidearms and personal property (including their horses) and return home.

which protects right of minorities to obtain an education in their own language. Finally, ties can credibly commit to an agreement by participating in international in utions that insist on the protection of minority rights. A government that is lling to join the European Union effectively constrains itself from exploiting ninority group because of the high costs to that government of being ejectec om the group.

OUTBIDDING: ZE OTS VERSUS SELLOUTS

Outbidding ari when two key conditions hold: two or more domestic parties are compet for leadership of their side, and the general population is uncertain abou hich of the groups best represents their interests.[77] The competition betwee Hamas and Fatah is a classic case where two groups vie for the support of t Palestinian citizens and where the average Palestinian is uncertain about w h side he or she ought to back.

If citizens h full information about the preferences of the competing groups, an out ding strategy would be unnecessary and ineffective; citizens would simply s port the group that best aligned with their own interests. In reality, howeve itizens cannot be sure if the group competing for power truly represent eir preferences. The group could be a strong and resolute defender of the use (zealots) or weak and ineffective stooges of the enemy (sellouts). If cit ns support zealots, they get a strong champion but with some risk that y will be dragged into a confrontation with the enemy that they end up los . If citizens support sellouts, they get peace but at the price of accepting a se outcome than might have been achieved with additional armed struggle roups competing for power have an incentive to signal that they are zealots ther than sellouts. Terrorist attacks can serve this function by signaling that a oup has the will to continue the armed struggle despite its costs.

Three reason elp to explain why groups are likely to be rewarded for being more milita rather than less. First, in bargaining contexts, it is often useful to be repres ed by an agent who is more hard-line than oneself. Hard-line agents will reje leals that one would accept, which will force the adversary

77. For the most e sive treatment of terrorism and outbidding, see Mia Bloom, *Dying to Kill: The Allure of Suici rrorism* (New York: Columbia University Press, 2005). See also Stuart J. Kaufman, "Spiralin Ethnic War: Elites, Masses, and Moscow in Moldova's Civil War," *International Security*, Vol. No. 2 (Fall 1996), pp. 108–138.

to make a better offer than one would get by representing oneself in the negotiations.[78] Palestinians might therefore prefer Hamas as a negotiating agent with Israel because it has a reputation for resolve and will reject inferior deals.

Second, uncertainty may also exist about the type of adversary the population and its competing groups are facing. If the population believes there is some chance that their adversary is untrustworthy (unwilling to compromise under any condition), then they know that conflict may be inevitable, in which case being represented by zealots may be advantageous.[79]

A third factor that may favor outbidding is that office-holding itself may produce incentives to sell out. Here, the problem lies with the benefits groups receive once in office (i.e., income and power). Citizens fear that their leaders, once in office, may betray important principles and decide to settle with the enemy on unfavorable terms. They know that holding office skews one's preferences toward selling out, but they remain unsure about which of their leaders is most likely to give in. Terrorist organizations exploit this uncertainty by using violence to signal their commitment to a cause. Being perceived as more extreme than the median voter works to the terrorists' benefit because it balances out the "tempering effect" of being in office.

An interesting aspect of the outbidding strategy is that the enemy is only tangentially related to the strategic interaction. In fact, an attack motivated by outbidding may not even be designed to achieve any goal related to the enemy, such as inducing a concession or scuttling a peace treaty. The process is almost entirely concerned with the signal it sends to domestic audiences uncertain about their own leadership and its commitment to a cause. As such, outbidding provides a potential explanation for terrorist attacks that continue even when they seem unable to produce any real results.

CONDITIONS FAVORABLE TO OUTBIDDING. Outbidding will be favored when multiple groups are competing for the allegiance of a similar demographic base of support. In Peru, the 1970s saw the development of a number of leftist groups seeking to represent the poor and indigenous population. When the military turned over power to an elected government in 1980, the Shining Path took up an armed struggle to distinguish itself from groups that chose to pur-

78. Abhinay Muthoo, *Bargaining Theory with Applications* (Cambridge: Cambridge University Press, 1999), p. 230.
79. Rui J.P. de Figueiredo Jr. and Barry R. Weingast, "The Rationality of Fear: Political Opportunism and Ethnic Conflict," in Barbara F. Walter and Jack Snyder, eds., *Civil Wars, Insecurity, and Intervention* (New York: Columbia University Press, 1999), pp. 261–302.

sue electoral p ics.[80] It also embarked on an assassination campaign designed to weak rival leftist groups and intimidate their followers. When organizations e unter less competition for the support of their main constituents, outbiddi will be less appealing.

BEST RESPONS TO OUTBIDDING. One solution to the problem of outbidding would be to e inate the struggle for power by encouraging competing groups to cons date into a unified opposition. If competition among resistance groups is minated, the incentive for outbidding also disappears. The downside of th ounterstrategy is that a unified opposition may be stronger than a divided . United oppositions, however, can make peace and deliver, whereas divide nes may face greater structural disincentives to do so.

An alternativ trategy for the government to pursue in the face of outbidding is to valid the strategy chosen by nonviolent groups by granting them concessions anc tempting to satisfy the demands of their constituents. If outbidding can be own to yield poor results in comparison to playing within the system, gro may be persuaded to abandon the strategy. As in the case of the Shining h, this may require providing physical protection to competing groups i ase the outbidder turns to intimidation in its competition with less viole ivals. In general, any steps that can be taken to make the non-outbidding oups seem successful (e.g., channeling resources and government servic o their constituents) will also help undermine the outbidders. The high t out in the December 2005 Iraqi election in Sunni-dominated regions may in ate that outbidding is beginning to fail in the communities most strongly c osed to the new political system.[81]

Conclusion

Terrorist violen is a form of costly signaling by which terrorists attempt to influence the b fs of their enemy and the population they represent or wish to control. The e violence to signal their strength and resolve in an effort to produce conces ns from their enemy and obedience and support from their followers. The lso attack both to sow mistrust between moderates who

80. James Ron, "Id gy in Context: Explaining Sendero Luminoso's Tactical Escalation," *Journal of Peace Research*, V 8, No. 5 (September 2001), p. 582.
81. Dexter Filkins, qis, Including Sunnis, Vote in Large Numbers on Calm Day," *New York Times*, December 1 05.

might want to make peace and to provoke a reaction that makes the enemy appear barbarous and untrustworthy.

In this article, we have laid out the five main goals terrorist organizations seek and the five most important terrorist strategies, and we have outlined when they are likely to be tried and what the best counterstrategies might look like. What becomes clear in this brief analysis is that a deeper study of each of the five strategies is needed to reveal the nuanced ways in which terrorism works, and to refine responses to it. We conclude by highlighting two variables that will be important in any such analysis, and by a final reflection on counterterror policies that are strategically independent or not predicated on the specific strategy being used.

The first variable is information. It has long been a truism that the central front in counterinsurgency warfare is the information front. The same is true in terrorism. Costly signaling is pointless in the absence of uncertainty on the part of the recipient of the signal. Attrition is designed to convince the target that the costs of maintaining a policy are not worth the gains; if the target already knew this, it would have ceded the issue without an attack being launched. Provocation is designed to goad the target into retaliating indiscriminately (because it lacks information to discriminate), which will persuade the population that the target is malevolent (because it is uncertain of the target's intentions). The other strategies are similarly predicated on uncertainty, intelligence, learning, and communication. Thus, it bears emphasizing that the problem of terrorism is not a problem of applying force per se, but one of acquiring intelligence and affecting beliefs. With the right information, the proper application of force is comparatively straightforward. The struggle against terrorism is, therefore, not usefully guided by the metaphor of a "war on terrorism" any more than policies designed to alleviate poverty are usefully guided by the metaphor of a "war on poverty" or narcotics policy by a "war on drugs." The struggle against terrorism can more usefully be thought of as a struggle to collect and disseminate reliable information in environments fraught with uncertainty.

The second important variable is regime type. Democracies have been the sole targets of attritional suicide bombing campaigns, whereas authoritarian regimes such as those in Algeria routinely face campaigns by rebel groups pursuing an intimidation strategy. Democracies also seem to be more susceptible to attrition and provocation strategies. This type of variation cries out for deeper analysis of the strengths and weakness of different regime types in the

face of differen rrorist strategies. Our analysis suggests that democracies are
more likely to b ensitive to the costs of terrorist attacks, to grant concessions
to terrorists so to limit future attacks, to be constrained in their ability to
pursue a length attritional campaign against an organization, but also to be
under greater p sure to "do something." This does not mean that all democracies will beha incorrectly in the face of terrorist attacks all the time. Democratic regimes y possess certain structural features, however, that make
them attractive gets for terrorism.

Finally, we r ze that our discussion is only a beginning and that further
elaboration of of the strategies and their corresponding counterstrategies
awaits future r arch. We also understand that not all counterterrorism policies are predica on the specific strategy terrorists pursue. Our analysis is at
the middling le of strategic interaction. At the tactical level are all the tools
of intelligence hering and target defense that make sense no matter what
the terrorist's st egy is. At the higher level are the primary sources of terrorism such as po ty, education, international conflict, and chauvinistic indoctrination that e le terrorist organizations to operate and survive in the first
place. Our aim his article has been to try to understand why these organizations choose c in forms of violence, and how this violence serves their
larger purpose he United States has the ability to reduce the likelihood of
additional atta on its territory and citizens. But it will be much more successful if it first nderstands the goals terrorists are seeking and the underlying strategic lo by which a plane flying into a skyscraper might deliver the
desired respon

Why Terrorism Does Not Work

Max Abrahms

Terrorist groups attack civilians to coerce their governments into making policy concessions, but does this strategy work?[1] If target countries systematically resist rewarding terrorism, the international community is armed with a powerful message to deter groups from terrorizing civilians. The prevailing view within the field of political science, however, is that terrorism is an effective coercive strategy. The implications of this perspective are grim; as target countries are routinely coerced into making important strategic and ideological concessions to terrorists, their victories will reinforce the strategic logic for groups to attack civilians, spawning even more terrorist attacks.[2]

This pessimistic outlook is unwarranted; there has been scant empirical research on whether terrorism is a winning coercive strategy, that is, whether groups tend to exact policy concessions from governments by attacking their

Max Abrahms is a doctoral candidate in political science at the University of California, Los Angeles. He wrote this article when he was a Research Associate in terrorism studies at the Belfer Center for Science and International Affairs in the John F. Kennedy School of Government at Harvard University.

The author would like to thank the following individuals for offering valuable advice and comments: Peter Krause, Deborah Larson, Marcy McCullaugh, David Rapoport, Steven Spiegel, Marc Trachtenberg, Micah Zenko, and especially Robert Goldenberg, Evan Spring, and the anonymous reviewers for *International Security*.

1. For decades, terrorism specialists and political scientists have recognized that groups use terrorism to achieve policy objectives. See, for example, Martha Crenshaw, "The Causes of Terrorism," *Comparative Politics*, Vol. 13, No. 4 (July 1981), p. 379.
2. The logic of this argument is explored in Ehud Sprinzak, "Rational Fanatics," *Foreign Policy*, No. 120 (September–October 2000), p. 68; Robert A. Pape, "The Strategic Logic of Suicide Terrorism," *American Political Science Review*, Vol. 97, No. 3 (August 2003), pp. 13–14; and Robert A. Pape, *Dying to Win: The Strategic Logic of Suicide Terrorism* (New York: Random House, 2005), pp. 61, 75–76. See also Alan Dershowitz, *Why Terrorism Works: Understanding the Threat, Responding to the Challenge* (New Haven, Conn.: Yale University Press, 2002). In recent years, numerous writers have argued that terrorism is both rational and effective. See, for example, David A. Lake, "Rational Extremism: Understanding Terrorism in the Twenty-first Century," *Dialogue-IO*, Vol. 1 (January 2002), p. 15; Andrew Kydd and Barbara Walter, "Sabotaging the Peace: The Politics of Extremist Violence," *International Organization*, Vol. 56, No. 2 (April 2002), p. 263; Andrew Kydd and Barbara Walter, "The Strategies of Terrorism," *International Security*, Vol. 31, No. 1 (Summer 2006), p. 49; Arie W. Kruglanski and Shira Fishman, "The Psychology of Terrorism: 'Syndrome' versus 'Tool' Perspectives," *Terrorism and Political Violence*, Vol. 18, No. 2 (Summer 2006), p. 207; Noam Chomsky, "The New War against Terror" (transcribed from audio), recorded at the Technology and Culture Forum at the Massachusetts Institute of Technology, October 18, 2001, http://www.chomsky.info/talks/20011018.htm; and Scott Atran, "Trends in Suicide Terrorism: Sense and Nonsense," paper presented to the World Federation of Scientists' Permanent Monitoring Panel on terrorism, Erice, Sicily, August 2004, http://www.sitemaker.umich.edu/satran/files/atran-trends.pdf.

International Security, Vol. 31, No. 2 (Fall 2006), pp. 42–78

civilian popula ıs. In the 1980s, Martha Crenshaw observed that "the outcomes of camp ns of terrorism have been largely ignored," as "most analyses have emph zed the causes and forms rather than the consequences of terrorism."[3] Tec obert Gurr added that terrorism's policy effectiveness is "a subject on whic ittle national-level research has been done, systematically or otherwise."[4] Th lacuna within terrorism studies is both a symptom and a cause of the lac of data sets with coded information on the outcomes of terrorist campaigr Within the past several years, numerous scholars have purported to shov that terrorism is an effective coercive strategy, but their research invari y rests on game-theoretic models, single case studies, or a handful of well own terrorist victories.[6] To date, political scientists have neither analyzed t outcomes of a large number of terrorist campaigns nor attempted to spec the antecedent conditions for terrorism to work. In light of its policy releva e, terrorism's record in coercing policy change requires further empirical a lysis.

This study a yzes the political plights of twenty-eight terrorist groups—the complete lis f foreign terrorist organizations (FTOs) as designated by the U.S. Departmer of State since 2001.[7] The data yield two unexpected findings. First, the group ccomplished their forty-two policy objectives only 7 percent of the time. Sec d, although the groups achieved certain types of policy objectives more th others, the key variable for terrorist success was a tactical one: target selec n. Groups whose attacks on civilian targets outnumbered attacks on militar rgets systematically failed to achieve their policy objectives, regardless of t r nature. These findings suggest that (1) terrorist groups rarely achieve t r policy objectives, and (2) the poor success rate is inherent

3. Martha Crensha ed., *Terrorism, Legitimacy, and Power: The Consequences of Political Violence* (Middletown, Con Vesleyan University Press, 1983), p. 5.
4. Ted Robert Gurr mpirical Research on Political Terrorism," in Robert O. Slater and Michael Stohl, eds., *Current spectives on International Terrorism* (New York: St. Martin's, 1988), p. 125.
5. See ibid., p. 120.
6. See, for exampl ax Abrahms, "Are Terrorists Really Rational? The Palestinian Example," *Orbis*, Vol. 48, No. ummer 2004), pp. 533–549; Max Abrahms, "Al-Qaida's Scorecard: A Progress Report on al-(la's Objectives," *Studies in Conflict and Terrorism;* Sprinzak, "Rational Fanatics," p. 68; Lake ational Extremism," p. 15; Kydd and Walter, "The Strategies of Terrorism," p. 49; Pape, *Dying Vin*, p. 40; and Pape, "The Strategic Logic of Suicide Terrorism," p. 13. The sample Pape used t etermine the motivations of suicide terrorist groups is impressive, incorporating data from ev suicide attack from 1980 to 2003. His secondary argument on terrorism's effectiveness relies or ess convincing sample of cases. For a critique of the methods Pape used to analyze the effecti ss of suicide terrorist groups, see Max Abrahms, "Dying to Win," *Middle East Policy*, Vol. 12, . 4 (Winter 2005), pp. 176–178.
7. U.S. Departmen State, "Foreign Terrorist Organizations (FTOs)," October 11, 2005, http://www.state.gov/s/ s/fs/37191.htm.

to the tactic of terrorism itself. Together, the data challenge the dominant scholarly opinion that terrorism is strategically rational behavior.[8] The bulk of the article develops a theory to explain why terrorist groups are unable to achieve their policy objectives by targeting civilians.

This article has five main sections. The first section summarizes the conventional wisdom that terrorism is an effective coercive strategy and highlights the deficit of empirical research sustaining this position. The second section explicates the methods used to assess the outcomes of the forty-two terrorist objectives included in this study and finds that terrorist success rates are actually extremely low. The third section examines the antecedent conditions for terrorism to work. It demonstrates that although terrorist groups are more likely to succeed in coercing target countries into making territorial concessions than ideological concessions, groups that primarily attack civilian targets do not achieve their policy objectives, regardless of their nature. The fourth section develops a theory derived from the social psychology literature for why terrorist groups that target civilians are unable to compel policy change. Its external validity is then tested against three case studies: the September 1999 Russian apartment bombings, the September 11, 2001, attacks on the United States, and Palestinian terrorism in the first intifada. The article concludes with four policy implications for the war on terrorism and suggestions for future research.

The Notion That Terrorism Works

Writers are increasingly contending that terrorism is an effective coercive strategy. In his 2002 best-seller, *Why Terrorism Works,* Alan Dershowitz argues that Palestinian gains since the early 1970s reveal that terrorism "works" and is thus "an entirely rational choice to achieve a political objective."[9] David Lake

8. Herbert Simon noted that there are two types of rationality. "Substantive rationality" is based on the actual "achievement of given goals." By contrast, "procedural rationality" depends only on "the [thought] process that generated it." In other words, substantive rationality is concerned with the consequences of the decision, whereas procedural rationality makes no claim that the actor correctly anticipates the consequences of his decision. Simon, "From Substantive to Procedural Rationality," in Spiro Latsis, ed., *Method and Appraisal in Economics* (Cambridge: Cambridge University Press, 1976), pp. 130–131; and Simon, *Models of Bounded Rationality,* Vol. 3: *Empirically Grounded Economic Research* (Cambridge, Mass.: MIT Press, 1997), pp. 8–9. My article addresses the question of whether terrorism is substantively rational behavior, not whether it is procedurally rational.
9. Dershowitz, *Why Terrorism Works,* p. 86. In the past several years, a flurry of editorials has likewise warned that the tendency for states to reward terrorism is encouraging other groups to use it. See John Derbyshire, "Terrorism Works," *National Review Online,* October 12, 2000; Evelyn Gordon, "Terrorism Works," *Jerusalem Post,* July 14, 2005; and R.W. Johnson, "Why Bush Might Yet Give In

recently adapte ımes Fearon's rationalist bargaining model to argue that terrorism is a "r ›nal and strategic" tactic because it enables terrorists to achieve a super bargain by increasing their capabilities relative to those of target countrie Based on their game-theoretic model and case study on Hamas, Andre Kydd and Barbara Walter likewise conclude that terrorist groups are "sur singly successful in their aims."[11] According to Scott Atran, terrorist group generally" achieve their policy objectives. As evidence, he notes that the l anese-based Shiite terrorist group, Hezbollah, successfully compelled the ited States and France to withdraw their remaining forces from Lebanon i 984 and that in 1990 the Tamil Tigers of Sri Lanka wrested control of Tami reas from the Sinhalese-dominated government.[12] For Ehud Sprinzak, the p hts of Hezbollah and the Tamil Tigers testify to terrorism's "gruesome eff veness," which explains its growing popularity since the mid-1980s.[13]

Robert Pape developed this thesis in a prominent article that was recently expande nto a major book.[14] Pape contends that "over the past two decades, suicid terrorism has been rising largely because terrorists have learned that it s."[15] He reports that from 1980 to 2003, six of the eleven terrorist campaig in his sample were associated with "significant policy changes by the rget state" and that "a 50 percent success rate is remarkable."[16] The pe ption that terrorism is an effective method of coercion, he affirms, is thus ounded in "reasonable assessments of the relationship between terrorist ercive efforts and the political gains that the terrorists have achieved."[17] Pa s research, although confined to suicide terrorist groups, is frequently cite evidence that terrorism in general is "effective in achieving a terrorist grou political aims."[18]

This emergin onsensus lacks a firm empirical basis. The notion that terrorism is an effecti coercive instrument is sustained by either single case studies or a few well-k wn terrorist victories, namely, by Hezbollah, the Tamil Tigers, and Pale ian terrorist groups. Pape's research appears to offer the

---

to the Terrorists," *L Telegraph* (London), September 29, 2001. See also Kruglanski and Fishman, "The Psychology o rrorism," p. 207; and Chomsky, "The New War against Terror."

10. Lake, "Rational tremism," pp. 20, 15.
11. Kydd and Walt 'Sabotaging the Peace," p. 264.
12. Atran, "Trends Suicide Terrorism."
13. Sprinzak, "Rati l Fanatics," p. 68.
14. Pape, "The Str ic Logic of Suicide Terrorism"; and Pape, *Dying to Win.*
15. Pape, "The Str ic Logic of Suicide Terrorism," p. 343.
16. Ibid., p. 9; and e, *Dying to Win*, pp. 64–65.
17. Pape, *Dying to* , pp. 61, 64–65.
18. See, for exampl Kydd and Walter, "The Strategies of Terrorism," p. 49.

strongest evidence that terrorist groups regularly accomplish their policy objectives, but on closer analysis his thesis is also empirically weak. Not only is his sample of terrorist campaigns modest, but they targeted only a handful of countries: ten of the eleven campaigns analyzed were directed against the same three countries (Israel, Sri Lanka, and Turkey), with six of the campaigns directed against the same country (Israel).[19] More important, Pape does not examine whether the terrorist campaigns achieved their core policy objectives. In his assessment of Palestinian terrorist campaigns, for example, he counts the limited withdrawals of the Israel Defense Forces from parts of the Gaza Strip and the West Bank in 1994 as two separate terrorist victories, ignoring the 167 percent increase in the number of Israeli settlers during this period—the most visible sign of Israeli occupation.[20] Similarly, he counts as a victory the Israeli decision to release Hamas leader Sheik Ahmed Yassin from prison in October 1997, ignoring the hundreds of imprisonments and targeted assassinations of Palestinian terrorists throughout the Oslo "peace process."[21] Pape's data therefore reveal only that select terrorist campaigns have occasionally scored tactical victories, not that terrorism is an effective strategy for groups to achieve their policy objectives. The two sections that follow are intended to help bridge the gap between the growing interest in terrorism's efficacy and the current weakness of empirical research on this topic.

Measuring Terrorism's Effectiveness

Terrorist campaigns come in two varieties: strategic terrorism aims to coerce a government into changing its policies; redemptive terrorism is intended solely to attain specific human or material resources such as prisoners or money.[22] Because my focus is on terrorism's ability to compel policy change, terrorism in this study refers only to strategic terrorism campaigns. Terrorism's effectiveness can be measured along two dimensions: combat effectiveness describes the level of damage inflicted by the coercing power; strategic effectiveness refers to the extent to which the coercing power achieves its policy objectives.[23] This study is confined to analyzing the notion that terrorism is strategically ef-

---

19. Pape, "The Strategic Logic of Suicide Terrorism," p. 9.
20. Abrahms, "Dying to Win," p. 177.
21. See Abrahms, "Dying to Win."
22. Gary C. Gambill, "The Balance of Terror: War by Other Means in the Contemporary Middle East," *Journal of Palestine Studies*, Vol. 28, No. 1 (Autumn 1998), p. 61.
23. Robert A. Pape, *Bombing to Win: Air Power and Coercion in War* (Ithaca, N.Y.: Cornell University Press, 1996), pp. 56–57.

fective, not whe :r it succeeds on an operational or tactical level.[24] Finally, because this stud s concerned with terrorism's effect on the target country, intermediate ob tives—namely, the ability of terrorist groups to gain international attention d support—are outside the scope of analysis.[25]

This study ar yzes the strategic effectiveness of the twenty-eight terrorist groups designa by the U.S. Department of State as foreign terrorist organizations since 20 The only selection bias would come from the State Department. Using thi st provides a check against selecting cases on the dependent variable, which ould artificially inflate the success rate because the most well known policy comes involve terrorist victories (e.g., the U.S. withdrawal from southern banon in 1984). Furthermore, because all of the terrorist groups have rei ined active since 2001, ample time has been allowed for each group to make ogress on achieving its policy goals, thereby reducing the possibility of a icially deflating the success rate through too small a time frame. In fact, t terrorist groups have had significantly more time than five years to accom h their policy objectives: the groups, on average, have been active since 19 the majority has practiced terrorism since the 1960s and 1970s; and only ur were established after 1990.

For terrorist ups, policy outcomes are easier to assess than policy objectives. Instead of bitrarily defining the objectives of the terrorist groups in this study, I define t n as the terrorists do. In general, the stated objectives of terrorist groups ar stable and reliable indicator of their actual intentions. This assumption und girds the widely accepted view within terrorism studies that groups use terr sm as a communication strategy to convey to target countries the costs o oncompliance.[26] Because these groups seek political change

---

24. See James T. Te chi, "A Reinterpretation of Research on Aggression," *Psychological Bulletin*, Vol. 81, No. 9 (Sept oer 1974), p. 562.
25. There is little de e that terrorism often facilitates the achievement of intermediate objectives. This position gaine cceptance after the 1967 Arab-Israeli war, when a spate of terrorist attacks galvanized Palestin nationalist sentiment and propelled the Palestinian cause onto the international agenda. In Se mber 1969, just three months after the Popular Front for the Liberation of Palestine hijacked a S. jet departing from Athens, the United Nations General Assembly recognized the "inaliena rights of the Palestinian people." Eighteen months after Palestinian terrorists killed eleven Isr Olympians at the 1972 Munich Games, Yassir Arafat was officially invited to speak before this ly. Bruce Hoffman has observed, "It is doubtful whether the terrorists could ever have received success had they not resorted to international terrorism." Hoffman, *Inside Terrorism* (New Yor Columbia University Press, 1998), p. 75. See also Abrahms, "Are Terrorists Really Rational?" p 1; and Thomas C. Schelling, "What Purposes Can 'International Terrorism' Serve?" in R.G. Fre nd Christopher W. Morris, eds., *Violence, Terrorism, and Justice* (New York: Cambridge Univer Press, 1991), p. 20.
26. See Crenshaw, e Causes of Terrorism," p. 379; Ronald D. Crelinsten, "Terrorism as Political Communication: Tl elationship between the Controller and the Controlled," in Paul Wilkinson and Alasdair M. St rt, eds., *Contemporary Research on Terrorism* (Aberdeen, Scotland: Aberdeen

and because their stated objectives represent their intentions, terrorism's effectiveness is measured by comparing their stated objectives to policy outcomes. A potential objection to this approach is that terrorists possess extreme policy goals relative to those of their supporters, and thus terrorist campaigns may be judged unsuccessful even when they compel policy changes of significance to their broader community. What distinguish terrorists from "moderates," however, are typically not their policy goals, but the belief that terrorism is the optimal means to achieve them.[27] As Pape has observed, "It is not that terrorists pursue radical goals" relative to those of their supporters. Rather, it is that "terrorists are simply the members of their societies who are the most optimistic about the usefulness of violence for achieving goals that many, and often most, support."[28] There are no broadly based data sets with coded information on the objectives of terrorist campaigns, but those ascribed to the terrorist groups in this study are all found in standard descriptions of them, such as in RAND's MIPT Terrorism Knowledge Base and the Federation of American Scientists' Directory of Terrorist Organizations (see Table 1).[29]

To capture the range of policy outcomes, this study employs a four-tiered rating scale. A "total success" denotes the full attainment of a terrorist group's policy objective. Conversely, "no success" describes a scenario in which a terrorist group does not make any perceptible progress on realizing its stated objective. Middling achievements are designated as either a "partial success" or a "limited success" in descending degrees of effectiveness. Several groups are counted more than once to reflect their multiple policy objectives. Hezbollah, for example, is credited with two policy successes: repelling the multinational peacekeepers and Israelis from southern Lebanon in 1984 and again in 2000. By contrast, Revolutionary Nuclei is tagged with two policy failures: its inability either to spark a communist revolution in Greece or to sever U.S.-Greek relations.

University Press, 1987), pp. 3–31; Bruce Hoffman and Gordon H. McCormick, "Terrorism, Signaling, and Suicide Attack," *Studies in Conflict and Terrorism,* Vol. 27, No. 4 (July/August 2004), pp. 243–281; Max Abrahms, "Al-Qaeda's Miscommunication War: The Terrorism Paradox," *Terrorism and Political Violence,* Vol. 17, No. 4 (Autumn 2005), pp. 529–549; and Kydd and Walter, "The Strategies of Terrorism," p. 59.

27. U.S. Department of Defense, "The National Military Strategic Plan for the War on Terrorism," February 1, 2006, p. 3.

28. Pape, "The Strategic Logic of Suicide Terrorism," p. 7.

29. Gurr, "Empirical Research on Political Terrorism," p. 120; RAND, MIPT Terrorism Knowledge Base: A Comprehensive Databank of Global Terrorist Incidents and Organizations, "Groups Subcategories," http://www.tkb.org/Category.jsp?catID?1; and Federation of American Scientists, "Liberation Movements, Terrorist Organizations, Substance Cartels, and Other Para-state Entities," http://www.fas.org/irp/world/para/. See also Kydd and Walter, "The Strategies of Terrorism," pp. 54–55.

Table 1. Terrorist Groups: Objectives, Targets, and Outcomes

Group	Objective	Type	Main Target	Outcome
Abu Nidal Organization	Destroy Israel	Maximalist	Civilian	No success
Abu Sayyaf Group	Establish Islamic state in Philippines	Maximalist	Civilian	No success
Al-Qaida	Expel the United States from Persian Gulf	Limited	Civilian	Limited success
Al-Qaida	Sever U.S.-apostate relations	Idiosyncratic	Civilian	No success
Al-Qaida	Spare Muslims from "Crusader wars"	Idiosyncratic	Civilian	No success
Armed Islamic Group	Establish Islamic state in Algeria	Maximalist	Civilian	No success
United Forces of Colombia	Eliminate left-wing insurgents	Idiosyncratic	Civilian	No success
Aum Shinrikyo	Establish utopian society in Japan	Maximalist	Civilian	No success
People's Liberation Front	Establish Marxism in Turkey	Maximalist	Civilian	No success
People's Liberation Front	Sever U.S.-Turkish relations	Idiosyncratic	Civilian	No success
Egyptian Islamic Jihad	Establish Islamic state in Egypt	Maximalist	Civilian	No success
National Liberation Army	Establish Marxism in Colombia	Maximalist	Civilian	No success
Revolutionary Armed Forces of Colombia	Establish peasant rule in Colombia	Maximalist	Military	Limited success
Fatherland and Liberty	Establish Basque state	Limited	Civilian	No success
Hamas	Establish state in historic Palestine	Maximalist	Civilian	Limited success
Hamas	Destroy Israel	Maximalist	Civilian	No success
Harakat ul-Mujahidin	Rule Kashmir	Limited	Military	No success
Harakat ul-Mujahidin	Eliminate Indian insurgents	Idiosyncratic	Military	No success
Hezbollah (Lebanese)	Expel peacekeepers	Limited	Military	Total success
Hezbollah (Lebanese)	Expel Israel	Limited	Military	Total success
Hezbollah (Lebanese)	Destroy Israel	Maximalist	Military	No success
Islamic Movement of Uzbekistan	Establish Islamic state in Uzbekistan	Maximalist	Military	No success
Islamic Group	Establish Islamic state in Egypt	Maximalist	Civilian	No success
Islamic Jihad	Establish state in historic Palestine	Maximalist	Civilian	Limited success
Islamic Jihad	Destroy Israel	Maximalist	Civilian	No success
Kach	Transfer Palestinians from Israel	Idiosyncratic	Civilian	No success
Mujahideen-e-Khalq	End clerical rule in Iran	Maximalist	Military	No success
Popular Front for the Liberation of Palestine (PFLP)	Destroy Israel	Maximalist	Civilian	No success
PFLP	Establish Marxist Palestine	Maximalist	Civilian	No success
PFLP–General Command	Destroy Israel	Maximalist	Military	No success
PFLP–General Command	Establish Marxist Palestine	Maximalist	Military	No success

Table 1. *Continued*

Group	Objective	Type	Main Target	Outcome
Kurdistan Workers' Party	Establish Kurdish state in Middle East	Limited	Civilian	No success
Kurdistan Workers' Party	Establish communism in Turkey	Maximalist	Civilian	No success
Palestine Liberation Front	Destroy Israel	Maximalist	Civilian	No success
Real Irish Republican Army	Establish Irish unification	Limited	Military	No success
Revolutionary Nuclei	Establish Marxism in Greece	Maximalist	Military	No success
Revolutionary Nuclei	Sever U.S.-Greek relations	Idiosyncratic	Military	No success
Seventeen November	Establish Marxism in Greece	Maximalist	Civilian	No success
Seventeen November	Sever U.S.-Greek relations	Idiosyncratic	Civilian	No success
Shining Path	Establish communism in Peru	Maximalist	Civilian	No success
Tamil Tigers	Establish Tamil state	Limited	Military	Partial success

SOURCES: RAND, MIPT Terrorism Knowledge Base, http://www.tkb.org/Home.jsp; and Federation of American Scientists, "Liberation Movements, Terrorist Organizations, Substance Cartels, and Other Para-state Entities," http://www.fas.org/irp/world/para.

To construct ıard test for the argument that terrorism is an ineffective means of coerci I afforded generous conditions to limit the number of policy failures. Firs or analytic purposes both a "total success" and a "partial success" are co ed as policy successes, while only completely unsuccessful outcomes ("no ıccesses") are counted as failures. A "limited success" is counted as neit a success nor a failure, even though the terrorist group invariably faces c cism from its natural constituency that the means employed have been ineff ive, or even counterproductive. Thus, a policy objective is deemed a succ even if the terrorist group was only partially successful in accomplishing whereas an objective receives a failing grade only if the group has not de any noticeable progress toward achieving it. Second, an objective is jud l successful even if the group accomplished it before 2001, the year the Sta Department assembled its official list of foreign terrorist organizations. Th , all policy successes are attributed to terrorism as the causal factor, regardle of whether important intervening variables, such as a peace process, may ha contributed to the outcome. Fourth, terrorist groups are not charged with a itional penalties for provoking responses from the target country that c d be considered counterproductive to their policy goals.[30] Fifth, the object s of al-Qaida affiliates are limited to their nationalist struggles. Groups s as the Kashmiri Harakat ul-Mujahidin and the Egyptian Islamic Jihad a ıot evaluated on their ability to sever U.S.-Israeli relations, for example, e ı though many of their supporters claim to support this goal.

Based on the olicy platforms, the twenty-eight terrorist groups examined in this study ha a combined forty-two policy objectives, a healthy sample of cases for analys Several well-known terrorist campaigns have accomplished their objectives. frequently noted, Hezbollah successfully coerced the multinational peac epers and Israelis from southern Lebanon in 1984 and 2000, and the Tamil T rs won control over the northern and eastern coastal areas of Sri Lanka fron 990 on. In the aggregate, however, the terrorist groups achieved their ıin policy objectives only three out of forty-two times—a 7 percent succ rate.[31] Within the coercion literature, this rate of success is considered extr ely low. It is substantially lower, for example, than even the success rate of nomic sanctions, which are widely regarded as only mini-

30. That the Israel ense Forces reoccupied large sections of the West Bank in April 2002 in response to terrorist ity, for example, is relevant only insofar as it may have prevented Palestinian terrorist organi ons from accomplishing their stated objectives.
31. Even when "li d successes" are counted as policy successes, the success rate is only 17 percent.

mally effective.[32] The most authoritative study on economic sanctions has found a success rate of 34 percent—nearly five times greater than the success rate of the terrorist groups examined in my study—while other studies have determined that economic sanctions accomplish their policy objectives at an even higher rate.[33] Compared to even minimally effective methods of coercion, terrorism is thus a decidedly unprofitable coercive instrument.[34]

When Terrorism Works: The Paramountcy of Target Selection

The terrorist groups in this study were far more likely to achieve certain types of policy objectives than others. Yet predicting the outcomes of terrorist campaigns based on their policy goals is problematic. The objectives of terrorist groups are sometimes difficult to code. More important, the terrorist groups did not tend to achieve their policy aims regardless of their nature. The key variable for terrorist success was a tactical one: target selection. Groups whose attacks on civilian targets outnumbered attacks on military targets systematically failed to achieve their policy objectives. Below I examine the effects of objective type and target selection on the outcomes of the forty-two terrorist campaigns included in this study.

IMPORTANCE OF OBJECTIVE TYPE

Since the mid-1960s, international mediation theorists have asserted that limited objectives are more conducive to locating a mutually acceptable resolution than disputes over maximalist objectives, which foreclose a bargaining range.[35] In the international mediation literature, limited objectives typically refer to demands over territory (and other natural resources); maximalist ob-

32. Robert A. Pape, "Why Economic Sanctions Do Not Work," *International Security*, Vol. 22, No. 2 (Fall 1997), p. 99.
33. Robert A. Hart, "Democracy and the Successful Use of Economic Sanctions," *Political Research Quarterly*, Vol. 53, No. 2 (June 2000), p. 279.
34. To say that the coercive skills of terrorist groups are poor relative to those of states because these groups are considerably weaker is to concede the point that compelling policy change is a low-probability affair for terrorist groups.
35. Robert A. Dahl, *Who Governs? Democracy and Power in an American City* (New Haven, Conn.: Yale University Press, 1961); Theodore J. Lowi, "American Business, Public Policy, Case Studies, and Political Theory," *World Politics*, Vol. 16, No. 3 (July 1964), pp. 677–715; and Marvin Ott, "Mediation as a Method of Conflict Resolution, Two Cases," *International Organization*, Vol. 26, No. 4 (Autumn 1972), p. 613. The distinction between limited and maximalist issues is also expressed in terms of tangible versus intangible issues, respectively. See John A. Vasquez, "The Tangibility of Issues and Global Conflict: A Test of Rosenau's Issue Area Typology," *Journal of Peace Research*, Vol. 20, No. 2 (Summer 1983), p. 179; and I. William Zartman, *Elusive Peace: Negotiating an End to Civil Conflicts* (Washington, D.C.: Brookings, 1995).

jectives, on the er hand, refer to demands over beliefs, values, and ideology, which are mor ifficult to divide and relinquish.[36] Empirical research on interstate bargain ; has demonstrated that limited issues are more likely to be resolved than d ıands over maximalist issues; in one study, Jacob Bercovitch, Theodore Anag son, and Donnette Willie showed that in the latter half of the twentieth centu only one out of ten Cold War disputes resulted in political compromise, c pared to thirteen of thirty-one nonideological disputes in which the coer ; party succeeded in winning concessions.[37] More recently, scholars have a lied the distinction between limited and maximalist objectives to civil w . Unlike traditional interstate conflicts, which often end in territorial com mise, civil wars were found to defy political resolution because they are f uently fought over competing ideologies where the costs of retreating are c paratively high.[38]

Disaggregati the terrorist campaigns by objective type offers preliminary evidence that it luences their success rate (see Figure 1). As in other political contexts, a terr t group is said to have limited objectives when its demands are over territo Specifically, the group is fighting to either (1) evict a foreign military from o pying another country, or (2) win control over a piece of territory for the p pose of national self-determination. By contrast, a terrorist group has max ılist objectives when its demands are over ideology. In this scenario, the g p is attacking a country to either (1) transform its political system (usuall either Marxist or Islamist), or (2) annihilate it because of its values.[39] The d suggest that, for terrorist groups, limited objectives are far more likely to b nciliated than maximalist objectives. Coercion succeeded in three out of eig ases when territory was the goal, but it failed in all twenty-two cases when oups aimed to destroy a target state's society or values. This

---

36. Kalevi J. Holst esolving International Conflicts: A Taxonomy of Behavior and Some Figures on Procedure,' rnal of Conflict Resolution, Vol. 10, No. 3 (September 1966), p. 272; Robert Jervis, *Perception and* erception in International Politics (Princeton, N.J.: Princeton University Press, 1976), p. 101; and D el Druckman and Benjamin J. Broome, "Value Differences and Conflict Resolution: Facilitation Delinking?" *Journal of Conflict Resolution*, Vol. 32, No. 3 (September 1988), p. 491.
37. Jacob J. Bercovi Theodore J. Anagnoson, and Donnette L. Willie, "Some Conceptual Issues and Empirical Tren n the Study of Successful Mediation in International Relations," *Journal of Peace Research*, Vol. No. 1 (June 1991), pp. 7–17; Druckman and Broome, "Value Differences and Conflict Resolution p. 489–510; and Jacob J. Bercovitch and Jeffrey Langley, "The Nature of the Dispute and the E iveness of International Mediation," *Journal of Conflict Resolution*, Vol. 37, No. 4 (Autumn 19 pp. 670–691.
38. Jacob J. Bercov and Karl DeRouen, "Managing Ethnic Civil Wars: Assessing the Determinants of Successful diation," *Civil Wars*, Vol. 7, No. 1 (Spring 2005), p. 100.
39. There is no sug tion that groups with limited objectives lack ideological convictions, only that the object of c ge is territorial possession, not the target country's ideology.

Figure 1. Terrorist Objectives Matter

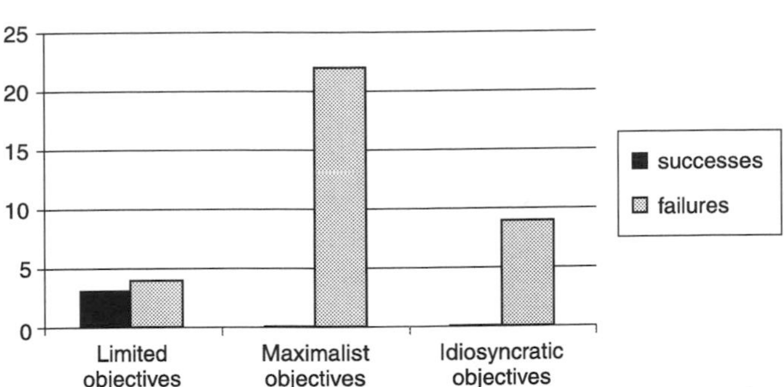

result is not only consistent with previous studies on interstate and civil conflict mediation; it is intuitively understandable that target countries would resist making concessions to groups believed to hold maximalist intentions.

There are, however, major limitations to predicting the outcomes of terrorist campaigns based on the nature of their policy objectives. First, even when their objectives are territorial, terrorist groups do not usually achieve them. The Kurdistan Workers' Party (PKK), Harakat ul-Mujahidin (HUM), Basque terrorists (ETA), and the Real Irish Republican Army (RIRA) have all failed to end what they regard as foreign occupations: the PKK's aspirations of an independent Kurdish state remain elusive; HUM has had little success establishing a Kashmiri state; the ETA has made some progress gaining civil and political rights, but not on its core demand of sovereignty; and Irish unification is not imminent. Second, in some cases terrorist objectives can be difficult to code. As an explanatory variable, objective type lacks robustness; terrorist objectives frequently do not conform to the territory-ideology organizing scheme. In this sample, 20 percent of the policy objectives are termed "idiosyncratic"; campaigns aiming to eliminate other militant groups (e.g., HUM) or sever relations between states (e.g., Revolutionary Nuclei) do not readily fit into the territory-ideology dichotomy (see Table 1). Furthermore, terrorist groups sometimes have ambiguous policy objectives. The al-Aqsa Martyrs Brigades, for example, routinely makes contradictory claims about whether its goal is to destroy Israel or merely establish a Palestinian state in the West Bank and Gaza Strip.[40]

40. The al-Aqsa Martyrs Brigades is not in the sample because the State Department began listing it as an FTO after 2001.

THE KEY: TARGE ELECTION

Target selection a superior explanatory variable for predicting the outcomes of terrorist cam gns. The Department of State defines "foreign terrorist organizations" as g ps that engage in "premeditated, politically motivated violence perpetrat against noncombatant targets."[41] Like other lists of terrorist groups, the Dep ment of State's does not distinguish between (1) groups that focus their attac primarily on civilian targets and (2) those that mostly attack military targets ut occasionally attack civilians. By convention, any group whose strategy ludes the intentional targeting of noncombatants is deemed a terrorist orga ation. This classification scheme may be defensible on normative grounds ut it obscures significant differences in the coercion rates of guerrilla group nd what I call "civilian-centric terrorist groups" (CCTGs). Guerrilla group y definition, mostly attack military and diplomatic targets, such as militar assets, diplomatic personnel, and police forces.[42] CCTGs, on the other d, primarily attack innocent bystanders and businesses. Conflating the t types of groups contributes to the view that attacking civilians is an effect tactic for groups to attain their policy goals.[43] In fact, for terrorist groups t targeting of civilians is strongly associated with policy failure.

RAND's MIP Terrorism Incident database provides statistics on the target selections of ev terrorist group.[44] When groups are classified by target selection, a trend nerges: guerrilla groups—that is, groups whose attacks on "military" and plomatic" targets outnumber attacks on "civilian" targets—accounted for of the successful cases of political coercion. Conversely, CCTGs never a mplished their policy goals, even when they were limited, ambiguous, or iosyncratic (see Figure 2). The remainder of the article develops a theo to explain why terrorist groups that target civilians systematically fail to hieve their policy objectives, even when they are not maximalist.

41. U.S. Departme State, "Foreign Terrorist Organizations (FTOs)."

42. The terms "gu a warfare" and "insurgency" are often used interchangeably to denote an asymmetric campai by subnational actors against a conventional army. I have opted against using the term "ins ncy" because it also denotes a separatist struggle. The term "guerrilla group," by contras ers only to a subnational group's target selection. See "Guerrilla," *Encyclopedia of Terrorism* (L on: Sage, 2003), p. 54; and Cathal J. Nolan, *The Greenwood Encyclopedia of International Relations* estport, Conn.: Greenwood, 2002), p. 669.

43. In Pape's resea for example, six of the thirteen terrorist campaigns are actually waged by guerrilla groups, w account for all of the terrorist victories in his sample. See Pape, *Dying to Win*, p. 40.

44. RAND, MIPT rism Knowledge Base, http://www.tkb.org/Home.jsp.

Figure 2. Paramountcy of Target Selection

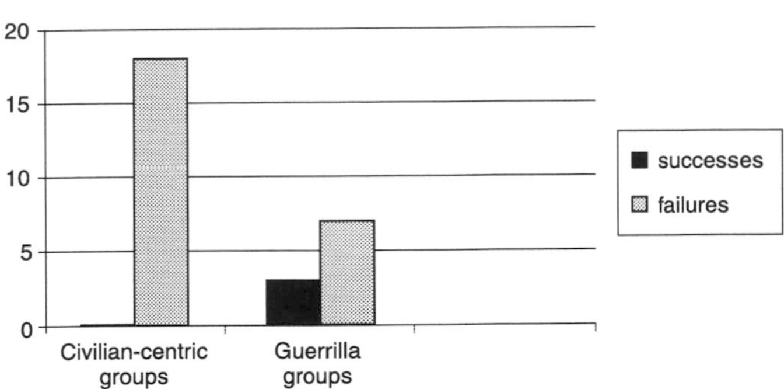

Why Attacking Civilians Is Strategically Ineffective

Terrorism is a coercive instrument intended to communicate to target countries the costs of noncompliance with their policy demands. This notion has important implications for explaining the poor track record of terrorist groups. The following analysis develops a theory for why terrorist groups—especially ones that primarily target civilians—do not achieve their policy objectives. The basic contention is that civilian-centric terrorist groups fail to coerce because they miscommunicate their policy objectives. Even when a terrorist group has limited, ambiguous, or idiosyncratic objectives, target countries infer from attacks on their civilians that the group wants to destroy these countries' values, society, or both. Because countries are reluctant to appease groups that are believed to harbor maximalist objectives, CCTGs are unable to win political concessions (see Figure 3).[45]

This model is grounded in two ways. First, it is consistent with attributional

45. Thomas C. Schelling makes a related point that coercion stands to work only when the coerced party understands the coercing party's demands. See Schelling, *Arms and Influence* (New Haven, Conn.: Yale University Press, 1966), p. 3. Several studies analyze how groups use terrorism to signal their capabilities and resolve. These studies tend to ignore the question of whether terrorism effectively conveys to the target government the terrorist group's policy objectives. See Harvey E. Lapan and Todd Sandler, "Terrorism and Signaling," *European Journal of Political Economy*, Vol. 9, No. 3 (August 1993), pp. 383–397; Per Baltzer Overgaard, "The Scale of Terrorist Attacks as a Signal of Resources," *Journal of Conflict Resolution*, Vol. 38, No. 3 (September 1994), pp. 452–478; and Hoffman and McCormick, "Terrorism, Signaling, and Suicide Attack," pp. 243–281.

Figure 3. Conting y Model of Civilian-centric Terrorist Groups

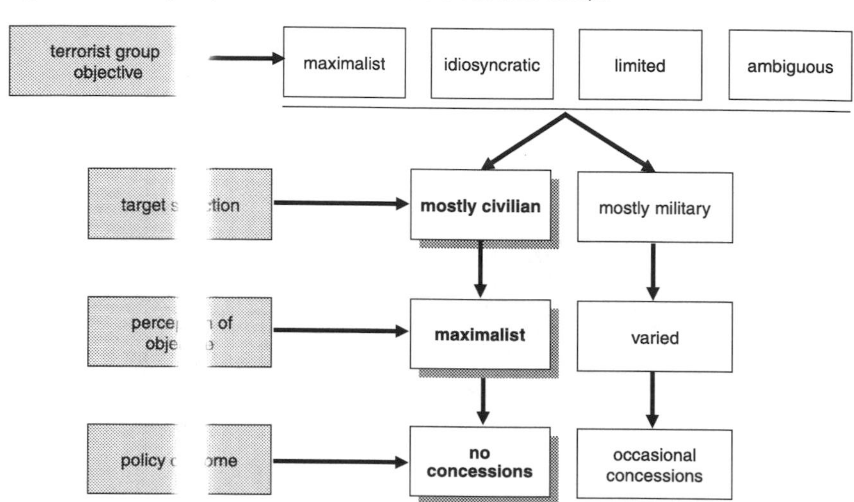

research in the ial psychology literature; correspondent inference theory offers a framewo o show that target countries infer that CCTGs—regardless of their policy der ıds—have maximalist objectives. Second, correspondent inference theory ıpplied to three case studies: the responses of Russia to the September 199 ıartment bombings, the United States to the September 11 attacks, and Isra o Palestinian terrorism in the first intifada. The three cases offer empirical dence that (1) target countries infer that groups have maximalist objectiv when they target civilians, and (2) the resultant belief that terrorist group ave maximalist objectives dissuades target countries from making politica oncessions. The two methodological approaches combine to offer an externa valid theory for why terrorist groups, when their attacks are directed agains vilians, do not achieve their policy goals regardless of their nature.

OBJECTIVES ENC ED IN OUTCOMES

Correspondent erence theory provides a framework for understanding why target countrie fer that CCTGs have maximalist objectives, even when their policy demand uggest otherwise. Correspondent inference theory was developed in the 0s and 1970s by the social psychologist Edward Jones to explain the cognitive process by which an observer infers the motives of an actor. The theory is derived from the foundational work of Fritz Heider, the father of attributional theory. Heider saw individuals as "naïve psychologists" motivated by a practical concern: a need to simplify, comprehend, and predict the motives of others. Heider postulated that individuals process information by applying inferential rules that shape their response to behavior. In laboratory experiments, he found that people attribute the behavior of others to inherent characteristics of their personality—or dispositions—rather than to external or situational factors.[46]

Correspondent inference theory attempted to resolve a crucial question that Heider left unanswered: How does an observer infer the motives of an actor based on its behavior?[47] Jones showed that observers tend to interpret an actor's objective in terms of the consequence of the action.[48] He offered the following simple example to illustrate the observer's assumption of similarity between the effect and objective of an actor: a boy notices his mother close the door, and the room becomes less noisy; the correspondent inference is that she wanted quiet.[49] The essential point is what Jones called the "attribute-effect linkage," whereby the objectives of the actor are presumed to be encoded in the outcome of the behavior.[50] Levels of correspondence describe the extent to which the objectives of the actor are believed to be reflected in the effects of the action.[51] When an action has high correspondence, the observer infers the objectives of the actor directly from the consequences of the action. With low correspondence, the observer either does not perceive the behavior as intentional or attributes it to external factors, rather than to the actor's disposition.[52]

46. Fritz Heider, *The Psychology of Interpersonal Relations* (New York: Wiley, 1958), p. 79.
47. Kathleen S. Crittenden, "Sociological Aspects of Attribution," *Annual Review of Sociology*, Vol. 9 (1983), p. 426.
48. Edward E. Jones and Daniel McGillis, "Correspondence Inferences and the Attribution Cube: A Comparative Reappraisal," in John H. Harvey, William J. Ickes, and Robert F. Kidd, ed., *New Directions in Attribution Research*, Vol. 1 (Hillsdale, N.J.: Erlbaum, 1976), pp. 389–420; and Edward E. Jones and Richard E. Nisbett, "The Actor and the Observer," in Jones, David E. Kanouse, Harold H. Kelley, Richard E. Nisbett, Stuart Valins, and Bernard Weiner, eds., *Attribution: Perceiving the Causes of Behavior* (Morristown, N.J.: General Learning Press, 1972), p. 87.
49. See "A Conversation with Edward E. Jones and Harold H. Kelley," in Harvey, Ickes, and Kidd, *New Directions in Attribution Research*, p. 378; and Edward E. Jones and Keith E. Davis, "From Acts to Dispositions: The Attribution Process in Person Perception," in Leonard Berkowitz, ed., *Advances in Experimental Social Psychology*, Vol. 2 (New York: Academic Press, 1965), p. 225.
50. Jones and Davis, "From Acts to Dispositions," p. 227.
51. Crittenden, "Sociological Aspects of Attribution," p. 427; and Jones and Davis, "From Acts to Dispositions," p. 263.
52. Jones and Davis, "From Acts to Dispositions," p. 264. Social psychologists stress two important points: first, that an observer believes an action has high correspondence does not mean the effect of the action actually reflects the actor's objectives (correspondent inferences can lead ob-

HIGH CORRESPO ENCE OF TERRORISM

The theory posi l here is that terrorist groups that target civilians are unable to coerce polic change because terrorism has extremely high correspondence.[53] Counti believe that their civilian populations are attacked not because the terroi group is protesting unfavorable external conditions such as territorial occu ion or poverty. Rather, target countries infer from the short-term conseque s of terrorism—the deaths of innocent citizens, mass fear, loss of confiden in the government to offer protection, economic contraction, and the inevit e erosion of civil liberties—the objectives of the terrorist group.[54] In sho target countries view the negative consequences of terrorist attacks on thei cieties and political systems as evidence that the terrorists want them dest ed. Target countries are understandably skeptical that making concessions ll placate terrorist groups believed to be motivated by these maximalist obj ves. As a consequence, CCTGs are unable to coerce target countries into ring a political compromise, even when their stated goals are not maxim t.

The three cas tudies that follow provide preliminary evidence that terrorism is a flawed ethod of coercion because (1) terrorism has high correspondence, and (2) ferences derived from its effects militate against political compromise. T ighlight the effect of the independent variable—terrorist attacks—on the oclivity of target states to bargain, a supporting case must conform to five npirical criteria: (1) the coercing party is not motivated by a maximalist obj ve, that is, the desire to destroy the target state's values or society; (2) the rcing party either uses terrorism or is suspected of doing so to further its p y objectives; (3) the target country fixates on the short-term effects of the t rist acts, rather than the coercing party's policy demands;

---

servers to assign mi ken objectives to the actor); and second, perceptions believed to be real have real consequences. ardless of their accuracy, inferences of the actor's objectives influence the observer's attitude ard the actor. See Jones and McGillis, "Correspondence Inferences and the Attribution Cube," 17; and Harold H. Kelley and John L. Michela, "Attribution Theory and Research," *Annual Re of Psychology*, Vol. 31 (New York: Academic Press, 1980), p. 494.

53. Attributional t ies have been empirically tested and confirmed in dozens of experiments since Heider intro d the basic framework almost fifty years ago. Relatively few applications have been made o de the laboratory, however, and fewer still have been applied to international relations. Th applied to international relations have tended to describe the cognitive forces impinging o e aggressor, specifically, how situational factors can induce seemingly normal people to part ate in depraved foreign policy behavior. See, for example, Christopher R. Browning, *Ordinar n: Reserve Policy Battalion 101 and the Final Solution in Poland* (New York: Harper Perennial, 1); Susan T. Fiske, Lasana T. Harris, Amy J.C. Cuddy, "Why Ordinary People Torture Enemy Pri rs," *Science*, Vol. 306, No. 5701 (Summer 2004), pp. 1482–1483; and Sam Keen, *Faces of the E y: Reflections of the Hostile Imagination* (New York: HarperCollins, 1991).

54. These common sequences of terrorist attacks are carefully explored in Ami Pedahzur, *Suicide Terrorism* (New rk: Polity, 2005).

(4) the target country infers from the effects of the terrorist acts that the coercing party has maximalist objectives; and (5) the target country's inference that the coercing party wants to destroy its society, values, or both impedes it from making political concessions.[55]

Russia's Response to the 1999 Apartment Bombings

Russia's response to the three apartment bombings that killed 229 Russian civilians in September 1999 helps illustrate why terrorist groups that target civilians are strategically ineffective. Before news of the bombings reverberated throughout Russia, there was widespread agreement among Russians that Chechen objectives were limited to establishing an independent Chechen state. During this period, most Russians favored territorial compromise. After the apartment bombings, however, large segments of Russian society fixated on their short-term consequences and inferred from them that the presumed perpetrators (the Chechens) surreptitiously wanted to destroy Russia. This view that the Chechens are irredeemably committed to destroying Russia has eroded support for granting Chechen independence. The attitudinal shift after the bombings offers preliminary evidence that (1) terrorism has high correspondence, and (2) inferences of Chechen objectives resulting from the terrorist attacks militated against making concessions. Below I detail this attitudinal shift by tracing the evolution of Russian opinion on Chechnya between the two Chechen wars.

THE FIRST CHECHEN WAR, 1994–96

With the collapse of the Soviet Union in the late 1980s, several North Caucasian republics declared sovereignty. In 1991 Chechnya's first president, Dzhokar Dudayev, took the additional step of declaring independence. Federal forces invaded Chechnya in December 1994 to reestablish control in the breakaway republic. For the next twenty months, Russian federal forces battled Chechen guerrillas in an asymmetric war based in Chechnya. During this period of guerrilla warfare, Russians recognized that Chechen objectives were

55. A potential objection to this framework is that it lacks a time dimension: terrorist groups, even if not initially motivated by maximalist intentions, may adopt them upon achieving more limited objectives. Violent means are often self-sustaining and can distort the ultimate goals of perpetrators, rendering ends and means conceptually indistinct. With this proviso in mind, the framework is not meant to imply that the publics of target countries are necessarily in a state of "false consciousness." Rather, the point is simply that the short-term consequences of terrorist acts inform target countries' understanding of the perpetrators' objectives and that this inference undercuts the terrorists' ability to win political concessions.

limited to self-c ərmination. John Russell has noted that in the first Chechen war, "the Russi public [believed] that Chechens perceived their struggle as one of national eration."[56] Michael McFaul has similarly observed that "the Russian militar nd the Russian people believed that the [Chechen] rationale for this war w self-defense."[57] The Russian military shared the view that Chechen object s were territorial, calling the first Chechen war the War for the Restoration Territorial Integrity.[58]

During this ıod, most Russians were prepared to make significant concessions over t status of Chechnya. When the war broke out, the Russian public and eve he secret police perceived it as precipitate, believing diplomatic solutions d not been exhausted.[59] Boris Yeltsin's position on the war did not gain p ılarity as it unfolded. Top military commanders openly resigned and con nned the president for not pursuing negotiations.[60] From the onset of militar perations until the cease-fire in August 1996, some 70 percent of Russian pposed the war.[61] Disdain for the war manifested itself most clearly in publ ıttitudes toward Defense Minister Pavel Grachev. Opinion polls rated his proval at only 3 percent, just a few points lower than the Russian public' ıpport for Yeltsin's handling of the Chechen problem in general.[62] By early 96, domestic opposition to fighting the guerrillas imperiled Yeltsin's electo prospects. The *Economist* predicted in February that "Mr. Yeltsin can scar y afford to let the conflict drift violently on if he hopes to win a second term ffice in June's presidential election."[63] Yeltsin folded to domestic pressure ılling for an end to all troop operations in Chechnya and the immediate con encement of negotiations with Dudayev over its future status. Yeltsin's pproval rating climbed from 21 percent in February 1996 to 52 percent thre onths later.[64] In May Yeltsin admitted in an interview that he

---

56. John Russell, " jahedeen, Mafia, Madmen: Russian Perceptions of Chechens during the Wars in Chechnya, 4–1996 and 1999–2001," *Journal of Post-Communist Studies and Transition Politics*, Vol. 18, No. 1 rch 2002), p. 80.
57. Michael McFau Russia under Putin: One Step Forward, Two Steps Back," *Journal of Democracy*, Vol. 11, No. 3 y 2000), p. 21.
58. Russell, "Mujal en, Mafia, Madmen," p. 77.
59. Mike Bowker, " sia and Chechnya: The Issue of Secession," *Nations and Nationalism*, Vol. 10, No. 4 (Winter 2004 p. 469, 473.
60. Liliia Federovn ıevtsova, *Yeltsin's Russia: Myths and Reality* (Washington, D.C.: Carnegie Endowment for Inter onal Peace, 1999), p. 117.
61. John Russell, rrorists, Bandits, Spooks, and Thieves: Russian Demonization of the Chechens before a ince 9/11," *Third World Quarterly*, Vol. 26, No. 1 (July 2005), p. 105.
62. Shevtsova, *Yelt Russia*, p. 117.
63. "Russia and C ınya: Yeltsin's Vietnam," *Economist*, February 10, 1996, p. 51.
64. "Mid-month P " VCIOM, posted by the Russian Independent Institute of Social and National Problems, ht /www.cs.indiana.edu/~dmiguse/Russian/polls.html.

would lose the upcoming election if he did not proceed with granting Chechnya de facto sovereignty.[65] The Khasavyurt agreement of August 1996 committed the Russian Federation to relinquishing Chechnya by December 2001.[66] In the interim period, Chechnya would have a de facto state with free elections, a parliament, a president, and autonomy over its finances and resources.[67] Noting the generous terms of the accord, the BBC remarked that the status reserved for Chechnya "essentially signified its independence."[68] In Khasavyurt, Yeltsin formally acknowledged that Russians preferred territorial compromise to fighting the guerrillas.

THE SECOND CHECHEN WAR, SEPTEMBER 1999–PRESENT

On September 8, 1999, Russia experienced its "first taste of modern-day international terrorism."[69] A large bomb was detonated on the ground floor of an apartment building in southeast Moscow, killing 94 civilians. On September 13, another large bomb blew up an apartment building on the Kashmirskoye highway, killing 118 civilians. On September 16, a truck bomb exploded outside a nine-story apartment complex in the southern Russian city of Volgodonsk, killing 17 civilians. The Kremlin quickly fingered the Chechens as the perpetrators.[70]

Russians responded to the terrorist attacks by fixating on their effects, while ignoring the Chechens' persistent policy demands. Russia watchers noted during the bombing campaign that "attention is being directed more at the actual perpetration of terrorist acts, their visible, external and horrific effects with

---

65. "Hope for Chechnya," *Economist*, June 1, 1996, p. 16.
66. Mark A. Smith, "The Second Chechen War: The All-Russian Context," Occasional Paper, No. 40 (London: Strategic and Combat Studies Institute, September 2000), p. 5.
67. "Chechnya's Truce," *Maclean Hunter*, June 10, 1996.
68. "Kremlin Deputy Chief of Staff Elaborates on Putin's Political Reform Proposals," *BBC Monitor*, October 4, 2004, http://www.russiaprofile.org/cdi/article.wbp?article-id=5FEB1101-585F-4CDB-841B-7D467FF7F83B.
69. Russell, "Mujahedeen, Mafia, Madmen," p. 77. The September 1999 apartment bombings were not the first terrorist attacks against Russian civilians, but there is general agreement that the bombings represented a watershed. Henceforth, Russian civilians would become a primary target. See Mia Bloom, *Dying to Kill: The Allure of Suicide Terror* (New York: Columbia University Press, 2005), p. 127.
70. Since the bombings, a conspiracy theory has continued to circulate that the Federal Security Services framed the Chechens to build support for a counteroffensive. Less than 10 percent of Russians accept this theory as credible. Even though the identity of the perpetrators has never been definitively established, the essential point is that the Russian public believed that the Chechens were responsible for the terrorist attacks. See A. Petrova, "The Bombing of Houses in Russian Towns: One Year Later," Public Opinion Foundation, poll conducted September 14, 2000, http://bd.english.form.ru/report/cat/az/A/explosion_house/eof003701.

perhaps not so ıch emphasis on the [stated] cause."[71] Indeed, polls showed that following ɛ terrorist acts only 15 percent of Russians believed the Chechens were ;hting for independence.[72] The Public Opinion Foundation reported that "t ; motive is mentioned less frequently now. . . . [It] is gradually dying out. As Timothy Thomas observed after the bombings, "The Chechens were ı longer regarded as a small separatist people struggling to defend their ter ɔry."[74] Yeltsin's successor, Vladimir Putin, contributed to the view that the C :hens ceased to be motivated by the desire for national self-determination, :laring that "the question of Chechnya's dependence on, or independence f n, Russia is of absolutely no fundamental importance anymore." Followi the terrorist attacks, he stopped referring to Chechens altogether, instead eling them as "terrorists." The campaign for the "restoration of territorial ir ;rity" became "the campaign against terrorism." Russian counterattacks l 'ame "counter-terrorist operations."[75] Putin's focus on the effects of Chechei iolence was most evident after September 11, 2001, when he told Western cc ıtries that "we have a common foe," given that the World Trade Center at :ks and the apartment bombings appear to "bear the same signature."[76]

After the boı ıngs, Russians concluded that Chechen objectives had suddenly become ı ximalist. Polls conducted after the terrorist attacks showed that Russians w : almost twice as likely to believe that Chechen motives were now to "kill Ru: ıns," "bring Russia to its knees," "destabilize the situation in

71. Quoted in Chaı W. Blandy, "Military Aspects of the Two Russo-Chechen Conflicts in Recent Times," *Central Asi. Survey*, Vol. 22, No. 4 (December 2003), p. 422.
72. Russell, "Mujal ɛen, Mafia, Madmen," p. 88.
73. Public Opinior ındation, "Chechen Labyrinth," June 6, 2002, http://bd.english.fom.ru/report/cat/az/A/c henian/ed022239.
74. Timothy Thom. 'Manipulating the Mass Consciousness: Russian and Chechen 'Information War' Tactics in the ɔnd Chechen-Russian Conflict," in A.C. Aldis, ed., *The Second Chechen War* (Washington, D.C.: ıflict Studies Research Center, 2000), p. 116.
75. Quoted in Rom Khalilov, "The Russian-Chechen Conflict," *Central Asia Survey*, Vol. 21, No. 4 (January/February)2), p. 411.
76. Quoted in Johr Loughlin, Gearoid O. Tuathail, and Vladimir Kolossov, "A 'Risky Western Turn?' Putin's 9/1 ript and Ordinary Russians," *Europe-Asia Studies*, Vol. 56, No. 1 (January 2004), p. 9. There i: endency to dismiss Putin's comparison of September 11 to the apartment bombings as instrı ıtal rhetoric designed to artificially shore up Russian relations with the West. This assertior ɔugh true, misses an important point: even Russians who opposed stronger relations with the V after September 11, 2001, believed the attacks were analogous to the apartment bombings, de e their belief that the Chechens were the perpetrators. See John O'Loughlin, Gearoid O. Tuath and Vladimir Kolossov, "Russian Geopolitical Storylines and Public Opinion in the W of 9-11," n.d., p. 13, http://www.colorado.edu/IBS/PEC/johno/pub/Russianstorylines.p

Russia," "destroy and frighten Russian society," and "bring chaos to Russian society" than to achieve "the independence of Chechnya."[77] Putin's public statements suggest that he too inferred Chechen objectives from the effects of the terrorism, asserting that the presumed perpetrators are attacking Russia so it "goes up in flames."[78] This post-bombing belief that Chechen objectives had become maximalist was accompanied by an abrupt loss of interest in making concessions and unprecedented support for waging war. The Public Opinion Foundation found that a strong majority of Russians (71 percent) supported the idea of trading land for peace but had come to believe that "the Chechens are not trustworthy."[79] When Russians were asked to explain why they no longer trusted the Chechens to abide by a land-for-peace deal, the most common explanation given was "because of the terrorist acts."[80] Whereas Russians had demanded Yeltsin's impeachment over the first Chechen conflict, after the apartment bombings they were "baying for blood."[81] In the first Chechen war, Russians favored, by a two to one margin, an independent Chechen state over battling the guerrillas in the breakaway republic; after the bombings, these numbers were reversed, even when respondents were told that federal forces would "suffer heavy losses."[82] Popular support for war remained remarkably stable after the bombings; six months after they occurred, 73 percent of Russians favored "the advance of federal forces into Chechnya," compared with only 19 percent of Russians who wanted "peaceful negotiations with the Chechen leadership."[83] Since 2000, support for President Putin's Chechnya policy has not dropped below 67 percent.[84]

THE APARTMENT BOMBINGS' HIGH CORRESPONDENCE

In the mid-1990s, foreign jihadists began using Chechen territory as a safe haven, but links between the two groups have been exaggerated. Russia scholars

77. "The Bombing of Houses in Russian Towns," Public Opinion Foundation, poll conducted September 14, 2000, http://bd.english.fom.ru/report/cat/az/A/explosion_house/eof003701.
78. Quoted in Yana Dlugy, "Putin Calls on Religious Leaders to Aid in Anti-terror Fight," Agence France-Presse, September 29, 2004.
79. S. Klimova, "Negotiating with Maskhadov," Public Opinion Foundation, poll conducted November 21, 2002, http://bd.english.fom.ru/report/cat/societas/chechnya/peace_conference/ed024629.
80. S. Klimova, "Attitude to Chechens: Pity and Fear," Public Opinion Foundation, January 30, 2003, http://bd.english.form.ru/report/cat/az/A/Chechenian/ed030429.
81. Graeme P. Herd, "Information Warfare and the Second Chechen Campaign," in Sally Cummings, ed., *War and Peace in Post-Soviet Eastern Europe* (Washington, D.C.: Conflict Studies Research Center, 2000), p. 32.
82. "Chechnya—Trends, 2000–2005," Levada Center (formerly VCIOM), poll conducted September 30, 2000, http://www.russiavotes.org/Mood_int_tre.htm.
83. Smith, "The Second Chechen War," p. 6.
84. O'Loughlin, Tuathail, and Kolossov, "Russian Geopolitical Storylines," p. 22.

widely agree t since the Soviet Union unraveled in the late 1980s, the Chechens' obje ve has remained constant—to establish an independent Chechen state.[8 ussian perceptions of Chechen aims changed profoundly, however, as a r lt of the apartment bombings. There is supporting evidence that the barrag f attacks on Russian civilians in September 1999 had high correspondence ussians fixated on the short-term consequences of the bombings and sudd y concluded that the suspected attackers evidently want Russia destroy Once Russians believed that the Chechens' goal was no longer confined achieving national self-determination, enthusiasm for compromise abrupt declined while support for a military solution increased.

U.S. Respons the September 11 Terrorist Attacks

The response he United States to the September 11 attacks further illustrates why terr st groups that target civilians are unable to coerce policy change. The U. esponse provides supporting evidence that (1) terrorism has high correspon ce, and (2) inferences derived from the effects of the attacks have not been ducive to offering concessions. The following case study shows that Am cans—especially in the immediate aftermath of the terrorist attacks—have ded to ignore al-Qaida's rationale for violence. Instead of focusing on al- ida's policy demands, they have fixated on the effects of the terrorist att s and inferred from them that the terrorists are targeting the United Sta to destroy its society and values. These inferences have hampered al-Q a from translating its violence into policy successes in the Muslim world.

AL-QAIDA'S STA OBJECTIVES

Al-Qaida descr s its use of terrorism as a communication strategy to demonstrate to the Un d States the costs of maintaining its unpopular foreign policies in the Mus world.[86] Osama bin Laden has implored Americans to rid

---

85. See Gail W. La s, "Putin's War on Terrorism: Lessons from Chechnya," *Post-Soviet Affairs*, Vol. 18, No. 3 (Janu /March 2002), p. 45; Roman Khalilov, "The Russian-Chechen Conflict," *Central Asia Survey*, Vol , No. 4 (January–February 2002), p. 411; Richard Pipes, "Give the Chechens a Homeland of Th wn," *New York Times*, September 9, 2004; and Pedahzur, *Suicide Terrorism*, p. 113.

86. In his May 199 terview with CNN, bin Laden described terrorism as a "message with no words." Four years r he characterized the coordinated strikes on Washington and New York as "speeches that ove dowed all other speeches." In his treatise for waging jihad, bin Laden's ideological counte t, Ayman al-Zawahiri, asserted that terrorism is "the only language understood by the est." An al-Qaida spokesman referred to the 2002 attack on a French

themselves of their "spiritless materialistic life," but a comprehensive perusal of al-Qaida's public statements reveals scant references to American popular culture. Bin Laden has threatened that "freedom and human rights in America are doomed," but American political values are also not a recurrent theme in al-Qaida communiqués. The relative silence on these issues suggests that American values are not a principal grievance.[87] In fact, bin Laden has explicitly rejected the claim that al-Qaida's goal is to change these values. On multiple occasions, he has warned American audiences that those who repeat this "lie" either suffer from "confusion" or are intentionally "misleading you."[88]

Since bin Laden declared war on the United States in February 1998, his policy demands have remained notably consistent.[89] First, his most well

---

tanker off the coast of Yemen as a "political message" to Washington. See CNN, "Interview with Osama bin Laden," May 10, 1997, http://fl1.findlaw.com/news.findlaw.com/cnn/docs/binladen/binladenintvw-cnn.pdf; videotape from Afghanistan made in November 2001, quoted in Brigitte L. Nacos, "The Terrorist Calculus behind 9/11: A Model for Future Terrorism?" *Studies in Conflict and Terrorism*, Vol. 26, No. 8 (January/February 2003), p. 1; and Ayman al-Zawahiri, *Knights under the Prophet's Banner—Meditations on the Jihadist Movement* (London: Al-Sharq al-Awsat, 2001), quoted in "Middle East/Afghanistan: Al Qaida Threat," *Oxford Analytica*, May 14, 2002, http://www.ciaonet.org/pbei/oxan/oxa05142002.html. For an almost identical statement, see "Al-Qaida Urges More Attacks, al-Zawahiri Tape," *Aljazeerah.com*, May 21, 2003.

87. Osama bin Laden's two-minute audiotape broadcast of October 6, 2002, on Aljazeera, quoted in Rohan Gunaratna, "Defeating Al Qaeda—The Pioneering Vanguard of the Islamic Movements," in Russell D. Howard and Reid L. Sawyer, eds., *Defeating Terrorism: Shaping the New Security Environment* (New York: McGraw-Hill, 2003), p. 26. See also Clark McCauley, "Psychological Issues in Understanding Terrorism and the Response to Terrorism," in Chris E. Stout, ed., *Psychology of Terrorism: Coping with the Continuing Threat* (Westport, Conn.: Praeger, 2004), p. 51. Several al-Qaida experts have remarked that al-Qaida leaders almost always emphasize their hatred of U.S. foreign policies, not American values. See, for example, Peter L. Bergen, *Holy War, Inc.: Inside the Secret World of Osama Bin Laden* (New York: Free Press, 2001), p. 223; and Rohan Gunaratna, *Inside Al Qaeda: Global Network of Terror* (New York: Columbia University Press, 2002), p. 45. For a detailed analysis of al-Qaida's objectives, see Max Abrahms, "Al-Qaeda's Scorecard: A Progress Report on al-Qaeda's Objectives," *Studies in Conflict and Terrorism*, Vol. 29, No. 4 (July–August, 2006), pp. 509–529.

88. "Bin Laden: 'Your Security Is in Your Own Hands,'" October 30, 2004, http://edition.cnn.com/2004/WORLD/meast/10/29/bin.laden.transcript.

89. Most terrorism experts believe that bin Laden's policy demands have stayed consistent since the late 1990s. Even those who place less emphasis on his policy demands do not dispute that the jihadists are committed to realizing them. The debate is over whether granting bin Laden's demands would alleviate the terrorism threat or merely transfer the violence to a new theater or cause. This article does not take a position on this important question. There is no suggestion here that the global jihadists would lay down their arms upon accomplishing the objectives laid out in bin Laden's 1998 fatwa. For a sample of works on this debate, see Anonymous (Michael Scheuer), *Imperial Hubris: Why the West Is Losing the War on Terror* (Washington, D.C.: Brassey's, 2004); Anonymous (Michael Scheuer), *Through Our Enemies' Eyes: Osama bin Laden, Radical Islam, and the Future of America* (Washington, D.C.: Brassey's, 2003); Daniel L. Byman, "Al-Qaeda as an Adversary: Do We Understand Our Enemy?" *World Politics*, Vol. 56, No. 1 (October 2003), pp. 139–163; Bergen, *Holy War, Inc.*; Jessica Stern, "Errors in Fighting Al Qaeda Have Worsened the Danger," *Boston*

known ultimat is for the United States to withdraw its troops from Saudi Arabia, "Land (he Two Holy Places." His statements indicate that he objects not only to the S. stationing of troops in "the holiest of places," but also to U.S. bases serv ; as a "spearhead through which to fight the neighboring Muslim people In al-Qaida communiqués, criticisms of U.S. military interference in Saud rabia have invariably been coupled with complaints about the treatment o s "neighbors," especially Iraq. For the al-Qaida leadership, deploying U.S. ops to Saudi Arabia during the lead-up to the 1991 Persian Gulf War was t only an egregious provocation in itself; the bases represented and faci ted the occupation of "its most powerful neighboring Arab state." Bin Lad and his lieutenants have thus threatened that the United States will rem a target until its military forces withdraw from the entire Persian Gulf.[90]

Second, al-Q a spokesmen say that its terrorist acts are intended to dissuade the Unit States from supporting military interventions that kill Muslims around th vorld. In the 1990s these interventions included "Crusader wars" in Chech a, Bosnia, and East Timor. Bloodshed in Israel and Iraq during this period ierated the most intense opposition. Since the September 11 attacks, al-Qaid condemnation of the United States has focused on events in these two coun s.[91]

Third, al-Qai communiqués emphasize the goal of ending U.S. support for pro-Western uslim rulers who suppress the will of their people. Al-Qaida leaders routin denounce the House of Saud and President Pervez Musharraf's P stan in particular as the most "oppressive, corrupt, and

Globe, March 25, 20 Assaf Moghadam, "The New Martyrs Go Global," *Boston Globe*, November 18, 2005; and Stev mon and Daniel Benjamin, "The Terror," *Survival*, Vol. 43, No. 4 (Winter 2001), pp. 5–17.

90. World Islamic nt, "Jihad against Jews and Crusaders," February 22, 1998, http://www .fas.org/irp/world ra/docs/980223-fatwa.htm; Osama bin Laden, "Declaration of War against the Americans Occ ing the Land of the Two Holy Places," August 1996, http://www.pbs.org/ newshour/terroris nternational/fatwa_1996.html; Middle East Media Research Institute, "Osama bin Lade eech Offers Peace Treaty with Europe, Says Al-Qa'ida 'Will Persist in Fighting' the U.S., ecial Dispatch, No. 695, posted April 15, 2004, http://memri.org/bin/ articles.cgi?Page=a ves&Area=sd&ID=\SP69504. Interview first broadcast on Aljazeera, April 15, 2004; and "Al-(la Urges More Attacks, al-Zawahiri Tape," Agence France-Presse, May 21, 2003.

91. See, for exampl Bin Laden Rails against Crusaders and UN," November 3, 2002, *BBC.com*, http://news.bbc.co 1/hi/world/monitoring/media_reports/1636782.stm. Statement first broadcast on *Aljaze om*, November 3, 2002. See also "Bin Laden's Warning: Full Text," October 7, 2001, *BBC.com*, p://news.bbc.co.uk/1/hi/world/south_asia/1585636.stm. Statement first broadcast on *Aljaz om*, July 7, 2001.

tyrannical regimes" whose very existence depends on the "supervision of America."[92] A prominent al-Qaida website has equated U.S. financial and political support of Saudi Arabia and Pakistan to colonization.[93]

Fourth, al-Qaida leaders describe Israel in similar terms, as a colonial outpost. Based on the organization's communiqués, al-Qaida's final objective is thus to destroy the "Zionist-Crusader alliance," which enables Israel to maintain its "occupation of Jerusalem" and "murder Muslims there."[94]

EFFECTS TRUMP RATIONALE

Americans have focused on the effects of al-Qaida violence, not on al-Qaida's stated purpose. Ronald Steel noted in the *New Republic* after the June 1996 attack on the Khobar Towers in Saudi Arabia, which killed 19 Americans, that American journalists fixated on "who or what bin Laden attacked" and "the method of attack." By contrast, "what bin Laden had been saying about why he and his al-Qaida forces were attacking was given short shrift."[95] The British journalist Robert Fisk similarly observed that after the August 1998 attacks on the U.S. embassies in Kenya and Tanzania, U.S. leaders emphasized the carnage and devastation, but "not in a single press statement, press conference, or interview did a U.S. leader or diplomat explain why the enemies of America hate America."[96] Since September 11, 2001, major Western journalists have devoted generous coverage to the fallout of terrorist attacks, but only since 2004, with the publication of Michael Schueur's *Imperial Hubris,* have they consistently published excerpts of al-Qaida's communiqués.[97]

---

92. *ABC News,* "Interview: Osama Bin Laden," May 1998, http://www.pbs.org/wgbh/pages/frontline/shows/binladen/who/interview.html; and Ayman Zawahiri, quoted in Bergen, *Holy War, Inc.*, p. 208. See also *Observer,* "Full Text: Bin Laden's 'Letter to America,'" November 24, 2002, http://observer.guardian.co.uk/worldview/story/0,11581,845725,00.html. The letter first appeared on the internet and was then circulated by supporters in Britain.
93. This statement is based on conclusions reported by the Center for Islamic Studies and Research in The Operation of 11 Rabi al-Awwal: *The East Riyadh Operation and Our War with the United States and Its Agents,* published in 2003. The book was translated by the Foreign Broadcast Information Service. For excerpts, see http://www.why-war.com/files/2004/01/qaeda_east_riyadh.html.
94. Middle East Media Research Institute, "Osama bin Laden Speech Offers Peace Treaty with Europe"; and World Islamic Front, "Jihad against the Jews and the Crusaders," February 23, 1998, http://www.fas.org/irp/world/para/ladin.htm.
95. Ronald Steel, "Blowback: Terrorism and the U.S. Role in the Middle East," *New Republic,* July 28, 1996, pp. 7–11.
96. Robert Fisk, "As My Grocer Said: Thank You Mr. Clinton for the Fine Words . . . ," *Independent* (London), August 22, 1998, p. 3.
97. See Anonymous, *Imperial Hubris,* p. 128.

HIGH CORRESPO ENCE OF SEPTEMBER 11

President Geor W. Bush's public pronouncements indicate that he deduces al-Qaida's moti directly from the short-term consequences of the terrorist attacks of Septe er 11. According to Bush, "We have seen the true nature of these terrorists he nature of their attacks," rather than in their professed political agenda.[98] r Bush, September 11 demonstrated that the enemy "hates not our policies ut our existence."[99] In the resulting panic weeks after the attacks, he conclu d, "These acts of mass murder were intended to frighten our nation into cha " With Americans hesitant to fly after the four planes were hijacked, he ass ed, "They [the terrorists] want us to stop flying."[100] The toppling of the W Trade Center and the economic contraction that followed revealed that " terrorists wanted our economy to stop." With American civil liberties i itably restricted in the wake of the attacks, he proclaimed that al-Qaida's als, inter alia, were to curtail "our freedom of religion, our freedom of spe , our freedom to vote and assemble and disagree with each other."[101] Give at al-Qaida and its affiliates are mute on these topics, it is difficult to ima e Bush ascribing them to the terrorists had Americans not been greatly fri ened for their safety, hesitant to fly, and worried about their political and ec omic future in the wake of the terrorist attacks.

For President sh, any group that deliberately attacks American civilians is evidently moti ed by the desire to destroy American society and its democratic values. W n asked by a reporter in October 2001 if there was any direct connection bet n the September 11 attacks and the spate of anthrax attacks that followed, eplied: "I have no direct evidence but there are some links . . . both series actions are motivated to disrupt Americans' way of life."[102] This interpretat of the motives of the unknown terrorist perpetrator(s) is revealing: the ide y of the person(s) who sent the anthrax is irrelevant because

98. George W. Bus eech by the president to the Warsaw Conference, Warsaw, Poland, November 6, 2001.

99. George W. Bus emarks by the president to the United Nations General Assembly, New York, November 1 01, http://www.usunnewyork.usmission.gov/01_162.htm.

100. Richard A. Cl , *Against All Enemies: Inside America's War on Terror* (New York: Free Press, 2004), p. 17; and Ge W. Bush, presidential speech to the California Business Association, Sacramento, November 2001.

101. Quoted in Cla *Against All Enemies*, p. 17; and George W. Bush, address by the president to a joint session of C ress, Washington, D.C., September 23, 2001.

102. George W. B remarks by the president to the Dixie Printing Company, Glen Burnie, Maryland, Octobe , 2001, http://www.globalsecurity.org/military/library/news/2001/10/mil-011024-usa03c.

all terrorists who disrupt the American way of life must be motivated by this maximalist objective.[103]

The American public has tended to share President Bush's interpretation of the terrorists' motives. Polls conducted after September 11 show that most Americans believed that al-Qaida was not responding to unpopular U.S. foreign policies. After the attacks, only one in five respondents agreed with the statement that "there is any way that the United States has been unfair in its dealings with other countries that might have motivated the terrorist attacks."[104] In a separate poll, only 15 percent of Americans agreed that "American foreign policies are partly the reason" for al-Qaida terrorism.[105] Instead of attributing al-Qaida terrorism to U.S. foreign policies, large segments of American society shared Bush's belief that the goal of the terrorists was to destroy American society and values. Since September 11, more Americans have polled that the terrorists are targeting the United States because of its "democracy," "freedom," "values," and "way of life" than because of its interference in the Muslim world.[106]

AL-QAIDA'S MISCOMMUNICATION STRATEGY

Bin Laden and his lieutenants frequently complain that the United States has failed to "understand" the "true reason" for the September 11 attacks. Instead of attacking because "we hate freedom," the attacks are a response to the fact that "you spoil our security" and "attack us."[107] Attributional research provides a framework to explain why al-Qaida's communication strategy has failed. As correspondent inference theory predicts, supporting evidence suggests that President Bush and large segments of American society focused on the disastrous effects of al-Qaida's behavior and inferred from them that the terrorists must want to destroy American society and its values—despite al-Qaida's relative silence on these issues.[108]

---

103. President Bush is not the only U.S. president to infer these objectives from terrorist attacks. The claim that al-Qaida struck the United States to destroy its society and values was also espoused by President Bill Clinton after the terrorist bombing of the World Trade Center in 1993. See Clarke, *Against All Enemies*, pp. 129–130.

104. Pew Research Center, Roper Center, September 21, 2001. Seventy percent of Americans rejected the idea that "unfair" U.S. foreign policies contributed to the terrorist attacks.

105. IPSOS-REID, Roper Center, September 21, 2001.

106. Roper Center, Harris poll, September 19–24, 2001, http://www.pollingreport.com/terror9.htm, October 20, 2005.

107. Quoted in Anonymous, *Imperial Hubris*, p. 153; and *Aljazeera.com*, "Bin Laden: 'Your Security Is in Your Own Hands.'"

108. Ronald Spiers, "Try Clearer Thinking About Terrorists," *International Herald Tribune*, January

To be sure, e n if terrorism had not delegitimized al-Qaida's policy demands, it is inc ceivable the United States would have ever fully complied
with them. Pau /ilkinson has observed that in deciding whether to negotiate
with terrorists, target government must first decide whether their demands
are "corrigible" "incorrigible." When demands are perceived as corrigible,
the target gove ent engages in a "roots debate"—an assessment of the pros
and cons of app ing the terrorists. When terrorists are perceived as incorrigible, concession e rejected outright because the demands are deemed so extreme that the all outside of the realm of consideration. In Wilkinson's
model, incorrig e terrorists are not categorically implacable, but placating
them would ex a prohibitive cost.[109] In the discourse of international relations theory, re ts would support the view that the United States has not entered a post–Se mber 11 roots debate because it is strategically wedded to
the Middle Eas

Realists are o trong ground in their prediction that the world's most powerful country w ld not willingly concede a geographically vital region of the
world to terror . But it is doubtful that had Americans viewed al-Qaida's
stated grievanc as credible, they would have embraced a counterterrorism
strategy after S ember 11 that systematically aggravated them. In response
to the Septemb 11 attacks, the United States took four steps: (1) increased
troop levels in Persian Gulf fifteenfold; (2) strengthened military relations
with pro-U.S. M lim rulers, especially in Pakistan and Saudi Arabia; (3) supported counter rorism operations—either directly or indirectly—that have
killed tens of t usands of Muslims around the world; and (4) became an
even less parti nediator in the Israeli-Palestinian conflict.[110] Although the

---

14, 2003; Bergen, *H* *Var, Inc.*, p. 223; and Gunaratna, *Inside Al Qaeda*, p. 45. See also Anonymous,
Imperial Hubris, p.

109. Paul Wilkinso ecurity Challenges in the New Reality," lecture, Tufts University, Medford,
Massachusetts, Oct 16, 2002.

110. For a detailed ysis of al-Qaida's effect on U.S. policies in the Muslim world, see Abrahms,
"Al-Qaeda's Score ." In this study, al-Qaida is tagged with failures in three of the core policy
objectives outlined ts 1998 declaration of war: ending U.S. support for Muslim "apostate" regimes, Israel, and t it derides as "Crusader wars," such as Operation Iraqi Freedom. Al-
Qaida's policy effe ness in the Persian Gulf is designated as a "limited success." Overall, the
September 11 attac lid not reduce U.S. involvement in the Gulf. On the contrary, the attacks
served as the critic npetus for the American public's decision to support the operation, which
has led to the long- occupation of Iraq and unprecedented U.S. military cooperation with the
Gulf monarchy co es. The one modest success was the U.S. decision to draw down its troop
presence in the Sa Arabian Peninsula after September 11, 2001. Al-Qaida does not regard this
policy outcome as worthy, for two reasons. First, the decision to withdraw hundreds of American troops from th udi desert after September 11 palls in comparison to the roughly 150,000
additional U.S. tro hat were deployed to the same theater during this period. Second, U.S. in-

September 11 attacks achieved al-Qaida's intermediate objectives of gaining supporters and attention, its post–September 11 policy failures are a testament, at least in part, to its flawed communication strategy.

Israel's Response to the First Intifada

The first intifada may seem like an unlikely case study to illustrate the limitations of terrorism as a coercive strategy. The mass uprising in the Gaza Strip and the West Bank was an exceptionally moderate period in the history of Palestinian terrorism. The revolt from December 1987 to January 1991 killed only twenty Israeli civilians. Compared with the "Revolutionary Violence" campaign of the 1970s and the outbreak of the second intifada in September 2000, the first intifada was a peaceful interlude.[111] Furthermore, the spontaneous insurrection was a bottom-up initiative. It circumvented Palestinian terrorist groups, which were ideologically opposed to a two-state solution. These groups were momentarily sidelined for three reasons. First, the Marxist groups (e.g., the Popular Front for the Liberation of Palestine and the PFLP–General Command) were reeling from the recent loss of their Soviet patron with the end of the Cold War. Second, the Islamist groups (e.g., Hamas and Islamic Jihad) did not yet pose a significant challenge to the Palestine Liberation Organization (PLO). Third, the PLO was based in Tunis during this period, largely detached from Palestinian life in the territories.[112] Facing relatively little competition from other Palestinian groups, the PLO co-opted the mass uprising in the late 1980s by recognizing the Israeli state within its pre-1967 borders and formally renouncing terrorism. Despite the unusually moderate tactics and objectives of the intifada, the Israeli response to it underscores that (1) the limited use of Palestinian terrorism had high correspondence, and (2) Israeli inferences of Palestinian objectives undermined support for making concessions.

Edy Kaufman has noted that "the primary purpose of the first intifada was

---

terference in the political affairs of the Saudi kingdom increased markedly after the September 11 attacks, owing to the joint U.S.-Saudi interest in fighting the jihadists. I thank Michael Knights of *Jane's Intelligence Review* for offering his expertise in this area. For supporting analysis, see Chaim Kaufmann, "Threat Inflation and the Failure of the Marketplace of Ideas: The Selling of the Iraq War," *International Security*, Vol. 29, No. 1 (Summer 2004), p. 31; and Pape, *Dying to Win*, pp. 46, 84.

111. B'Tselem, "Fatalities in the First Intifada," http://www.btselem.org/english/statistics/first_Intifada_Tables.asp.

112. See Bloom, *Dying to Kill*, p. 24; and Council on Foreign Relations, "Terrorism: Questions and Answers," October 31, 2005, http://cfrterrorism.org/groups/pflp.html.

to communicat Israelis the need to end the occupation of the territories."[113] Terrorist acts, e in small numbers, interfered with the message. Throughout the intifada, on 5 percent of Palestinian demonstrations were violent.[114] Yet an absolute ma ty of Israelis (80 percent) believed that the means employed by the Palestini to protest Israeli rule were "mainly violent." Of the violent Palestinian acts e vast majority consisted of rock throwing against the Israel Defense Forces the territories, with few incidences of terrorism inside the Green Line. An en broader consensus of Israelis (93 percent) felt that the intifada was direct "both towards civilians and towards the army."[115] Notwithstanding the i ada's restrained use of violence, Israelis appear to have fixated on the i rmittent attacks against Israeli civilians.

The Louis G nan Israel Institute of Applied Social Research conducted a series of polls i ecember 1990 to assess the Israeli public's views of Palestinian objectives i e first intifada. As correspondent inference theory predicts, a strong majori of the respondents surveyed (85 percent) believed its purpose was to "c e damage and injury"—as it surely did—while only a fraction (15 percen believed the goal was to "express protest." Similarly, the majority (66 pe nt) believed that the intifada was directed against "the existence of the stat f Israel," while a minority (34 percent) believed the purpose was to liberate West Bank and Gaza Strip.[116] The disconnect between the PLO's policy d ands and Israeli perceptions of Palestinian objectives has been explained (1) inconsistent rhetoric on the part of Palestinian leaders about the aims he intifada, and (2) Jewish apprehension that contemporary violence agains rael is akin to previous traumatic experiences in which Jewish survival in Diaspora was threatened.

Compelling lence suggests, however, that terrorism informed the Israeli view of Palesti objectives. In a fascinating study based on the polling data contained in th uttman report, Kaufman observed that the respondents who perceived Pale ian tactics as "mainly violent" were more likely to believe that the Palesti n goal was to "destroy Israel." Conversely, the more Israelis perceived Pale ian tactics as nonviolent, the more they believed the goal

113. Edy Kaufman, raeli Perceptions of the Palestinians' 'Limited Violence' in the Intifada," *Terrorism and Political ence*, Vol. 3, No. 4 (Winter 1991), p. 4.
114. Gene Sharp, " Intifada and Nonviolent Struggle," *Journal of Palestine Studies*, Vol. 19, No. 1 (Autumn 1989), p.
115. Kaufman, "Isr Perceptions of the Palestinians 'Limited Violence' in the Intifada," p. 4.
116. Louis Guttma ael Institute of Applied Social Research, Jerusalem, "Public Assessment of the Activities and ence of the Intifada," No. (s)IK1124/E&H (December 1990).

was to liberate the territories. The positive correlation between perceived Palestinian terrorism and maximalist objectives existed independent of the respondents' political affiliation, suggesting that the association was not a function of their preexisting political attitudes.[117] Not surprisingly, Israelis were twice as likely to believe "less in the idea of peace" than before the intifada.[118] Because the majority of Israelis regarded the intifada as a protracted terrorist campaign, and Israelis inferred from Palestinian terrorism their intentions of wanting to destroy Israel, the intifada undermined Israeli confidence in the Palestinians as a credible partner for peace.

In the early 1990s, Israeli Prime Ministers Yitzhak Shamir and Yitzhak Rabin came under increased pressure to trade "land for peace" with the Palestinians. The sources of pressure were twofold. First, President George H.W. Bush, determined to improve U.S.-Arab relations after Israel had lost its strategic utility as a Cold War satellite, "forced the Israelis to the negotiating table" by linking U.S. financial assistance to Shamir's participation in the Madrid peace conference in October 1991. Second, Israeli military strategists recognized that the Jewish state faced a long-term demographic problem in occupying a growing and restive Palestinian population.[119] In September 1993 Israel consented to the land-for-peace formula outlined in the Declaration of Principles known as the Oslo accords, but the pattern persisted: although Palestinian terrorism demonstrated to Israel the costs of the occupation, it undercut Israeli confidence in the Palestinians as a credible partner for peace, reducing support for making territorial concessions.[120] Throughout the 1990s, the Jaffee Center

117. Kaufman, "Israeli Perceptions of the Palestinians 'Limited Violence' in the Intifada," p. 13.
118. *Jerusalem Post International Edition*, No. 1 (weekend ed., August 27, 1988), p. 451.
119. Avi Shlaim, "When Bush Comes to Shove: America and the Arab-Israeli Peace Process," *Oxford International Review*, Vol. 3, No. 2 (Spring 1992), p. 4.
120. The limited objectives of the first intifada should not be confused with the maximalist objectives of the Palestinian terrorist organizations. The six Palestinian terrorist organizations in this study have been largely ineffective in accomplishing their policy objectives. Hamas is typically regarded as the greatest beneficiary of Palestinian terrorism. Even for Hamas, however, the gulf between its policy demands and their outcome is vast. Its Covenant of the Islamic Resistance Movement stresses two goals. First, Israel "or any part of it should not be squandered; it or any part of it should not be given up." According to Hamas, all of historic Palestine is an Islamic *waqf*, which translates as a "prohibition from surrendering or sharing." Hamas's only territorial acquisition is in the Gaza Strip, which represents less than 2 percent of the total land area Hamas claims as its own. Even if one assumes that Hamas may ultimately accept a Palestinian state in the West Bank and Gaza Strip, its territorial achievements to date have been minor. The Gaza Strip—one-nineteenth the size of the West Bank—represents less than 6 percent of the disputed land outside the Green Line. Even the most moderate Palestinian nationalist would be categorically opposed to establishing a Palestinian state in such a small territory. Furthermore, according to international law Gaza remains under occupation because Israel still controls the airspace and Palestinian movement on land and by sea. Palestinians share the view that Gaza remains under occupation, commonly referring to it as "the prison." The second major policy objective is to destroy Israeli so-

for Strategic St es periodically polled Israeli respondents on their perceptions of Palest an aspirations. The "dominant" response was that the Palestinians wa ed to "conquer Israel" and "destroy a large portion of the Jewish populati ," a position that peaked during heightened levels of terrorist activity.[121] T perception that the Palestinians hold maximalist aspirations has been the pr ipal impediment to Israel's willingness to make significant territorial conc ions. Since 1994 the Tami Steinmetz Center for Peace Research has poll a representative sample of Israelis on two questions: Do you believe the Pale nians are viable partners for peace? And do you support the peace process? tances of Palestinian terrorism systematically incline Israelis to answer "no" both questions.[122]

In sum, since e first intifada, Palestinian violence has created pressure on Israel to chang he status quo. Paradoxically, terrorism has simultaneously convinced Israe that the Palestinians are not committed to a two-state solution, which has oded support for making the territorial concessions necessary to achievi it.

Conclusion

Thomas Schelli asserted more than a decade ago that terrorists frequently accomplish "int nediate means toward political objectives . . . but with a few exceptions it is rd to see that the attention and publicity have been of much value except as ds in themselves."[123] This study corroborates that view; the twenty-eight g ps of greatest significance to U.S. counterterrorism policy have achieved t r forty-two policy objectives less than 10 percent of the time. As the political ediation literature would predict, target countries did not make concessio when terrorist groups had maximalist objectives. Yet even

---

ciety. Despite Pales an violence, Israel's gross domestic product per capita ($18,000) is higher than those of New land, Spain, Portugal, and Greece. Far from destroying Israel, Palestinians consistently rate Is as the country to which the goal of Palestinian statehood should most aspire. See Central In gence Agency, "Gaza Strip," *The World Fact Book*, http://www.cia.gov/cia/publications/factb /index.html; "Covenant of the Islamic Resistance Movement," August 18, 1988, http://www. edu/lawweb/avalon/mideast/hamas.htm; and Palestinian Center for Policy and Survey Res ch, "Palestinians Expect It to Grow," June 6, 2005, http://www.pcpsr .org/survey/polls/2005 6ejoint.html.

121. Asher Arian, *I li Public Opinion on National Security, 2000* (Tel Aviv: Jaffee Center for Strategic Studies, 2000), 4.

122. Tami Steinme Center for Peace Research, Tel Aviv University, "Peace Index," http://www.tau.ac.il/pea See also David Fielding and Madeline Penny, "What Causes Changes in Opinion about the aeli-Palestinian Peace Process?" Economics Discussion Paper, No. 0601 (Dunedin, New Ze d: School of Business, University of Otago, March 2006), p. 8.

123. Schelling, "W Purposes Can 'International Terrorism' Serve?" p. 20.

when groups expressed limited, ambiguous, or idiosyncratic policy objectives, they failed to win concessions by primarily attacking civilian targets. This suggests not only that terrorism is an ineffective instrument of coercion, but that its poor success rate is inherent to the tactic of terrorism itself.

Why are terrorist groups unable to coerce governments when they primarily attack civilian targets? Terrorism miscommunicates groups' objectives because of its extremely high correspondence. The responses of Russia to the September 1999 apartment bombings, the United States to the attacks of September 11, and Israel to Palestinian terrorism in the first intifada provide evidence that target countries infer the objectives of terrorist groups not from their stated goals, but from the short-term consequences of terrorist acts. Target countries view the deaths of their citizens and the resulting turmoil as proof that the perpetrators want to destroy their societies, their publics, or both. Countries are therefore reluctant to make concessions when their civilians are targeted irrespective of the perpetrators' policy demands.

Four policy implications follow for the war on terrorism. First, terrorists will find it extremely difficult to transform or annihilate a country's political system. Second, the jihadists stand to gain from restricting their violence to military targets. Already, mounting U.S. casualties in Iraq and the absence of a post–September 11 attack on the homeland have eroded U.S. support for maintaining a military presence in Iraq.[124] Terrorist strikes on the U.S. homeland will only undermine the terrorists' message that their purpose is to alter unpopular U.S. policies in the Muslim world. Even sporadic attacks on American civilians—if seen as the dominant component of al-Qaida's overall strategy—will undermine support for an exit strategy. Third, the self-defeating policy consequences of terrorism will ultimately dissuade potential jihadists from supporting it. Although guerrilla attacks against U.S. forces in Iraq show no signs of abating, polling data from Muslim countries suggest that the terrorism backlash is already under way. The Pew Research Center reported in its July 2005 Global Attitudes Project that compared with its polls conducted in 2002, "In most majority-Muslim countries surveyed support for suicide bombings and other acts of violence in defense of Islam has declined significantly," as has "confidence in Osama bin Laden to do the right thing in world affairs."[125] Similarly, major Islamist groups and leaders are increasingly denouncing terrorist

124. See "Bush Urges Patience as Support for War Shrinks," *CNN.com*, October 30, 2005.
125. Since 2002, public support for terrorism has dropped by 64 percent in Pakistan, 80 percent in Indonesia, 87 percent in Lebanon, and 200 percent in Morocco. Pew Global Attitudes Project, "Support for Terror Wanes among Muslim Publics," July 14, 2005, pp. 2, 6, http://www.pewglobal.org.reports/pdf/248.pdf.

attacks as coun productive, even as they encourage guerrilla warfare against the Iraqi occup on.[126] Fourth, it is commonly said that terrorists cannot be deterred becau hey are willing to die for their cause and that they lack a "return address" t hreaten with a retaliatory strike.[127] But perhaps the greatest reason deterren breaks down is because of the widespread, albeit erroneous, belief that attac g civilians is an effective strategy for terrorist groups to advance their pol goals. Disabusing terrorists of this notion would go a long way toward de ing the cycles of violent reprisal.

Further resea is needed in three areas. First, why do terrorist groups target civilians if ing so is strategically ineffective? Testing of the following four hypothese ould yield useful results: (1) groups have an exaggerated sense of terrori 's ability to coerce policy change;[128] (2) terrorist groups attach equal im tance to achieving their intermediate objectives; (3) even though terroris lmost never pays, it is a superior strategy to the alternatives, such as condu ng a peaceful protest; and (4) only comparatively weak groups target lians, because attacking military targets requires a higher level of comba phistication. Of these hypotheses, only the fourth one appears empirica dubious. Nascent terrorist groups generally focus their attacks on milita targets and then graduate to attacking civilian targets. This progression fr military to civilian targets was evident between the two Chechen wars, ween al-Qaida's declaration of war on the United States in 1998 and the Se mber 11 attacks, and from the beginning of the first intifada to its more vi nt conclusion. In each campaign, the terrorists initially confined their a cks to military targets and then, upon becoming stronger organizationally technologically, took aim at civilians.

Second, futu esearch may demonstrate that in international relations the attribute-effect kage diminishes over time. In this study, the target countries inferred from a cks on their civilians that the perpetrators held maximalist objectives that ld not be satisfied. As time elapsed from the terrorist attacks, however, e publics of Russia and the United States began expressing

126. Fareed Zakari How We Can Prevail," *Newsweek*, July 18, 2005, p. 38.
127. See, for examp George W. Bush, "National Security Strategy of the United States of America" (Washington, .: White House, September 17, 2002), http://www.whitehouse.gov/nsc/nss.html.
128. Bin Laden, fo ample, has frequently said that terrorism works, especially against the United States, such when it withdrew from Lebanon following the 1983 U.S. Marine barracks bombing and from alia in 1993 after the deaths of the eighteen U.S. Army Rangers. See Bruce Hoffman, "Rethink Terrorism and Counterterrorism since 9/11," *Studies in Conflict and Terrorism*, Vol. 25, No. 5 tember 2002), p. 310.

greater receptivity to curtailing their country's influence in Chechnya and the Muslim world, respectively.[129]

Third, correspondent inference theory may have prescriptive utility for conducting a more strategic and humane war on terrorism. If countries impute terrorists' motives from the consequences of their actions, then the communities in which terrorists thrive may impute states' motives from the consequences of their counterterrorism policies, reinforcing the strategic logic of minimizing collateral damage. Correspondent inference theory can explain not only why terrorist campaigns rarely work, but also perhaps why counterterrorism campaigns tend to breed even more terrorism.

129. See A. Petrova, "Approval for Russian Military Actions in Chechnya Is Steadily Declining," Public Opinion Foundation Database, September 5, 2002, http://bd.english.fom.ru/report/cat/societas/Chechnya/truck_war/eof023305; and Susan Page, "Poll: American Attitudes on Iraq Similar to Vietnam Era," *USA Today*, December 15, 2005.

C orrespondence

Does Te rism Ever Work? The 2004 Madrid Train Bombings

William Rose and Rysia Murphy
Max Abrahms

To the Editors

Max Abrahms's gument that terrorism rarely works is compelling.[1] He is not correct, howev that terrorist groups that primarily attack civilians never achieve their p ical objectives. The March 2004 Madrid train bombings offer an exception to brahms's thesis. The terrorist group that carried out the attack sought to pel Spain to withdraw its troops from Afghanistan and especially Iraq. T result was a partial success, because Spain did withdraw its forces from Ira This case study, developed below, helps to identify the uncommon condi s under which at least partial terrorist success is possible, and the finding ave implications for counterterrorism policy.

Two addition rguments follow from this case. First, Abrahms's concentration on official eign terrorist organizations (FTOs) is too narrow to capture the emerging p omenon of ad hoc terrorist networks that do not have formal affiliation cell of a recognized FTO. Second, his focus on compelling governments t ake policy concessions misses an important distinction between the impa f a terrorist attack on a government and on a country's citizens. The Mad attack never compelled the government led by the Popular Party to change licy on Spanish troops in Iraq. Instead it mobilized voters to elect a new go nment led by the Socialist Party because, in large part, this party campaign on the promise to pull Spanish troops from Iraq.[2]

To be fair, t strengths of Abrahms's analysis outweigh its weaknesses. Contrary to so recent scholarship on terrorism, he convincingly shows that terrorist o nizations rarely achieve their political objectives. Although he is not the on scholar to argue that terrorism usually fails, he is the first to analyze system cally a large number of terrorist organizations and cam-

William Rose is Prof and Chair of the Government Department at Connecticut College. Rysia Murphy is a recent graduate he college. *The authors thank Julie Berson, Raj Chari, Nicholas Culver, Bruce Hoffman, Javier Jord Chaim Kaufmann, Arang Keshavarzian, Petter Nesser, and David Patton for their comments on an earl draft.*

Max Abrahms is a d ral candidate in political science at the University of California, Los Angeles.

1. Max Abrahms, " Terrorism Does Not Work," *International Security*, Vol. 31, No. 2 (Fall 2006), pp. 42–78.
2. For a more exte e treatment of this case study, see http://www.conncoll.edu/academics/web_profiles/rose- phy_long_IS_letter.pdf.

International Security, 32, No. 1 (Summer 2007), pp. 185–192

paigns. Further, he clarifies the conditions under which success can occur: when terrorist groups have limited objectives and, more important, when their main targets are military and not civilian. His analysis is theory informed, as he adapts correspondent inference theory to explain his observations. His article also stimulates contemplation, discussion, and new research projects—including our Madrid case study.

Abrahms asserts that terrorism rarely succeeds in achieving its political objectives, especially when a terrorist organization primarily targets civilians. To support his thesis, he sensibly forwards historical examples that demonstrate the argument's plausibility. All twenty-eight FTOs that he examines meet his expectations. He then turns to three case studies that match his predictions perfectly, and he explores them in depth to show how causation unfolded. His research is a shining example of a plausibility probe. We looked in vain for any acknowledgment that his thesis might be wrong at least sometimes, however, or that the degree of certainty of his conclusions is not high. Likewise, we hoped to find a section in which he would encourage scholars to find cases that challenge his thesis. Finding none, in a brainstorming session we thought of a case that does not fit: the Madrid train bombings.

On March 11, 2004, Spain was the site of the most devastating terrorist attack in Europe since World War II. Ten bombs exploded on three commuter trains full of passengers making the morning trip into Madrid. The attack resulted in 191 deaths and 1,500 wounded.[3]

Suspicion initially fell on the Basque separatist movement ETA, which had been the only active terrorist group in Spain. Evidence soon indicated, however, that an Islamic terrorist organization was responsible for the attack. The reality was that the individuals who helped plan, fund, and carry out the attack constituted an ad hoc jihadist network and not a particular terrorist organization.[4] A number of these individuals had ties with high-profile members of the Moroccan Islamic Combatant Group, but some were linked to other groups or were unaffiliated. Many were homegrown radicals acting on their own rather than being directed by al-Qaida, the Moroccan Group, or any other organization. Spanish journalists and scholars refer to the ad hoc group that carried out the March 11, 2004, attacks as the 11-M network.

3. Raj S.Chari, "The 2004 Spanish Election: Terrorism as a Catalyst for Change?" *West European Politics*, Vol. 27, No. 5 (November 2004), p. 954.
4. Javier Jordán and Nicola Horsburgh, "Spain and Islamism: Analysis of the Threat and Response 1995–2005," *Mediterranean Politics*, Vol. 11, No. 2 (July 2006), pp. 209–229; and Gordon Corera, "The Legacy of the Madrid Bombings," *BBC News*, February 14, 2007.

The primary litical objective of the perpetrators was to compel Spain to end its military pport for the U.S.-led occupations in Afghanistan and especially Iraq.[5] The rrorists may also have hoped that Spain would be the weakest link in the U coalition in Iraq, whereby its withdrawal would cause other coalition partn to follow.[6] The document supporting this latter assertion was posted on Islamist message board four months before the 11-M attack, and it containe rational analysis of politics in Britain, Poland, and Spain and implications fo e jihadist policy agenda. For two reasons, the document's author sensibly ncluded that attacks on the Spanish would be most effective: public oppositi to the war was greatest in Spain, and Spain was thought to have lower tole ice for casualties than Britain or Poland. Although the analysis focused on h ming Spaniards in Iraq rather than in Europe, it set the stage for the 11-M ne ork to predict at least some success.

Translating t terrorists' desire to compel Spanish troop withdrawal into terms consisten ith Abrahms's analysis, it was a "limited objective" associated with dema s over territory.[7] Spain complied partially when it pulled its troops out of q. This response does not follow two key predictions of Abrahms's the First, with civilians as the primary target, the public is expected to inter the attack in maximalist terms. This predicted consequence did not occur. ay after the attack, newspapers throughout Spain conveyed that many peo viewed the attack as a result of Spain's involvement in Iraq war.[8] One Elca poll found that 49 percent of Spaniards believed that troop withdrawal wo make Islamist attacks less likely. This finding supports the assertion that a nificant segment of the Spanish public correctly saw the limited objectives he terrorist group.[9] Second, Abrahms's theory predicts that countries whos itizens are targeted will not make policy concessions. Again

5. Javier Jordán an obert Wesley, "The Madrid Attacks: Results of Investigations Two Years Later," *Terrorism M or*, Vol. 4, No. 5 (March 9, 2006), pp. 1–4.
6. See Brynjar Lia a Thomas Hegghammer, "Jihad Strategic Studies: The Alleged Al Qaida Policy Study Preceding Madrid Bombings," *Studies in Conflict & Terrorism*, Vol. 27, No. 5 (September–October 2004), 368–371.
7. Abrahms writes, terrorist group is said to have limited objectives when its demands are over territory. Specificall e group is fighting to either (1) evict a foreign military from occupying another country, or (2 n control over a piece of territory for the purpose of national self-determination." Abrahms, hy Terrorism Does Not Work," p. 53.
8. Quotations fron o newspapers can be found in Jose A. Olmeda, "Fear or Falsehood? Framing the 3/11 T rist Attacks in Madrid and Electoral Accountability," Defense and Security Working Paper, Nc (Madrid: Real Instituto Elcano, May 5, 2005), p. 25.
9. Charles Powell, id Terrorism Sway Spain's Election?" *Current History*, November 2004, p. 380.

it is wrong. In national elections three days after the attack, voters defied earlier polls and voted out the government (led by the People's Party) that supported Spain's intervention in Iraq. The surprise winner was the Socialist Party, which during the campaign had called for removing Spanish troops from Iraq. The troops were withdrawn several months later.

Earlier in March the incumbent Popular Party led the polls by 5 percent, and commentators agree that it would have won the election had it not been for the terrorist attack. The opposition Socialist Party, headed by José Luis Rodríguez Zapatero, won 42.64 percent of the votes compared with 37.64 percent for the Popular Party. With 164 out of 350 seats in the Congress of Deputies, the Socialists were in a position to form a minority government.[10] During the campaign Zapatero had promised to remove Spanish troops from Iraq by June 30, 2004. Twenty-eight percent of voters said that the bombings had influenced their vote; and when Spanish troops were withdrawn a month earlier than expected, a strong majority supported the move.[11] A methodical analysis concludes that the Madrid attack and the political atmosphere surrounding it affected election results by mobilizing about 1,700,000 voters who had not planned to vote and by discouraging approximately 300,000 voters from voting—leading to a net 4 percent increase in voter turnout. In addition, more than 1 million voters switched their vote to the Socialist Party.[12]

Scholars highlight three factors to explain the surprise election outcome, although they may disagree on their relative importance. First, the Popular Party continued to blame ETA even after the leadership learned that an Islamic group was responsible for the attack. Admitting that Islamists were to blame would have exposed Prime Minister José María Aznar to the charge that his foreign policy contributed to the terrorist attack. Segments of the Spanish population sought to punish his party for the apparent deception. This factor is linked to a highly partisan "framing contest" between the government and the opposition, whereby the opposition presented the situation to the public more effectively than did the government.[13] Second, a significant part of the public

10. Chari, "The 2004 Spanish Election," pp. 957–958.
11. Powell, "Did Terrorism Sway Spain's Election?" pp. 379, 381.
12. Narciso Michavila, "War, Terror and Elections: Electoral Impact of the Islamist Terror Attacks on Madrid," Public Opinion Working Paper, No. 13 (Madrid: Real Instituto Elcano April 6, 2005), p. 31.
13. Olmeda, "Fear or Falsehood?" pp. 3–4. Narciso Michavila calls this circumstance the "dual news manipulation hypothesis." Michavila, "War, Terrorism, and Elections," pp. 20–22. Javier Jordán and Nicola Horsburgh are concerned about the partisan politics that this factor revealed, whereby the two parties were "playing politics with terrorism." Jordán and Horsburgh, "Politics

mistrusted the] ular Party even before the Madrid attack. In reaction to several negative e its since the party assumed an absolute majority in 2000, many Spaniard ad begun to sense that the party was complacent and arrogant and that i lecisionmaking process lacked transparency.[14] Third, when the terrorists ef tively signaled devastating punishment for Spain's involvement in Iraq, t public's antiwar views became more pressing. Previously, many had opp d the war but supported Aznar. Following the 11-M attack, however, a sigr cant segment was no longer willing to support the Popular Party and its w policy.

The confluen of conditions present in the Madrid case is probably quite rare and possib unique. There may be additional, less obvious factors, and perhaps someti s they carry more causal weight than these three. Although the generalizab y of our findings is low, the case does show that Abrahms's theory is not al ys right. Further research is needed to learn more about the reliability of hi ndings. We encourage scholars to conduct studies with a larger collectior cases as well as to seek out cases that may be exceptions to the rule. If mor xceptions can be found, scholarly understanding of variations in outcom can widen and deepen.

If successful t orist attacks against civilians are indeed rare like we expect, then the impact our findings on Abrahms's four policy implications would not be extensiv Our findings, however, suggest additional policy implications. They deri from the above-mentioned observation that the 11-M terrorist network pro bly targeted Spain because it was the weakest link among European mem s of the U.S.-led coalition in Iraq. To the extent that such an analysis influer d the terrorists, therefore, several implications follow. First, more such atta are likely in the future, because even partial success breeds support for the Thus at least some terrorist groups will concentrate on targets where suc is believed possible. Second, several relevant elements for countering terr m are prescribed. One is that scholars and analysts worried about terrorism hould conduct parallel analyses that could provide early warning signal r countries at higher risk for terrorist attacks. Because the terrorists are s ewhat more likely to succeed in such countries, another recommendatio s to give higher priority to preventing or foiling attacks. If

and Terrorism: The idrid Attacks Case," in George Kassimeris, ed., *Playing Politics with Terrorism: A User's Guide* ndon: Hurst, 2007), p. 2.

14. For an elaborat of these negative events, see Chari, "The Spanish 2004 Election," pp. 954–955.

an attack occurs, it should be handled with less partisanship over framing the issue than occurred after the 11-M attack. Finally, because distrust of the government led by the Popular Party contributed to the terrorists' success, governments have an interest in building and maintaining the trust of their publics.

—*William Rose*
New London, Connecticut

—*Rysia Murphy*
New London, Connecticut

The Author Replies:

I appreciate William Rose and Rysia Murphy's thoughtful comments on my recent article in *International Security.*[1] We agree on two main points: (1) terrorist groups that primarily target civilians fail to coerce their governments into making policy concessions; and (2) future research is needed to determine if there are any exceptions to the rule. Rose and Murphy focus on the second point and purport to identify an important outlier that "does not fit" the rule: the March 2004 Madrid train bombings.

The authors claim that the Madrid case undermines my article in two ways. First, they believe the attack shows that democracies are uniquely vulnerable to coercion because terrorists can sometimes influence policies by scaring the electorate into ousting the incumbent leader. Specifically, they argue that the Madrid attack represents a successful case of coercion because it bombed to power the antiwar candidate for prime minister, José Luis Rodríguez Zapatero, who kept his campaign pledge to withdraw Spanish troops from Iraq. Second, the authors assert that the Madrid case does not conform to correspondent inference theory because the Spanish public interpreted the bombings as evidence of 11-M's intent to end the occupation, rather than to destroy the Spanish way of life, making coercion possible. The first claim is weaker than the second: the Madrid case is an empirically problematic example of terrorist coercion, but it helps to delimit the antecedent conditions in which terrorist attacks on civilians might theoretically be effective.

The Madrid case is an empirically problematic example of terrorist coercion

1. Max Abrahms, "Why Terrorism Does Not Work," *International Security,* Vol. 31, No. 2 (Fall 2006), pp. 42–78.

for three reasor First, the argument that the 11-M attack coerced Spain into withdrawing fr Iraq is questionable, because Zapatero might have won the election and the altered Spanish policy even in the absence of the attack. The "surprise" defe of Prime Minister José María Aznar was actually not that surprising. In tl days preceding the attack, Aznar held a narrow lead in most surveys, but th lifferences between the candidates' voter estimates usually fell within the rgin of error.[2] Indeed, by early March the gap between the two candidates d closed: some surveys put Aznar ahead by a single point, while others ha Zapatero winning by a razor-thin margin. In their study on the 2004 Spani election, Ignacio Lago and José Ramón Montero state, "It must be remen red that if the attacks had not taken place, either the PP [Aznar's Popul Party] or the PSOE [Zapatero's Socialist Party] could have won the electio nly days before 11-M, the polls pointed to a 'technical tie.'"[3] Furthermore, ir e lead-up to the attack, the majority of Spaniards believed the country nee d a "change of government"; a large percentage of the electorate was und led; and in Spain undecided voters tend to vote for left-wing candidates suc Zapatero.[4] Postelection returns confirm that Aznar did not lose any electo support after the attack; as expected, the undecided voters gravitated tow the left-leaning candidates.[5] The extent of electoral change or interelectora latility was not atypical for Spanish national elections.[6] The claim that the M attack successfully coerced Spain into withdrawing from Iraq is based or e counterfactual argument that without the attack, Zapatero would have los e election, which is uncertain from the polling data.

Second, Rose d Murphy imply that undecided voters gravitated toward Zapatero after attack because it revealed the escalating costs of maintaining troops in Ir but Aznar compromised his electoral viability primarily by blaming the bo ings on ETA. In testimony before the U.S. Senate Foreign Relations Commit , Philip Gordon stated, "The [Aznar] government appears to have paid mor f a price for misleading the public than for its policy on Iraq."[7] In her s y on the 2004 election, Georgina Blakeley found that "the

2. Ignacio Lago an sé Ramón Montero, "The 2004 Election in Spain: Terrorism, Accountability, and Voting," *Taiwa urnal of Democracy*, Vol. 2, No. 1 (July 2006), p. 17.
3. Ibid., p. 34.
4. Georgina Blakel 'It's Politics, Stupid! The Spanish General Election of 2004," *Parliamentary Affairs*, Vol. 59, No. March 2006), p. 339.
5. See Enric Ordeix igo, "Aznar's Political Failure or Punishment for Supporting the Iraq War? Hypotheses About Causes of the 2004 Spanish Election Results," *American Behavioral Scientist*, Vol. 49, No. 4 (Dec er 2005), p. 613.
6. Ingrid van Biez 'Terrorism and Democratic Legitimacy: Conflicting Interpretations of the Spanish Elections," *diterranean Politics*, Vol. 10, No. 1 (March 2005), p. 107.
7. Philip H. Gordo Madrid Bombings and U.S. Policy," testimony before the Senate Foreign Re-

point, therefore, is not that the bombings affected the general election, but rather, that the government's handling of the bombings had such profound consequences."[8] The BBC likewise reported, "It is sometimes wrongly claimed that the bombings themselves led directly to the defeat of the Conservative government and its replacement just days later by the Socialists. In fact, it was the perception that the government was misleading the public about who was responsible that did [the] most damage."[9] Other foreign outlets, including Spanish television networks and the French newspaper *Le Monde,* reached the same conclusion.[10] In sum, the dominant interpretation is that Zapatero's postattack election gains were due mostly to Aznar's mismanagement of the attack—not the Iraqi occupation that elicited it—undermining the claim that the attack itself bombed Zapatero into power and effectively coerced the Spanish withdrawal.

Third, it is doubtful that enlarging my sample of terrorist organizations or including ad hoc groups affiliated with al-Qaida would lend support to the claim that democracies are uniquely vulnerable to terrorist coercion. I agree with Rose and Murphy that "the Madrid case is probably quite rare and possibly unique" because terrorism historically shifts the electorate to the right not the left—thereby empowering hard-liners who oppose accommodating the perpetrators.[11] The most obvious example is in Israel, but the trend is also evident in the United States, where the mere release of Osama bin Laden's videotape the weekend before the 2004 presidential election boosted George W. Bush's electoral lead by two percentage points over his comparatively dovish opponent, John Kerry.[12]

Rose and Murphy's stronger claim is that the Madrid case does not conform to correspondent inference theory. They point out that the train bombings targeted Spanish civilians, and yet the public did not revise its perception that al-

lations Committee, 108th Cong., 2d sess., March 31, 2004, p. 2, http://www.senate.gov/?foreign/testimony/2004/GordonTestimony040331.pdf.

8. "The Legacy of the Madrid Bombings," *BBC News,* February 15, 2007, http://news.bbc.co.uk/2/hi/europe/6357599.stm.

9. Blakeley, "It's Politics, Stupid!" p. 342.

10. See Ray Suarez, José Gijon, and Salvador Sala, "Terrorism and Politics in Spain," *NewsHour with Jim Lehrer,* March 16, 2004; and "L'Espagne Sanctionne le Mensonge d'Etat" [Spain punishes the government's lie], *Le Monde,* March 16, 2004, http://www.pbs.org/newshour/bb/international/jan-june04/spain_03-16.html.

11. See Christopher Hewitt, *Consequences of Political Violence* (Sudbury, Mass.: Dartmouth, 1993), pp. 80, 97–98.

12. Claude Berrebi and Esteban F. Klor, "On Terrorism and Electoral Outcomes: Theory and Evidence from the Israeli-Palestinian Conflict," *Journal of Conflict Resolution,* Vol. 50, No. 6 (January 2006), pp. 899–925. See also David Paul Kuhn, "Who Will 'Osama Surprise' Help?" *CBSNews.com,* October 30, 2004, http://www.cbsnews.com/stories/2004/10/30/politics/main652438.shtml.

Qaida and its a iates aimed to achieve the limited policy goal of ending the occupation of I . The Madrid case suggests that when a target country has strong preexisti beliefs that the terrorists are motivated by limited policy objectives, it will always infer from attacks on its civilians that the terrorists are driven by i logical or maximalist objectives.

Before the Se mber 11 attacks, most Americans had little knowledge of al-Qaida. They th fore inferred from the consequences of the terrorist acts that the perpet ors aimed to harm American society and its values. Similarly, until the tember 1999 apartment bombings, the Russian public knew little about the echnya campaign and therefore inferred from them that the Chechens had aximalist objectives. By contrast, Spanish opinion of al-Qaida's limited licy objectives was broadly and intensely established prior to the train bo ings. Before the attack, 90 percent of the public disagreed with Aznar's p ion that participating in the Iraq war made Spain safer from terrorism, an e nched disconnect highlighted by two of the largest antiwar protests in hist [13] Whereas news of the Chechnya occupation was withheld from the Russia ublic until it was targeted in September 1999, Spanish combat deaths in I in August, October, and November 2003 were front-page news, reinforci the perception that the terrorists aimed to end the occupation rather thar pain's way of life.[14]

The Madrid mple suggests that, in theory, terrorist attacks on civilians may potentiall ad to policy concessions if the target country has extremely firm preexistin eliefs that the enemy is motivated by limited policy objectives. When thi the case, attacks—regardless of target selection—will communicate the e lating costs of defying the terrorists' limited policy goals, making coercio ossible. Future research is still needed, however, to identify a case of coerci where these antecedent conditions are present. Such a case would demons e not only that the attack(s) on civilians stoked the public's preexisting fea f defying the terrorists' limited policy objectives, but that these fears act y changed the country's policy. Rose and Murphy's case study on the 11 attack provides convincing evidence of the former, but not the latter. It is asic truism that insurgency works, but terrorism does not.

—*Max Abrahms*
Los Angeles, California

13. Mar Roman, "S Won't Bow to Calls to Pull Troops," Associated Press, December 1, 2003.
14. Ibid.

What Terrorists Really Want

Terrorist Motives and Counterterrorism Strategy

Max Abrahms

What do terrorists want? No question is more fundamental for devising an effective counterterrorism strategy. The international community cannot expect to make terrorism unprofitable and thus scarce without knowing the incentive structure of its practitioners.[1] The strategic model—the dominant paradigm in terrorism studies—posits that terrorists are rational actors who attack civilians for political ends. According to this view, terrorists are political utility maximizers; people use terrorism when the expected political gains minus the expected costs outweigh the net expected benefits of alternative forms of protest.[2] The strategic model has widespread currency in the policy community; extant counterterrorism strategies are designed to defeat terrorism by reducing its political utility. The most common strategies are to mitigate terrorism by decreasing its political benefits via a strict no concessions policy; decreasing its prospective political benefits via appeasement; or decreasing its political benefits relative to nonviolence via democracy promotion.

Are any of these counterterrorism strategies likely to work? Can terrorism be neutralized by withholding political concessions, granting political conces-

Max Abrahms is a doctoral candidate in political science at the University of California, Los Angeles. He conducted research for this article when he was a Research Associate at the Belfer Center for Science and International Affairs in the John F. Kennedy School of Government at Harvard University.

The author would like to thank the following individuals for their time and comments: Robert Goldberg, Matthew Gottfried, Rex Hudson, Peter Krause, Deborah Larson, Karen Levi, Charles Mahoney, David Rapoport, Steven Spiegel, Arthur Stein, Marc Trachtenberg, Robert Trager, Jeff Victoroff, and the anonymous reviewers.

1. See Louise Richardson, *What Terrorists Want: Understanding the Enemy, Containing the Threat* (New York: Random House, 2006), p. 44.
2. Martha Crenshaw refers to what I call the strategic model as the "instrumental model." For summaries of this model, see Crenshaw, "Theories of Terrorism: Instrumental and Organizational Approaches," in David C. Rapoport, ed., *Inside Terrorist Organizations* (New York: Columbia University Press, 1988), pp. 13–31; Crenshaw, "The Logic of Terrorism: Terrorist Behavior as a Product of Strategic Choice," in Walter Reich, ed., *Origins of Terrorism: Psychologies, Ideologies, Theologies, States of Mind* (New York: Cambridge University Press, 1990), pp. 7–24; Gordon H. McCormick, "Terrorist Decision Making," *Annual Review of Political Science*, Vol. 6 (June 2003), p. 482; and Gary C. Gambill, "The Balance of Terror: War by Other Means in the Contemporary Middle East," *Journal of Palestine Studies*, Vol. 28, No. 1 (Autumn 1998), pp. 51–66. For applications of the strategic model, see Robert A. Pape, *Dying to Win: The Strategic Logic of Suicide Terrorism* (New York: Random House, 2005); Max Abrahms, "Why Terrorism Does Not Work," *International Security*, Vol. 31, No. 2 (Fall 2006), pp. 42–78; Andrew H. Kydd and Barbara F. Walter, "The Strategies of Terrorism," *International Security*, Vol. 31, No. 1 (Summer 2006), pp. 49–80; and James DeNardo, *Power in Numbers: The Political Strategy of Protest and Rebellion* (Princeton, N.J.: Princeton University Press, 1985), p. 3.

International Security, Vol. 32, No. 4 (Spring 2008), pp. 78–105

sions, or provic ; peaceful outlets for political change? In other words, does the solution to orism reside in diminishing its political utility? The answer depends on wh er the strategic model is externally valid, that is, on whether terrorists are in t rational people who attack civilians for political gain. If the model is empiri ly grounded, then the international community can presumably combat ter ism by rendering it an ineffective or unnecessary instrument of coercion. If t model is unfounded, however, then current strategies to reduce terrorism' olitical utility will not defuse the terrorism threat.

Despite its p y relevance, the strategic model has not been tested. This is the first study omprehensively examine its empirical validity.[3] The strategic model rests three core assumptions: (1) terrorists are motivated by relatively stable a consistent political preferences; (2) terrorists evaluate the expected politi payoffs of their available options, or at least the most obvious ones; and (errorism is adopted when the expected political return is superior to those alternative options.

Does the terr st's decisionmaking process conform to the strategic model? The answer ap rs to be no. The record of terrorist behavior does not adhere to the model's ee core assumptions. Seven common tendencies of terrorist organizations fl y contradict them. Together, these seven terrorist tendencies represent impo nt empirical puzzles for the strategic model, posing a formidable challenge the conventional wisdom that terrorists are rational actors motivated fore st by political ends. Major revisions in the dominant paradigm in terror studies and the policy community's basic approach to fighting terroris are consequently in order.

This article h our main sections. The first section summarizes the strategic model's core as mptions and the empirical evidence that would disconfirm them.[4] The sec section demonstrates the empirical weakness of the strategic model. In t section, I present the seven puzzles—based on the records of dozens of orist organizations from the late 1960s to the present,

3. Martha Crensha s raised important questions about the strategic model's empirical validity. See, for example, C shaw's "Theories of Terrorism" and "The Logic of Terrorism."
4. There is a debat thin the social sciences about whether a hypothesis's assumptions need to be empirically vali Milton Friedman famously argued that the merit of a hypothesis depends strictly on its predi e power, whereas many other theorists believe that the core assumptions of a hypothesis must be grounded in reality. For a summary of this theoretical debate, see Jack Melitz, "Friedman Machlup on the Significance of Testing Economic Assumptions," *Journal of Political Economy*, V 73, No. 1 (February 1965), pp. 37–60. In the field of international relations, most theory testing es the assumptions as exogenous, but this is not always the case. For two important exceptio hat criticize realism because of its assumption of anarchy, see David A. Baldwin, ed., *Neore n and Neoliberalism: The Contemporary Debate* (New York: Columbia University Press, 1993); an lexander Wendt, "Anarchy Is What States Make of It: The Social Construction of Power Polit *International Organization*, Vol. 46, No. 2 (Spring 1992), pp. 391–425.

supplemented with theoretical arguments from the bargaining and coercion literatures—that cannot be reconciled with the model's underlying assumptions. The third section develops an alternative explanation for terrorism. The argument is not that terrorists are crazy or irrational; as Louise Richardson notes, psychiatric profiles of terrorists are "virtually unanimous" that their "primary shared characteristic is their normalcy."[5] Rather, I contend that the strategic model misspecifies terrorists' incentive structure; the preponderance of empirical and theoretical evidence reveals that terrorists are rational people who use terrorism primarily to develop strong affective ties with fellow terrorists.[6] If terrorists generally attach utmost importance to the social benefits of using terrorism, then extant strategies to reduce its political benefits will fail to counter the terrorism threat. In the final section, I suggest a reorientation of counterterrorism strategy in light of what terrorists really seem to want.

The Strategic Model

In classical economic theory, rational agents (1) possess stable and consistent preferences; (2) compare the costs and benefits of all available options; and (3) select the optimal option, that is, the one that maximizes output.[7] Modern decision theory recognizes that decisionmakers face cognitive and informational constraints. Rational actor models therefore typically relax each assumption such that the rational agent must only (1) possess relatively stable and consistent goals; (2) weigh the expected costs and benefits of the most obvious options; and (3) select the option with the optimal expected utility.[8] The strategic model is explicitly predicated on this trio of assumptions.

First, the strategic model assumes that terrorists are motivated by relatively stable and consistent political goals, which are encoded in the political plat-

5. Richardson, *What Terrorists Want*, p. 14.
6. Sociologists routinely treat social objectives as rational. See, for example, Jeffrey Pfeffer, *Organizations and Organization Theory* (Boston: Pitman, 1982), pp. 9, 42–43, 62, 72, 256. Rational choice theorists in economics and political science also frequently treat social objectives as rational. See, for example, Jon Elster, "Introduction," in Elster, ed., *Rational Choice* (Oxford: Basil Blackwell, 1986), p. 1; Gary Becker, "The Economic Approach to Human Behavior," in Elster, *Rational Choice*, pp. 115, 119; and John C. Harsanyi, "Rational Choice Models of Political Behavior vs. Functionalist and Conformist Theories," *World Politics*, Vol. 21, No. 4 (July 1969), pp. 513–538.
7. See David M. Kreps, *A Course in Microeconomic Theory* (Princeton, N.J.: Princeton University Press, 1990), p. 480; Elster, "Introduction," pp. 4, 16; Sidney Verba, "Assumptions of Rationality and Non-Rationality in Models of the International System," *World Politics*, Vol. 14, No. 1 (October 1961), pp. 93–117; and Graham Allison and Philip Zelikow, *Essence of Decision: Explaining the Cuban Missile Crisis*, 2d ed. (New York: Longman, 1999), pp. 17–18.
8. Elster, "Introduction," p. 5; and Allison and Zelikow, *Essence of Decision*, p. 18.

form of the ter ist organization. That West Germany's Red Army Faction (RAF) identifie self as Marxist, for example, implies that RAF members participated in th rganization to achieve its stated revolutionary agenda.[9] Disconfirming dence would therefore reveal that the RAF expressed a protean set of pol al objectives, fought mainly against other groups with its identical politic platform, or continued using terrorism after its stated political grievances l been resolved.

Second, the s egic model assumes that terrorism is a "calculated course of action" and tha efficacy is the primary standard by which terrorism is compared with otl methods of achieving political goals."[10] Specifically, the model assumes at terrorist groups weigh their political options and resort to terrorism only fter determining that alternative political avenues are blocked.[11] Disc rming evidence would therefore demonstrate that terrorism is not a strateg last resort and that terrorist groups reflexively eschew potentially promi nonviolent political alternatives.

Third, the st egic model assumes that the decision to use terrorism is based on "the l c of consequence," that is, its political effectiveness relative to alternative o ons.[12] Specifically, it is assumed that terrorist organizations achieve their pc cal platforms at least some of the time by attacking civilians; that they posse "reasonable expectations" of the political consequences of using terrorisn ased on its prior record of coercive effectiveness; and that they aban the armed struggle when it consistently fails to coerce policy concess s or when manifestly superior political options arise.[13] Disconfirming dence would therefore reveal that terrorist organizations do not achieve eir political platforms by attacking civilians; that they do not renounce t orism in spite of consistent political failure or manifestly superior politic ptions; or that they do not even use terrorism in a manner that could pote lly coerce policy concessions from the target country. Below I identify and n describe seven tendencies of terrorist organizations that challenge the ategic model with disconfirming evidence of its core assumptions.

9. See McCormick, rrorist Decision Making," p. 482; and Crenshaw, "Theories of Terrorism," pp. 15, 27.
10. McCormick, "T rist Decision Making," p. 481.
11. Crenshaw, "The s of Terrorism," p. 16. See also Alex P. Schmid and Albert J. Jongman, *Political Terrorism* (Ams am: North-Holland, 1988), pp. 122–123.
12. See James G. M , *A Primer on Decision Making: How Decisions Happen* (New York: Free Press, 1994), pp. 2–3. See Crenshaw, "The Logic of Terrorism," p. 20.
13. See Pape, *Dyin Win*, p. 62. See also Crenshaw, "Theories of Terrorism," p. 16; and Schmid and Jongman, *Polit Terrorism*, pp. 122–123.

The Seven Puzzling Tendencies of Terrorist Organizations

Seven empirical puzzles vitiate the strategic model's premise that terrorists are rational people who are motivated mainly to achieve their organization's stated political goals. The seven puzzles contradicting the strategic model are (1) terrorist organizations do not achieve their stated political goals by attacking civilians; (2) terrorist organizations never use terrorism as a last resort and seldom seize opportunities to become productive nonviolent political parties; (3) terrorist organizations reflexively reject compromise proposals offering significant policy concessions by the target government; (4) terrorist organizations have protean political platforms; (5) terrorist organizations generally carry out anonymous attacks, precluding target countries from making policy concessions; (6) terrorist organizations with identical political platforms routinely attack each other more than their mutually professed enemy; and (7) terrorist organizations resist disbanding when they consistently fail to achieve their political platforms or when their stated political grievances have been resolved and hence are moot.

PUZZLE #1: COERCIVE INEFFECTIVENESS

In the strategic model, people participate in a terrorist organization because they are deeply committed to achieving its political platform. The strategic model is explicit that success for a terrorist organization requires the attainment of its stated political goals.[14] Even if all other strategies are blocked, terrorism is not based on the logic of consequence and is thus irrational according to the model unless organizations achieve their political platforms at least some of the time by attacking civilians.[15] A major puzzle for the model then is that although terrorism is by definition destructive and scary, organizations rarely if ever attain their policy demands by targeting civilians.[16]

The Rand Corporation reported in the 1980s that "terrorists have been unable to translate the consequences of terrorism into concrete political gains. . . . In that sense terrorism has failed. It is a fundamental failure."[17] Martha

14. Crenshaw, "Theories of Terrorism," p. 15.
15. Sun-Ki Chai, "An Organizational Economics Theory of Antigovernment Violence," *Comparative Politics*, Vol. 26, No. 1 (October 1993), p. 100.
16. The strategic model focuses on strategic terrorism, not redemptive terrorism. The former aims to coerce a government into changing its policies, whereas the latter is intended solely to obtain specific human or material resources such as prisoners or money. On this distinction, see Abrahms, "Why Terrorism Does Not Work," p. 46.
17. Bonnie Cordes, Bruce Hoffman, Brian M. Jenkins, Konrad Kellen, Sue Moran, and William Sater, *Trends in International Terrorism, 1982 and 1983* (Santa Monica, Calif.: RAND, 1984), p. 49.

Crenshaw rema ed at the time that terrorist organizations do not obtain "the long-term ideo ical objectives they claim to seek, and therefore one must conclude that t orism is objectively a failure."[18] Thomas Schelling reached the same conclu n in the 1990s, noting that terrorist attacks "never appear to accomplish any ng politically significant."[19] In a study assessing terrorism's coercive effecti ess, I found that in a sample of twenty-eight well-known terrorist campa s, the terrorist organizations accomplished their stated policy goals zero p nt of the time by attacking civilians.[20] Although several political scientists ve developed theoretical models predicated on the notion that terrorism is effective coercive instrument, their research fails to identify a single terroris ganization that has achieved its political platform by attacking civilians.[21]

Terrorist orga ations may not realize their policy demands by targeting civilians, but do se attacks generally advance their political cause? Walter Laqueur notes t for terrorist organizations, the political consequences of their violence is arly always "negative."[22] Polls show, for example, that after the Irish Repub n Army (IRA) attacked the British public, the British people became signific ly less likely to favor withdrawing from Northern Ireland.[23] Similar trends public opinion have been registered after groups attacked civilians in Eg , Indonesia, Israel, Jordan, the Philippines, and Russia.[24] Although the in national community frequently appeals for target countries to appease terr ts, terrorist attacks on civilians have historically empowered hard-liners wh ppose, as a matter of principle, accommodating the perpetrators. For this re n, numerous studies have shown that terrorist attacks tend to close—not n—the bargaining space between what terrorist groups

18. Crenshaw, "Th es of Terrorism," p. 15.
19. Thomas C. Sch g, "What Purposes Can 'International Terrorism' Serve?" in R.G. Frey and Christopher W. M , eds., *Violence, Terrorism, and Justice* (New York: Cambridge University Press, 1991), p. 20.
20. Abrahms, "Wh rrorism Does Not Work," pp. 42–78.
21. Proponents of t trategic model claim that terrorism is an effective coercive instrument. Yet their confirming e ples are limited to successful guerrilla campaigns, which are directed against military an plomatic—not civilian—targets. See, for example, Pape, *Dying to Win*, p. 39; and Kydd and Wal "The Strategies of Terrorism," p. 49. On the distinction between terrorist and guerrilla camp s, see Abrahms, "Why Terrorism Does Not Work," pp. 44–46.
22. Walter Laqueu *rrorism* (Boston: Little, Brown, 1977), p. 117.
23. Peter R. Neum and Mike Smith, "Strategic Terrorism: The Framework and Its Fallacies," *Journal of Strategic ies*, Vol. 28, No. 4 (August 2005), p. 587.
24. See, for exampl hn Mueller, *Overblown: How Politicians and the Terrorism Industry Inflate National Security Thre nd Why We Believe Them* (New York: Free Press, 2006), p. 184; and Claude Berrebi and Esteba Klor, "On Terrorism and Electoral Outcomes: Theory and Evidence from the Israeli-Palestini Conflict," *Journal of Conflict Resolution*, Vol. 50, No. 6 (Spring 2006), pp. 899–925.

demand and what target governments are willing to offer.[25] In sum, the strategic model posits that rational people participate in terrorist organizations to achieve their stated political goals. In practice, however, terrorism does not accomplish them. Predictably, terrorism's political ineffectiveness has led scholars to question its rationality and motives.[26]

PUZZLE #2: TERRORISM AS THE FIRST RESORT

The strategic model assumes that groups turn to terrorism only after weighing their political options and determining they are blocked. In the parlance of the model, the decision to use terrorism is a "last resort," a "constrained choice" imposed by the absence of political alternatives.[27] In reality, terrorist groups do not embrace terrorism as a last resort and seldom elect to abandon the armed struggle to become nonviolent political parties.

Terrorist groups never lack political alternatives.[28] Large-*n* studies show, first, that only the most oppressive totalitarian states have been immune from terrorism, and second, that the number of terrorist organizations operating in a country is positively associated with its freedom of expression, assembly, and association conditions conducive to effecting peaceful political change.[29] The "paradox of terrorism" is that terrorist groups tend to target societies with the greatest number of political alternatives, not the fewest.[30] Case studies on terrorist organizations confirm that the decision to use terrorism is not a last resort.[31] In their study of Italian terrorist organizations in the mid-1960s and early 1970s, for example, Donatella Della Porta and Sidney Tarrow found that terrorism was "part of the protest repertoire from the very beginning," even

25. See, for example, Alan B. Krueger, *What Makes a Terrorist: Economics and the Roots of Terrorism* (Princeton, N.J.: Princeton University Press, 2007), pp. 130–131; and Christopher Hewitt, *Consequences of Political Violence* (Sudbury, Mass.: Dartmouth, 1993), pp. 80, 97–98.
26. See Ariel Merari, "Terrorism as a Strategy of Insurgency," *Terrorism and Political Violence*, Vol. 5, No. 4 (Winter 1993), p. 229; Richardson, *What Terrorists Want*, p. 75; and Martha Crenshaw, "How Terrorists Think: What Psychology Can Contribute to Understanding Terrorism," in Lawrence Howard, ed., *Terrorism: Roots, Impact, Responses* (New York: Praeger, 1992), p. 75.
27. See McCormick, "Terrorist Decision Making," p. 483; Crenshaw, "How Terrorists Think," p. 72; and DeNardo, *Power in Numbers*, p. 242.
28. Crenshaw, "How Terrorists Think," p. 71.
29. See, for example, William L. Eubank and Leonard B. Weinberg, "Does Democracy Encourage Terrorism?" *Terrorism and Political Violence*, Vol. 6, No. 4 (Winter 1994), pp. 417–443; and Leonard B. Weinberg and William L. Eubank, "Terrorism and Democracy: What Recent Events Disclose," *Terrorism and Political Violence*, Vol. 10, No. 1 (Spring 1998), pp. 108–118. See also Laqueur, *Terrorism*, p. 220.
30. Bonnie Cordes, "When Terrorists Do the Talking: Reflections on Terrorist Literature," in Rapoport, *Inside Terrorist Organizations*, p. 150. See also Walter Laqueur, "Interpretations of Terrorism: Fact, Fiction, and Political Science," *Journal of Contemporary History*, Vol. 12, No. 1 (January 1977), p. 1.
31. Laqueur, "Interpretations of Terrorism," p. 1; and Laqueur, *Terrorism*, p. 80.

though opportu y abounded for nonviolent, constitutionally protected political protest.[32] M generally, the authors concluded that terrorism "tended to appear from th ry beginning of the protest cycle" for the dozens of terrorist organizations o ating in Western Europe during this period.[33]

Relatively fe errorist organizations have elected to abandon the armed struggle to beco normal political parties.[34] More commonly, terrorist organizations toil alo de peaceful parties, refuse to lay down their arms after participating in na nal elections, or sabotage open elections that would have yielded major itical gains for the group, such as today's militant Sunni groups in Iraq. n many instances, nonviolent strategies are believed to be more policy eff ve, but terrorist organizations tend to retain, in one form or another, the pa of armed resistance.[36]

For these rea s, Crenshaw has sensibly asked, "Why use terrorism when it cannot be justif . . . as a last resort?"[37] The answer of most terrorism experts is that terrorist oups seem to possess "an innate compulsion" to engage in terrorism and a unswerving belief" in its desirability over nonviolence, contradicting the st egic model's assumption that groups employ terrorism only as a last resort on evaluating their political options.[38]

PUZZLE #3: REFL VELY UNCOMPROMISING TERRORISTS

As a rule, terro t organizations do not compromise with the target country. Bruce Hoffman s observed that terrorist organizations are notorious for their

---

32. Donatella Della rta and Sidney Tarrow, "Unwanted Children: Political Violence and the Cycle of Protest in Ital 966–1973," *European Journal of Political Research,* Vol. 14, Nos. 5–6 (November 1986), p. 616. See a Peter H. Merkl, ed., *Political Violence and Terror: Motifs and Motivations* (Los Angeles: Universit California Press, 1986), p. 146.
33. Della Porta and rrow, "Unwanted Children," pp. 14, 53.
34. Paul Wilkinson *rrorism versus Democracy: The Liberal State Response* (London: Frank Cass, 2000), p. 59.
35. Examples of th st point include the dozens of United States– and European-based Marxist terrorist organizati from the late 1960s to the late 1980s, such as Action Directe, the Communist Combatant Cells, t AF, the Red Brigades, and the Weather Underground. Examples of the second point, includi errorist organizations overtly aligned with a "parent" political wing, are Aum Shinrikyo, th mmunist Party of Nepal, the Communist Party of the Philippines, Dev Sol, ETA, Fatah, Hamas rakat ul-Mujahidin, Hezbollah, the IRA, the Japanese Red Army, Kach, the PKK, the Revolutio y Armed Forces of Colombia, and the Revolutionary United Front. On the relationship betwe rrorist organizations and political parties, see Leonard Weinberg and Ami Pedahzur, *Political ies and Terrorist Groups* (London: Routledge, 2003).
36. See Maria Step and Erica Chenoweth, "Does Terrorism Work? Comparing Strategies of Asymmetric Warfa presentation to the Centre for Defence Studies, King's College, London, March 2007. See al Crenshaw, "How Terrorists Think," p. 71; and Laqueur, "Interpretations of Terrorism," p. 1.
37. Crenshaw, "Ho errorists Think," p. 72.
38. Bruce Hoffman *side Terrorism* (New York: Columbia University Press, 1998), p. 174; and Audrey Kurth Cro "How al-Qaida Ends: The Decline and Demise of Terrorist Groups," *International Security,* V 1, No. 1 (Summer 2006), p. 11. See also Laqueur, *Terrorism,* p. 119.

"resolutely uncompromising demands."[39] Crenshaw has likewise noted that terrorist organizations are characterized by "an intransigent refusal to compromise."[40] It is far more common for them to derail negotiations by ramping up their attacks.[41] In fact, no peace process has transformed a major terrorist organization into a completely nonviolent political party.[42] Proponents of the strategic model claim that terrorists are acting rationally in opposing compromise because their policy preferences are inherently extreme, precluding a mutually acceptable bargain solution with the target country.[43] This argument is empirically and theoretically flawed.

First, terrorism is an extremism of means, not ends.[44] Many terrorist organizations profess surprisingly moderate political positions. Russian terrorist groups of the mid-nineteenth century were known as "liberals with a bomb" because they sought a constitution with elementary civil freedoms.[45] The expressed goal of the al-Aqsa Martyrs Brigades is to achieve a Palestinian state in the West Bank and Gaza Strip—a policy preference held by most of the international community. Robert Pape points out that even in his sample of contemporary suicide terrorist organizations, "the terrorists' political aims, if not their methods, are often more mainstream than observers realize; they generally reflect quite common, straightforward nationalist self-determination claims of their community . . . goals that are typically much like those of other nationalists within their community."[46] Yet terrorist organizations rarely commit to negotiations, even when these would satisfy a significant portion of their stated political grievances. The al-Aqsa Martyrs Brigades, for example, responded with an unprecedented wave of terror to Israeli Prime Minister Ehud Barak's January 2001 offer of the Gaza Strip and most of the West Bank.[47]

Second, even when terrorist groups are motivated by extreme policy preferences, a negotiated settlement is always preferable to political deadlock, ac-

---

39. Hoffman, *Inside Terrorism*, p. 128.
40. Martha Crenshaw, "An Organizational Approach to the Analysis of Political Terrorism," *Orbis*, Vol. 29, No. 3 (Fall 1985), p. 481.
41. See Andrew Kydd and Barbara F. Walter, "Sabotaging the Peace: The Politics of Extremist Violence," *International Organization*, Vol. 56, No. 2 (Spring 2002), pp. 263–296. See also Stephen John Stedman, "Spoiler Problems in Peace Processes," *International Security*, Vol. 22, No. 2 (Fall 1997), pp. 5–53.
42. Wilkinson, *Terrorism versus Democracy*, p. 59.
43. See, for example, David A. Lake, "Rational Extremism: Understanding Terrorism in the Twenty-first Century," *Dialog-IO*, Vol. 1, No. 1 (Spring 2002), pp. 15–29.
44. Anthony Oberschall, "Explaining Terrorism: The Contribution of Collective Action Theory," *Sociological Theory*, Vol. 22, No. 1 (March 2004), p. 26. On the types of political demands that terrorist organizations make, see Abrahms, "Why Terrorism Does Not Work," pp. 53–54.
45. Laqueur, *Terrorism*, p. 37.
46. Pape, *Dying to Win*, p. 43.
47. See Dennis Ross, *The Missing Peace: The Inside Story of the Fight for Middle East Peace* (New York:

cording to the l c of the strategic model.[48] Most bargaining theorists do not accept "issue ir visibility" between rational adversaries as a viable explanation for conflic ecause contested issues are typically complex and multidimensional, ena ng the warring parties to find linkages and side payments that create a m ually beneficial bargain solution.[49] Hamas, for example, has opposed surre ring claims to all of historic Palestine, but the Islamist group professes value the West Bank and Gaza Strip. If acting solely to optimize its politic platform, Hamas would therefore be expected to accept the Palestinian terri ies in exchange for peace. Hamas, however, acts as a spoiler, depriving its m bers of policy goals that the organization purports to support. In sum, ba aining theory dictates that the rational course of action is for terrorist organi ions to compromise—even if that means securing only partial concessions ver continued deadlock—but they rarely do. The tendency for terrorist or izations to reflexively oppose compromise undercuts the strategic model ssumptions that terrorists weigh the most obvious political options and sel terrorism because of its relative political effectiveness.

PUZZLE #4: PRO N POLITICAL PLATFORMS

The strategic m el assumes that terrorists are motivated by relatively stable and consistent als reflected in their organization's political platform. But terrorist organi tions often have protean political platforms.[50] The Rand Corporation de ibed France's Action Directe in the 1980s as a "chameleon organization" t "rapidly refocused" on a host of faddish policy issues, from opposing Israel nuclear energy to the Catholic Church.[51] For Ely Karmon, Action Directe's dgepodge of stated goals reflected the organization's inability to agree on ic ideological principles.[52] Action Directe was an unusually

---

Farrar, Straus and ux, 2004). See also Robert Malley, "Israel and the Arafat Question," *New York Review of Book* ol. 51, No. 15 (October 7, 2004), pp. 19–23.
48. See DeNardo, *r in Numbers*, p. 90; and Navin A. Bapat, "State Bargaining with Transnational Terrorist Gro ," *International Studies Quarterly*, Vol. 50, No. 1 (March 2006), p. 214. For a seminal work on c romise from a rationalist bargaining perspective, see Robert Powell, "Bargaining Theory an ternational Conflict," *Annual Review of Political Science*, Vol. 5 (June 2002), pp. 1–30.
49. See James D. Fe n, "Rationalist Explanations for War," *International Organization*, Vol. 49, No. 3 (Summer 1995), p 82, 390; and Robert Powell, "War as a Commitment Problem," *International Organization*, Vol. 6 o. 1 (Winter 2006), pp. 176–178, 180. For a contrarian perspective on issue indivisibility, see M ca Duffy Toft, "Issue Indivisibility and Time Horizons as Rationalist Explanations for War," *S ity Studies*, Vol. 15, No. 1 (January–March 2006), pp. 34–69.
50. See Crenshaw, eories of Terrorism," p. 20. See also Cordes et al., *Trends in International Terrorism*, p. 50.
51. Quoted in Cre w, "Theories of Terrorism," p. 20.
52. Ely Karmon, *C ions between Terrorist Organizations: Revolutionaries, Nationalists, and Islamists* (Leiden, The Neth ds: Koninklijke Brill, 2005), p. 141.

capricious terrorist organization, but even the crucial case of al-Qaida has purported to support a highly unstable set of political goals.[53] In "The Protean Enemy," Jessica Stern charts al-Qaida's transitory political agenda, as the movement morphed rapidly and unpredictably from waging defensive jihad against the Soviets in Afghanistan to fighting local struggles in Bosnia, the Philippines, Russia, Spain, and in Muslim countries to its eventual targeting of the "far enemy" in the late 1990s. The marked fluidity of al-Qaida's political rationale is reflected in the fatwas Osama bin Laden issued throughout the 1990s, which contain a litany of disparate grievances against Muslims.[54] Only in his fourth call to arms on October 7, 2001, did he emphasize the Israeli occupation, which is known in policy circles as his "belated concern."[55] Al-Qaida members have frequently criticized the inconsistency of their organization's jihadi message. The al-Qaida military strategist, Abul-Walid, complained that with its "hasty changing of strategic targets," al-Qaida was engaged in nothing more than "random chaos."[56] Other disgruntled al-Qaida members have reproached the organization for espousing political objectives that "shift with the wind."[57] Not surprisingly, the "opportunistic" nature of al-Qaida's political platform has led scholars to question the movement's dedication to achieving it.[58]

Some of the most important terrorist organizations in modern history have pursued policy goals that are not only unstable but also contradictory. The Basque separatist group ETA, for example, is criticized for failing to produce "a consistent ideology," as its political goals have wavered from fighting to overturn the Franco dictatorship in Spain to targeting the emergent democratic government—a progression similar to that of the Shining Path, Peru's most notorious terrorist organization.[59] The Kurdistan Workers' Party— Turkey's most dangerous contemporary terrorist group (known by the Kurdish acronym PKK)—has likewise vacillated between advocating jihad, a Marxist revolution, and a Kurdish homeland governed without Islamist or

53. For an excellent recent study on al-Qaida's protean nature, see Vahid Brown, "Cracks in the Foundation: Leadership Schisms in al-Qaida from 1989–2006," CTC Report (West Point, N.Y.: Combating Terrorism Center, September 2007), p. 2.
54. Jessica Stern, "The Protean Enemy," *Foreign Affairs*, Vol. 82, No. 4 (July/August 2003), p. 1.
55. Samuel R. Berger and Mona Sutphen, "Commandeering the Palestinian Cause: Bin Laden's Belated Concern," in James F. Hoge Jr. and Gideon Rose, eds., *How Did This Happen? Terrorism and the New War* (New York: PublicAffairs, 2001), p. 123.
56. Quoted in Brown, "Cracks in the Foundation," p. 10.
57. Omar Nasiri, *Inside the Jihad: My Life with Al Qaeda, A Spy's Story* (New York: Basic Books, 2006), p. 295.
58. Cronin, "How al-Qaida Ends," pp. 41–42.
59. Crenshaw, "An Organizational Approach to the Analysis of Political Terrorism," p. 71.

Marxist princip .[60] The Abu Nidal Organization staged countless attacks against Syria in e 1980s and then "almost overnight switched allegiance" by becoming a Sy n proxy.[61] According to Leonard Weinberg, the most feared international te rist group of the 1980s was willing to carry out a terrorist attack "on behal f any cause," even conflicting ones.[62] Similarly, Laqueur points out that any well-known groups that began on the extreme right—such as the Arg ine Montoneros, Colombian M-19, and the Popular Front for the Liberation Palestine—ended up on the left as far as their phraseology was concerned. Hoffman has likewise noted that in the 1980s, right-wing terrorist groups in est Germany temporarily adopted left-wing rhetoric and began attacking gets that are the traditional choice of left-wing groups. Predictably, the lice initially suspected that dozens of their attacks were the work of comm st groups.[64] That terrorist organizations often pursue unstable, even incon ent, political goals undermines the assumption that terrorist members are m vated by a stable and consistent utility function encoded in their organizati 's political platform.

PUZZLE #5: ANO MOUS ATTACKS

The strategic m el assumes that terrorism is based on the logic of consequence, specifi y, its ability to coerce policy concessions from the target country by con ing the costs of noncompliance. For this reason, proponents of the model de ibe terrorism as a form of "credible signaling" or "costly signaling."[65] A bas principle of coercion, however, is that the coercer must convey its policy d ands to the coerced party.[66] A puzzle for the strategic model is that most of time terrorist organizations neither issue policy demands nor even take c lit for their attacks.

Since the em ence of modern terrorism in 1968, 64 percent of worldwide terrorist attacks ve been carried out by unknown perpetrators. Anonymous terrorism has b rising, with three out of four attacks going unclaimed since September 11, 1.[67] Anonymous terrorism is particularly prevalent in Iraq,

60. See Ami Pedah *Suicide Terrorism* (Cambridge: Polity, 2005), pp. 87, 89. See also Mia Bloom, *Dying to Kill: The A e of Suicide Terror* (New York: Columbia University Press, 2005), p. 112.
61. Walter Laqueu *e Age of Terrorism* (Boston: Little, Brown, 1987), pp. 287–288.
62. Leonard Weinb *Global Terrorism: A Beginner's Guide* (Oxford: Oneworld, 2005), p. 83.
63. Laqueur, *The A f Terrorism*, p. 205.
64. Bruce Hoffman ight-Wing Terrorism in West Germany," No. P-7270 (Santa Monica, Calif.: RAND, 1986), pp.
65. Pape, *Dying to* , p. 29; and Kydd and Walter, "Strategies of Terrorism," p. 50.
66. Robert J. Art a Patrick M. Cronin, eds., *The United States and Coercive Diplomacy* (Washington, D.C.: United S s Institute of Peace Press, 2003), p. 371.
67. Author's calcul ns from RAND's MIPT data set, http://www.tkb.org.

where the U.S. military has struggled to determine whether the violence was perpetrated by Shiite or Sunni groups with vastly different political platforms.[68]

Policy demands are rarely forthcoming, even when the terrorist organization divulges its identity to the target country.[69] In the early 1990s, Schelling captured this point: "Usually there is nothing to negotiate. A soldier is killed in a disco in Germany. A bomb explodes in front of an Israeli consulate. Japanese Black Septembrists unpack automatic weapons in the Lod airport and start shooting. The perpetrators don't ask anything, demand anything."[70] The tendency for terrorist organizations to refrain from issuing policy demands increased in the late 1990s, leading Hoffman to conclude that the coercive logic of terrorism is "seriously flawed."[71] After the attacks of September 11, David Lake also observed that the terrorists "did not issue prior demands," and therefore a theory premised on coercion "would seem ill-suited to explaining such violence."[72] In sum, the strategic model assumes that terrorism is an effective coercive instrument. Yet terrorist groups rarely convey through violence their policy preferences to the target country, precluding even the possibility of successful coercion.

PUZZLE #6: TERRORIST FRATRICIDE

The strategic model assumes that terrorists are motivated by a consistent utility function reflected in their organization's political platform, but terrorist organizations with the same political platform routinely undercut it in wars of annihilation against each other. Particularly in the early stages of their existence, terrorist organizations purporting to fight for a common cause frequently attack each other more than their mutually declared enemy.

The Tamil Tigers, for example, did not target the Sinhalese government in the mid-1980s. Instead, it engaged in a "systematic annihilation" of other Tamil organizations "espousing the same cause" of national liberation.[73] Pape

68. See Pedahzur, *Suicide Terrorism,* pp. 114–115.
69. See Eqbal Ahmad, "Comprehending Terror," *MERIP,* No. 140 (May–June 1986), p. 3; and Bonnie Cordes, "Euroterrorists Talk about Themselves: A Look at the Literature," in Paul Wilkinson and Alasdair M. Stewart, eds., *Contemporary Research on Terrorism* (Aberdeen, Scotland: Aberdeen University Press, 1987), p. 331.
70. Schelling, "What Purposes Can 'International Terrorism' Serve?" p. 24.
71. Bruce Hoffman, "Why Terrorists Don't Claim Credit," *Terrorism and Political Violence,* Vol. 9, No. 1 (Spring 1997), p. 1. See also Mark Juergensmeyer, "The Logic of Religious Violence," in Rapoport, *Inside Terrorist Organizations,* p. 172.
72. Lake, "Rational Extremism," p. 15.
73. Shri D.R. Kaarthikeyan, "Root Causes of Terrorism? A Case Study of the Tamil Insurgency and

observes that tl 'apparent implication" of the Tigers' target selection is that the violence ha little to do with the political grievances of Tamil society or the relationshiṛ etween the Tamils and their Sinhalese opponents."[74] Ami Pedahzur allud to the fact that the Tigers' target selection is difficult to reconcile with the ategic model: "In contrast to what might be expected from a guerrilla or a te rist organization whose [expressed] goals were national liberation, the firs iolent actions initiated by the Tigers were not aimed at any army forces or halese politicians. . . . The Tigers systematically liquidated leaders and sor imes activists of other [Tamil] organizations."[75] Similarly, in the early years he Algerian War, the National Algerian Movement (known by the French a nym MNA) and the National Liberation Front (FLN) mainly attacked each c r, not their French occupiers.[76] Proponents of the strategic model might re n that the MNA and the FLN were battling to determine the political future Algeria. Benjamin Stora points out, however, that "for both organizations tl nature of the future independent Algerian society was not at issue."[77] Predic ly, the interorganizational violence had a "devastating" effect on the mu lly expressed goal of the MNA and the FLN to end the French occupat 1.[78] Terrorist organizations also undermined their political platforms by ta ting each other more than their mutually declared enemy in the violent clas in Aden between the Liberation of Occupied South Yemen and the Nation iberation Front in 1967; in Argentina between Marxist terrorist organizat s in the late 1970s; and in the Gaza Strip between Palestinian groups "fightin for a common cause" during the first intifada.[79] In recent years, the sam phenomenon has been endemic in terrorist hot spots. In Chechnya, loca rrorist organizations have been terrorizing each other despite their joint litical platform to establish Chechen independence. And in southern Iraq, iite militias with a shared ideological stance have been mainly blowing ch other up, to the obvious benefit of the Sunnis.[80] That ter-

the LTTE," in Tore rgo, ed., *Root Causes of Terrorism: Myths, Reality, and Ways Forward* (New York: Routledge, 2(, p. 134.
74. Pape, *Dying to* , pp. 139–140.
75. Pedahzur, *Suic errorism*, pp. 81–82.
76. Martha Crensh ed., *Terrorism in Context* (University Park: Penn State University Press, 1995), p. 483.
77. Benjamin Stora *eria, 1830–2000: A Short History*, trans. Jane Marie Todd (Ithaca, N.Y.: Cornell University Pre 001), p. 59.
78. Crenshaw, *Terr n in Context*, p. 484.
79. Pedahzur, *Sui Terrorism*, p. 44. See also Jonathan Schanzer, "Palestinian Uprisings Compared," *Middl st Quarterly*, Vol. 9, No. 3 (Summer 2002), pp. 27–38; and Peter H. Merkl, "Approaches to th dy of Political Violence," in Merkl, *Political Violence and Terror*, p. 45.
80. Ann Scott Tyso Attacks in Iraq Continue to Decline," *Washington Post*, October 31, 2007; and Anthony H. Corde n, "Still Losing? The June 2007 Edition of 'Measuring Stability in Iraq,'"

rorist organizations frequently undercut their stated political agenda is puzzling for the strategic model because terrorists are presumed to be primarily motivated to achieving it.

PUZZLE #7: NEVER-ENDING TERRORISM

The strategic model assumes that terrorist organizations disband or renounce terrorism when it continuously fails to advance their political platforms.[81] To act otherwise, Pape says, is "deeply irrational" because "that would not constitute learning."[82] Yet terrorist organizations survive for decades, notwithstanding their political futility.[83]

The primary explanation for war in the bargaining literature is that rational actors miscalculate the capability and resolve of their opponents.[84] Proponents of the strategic model might speculate that terrorist organizations are acting rationally; they simply overestimate the likelihood that attacking civilians will coerce their governments into making policy concessions. The problem with this argument is that informational explanations provide a poor account of protracted conflict. James Fearon has shown that after a few years of war, fighters on both sides are expected to develop accurate understandings of their relative capabilities and resolve.[85] The idea that terrorists misjudge the coercive effectiveness of their violence therefore does not obtain because terrorist organizations exist for decades despite their political hopelessness. As Loren Lomasky observes, the strategic model "impute[s] to terrorists no lesser rationality than that which social analysts routinely ascribe to other actors. . . . Rational agents are not systematically unable to distinguish efficacious from inefficacious activity."[86] The longevity of terrorist organizations relative to

---

Working Paper (Washington, D.C.: Center for Strategic and International Studies, June 20, 2007), http://www.thewashingtonnote.com/archives/IraqStab&Security06-20%5B1%5D.htm.

81. See Bruce Hoffman and Gordon H. McCormick, "Terrorism, Signaling, and Suicide Attack," *Studies in Conflict and Terrorism*, Vol. 27, No. 4 (July 2004), p. 252. See also Crenshaw, "Theories of Terrorism," p. 16.

82. Pape, *Dying to Win*, pp. 63–64.

83. Abrahms, "Why Terrorism Does Not Work," p. 47. See also Martha Crenshaw, "How Terrorism Declines," in Clark McCauley, ed., *Terrorism Research and Public Policy* (London: Frank Cass, 1991), p. 79.

84. Erik Gartzke, "War Is in the Error Term," *International Organization*, Vol. 53, No. 3 (Summer 1999), p. 573.

85. James D. Fearon, "Why Do Some Civil Wars Last So Much Longer than Others?" *Journal of Peace Research*, Vol. 41, No. 3 (May 2004), p. 290. See also Branislav L. Slantchev, "The Power to Hurt: Costly Conflict with Completely Informed States," *American Political Science Review*, Vol. 97, No. 1 (February 2003), p. 123.

86. Loren E. Lomasky, "The Political Significance of Terrorism," in Frey and Morris, *Violence, Terrorism, and Justice*, p. 90.

their political a omplishments therefore conflicts with the strategic model's assumption tha errorism is based on the logic of consequence.

Conversely, t strategic model assumes that because terrorists are motivated by relativ stable policy aims, the violence will cease when the organization's stated evances have been lifted.[87] A puzzle for the model then is that terrorist o nizations resist disbanding when their political rationales have become n t.[88] Pape's research demonstrates that contemporary guerrilla campaigns ve coerced major policy concessions from target countries; yet none of th organizations that also use terrorism have disbanded.[89] Hezbollah, for ample, remains an operational terrorist group, despite the fact that its gue lla attacks on the Israel Defense Forces achieved the stated goal of liberati southern Lebanon in May 2000. When their political rationale is losing r vance, terrorist organizations commonly invent one. Klaus Wasmund's cas tudy of the RAF shows, for example, that the German terrorists were "aggr ited" when the Vietnam War ended because they suddenly faced a "dilemr of finding a suitable revolutionary subject." Instead of abandoning the arm struggle, the RAF turned overnight into a militant advocate of the Palestini cause.[90] Similarly, the 9/11 commission explains that upon discovering in ril 1988 that the Soviets were planning to withdraw from Afghanistan, th mujahideen made the collective decision to remain intact while they hun for a new political cause.[91] In this way, terrorist organizations contrive a w political raison d'être, belying the assumption that terrorists are motiva by relatively stable policy preferences reflected in their organizations' itical platforms.

What Terroris Really Want

These seven p les challenge the strategic model with disconfirming evidence of its core sumptions that terrorists (1) are motivated by relatively consistent and stab political goals issued by the terrorist organization; (2) weigh the expected p ical costs and benefits of the most obvious options; and (3) opt for a strate of terrorism because of its expected political effectiveness

87. See Pape, *Dyin Win*, p. 94.
88. See Crenshaw, w Terrorism Ends," p. 80. See also Martha Crenshaw, "The Causes of Terrorism," *Comparati olitics*, Vol. 13, No. 4 (July 1981), p. 397.
89. Pape, *Dying to* , p. 109.
90. Klaus Wasmun The Political Socialization of West German Terrorists," in Merkl, *Political Violence and Terror*, p. . See also Hoffman, *Inside Terrorism*, p. 179.
91. *The 9/11 Commi n Report: Final Report of the National Commission on Terrorist Attacks upon the United States* (New k: W.W. Norton, 2004), p. 56.

Figure 1. The Empirical Weakness of the Strategic Model

Seven Puzzles of Terrorist Organizations	Assumption 1: Terrorists have consistent and stable political goals.	Assumption 2: Terrorists evaluate their political options.	Assumption 3: Terrorism offers a superior political return.
	protean political goals	reflexively uncompromising	coercive ineffectiveness
	terrorist fratricide	terrorism as the first resort	anonymous attacks
	never-ending terrorism		

NOTE: The strategic model's assumptions are obviously interrelated; there is no implication that each puzzle violates only one of them.

(see Figure 1). The puzzles suggest that the strategic model is flawed in one of two ways: either terrorists are irrational people who minimize their utility or the model misspecifies their incentive structure. Psychiatric studies reveal that terrorists are not irrational.[92] This implies that the foremost objective of terrorists may not be to achieve their organization's political platform.

The tremendous number and variation of terrorist organizations in the world preclude a single causal explanation for terrorism that obtains in every situation. The equifinality of terrorism ensures that any causal explanation is necessarily probabilistic, not deterministic.[93] This section demonstrates, however, that an alternative incentive structure has superior explanatory power. There is comparatively strong theoretical and empirical evidence that people become terrorists not to achieve their organization's declared political agenda, but to develop strong affective ties with other terrorist members. In other words, the preponderance of evidence is that people participate in terrorist organizations for the social solidarity, not for their political return.

Organization theories are potentially useful for explaining terrorist motives because nearly all terrorist attacks are perpetrated by members of terrorist organizations.[94] The natural systems model, a leading approach in organization theory, posits that people participate in organizations not to achieve their

92. Richardson, *What Terrorists Want*, p. 14. See also Marc Sageman, *Understanding Terror Networks* (Philadelphia: University of Pennsylvania Press, 2004), p. 81.
93. Karen Rasler, "Review Symposium: Understanding Suicide Terror," *Perspectives on Politics*, Vol. 5, No. 1 (February 2007), p. 118. See also Krueger, *What Makes a Terrorist*, p. x.
94. See Christopher Hewitt, *Understanding Terrorism in America: From the Klan to al-Qaida* (London: Routledge, 2003), p. 57. See also Krueger, *What Makes a Terrorist*, p. 71.

official goals, b to experience social solidarity with other members. After briefly describi the natural systems model, I demonstrate its applicability to understanding rorists' motives.[95]

THE NATURAL S EMS MODEL

Organization t ry has been dominated by two dueling models since the 1930s: the classi model and the natural systems model, which counts many more adherent Classical organization theorists such as Max Weber and Frederick Taylo onceived of the organization as a set of arrangements oriented toward m imizing output. In the classical model, members participate in an organizati solely to achieve its stated goals. According to this view, the effectiveness ar rationality of an organization therefore depend entirely on the degree to w h its actions advance its official aims.[97] In assuming that terrorists are mot ted to achieving their organizations' stated political goals, the strategic m el is predicated on the antiquated views of the classical model, which f d almost immediate opposition.

Chester Barn , the father of the natural systems model, exposed the classical fallacy of eq ing the official goals of an organization with the goals of its members. Barn demonstrated that most individuals engage in a cost-benefit analysis whether to participate in an organization based on its personal inducem , which have little if any connection to the organization's stated goals. Fo Barnard, the most important incentive is what he called the "condition of c munion," the sense of solidarity from participating in a social collectivity.

The natural s ems model stresses that there is often a disconnect between the official goal an organization and the latent social goals governing its behavior. The loo coupling of organizational practices with official goals implies that the f re to achieve them may be entirely satisfactory from the perspective of i nembers.[99] In fact, the model emphasizes that organizations

---

95. In the select cas vhere terrorism scholars have explicitly employed a variant of organization theory, they invari present it as a secondary lens to complement—not contest—the strategic model. See, for exa le, Bloom, *Dying to Kill*, p. 3; Richardson, *What Terrorists Want*, p. 79; and Pedahzur, *Suicide T rism*, pp. 11, 25.
96. See Charles Pe v, *Complex Organizations: A Critical Essay* (Glenview, Ill.: Scott, Foresman, 1972), p. 75; and Pf r, *Organizations and Organization Theory*, p. 72.
97. Gibson Burrell Gareth Morgan, *Sociological Paradigms and Organisational Analysis* (London: Heinemann, 1988), 49; Paul S. Goodman and Johannes M. Pennings, eds., *New Perspectives on Organizational Effec ness* (London: Jossey-Bass, 1981), p. 3; and W. Richard Scott, "Effectiveness of Organizational E tiveness Studies," in Goodman and Pennings, *New Perspectives on Organizational Effectiveness*, 5.
98. Chester I. Barn *The Functions of the Executive* (Cambridge, Mass.: Harvard University Press, 1938), pp. 17, 85, 1 46, 148.
99. Ibid., pp. 145–1 48. See also W. Richard Scott, *Organizations: Rational, Natural, and Open Sys-*

will act to perpetuate their existence—even when doing so undermines their official goals—whenever members attach utmost importance to the social benefits of the organization.[100]

If people participate in terrorist organizations primarily to achieve social solidarity, one would therefore expect to find (1) evidence at the individual level that people are mainly attracted to terrorist organizations not to achieve their official political platforms, but to develop strong affective ties with other terrorist members; and (2) evidence at the organizational level that terrorist groups consistently engage in actions to preserve the social unit, even when these impede their official political agendas. There is compelling evidence at both levels of analysis.

TERRORISTS AS SOCIAL SOLIDARITY SEEKERS

Empirical evidence is accumulating in terrorism studies and political psychology that individuals participate in terrorist organizations not to achieve their political platforms, but to develop strong affective ties with fellow terrorists.

First, psychologist Jeff Victoroff has concluded in a précis of the terrorism literature that "the claim that no individual factors identify those at risk for becoming terrorists is based on completely inadequate research."[101] Terrorist organizations appeal disproportionately to certain psychological types of people, namely, the socially alienated. Melvin Seeman defines alienation broadly as the feeling of loneliness, rejection, or exclusion from valued relationships, groups, or societies.[102] Demographic data show that the vast majority of terrorist organizations are composed of unmarried young men or widowed women who were not gainfully employed prior to joining them.[103] Other demographic

tems, 3d ed. (Englewood Cliffs, N.J.: Prentice Hall, 1992), pp. 5, 51; and Walter W. Powell, "Expanding the Scope of Institutional Analysis," in Walter W. Powell and Paul J. DiMaggio, eds., *The New Institutionalism in Organizational Analysis* (Chicago: University of Chicago Press, 1991), p. 183.

100. See David M. Austin, "The Political Economy of Social Benefit Organizations: Redistributive Services and Merit Goods," in Herman D. Stein, ed., *Organization and the Human Services: Cross-Disciplinary Reflections* (Philadelphia: Temple University Press, 1981), p. 170. See also David L. Clark, "Emerging Paradigms: In Organizational Theory and Research," in Yvonna S. Lincoln, ed., *Organizational Theory and Inquiry: The Paradigm Revolution* (Beverly Hills, Calif.: Sage, 1985), p. 59.

101. See Jeff Victoroff, "The Mind of the Terrorist: A Review and Critique of Psychological Approaches," *Journal of Conflict Resolution*, Vol. 49, No. 1 (February 2005), p. 34.

102. Melvin Seeman, "Alienation and Engagement," in Angus Campbell and Philip E. Converse, eds., *The Human Meaning of Social Change* (New York: Russell Sage, 1972), pp. 472–473.

103. For research on the prevalence of these demographic characteristics in a wide variety of terrorist organizations, see Pedahzur, *Suicide Terrorism*, pp. 151–152; Alex P. Schmid, "Why Terrorism? Root Causes, Some Empirical Findings, and the Case of 9/11," presentation to the Council of Europe, Strasbourg, France, April 26–27, 2007, p. 12; Ariel Merari, "Social, Organizational, and Psychological Factors in Suicide Terrorism," in Bjorgo, *Root Causes of Terrorism*, p. 75; Sageman, *Understanding Terror Networks*, p. 95; Rex A. Hudson, "The Sociology and Psychology of Terrorism" (Washington, D.C.: Federal Research Division, Library of Congress, September 1999); Charles

studies show tl terrorist organizations are frequent repositories for people undergoing dis :ation from their native homeland who are therefore detached from fa y, friends, and the host society they are attempting to join. Marc Sageman' tudy of 172 global Salafi jihadists demonstrates that these risk factors ar articularly prevalent among the crucial case of al-Qaida members, 80 p ent of whom are "cultural outcasts living at the margins of society" as un imilated first- or second-generation immigrants in non-Muslim countr [104] Analysts who study al-Qaida are increasingly finding that European M slims are unassimilated in their host countries and represent a core constitue of al-Qaida, whereas Muslims in the United States are comparatively assir ated and detached from the al-Qaida network.[105] Variation on the indepen nt variable of alienation or social isolation can therefore explain variation the dependent variable for joining al-Qaida. The high correlation of what ert Bandura calls "conducive social conditions" among the hundreds of ter ist members for whom data exist is consistent with my argument that most lividuals participate in terrorist organizations to achieve social solidarity.[10

Second, mem rs from a wide variety of terrorist groups—including ETA, the IRA, the Ita Communist Party, the RAF, the Red Brigades, Turkish terrorist organiza s, and the Weather Underground—say that they joined these armed str gles not because of their personal attachment to their political or ideologi agendas, but to maintain or develop social relations with other terrorist r nbers.[107] These are not the statements of a small number of terrorists; in th urkish sample, for instance, the 1,100 terrorists interviewed

---

A. Russell and Bow n A. Miller, "Profile of a Terrorist," in John D. Elliott and Leslie K. Gibson, eds., *Contemporary rorism: Selected Readings* (Gaithersburg, Md.: International Association of Chiefs of Police, 1 , pp. 81–95; and Stern, "The Protean Enemy," p. 6. In Sageman's sample, many of the jihadis e married, but most researchers believe that the jihadist population is overwhelmingly single.

104. Sageman, *Un tanding Terror Networks*, p. 92. See also Olivier Roy, "Terrorism and Deculturation," in ise Richardson, ed., *The Roots of Terrorism* (New York: Routledge, 2006), pp. 159–160; Stern, e Protean Enemy," p. 7; and *The 9/11 Commission Report*, p. 231.

105. See Roy, "Terr m and Deculturation," p. 166.

106. Albert Bandu Psychological Mechanisms of Aggression," in Mario von Cranach, ed., *Human Ethology: Clai d Limits of a New Discipline* (Cambridge: Cambridge University Press, 1979). Proponents of the tegic model reject the idea that individuals turn to terrorism because they are socially alienat heir evidence, ironically, is that people who join a terrorist organization are sometimes embrac ven celebrated, by their surrounding communities. See, for example, Pape, *Dying to Win*, chap

107. See, for exam Schmid, "Why Terrorism?" p. 11; Robert W. White, "Political Violence by the Nonaggrieved, Donatella Della Porta, ed., *International Social Movement Research*, Vol. 4 (Greenwich, Conn. Press, 1992), p. 92; Wasmund, "The Political Socialization of West German Terrorists," pp. 209 2; Hudson, "The Sociology and Psychology of Terrorism," p. 37; and Richard G. Braungart a Margaret M. Braungart, "From Protest to Terrorism: The Case of the SDS and the Weathermen," Della Porta, *International Social Movement Research*, p. 73.

were ten times more likely to say that they joined the terrorist organization "because their friends were members" than because of the "ideology" of the group.[108]

Third, recent studies on al-Qaida, Fatah, Hamas, Hezbollah, Palestinian Islamic Jihad, and Turkish terrorists have found that the key scope condition for their joining the terrorist organization was having a friend or relative in it—a conclusion consistent with prior research on ETA, the IRA, and both Italian and German right-wing and Marxist terrorist groups.[109] These findings are also consistent with a fascinating July 2007 study of Guantanamo Bay detainees. Researchers from West Point's Combating Terrorism Center found in their sample of 516 detainees that knowing an al-Qaida member was a significantly better predictor than believing in the jihad for turning to terrorism—even when a militant definition of jihad was used and other variables were held constant.[110] The strategic model cannot explain why the vast majority of politically discontented people do not use terrorism. Yet the requirement of social linkages to the terrorist organization can explain the difference between the large pool of socially isolated people and the relatively small number who become terrorists.[111]

Fourth, case studies of al-Qaida, Aum Shinrikyo, Hezbollah, the IRA, the RAF, the Weather Underground, and Chechen and Palestinian terrorist groups have concluded that most of the terrorists in these groups participated in the armed struggle to improve their relationships with other terrorists or to reduce their sense of alienation from society, usually both.[112] These studies emphasize that social bonds preceded ideological commitment, which was an effect, not a cause, of becoming a terrorist member.[113]

---

108. See Schmid, "Why Terrorism?" p. 11.
109. See, for example, White, "Political Violence by the Nonaggrieved," p. 93; Jerrold M. Post, Ehud Sprinzak, and Laurita M. Denny, "The Terrorists in Their Own Words: Interviews with 35 Incarcerated Middle Eastern Terrorists," *Terrorism and Political Violence*, Vol. 15, No. 1 (March 2003), pp. 171–184; Sageman, *Understanding Terror Networks*, p. 92; and Schmid, "Why Terrorism?" p. 11.
110. Joseph Felter and Jarret Brachman, "An Assessment of 516 Combatant Status Review Tribunal Unclassified Summaries," CTC Report (West Point, N.Y.: Combating Terrorism Center, July 15, 2007), pp. 24–25, 34.
111. For discussion of the fundamental problem of specificity in terrorism studies, see Sageman, *Understanding Terror Networks*, chap. 4. See also Weinberg, *Global Terrorism*, p. 82.
112. See, for example, Hudson, "The Sociology and Psychology of Terrorism," p. 148; Sageman, *Understanding Terror Networks*, p. 95; Merkl, "Approaches to the Study of Political Violence," p. 42; Jerrold M. Post, "The Socio-cultural Underpinnings of Terrorist Psychology: 'When Hatred Is Bred in the Bone,'" in Bjorgo, *Root Causes of Terrorism*, p. 55; *The 9/11 Commission Report*, p. 231; and Braungart and Braungart, "From Protest to Terrorism," p. 68.
113. The studies on suicide terrorists devote extra attention to this point. One explanation for why suicide terrorists appear relatively apolitical is that organization leaders prefer expending members with no prior connection to the organization or its political cause. See Pedahzur, *Suicide Terrorism*, pp. 126, 131–133, 152–154. See also Sageman, *Understanding Terror Networks*, pp. 93, 135.

Fifth, many t ɔrist foot soldiers and even their leaders never develop a basic understand ; of their organization's political purpose. This finding strengthens th rgument that ideological commitment enters through the back door, if at of terrorist organizations. In his study of the IRA, for example, Robert Wh found that nearly half of the terrorists he interviewed were unaware of the scrimination in Northern Ireland against Catholics, despite the salience of s issue in IRA communiqués.[114] According to Olivier Roy, Mia Bloom, anc former mujahideen, al-Qaida foot soldiers and their leaders are often ignor about the basic tenets of Islam, if not bin Laden's political vision.[115] Al-Q a is unexceptional in this regard; Richardson's research shows that "a king and quite surprising" aspect of terrorism is that the leaders of "ver ifferent terrorist movements" are unable to explain their basic political pur se.[116] When asked to describe the society that their organizations hoped to ieve, the leader of the Shining Path conceded, "We have not studied the que ɔn sufficiently"; the founder of the RAF responded, "That is not our concern the leader of the Japanese Red Army replied, "We really do not know wha will be like"; and the spokesman for the Revolutionary Armed Forces Colombia acknowledged, "I must admit that we have yet to define this aspe "[117] Audrey Cronin has found that leaders of both left-wing and anarchist t ɔrist groups are also "notorious for their inability to articulate a clear visi of their [political] goals."[118] That even terrorist leaders frequently cannot xplain their organizations' political purpose suggests that members have lifferent motive for participating in them.[119]

Sixth, terroris rganizations focus their recruitment on the socially isolated, not on people ı a demonstrable commitment to their given political cause.

114. White, "Politi Violence by the Nonaggrieved," p. 83. See also Christopher Dobson and Ronald Payne, *The rorists: Their Weapons, Leaders, and Tactics* (New York: Facts on File, 1981), p. 32.

115. Roy, "Terroris ıd Deculturation," pp. 159–160; Mia Bloom, "The Transformation of Suicide Bombing Campaig ectarian Violence and Recruitment in Pakistan, Afghanistan, and Iraq," paper presented at th Terrorist Organizations: Social Science Research on Terrorism" conference, University of Calif a, San Diego, May 4, 2007; and Nasiri, *Inside the Jihad*, p. 279.

116. Richardson, *W Terrorists Want*, pp. 85–86. See also Laqueur, *Terrorism*, p. 81.

117. Quoted in Ric dson, *What Terrorists Want*, pp. 86–87.

118. Cronin, "How Qaida Ends," p. 23. See also Hoffman, *Inside Terrorism*, p. 172.

119. That terrorist ı nbers often appear uninterested and uninformed regarding their organization's official politi genda is actually not surprising. Terrorists—be it al-Qaida operatives, Red Brigadists, RAF m ers, the Weathermen, or the Tupamaros of Uruguay—have rarely hailed from the constituen they claim to represent; many terrorist organizations do not train or indoctrinate their memb n any ideology; and terrorists are often "walk-ins" who have no prior association with the te st organization or its political cause before volunteering for an operation. See *The 9/11 Comm n Report*, pp. 228, 232; Dipak K. Gupta, "Exploring Roots of Terrorism," in Bjorgo, *Root Causes rrorism*, p. 19; Pedahzur, *Suicide Terrorism*, pp. 132–133; Crenshaw, *Terrorism in Context*, p. 15; a Crenshaw, "How Terrorists Think," p. 73.

Pedahzur's research, for example, shows that Hezbollah, the PKK, and Chechen and Palestinian groups recruit young, unemployed men "who have never found their place in the community," not fervent nationalists committed to political change.[120] Similarly, Peter Merkl shows that Marxist terrorist groups have historically recruited unemployed youth with "failed personal lives" who lacked "political direction."[121] Gregory Johnsen likewise suggests that al-Qaida, at least in Yemen, focuses its recruitment not on committed jihadists, but on "young and largely directionless" socially marginalized Muslim men.[122]

Seventh, terrorist organizations are particularly attractive outlets for those seeking solidarity. According to political psychologists, terrorist groups are far more tight-knit than other voluntary associations because of the extreme dangers and costs of participation, as well as their tendency to violate societal expectations.[123] This observation may account for the fact that even when terrorist organizations fail to achieve their political platforms, committing acts of terrorism tends to generate new recruits, boost membership morale, and otherwise strengthen the social unit.[124]

Eighth, terrorists seem to prefer participating in terrorist groups and activities most conducive to developing strong affective ties with fellow terrorists. Jacob Shapiro has found that within the al-Qaida network, terrorists prefer operating in more centralized, cohesive clusters of cliques.[125] Indeed, since the emergence of modern international terrorism, terrorists have flocked to where other terrorists—regardless of their political orientation—were gathered. In the 1970s, thousands of terrorists from dozens of countries and organizations descended on training camps run by the Palestine Liberation Organization; in the 1980s and mid-1990s, the locus of terrorist activity shifted first to Afghanistan to train with the Afghan mujahideen and then to al-Qaida camps. Based on her interviews with terrorists, Jessica Stern has likened these adventures to an "Outward Bound" experience for young men seeking challenges, excitement, and above all "friendship" with fellow terrorists of diverse political

120. Pedahzur, *Suicide Terrorism*, pp. 137–138, 168.
121. Merkl, *Political Violence and Terror*, p. 42.
122. Gregory Johnsen, "Securing Yemen's Cooperation in the Second Phase of the War on al-Qa'ida," *CTC Sentinel*, Vol. 1, No. 1 (December 2007), p. 34.
123. Crenshaw, "How Terrorists Think," p. 73; and Crenshaw, "The Psychology of Political Terrorism," in M.G. Hermann, ed., *Political Psychology: Contemporary Problems and Issues* (San Francisco, Calif.: Jossey-Bass, 1986), p. 394. See also Shira Fishman, "Perceptions of Closeness as a Function of Group Importance," University of Maryland, 2007.
124. See Richardson, *What Terrorists Want*, p. 301; Bloom, *Dying to Kill*, pp. 19, 39; and Hoffman, *Inside Terrorism*, pp. 73–75.
125. Jacob N. Shapiro, "The Terrorist's Challenge: Security, Efficiency, Control," paper presented at the "Terrorist Organizations: Social Science Research on Terrorism" conference.

backgrounds.12(rst-hand accounts from these camps confirm that the terrorists often had li idea or preference where they would fight upon completing their training.12

Ninth, there ircumstantial evidence that terrorist organizations collapse when they ceas be perceived as desirable social collectivities worth joining. David Rapopor research demonstrates that throughout history terrorist organizations hav disbanded when their members grew old, tired of waging the armed stru e, and their group failed to appeal to the younger generation.[128] Cronin' search on the decline of terrorist groups also lists "generational transitio ilure" as their leading cause of death.[129] The tendency for terrorist groups die out in the course of a "human life cycle"—irrespective of the state of ir political grievances—suggests that they appeal to new members prim y for social, not political, reasons.

The research ndscape is constrained by the limited reliable demographic data on terroris representative samples, and controlled studies to firmly establish causatio In the aggregate, however, there is mounting empirical evidence that peo may participate in terrorist organizations mainly to achieve social solidarit ot their official political agendas. This incentive structure is testable. The na al systems model posits that when members attach utmost importance to organization's social benefits, the organization will seek to prolong its exi nce, even when doing so impedes its official goals. This is precisely the w terrorist organizations typically behave.

THE PUZZLES RE ITED

The seven puzz are perplexing for the strategic model because they demonstrate that terro t organizations behave more as social solidarity maximizers than as politica aximizers. The puzzles are easily resolved from the vantage of organization eory. The natural systems model predicts that terrorist organizations will r inely engage in actions to perpetuate and justify their exis-

126. Stern, *Terror i* *Name of God*, p. 5.
127. Nasiri, *Inside* *ihad*, pp. 151, 178, 217.
128. David C. Rap rt, "The Fourth Wave: September 11 in the History of Terrorism," *Current History*, Vol. 100, N 50 (December 2001), pp. 419–424. See also David C. Rapoport, "Generations and Waves: The to Understanding Rebel Terror Movements," paper presented at the "Seminar on Glob ffairs," Ronald W. Burkle Center for International Affairs, University of California, Los A les, November 7, 2003, http://www.international.ucla.edu/cms/files/David_Rapoport_W s_of_Terrorism.pdf.
129. Cronin's supe tudy identifies seven reasons why terrorist organizations have historically gone out of busine More terrorist organizations suffered from the failure to make the "generational transition" t from any of the other six reasons explored. It should be noted that Cronin does not purport t egorize the universe of terrorist groups. See Cronin, "How al-Qaida Ends," p. 19.

tence, even when these undermine their official political agendas. True to the model, terrorist organizations (1) prolong their existence by relying on a strategy that hardens target governments from making policy concessions; (2) ensure their continued viability by resisting opportunities to peacefully participate in the democratic process; (3) avoid disbanding by reflexively rejecting negotiated settlements that offer significant policy concessions; (4) guarantee their survival by espousing a litany of protean political goals that can never be fully satisfied;[130] (5) avert organization-threatening reprisals by conducting anonymous attacks, even though they preclude the possibility of coercing policy concessions; (6) annihilate ideologically identical terrorist organizations that compete for members, despite the adverse effect on their stated political cause; and (7) refuse to split up after the armed struggle has proven politically unsuccessful for decades or its political rationale has become moot.

None of these common tendencies of terrorist organizations advances their official political agendas, but all of them help to ensure the survival of the social unit. Together, they reveal the operating decision rules of terrorist members. Whereas the strategic model locates the motives of terrorists in the official goals of the terrorist organization, the trade-offs it makes provides direct insight into its members' incentive structure. Just as economists measure utility functions through revealed preferences, terrorism scholars need not make comparisons among utilities.[131] The seven puzzles discussed above contradict the strategic model because terrorists already make such trade-offs by regularly prioritizing the maintenance of the terrorist organization over the advancement of its official political agenda as predicted by the natural systems model.[132]

---

130. The tendency for terrorist organizations to issue protean political demands may dissuade target countries from making policy concessions. See Paul Wilkinson, "Security Challenges in the New Reality," paper presented at the 33d IFPA-Fletcher Conference on National Security Strategy and Policy, Washington, D.C., October 16, 2002, http://www.ifpafletcherconference.com/oldtranscripts/2002/wilkinson.htm.

131. For a similar argument unrelated to terrorist motivations, see Jeffrey Pfeffer, "Usefulness of the Concept," in Goodman and Pennings, *New Perspectives on Organizational Effectiveness,* p. 137. On revealed preferences, see Amartya Sen, "Behaviour and the Concept of Preference," in Elster, *Rational Choice,* pp. 61, 67.

132. In this way, the role of social solidarity is very different in terrorist organizations than in conventional armies. In the military, training is designed to foster in-group cohesion not as the end goal, but as a means to enhance battlefield performance. Unlike terrorist organizations, conventional armies therefore do not regularly sacrifice their political goals for the social benefit of the fighting unit. On the complementary relationship between small unit cohesion and military performance, see James Griffith, "Institutional Motives for Serving in the U.S. Army National Guard," *Armed Forces and Society,* Vol. 20, No. 10 (May 2007), pp. 1–29; and Guy L. Siebold, "The Essence of Military Group Cohesion," *Armed Forces and Society,* Vol. 33, No. 2 (January 2007), pp. 286–295.

In sum, the s en puzzles for the strategic model challenge the prevailing view that terro s are rational people who use terrorism for political ends. The prepondera e of theoretical and empirical evidence is that people participate in terrorist ganizations not to achieve their official political platforms, but to develop ong affective ties with fellow terrorists—an incentive structure reflected in e trade-offs terrorist organizations typically make to maintain their surviv If terrorists generally attach greater importance to the social benefits than to e political benefits of using terrorism, then extant counterterrorism strate s require fundamental change.

Counterterror n Implications

The most comm n counterterrorism strategies are designed to reduce terrorism by divestin t of its political utility. The predominant strategy is to deter terrorism b decreasing its political utility via a strict no concessions policy.[133] Like m t heads of state, President George W. Bush believes that terrorism will des when its practitioners realize that "these crimes only hurt their [political] use."[134] Although target governments rarely appease terrorists, there is als widespread belief in the international community that they can be defused ough political accommodation.[135] Proponents of this second strategy urge re ndling stalled peace processes, for example, to deny prospective political nefits from using terrorism. The third most common counterterrorism strategy is democracy promotion, which is intended to decrease terrorism utility by empowering citizens to peacefully address their country's politi problems.[136] All three strategies have poor track records. As I have shown, t orist organizations often resist disbanding in the face of consistent political lure, in spite of the ending of their immediate political grievances, and even when presented with peaceful alternatives for political gain.

Why does wi nolding political concessions, granting political concessions, or providing no violent political alternatives fail so often to eradicate terrorism? The strate model's premise that terrorists are political maximizers is empirically wea Strategies to dry up the demand for terrorism by minimizing its political lity are misguided and hence unlikely to work on any sys-

133. See Martha C haw, *Terrorism, Legitimacy, and Power: The Consequences of Political Violence* (Middletown, Conn Wesleyan University Press, 1983), p. 10.
134. Quoted in Ala I. Dershowitz, *Why Terrorism Works: Understanding the Threat, Responding to the Challenge* (New ven, Conn.: Yale University Press, 2002), p. 17.
135. Laqueur, *Terro n*, p. 5.
136. See George W ush, "President Discusses War on Terror," National Defense University, Washington, D.C. March 8, 2005, http://www.whitehouse.gov/news/releases/2005/03/20050308-3.html.

tematic basis. The evidence is stronger that terrorists tend to think and act more as social solidarity maximizers, which requires a different counterterrorism approach.

Both supply-side and demand-side counterterrorism strategies must be informed by the terrorist's incentive structure. Supply-side strategies can help law enforcement identify potential terrorists, unravel covert networks, and even thwart terrorist attacks by exploiting the knowledge that people tend to participate in terrorist groups to develop strong affective ties with fellow terrorists. There is no single "terrorist personality," but certain communities are prone to terrorism. Law enforcement must pay greater attention to the socially marginalized than to the politically downtrodden. This includes diaspora communities in Western countries that host large unassimilated, dislocated populations such as the Maghrebin in France; single, unemployed, Islamist men residing in comparatively secular Muslim countries such as in Pakistan; restive, youthful populations that feel estranged from the state such as in Saudi Arabia; and prison populations, which, by definition, are home to the socially isolated and dislocated. These are impossibly large groups of people to monitor. Law enforcement can tighten the noose considerably by exploiting the fact that terrorist groups are composed of networks of friends and family members, and that knowing one of them is the key scope condition for entry into the group. Governments should utilize this knowledge to aggressively boost funding of social network analysis (SNA) research. SNA is a mathematical method for mapping and studying relationships between people, with untapped counterterrorism potential. The basic idea is to trace the social relations or "links" emanating from known terrorists or suspects, and then connect the dots between these "nodes" of people, to estimate the probability of their involvement in the terrorist network. People who email, talk on the phone, or intentionally meet with terrorists or their close friends are statistically more likely to be complicit. In this way, SNA can help law enforcement identify and then surveil the inner circle. Because acquaintances can also play a critical role in the network, greater data-mining power and accuracy need to be developed to expose these weak ties without undue infringements on civil liberties.[137]

Demand-side strategies should focus on divesting terrorism's social utility, in two ways. First, it is vital to drive a wedge between organization members. Since the advent of modern terrorism in the late 1960s, the sole counterterrorism strategy that was a clear-cut success attacked the social bonds of the

137. For a useful primer on SNA, see Patrick Radden Keefe, "Can Network Theory Thwart Terrorists?" *New York Times*, March 12, 2006. See also Sageman, *Understanding Terror Networks*, pp. 163, 169, 178.

terrorist organi ion, not its utility as a political instrument. By commuting prison sentenc in the early 1980s in exchange for actionable intelligence against their fe v Brigatisti, the Italian government infiltrated the Red Brigades, bred mi ist and resentment among the members, and quickly rolled up the organiz on.[138] Similar deals should be cut with al-Qaida in cases where detainee rior involvement in terrorism and their likelihood of rejoining the undergr nd are minor. Greater investment in developing and seeding double agents also go a long way toward weakening the social ties undergirding terroris rganizations and cells around the world. Second, counterterrorism strate s must reduce the demand for at-risk populations to turn to terrorist organi ions in the first place. To lessen Muslims' sense of alienation from democrati ocieties, these societies must improve their records of cracking down on b try, supporting hate-crime legislation, and most crucially, encouraging m rate places of worship—an important alternative for dislocated youth to velop strong affective ties with politically moderate peers and mentors. I uthoritarian countries, an abrupt transition to democracy risks empower extremists.[139] These regimes must, however, permit the development o vil society to provide opportunities for the socially disenfranchised to b l in peaceful voluntary associations. Counterterrorism operations must als edouble their efforts to minimize collateral damage, which invariably creat dislocation, social isolation, and calls for revenge. Such policies will help uce the incentive and therefore incidence of terrorism by diminishing its cial benefits, which are what its practitioners apparently value most.

138. See Bruce Ho n, "Foreword," in Cindy C. Combs, *Twenty-first Century Terrorism* (New York: Prentice Hall 96), pp. v–18.
139. F. Gregory Ga III, "Can Democracy Stop Terrorism?" *Foreign Affairs*, Vol. 84, No. 5 (September/October 20 pp. 62–76.

Correspondence

What Makes Terrorists Tick

Erica Chenoweth, Nicholas Miller, and Elizabeth McClellan
Hillel Frisch
Paul Staniland
Max Abrahms

To the Editors (Erica Chenoweth, Nicholas Miller, and Elizabeth McClellan write):

Max Abrahms's article "What Terrorists Really Want: Terrorist Motives and Counterterrorism Strategy" is a welcome critique of the many points taken for granted by rational choice interpretations of terrorist group behavior.[1] His systematic review of the observable implications of rational choice perspectives on terrorism reveals some of the important shortfalls in the current literature. Abrahms overreaches, however, in rejecting strategic models of terrorism without providing ample empirical evidence or qualifications to his claims.

Abrahms presents seven "puzzling" tendencies of terrorist organizations as anomalies for the strategic model. We argue, however, that a strategic perspective can account for these anomalous behaviors when one examines the group's internal dynamics—particularly the relationship between the group's leadership and its constituents—which may require scholars to consider this level of analysis to explain terrorist group behavior. We consider each of Abrahms's puzzles in turn.

Erica Chenoweth is Assistant Professor of Government at Wesleyan University. Nicholas Miller is an undergraduate Government major at Wesleyan. Elizabeth McClellan is an undergraduate Comparative Government and Studio Art double major at Wesleyan. For a longer, more detailed version of this letter, see Erica Chenoweth's website, http://wesfiles.wesleyan.edu/home/echenoweth/web/home.htm.

Hillel Frisch is Associate Professor in the Departments of Political Studies and Middle East History at Bar-Ilan University. He thanks Stuart Cohen, Efraim Inbar, and Gordon McCormick for their helpful comments.

Paul Staniland is a Ph.D. candidate in the Department of Political Science and member of the Security Studies Program at the Massachusetts Institute of Technology, and a Research Fellow at the Belfer Center for Science and International Affairs in the Harvard Kennedy School at Harvard University. The author would like to thank Brendan Green, Vipin Narang, Joshua Rovner, and Cyrus Samii for helpful comments.

Max Abrahms is a Social Science Predoctoral Fellow in the Center for International Security and Cooperation at Stanford University, and a Ph.D. candidate in the Department of Political Science at the University of California, Los Angeles. He would like to thank Mia Bloom, Martha Crenshaw, Matthew Gottfried, Peter Krause, Jessica Stern, Paul Stockton, and Robbie Totten for their helpful comments. He is especially grateful to Richard English for sharing his expertise over the years on the Irish Republican Army.

1. Max Abrahms, "What Terrorists Really Want: Terrorist Motives and Counterterrorism Strategy," *International Security*, Vol. 32, No. 4 (Spring 2008), pp. 78–105. Further references to this article appear parenthetically in the text.

International Security, Vol. 33, No. 4 (Spring 2009), pp. 180–202

PUZZLE #1: COEI VE INEFFECTIVENESS

Abrahms's argu ent that terrorism is ineffective, and therefore not rational, has two main fl 's. First, by relying on the State Department's current list of foreign terroris rganizations, Abrahms misses the large number of terrorist groups that hav eased to exist and inherently selects groups that are still operating precisel because they have not yet achieved their goals. Seth Jones and Martin Lib i have found that since 1968, 268 terrorist groups have disbanded and an ditional 136 have splintered into other violent groups.[2] Indeed, Jones anc ibicki found that 27 groups disbanded after achieving their goals, for a succ rate of 10 percent.[3] Although not an overly impressive rate, there is a critica ifference between never succeeding and succeeding one out of ten times wh an organization surveys its strategic options.

Second, Abra s does not explore alternative measures and perceptions of success upon w h terrorist organizations may rely. There may not be a clear causal link betw n the terrorist campaign and the realization of the organization's goals, bu leaders perceive that terrorism can be successful relative to other alternativ then choosing terrorism is rational. This is an issue that Robert Pape ad esses in his discussion of suicide terrorism, noting that "in this search for effective strategy, coercers' assessments are likely to be largely a functi of estimates of the success of past efforts; for suicide terrorists, this means essments of whether past suicide campaigns produced significant concess s."[4] Because it is often ambiguous whether a government's decisions are dr n by terrorism or unrelated factors, it is rational to consider terrorism succe ul as long as this interpretation is "shared by a significant portion of othe bservers."[5] For instance, Abrahms was probably right that the 2004 Madri bombings had a "questionable" effect on the results of the Spanish electio and Spain's subsequent withdrawal of its military forces from Iraq. But m y observers have interpreted these outcomes as examples of terrorist success an opinion likely shared by many terrorists and leaders who are contemplat adopting a terrorist strategy.[6] Many terrorist leaders cite prominent exan es of perceived terrorist successes in explaining their tactics,

2. Seth G. Jones an Martin C. Libicki, *How Terrorist Groups End: Lessons for Countering al Qa'ida* (Washington, D.C.: ND, 2008), p. 19.
3. Ibid.
4. Robert A. Pape, e Strategic Logic of Suicide Terrorism," *American Political Science Review*, Vol. 97, No. 3 (Aug 2003), pp. 343–361, at p. 350.
5. Ibid., p. 351.
6. Max Abrahms, W am Rose, and Rysia Murphy, "Correspondence: Does Terrorism Ever Work? The 2004 Madrid T Bombings," *International Security*, Vol. 32, No. 1 (Spring 2007), pp. 185–192. p. 189.

whether they refer to Irgun, Hezbollah, the African National Congress (ANC), the Tamil Tigers, or al-Qaida.[7]

PUZZLE #2: TERRORISM AS THE FIRST RESORT

Abrahms argues that "terrorist groups do not embrace terrorism as a last resort and seldom elect to abandon the armed struggle to become nonviolent political parties," and that this undermines the strategic model (p. 84). But the strategic model does not require groups to adopt a number of other alternatives before adopting terrorism. They only consider other alternatives and decide that terrorism is the optimal strategy. This was the case with the ANC, which "considered four types of violent activities" before judging that "open revolution was inconceivable."[8] That terrorists' assessments are rarely correct or justifiable does not mean that they have made a priori irrational choices.

Furthermore, Abrahms's assertion that terrorist groups rarely transform into "nonviolent political parties" is empirically weak. Jones and Libicki found that the most common way for terrorist groups to end was by joining the political process—either through a peace settlement with the government and abandonment of violence or through "civic action" in the absence of an explicit agreement.[9] Of 268 groups that have ended since 1968 without splintering, 114 (or 43 percent) did so by entering nonviolent politics in one way or another.[10] Examples include the Irish Republican Army (IRA), the Farabundo Martí National Liberation Front in El Salvador, and the Mozambican National Resistance.[11]

Even if such empirics were absent, Abrahms's claim that terrorist groups "toil alongside peaceful parties" and "sabotage open elections that would have yielded major political gains for the group" is not a disconfirmation of the strategic model (p. 85). Just because political parties with the same general ideology gain power does not suggest that extremist groups will be satisfied. Indeed, slight variations in political agendas may give the groups sufficient reason to remain dubious about the parties' intentions and capabilities to address group grievances. For instance, Abrahms uses the Italian left-wing

7. For a collection of original terrorist documents, see Walter Laqueur, ed., *Voices of Terror: Manifestos, Writings, and Manuals of al-Qaeda, Hamas, and Other Terrorists from around the World throughout the Ages* (New York: Sourcebooks, 2005). See, for instance, excerpts of Ayman al-Zawahiri's "Knights under the Prophet's Banner," pp. 426–433.
8. Nelson Mandela, *Long Walk to Freedom: The Autobiography of Nelson Mandela* (Boston: Little, Brown, 1994), p. 240.
9. Jones and Libicki, *How Terrorist Groups End*, pp. 20–22.
10. Ibid., p. 19.
11. Ibid., pp. 22–23.

terrorists of th 970s as an example of this phenomenon. These terrorists, however, view the Italian Communist Party as having sold out to the Christian Dem ıts to form a governing coalition, especially when grievances about labor an vages were not immediately satisfied.[12] Once these grievances were add ssed, members of the groups became introspective.[13] Effective counterter ism policies subsequently brought the terrorist groups to their demise.

PUZZLE #3: REFL VELY UNCOMPROMISING TERRORISTS

There are at lea hree problems with Abrahms's claim that terrorists' unwillingness to com omise with governments undermines the strategic model. First, some terr st groups have attempted to compromise by declaring unilateral cease-fir as the Basque terrorist group ETA did in 2006. As mentioned above, since 19 43 percent of terrorist groups have ended by entering the political proces often due to negotiations.[14]

Second, failin o compromise is not in itself evidence of irrationality. Terrorist groups ma ave extreme aims that preclude compromise. Jones and Libicki's findin support this claim, as groups with limited aims were far more likely to ounce violence and enter politics.[15] Furthermore, although Abrahms claim at "many terrorist organizations profess surprisingly moderate political itions" such as separatism and self-determination, he does not acknowled hat these "moderate political positions" often seem extreme to the governm s that terrorists are targeting (p. 86). Historical instances of states willingly rrendering control over territory are rare indeed, especially in the absence a protracted struggle.

Even among rorists with limited goals, there are strategic reasons to be uncompromisi and to attack at seemingly counterproductive times. These reasons includ utbidding among groups,[16] suspicions about the government's credibil [17] and the number of combatant groups—in nearly every case of the un promising terrorists mentioned in this section, other rival

12. Donatella della rta, "Left-wing Terrorism in Italy," in Martha Crenshaw, ed., *Terrorism in Context* (University rk: Penn State University Press), pp. 105–159.
13. Erica Chenowe "The Inadvertent Effects of Democracy on Terrorist Group Proliferation," Ph.D. dissertation, versity of Colorado, Boulder, 2007, pp. 175–245.
14. Jones and Libic *How Terrorist Groups End*, p. 18.
15. Ibid., p. 20.
16. Mia Bloom, *Dy to Kill: The Allure of Suicide Terror* (New York: Columbia University Press, 2005).
17. Dan Reiter, "E ring the Bargaining Model of War," *Perspectives on Politics*, Vol. 1, No. 1 (March 2003), pp. 3.

terrorist groups existed. Terrorist groups may attempt to hold peace processes hostage (e.g., Real IRA Omagh bombing in 1998) because they are dubious of their competitors' abilities to extract sufficient concessions rather than "selling out," or because holding out for the end of the peace talks may enable the group to extract more concessions.[18]

Third, Abrahms does not address the role of the government in negotiations with terrorist groups. In addition to all of the standard difficulties with negotiations (e.g., cheating, indivisibility, and domestic pressures), negotiating with terrorists can pose further challenges to the state. In fact, Peter Neumann notes that most governments are reflexively uncompromising toward terrorists.[19] As Abrahms argues previously, "Target countries view the negative consequences of terrorist attacks on their societies and political systems as evidence that the terrorists want them destroyed. Target countries are understandably skeptical that making concessions will placate terrorist groups believed to be motivated by these maximalist objectives."[20] If he is right, governments will hesitate to compromise with terrorists who target civilians because they infer from their tactics that their extreme goals preclude a settlement. This indeed seems plausible, but it demands qualification from Abrahms's later claim of "reflexively uncompromising terrorists" (pp. 85–87). If governments are generally unwilling to make concessions to terrorist groups, then it is inaccurate to blame terrorists solely for failing to reach compromises with the government.

PUZZLE #4: PROTEAN POLITICAL PLATFORMS

Abrahms argues that the tendency of terrorist groups to change their goals over time refutes strategic models of terrorism. Changing stated platforms, however, is not a disconfirmation of the strategic model, especially when one relaxes the assumption that terrorist groups are unitary actors.

Terrorist groups may "make up" political goals to survive because, at the group level of analysis, survival may be a stable preference over time. According to Daniel Byman, "Over 90 percent of terrorist groups do not survive their first year,"[21] while those that do survive have flexible organizational structures and are able to remain discrete. Terrorist organizations that do not place a high

18. David E. Cunningham, "Veto Players and Civil War Duration," *American Journal of Political Science*, Vol. 50, No. 4 (September 2006), pp. 875–892.
19. Peter Neumann, "Negotiating with Terrorists," *Foreign Affairs*, Vol. 86, No. 1 (January/February 2007), pp. 128–138.
20. Max Abrahms, "Why Terrorism Does Not Work," *International Security*, Vol. 31, No. 2 (Fall 2006), p. 59.
21. Daniel Byman, *Deadly Connections: States That Sponsor Terrorism* (Cambridge: Cambridge University Press, 2005), p. 63.

priority on grou maintenance are likely to dissolve, so leaders may sacrifice some stated ain or the benefits of flexibility and continuity. For instance, because joining a rrorist group is often an irreversible decision, the group's leadership may vent new causes to appease their most devoted members, donors, and sp ors (pp. 86–89). Indeed, remaining united may be the only alternative for ne terrorists given the high costs of exit.

PUZZLE #5: ANO MOUS ATTACKS

Abrahms argu that terrorists often do not claim responsibility for their attacks, and tha is strategy is illogical because it "pre[cludes] even the possibility of succes l coercion" (p. 90). There are numerous strategic explanations, however, r this behavior.

First, one of e major goals of terrorist violence—to provoke a disproportionate gov nment reaction to the violence—is often best served through anony us attacks that provoke the government into cracking down on the pulation indiscriminately.[22] If this is part of the terrorist group's intenti , then claiming attacks is unnecessary and may even be counterproduct .

A strategy of iling may also be effectively carried out anonymously.[23] If a country seeks t argain with moderates on terms that are unacceptable to terrorist organizat s, the organizations may have strategic interests in disrupting the talks. A nymous attacks may even be more effective at disrupting negotiations be se they create suspicion that the moderates themselves may support terrori

Anonymity also protect terrorist organizations from loss of popular support. An ira ublic may be more likely to back fierce government retaliation through v le counterterrorist responses.[24] Mia Bloom, for instance, has documente number of unclaimed attacks that groups avoid claiming because of neg e public reactions.[25] On the other hand, highly visible public actions can liver recruits and resources. Correspondingly, sometimes multiple group aim an attack after their constituents respond favorably to

22. Andrew H. Ky nd Barbara F. Walter, "The Strategies of Terrorism," *International Security,* Vol. 31, No. 1 (Sun r 2006), pp. 49–79.
23. Ibid.
24. James D. Fearo Domestic Political Audiences and the Escalation of International Disputes," *American Political S e Review,* Vol. 88, No. 3 (September 1994), pp. 577–592; and Max Abrahms, "Why Democracies ke Superior Counterterrorists," *Security Studies,* Vol. 16, No. 2 (April–June 2007), pp. 223–253.
25. Bloom, *Dying t ll.*

it.[26] Because of the uncertainty of the public response, anonymity can help terrorist groups survive unpopular miscalculations.

PUZZLE #6: TERRORIST FRATRICIDE

Abrahms claims that the strategic model cannot explain why "organizations purporting to fight for a common cause frequently attack each other more than their mutually declared enemy" (p. 90). On the contrary, "liquidating" groups with similar ideologies is rational given that the groups are competing for the same "market share" of recruits, sponsorship, sympathy, and attention.[27] The Tamil Tigers viciously pursued rivals in the early years and have evolved to be the hegemonic violent nationalist movement in Tamil Eelam. Consequently, the Tamil Tigers have become synonymous with the Tamil nationalist movement, so that governments are unable to address policy issues regarding Tamil Eelam without considering the Liberation Tigers of Tamil Eelam. The National Liberation Front in Algeria also dominated its competition and eventually negotiated the terms of the French departure.[28] From a strategic standpoint, establishing dominance enables a group to control the terms of negotiation if it reaches negotiations with the government.

Regardless, terrorists spend less time attacking their rivals than they do their primary opponents. According to Christopher Hewitt, fratricidal attacks in the United States account for only 17 percent of terrorist activities, whereas terrorist targets are linked to stated aims more than 65 percent of the time.[29] In fact, terrorist fratricide would be more puzzling from the perspective of natural systems theory, where terrorist recruits seek camaraderie and companionship through social solidarity within a violent group. Attacking colleagues with similar political platforms inside or outside the group may not necessarily serve this goal either. Such behavior can be attributed to strategic calculations of relative gain and loss and, therefore, conforms more to strategic models than Abrahms suggests.

PUZZLE #7: NEVER-ENDING TERRORISM

Abrahms argues that the persistence of terrorist groups after their stated aims have become obsolete challenges the strategic model. Importantly, however, re-

26. Ibid.
27. Ibid.
28. Martha Crenshaw, "The Effectiveness of Terrorism in the Algerian War," in Crenshaw, *Terrorism in Context*, pp. 473–513, at pp. 511–513.
29. Christopher Hewitt, *Understanding Terrorism in America: From the Klan to al Qaeda* (New York: Routledge, 2003), pp. 66–67.

searchers at RA[illegible] found that 404 terrorist groups have ended since 1968; 136 of these splintered [illegible]o other terrorist groups, and 268 have renounced violence.[30]

CONCLUSION

Although his ar[illegible]e is an important, insightful, and creative critique, Abrahms goes too far in r[illegible]cting strategic models of terrorism. The puzzles that he presents are not pu[illegible]es for the strategic model. Instead, these anomalies are opportunities to [illegible]ineate the levels of analysis at which rational behavior is failing. What i[illegible]ational for a terrorist recruit may not be rational for the group's leader[illegible]p, and vice versa. Abrahms's alternative to the strategic model—natura[illegible]stems theory—concerns only the individual's incentives for joining a group [illegible]atural systems theory does not describe how terrorist leaders organize, ap[illegible]y ideology, and select strategy, but rather deals exclusively with foot soldie[illegible] Abrahms may be right that the strategic model does not adequately addre[illegible]he interests of the rank-and-file (p. 95). But it may be necessary to apply t[illegible] strategic model to the internal dynamics of the groups by disaggregating [illegible]ot soldiers from strategists rather than rejecting the model outright.

Abrahms's m[illegible]n contribution may be to explain the types of individuals who are attract[illegible] to terrorist groups—in other words, how the preferences of terrorist recruit[illegible]rm. His article reinforces this need to reconsider the unitary actor assumpti[illegible]n rational choice models, which may provide many fruitful avenues for fu[illegible]e research.[31] Indeed, strategic models and natural systems theory can be c[illegible]plementary, particularly if they unify the different levels of analysis discus[illegible] above. But at the level of the group's strategy, the natural systems perspe[illegible]ve does not outperform the strategic model in generating a unique set of p[illegible]ictions that enhance scholars' theoretical understandings or policy choices.

—*Erica Chenoweth*
Middletown, Connecticut

—*Nicholas Miller*
Middletown, Connecticut

—*Elizabeth McClellan*
Middletown, Connecticut

30. Jones and Libic[illegible] *How Terrorist Groups End*, p. 19.
31. For one such [illegible]plication, see Wendy Pearlman, "Fragmentation and Violence: Internal Influences on Tacti[illegible] the Case of the Palestinian National Movement, 1920–2006," Ph.D. dissertation, Harvard Un[illegible]rsity, 2007.

To the Editors (Hillel Frisch writes):

Max Abrahms's article "What Terrorists Really Want: Terrorist Motives and Counterterrorism Strategy" constitutes a well-written, thought-provoking critique of the assumption that terrorist groups are strategic in their pursuit of political goals and hence amenable to political concessions.[1] Nevertheless, the evidence Abrahms presents to support his argument, his alternative explanation for why terrorists pursue terrorism, and the policy implications he draws from his analysis are all open to question.

Abrahms claims that members of terrorist organizations are motivated primarily by the quest for social solidarity rather than by the desire to achieve clearly defined political goals. As Gordon McCormick notes, however, the truth is that there are movements that are either strategic or motivated by social solidarity, or both: "Terrorist groups, in this respect—as in many others—are not created equal. Nor is their behavior necessarily consistent over the course of their operational life. Some (otherwise distinctive) groups, such as the contemporary Irish Republican Army (IRA), al-Qaeda, Hamas, and the Tamil Tigers, have largely managed to subordinate their actions to their political objectives. . . . Others, such as the late November 17, the Popular Forces of 25 April, the Justice Commandos of the Armenian Genocide, or any number of today's 'amateur' terrorists, have effectively subordinated their political objectives to their need to act."[2] Albert Camus, in his intriguing play on a Russian terrorist cell in 1905, *The Just Assassins,* effectively demonstrates this duality down to the level of the two main characters, Stephan and Yanek.[3]

A more serious problem is Abrahms's assumption that the behavior of terrorist organizations is irrational and therefore a puzzle for the strategic paradigm. Take, for example, his puzzle that "terrorist organizations with identical political platforms routinely attack each other more than their mutually professed enemy" (p. 82). Is this indeed irrational, nonstrategic behavior? Not when one considers that most terrorist movements have two basic objectives: to wring concessions from the government but, no less, to achieve hegemony in the rebel camp. Movements such as Fatah, for example, not only strive to

1. Max Abrahms, "What Terrorists Really Want: Terrorist Motives and Counterterrorism Strategy," *International Security,* Vol. 32, No. 4 (Spring 2008), pp. 78–105. Additional references to this article appear parenthetically in the text.
2. Gordon H. McCormick, "Terrorist Decision Making," *Annual Review of Political Science,* Vol. 6 (June 2003), p. 480.
3. See David C. Rapoport, "Inside Terrorist Organizations," in Rapoport, ed., *Inside Terrorist Organizations* (New York: Columbia University Press, 1988), p. 2.

gain independe e; they also aim to constitute the government of the future state. This is w so many "wars of national liberation" are also civil wars. Therefore, "frat ide" is often motivated by strategic thinking, as the recent struggle for dor iance between Hamas and Fatah over control of the Palestinian Authority (I suggests. Prior to their brief civil war, the Fatah Tanzim and the al-Aqsa Ma rs Brigade undermined PA institutions to correct what activists from the "ir le" (i.e., those who fought the Israelis while the PLO leadership was far av y in Tunis) felt was an unfair share of positions of power allocated to the with the establishment of the Palestinian Authority in 1994. Regarding al-Q la, since 2003, at least, it has almost exclusively targeted states with a r tary presence in Iraq, demonstrating its strategic motivations.[4] The Afr n National Congress employed terrorism only late in its struggle agains he white government of South Africa, effectively refuting Abrahms's clai that terrorist organizations never use terrorism as a last resort.

Whether terr st organizations can be assumed to be nonstrategic because of changing pr an political platforms can also be questioned. One wonders whether the po cal platforms of terrorist groups are more protean than those of regular polit l parties or movements. The Basque, Fatah, and PKK terrorist movements ift in their political objectives according to calculations of what is achiev e, similar to the mainstream Zionist political movement, which did not e age in terrorism. Although Theodor Herzl, who founded the World Zionist C anization, wrote about Jewish statehood even before the creation of the Zic st movement, statehood was never mentioned again as the movement's go by mainstream Zionists at least until the Holocaust. The reason was becaus he leadership believed that disclosure of its ultimate objective of a Jewish ite was not politically expedient. A terrorist movement that ratchets up its jective from achieving autonomy to statehood or ratchets down its dema s from statehood to autonomy might be making a rational (re)assessment ween its goals and its capabilities relative to those of the state. Yasir Ara for example, accepted the autonomy plan in 1993, to which he had been bit ly opposed for more than twenty years, when he signed the Declaration of rinciples along with Prime Minister Yitzhak Rabin on the White Hous awn, for fear that Israel might make a deal with the leadership within the rritories. Hamas prefers controlling Gaza compared to the

4. Robert A. Pape, *ig to Win: The Strategic Logic of Suicide Terrorism* (New York: Random House, 2005), p. 57.

much smaller probability that it would be allowed to build a radical Islamist Palestinian state. In short, terrorist movements can be strategic even when changing their political platforms over time.[5]

Abrahms also conflates the motivations of terrorists with those of the movement's leadership. Just as techniques used to motivate individual soldiers or small units do not necessarily reflect the strategic objectives of the national and military leadership, neither can one necessarily assume correspondence between the factors motivating terrorists and the strategic objectives of the terrorist movement. Terrorists might indeed join the movement in search of companionship, as Abrahms suggests, but this hardly reflects on the strategic goals of the movement itself.

Equally problematic is Abrahms's proposal that the social model is more relevant than the strategic model when assessing terrorists' motivations. If indeed "terrorists are rational people who use terrorism primarily to develop strong affective ties with fellow terrorists," collective terrorism should be more prevalent in Western states, as alienated individuals seek friendship and social interaction (p. 80). Nor can the social model account for why, in the Palestinian political-terrorist arena, organizations such as the Abu Nidal Organization and the Popular Front for the Liberation of Palestine–General Command pursued violence at all costs, whereas the Fatah mainstream movement sharply reduced its terrorist activity during the Oslo years (1994–2000) and then returned to it with a vengeance once the al-Aqsa intifada broke out. Abrahms's explanation might account for why the Abu Nidals of the world exist (although even Abrahms concedes that they became guns for hire and thus might have been acting strategically, assuming the alternative would have meant a life sentence), but it cannot account for why Fatah, the dominant group in the Palestinian arena for decades, was strategic. Even in the life cycle of a single terrorist group, the salience of visceral psychological or social explanations might vary over time. Forty years ago, Fatah members were heavily influenced by Franz Fanon's thesis of violence as catharsis. Fanon's name and his legacy find almost no echo in more recent Fatah writings.

Instead of seeking to determine whether the strategic model or the social/psychological paradigm is correct—they are both right in the sense that some

5. Harvey Kushner, *Terrorism in America: A Structured Approach to Understanding the Terrorist Threat* (New York: Charles and Thomas, 1998), pp. 81–83. See also Leonard Weinberg and William Lee Eubank, "Cultural Differences in the Behavior of Terrorists," *Terrorism and Political Violence*, Vol. 6, No. 1 (Spring 1994), pp. 6–8.

organizations a ccording to the expectations of the strategic model and others because of ial/psychological expectations—scholars should be asking why some orga ations seem to be more strategic and others less so or not at all.

An initial ex nation can be derived from the works of Barry Collins and Harold Guetzk as well as Martha Crenshaw.[6] These scholars observed that, as movements deeper underground, the "interpersonal" rewards of group membership be ne more important than the strategic goals of their political mission. One w ld assume that as long as organizations are able to grow more politicall lient, they will maintain or cultivate a strategy to achieve definable politi goals. Conversely, failure, setback, or prolonged marginality will make orga ations less strategic, as their immediate social environment overwhelms th . The seeds of a competing argument to that proposed by Abrahms may e emerged. Abrahms argues that it is the quest for affective ties that drives rorist organizations, whereas this alternative explanation is based on the pr ise that it is the competitive environment between terrorists and governme nd the relative success achieved by the terrorists over time that predicts h strategic or nonstrategic they may become. This is only one of many poten alternative explanations, however. What is important is the need to tak p the challenge to explain the puzzle of why some terrorist organizatio eem to be strategic, others not, and still others seem to be both over diffe t time periods. One can then tease out the policy implications of the fi gs for conflict resolution or, short of that, for successful counterinsurge .

Abrahms has ade a valuable contribution to explaining why some terrorist organizations a not necessarily motivated by political goals, and many more at some time d g their life cycles. The puzzle of why this is true of some organizations mo f the time, or most organizations some of the time, remains a challenge tha udents of terrorism should endeavor to meet.

—*Hillel Frisch*
Ramat Gan, Israel

6. Barry E. Collins d Harold Guetzkow, *The Social Psychology of Group Processes for Decision Making* (New York: n Wiley and Sons, 1964); and Martha Crenshaw, "An Organizational Approach to the Anal of Political Terrorism," *Orbis*, Vol. 29, No. 3 (Fall 1985), pp. 465–489. These works are analyze McCormick, "Terrorist Decision Making," p. 489.

To the Editors (Paul Staniland writes):

In "What Terrorists Really Want: Terrorist Motives and Counterterrorism Strategy,"[1] Max Abrahms argues that terrorists are "social solidarity maximizers" (p. 101), rather than strategic political actors, meaning that individuals join terrorist groups "to develop strong affective ties with other terrorists" (p. 96). As a result, terrorist groups "routinely engage in actions to perpetuate and justify their existence, even when these undermine their official political agendas" (pp. 101–102). Abrahms argues that the seven predictions of the natural systems model find support in "the preponderance of theoretical and empirical evidence" (p. 103).

Abrahms makes a valuable contribution to scholars' understanding of terrorism. His argument, however, has significant theoretical and empirical shortcomings. I focus on three issues: the diverse motivations of individual participants, armed group elites' use of organizations to shape the actions of foot soldiers, and the behavior of terrorist organizations in Northern Ireland and Sri Lanka, two cases that Abrahms repeatedly refers to in support of his claims.

THE MULTIPLE LOGICS OF PARTICIPATION IN MILITANCY

Research on civil wars suggests that it is impossible to offer a single answer to the question, "What do terrorists want?"[2] This work shows that there is no dominant logic of participation in militancy. In a study of combatants in Sierra Leone's civil war, Macartan Humphreys and Jeremy Weinstein find that "different logics of participation may coexist in a single war."[3] Social sanction, grievances, and selective incentives all provided motivation to join. Stathis Kalyvas and Ana Arjona's survey of former combatants in the Colombian civil

1. Max Abrahms, "What Terrorists Really Want: Terrorist Motives and Counterterrorism Strategy," *International Security*, Vol. 32, No. 4 (Spring 2008), pp. 78–105. Further references to this article appear parenthetically in the text.
2. It is possible that insurgent groups differ from purely terrorist groups; indeed Abrahms draws such a distinction on page 83 of his article. Still, he repeatedly references insurgents such as the Tamil Tigers; Hezbollah; PKK; Hamas; Afghan, Iraqi, and Chechen guerrillas; and FARC in support of his argument. Thus there does not appear to be an empirically relevant distinction. There are few major organizations that do not kill both civilians and agents of the state.
3. Macartan Humphreys and Jeremy M. Weinstein, "Who Fights? The Determinants of Participation in Civil War," *American Journal of Political Science*, Vol. 52, No. 2 (April 2008), p. 437.

war reveals tha evenge, ideology, and material rewards were the dominant motivations for rticipation.[4]

Qualitative fi work makes similar points. Lucian Pye explores the varied reasons people ned communist guerrilla groups in Malaya.[5] Elisabeth Wood highlights mult e mechanisms that encourage participation, particularly oppressive state p cy and the pleasure of agency.[6] Weinstein's work on insurgent organizati suggests at least two types of participants—investors and consumers.[7] Ro r Petersen's study of insurgent mobilization reveals several mechanisms th ncourage participation, including community norms, rational calculations sychological hopes, and a lack of other options.[8]

ELITE GOALS AN ORGANIZATIONAL CONTROL

Abrahms assun that individuals' motives for joining a group determine the goals and actio of the organization. The problem with this assumption is that insurgent e es often have political goals distinct from foot soldiers' varied motivations lites use organizational mechanisms to bring cadre behavior in line with lea rship aims.

For instance, cruits joined the Provisional Irish Republican Army (PIRA) for many reas (though only after the political crisis of the late 1960s). PIRA's ranks ir ided thugs, intellectuals, ordinary people, criminals, Marxists, Catholics, l dozens of other types of individuals.[9] But throughout the conflict, the PIR leadership pursued the political goal of unifying Ireland by calibrating offe ves, strategizing about how to use the Sinn Féin political party, negotiati with other parties and the British government, and finally agreeing to a p ical settlement and disbandment. The leadership used coercion, material r rds, persuasion, and social pressures to largely keep its cadres in line, rega less of their original motivations for joining.[10]

---

4. Stathis Kalyvas Ana Arjona, "Preliminary Results of a Survey of Demobilized Combatants in Colombia," unp shed paper, Yale University, 2006.
5. Lucian Pye, *Gu a Communism in Malaya: Its Social and Political Meaning* (Princeton, N.J.: Princeton Universi ress, 1956).
6. Elisabeth Jean W l, *Insurgent Collective Action and Civil War in El Salvador* (Cambridge: Cambridge University s, 2003).
7. Jeremy M. Wein n, *Inside Rebellion: The Politics of Insurgent Violence* (Cambridge: Cambridge University Press, 2 .
8. Roger D. Peterse *Resistance and Rebellion: Lessons from Eastern Europe* (Cambridge: Cambridge University Press, 2 .
9. Eamon Collins p ides an inside picture of the range of personalities in the PIRA. See Collins with Mick McGov *Killing Rage* (London: Granta, 1998).
10. Rogelio Alonso hlights "internal repression" as central to PIRA operations. See Alonso, *The IRA and Armed Str e* (London: Routledge, 2007), especially pp. 3–4.

Foot soldiers similarly end up in the Liberation Tigers of Tamil Eelam (LTTE, or Tamil Tigers) through numerous mechanisms, but the core leadership has resolutely pursued the goal of an independent Eelam despite heterogeneous cadre-level motivations. Some foot soldiers were abducted as children; others fervently believe in the need for a Tamil state; others are in thrall to the personality cult of LTTE leader Velupillai Prabhakaran; others need a job; still others joined after seeing their mothers raped by soldiers.[11] The Tigers' leadership has harnessed these diverse motivations toward a consistent separatist goal.

Abrahms emphasizes organization theory, but he does not deal with the vast literature on the control, indoctrination, and incentives that leaders use to create coordinated outcomes from disparate individuals.[12] The Tigers and PIRA are fundamentally political, not affective. In the next section I show that both groups' leaders have used their organizational control to pursue strategic and political goals.[13]

HOW DO ARMED GROUPS BEHAVE?

Below I briefly survey the accuracy of Abrahms's seven predictions of group behavior. I find little support for his argument in Northern Ireland and Sri Lanka, where I have done detailed field research on armed groups. The failure of the natural systems model to illuminate these cases casts doubt on its broader accuracy. I focus on the Provisional IRA and LTTE but also discuss the other major groups in each war.

Abrahms's first prediction is that armed groups "prolong their existence by relying on a strategy that hardens target governments from making policy concessions" (p. 102). By contrast, the LTTE has repeatedly brought the government of Sri Lanka to the negotiating table. It won some concessions from the government in 1989–90 and 2002, though neither set of concessions went far enough for the Tigers. The PIRA extracted concessions from the British and then disbanded. There is little evidence that either group intentionally stopped the government from making concessions that it believed would advance its

11. A knowledgeable aid worker in Sri Lanka listed six major motivations for individuals to join the Tigers, in addition to forced conscription. Interview by author, Colombo, March 2008.

12. A pioneering study is Nathan Leites and Charles Wolf Jr., *Rebellion and Authority: An Analytical Essay on Insurgent Conflicts* (Chicago: Markham, 1970).

13. Between 1923 and 1968, the IRA was a peripheral and largely inactive organization. The LTTE was formed in 1972, the other Tamil militant groups between 1975 and 1980; major combat did not occur until 1983. It is hard to understand how the quest for affective ties explains this over-time variation, unless there were no socially alienated single males in these societies prior to the late 1960s. This seems unlikely. Abrahms is trying to explain a variable with a constant.

strategic goal. C ıflicts endured because of fluctuating power and distrust between the state ıd its foe.

This is also tı of the other armed groups. In Northern Ireland, the Official IRA (OIRA) un terally declared a cease-fire in 1972 despite the absence of concessions, an he Ulster Volunteer Force (UVF) signed on to the 1998 Good Friday agreeme In Sri Lanka the other major Tamil militant groups—Eelam People's Revol onary Liberation Front (EPRLF), Tamil Eelam Liberation Organization (T .O), Eelam Revolutionary Organization of Students (EROS), and People's L ration Organization of Tamil Eelam (PLOT)—all agreed to the 1987 Indo-L ka accord.[14]

Abrahms's s nd prediction is that armed groups "ensure their continued viability by resi ng opportunities to peacefully participate in the democratic process" (p. 102 Cross-national research casts doubt on this claim.[15] Northern Ireland's histor is similarly disconfirming. The PIRA's Sinn Féin political wing has enga l in the democratic process and now shares power in the Northern Irelaı Assembly. The OIRA entered mainstream politics as the Workers' Party. e UVF declared a cease-fire in 1994 and put forward the Progressive Union Party as its electoral face. In Sri Lanka, EPRLF, PLOT, and TELO all agree to lay down their arms and entered the democratic mainstream via the 1 7 Indo-Lanka accord. Even after rearming during 1987–90 to protect themsel , EPRLF and TELO are now unarmed parties that regularly contest election The armed parties keep their weapons to protect themselves from the Tigers who have deemed them political traitors.[16]

Abrahms's t d prediction is that armed groups "avoid disbanding by reflexively rejec g negotiated settlements that offer significant policy concessions" (p. 102). Northern Ireland, the PIRA and the OIRA have disbanded, and the UVF is the process of doing so. The Irish National Liberation Army (INLA) and Uls Defence Association (UDA) remain intact, but have become fractious drug ılers, not seekers of social solidarity.

In Sri Lanka, 'RLF, TELO, and a faction of EROS have disbanded as combatants. Group ıat have not disbanded have plausible strategic rationales.

---

14. M.R. Narayan ımy, *Tigers of Lanka: From Boys to Guerrillas* (Delhi: Konark, 1994), pp. 240–250.

15. Abrahms asser "No peace process has transformed a major terrorist organization into a completely nonviol political party" (p. 86). A study of 648 terrorist groups between 1968 and 2006, however, reve that "a transition to the political process is the most common way in which terrorist groups en (43 percent)." Seth G. Jones and Martin C. Libicki, *How Terrorist Groups End: Lessons for Counter l Qa'ida* (Washington, D.C.: RAND, 2008), p. xiii.

16. There are three -state Tamil armed groups that contest elections: the PLOT, the Eelam People's Democratic P (EPDP), and Tamil Makkal Viduthalaip Puligal (TMVP).

The LTTE does not trust a Sinhalese-dominated government to deliver on the terms of a settlement, much less grant independence. PLOT, EPDP, and TMVP remain armed to protect themselves and reap rewards from extortion.[17]

Abrahms's fourth prediction is that armed groups "guarantee their survival by espousing a litany of protean political goals that can never be fully satisfied" (p. 102). Although protean political goals certainly are espoused by some groups around the world, in Northern Ireland and Sri Lanka, organizations have advanced clear separatist goals. The IRA wanted the unification of Ireland—an unlikely goal, but given the history of 1916–22, the isolation of Northern Ireland from the British mainstream, and demographic trends, not unthinkable.[18] The OIRA was willing to settle for democratization and popular participation, and the PIRA showed it would settle for power sharing. The Protestant paramilitaries wanted to maintain union with the United Kingdom.[19] In Sri Lanka, even the hardest-line Tamil groups have sought a straightforward goal—an independent Tamil homeland. As shown in 1987 and since, several Tamil groups have been willing to settle for power devolution.

Abrahms's fifth prediction is that armed groups "avert organization-threatening reprisals by conducting anonymous attacks" (p. 102). In Northern Ireland, the PIRA, OIRA, and INLA often claimed responsibility for their attacks. When they did not, it was because they did not want to lose support or be condemned internationally for an operation that went wrong. The INLA took credit for killing Member of Parliament Airey Neave, but not for the "Darkley massacre." The PIRA tried to distance itself from the Enniskillen bombing, but took credit for bombing Thiepval Barracks.[20] The Protestant paramilitaries claimed responsibility when it suited their purposes. In Sri Lanka in the 1980s, the competition between Tamil groups encouraged them to take credit for attacks. Since the LTTE gained primacy, it has publicized and claimed credit for many of its suicide attacks.

Abrahms's sixth prediction is that armed groups "annihilate ideologically identical terrorist organizations that compete for members" (p. 102). It is un-

17. Human Rights Watch, "Sri Lanka: Political Killings during the Ceasefire," Human Rights News (New York: Human Rights Watch, August 7, 2003), http://hrw.org/backgrounder/asia/srilanka080603.htm.

18. For an analysis, see M.L.R. Smith, *Fighting for Ireland? The Military Strategy of the Irish Republican Movement* (London: Routledge, 1995).

19. Steve Bruce, *The Red Hand: Protestant Paramilitaries in Northern Ireland* (Oxford: Oxford University Press, 1992).

20. The name used to take credit for PIRA attacks was P. O'Neill. After the disastrous Enniskillen bombing (which killed eleven civilians), the PIRA leadership blamed local mistakes by the Fermanagh Brigade.

clear what behа ›r this would refer to in either case. The PIRA was ideologically different f n the OIRA, which it split from in 1969. The Irish National
Liberation Arm differed from the OIRA leadership, resulting in a break in
1974.[21] The PIR espoused a hard-line Irish nationalism, in contrast to the
mass mobilizin 'iolence-averse focus of the OIRA or the far-left vision of the
INLA.[22] These ological differences help to account for why the PIRA and
the INLA broke vay from the OIRA and why the OIRA stopped fighting. Despite feuds betv en these groups, there was no "annihilation."

Abrahms's d ussion of Sri Lanka is empirically suspect. First, he incorrectly claims th he Tamil Tigers "did not target the Sinhalese government in
the mid-1980s" . 90). The LTTE's initial killings in the 1970s targeted pro-
government po cal figures—the mayor of Jaffna in 1975, two policemen in
1977, and two lice inspectors and a member of Parliament in 1978. The
LTTE's June 198 ambush of a convoy in Jaffna, which killed thirteen soldiers,
triggered a maj escalation of violence between the Tigers and the state. The
LTTE did make id for dominance (primarily between April 1986 and March
1987) by target , other groups, but it was simultaneously involved in antigovernment in gency throughout northeastern Sri Lanka. Second, there
were important eological differences among Tamil groups. The LTTE's closest ideological 1 tch was TELO, but it was an Indian proxy army. The LTTE,
by contrast, dis isted the Indian state. PLOT broke away from the LTTE in
part because of OT supporters' left-wing vision of Sinhalese-Tamil cooperation in seeking forge an island-wide revolution.[23] EPRLF and EROS espoused leftist 'ologies and emphasized lower-caste mobilization. These
differences mat ed in the negotiation and (failed) implementation of the
Indo-Lanka acc l of 1987: EPRLF and TELO supported it, the LTTE opposed
it, and PLOT t 1 to remain neutral.[24] The remnants of PLOT and parts of
EPRLF and ER(now support the Sri Lankan government; another faction of
EROS was inte ted into the Tigers.

Abrahms's se nth prediction is that armed groups "refuse to split up after
the armed strug has proven politically unsuccessful for decades or its politi-

21. Jack Holland a Henry McDonald, *INLA: Deadly Divisions* (Dublin: Torc, 1994).
22. Peter Taylor, *Th rovos: The IRA and Sinn Fein* (London: Bloomsbury, 1998); and Richard English, *Armed Struggl ie History of the IRA* (Oxford: Oxford University Press, 2003).
23. For discussion LOT ideology, see Mark P. Whitaker, *Learning Politics from Sivaram: The Life
and Death of a Revo nary Tamil Journalist in Sri Lanka* (London: Pluto, 2007).
24. Rohan Gunarat *Indian Intervention in Sri Lanka: The Role of India's Intelligence Agencies* (Colombo: South Asia etwork on Conflict Research, 1993); and University Teachers for Human
Rights (Jaffna), *Th oken Palmyrah* (Jaffna, Sri Lanka: University Teachers for Human Rights,
1990).

cal rationale has become moot" (p. 102). Contrary to Abrahms's emphasis on social solidarity, most of these organizations have suffered a variety of elite splits and internal conflict over politics and personalities. The origins of PIRA and INLA lie in disagreement with the OIRA leadership over how to respond to sectarian violence in Belfast and Derry.[25] In 1997 the Real IRA broke away from PIRA because of discontent with its growing politicization.[26] The Loyalist Volunteer Force split from the UVF in 1996 in part over the peace process.[27] Splits and clashes within the UDA and INLA have occurred because of personal and criminal rivalries.

In Sri Lanka, the LTTE suffered a major split when its eastern commander, Karuna Amman, broke away in 2004. This split was driven by personal rivalry and disagreement over the desirability of armed struggle.[28] Internal factional struggles within the LTTE occurred in 1980 (leading to PLOT's formation) and the early 1990s. EPRLF broke from EROS in 1980, and the EPDP in turn from the EPRLF in 1987, partly because of disagreements about politics. EROS broke in two in the late 1980s over joining the LTTE. TELO was in the midst of an internal war when targeted by the Tigers in 1986.[29] Given the pervasiveness of intra-organizational splits, feuds, and factionalism, the idea that militants seek Chester Barnard's "condition of communion" (p. 95) is bizarre.

THE COMPLEXITY OF MILITANCY

Rather than apolitical but solidaristic collections of lonely men, many militant groups bear resemblance to militaries and even states—organizationally complex, often internally divided, driven by political goals, and sometimes willing to abandon violence. Individuals join for numerous reasons and, in turn, are shaped by mechanisms of discipline and indoctrination. This does not mean that either militants or armed groups are purely strategic or rational actors, but it does suggest that they are not simplistic solidarity maximizers.

—*Paul Staniland*
Cambridge, Massachusetts

25. Patrick Bishop and Eamon Mallie, *The Provisional IRA* (London: Corgi Books, 1987), pp. 119–138.
26. On the Continuity split, see Robert W. White, *Ruarí Ó Brádaigh: The Life and Politics of an Irish Revolutionary* (Bloomington: Indiana University Press, 2006). On the Real split, see Ed Moloney, *A Secret History of the IRA* (New York: W.W. Norton, 2002), chap. 17; and English, *Armed Struggle*, pp. 316–318.
27. Jim Cusack and Henry McDonald, *UVF* (Dublin: Poolbeg, 1997).
28. "Situation Report: The Rise and Fall of Karuna," *Sunday Times* (Colombo), April 11, 2004.
29. This history is based on Swamy, *Tigers of Lanka*.

Max Abrahm eplies:

I appreciate the oughtful comments of Erica Chenoweth and her coauthors, Paul Staniland, d Hillel Frisch to my recent article, as well as this opportunity to address em.

In my article presented a test of the strategic model, the dominant paradigm in the aca mic and policy communities on terrorist motives, behavior, and counterter sm strategy. This model holds that rational people use terrorism to achie a political return; terrorist groups hence operate as political maximizers; an overnments can therefore combat terrorism by reducing the political utility its practitioners. Contrary to the strategic model, I found that in practice rorist groups engage in seven politically counterproductive behavioral tend cies that perpetuate the existence of the group at the expense of its official pc cal goals. According to the natural systems model in the organization liter re, this behavioral trade-off reveals that members of an organization attach ater importance to its social benefits than to its official ones. I concluded tha terrorists likewise prioritize the social benefits over the political benefits c articipating in terrorist groups, then extant counterterrorism strategies requi reform.[1]

Erica Chenov h, Nicholas Miller, and Elizabeth McClellan raise three main objections to m rgument.[2] First, they claim that my analysis of terrorist motives pertains o to foot soldiers, and not to their leaders. Second, they draw upon a recent R ND study to contest the empirical basis of the seven puzzling terrorist tenden s for the strategic model that I identified.[3] Third, they maintain that these ative puzzles, even if empirically valid, are not evidence of irrationality gi the internal dynamics of terrorist groups. Each objection is misplaced.

First, demog hic studies routinely find that terrorist foot soldiers are motivated by tl ocial—not the political—return.[4] This is consistent with de-

---

1. Max Abrahms, at Terrorists Really Want: Terrorist Motives and Counterterrorism Strategy," *International rity,* Vol. 32, No. 4 (Spring 2008), pp. 78–105.
2. Erica Chenowet icholas Miller, and Elizabeth McClellan, "Correspondence: Politics, Motivation, and Organiza in the Study of Terrorism," *International Security,* Vol. 33, No. 4 (Spring 2009), pp. 180–202.
3. Seth G. Jones ar Iartin C. Libicki, *How Terrorist Groups End: Lessons for Countering al Qa'ida* (Washington, D.C.: ND, 2008).
4. See, for exampl Iarc Sageman, *Understanding Terror Networks* (Philadelphia: University of Pennsylvania Press 04), p. 92; Olivier Roy, "Terrorism and Deculturation," in Louise Richardson, ed., *The Roots errorism* (New York: Routledge, 2006), pp. 159–160; and Joseph Felter and Jarret Brachman, " Assessment of 516 Combatant Status Review Tribunal (CSRT) Unclassified Summaries," CTC ort (West Point, N.Y.: Combating Terrorism Center, July 15, 2007), pp. 24–25, 34.

mographic research on national militaries, which finds that troops are also generally motivated by the social benefits of participation rather than by the mission's official political purpose.[5] In keeping with the strategic model, however, my study ascertained the motives of terrorists by analyzing the behavioral tendencies of terrorist groups. This approach helps to account for the motives of their leaders because they, by definition, influence the core decisions of the group.[6] My research shows that the behavior of terrorist groups is fundamentally different from that of national militaries. Unlike militaries, terrorist groups tend to act in ways that keep the fighting unit intact, even when these actions undercut these groups' given political rationale. This behavioral trade-off implies that terrorist members with the greatest capacity to influence the core decisions of the group attach utmost value to perpetuating the social unit.

Second, rather than undermining the seven puzzles to the strategic model, the RAND study lends empirical support to these politically irrational terrorist tendencies. In my article I demonstrated, for example, that the use of terrorism is itself an unproductive behavior for groups to achieve their political platforms, an obvious puzzle for the strategic model. Chenoweth, Miller, and McClellan cite the study to declare that terrorist groups have a political "success rate of 10 percent," and hence terrorism is perhaps a rational political strategy. In fact, what Seth Jones and Martin Libicki found is that 10 percent of terrorist groups that have ended since 1968 accomplished their political platforms. An additional 244 groups still use terrorism, and another 136 groups have morphed into other terrorist groups. All told, the RAND study concluded that only 4 percent of terrorist groups since 1968 have attained their policy demands. Even more important, the study stresses that these outlying groups did not tend to accomplish these demands due to terrorism. For example, several Armenian groups achieved their political platforms only by dint of the Soviet Union's unraveling.[7] The study thus affirms the empirical puzzle for the strategic model that terrorism is ineffective in achieving terrorist groups'

5. See Benjamin A. Valentino, *Final Solutions: Mass Killing and Genocide in the 20th Century* (Ithaca, N.Y.: Cornell University Press, 2005), p. 58.
6. Inferring the motives of terrorists through their behavior makes additional sense as terrorist groups have become increasingly networked, blurring the distinction between leaders and foot soldiers. This trend applies not only to religious groups such as al-Qaida and its affiliates but also to ethnonationalist groups such as Fatah and Hamas. On the increasingly networked nature of even ethnonationalist terrorist groups, see Ami Pedahzur and Arie Perliger, "The Changing Nature of Suicide Attacks: A Social Network Perspective," *Social Forces*, Vol. 84, No. 4 (June 2006), pp. 1987–2008.
7. Jones and Libicki, *How Terrorist Groups End*, p. 15.

platforms. In th ırticle I also demonstrated why it is politically irrational for terrorist groups reflexively eschew peace processes, elections, and other potentially effecti ıonviolent political avenues. To challenge the external validity of these pu es, Chenoweth, Miller, and McClellan repeatedly reference the RAND stuc as claiming that "since 1968, 43 percent of terrorist groups have ended by tering the political process," broadly defined. They seize on this figure to su est that terrorist groups are rational political actors that survey their strate options, often pursuing nonviolent alternatives when these serve their polit l ends. This figure, however, again excludes hundreds of terrorist groups t are hardest for the strategic model to explain, including those that have ılintered for the purpose of derailing peace processes, elections, and other storically productive nonviolent political alternatives. When the universe of rrorist groups is included in the analysis, the RAND study found that sinc 68 fewer than one in five groups have embraced any type of nonviolent poli al path, a strikingly low percentage given terrorism's manifest political im tence. In sum, a careful analysis of the RAND study bolsters my contention t terrorist groups tend to engage in behaviors that prolong their existence, n when these impede progress on their stated political aims. This trade-off c account for the pronounced disparity between the longevity of terrorist gro and their negligible political accomplishments.[8]

Third, Chenc th, Miller, and McClellan also assert that the seven behavioral tendencie discuss in my article are not evidence of terrorist irrationality. I agree; th even politically counterproductive terrorist tendencies are irrational only m the vantage of the strategic model. They make perfect sense if terroris roups are driven not to coerce government compliance, but to perpetuate t social unit. Indeed, Chenoweth and her coauthors note that terrorist groups ly on anonymous attacks both to prevent the target government from elim ıting the organization and to generate new recruits by provoking govern nt overreaction; that terrorist groups abruptly change their political platfor to retain current members and to attract new ones; and that to win recruits, rorist groups often attack other groups that share their platform. Chenowe Miller, and McClellan ultimately reject a social explanation for terrorism, h ever, claiming that these terrorist behaviors are reconcilable with what they n as "strategic models of terrorism." Yet they neither define this nomenclat nor demonstrate that prolonging the life span of terrorist

8. See Max Abrahn 'Why Terrorism Does Not Work," *International Security*, Vol. 31, No. 2 (Fall 2006), pp. 42–78.

groups helps to advance their policy demands—a necessary, empirically invalid assumption for their behaviors to be politically rational.[9]

Paul Staniland raises three other objections with my article.[10] First, he draws upon the civil war and guerrilla warfare literatures to argue that many "militant groups" do not behave in the manner I described. This was not my unit of analysis, however. Within terrorism studies, there is a widespread belief that for maximum analytic leverage, terrorist groups, as traditionally defined, should be distinguished from other types of violent substate groups.[11] This is precisely the reason we have the field of terrorism studies.

Second, Staniland states that "it is impossible to offer a single answer to the question, 'What do terrorists want?'" My goal, however, was more modest—to compare the power of a social explanation for terrorism to a political one by analyzing the behavioral tendencies of terrorist groups.

His third point, ironically, is that the behavior of the Irish Republican Army (IRA), Tamil Tigers, and affiliates reveals that their leaders used terrorism rationally for a single purpose—to achieve concrete political aims. In defense of the conventional wisdom, Staniland claims to show that the seven politically counterproductive habits of terrorist groups are nowhere to be found in the histories of the IRA, Tigers, or associated groups, casting doubt on the broader accuracy of my study. His assessment is problematic for four reasons.

First, Staniland compares apples to oranges by testing slightly different terrorist group behaviors than I did. He quotes my work extensively, but none of the terrorist tendencies that he tests is culled from the sections that dealt with the strategic model. In fact, Staniland does not purport to test this model, even though that was the purpose of my study. Instead, he treats the deracinated variants of the terrorist tendencies as testable "predictions" to falsify the natural systems model. This model makes no such predictions, however. The natural systems model is not a terrorism model at all; it is a methodological device for assessing the social basis of organizational behavior.[12]

---

9. See Abrahms, "Why Terrorism Does Not Work."
10. Paul Staniland, "Correspondence: Politics, Motivation, and Organization in the Study of Terrorism," *International Security*, Vol. 33, No. 4 (Spring 2009), pp. 189–195.
11. On this distinction, see Abrahms, "Why Terrorism Does Not Work," pp. 52–54; Jeff Goodwin, "A Theory of Categorical Terrorism," *Social Forces*, Vol. 84, No. 4 (June 2006), pp. 2027–46; Assaf Moghadam, "Suicide Terrorism, Occupation, and the Globalization of Martyrdom: A Critique of *Dying to Win*," *Studies in Conflict and Terrorism*, Vol. 29, No. 6 (August 2006), p. 710; and Jones and Libicki, *How Terrorist Groups End*, appendix.
12. On the perils of testing empirical relationships outside of their theoretical context, see David A. Lake, "Fair Fights? Evaluating Theories of Democracy and Victory," *International Security*, Vol. 28, No. 1 (Summer 2003), p. 154.

Second, in tı :ing the seven terrorist tendencies as discrete predictions, Staniland stron ' implies that a group's failure to engage in all of them constitutes disconfi ıing evidence of its political irrationality. The strategic model is clear, howev(:hat a terrorist group is politically irrational whenever it engages in any of ·se seven tendencies. Sun-Ki Chai has pointed out, for example, that if ter ısm is itself politically ineffective behavior, then it is not politically ratio , regardless of whether there exist alternative methods of inducing politica ıange.[13] Conversely, if terrorist groups do not seize superior political outlets eir behavior is also politically irrational, even if it is true that a very limited n ıber of groups that have used terrorism happened to accomplish their polit l platforms. A large portion of Staniland's test is thus irrelevant for demoı ·ating that a terrorist group did not behave as a political maximizer in a ·rdance with the strategic model, even when its underlying rationality assu ›tions are relaxed.

Third, Stanila uses his case studies in a methodologically unorthodox and suspect way. Tc ·monstrate the tendency of terrorist groups to engage in the seven politicall rational behaviors, I relied on large-*n* studies, citing my own and those of ot s. Staniland charges that his two cases disconfirm these terrorist tendenci Case studies offer a number of methodological advantages over large-*n* stu ·s, but generalizing empirical relationships is not considered one of them.[14] ; is a particular concern because several of the actions highlighted in his t cases are seen as "exception[s]" that are "contextually specific" and thus nlikely to be widely replicable."[15]

Fourth, Stani d is mistaken to conclude that none of the seven politically counterproduct · tendencies was evident in the Irish or Tamil campaigns. In both cases, his ıpirical analysis suffers from problems of commission and omission. For r(ons of space, I will restrict my analysis to the IRA and its republican affilia groups that Staniland claims to know best.[16] I will set aside

13. Sun-Ki Chai, " Organizational Economics Theory of Antigovernment Violence," *Comparative Politics*, Vol. 26 ›. 1 (October 1993), p. 100.
14. See Gary King, ›ert O. Keohane, and Sidney Verba, *Designing Social Inquiry: Scientific Inference in Qualitative I ırch* (Princeton, N.J.: Princeton University Press, 1994), chap. 6.
15. Donald L. Hor(z, "Explaining the Northern Ireland Agreement: The Sources of an Unlikely Constitutional Con ·us," *British Journal of Political Science*, Vol. 32, No. 2 (April 2002), p. 193; Andrew Reynolds, "A ıstitutional Pied Piper: The Northern Irish Good Friday Agreement," *Political Science Quarter* Vol. 114, No. 4 (Winter 1999–2000), p. 617; and Ami Pedahzur, *Suicide Terrorism* (Cambrid Polity, 2005), p. 72. These quotations refer to the Good Friday agreement and the Tigers' mil / capabilities, which greatly exceed those of typical groups that have used terrorism.
16. For two excelle ccounts of organizational goals trumping political goals in the Tamil cam-

the demographic studies of their members who were found to be principally motivated by social solidarity and not the political return.[17] Instead, I will focus on the first three politically irrational terrorist group behaviors that I identified, which the Irish case allegedly disconfirms.

Large-*n* studies show that terrorism is an ineffective coercive strategy.[18] Staniland argues that the 1998 Good Friday power-sharing agreement is countervailing evidence. His view of this agreement (or executive) is at odds, however, with that of longtime IRA experts. Louise Richardson explains, "Those who argue, for example, that the establishment of the power-sharing executive in Northern Ireland has rewarded the terrorism of the IRA are quite wrong. The IRA did not wage a terrorist campaign to share power with Protestants in Northern Ireland. . . . The IRA campaign was fought to bring about a united Ireland, which they have not succeeded in achieving."[19] Other IRA experts agree with Richardson that Irish republican terrorism was a political failure. In fact, a recurrent observation in the literature is that the attacks on civilians steeled London's resolve against making territorial concessions.[20]

In addition, large-*n* studies demonstrate that terrorist groups do not tend to use terrorism as a last resort, even when democratic political alternatives exist.[21] Staniland argues that the Irish case is again disconfirming. Yet the

paign, see Mia Bloom, *Dying to Kill: The Allure of Suicide Terror* (New York: Columbia University Press, 2005), chap. 3; and Pedahzur, *Suicide Terrorism*, chap. 4. These accounts detail the Tigers' target selection, offering strong evidence that they did not behave as political maximizers.

17. See, for example, Robert W. White, "Political Violence by the Nonaggrieved," in Donatella della Porta, ed., *International Social Movement Research*, Vol. 4 (Greenwich, Conn.: Jai Press, 1992), p. 92; Robert W. White, "From Peaceful Protest to Guerrilla War: Micromobilization of the Provisional Irish Republican Army," *American Journal of Sociology*, Vol. 94, No. 6 (May 1989), pp. 1277–1302; and Edgar O'Ballance, *Terror in Ireland: The Heritage of Hate* (Novato, Calif.: Presidio, 1981), p. 138.

18. See Abrahms, "Why Terrorism Does Not Work." In her comprehensive study on how terrorist campaigns end, Audrey Kurth Cronin also finds that terrorism has not paid politically. See Cronin, *How Terrorism Ends: Understanding the Decline and Demise of Terrorist Campaigns* (Princeton, N.J.: Princeton University Press, forthcoming).

19. Louise Richardson, *What Terrorists Want: Understanding the Enemy, Containing the Threat* (New York: Random House, 2006), p. 75.

20. See, for example, Paul Wilkinson, *Terrorism and the Liberal State*, 2d ed. (New York: New York University Press, 1986), p. 163; Rogelio Alonso, "The Modernization in Irish Republican Thinking toward the Utility of Violence," *Studies in Conflict and Terrorism*, Vol. 24, No. 2 (January 2001), pp. 136–137, 141; and Caroline Kennedy-Pipe, "From War to Uneasy Peace in Northern Ireland," in Michael Cox, Adrian Guelke, and Fiona Stephen, eds., *A Farewell to Arms? Beyond the Good Friday Agreement*, 2d ed. (New York: Manchester University Press, 2006), p. 51.

21. See Abrahms, "What Terrorists Really Want," pp. 84–85. For an important related study, see Maria J. Stephan and Erica Chenoweth, "Why Civil Resistance Works: The Strategic Logic of Nonviolent Conflict," *International Security*, Vol. 33, No. 1 (Summer 2008), pp. 7–44. See also Jones and Libicki, *How Terrorist Groups End*.

Sinn Féin regul y complained that republican terrorist groups were not only "non-electoral" ıt militantly "anti-electoral."[22] Following the Sunningdale agreement of 1 , Irish Catholics gravitated toward constitutional political parties. And the terrorism persisted vigorously for decades.[23] As Richardson poi out, "It is surely reasonable to expect that the same [political] result coul ave been achieved through concerted peaceful political action over the t thirty years and without any significant loss of life."[24] Former IRA me ers go further, believing that a peaceful democratic strategy would have be politically superior.[25] This was eminently knowable even at the time, in the inion of many authorities on the subject.[26]

Large-*n* studi suggest as well that terrorist groups tend to eschew compromise at the exp se of their stated political goals.[27] Staniland maintains that the Irish case d roves this terrorist tendency. Yet a bevy of rejectionist splinter groups eme d after Sunningdale. Most of them developed for social reasons, not politi ones.[28] Bruce Hoffman has likened these spoilers to sharks in the water th kept moving for no instrumental purpose other than to remain intact an vert their demise.[29] Irish leaders corroborate Hoffman's account. In an a le entitled "The Futile Path of Militarism," the leading republican new aper explained that "the tactic of armed struggle— rather than the politic bjective for which it is [supposedly] carried out—has been elevated to a pr iple."[30] Other authorities have likewise concluded that after Sunningdale, t IRA and its affiliates "ignored the political objective for which they clai d to be struggling and raised military actions to an end in itself."[31]

22. Quoted in Bria eney, *Sinn Féin: A Hundred Turbulent Years* (Madison: University of Wisconsin Press, 2003), pp 9–270.
23. See Alonso, "T lodernization in Irish Republican Thinking toward the Utility of Violence," p. 135.
24. Richardson, *Wl Terrorists Want*, p. 17.
25. See, for examp amon Collins with Mick McGovern, *Killing Rage* (London: Granta, 1997), p. 4.
26. See, for exampl oren E. Lomasky, "The Political Significance of Terrorism," in R.G. Frey and Christopher W. M , eds., *Violence, Terrorism, and Justice* (New York: Cambridge University Press, 1991), p. 90.
27. See, for exampl ndrew Kydd and Barbara F. Walter, "Sabotaging the Peace: The Politics of Extremist Violence, *ternational Organization*, Vol. 56, No. 2 (Spring 2002), pp. 263–296. See also Stephen John Stedr "Spoiler Problems in Peace Processes," *International Security*, Vol. 22, No. 2 (Fall 1997), pp. 5–5 nd Jones and Libicki, *How Terrorist Groups End*, p. 19.
28. Richardson, *Wl Terrorists Want*, p. 211.
29. Bruce Hoffman *side Terrorism* (New York: Columbia University Press, 1998), p. 162.
30. "The Futile Pat Militarism," *An Phoblacht*, August 20, 1998, at http://republican-news.org/archive/1998/Aug 0/20pol.html.
31. Ibid.

In sum, the historical record is replete with empirical evidence that Irish republican terrorist groups did not even remotely behave as political maximizers, notwithstanding the widespread belief in the strategic model. These terrorist groups acted in ways that served not to advance their political platform, but to sustain themselves, providing insight into the incentive structure of their leaders.

Hillel Frisch levels two other objections. First, he maintains that the terrorist behaviors that I identified are in fact consistent with the strategic model. As evidence, he purports to show how certain terrorist groups were acting in a politically rational manner by engaging in these seemingly puzzling behaviors for the strategic model. Yet none of his cases exemplify the behavioral tendencies that I described. To demonstrate that it is actually politically rational for terrorist groups with the same political platform to fight each other, Frisch lists several well-known cases of groups with different platforms that have done so. Similarly, to demonstrate that it is actually politically rational for terrorist groups to abruptly alter the entire nature of their political demands, he lists examples of groups that have only minimally "ratchet[ed] down" their original demands. His examples serve to demonstrate only that terrorist groups do not always engage in all of the behavioral tendencies that I enumerated. In highlighting cases that deviate from the puzzling terrorist tendencies, he fails to demonstrate how these puzzles conform to the strategic model.

Frisch's second contention is that whereas some terrorist groups are motivated by the social benefits, others are motivated by the political benefits.[32] He asserts that the former applies to defunct groups of marginal historical importance, such as the November 17 group and the Popular Forces of 25 April, and that the latter applies to the most dangerous contemporary groups, such as al-Qaida and its affiliates. Frisch does not explain why he believes that such group types exist or how to discern them from each other.

The evidence is accumulating, however, that the terrorist groups of greatest concern to the United States and its allies are not rational political actors. Based on their behavior, al-Qaida and its affiliates do not appear (1) to be motivated by relatively stable and consistent political preferences; (2) to evaluate the expected political payoffs of the available options; or (3) to adopt terrorism because of its superior political return. On the contrary, terrorism is having a deleterious impact on al-Qaida's political platform, and the likelihood of ad-

32. Hillel Frisch, "Correspondence: Politics, Motivation, and Organization in the Study of Terrorism," *International Security*, Vol. 33, No. 4 (Spring 2009), pp. 180–202.

vancing it with rorism is "close to zero";[33] its leadership opposes elections, even when the vould further its given political cause, such as in Iraq;[34] al-Qaida is reflex ly averse to politically compromising;[35] it possesses what Jessica Stern h dubbed "protean" political demands, which constantly change to the b ıddlement of even its military leadership;[36] al-Qaida attacks are generally aı ymous, or at least we suspect this to be so;[37] it targets other Muslim groups ven when they share major elements of its political platform;[38] and al- ıida has resisted disbanding after consistently failing to achieve its poli demands or even when they have become moot for reasons that have nothi to do with terrorism.[39] These are rational behaviors only if the endgame fo l-Qaida is to stay intact.

The future p s a natural experiment. Will al-Qaida and its affiliates immediately disban ıd renounce terrorism now that they have unambiguously failed to advan their political demands? Will their leaders finally embrace the ballot? Will y offer a credible compromise in the interests of achieving at least part of the ever-changing demands? If the Irish case is at all generalizable, do not ho your breath.

—*Max Abrahms*
Palo Alto, California

33. Jones and Libic *How Terrorist Groups End*, p. xvii.
34. Abrahms, "Wh errorists Really Want," p. 85.
35. Ashton B. Cart hn Deutch, and Philip Zelikow, "Catastrophic Terrorism: Tackling the New Danger," *Foreign A*, Vol. 77, No. 6 (November/December 1998), p. 85.
36. Jessica Stern, " Protean Enemy," *Foreign Affairs*, Vol. 82, No. 4 (July/August 2003), p. 1. See also Vahid Brown, acks in the Foundation: Leadership Schisms in al-Qaida from 1989–2006," CTC Report (West ıt, N.Y.: September 2007), p. 10.
37. See Assaf Mog am, *The Globalization of Martyrdom: Al Qaeda, Salafi Jihad, and the Diffusion of Suicide Attacks* (Bal re, Md.: Johns Hopkins University Press, 2008), pp. 49–51.
38. Ibid., p. 34.
39. See Stern, "The tean Enemy," p. 14.

Part III: Countering Terrorism

Deterring Terrorism

It Can Be Done

Robert F. Trager and Dessislava P. Zagorcheva

Can deterrence work against contemporary terrorists? Many prominent international relations scholars and analysts have argued that deterrent strategies have no significant role to play in countering the new terrorist threat. Richard Betts, for example, writes that deterrence has "limited efficacy . . . for modern counterterrorism."[1] A RAND study asserts, "The concept of deterrence is both too limiting and too naïve to be applicable to the war on terrorism."[2] And the belief that deterrence is inadequate as a counterterrorist strategy is also shared by President George W. Bush and his administration, whose National Security Strategy states, "Traditional concepts of deterrence will not work against a terrorist enemy."[3]

The case against the use of deterrence strategies in counterterrorist campaigns appears to rest on three pillars. First, terrorists are thought to be "irrational," and therefore unresponsive to the cost-benefit calculation required for deterrence.[4] Second, as Robert Pape argues, many terrorists are said to be so highly motivated that they are "willing to die, and so not deterred by fear of punishment or of anything else."[5] Third, even if terrorists were afraid of punishment, they cannot be deterred because they "lack a return address against

Robert F. Trager is a Fellow in the Department of Politics and International Relations at Oxford University. Dessislava P. Zagorcheva is a Ph.D. candidate in political science at Columbia University.

The authors would like to thank Richard Betts, Maria Fanis, Tanisha Fazal, Robert Jervis, Brigitte Nacos, Stephanie Neuman, William Karl Riukas, Sebastian Rosato, Anne Sartori, Sean Smeland, Jack Snyder, and two anonymous reviewers for their helpful comments and advice. They are also grateful to seminar participants at the Institute for Social and Economic Research and Policy at Columbia University, and the 2003 Summer Workshop on the Analysis of Military Operations and Strategy.

1. Richard K. Betts, "The Soft Underbelly of American Primacy: Tactical Advantages of Terror," in Demetrios James Caraley, ed., *September 11, Terrorist Attacks, and U.S. Foreign Policy* (New York: Academy of Political Science, 2002), p. 46.
2. Paul K. Davis and Brian Michael Jenkins, *Deterrence and Influence in Counterterrorism: A Component in the War on al-Qaeda* (Santa Monica, Calif.: RAND, 2002), p. xviii.
3. George W. Bush, *The National Security Strategy of the United States of America* (Washington, D.C.: U.S. Government Printing Office, September, 2002), p. 15.
4. The claim that terrorists are irrational is more commonly found in the popular press, but it is also a key argument against deterrence strategies generally, and therefore must be addressed in any discussion of the use of deterrence in counterterrorism.
5. Robert A. Pape, *Dying to Win: The Strategic Logic of Suicide Terrorism* (New York: Random House, 2005), p. 5.

International Security, Vol. 30, No. 3 (Winter 2005/06), pp. 87–123

which retaliatio :an be visited."[6] (The claim that terrorists are "fanatical" appears to repres a combination of the first and second pillars.)

If these argur ıts are correct, not only will deterrence prove ineffective but the world—anc ıe United States in particular—faces a grim and unpreventable onslaught errorist attacks. If terrorists cannot be found, the use of force against them is ·ffective. Counterterrorist strategies that attempt to address root causes, su as "winning hearts and minds" and economic aid and democratization, strategies for the long run. In the meantime, religious terrorism is on the ·,[7] and the rate of suicide terrorist attacks has increased significantly: fr 41 in the 1980s, to 100 in the 1990s, to 174 in 2000–03 alone.[8] These trends ar ·articularly dangerous because many scholars, analysts, and policymakers ir ·asingly worry that terrorists could acquire and use mass casualty weapon: ırguably the gravest threat to developed countries and to world order.[9]

In this article ·e argue that the claim that deterrence is ineffective against terrorists is wro . Many terrorists can be deterred from actions that harm targeted states, a deterrence should remain an important weapon in the counterterrorisı ırsenal. Moreover, even seemingly fanatical terrorists, intensely motivat by religious beliefs, are not irrational in a sense that makes them impossibl) deter. Further, some essential elements of terrorist support systems are like to be less motivated and therefore vulnerable to traditional forms of deterr e, particularly at early decision nodes in the lengthy process of preparation ı ıuired for major attacks.

Even the mo ıighly motivated terrorists, however, can be deterred from certain courses ıction by holding at risk their political goals, rather than life or liberty. We sl v that this is possible for two reasons: (1) terrorist-state rela-

---

6. Betts, "The Soft ·lerbelly of American Primacy," p. 45.
7. According to th S. State Department's classification, the number of religiously motivated foreign terrorist or zations rose from nearly zero in 1980 to almost half of all such organizations by 1998. See M : Juergensmeyer, *Terror in the Mind of God: The Global Rise of Religious Violence* (Berkeley: Universi ıf California Press, 2000), p. 6; and Bruce Hoffman, *Inside Terrorism* (New York: Columbia Ur rsity Press, 1999).
8. Compiled from in Pape, *Dying to Win*, app. 1, pp. 253–264. From 2000 to 2003, 20 of the 174 total attacks were ı ·etrated by Iraqi rebels against U.S. and allied forces.
9. Jessica Stern has ued that terrorists or their state sponsors could obtain nuclear and chemical materials from poo guarded former Soviet facilities as well as the expertise of underpaid nuclear scientists. Se ·rn, *The Ultimate Terrorist* (Cambridge, Mass.: Harvard University Press, 1999). Graham All states that "a nuclear terrorist attack on America in the decade ahead is more likely than n Allison, *Nuclear Terrorism: The Ultimate Preventable Catastrophe* (New York: Times Books, 2004)

tionships, while adversarial, are often not zero sum; and (2) although terrorists are difficult to find, powerful states still have the ability to influence their political aims. From a policy perspective, the ability to hold political ends at risk is a crucial point, because doing so stands by far the best chance of fracturing the global terrorist network, one of the most important objectives of counterterrorism policy. Policymakers should be sensitive to this central objective of grand strategy, namely, preventing terrorist adversaries from cooperating with one another.

This article has six main sections. In the first, we define deterrence in the context of the interactions between states and nonstate actors and examine why critics believe that it is an ineffective means of counterterrorism. The next three sections address each of the purported impediments to deterring terrorists. In the section on terrorist motivation, we develop a framework based on terrorist goals and levels of motivation that clarifies the strategies available to states to associate costs and benefits with courses of action of different types of groups. In the fifth section, we illustrate the effectiveness of coercion even against highly motivated groups by analyzing the results of its use against elements of terrorist networks in the Southern Philippines. We argue that the current approach of the U.S. and Philippine governments vis-à-vis the Moro Islamic Liberation Front (MILF)—accommodating some of the group's political goals and then holding that accommodation at risk to prevent the MILF from cooperating with al-Qaida and Jemaah Islamiah—is the best means of achieving the principal U.S. objective of denying all forms of support to groups intent on mass casualty attacks against the United States. In the concluding section, we apply our theoretical framework to current U.S. efforts to counter global terrorism and provide policy recommendations based on our findings.

The Meaning of Deterrence in the Context of Counterterrorism

Deterrence approaches are only one of several classes of strategies for countering terrorism. Other strategies include persuasion (or "winning hearts and minds"), economic aid and democratization, appeasement, and military force.[10] A deterrence strategy, by contrast, consists of the following two ele-

10. Our focus on deterrence does not imply that other strategies do not have important roles to play as well. On the contrary, the realm of ideas will be a key battleground over the long run. On persuasion, see, for example, Helena K. Finn, "The Case for Cultural Diplomacy: Engaging For-

ments: (1) a th t or action designed to increase an adversary's perceived costs of engagi in particular behavior, and (2) an implicit or explicit offer of an alternative s of affairs if the adversary refrains from that behavior.[11] Additionally, to b alled a deterrence strategy, this increase in the adversary's perceived costs ist be the result of costs imposed, at least in some contingencies, by the det er itself.[12]

This definitio of deterrence subsumes what Glenn Snyder has called "deterrence by pun ment" and "deterrence by denial."[13] Generalizing these concepts so that th apply to the interactions between state and nonstate actors as well as to in actions among states, we take deterrence by punishment to

---

eign Audiences," F gn *Affairs*, Vol. 82, No. 6 (November/December 2003), pp. 15–20; Peter G. Peterson, "Diplom and the War on Terrorism," *Foreign Affairs*, Vol. 81, No. 5 (September/ October 2002), pp. 6; and Michael Mousseau, "Market Civilization and Its Clash with Terror," *International Securit* ol. 27, No. 3 (Winter 2002/03), pp. 5–29. On economic aid and democratization, see Carol Gr m, "Can Foreign Aid Help Stop Terrorism? Not with Magic Bullets," *Brookings Review*, V 0, No. 3 (Summer 2002), pp. 28–32; Ivo H. Daalder and James M. Lindsay, "Nasty, Brutish, an ng: America's War on Terrorism," *Current History*, December 2001, pp. 403–408; and Alan B. K ger and Jitka Maleckova, "The Economics and the Education of Suicide Bombers: Does Po Cause Terrorism?" *New Republic*, June 20, 2002, pp. 27–33.

11. This second ele at defines the magnitude of the political objectives sought by the coercing state. Other works also address this issue include Barry M. Blechman and Tamara S. Cofman, "Defining Moment e Threat and Use of Force in American Foreign Policy," *Political Science Quarterly*, Vol. 114, 1 (Spring 1999), pp. 1–30; and Alexander L. George, *Forceful Persuasion: Coercive Diplomacy as lternative to War* (Washington, D.C.: United States Institute of Peace, 1991).

12. This last requir nt distinguishes deterrence from other forms of diplomacy, such as persuasion, where no cost e imposed. Although we regret the need for yet another definition of deterrence, existing def ons are inadequate because they do not encompass both deterrence by punishment and d ence by denial; they are too closely tied to the interstate context; or they do not clearly disting deterrence from persuasion. For classic writings on coercion and deterrence, see Thomas chelling, *The Strategy of Conflict* (New York: Oxford University Press, 1963); Thomas C. Schellin *rms and Influence* (New Haven, Conn.: Yale University Press, 1966); Glenn H. Snyder, *Deterre nd Defense: Toward a Theory of National Security* (Princeton, N.J.: Princeton University Press, 1 ; Alexander L. George and Richard Smoke, *Deterrence in American Foreign Policy: Theory and P ce* (New York: Columbia University Press, 1974); Patrick M. Morgan, *Deterrence: A Conceptual lysis* (Beverly Hills, Calif.: Sage, 1977); Robert Jervis, Richard Ned Lebow, and Janice Gross St *Psychology and Deterrence* (Baltimore, Md.: Johns Hopkins University Press, 1985); John J. Mear mer, *Conventional Deterrence* (Ithaca, N.Y.: Cornell University Press, 1983); and Herman Kahn, *Escalation: Metaphors and Scenarios* (New York: Frederick A. Praeger, 1965). Recent works on c ion include Robert A. Pape, *Bombing to Win: Air Power and Coercion in War* (Ithaca, N.Y.: Corn niversity Press, 1996); and Daniel Byman, *The Dynamics of Coercion: American Foreign Policy a e Limits of Military Might* (New York: Cambridge University Press, 2002).

13. Snyder, *Deterre nd Defense*, pp. 14–16. Thomas Schelling, *Arms and Influence*, pp. 70–71, contrasts deterrence (t threat to take hostile action *if* the adversary acts) with compellence (the threat to take hosti ction *unless* the adversary acts). Because of the close relationship between these two terms, h of what we say about deterrence by punishment can be applied to compellence as we ee Patrick M. Morgan, *Deterrence Now* (New York: Cambridge University Press, 2003), p. 3; a Robert J. Art, "To What Ends Military Power?" *International Security*, Vol. 4, No. 4 (Spring 1989 . 3–35.

refer to the threat of harming something the adversary values if it takes an undesired action. Such a threatened trigger of punishment might be a terrorist attack, but it might also be an action believed to be a precursor to an attack.[14] Deterrence by denial involves "hardening" targets in the hope of making an attack on them too costly to be tried and convincing terrorists of the state's determination not to make concessions in the face of terror tactics. Thus, it is generally true that "where punishment seeks to coerce the enemy through fear, denial depends on causing hopelessness."[15]

For both deterrence by punishment and deterrence by denial strategies to be successful, two conditions must hold: the threatened party must understand the (implicit or explicit) threat, and decisionmaking by the adversary must be sufficiently influenced by calculations of costs and benefits. Because terrorists can appear fanatical, some analysts believe that, in general, neither of these conditions can be met. We term this the "problem of irrationality."

Deterrence by punishment also requires that several additional conditions hold: the deterrer must be able to hold something the adversary values at risk; the adversary must value what is held at risk over the expected value of taking action; and both the threat of retaliation and the deterrer's promise not to take action if its conditions are met must be credible. These conditions depend on the capabilities of the two sides; the deterrer must be able to carry out its threat. They also depend on the deterrer's having an incentive to follow through; the deterrer must not be made worse off by carrying out a threat than if it had simply not responded to the provocation.[16] Thus, the conditions for deterrence by punishment strategies depend on the existence of a state of the world that both sides prefer to the state in which the deterrer takes action against the adversary and the adversary responds as best it can, often by doing

---

14. According to Glenn Snyder, deterrence by punishment primarily affects "the aggressor's estimate of possible costs," rather than "[the aggressor's] estimate of the probability of gaining his objective." Snyder, *Deterrence and Defense*, p. 15. A question thus arises: How should threats to take offensive action against groups in response to precursors to terrorist acts be classified? Although such threats may primarily influence terrorists' calculations of the probability of attaining an objective later on, we call this "deterrence by punishment" because it involves a choice of triggers for actions whose credibility must be demonstrated.

15. David Johnson, Karl Mueller, and William Taft V, *Conventional Coercion across the Spectrum of Conventional Operations: The Utility of U.S. Military Forces in the Emerging Security Environment* (Santa Monica, Calif.: RAND, 2002), http://www.rand.org/publications/MR/ MR1494/, pp. 16–17. Defense is distinct from deterrence by denial because it merely aims at "reducing . . . costs and risks in the event deterrence fails," rather than influencing the behavior of the adversary. Snyder, *Deterrence and Defense*, p. 3.

16. This last condition must hold over the long run. Deterrence is consistent with, and often requires, short-term sacrifice.

its worst again ne deterrer. This in turn requires that there be some overlap in the preferenc of both sides over states of the world. If their preferences are precisely oppos , deterrence is impossible.[17] As Thomas Schelling puts it, "If his pain were greatest delight and our satisfaction his greatest woe, we would just pro d to hurt and frustrate each other."[18]

Viewed in th vay, deterrence resembles a bargain: both sides agree to co-operate on a st of affairs that both prefer to alternatives. Deterrence, therefore, is not just ut making threats; it is also about making offers. Deterrence by punishment about finding the right combination of threat and offer that meets the cond ns listed here.[19]

In the case of te-terrorist interaction, these conditions seem difficult or impossible to me Because of their ideological and religious beliefs, many terrorists place ex me value on their political objectives relative to other ends (e.g., life and p erty). For this reason, it appears impossible that a deterrer could hold at ri something of sufficient value to terrorists such that their behavior would b ffected. Similarly, deterrence by denial strategies seem destined to fail for same reason, because they require that terrorists prefer the status quo to ta g action given the dangers. Put differently, if the terrorists' motivation is hi enough, then even a small probability of a successful operation and a hig robability of punishment will not deter them. Further, because the inter of terrorists and states seem so opposed, it also appears impossible that e two sides could agree on a state of affairs that both prefer

17. When preferen re nearly opposite, relations are adversarial, but when preferences are precisely opposed, rel s are zero sum. See Robert Axelrod, *Conflict of Interest: A Theory of Divergent Goals with Applicati to Politics* (Chicago: Markham, 1970).
18. Schelling, *Arms l Influence*, p. 4.
19. Whether in a t rist context or not, this highlights the need for the second element in our definition of deterr . When analysts have attempted to study threats but ignored the offer implicit in any threat, y have been led astray. To take one example from the Cold War: Would additional nuclear ca ilities be more likely to deter a first strike? When we consider only the severity and credib of the threat, the answer appears to be that at least additional capability can do no harm. W we also consider the credibility of the offer in the event the adversary complies, however, our clusions may change radically. Increased capability may give the deterrer a greater incentive to ke first, decreasing the credibility of the offer not to attack. This in turn may give the adversary increased incentive to strike first itself, reversing our original conclusion that increased capa ties would aid in deterring a first strike. See Snyder, *Deterrence and Defense*, p. 10. For related li ture on provocation and deterrence, see, for example, Richard Ned Lebow, "Provocative Deter e: A New Look at the Cuban Missile Crisis," *Arms Control Today*, Vol. 18, No. 6 (July/Augus 88), pp. 15–16; Janice Gross Stein, "Reassurance in International Conflict Management," *Poli Science Quarterly*, Vol. 106, No. 3 (Autumn 1991), pp. 431–451; and Robert Jervis, "Rational D rence: Theory and Evidence," *World Politics*, Vol. 41, No. 2 (January 1989), pp. 183–207.

to that in which each does its worst against the other. We call these issues the "problem of terrorist motivation."

Even if this problem were solved, and targets for retaliation valued by terrorists discovered, a practical problem for deterrence by punishment strategies seems to remain. The capability to impose sufficient costs such that terrorists are deterred may require the ability to find the members of the terrorist group responsible. We call this the "return address problem."

Other doubts about the efficacy of deterrence strategies are still subject to ongoing debate. Even during the Cold War, analysts pointed out numerous difficulties with deterrence strategies, as well as a variety of factors that could lead to deterrence failure.[20] Although we disagree with the stronger claims against the efficacy of conventional deterrence, we do not try to resolve these debates here.[21] Instead, we focus on the three arguments that pertain particularly to deterrence in the terrorist context.[22]

The Problem of Irrationality

The assertion that terrorists are highly irrational is contradicted by a growing body of literature that shows that terrorist groups (though not necessarily every individual who engages in terrorist activities) usually have a set of hier-

20. As Edward Rhodes wrote in his review of empirical studies of conventional deterrence, "The nature of conventional deterrence is that it will regularly fail, even in cases where commitments to respond are 'clearly defined, repeatedly publicized, and defensible, and the committed state [gives] every indication of its intention to defend them by force if necessary.'" Richard Ned Lebow, "Conclusions," in Jervis, Lebow, and Stein, *Psychology and Deterrence*, p. 211, quoted in Rhodes, "Can the United States Deter Iraqi Aggression? The Problems of Conventional Deterrence," 2002, Rutgers University, p. 4. See also Lebow, "Miscalculation in the South Atlantic: The Origins of the Falklands War," in Jervis, Lebow, and Stein, *Psychology and Deterrence*, pp. 89–124; Lebow, "The Deterrence Deadlock: Is There a Way Out?" in Jervis, Lebow, and Stein, *Psychology and Deterrence*, pp. 180–202; and Joseph Lepgold, "Hypotheses on Vulnerability: Are Terrorists and Drug Traffickers Coercible?" in Lawrence Freedman, ed., *Strategic Coercion: Concepts and Cases* (New York: Oxford University Press, 1998).

21. For a review of methodological difficulties that have beset past studies of deterrence, see Christopher Achen and Duncan Snidal, "Rational Deterrence Theory and Comparative Case Studies," *World Politics*, Vol. 41, No. 2 (January 1989), pp. 143–169; James Fearon, "Signaling versus the Balance of Power and Interests," *Journal of Conflict Resolution*, Vol. 38, No. 2 (June 1994), pp. 236–269; Curtis S. Signorino and Ahmer Tarar, "A Unified Theory and Test of Extended Immediate Deterrence," working paper, University of Rochester, December 7, 2001, http://www.rochester.edu/college/psc/signorino/papers/SigDeter.pdf; and Bear F. Braumoeller, "Causal Complexity and the Study of Politics," *Political Analysis*, Vol. 11, No. 3 (Summer 2003), pp. 209–233.

22. Throughout we also focus attention on deterrence strategies that target classes of individuals who are essential for the functioning of a terrorist group as a whole. Deterring specific individuals retards the capacity of groups only when the supply of individuals willing to fill their roles is a constraining factor. In contemporary terrorist networks, this is often true to only a limited degree.

archically orde goals and choose strategies that best advance them.[23] The resort to terror tics is itself a strategic choice of weaker actors with no other means of furth g their cause.[24] Suicide tactics in particular, as Pape shows, are practiced in e context of coercive campaigns and were adopted because they proved to remarkably successful for coercing liberal democracies.[25] In addition, terror groups have often put interest ahead of strictly interpreted ideology, for in nce, in cooperating with groups and states with opposed beliefs.[26]

Therefore, ev though terrorist decisionmaking processes are certain to consist of both onal and nonrational elements, this is neither peculiar to terrorists nor pre des deterrence. Deterrence requires only that terrorists be sufficiently infl nced by cost-benefit calculations. As Robert Jervis argued more than a qu r century ago, "Much less than full rationality is needed for the main lines deterrence] theory to be valid."[27]

The Problem Terrorist Motivation

The issue of ter ist motivation is the most serious difficulty facing powerful states attemptin o implement deterrence strategies. To address this issue, we have develope framework that specifies the types of deterrence strategies that can be effe e against particular classes of groups and elements of terrorist networks.[28] s framework is represented in Figure 1, where the intensity of the terrorists otivation is on the vertical axis.[29] We define "motivation" as

23. See Martha Cre aw, "The Causes of Terrorism," in Charles W. Kegley, ed., *International Terrorism: Characteristi Causes, Controls* (New York: St. Martin's, 1990), p. 117; Betts, "The Soft Underbelly of Ameri Primacy"; Robert A. Pape, "The Strategic Logic of Suicide Terrorism," *American Political S e Review*, Vol. 97, No. 3 (August 2003), pp. 343–361; Jonathan Schachter, *The Eye of the Believer: hological Influences on Counter-terrorism Policy-Making* (Santa Monica, Calif.: RAND, 2002), p. 96 d Andrew Kydd and Barbara Walter, "The Politics of Extremist Violence," *International Organi n*, Vol. 56, No. 2 (Spring 2002), pp. 279–289.
24. Betts, "The Sof derbelly of American Primacy."
25. Pape, *Dying to* , pp. 44–45.
26. Consider, for i nce, al-Qaida's decision before the 2003 Iraq war to cooperate with Iraqi Baathists against th nited States.
27. Robert Jervis, terrence Theory Revisited," *World Politics*, Vol. 31, No. 2 (January 1979), p. 299.
28. Other authors suggested a variety of taxonomies of terrorist groups, based on different criteria, that may e useful for particular applications. In general, experts have identified the following types of rism: nationalist, religious, anarchist, state sponsored, left wing, and right wing.
29. We have drawn r categories, but each axis is better thought of as representing a continuum. The more motivate e group, for instance, the less susceptible it will be to the deterrence strategies listed in quad s 1 and 2.

Figure 1. Potential Deterrence Strategies Based on the Intensity of Terrorist Motivation and the Similarity of Preferences over Outcomes

Intensity of motivation		Goals that can be accommodated?[a] Yes	Goals that can be accommodated?[a] No
	Low (terrorists value life over goals)	1 deterrence by punishment: political and nonpolitical ends held at risk; deterrence by denial	2 deterrence by punishment: political ends held at risk; deterrence by denial
	High (terrorists value goals over life)	3 deterrence by punishment: political ends held at risk; temporary deterrence by punishment;[b] deterrence by denial	4 temporary deterrence by punishment; deterrence by denial

[a]Some terrorist groups have objectives that could be at least partially accommodated either by the deterring state or by actors over whom the deterring state has leverage. In this sense, the relationship is not zero sum.

[b]"Temporary deterrence" implies that groups can be influenced to refrain from taking action while they build capability for larger strikes. This is sometimes to the advantage of the deterrer because it provides a greater window of opportunity for the use of offensive strategies against the group.

the extent to which terrorists value their political goals over nonpolitical ends. Examples of the latter may include life, liberty, property, and social standing (when not derived directly from terrorist activity). The degree to which terrorist groups have some political goals that could be accommodated by deterring states is on the horizontal axis.

We first discuss the potential of deterrence by punishment strategies targeted at less motivated elements of terrorist networks at stages in the terror process when they are most susceptible to influence. This corresponds to quadrants 1 and 2 in Figure 1. We show that by considering only the possibility of deterring a suicide terrorist the moment before he (or, more rarely, she) commits the act, analysts have overlooked deterrence strategies that could prove effective. We then consider the possibility of deterring the most highly motivated terrorists, that is, those willing to run any risk in pursuit of their goals (quadrant and 4). We show that by holding at risk political ends, states can deter such t orists from certain courses of action. We then argue that despite the proble of terrorist motivation, deterrence by denial strategies can be effective agains l classes of terrorist groups, and conclude the section by applying the theo cal framework developed here to the issue of deterring multiple groups at ce.

DETERRING LESS OTIVATED ELEMENTS OF TERRORIST NETWORKS

The higher the ue terrorists place on what is not gained through terror relative to what is, e more compelling is a threat against the former, and the more likely det ence will succeed. It is less obvious that, through careful attention to the m y different elements of terrorist systems and an understanding of the proc es that lead to attacks, even apparently highly motivated groups may be usceptible to the deterrence strategies listed in quadrants 1 and 2.

To produce a ge-scale attack, terrorists must constitute a system of actors fulfilling specifi unctional roles. As Paul Davis and Brian Jenkins characterize it, such a s em "comprises leaders, lieutenants, financiers, logisticians and other facili rs, foot soldiers, supporting population segments, and religious or otherw ideological figures."[30]

Some elemen of the terrorist system are more difficult to deter than others. Financiers, for e mple, are sometimes less fanatically motivated than other elements of the tem and thus easier to deter. Although states often have difficulty tracki them down,[31] they have had success when making this a priority.[32] The atest difficulties are often political rather than a matter of finding perpet rs, and the resolution of political difficulties usually depends on the le l of diplomatic resources that states are willing to commit. Although findi all financiers of all groups prior to terrorist attacks is impossible, once larg cale attacks are committed, it is sometimes possible to con-

30. Davis and Jenk *Deterrence and Influence in Counterterrorism*, p. xi.
31. See, for exampl ouise Branson, "Cutting Off Terrorists' Funds," *Straits Times*, September 26, 2001.
32. For instance, t J.S. government has closed down several important sources of terrorist financing since the cks of September 11, 2001; and in November 2002, the CIA together with financial investigat announced that they had traced tens of millions of dollars flowing to al-Qaida, mostly from udi sources. See, for example, "U.S.: Al Qaida Funded by Only 12 Individuals, Most Saudis," *orldTribune.com*, October 20, 2002, http://www.hvk.org/articles/1002/194.html. See also *The Commission Report: Final Report of the National Commission on Terrorist Attacks upon the Unite tes* (Washington, D.C.: U.S. Government Printing Office, July 2004), p. 382.

centrate investigative resources and uncover the source of financing in particular cases. A demonstrated policy of committing significant resources to find and punish financiers may therefore deter an essential part of the system from engaging in terrorist activity.

This example highlights an underrecognized contrast between brute force and deterrence strategies. When a government weighs the benefits of using force against the costs of diplomatic and material concessions to states whose assistance is required to punish terrorist militants and financiers, it may decide that the price is too high. The possibility of deterring future terrorists, however, provides a strong additional incentive. Thus, a deterrence approach implies an even more aggressive policy than a brute force approach if deterrence is unsuccessful in a particular case.

State sponsors represent another element of terrorist systems that many view as less motivated and easier to find, and therefore susceptible to deterrence.[33] Scholars and policymakers who are skeptical of using deterrence against terrorists often believe that, on the contrary, their state sponsors are deterrable. The Bush administration's National Strategy for Combating Terrorism contains a long discussion of the administration's policy of deterring state sponsors of terrorism, though it makes no other explicit reference to a deterrence approach.[34] Other scholars argue, however, that failing states may be highly motivated to sell their capabilities and provide other assistance for financial gain. Nevertheless, because the response of a powerful state to a terrorist attack will likely be proportional to the scale of the attack, even highly motivated potential state sponsors with advanced capabilities and other countercoercive instruments will be forced to exercise restraint. The capabilities of state sponsors may enable them to avoid being deterred from supporting smaller-scale international terrorism, but powerful states will likely retain the ability to deter would-be state sponsors from supporting larger-scale attacks.[35]

In addition to paying attention to the diverse elements that make up terrorist systems, as Michael Powers has argued in the context of WMD terrorism,

---

33. Currently Cuba, Iran, Libya, North Korea, Sudan, and Syria are on the U.S. list of states that sponsor terrorism. Office of the Coordinator for Counterterrorism, U.S. Department of State, *Country Reports on Terrorism, 2004* (Washington, D.C.: U.S. Government Printing Office, 2005), pp. 88–90.
34. *National Strategy for Combating Terrorism,* (Washington, D.C.: U.S. Government Printing Office, February 14, 2003), http://www.whitehouse.gov/news/releases/2003/02/counter_terrorism/counter_terrorism_strategy.pdf.
35. We are not implying that all terrorist groups have state sponsors or that the Bush administration's focus on states over nonstate actors is appropriate.

deterrers shoul ıink of terrorist activity as a process, or series of actions culminating in vio ıce, rather than a single act or event such as the terrorist attacks of Septe ›er 11, 2001.[36] Consider, for example, the process that culminated in ı se attacks. As early as 1996, Mohammed Atta began planning and recrui g for them in Hamburg. Over the next five years, he and his associates arran d for financing, visas, accommodation, and flight lessons; selected targets; tinued to recruit; and ultimately carried out the attacks.[37] Each stage pres s an opportunity for detection by intelligence networks and law enforcemer ›r for a military response. When, at a particular stage in the process leading an attack, the risks of detection and punishment outweigh the benefits of ıccessful attack multiplied by the probability of success, the terrorist or terr st supporter will be deterred. Deterrence is possible when the benefits of ıccessful attack are not too high, as in quadrants 1 and 2 of Figure 1.

In analyzing decision calculus of elements of terrorist systems at each point in the pr ss, we can see the usefulness of developing a deterrence strategy that s triggers for action that occur early in that process. Even though the earl tages are often the most difficult to detect, the punishment need not be as vere, nor the probability of detection as high, to have an equivalent dete nt effect. This is because, in the early stages, the prospects of achieving a suc sful attack are more uncertain. Even those willing to give their lives wher e success of an attack is assured may be unwilling to begin a process that ma ıot, in the end, advance their cause. Thus, to deter terrorists, states should s ch for less motivated or more visible elements of terrorist networks and t aten retaliation at early or more easily detectable stages of the terror proc

DETERRING TER ISTS WHOSE GOALS CAN BE PARTIALLY ACCOMMODATED

In some cases, t orists are so motivated that deterrence by punishment strategies that targe ıe nonpolitical ends of terrorists are insufficient. Nevertheless, overlap in preferences of terrorists and deterring states can still create a range of agre ents that deterrence strategies can enforce (see quadrant 3). This is a type leterrence by punishment where political ends are held at risk. Whereas tl previous discussion emphasized the potential of the deterrer

36. Michael J. Pov , "Deterring Terrorism with CBRN Weapons: Developing a Conceptual Framework," occas ıl paper no. 2, CBACI (February 2001), http://knxas1.hsdl.org/homesec/docs/nonprof/nps 91704-01.pdf, p. 5.

37. See, for examp "Al-Jazeera Offers Accounts of 9/11 Planning," *CNN.com*, September 12, 2002, http://www. com/2002/WORLD/meast/09/12/alqaeda.911.claim.

to harm members of the terrorist group, here we also consider the alternative to the threat, that is, the deterring state's offer made to the group in the event it refrains from the undesired behavior.

Terrorists usually have a range of objectives, some dearer than others. States also have preferences over these same objectives. When the preference orderings of terrorists and states are precisely opposed, deterrence is impossible.[38] Even a small overlap in the preferences of the two sides, however, can be exploited in the cause of deterrence. We highlight this possibility by focusing on two areas of common ground.

First, many terrorist organizations with global objectives have local concerns even closer to heart. In fact, some organizations merely advance the agenda of other groups in return for resources and expertise they can apply locally. For instance, three members of the Irish Republican Army (IRA) arrested in Colombia in 2001 were "suspected of training the Revolutionary Armed Forces of Colombia (FARC) in how to conduct an urban bombing campaign."[39] It is unlikely that the IRA had taken up the cause of Marxist insurgency in Colombia. Rather, some trade must have occurred between the IRA and the FARC, such that the interests of both were furthered. In the jargon of the U.S. National Strategy for Combating Terrorism, the two must have achieved synergies.

Terrorist preferences of this sort are represented in the upper half of Figure 2. Such terrorists would like to cooperate with groups intent on striking the deterring state, or they might like to strike the deterring state themselves. There are several reasons why this might be the case: a strike might further the goals of groups directly; the response of the deterring state might be thought likely to galvanize support for their cause; or assistance on the part of one group might have been traded for another form of assistance from the other. The group whose preferences are represented in Figure 2, however, is even more interested in advancing a local agenda through acts targeted at a domestic audience. Of the forty-two foreign terrorist organizations (FTOs) currently designated by the U.S. Department of State, the vast majority fall into this category to a greater or lesser degree.[40]

The terrorists' local agenda may have nothing in common with the foreign policy goals of the deterring state, but if some aspects of this agenda can be

38. We discuss one partial exception to this rule below, which we term "temporary deterrence."
39. *National Strategy for Combatting Terrorism*, p. 8.
40. See Office of Counterterrorism, U.S. Department of State, "Fact Sheet: Foreign Terrorist Organizations," March 23, 2005, http://www.state.gov/s/ct/rls/fs/37191.htm.

Figure 2. An Example of Overlapping Preferences between Terrorists and a Deterring State

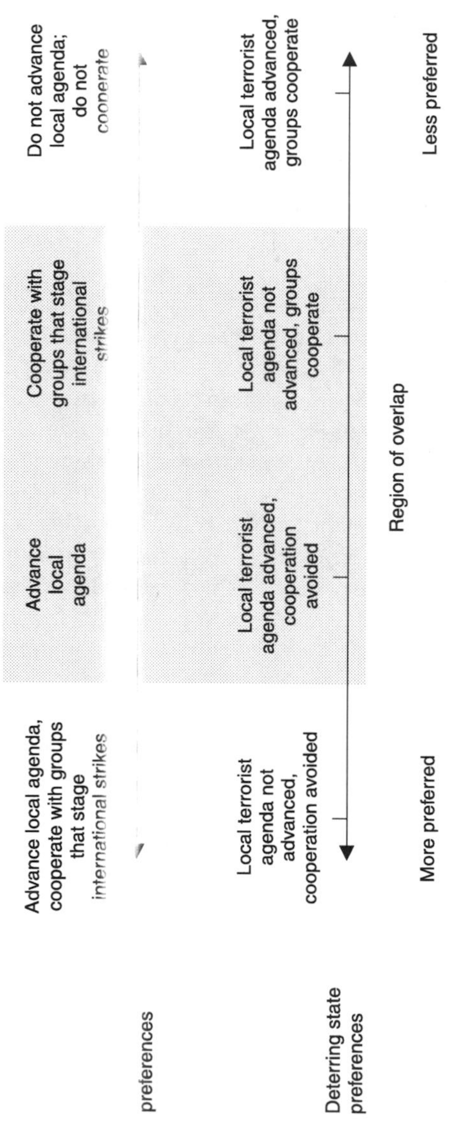

even partially accommodated, there is overlap between the preferences of the two sides. This presents the state with strategic opportunity. Consider, for instance, the interests of the United States vis-à-vis terrorist groups such as Sendero Luminoso (Shining Path), the Liberation Tigers of Tamil Eelam, Hamas, and the Basque Fatherland and Liberty. While the interaction between these groups and the local states may be zero sum—one's pain is strictly the other's gain—their relationship with the United States may not be.[41] Each of these groups may be able to achieve synergies through cooperation with other transnational groups, but they may prefer not to cooperate with such groups if that induces the U.S. government to refrain from devoting significant resources to intervening in their local conflicts. The United States, in turn, may prefer not to devote significant resources to targeting groups that do not cooperate with those it considers most threatening.

Thus, if the local agenda does not sufficiently conflict with the interests of the deterring state, the local interests of the terrorist group can serve as an effective hostage for a policy of deterrence. Often, the deterring state can threaten to tip the scales in the local conflict. Terrorist groups whose primary concern is the local theater may be willing to refrain from certain actions (e.g., cooperating with groups considered more dangerous by the deterring state) in return for less interference by the deterring state in the local conflict. In such cases, terrorists would be coerced into courses of action not just out of fear for their lives and property, but also out of fear for their cause. This in turn implies that designing an effective strategy for combating terrorism requires an in-depth understanding of terrorist adversaries, not only their capabilities and intentions toward a particular state but also their stakes in other configurations.

If, instead, force is actually used by a state against the terrorist group, this can create a harmony of interest between the group and more dangerous terrorist organizations or even change the preferences of the group such that local concerns seem less important. If the local agenda is put out of reach, members of the group may even turn their focus to international terrorism. More important, by using force against terrorist groups, states give these groups every incentive to cooperate with other groups and organizations whose interests are similarly opposed by the target state. This is a dangerous possibility because local terrorist groups can provide "intelligence, personnel, expertise, resources, and safe havens" to groups and individuals who may be even more

41. For a discussion of the bargaining relationship between terrorist groups and local states, see Paul Pillar, *Terrorism and U.S. Foreign Policy* (Washington, D.C.: Brookings, 2001), pp. 145–148.

threatening.[42] A olicy that makes action by the deterring state contingent on the creation of h links would have the opposite effect. Rather than creating a harmony of in rests among terrorist groups opposed to the deterrer, such a policy would h to fracture the global terrorist network. In fact, in addition to being deterr from cooperating, some groups might even be coerced into providing local telligence on other groups, as in the case of the MILF discussed below.

A second exa le of overlapping preferences that can produce a deterrence equilibrium occ s when both sides prefer bounding the scope of violence to the state of affa when each side does its worst against the other. Sometimes, by tacitly perm ng smaller-scale attacks, or those of a particular type, a state can deter those larger scale, or of an alternative variety. Suppose a state can credibly threat o inflict substantial damage on the capabilities of the terrorist group, in the ent the group carries out an attack. If the state makes such a threat, so that i actions are contingent on the actions of the terrorist group, what would be e likely response of the group? If the threat is sufficiently credible, and if ver levels of violence also advance the group's aims but do not elicit such a rong response from the target, then the group's best option would be to mo rate the destruction it causes. The group would be partially deterred, not fo ear of losing life or property, but for fear of losing the ability to prosecute its use altogether.[43]

The conflict b veen the Israeli Defense Forces (IDF) and the South Lebanon Army (SLA), the one hand, and the Lebanese liberation movement Hezbollah, on e other, may provide an example of these dynamics.[44] Throughout the st half of the 1990s, both sides retaliated following successful attacks on t r forces by targeting civilians identified with the opposing

42. *National Strateg r Combatting Terrorism*, p. 9.

43. This is similar ne argument in the literature on intrawar deterrence and limited war that, even in intense con ts, states may limit the severity of their attacks to avoid provoking retaliation in kind. On the tention of both sides from using chemical weapons in World War II, see, for example, Jeffrey W egro, *Cooperation under Fire: Anglo-German Restraint during World War II* (Ithaca, N.Y.: Corne niversity Press, 1995), chap. 4, especially p. 201. On the geographical limits on fighting during Korean War, see Stephen J. Cimbala, *Military Persuasion in War and Policy: The Power of Soft* (N York: Praeger, 2002), pp. 100–101.

44. See Clive Jones sraeli Counter-insurgency Strategy and the War in South Lebanon, 1985–97," *Small Wars a nsurgencies*, Vol. 8, No. 3 (Winter 1997), pp. 82–108; Daniel Sobelman, "Hizbollah Two Ye after the Withdrawal: A Compromise between Ideology, Interests, and Exigencies," *Strategic sessment*, Vol. 5, No. 2 (August 2002), http://www.tau.ac.il/jcss/sa/v5n2p4Sob.html; a Augustus Richard Norton, "Hizballah and the Israeli Withdrawal from Southern Lebanon," *urnal of Palestinian Studies*, Vol. 30, No. 1 (Autumn 2000), pp. 22–35.

side. In 1994 Hezbollah even attacked Jewish targets in London and Buenos Aires. In 1996 Israel hoped to use force to "break Hezbollah," in the words of an Israeli general, in an extensive operation code-named Grapes of Wrath.[45] As a result of Israeli air and artillery bombardment, 400,000 Lebanese fled north, creating a massive refugee problem for the Lebanese government. Many Lebanese civilians were also killed, including 102 sheltered in a United Nations compound. Israel's attacks put pressure on Hezbollah through several channels: group members were killed during the operation; refugees created difficulties for the Lebanese government, which in turn pressured Hezbollah to make concessions to end the violence (or pressured Damascus to pressure Hezbollah); there was also a danger that the Lebanese population would cease its support of Hezbollah to halt the violence.

As a strategy of brute force, the operation was a failure, as hundreds of Katyusha rockets launched from Southern Lebanon continued to fall on Northern Israel throughout the conflict. The operation also failed to deter Hezbollah from future actions against Israeli interests in Southern Lebanon. Thus, because of Hezbollah's high level of motivation, Israeli coercion was insufficient to compel Hezbollah to give up its objectives entirely. The escalating cycle of violence was broken, however, by an agreement in 1996, brokered by former U.S. Secretary of State Warren Christopher. In it, Hezbollah agreed to refrain from attacking targets inside Israel, and the IDF and SLA committed to refrain from attacking Lebanese civilians. This agreement appears to have been generally successful in bounding the scope of the conflict to the present day. Thus, although Hezbollah could not be deterred from pressing its interests by violent means, it was deterred from terrorist activities within Israel.

A limited strategy of this sort may be optimal for states that have the capability to retaliate effectively but also have other pressing uses for intelligence and operational and other material resources, or whose retaliation would be associated with extreme costs, such as inflaming resentment against the state. This approach might be the best strategy against some of the terrorist groups that Ian Lustick has labeled "solipsistic."[46] Such groups use terror partly or primarily as a means of affecting the behavior of groups and individuals with whom the perpetrators identify. Thus, because their use of terror is not meant

45. Eitam Rabin, "Interview with IDF Major-General Amiram Levine, OC Northern Command," *Haaretz*, August 7, 1996.
46. Ian Lustick, "Terrorism in the Arab-Israeli Conflict: Targets and Audiences," in Martha Crenshaw, ed., *Terrorism in Context* (State College: Pennsylvania State University Press, 1995), pp. 514–552.

to coerce, lowe :vels of violence may sufficiently advance their objectives, and they may r wish to incite the retaliation that a large-scale attack would bring.[47]

The sort of pr :rence overlap represented in Figure 2 is also a plausible description of the te of affairs for the United States and other nations vis-à-vis certain terrorist oups prior to September 11. Consistent with this interpretation, the U.S. r onse to the 2,400 anti-U.S. terrorist incidents from 1983 to 1998 was fairly ıoderate: the United States retaliated militarily only three times.[48] In the 1)s, the United States experienced a series of terrorist attacks, some of which re allegedly tied to Osama bin Laden and al-Qaida. Among these were the tack on the USS *Cole* off the coast of Yemen in 2000, the Khobar Towers mbing in Saudi Arabia in 1996, and the first World Trade Center bombin 1993. The U.S. response focused primarily on pursuing the individuals dir y involved in the attacks rather than the group responsible.

Although U.S ıctions may have been consistent with a policy of deterring more serious th ıts, they may also have been interpreted as a sign of unwillingness to bear : costs of a more vigorous response. Bin Laden may have interpreted U.S. v ıdrawals from Beirut in 1983, following the bombings of the U.S. embassy a marine barracks, and from Somalia in 1993, six months after eighteen U.S. s liers were killed in a fierce firefight in Mogadishu, in this way.[49] If this ir pretation is correct, it may be that deterrers must demonstrate capability ıd resolve before deterrence can function effectively. The implications of ar dversary developing a perception that a deterrer lacks the willingness to r ond are serious because, once established, such reputations are difficult to ınge.[50]

From a theo cal perspective, the discussion here highlights the importance of the off nade to the challenging state or terrorist group if it complies with the deterr demands, and the possibility of using leverage over one po-

47. Determining w ı groups should be classified as "solipsistic" requires intensive analysis. Ian Lustick, "Terrorism d the Arab-Israeli Conflict," pp. 514–552, convincingly argues that Palestinian violence in the 0s and Zionist violence in the 1940s deserve this title.
48. Michele Malves 'Explaining the United States' Decision to Strike Back at Terrorists," *Terrorism and Political Vio e,* Vol. 13, No. 2 (Summer 2001), pp. 85–106.
49. See Osama bin len, "Declaration of War against the Americans Occupying the Land of the Two Holy Places," gust 23, 1996; and John Miller, "To Terror's Source," interview with Osama bin Laden, Afghani ı, *ABC News*, May 28, 1998.
50. As Robert Jerv rgues, "One of the basic findings of cognitive psychology is that images change only slowly l are maintained in the face of discrepant information. This implies that trying to change a rep ion of low resolve will be especially costly." Jervis, "Deterrence and Perception," *International ırity,* Vol. 7, No. 3 (Winter 1982/83), p. 9.

litical end for leverage over the actions a group takes in pursuit of another. By altering the offer, such as by refraining from intervening in local conflicts or even tacitly permitting lower-level violence, states can wholly or partially deter even highly motivated groups. At times, therefore, deterring states should consider limiting their demands.

Furthermore, certain sorts of accommodations are likely to be more effective than others. In particular, accommodations that can be held at risk serve the cause of deterrence. Those that do not may reduce terrorist grievances and therefore motivation, but they do not serve deterrence directly. As an example, consider a state's decision to release captured militants. On the one hand, this strengthens the capabilities of the militants' organization but does not address their core concerns. On the other hand, if the group is highly motivated, it is by definition undeterred by fear of capture. Thus, in many cases, the release of militants will not provide any leverage over the organization's behavior because this accommodation, unlike the two other examples given above, cannot be held at risk.

Any accommodation also carries the risk that it will encourage other groups to demand similar treatment. The deterring state must therefore be clear in signaling the different approach it intends to use with different groups. Groups that fall into quadrant 1 in Figure 1 should not be treated like those that fall into quadrant 3, and the groups must be made to understand this. States will have to weigh the risks associated with (publicly observable) accommodation in individual cases.[51]

DETERRING TERRORISTS WITH PRECISELY OPPOSED PREFERENCES

Highly motivated terrorists whose preferences are precisely opposed to those of the deterring state cannot be deterred, though they can be influenced.[52] They cannot be deterred because their high level of motivation means that no matter what threat is leveled against them, they will always pursue their objectives, and because their preferences are precisely opposed, no bargaining space exists. Such terrorists cannot be made to refrain from taking hostile action.

Different groups fall into this category for different states, but in general few groups belong in quadrant 4. From the perspective of the United States, because the vast majority of terrorist groups are primarily concerned with lo-

51. On the trade-offs between clarity and ambiguity in signaling, see Snyder, *Deterrence and Defense*, pp. 246–249.
52. Davis and Jenkins make a similar point in *Deterrence and Influence in Counterterrorism*, p. 9.

cal conflicts, o certain parts of the al-Qaida network seem to fit this classification.

When states mpt to deter such groups, there is a significant danger that deterrence may pear to succeed in the short run, lulling the state into complacency. If the te has even a chance of retaliating effectively, the terrorist group may hav centive to bide its time, building its capabilities in preparation for a more ssive strike.[53] The radicalization of terrorist discourse in the 1990s may ther re explain both the higher number of casualties per attack and the decrea in the number of individual attacks.[54] Still, in some cases, such "tempora deterrence" can be useful if it provides the deterring state with time to ap offensive strategies. Unfortunately, the temporary lull in attacks is likely t e followed by attacks of greater severity.

USING DETERRE BY DENIAL

Deterrence by ial strategies have the potential to be effective against all four types of te rist groups. By hardening targets (e.g., fortifying embassies, reinforcing coc doors, upgrading border security, and tightening immigration controls) a demonstrating resolve not to make concessions, the deterring state can l en terrorists' motivation by reducing the benefits of terror tactics. Thus, a ough defensive strategies cannot protect every target, they can minimize terrorists' power to hurt, thereby lessening the coercive power of terror action. This in turn reduces terrorist motivation, increasing the effectivenes f many of the strategies described above.

As some ana ts have pointed out, one of the reasons for the 1998 attacks on U.S. embass in Tanzania and Kenya was that terrorists believed that U.S. assets in Africa ere easier targets compared with better-secured facilities in

53. Terrorists are u ely to wait too long before striking because the process of building greater capability runs the of being discovered before it is utilized. A failed deterrence strategy, however, is consistent low levels of terrorist activity in the near term.
54. On the radicali on of terrorist groups, see Rex A. Hudson, *The Sociology and Psychology of Terrorism: Who Beco a Terrorist and Why?* (Washington, D.C.: Federal Research Division, Library of Congress, 1999) . 1–3; and Ian Lesser, Bruce Hoffman, John Arquilla, David Rondfeldt, Michelle Zanini, a rian Michael Jenkins, *Countering the New Terrorism* (Santa Monica, Calif.: RAND, 1999), http ww.rand.org/publications/MR/MR989/. On trends in international terrorism, see U.S. De tment of State, *Patterns of Global Terrorism: 2001*, app. 1: Statistical Review, http://www.state.g s/ct/rls/pgtrpt/2001/html/10265.htm; and Bruce Hoffman, "The Confluence of Inte onal and Domestic Trends in Terrorism," working paper (Edinburgh: Center for the Study Terrorism and Political Violence, St. Andrew's University, 1996), http://www.ciaonet.org/ /hob01/.

the Middle East and elsewhere.[55] This has been taken as a sign of the futility of defensive strategies, but in some ways it is just the opposite. Terrorist motivation, and with it terrorist actions, would likely increase if the terrorists were able to strike higher-value targets more easily. Thus, although defensive strategies are inadequate in themselves, they form an important component of a deterrence approach.

DETERRING MULTIPLE GROUPS AT ONCE

During the Cold War, deterrence was mainly considered in the context of the interaction between the United States and the Soviet Union. Today, however, governments are faced with the challenge of deterring multiple groups at once. This presents both difficulties and strategic opportunities. Investigating and targeting multiple groups in disparate areas of the globe that use different languages and operating procedures will severely tax the intelligence, diplomatic, administrative, and military resources of deterring states. States' activities in different countries require separate negotiations with local authorities. These factors limit the ability of the deterrer to threaten focused retaliation against terrorist groups. In fact, a deterrence by punishment policy that would be successful against a single group may not be credible against multiple groups because of the resource constraints of the deterring state.[56]

Rather than attempting or threatening to use force against all terrorist groups at once, a more credible policy might produce the desired result by committing to focus resources only on those considered the most dangerous. Suppose there are two groups that a state wishes to deter. Both are highly motivated, but they do see intermediate levels of violence as furthering their cause. The deterring state has several options. First, it might threaten both of them, but the groups might realize that if they both attack, the state's resources would not be sufficient to retaliate effectively against the two at once. Second, the state could threaten only one, in which case the other would be completely undeterred. A third option is more attractive, though not without practical difficulties. The deterring state could threaten to concentrate its resources against whichever group shows itself to be more dangerous. Each group

55. Richard A. Falkenrath and Philip B. Heymann made a similar argument that soft targets in U.S. cities would be attacked if embassies were fortified. Falkenrath and Heymann, "We'd Better Be Ready for an Escalation," *Boston Globe,* August 27, 1998.
56. For a discussion of the problem of deterring multiple adversaries, see Daniel S. Treisman, "Rational Appeasement," *International Organization,* Vol. 58, No. 2 (April 2004), pp. 345–373.

would then hav n incentive to be slightly less violent than the other. To plan operations that deterrer would perceive as less worthy of retaliation, each would have to ss the actions that the other group is likely to take. If the two groups thought coordinating, they would have no reason to trust each other. Therefore, beca each would be evaluating the likely actions of the other, and expecting e evaluated in turn, both would be forced to significantly moderate their avior.

In practice, p ymakers' resource allocation decisions require considerable judgment, and ferent terrorist groups must be dealt with in different ways. In attempting t leter multiple groups at once, the deterring state might decide to signal a tention to focus resources on several of the most dangerous groups. There also be relatively low-cost actions, such as blocking assets and restricting travel of individuals, that could be taken against many terrorist groups. I in other cases, effective measures against groups may require significa ntelligence, diplomatic, and special operations resources. When signalin ynamics allow, these resources should be reserved for a smaller set of g ps, as described here. Inclusion on this short list should be as fluid as poss so that even groups that are not on it are still under threat.

The Return A ress Problem

Terrorists are u lly difficult to find, which reduces the degree of coercive leverage of cert sorts of threats. It does not follow from this, however, that attempts at det ence by punishment will fail. Rather, this observation highlights the impo nce of matching the demands that states make of particular terrorist group ith the level of threat that can credibly be brought to bear against them. T question then is whether significant demands can be made. We submit that ey can be, despite terrorists' lack of a "return address."

First, when s s devote sufficient resources, they can find members of terrorist organizat s. Many terrorist groups operate partly or wholly out of known base a —for instance, al-Qaida in Afghanistan (before the 2001 war), Abu Say on the Philippine islands of Basilan and Jolo, and the Mujahedin-e K in Iraq. The armed forces of the Philippines, assisted by the United States, e able to find and kill many Abu Sayyaf Group members. Other terrorist ganizations, however, do not have large and identifiable bases. Some ha road areas of operation, or they may be dispersed in particular population Examples include Aum Shinrikyo, Sendero Luminoso, and al-Qaida after the Afghan war. These groups tend to be smaller and, because they are dispersed among the population, are more difficult to find.[57] Still, members of such groups have been found in the past and punished for their activities when states have made this a priority.[58] A deterrence approach that reserves intelligence and other resources for use in cases of deterrence failure would only increase the ability of states to find group members.

Second, even though targeted states cannot find every terrorist and terrorist facilitator, they almost always have the ability to increase the costs to terrorist groups of achieving their political goals.[59] States therefore can put these political goals further from reach, decreasing the likelihood that the group will achieve any of its objectives. Some mechanisms for frustrating a group's political goals require that its members be found; others do not. Counterinsurgency and law enforcement operations are principal examples of the former. Examples of the latter include a deterring state providing economic and military aid to governments targeted by insurgents, pressuring targeted states not to make concessions to terrorists, aiding other groups with goals that are opposed to those of the terrorist group, and imposing travel and fund-raising restrictions on terrorist group members.[60]

Furthermore, uses of force such as counterinsurgency operations need not result in the capture of every terrorist to seriously harm both the political and

---

57. Al-Qaida is an exception to the rule that baseless groups are relatively small, partly because it did have a base in Afghanistan until the 2001 Afghan war.
58. The U.S. response following the hijacking of the *Achille Lauro* cruise ship in 1985 is instructive. Although the hijackers were found and captured, Italian authorities released the leader of the group responsible because the U.S. government was unwilling to pay the diplomatic costs of prevailing upon the Italians to act differently. Following the September 11 attacks, however, the United States began to dedicate more resources to this area and, as a result, has achieved some successes in the war on terror. See Federal Bureau of Investigation, "War on Terrorism," http://www.fbi.gov/terrorinfo/counterrorism/waronterrororhome.htm (accessed April 2003); and "Al Qaeda's Most Wanted," *USAToday.com*, March 2, 2003, http://www.usatoday.com/news/world/2003-03-02-alqaeda-list_x.htm. According to President Bush, nearly half of al-Qaida's leadership had been captured or killed by May 1, 2003. See "President Bush Announces Combat Operations in Iraq Have Ended," speech delivered on the USS *Abraham Lincoln*, May 1, 2003, http://www.state.gov/p/nea/rls/rm/20203.htm.
59. Scholars who have doubted the efficacy of deterrence strategies have concurred in this. Robert Pape, for example, notes that "military action can disrupt a terrorist group's activities temporarily." Pape, *Dying to Win*, p. 239.
60. Because terrorists depend on support from the communities they live in, it might also be possible to target the community as a whole, which would also not require finding individual terrorists. Individuals who terrorists hold dear, such as family members, might also be threatened. We do not explore these options further except to note that, in many cases, they stand a significant chance of galvanizing support for the terrorists' cause.

nonpolitical int sts of the terrorist group. In fact, uses of force that fail to obtain a state's po cal objectives may still hurt the interests of the group and its members. Once ;ain, the Balikatan Operation against the Abu Sayyaf Group is a telling exar le.

This point is ticularly important because it is in cases where other strategies such as for cannot achieve the ends of states that a "bargaining range" exists. In these ations, the sides may agree to refrain from doing their worst against the oth ecause terrorist-state interaction is not zero sum, making a deterrence equi rium possible. Conversely, if deterrence strategies are ineffective in partic r cases because terrorists cannot be found, the use of force will be ineffecti as well. Therefore, deterrence strategies that threaten the use of force are pr uctive when the effectiveness of force occupies a middle range, when fo cannot easily achieve the ends of states but can at least disrupt terrorist g p operations.

Third, the dif ulty of finding terrorists poses a problem for deterrence only when their mot tion is high, and high levels of motivation often make terrorists more susce ble to deterrence strategies that target political ends. Less motivated pote l terrorists will be deterred just as less motivated potential criminals are d red, even though the police cannot catch every one. Highly motivated terro ts, because they hold their political goals so dearly, are loath to run even low level risks to these goals. This magnifies the coercive leverage of strategie at target political ends.

A related arg ent made by some scholars is that because terrorists easily blend into the cal population, collateral damage caused by attempts at retaliation agai them inflames hatred of the retaliating state and galvanizes support for the rorists' cause. Indeed, inciting such retaliation may be an explicit terrorist c ctive, so threatened retaliation would hardly deter.[61] States have a variety c taliatory options, however, and some of these are more narrowly focused terrorists than others. Although lessons from the Israeli-Palestinian con t are difficult to draw, it seems intuitively clear that tactics that harm or ki rge numbers of noncombatants have radicalized more mod-

---

61. For a similar ar ent, see David Lake, "Rational Extremism: Understanding Terrorism in the 21st Century," *Dia -IO*, Spring 2002, pp. 15–29. Also, as Andrew Kydd and Barbara Walter show, extremist Pa nian violence against Israelis often occurred when the prospects of peace seemed highest. O ossible interpretation is that Palestinian extremists actually desired Israeli retaliation (either d t or indirect through halting the peace process) to win Palestinian moderates to their side. K and Walter's interpretation is slightly different: in their view, extremist violence reveals info tion about the trustworthiness of the other side. Kydd and Walter, "The Politics of Extremis olence."

erates than tactics that focus squarely on the perpetrators of violence. As an example of a more focused approach, consider the Israelis' reaction to their athletes being taken hostage by the Palestinian Liberation Organization at the 1972 Summer Olympics in Munich: two of three surviving PLO members were assassinated without significant collateral damage.[62] Interestingly, it is often resource constraints that prevent states from adopting a more focused response, and critics have argued that the Israeli response to the Munich attack "came with considerable costs in terms of manpower, [and] resources."[63]

The danger that, in some instances, punishment could be counterproductive applies equally to the use of force. Further, deterrence does not require that retaliation be in the near-term interests of the side that undertakes it. Rather, as discussed above, retaliation must hurt the individuals to be deterred, and the threat of retaliation must be credible. Credibility requires that the benefits of a successful deterrence policy (postretaliation), in addition to the direct benefits of retaliating, outweigh the near-term costs of retaliating. Thus, if Israeli retaliation hurts the perpetrators of terrorist acts, this can serve a policy of deterrence even if near-term Israeli interests are also hurt.

Fracturing the Global Terrorist Network in the Southern Philippines

In this section, we test our central argument that important elements of the global terrorist network can be deterred from actions that harm states. In particular, groups that have provided essential training and other assistance to the most dangerous terrorists can be deterred from doing so in the future. We accomplish this by examining one case where coercion is being attempted—against the Moro Islamic Liberation Front—and one case where force was tried—in the 2002 Operation Balikatan against the Abu Sayyaf Group. These cases offer useful lessons for U.S. counterterrorism policy because, as one study suggests, "the Philippines has become the model for additional fronts in the war on terrorism," and George W. Bush's administration intends to use similar strategies in Indonesia and elsewhere.[64] By comparing the outcomes in

62. The other kidnappers were killed by German police at the Munich airport.
63. Schachter, *The Eye of the Believer*, p. 109; and Dan Raviv and Yossi Melman, *Every Spy a Prince: The Complete History of Israel's Intelligence Community* (Boston: Houghton Mifflin, 1990), pp. 184–194.
64. Gaye Christofferson, "The War on Terrorism in South East Asia: Searching for Partners, Delimiting Targets," *Strategic Insight*, Vol. 1, No. 1 (March 2002), http://www.ccc.nps.navy.mil/rsepResources/si/mar02/eastAsia.asp; John Gershman, "Is South East Asia the Second Front?"

the MILF and / ı Sayyaf Group cases, we illustrate some of the critical dynamics of the p cy choice.

The MILF ca: ıvoids methodological problems commonly associated with empirical tests deterrence theories. Testing theories of general deterrence (where the acti taken by the deterrer are not in the context of an ongoing crisis) is difficu ecause adversaries that seem to have been deterred may not have wanted to e action in the first place. Examining cases of immediate deterrence (where leterrent threat is made in the context of a crisis) ameliorates the problem of aluating the intentions of the adversary but creates a new difficulty: actu dversaries are unlikely to be representative of the class of potential adve ries. Thus, inferences drawn from immediate deterrence cases may not ply to cases of general deterrence. Similarly, the very existence of a terro group marks the group as different from the class of potential terrorists. S ıe experience of deterring existing groups that have already demonstrated a illingness to carry out attacks may not provide lessons that are immediatel ansferable to questions concerning the whole class of terrorists and potent terrorists.

Because the LF is known to have cooperated with al-Qaida and Jemaah Islamiah in the st, we can infer that, under some circumstances, it would do so again. The ca thus avoids the problem of testing for general deterrence because we know ıt the action to be deterred is desirable in some instances. At the same time, U.S. and Philippine governments began an aggressive campaign to coerce MILF to sever its ties to Jemaah Islamiah and al-Qaida only after Septembe and the string of attacks in 2002 linked to these two other groups.[65] Thus, e case also avoids the problem of testing for immediate deterrence becaus f both the unanticipated change in policy by the deterring governments a the increased resources these governments could credibly threaten to dep to enforce compliance.

The MILF ca demonstrates each aspect of our argument. First, governments often ha he ability to impose costs on terrorist groups or elements of terrorist suppo ıetworks, even those that are highly motivated. Second, such groups/elemen espond to these incentives. Third, states can achieve important goals, such preventing cooperation among terrorist groups, through de-

---

Foreign Affairs, Vol. No. 4 (July/August 2002), pp. 60–74; and Walden Bello, "A 'Second Front' in the Philippines," *tion*, March 18, 2002, pp. 18–22.

65. Among the 200 tacks by Jemaah Islamiah and al-Qaida in Asia are the Bali bombing, which killed more than 2 people, the Zamboanga bombings (in the Southern Philippines), and the Metro Manila bom s.

terrence. The Abu Sayyaf Group case illustrates both the capacity of states to harm terrorist groups, and the limitations of force in achieving the true ends of states that employ it.

DETERRENCE OF THE MORO ISLAMIC LIBERATION FRONT

In 1977 Hashim Salamat challenged Nur Misuari for leadership of the Moro National Liberation Front (MNLF), a group that views itself as carrying on a several-hundred-year struggle for the rights of Muslims in the Southern Philippines.[66] Although Salamat's bid for leadership was unsuccessful, several thousand fighters remained loyal to him, calling themselves the "new MNLF." In 1984 this group renamed itself the Moro Islamic Liberation Front. In the 1980s and early 1990s, the MNLF negotiated with the Philippine government as the representative of the Moro people, while the MILF concentrated on building its capabilities and support at the grassroots level. In 1996 the government and the MNLF signed a peace agreement, still in place, that promised greater autonomy for Muslim regions. Within a month, however, fighting broke out between the MILF and government forces.[67] Battles of varying intensities between the two sides, punctuated by several cease-fire agreements, have continued almost to the present day.[68]

In March 2000, President Joseph Estrada ordered all-out military action against the MILF that culminated in July when government forces overran the group's main base, Camp Abubakar. Despite this use of massive military force, the group continued to pursue its objectives (principally greater autonomy for Moros), indicating a high level of motivation. Thus, if the MILF is to be coerced

---

66. See "Guide to the Philippines Conflict," *BBC News,* http://newsvote.bbc.co.uk/mpapps/pagetools/print/news.bbc.co.uk/2/hi/asia-pacific/1695576.stm; Anthony Davis, "Attention Shifts to Moro Islamic Liberation Front," *Jane's Intelligence Review,* April 2002, pp. 20–23; Kristina Gaerlan and Mara Stankovitch, eds., *Rebels, Warlords, and Ulama* (Quezon City, Philippines: Institute for Popular Democracy, 2000); Alonto Norodin Lucman, *Moro Archives: A History of Armed Conflicts in Mindanao and East Asia* (Quezon City, Philippines: FLC Press, 2000); Abaton Macapado Muslim, *The Moro Armed Struggle in the Philippines: The Nonviolent Autonomy Alternative* (Marawi City, Philippines: Mindanao State University, 1994); and Hilario M. Gomez, *The Moro Rebellion and the Search for Peace: A Study on Christian-Muslim Relations in the Philippines* (Zamboanga City, Philippines: Silsilah, 2000).

67. See, for example, "Chronology for Moros in the Philippines," Minorities at Risk Project (College Park: Center for International Development and Conflict Management, University of Maryland, 2004), http://www.cidcm.umd.edu/inscr/mar/chronology.asp?groupId?84003.

68. After a brief suspension of the peace talks in 2005, the Philippine government and the MILF have started work on a preliminary draft of a peace settlement. The final draft is expected by mid-2006. See, for example, Barbara Mae Decanay, "Negotiators Begin Work on Initial Peace Pact," *Gulf News,* September 24, 2005. Negotiations between the Philippine government and the MILF have been ongoing since November 2001, when the two entered into a cease-fire agreement.

into ending its)ellion, either greater force than the Philippine government can muster alo must be brought to bear, or some political demands of the group must be :ommodated and the accommodation held at risk.

The Philippi government has repeatedly accused the MILF of terrorist activities,[69] inc ling bus and airport bombings and numerous hostage takings.[70] But tl validity of these reports is difficult to determine because the government als ias incentive to undermine the legitimacy of the group. The rebels themsel have repeatedly denied these charges.[71] Still, independent sources have al accused the group of using terror tactics, mainly against the Christian comn ity and businesspeople refusing to pay "tolls" for travel in areas controlle y the rebels.[72] Therefore, it appears likely that the MILF or some affiliated ments have engaged in some level of terrorism.

There is less ubt that elements of the group have cooperated with other terrorist organi tions.[73] Reports of MILF cooperation with al-Qaida and Jemaah Islamia ome not just from Philippine intelligence sources,[74] but also from many otl analysts.[75] According to Western and Asian intelligence sources, "Al Qa a's relationship with the Moro Islamic Liberation Front was . . . fruitful. At N bin Laden's request, the front opened its Camp Abubakar to foreign jihadist which meant they did not all have to go to Afghanistan.

---

69. Most of the vi ce perpetrated by the MILF has been against government forces.

70. See, for examp Rajiv Chandrasekaran, "Military Finds 2 Beheaded by Philippine Rebels," *Washington Post*, M 7, 2000; "Philippine Officials Link Bombings to Muslim Rebels, as Third Hostage-Taking Un ls," CNN, *World News*, May 3, 2000; "A Hostage Crisis Confronts Estrada," *Economist*, May 6, 2 pp. 42–43; and Ellen Nakashima, "Five Detained in Philippine Bombing," *Washington Post*, M 6, 2003.

71. See MILF press ases from May 13, May 8, April 3, and February 15, all in 2003; June 21 and May 3, 2002; June 001; and July 12, 2000, http://www.luwaran.com/press.htm. The case of Koronadal City is o f many examples of the differing accounts of specific incidents. See, for example. "Governme Nearing Decision on Whether to Tag MILF as Terrorist, Says GMA," http://www.news.ops.go /archives 2003/may13.htm#MILF

72. See, for exampl Muslim Separatist Movements in the Philippines and Thailand," in Angel Rabasa and Peter C k, *Indonesia's Transformation and the Stability of Southeast Asia* (Santa Monica, Calif.: RAND, 2001

73. See, for examp Daljit Singh, "The Terrorist Threat in Southeast Asia," in Russell Heng and Denis Hew, eds., *I nal Outlook, 2003–2004* (Singapore: Institute of Southeast Asian Studies, 2003), p. 4.

74. Philippine sou have in fact reversed themselves on the question of MILF links with other Southeast Asian I iic groups, seemingly as Manila's political needs change. See Patrick Goodenough, "Lin between Al Qaeda and Filipino Militants Probed," September 19, 2002, http://www.cnsne om/ForeignBureaus/Archive/200209/FOR20020919a.html.

75. For a detailed scussion of links among these groups, see Barry Desker and Kumar Ramakrishna, "For an Indirect Strategy in Southeast Asia," *Washington Quarterly*, Vol. 25, No. 2 (Spring 2002), pp 1–176.

Three other camps for foreigners were opened in the 1990's—Camp Palestine, primarily for Arabs; Camp Vietnam and Camp Hudaibie, for Malaysians and Indonesians."[76] MILF officials have themselves acknowledged that members of their group trained in Afghanistan and fought against the Soviets there.[77]

Singaporean officials have detailed kinship ties between MILF and Jemaah Islamiah members,[78] as well as an attempt by Jemaah Islamiah operations chief, Riduan Isamuddin (also known as Hambali), to establish a coalition of Southeast Asian Islamic groups that included the MILF. According to these officials, "The alliance sought to promote cooperation among the separate militant groups in obtaining arms, training and financial support, as well as conducting terrorist attacks."[79] In 2003 Fathur Rohman al-Ghozi, a member of Jemaah Islamiah known to have "trained terrorists from all over the Islamic world in bomb-making at a camp run by the Moro Islamic Liberation Front," was captured and killed by the Philippine military.[80] Interrogations of captured Jemaah Islamiah terrorists, such as Hambali in 2003, though unreliable in themselves, confirm the evidence of cooperation between the two groups.[81]

Differences between groups such as the MILF, on the one hand, and Jemaah Islamiah and al-Qaida, on the other, make the former more susceptible to certain kinds of deterrence strategies. Despite MILF cooperation with Jemaah Islamiah and al-Qaida in the past, the global objectives of these two groups are not part of the MILF's core agenda. The MILF explicitly rejected the Taliban's call for a jihad against the United States and its allies after the terrorist attacks on the World Trade Center and the Pentagon.[82] It specifically condemned the attacks, as well as the Abu Sayyaf Group and the other "terrorists" in the Southern Philippines.[83] Further, the Philippine government appears willing to

76. Raymond Bonner, "Threats and Responses: Foreign Correspondents; Southeast Asia Remains Fertile for Al Qaeda," *New York Times*, October 28, 2002.
77. See "Philippines: Island under Siege," PBS, *Frontline*, http://www.pbs.org/frontlineworld/stories/philippines/thestory.html.
78. Helmi Yusof, "Nabbed: Two Groomed to Head Jemaah Islamiah Group," *Straits Times*, December 19, 2003.
79. Alan Sipress and Ellen Nakashima, "Militant Alliance in Asia Is Said to Seek Regional Islamic State," *Washington Post*, September 20, 2002.
80. Richard C. Paddock and Al Jacinto, "Bomb Maker Gunned Down in Philippines," *Los Angeles Times*, October 13, 2003.
81. Sol Jose Vanzi, "Jamaah Islamiyah Still Working with MILF," Philippine Headline News Online, October 7, 2003, http://www.newsflash.org/2003/05/ht/ht003782.htm.
82. The Taliban, which was in close alliance with Osama bin Laden, ruled Afghanistan from 1996 to 2001, when it was overthrown by U.S. troops in response to the September 11 attacks.
83. See Christina Mendez, "MILF Rejects 'Holy War' vs. US," *Philippine Star*, September 17, 2001,

accommodate r ıy of the goals the MILF is seeking in the ongoing negotiations, and the ; ›up's goals can certainly be accommodated by the United States, which h little stake in the conflict. Thus, despite the relatively high level of motiva n of MILF members, there appears to be an opportunity to deter the grour om particular courses of action, such as pursuing an independent state a l using terror tactics. Even if an ultimate resolution of the conflict cannot l reached, however, the threat of U.S. involvement could deter MILF cooperati with al-Qaida, Jemaah Islamiah, and the Abu Sayyaf Group.

Following th eptember 11 attacks, the U.S. and Philippine governments used the threat inclusion on the U.S. FTO list as a means of coercing the MILF.[84] In early ay 2003, the United States explicitly linked this threat to the cessation of M violence against civilians. As the U.S. ambassador to the Philippines, Fra is Ricciardone, stated, "If they continue with acts of terrorism, everybody ill consider them terrorists."[85] He further warned the rebels that they woulc se $30 million earmarked by the U.S. Congress for their area if they did not t their links to Jemaah Islamiah.[86] Other threats were likely communicated the MILF through channels that have not yet been documented or ma public, and the coordinated U.S.-Philippine use of force against the Abı ayyaf Group must have been at least implicitly threatening. The MILF has ı bably been under threat (implicitly and explicitly) from the United States a the European Union for several years.

The positive n that peace talks appear to have taken in the last couple of years may be t result of a combination of promised rewards and the increased severit the threats that Philippine negotiators can credibly bring to bear in an env ıment of heightened U.S. concerns about terrorist activity. However, becaı sporadic peace talks began several years prior to the Sep-

---

cited in Larry Niks "Abu Sayyaf: Target of Philippine-U.S. Anti-terrorism Cooperation," CRS report (Washington C.: Congressional Research Service, January 25, 2002), p. 5; and MILF press release, February 1 003.

84. "GMA Inclinec Tag MILF Terrorist," Philippine Headline News Online, May 11, 2003, http://www.newsfl .org/2003/05/pe/pe002597.htm. As discussed above, inclusion on the U.S. FTO list places resı ions on the ability of a group to raise funds abroad.

85. Norman Borda a and Carlito Pablo, "Ricciardone: U.S. May Declare MILF a Terrorist Group," Inquirer n service, May 6, 2003, http://www.inq7.net/nat/2003/may/07/nat_2-1.htm; and "U.S. Wanted M F on Terror List," Sun.Star Network Online, November 6, 2002,http://www .sunstar.com.ph/sta net/2002/11/06/us.wanted.milf.on.terror.list.official.html; and Cartilo Pablo, Norman Bordadora d Armand N. Nocum, "RP Won't Ask U.S. to Recall Terrorist Tag," Inquirer news service, Janu 28, 2003, http://ebalita.net/go/news/news.php?id=861.

86. "U.S. to MILF: Terror Ties or Lose Aid," October 2, 2003, Sun.Star Network Online, http://www.sunstar.com.ı static/net/2003/10/02/us.to.milf.cut.terror.ties.or.lose.aid.html.

tember 11 attacks, we can only speculate about this. But on the issue of deterring cooperation between the MILF and Jemaah Islamiah, the Abu Sayyaf Group, and al-Qaida, a significant change in the MILF's position does appear to have occurred, with its causal roots in the changed post–September 11 environment. In November 2002, as a result of negotiations between the U.S. and Philippine governments and the MILF, the latter promised to help local authorities arrest about 100 suspected al-Qaida and Jemaah Islamiah operatives. As one of the negotiators explained, the MILF "is more than willing to provide concrete proof that it's not a terrorist group by helping us root out terrorists in the country."[87] The group also agreed to assist the Philippine government in fighting the Abu Sayyaf Group. To this end, it warned the group's members against entering the territories the MILF controls and directed its armed forces to go after "bandits" and other criminal elements in these areas.[88]

Cooperation against the Abu Sayyaf Group continues, and according to Philippine Maj. Gen. Raul Relano, the government, "will not stop tracking [the Abu Sayyaf Group] down with the help of our MILF friends."[89] The Philippine government and the MILF have also coordinated in strikes against the Abu Sayyaf Group and the "Pentagon Gang" (a Filipino terrorist group that broke away from the MILF in 2001 and has continued its involvement in kidnappings and extortion and is currently on the U.S. State Department's Terrorist Exclusion List[90]). What is significant about these latest examples of cooperation with the government is not only that the targeted area is an MILF stronghold, but that the rebels provided the Philippine military with critical intelligence, including information on former MILF members, and even with operational support.[91]

Antiterrorist cooperation between the Philippine government and the MILF was formalized in May 2002 with the creation of the Ad Hoc Joint Action

87. Quoted in Carlito Pablo, "More Rebels to Hunt Jemaah Islamiah Agents," Inquirer news service, November 5, 2002, http://www.inq7.net/nat/2002/nov/06/nat_1-1.htm.
88. Keith Bacongo, "MILF to Help Government Crush Abu Sayyaf," *MindaNews.com,* June 12, 2002, http://www.mindanews.com/2002/06/3rd/nws12abu.html; and Florante Solmerin, "AFP, MILF Team Up vs. Sayyaf," *Manila Standard,* September 16, 2005.
89. "GMA Adviser Sees No Obstacle to Pact with MILF," *Philippine Daily Inquirer,* December 1, 2004.
90. U.S. Department of State, *Patterns of Global Terrorism—2003,"* http://www.state.gov/s/ct/rls/pgtrpt/2003/31747.htm, app. D.
91. "Philippine Military Chief: Abu Sayyaf Leader Hiding in Moro Rebel Area," BBC, December 6, 2004; and BBC, "Philippine MORO Group Confirms Support for Operation against Kidnap Gang," August 15, 2004. See also Raymond Bonner and Carlos H. Conde, "U.S. and the Philippines Join Forces to Pursue Terrorist Leader," *New York Times,* July 22, 2005.

Group, which i sked with carrying out a joint operation to isolate "criminal syndicates, kid p-for-ransom groups and other criminal elements within MILF-controlle reas."[92] At that time, negotiations failed to establish guidelines for action, t in late December 2004, this hurdle was overcome. According to MILF sp sman, Eid Kabalu, "The joint effort to fight terrorism" now includes "comp hensive coverage of the Southern Philippines."[93]

This case ill ates the potential of coercion even against nonstate actors and highly mot ted groups that have engaged in terrorist activities. The case also demonstra the importance of tailoring the coercive approach to the goals and situa n of particular groups. It is therefore essential that faraway powers unders d local conflicts intimately before becoming involved.

JOINT MILITARY TION AGAINST THE ABU SAYYAF GROUP

To fully unders d the dynamics of deterrence in the MILF case, it is helpful to consider bot des' evaluations of a counterfactual, namely, what the state of affairs woul e if the U.S. and the Philippine governments used force against the MI As discussed above, for a deterrence equilibrium to exist, both sides mus ew this outcome as less preferable to the terms of a negotiated solution. S h counterfactuals are always difficult to know. We can gain some insight i these questions, however, by briefly considering a case known to all pa s to the negotiations: the joint U.S.-Philippine military operation against t Abu Sayyaf Group.

Like the MIL he Abu Sayyaf Group also split from the MNLF, and the region of its basi areas is known. Definitive information is difficult to obtain, but the group a ears to number in the hundreds and to be motivated primarily by the profit gains from kidnapping ransoms.[94] Its ties to bin Laden date back to fighting Afghanistan in the 1980s. From January to July of 2002, the U.S. and Philip e armed forces conducted Operation Balikatan against the Abu Sayyaf G p. Approximately 1,300 U.S. troops, including 160 special forces, and mo han 3,000 Philippine soldiers participated in the operation,

92. See "Joint Com nique between the Government of the Republic of the Philippines and the Moro Liberation y," signed on May 6, 2002, http://www.mindanews.com/peprcs/milf/may6.shtml.
93. Barbara Mae D ay, "Manila and Moros Step Up Campaign against Terrorists," *Gulf News*, December 31, 2004.
94. U.S. Departme f State, *Patterns of Global Terrorism—2003*, app. B.

whose main goal was to neutralize the group and to free three hostages (two Americans and one Filipino).[95]

This operation exemplifies some of the inherent limitations of using force against terrorists, even though states can harm terrorist groups. Although several hundred Abu Sayyaf Group members were killed, its leadership remained largely intact and capable of planning and conducting new attacks. One of the American hostages was rescued, but the other two (an American missionary and a Filipino nurse) were killed. Basilan island, a stronghold of the group, was pacified, but the Abu Sayyaf Group moved to Jolo island, which became the new center of violence.[96] Following the operation, Abu Sayyaf Group activities included a series of bombings, one of which killed a U.S. Green Beret.[97] The presence of U.S. troops in the Philippines also "caused widespread resentment and apprehensions that the U.S. presence may become permanent as it was before 1992."[98] This presence may radicalize some moderate Muslims in the area, who have historically been supportive of the United States.[99]

For the past several years, the U.S. and Philippine governments have been considering further joint operations against the Abu Sayyaf Group, undertaking one in July 2005.[100] Like previous operations, these are likely to kill some militants, but not all. Those remaining may become more radicalized, and they may seek to join global terrorist groups when their local objectives are put out of reach.

Were coordinated U.S.-Philippine military action to be taken against the MILF, the results would likely be similar, though on a much larger scale given its greater size. When President Estrada declared "all out war" on the group in January 1999, 90,000 civilians lost their homes; the operational capabilities of

95. For more details, see C.S. Kuppuswamy, "Abu Sayyaf: The Cause for the Return of U.S. Troops to Philippines?" *South Asia Analysis Group*, No. 417 (February 2002); and C.S. Kuppuswamy, "Philippines: The U.S. Campaign against Abu Sayyaf," *South Asia Analysis Group*, paper no. 498, July 2002.
96. Eric Schmitt with Carlos H. Conde, "U.S. and the Philippines May Start New Training Mission," *New York Times*, December 1, 2002.
97. Ellen Nakashima, "Island in Philippines Poses Counterterrorism Challenge," *Washington Post*, December 21, 2002; and "Abu Sayyaf Launches New Attacks," Inquirer news service, July 4, 2003, http://www.inq7.net/reg/2003/jul/04/reg_9-1.htm.
98. Kuppuswamy, "Abu Sayyaf."
99. See, for example, Mark Landler, "A Nation Challenged: The Philippines; The Temperature's a Lot Warmer but the Mission's the Same: Hunting Down Terrorists," *New York Times*, November 4, 2001.
100. Bonner and Conde, "U.S. and the Philippines Join Force to Pursue Terrorist Leader," p. 4.

the group were tarded but not destroyed; and it was encouraged to adopt more extreme t ics, including an apparent alliance with another insurgent group, the New 'hilippines Army, in Southern Mindanao. (The two groups agreed to "con ct joint attacks and training exchanges and to share weapons."[101]) The us f military force thus has both benefits and costs. Its periodic use may be nec ary to make threats credible, but in particular situations, deterrence appear o be a preferred alternative.

Conclusions a Recommendations for U.S. Counterterrorism Policy

Our analysis le s to several conclusions for U.S. counterterrorism policy. First, when ade ate resources are devoted to deterrence, traditional targeting of nonpolitical ls can sometimes deter critical elements of terrorist networks from participati in terrorist enterprises. Significant resources should therefore be devoted pursuing all elements of terrorist systems responsible for attacks after the f to demonstrate the capability and will to do so and thereby increase the like ood of future deterrence success. This implies a higher level of resource con itment than would be the case if the policy objective were merely to brin individuals responsible to justice.[102] Particular emphasis should be plac on terrorist financiers because they have targetable assets (nonpolitical en) that stand a reasonable chance of being found.

Second, even e most highly motivated terrorist groups can be deterred from certain co es of action. Of principal importance to the U.S. campaign against al-Qaid nd like-minded groups is the ability to prevent them from cooperating wi each other to achieve synergies. As in the case of the MILF, groups that are imarily focused on local concerns can be coerced into denying sanctuary (a other assistance) to members of more dangerous groups.[103]

When the Ur d States moves beyond a deterrence posture and becomes even more dee involved in local conflicts, it will confront a number of important costs ar risks. As Robert Pape and others have shown, U.S. presence abroad can pro te the spread of extremist ideologies.[104] The use of military

101. Antonio Lope Mindanao's Chance," *AsiaWeek*, March 5, 1999, p. 1.
102. On the effects demonstrations of force on conventional deterrence, see Snyder, *Deterrence and Defense*, pp. 25 58.
103. Denying terro sanctuary is a key recommendation of *The 9/11 Commission Report*, pp. 365–367.
104. Pape, *Dying to n*. See also Evan Eland, "Does U.S. Intervention Overseas Breed Terrorism? The Historical Rec " Cato Institute Foreign Policy Briefing no. 50, December 17, 1998, http://www.cato.org/pub briefs/fpb50.pdf; U.S. Department of State, *Patterns of Global Terrorism:*

force, in addition to carrying direct costs in lives and resources, can become a critical source of disagreement between allies, as the lead-up to the 2003 Iraq war showed. Similar disagreements in the future could jeopardize critical U.S. efforts to maintain a broad antiterrorist coalition. Further, the use of force against terrorists and insurgencies often fails to achieve political objectives (as the Abu Sayyaf case shows), and as Martha Crenshaw warns, "may radicalize the whole movement or some splinter faction."[105]

The application of force, and other aggressive policies, against a set of adversaries can also create powerful common interests, driving them to cooperate.[106] For instance, in apparent reaction to being branded a terrorist group and having its foreign assets frozen by Western governments, the communist New People's Army of the Philippines announced it would combine forces with the MILF.[107] In fact, the very effectiveness of local antiterrorism efforts may even turn a local movement into a global one. When primary local goals are put out of reach, militants may shift their focus to secondary global goals. Thus, Egypt's effectiveness in eliminating the threat posed by Islamic Jihad may have been a reason militants such as Ayman al-Zawahiri refocused their efforts on new targets,[108] linking up with bin Laden and al-Qaida.[109]

In choosing among policy options, decisionmakers must bear these costs in mind. This is not to say that the United States should not consider strong measures, such as the use of military force, in the war on terror. By holding at risk the local agendas of local groups, however, the United States can often more effectively achieve its ends of preventing cooperation between groups and denying sanctuary to those against which force will have to be used. Because this sort of deterrence strategy is also less resource intensive, and less likely to

---

1997, Department of State Publication 10535 (Washington, D.C.: Office of the Coordinator for Counterterrorism, Office of the Secretary of State, April 1998), http://www.state.gov/www/global/terrorism/1997Report/1997index.html, p. 2; "Professor Chaos: Consultant Brian Jenkins Deconstructs Terrorism's Big Picture," *Washington Post*, June 1, 2003; and Christopher Marquis, "World's View of U.S. Sours after Iraq War, Poll Finds," *New York Times*, June 4, 2003.

105. "How Terrorism Ends," special report no. 48 (Washington, D.C.: United States Institute of Peace, May 25, 1999). See also Ehud Sprinzak, "The Great Superterrorism Scare," *Foreign Policy*, No. 112 (Fall 1988), pp. 110–124.

106. For the opposite argument, see James S. Robbins, "Freedom Eagle," *National Review*, January 18, 2002, http://www.nationalreview.com/contributors/robbins011802.shtml.

107. Erin Prelypchan, "Manila's Twin Nightmare," *Newsweek*, March 24, 2003, p. 36.

108. The founder of Egyptian Islamic Jihad, al-Zawahiri allegedly played a key role in the 1988 bombings of the U.S. embassies in Tanzania and Kenya. He is believed to continue to serve as a doctor and close adviser to Osama bin Laden.

109. Nimrod Raphaeli, "Ayman Muhammad Rabi' Al-Zawahiri: The Making of an Arch-Terrorist," *Terrorism and Political Violence*, Vol. 14, No. 4 (Winter 2002), pp. 1–22.

cause disagreer its among U.S. allies, spread extremism, and drive terrorist
groups togethe t is often likely to prove more effective.

Third, most t orist groups can be deterred from cooperating with al-Qaida
because it is nc he archetypal terrorist group. The breadth of its reach, the
fanaticism of its embers, and the sweeping nature of its goals make it the exception rather t n the rule. Policymakers should not assume that the experience of the figh gainst al-Qaida is transferable to other groups.

Fourth, the fc s of applied resources in the antiterrorist campaign should
be narrowly on -Qaida and its few current and potential allies whose ideological affinity i o strong or whose gains from cooperation so great that they
cannot be deter . The threat that groups that target the United States directly
will develop or quire the means of causing mass casualties far outweighs all
other terrorist t ats the United States faces. Because of the magnitude of the
resource comm ent required to achieve U.S. objectives against these groups,
and the gravity the threat they pose, no resources should be unnecessarily
squandered on s essential tasks (except perhaps for purposes of demonstrating capability l resolve in the event of deterrence failure). By deterring
other groups fr cooperating with those judged most dangerous, the United
States can signi ntly decrease the capacity of groups such as al-Qaida, while
still preserving resources for use against al-Qaida directly.

Fifth, deterre by denial strategies decrease the coercive leverage of terrorist tactics and t efore the motivation to carry out attacks. The United States
should apply su strategies against groups that directly target it. Soft terrorist
targets should l hardened, and resolve not to back down in the face of anti-
U.S. terrorism s uld be demonstrated whenever possible.[110]

These conclu ns and recommendations are particularly timely because of
the debate with the Bush administration regarding the appropriate scope of
the global war c terrorism. In the spring of 2005, the administration started a
high-level revie of its overall counterterrorism policy.[111] Taking into account
the lessons fron he last three years and changes in the nature of al-Qaida it-

---

110. Recent policy ements have recognized the deterrent potential of defensive measures. See, for example, Depa nt of Defense, *The National Defense Strategy of the United States of America* (Washington, D.C.: . Government Printing Office, March 2005), http://www.defenselink.mil/news/Mar2005/d2 0318nds2.pdf.

111. See, for exam Susan B. Glasser, "Review May Shift Terror Policies; U.S. Is Expected to Look beyond Al Qa ," *Washington Post*, May 29, 2005; Jim Hogland, "A Shifting Focus on Terrorism," *Washington P* April 24, 2005; and Linda Robinson, "Plan of Attack," *U.S. News and World Report*, August 1, 2 , p. 26.

self, the U.S. government is considering comprehensive changes in its counterterrorism strategy. Although it is too early to know for certain, early reports suggest the likelihood of several key shifts.[112] The new policy will emphasize the need to broaden the tools used to fight terrorism to more fully include the use of all instruments of power—diplomatic, economic, and political. This is all to the good, particularly as it will include resources to more directly confront the spread of extremist ideas. At the same time, however, a debate continues within the administration on the optimal scope of the antiterrorist campaign, especially once fewer military and intelligence resources are focused on Iraq. A significant broadening of the scope of the campaign to include more aggressive policies targeted at a wider range of terrorist groups will run the risks of high levels of U.S. involvement in local conflicts described above. To the extent the United States is able to minimize the resources required to achieve these additional objectives by working indirectly through partner nations, the risks will be reduced but not eliminated. Given that the central policy objective in targeting these groups is to prevent them from increasing al-Qaida's global reach, a deterrence policy may be a better option.

112. Important bureaucratic changes will also be made. See, for example, Hogland, "A Shifting Focus on Terrorism."

Fri nds Like These

Co iterinsurgency and the War on Terrorism

Daniel L. Byman

Throughout the 1980s, the United Stat poured money into El Salvador to check communist expansion in Central nerica. Although at that time the Salvador conflict was the costliest U.S. m ary effort since Vietnam, at the end of the decade the United States found it spinning its wheels. Despite almost a decade of training, aid, and high-le l pushes for reform, the Salvador armed forces still suffered basic flaws suc a mediocre and disengaged officer corps, widespread corruption, a poor omotion system, and conscripts who did not want to fight. These military aknesses were only part of a broader problem. The armed forces perpetra or supported blatant and brutal oppression such as the killing of moderat olitical opponents and Catholic Church officials, including priests and nu The military also was a strong voice against much-needed economic, poli l, and social reforms that, had they been implemented, would have hi red the insurgents' ability to recruit and operate. Not surprisingly, as th ecade ended, U.S. military officials concluded that an outright military v ory over the communist insurgents was unlikely and that a political settlen t was required.

In his landm study of El Salvador, Benjamin Schwarz found that the problem was n hat the United States was fighting the wrong war or otherwise repeating tnam-era mistakes of using conventional military power to fight an uncon tional war. Rather, the United States did not understand its own allies. El S ador's military mirrored the country as a whole, complete with the same f tures, weaknesses, and pathologies. Indeed, U.S. attempts to initiate reform n failed because they relied on the Salvadoran military and government e though they had interests quite distinct from the U.S. agenda.[1] Nor i l Salvador an exception. In his study of various Cold War

---

Daniel L. Byman is ctor of the Center for Peace and Security Studies and Associate Professor in the Edmund A. Walsh S l of Foreign Service at Georgetown University. He is also a nonresident Senior Fellow in the Saban Ce for Middle East Policy at the Brookings Institution.

The author would e to thank Sunil Dasgupta, David Edelstein, Alan Kuperman, Kathleen McNamara, Sara B Moller, Jeremy Shapiro, Benjamin Valentino, and two anonymous reviewers. The piece dra part on his 2005 monograph *Going to War with the Allies You Have: Allies, Counterinsurgency, the War on Terror* (Carlisle, Pa.: U.S. Army War College).

1. For a superb o iew of the U.S. counterinsurgency program and its many problems, see Benjamin C. Schwa *American Counterinsurgency Doctrine and El Salvador: The Frustrations of Re-*

International Security, 31, No. 2 (Fall 2006), pp. 79–115

insurgencies, Douglas Blaufarb found that the United States consistently had little leverage with its allies, which frequently pursued policies that both hindered counterinsurgency (COIN) and went contrary to U.S. interests.[2]

The El Salvador and other Cold War experiences are relevant to policymakers today as well as to historians, for the September 11, 2001, terrorist attacks on the United States not only ushered in a new era of counterterrorism, but they also forced the return of the counterinsurgency era. The global effort against al-Qaida has meant closer ties with a number of governments involved in fighting Islamist insurgents that, to different degrees, have ties to al-Qaida. Since the attacks, the United States has forged closer relations with Algeria, Pakistan, and other countries fighting insurgent groups that have relations with the global Sunni jihadist movement that al-Qaida champions, as well as having become embroiled in a costly counterinsurgency campaign in Iraq that has become linked to the global jihad. In most of these struggles, local security forces are the tip of the spear. And in Iraq, one of the most important U.S. problems is that Iraqi security forces are too inept to take over from the United States.

Despite this central importance, thinking and scholarship on counterinsurgency tends to ignore the role of allies. Analyses are typically divided into two kinds: those that focus on the insurgents, and those that examine COIN forces, with the latter including both the United States and the host government and thus wrongly assuming they both share the same interests. Even the U.S. counterinsurgency doctrine issued in 2004 mentions the role of the host nation only in passing, without any serious discussion given to problems that may be encountered.[3]

What obstacles do potential U.S. allies face when fighting insurgents? What are the sources of these challenges? What influence can the United States exert to compensate for its allies' weaknesses? These are the questions this article seeks to answer.

---

form and the Illusions of Nation Building (Santa Monica, Calif.: RAND, 1991). Another valuable study of the U.S. problems in El Salvador with regard to reform is Andrew J. Bacevich, James D. Hallums, Richard H. White, and Thomas F. Young, *American Military Policy in Small Wars: The Case of El Salvador* (Washington, D.C.: Pergamon-Brassey's, 1988).

2. Douglas Blaufarb, *The Counterinsurgency Era: U.S. Doctrine and Performance* (New York: Free Press, 1977). This proved a particular problem for the United States in Vietnam where, as in Iraq today, the goal was to stand the Vietnamese up while U.S. forces stood down. For a review, see Scott Sigmund Gartner, "Differing Evaluations of Vietnamization," *Journal of Interdisciplinary History*, Vol. 29, No. 2 (Autumn 1998), pp. 243–262.

3. U.S. Army, "Counterinsurgency Operations," FMI3-07.22 (Washington, D.C.: U.S. Army Headquarters, 2004), section 2-16, notes that the United States seeks to improve host-nation security forces, but it does not discuss their common problems and weaknesses.

This article d vs on several bodies of research to better understand why allies often perf poorly, including principal-agent theory, work on moral hazards, and t vast body of research on the general problems facing alliances.[4] The pri pal-agent approach and work on alliances suggest that allies often have high divergent objectives and that they can effectively manipulate information to loit the United States. When trying to exert control over its allies, the Unit tates frequently faces problems identified by scholars working on moral ards: the very words Washington uses to demonstrate its commitment to ally have the unintended effect of making the ally more reckless and le ikely to heed the wishes of the United States.

U.S. allies tha re fighting al-Qaida-linked insurgencies often have four categories of struc al problems that explain some of their distinct interests and lead to particul challenges against insurgents: illegitimate (and often repressive) regimes; l-military tension manifested by fears of a coup; economic backwardness; d discriminatory societies.[5] Because of these problems, allies frequently stra r from the counterinsurgency ideal, both militarily and politically. Their itary culture often is characterized by poor intelligence; a lack of initiativ little integration of forces across units; soldiers who do not want to fight; l officers and noncommissioned officers (NCOs); and difficulties with t ning, learning, and creativity. In addition, the structural weaknesses ha direct political effect that can aid an insurgency by hindering the develo nt and implementation of a national strategy, encouraging widespread co ption, alienating the military from the overall population,

---

4. This article does claim to systematically test these literatures. Rather, it selectively draws on their insights to she ght on the problems the United States faces when confronting insurgencies.
5. The forces exam l include not only regular military forces but also those involved in fighting the insurgency, suc special police and intelligence units. In Saudi Arabia, for example, the regular army is exclu from many sensitive duties linked to counterterrorism and counterinsurgency, with the Sau rabian National Guard playing the key role. The special security forces and the special emerge forces play particularly important roles in the effort against al-Qaida. See Anthony H. Cord an and Nawaf Obaid, "Saudi Internal Security: A Risk Assessment," Working Draft (Wa gton, D.C.: Center for Strategic and International Studies, May 2004), p. 18. In Algeria, initial f res led to the formation of elite COIN units that over time became quite large. Luis Martine *e Algerian Civil War, 1990–1998*, trans. Jonathan Derrick (New York: Columbia University Pres 000), p. 149. India has numerous forces involved in fighting insurgents in Kashmir, including regular and special police, village defense committees, the central reserve police force, the Inc reserve police force, the central industrial security force, and the border security force. For a w, see Thomas A. Marks, "At the Frontlines of the GWOT: State Response to Insurgency in Ja u," *Journal of Counterterrorism & Homeland Security International*, Vol. 10, No. 1 (Fall 2003), pp. 3 . In many countries, the paramilitary forces are as large or larger than the regular army force Uzbekistan, the paramilitary forces number approximately 20,000, and those in the regula my and air force account for another 55,000. Roger N. McDermott, "The Armed Forces of th epublic of Uzbekistan, 1992–2002: Threats, Influence, and Reform," *Journal of Slavic Military St s*, Vol. 16, No. 2 (June 2003), p. 29.

and offering the insurgents opportunities to penetrate the military. Taken together, these problems and divergent interests explain in part why allies often have security services that are poorly postured to fight insurgencies and why allies do not make the necessary reforms to improve their performance.

The United States is on the horns of a dilemma when working with allies to fight insurgents. Allies experience insurgencies because of the weakness of the state, as well as other factors such as discrimination and corruption.[6] These problems create tremendous difficulties when the United States expects allied militaries to fight on its behalf—the structural problems that cause the insurgencies also shape how well allies fight them.

The implications of these weaknesses go beyond the ability (or lack thereof) of local forces to fight the insurgents and shape the relationship between the regime and the United States. Washington must recognize that its allies, including those in allied militaries, are often ineffective at fighting insurgents and at times can make the problem worse. U.S. COIN doctrine, no matter how well thought out, cannot succeed without the appropriate political and other reforms from the host nation, but these regimes are likely to subvert the reforms that threaten the existing power structure. The influence of the United States is often limited, as the allies recognize that its vital interests with regard to fighting al-Qaida-linked groups are likely to outweigh any temporary disgust or anger of an ally's brutality or failure to institute reforms.

These conflicting interests are painfully relevant to Iraq today. The United States seeks to shift the primary burden for fighting the Iraqi insurgency to Iraqi forces. Should this happen, the broader problems in Iraqi society and the distinct interests of those who make up the regime are likely to cause severe problems for the Iraqi forces fighting the insurgency, suggesting that the U.S. strategy to "hand off" the fight to local allies may fail.

To help overcome these problems, the United States should try to increase its intelligence on allied security forces so that it can better understand the true nature of their activities. To reduce its vulnerability to manipulation, the United States should also try to diversify its intelligence sources to ensure that it does not rely exclusively on the local ally for information. At times, Washington should try to act more like a third party to a conflict rather than an open and strong ally of government forces. In doing so, it can better exert lev-

6. James D. Fearon and David D. Laitin believe that factors that indicate a country is vulnerable to insurgency include poverty (which suggests states that are poor and bureaucratically weak), instability, inaccessible terrain, and a large population. See Fearon and Laitin, "Ethnicity, Insurgency, and Civil War," *American Political Science Review*, Vol. 97, No. 1 (February 2003), pp. 75–90.

erage over the ernment to make useful reforms and other concessions that might help solv undamental problems.

In all of its C N programs, the United States must have realistic expectations. Training, ilitary-to-military contacts, education programs, and other efforts to bolste s COIN capabilities all can be beneficial. Indeed, these capabilities are ofte ne best available options for the United States to shape and help allied effo . Washington must recognize, however, that the effects of various COIN grams are likely to be limited at best because of the structural problems d divergent interests noted above: even massive amounts of aid cannot crea healthy economy where the preconditions of the rule of law and social stabi do not exist, and U.S. programs for developing honest government can at st help around the margins. At times, the brutality and incompetence of local regime may simply be too much to overcome. In these cases, the Unite tates may damage its image profoundly yet achieve little on the ground, wh suggests that the United States should carefully pick its battles and not em ace every counterinsurgency effort uncritically.

The article h seven main sections. The first section discusses the overlap between count nsurgency and counterterrorism. The second section describes the role allies in counterinsurgency, with a particular focus on countries fighting a aida-linked insurgencies. To identify likely problems, this section draws n research on alliances made during conventional wars and by looking at w on principal-agent problems that have plagued many businesses and inte tional organizations. The third section offers an "ideal type" COIN force an hen assesses how allied militaries involved in the struggle against al-Qaid are against this hypothetical force. The fourth section discusses the struc al factors that shape allies' military cultures and their political profiles and plains how these general factors in turn affect the politics of counterinsurge and the military cultures of the countries in question as they are releva o COIN. The fifth examines the implications for the United States and disc s the limits of U.S. influence over its allies. The sixth section discusses the i lications of many of these problems for Iraq, should the United States t sfer more of the burden of fighting the insurgency to the Iraqi forces. Th rticle concludes with recommendations for how to mitigate some of the pr ems.

Counterterror , Counterinsurgency, and al-Qaida

Counterinsurge y and counterterrorism overlap considerably both in theory and in practice. is article uses the definition of "insurgency" provided in the

Central Intelligence Agency pamphlet "Guide to the Analysis of Insurgency," which reads as follows:

Insurgency is a protracted political-military activity directed toward completely or partially controlling the resources of a country through the use of irregular military forces and illegal political organizations. Insurgent activity—including guerrilla warfare, terrorism, and political mobilization, for example, propaganda, recruitment, front and covert party organization, and international activity—is designed to weaken government control and legitimacy while increasing insurgent control and legitimacy. The common denominator of most insurgent groups is their desire to control a particular area. This objective differentiates insurgent groups from purely terrorist organizations, whose objectives do not include the creation of an alternative government capable of controlling a given area or country.[7]

Insurgents' primary method is usually guerrilla war, which is often supplemented by terrorism—defined as the use of violence or the threat of violence against civilians to achieve a political purpose and have a psychological effect. Terrorism offers insurgents another method of weakening a state and can give more narrow advantages in the broader struggle. For example, killing civilians may lead a rival ethnic group to flee a contested area, demonstrate that the government cannot impose order and protect its people, and convince officials and the populace as a whole to collaborate out of fear.[8]

The relationship between counterterrorism and counterinsurgency is not new. Many of the state-supported terrorist groups are also insurgencies—there is no clear dividing line, and in fact tremendous overlap exists. Although the exact percentage depends heavily on coding decisions, in my judgment approximately half of the groups listed by the U.S. Department of State as foreign terrorist organizations in 2005 were insurgencies as well as terrorist groups.[9] Even more important, the majority of the most worrisome terrorist groups in the world today are also insurgencies. The Liberation Tigers of Tamil Eelam (LTTE), the Kurdish Workers' Party, the Lebanese Hezbollah, and the Revolu-

7. Central Intelligence Agency, "Guide to the Analysis of Insurgency" (Washington, D.C.: Central Intelligence Agency), p. 2. The pamphlet was published in the 1980s. For an alternative definition that emphasizes the importance of guerrilla war and the spirit of peasant rebellion, see Raj M. Desai and Harry Eckstein, "Insurgency: The Transformation of Peasant Rebellion," *World Politics*, Vol. 42, No. 4 (July 1990), p. 442. Fearon and Laitin define "insurgency" as involving guerrilla warfare from rural base areas, whereas the U.S. Army definition emphasizes that "political power is the central issue in an insurgency." Fearon and Laitin, "Ethnicity, Insurgency, and Civil War"; and U.S. Army, "Counterinsurgency Operations," sec. 1-1.
8. See Daniel L. Byman, "The Logic of Ethnic Terrorism," *Studies in Conflict and Terrorism*, Vol. 21, No. 2 (April/June 1998), pp. 149–169.
9. U.S. Department of State, *Country Reports on Terrorism, 2005* (Washington, D.C.: U.S. Department of State, April 2006), pp. 183–228.

tionary Armed rces of Colombia all use guerrilla war as a major component in their struggl ust as the Palestine Liberation Organization attempted to do in the 1960s anc 70s. Indeed, many terrorist groups that did not use guerrilla warfare, such a he Provisional Irish Republican Army and Hamas, had attempted to do but found they were not strong enough. Other insurgent groups often e nd their activities to include terrorism. Lashkar-e-Taiba, an insurgent grou ghting in Kashmir, also began to conduct terrorist attacks in the rest of Indi s its campaign wore on.[10]

Al-Qaida rec nizes the importance of insurgencies. Michael Scheuer, a prominent cou rterrorism expert, argues that its leader, Osama bin Laden, has promoted (l at times directed) a "worldwide, religiously inspired, and professionally ded Islamist insurgency."[11] Support for insurgencies in Chechnya, Afg istan, Iraq, and elsewhere has long been an al-Qaida priority as is shown its rhetoric, recruitment, and spending.[12] Understandably, the United Stat focuses on terrorist attacks, but with regard to both body counts and des ilization, these lower-profile insurgencies are causing much greater sufferin

Insurgencies ve several vital organizational functions for al-Qaida beyond its broad mbition of wanting them to triumph and replace local governments. Insu nt veterans are often at the core of the terrorist organization. The long strug against the Soviet Union in Afghanistan, of course, was a uniting expe nce for much of the al-Qaida leadership. Many members also came toge r and were vetted in struggles in the Balkans, Chechnya, Kashmir, and n Iraq.[13] Because al-Qaida can tap into these insurgencies for recruits and its gistics network, it is able to conduct operations far beyond where its narr core is located and can replenish cadre as they are lost.[14] Insurgencies al add legitimacy to al-Qaida as Muslims around the world support many these struggles, even though they might otherwise oppose al-Qaida's ideo ical agenda and use of terrorism. Thus, defeating al-Qaida

10. Thomas A. Ma "India: State Response to Insurgency in Jammu & Kashmir—The Jammu Case," *Low Intensit nflict & Law Enforcement*, Vol. 12, No. 3 (Autumn 2004), p. 137.

11. See Anonymou *hrough Our Enemies' Eyes: Osama bin Laden, Radical Islam, and the Future of America* (Washingt .C.: Brassey's, 2002), p. xviii. "Anonymous" was subsequently revealed as Michael Scheuer.

12. Ibid., p. 207.

13. National Comn on on Terrorist Attacks Upon the United States, *The 9/11 Commission Report* (New York: W.W. ton, 2004), pp. 47–70; and Marc Sageman, *Understanding Terror Networks* (Philadelphia: Uni ty of Pennsylvania Press, 2004).

14. The ability to r it and replace lost cadre is vital for successful terrorist organizations. Kim Cragin and Sara A. y, *The Dynamic Terrorist Threat: An Assessment of Group Motivations and Capabilities in a Changin orld* (Santa Monica, Calif.: RAND, 2003), pp. 34–36.

requires defeating, or at least inhibiting, its ability to tap into insurgencies around the world.

Al-Qaida maintains links to several insurgencies and proto-insurgencies around the globe. Insurgent fighters in Algeria (the Salafist Group for Preaching and Combat), Iraq (various Sunni groups), Afghanistan (the Taliban), India (groups fighting in Kashmir such as Lashkar-e-Taiba), Chechnya, Pakistan (former Taliban and their sympathizers among Pakistani domestic groups), Somalia (various Islamist fighters), and Uzbekistan (the Islamic Movement of Uzbekistan) all have varying degrees of ties to al-Qaida and the movement it supports. Size is a key criteria for an insurgency, and several groups examined in this study are not yet strong enough to be deemed insurgencies, but may move in that direction. They include the anti-Saudi al-Qaida on the Arabian Peninsula, the Jemaah Islamiyah in Southeast Asia, the Abu Sayyaf Group in the Philippines, and the Islamic Group and Egyptian Islamic Jihad in Egypt.[15]

To be clear, al-Qaida did not "cause" any of these insurgencies, and in almost all the cases the insurgents have agendas that are in many ways distinct from al-Qaida's. Nevertheless, individuals affiliated with these groups are often members of al-Qaida, and the terrorist organization in turn exploits these groups' networks and personnel for its own purposes. It is thus plausible that a "war on terrorism" might lead to greater U.S. involvement with these countries, and in most cases it already has.[16] As Steven Metz and Raymond Millen note, "The United States is more likely to assist regimes threatened by insurgents linked to al-Qaeda or its affiliates."[17]

Iraq is excluded from the analysis section of the article because the focus is on allied militaries and their relations to their societies, which in Iraq is complicated by the U.S. occupation and heavy role in the post-occupation. Since the insurgency began in 2003, U.S. forces have done the bulk of the fighting, not local Iraqis.[18]

The arguments in this article, however, have tremendous implications for

---

15. Somalia is excluded from this study because it lacks a true government. The United States, however, appears to have allied with local militias fighting those tied to jihadists. See Emily Wax and Karen DeYoung, "United States Secretly Backing Warlords in Somalia," *Washington Post*, May 17, 2006.
16. Bruce Hoffman notes that the United States repeatedly fails to detect the development of insurgencies until it is too late. Hoffman, "Insurgency and Counterinsurgency in Iraq," Occasional Paper OP-127-IPC/CMEPP (Santa Monica, Calif.: RAND, June 2004), pp. 1–4.
17. Steven Metz and Raymond Millen, *Insurgency and Counterinsurgency in the 21st Century: Reconceptualizing Threat and Response* (Carlisle Barracks, Pa.: Strategic Studies Institute, U.S. Army War College, November 2004), p. 18.
18. Using preliberation forces, however, would skew the data as well. For a superb review of the

the future of Ir once U.S. forces depart or draw down: objectives that both the George W. sh administration and its critics seek. As the Bush administration's Natior Strategy for Victory in Iraq makes clear, the United States aims to build u he capabilities of the Iraqi security forces and steadily shift responsibility f the fight to them.[19] Thus, the findings from other struggles are applied to I briefly in the article's conclusion.

Although co terterrorism and counterinsurgency overlap, they are far from identical. me components of the U.S. global counterterrorism campaign have littl alue for counterinsurgency. The United States tries to inhibit the internationa ravel of terrorists, track cells operating in otherwise peaceful countries, rend uspects from one country to another, and construct barriers around nationa cons in the United States. All of these are done primarily against the relat ly small number of international terrorists (or those they inspire) and have le to do with guerrilla war or the broader popular struggles noted above. Tl require the United States to develop ties to many countries in Europe and a, use its intelligence services to monitor radicals around the world, and con uct effective defenses. All of these steps require capabilities different from t se needed for counterterrorism.

Similarly, ma insurgents, including some Islamist ones, have a local focus and do not see ir insurgency as inherently involving the United States. The LTTE, for exan e, is a vicious terrorist group and a highly capable insurgency. Its actio though violent, are primarily directed against the government of Sri La a and do not involve U.S. interests. Similarly, the United States can parti ate in or avoid struggles against Maoist rebels in Nepal or even Islamist r ls such as those found in Hamas, who have shunned al-Qaida, but thes e not part of the struggle against bin Laden and his allies.

Allies' Centra y in Counterinsurgency

Successful cou insurgency against anti-U.S. groups linked to al-Qaida depends heavily c llies' military forces. In addition to establishing government control and elir ating insurgent combatants, military forces act to secure an area so that pol al and other reforms can be carried out.[20] Allies are also vital

---

Iraqi military perfo nce through the 1991 Gulf War, see Kenneth M. Pollack, *Arabs at War: Military Effectiveness, 1* *1991* (Lincoln: University of Nebraska Press, 2002), pp. 155–266.

19. National Securi Council, "National Strategy for Victory in Iraq" (Washington, D.C.: National Security Council, N ember 2005), pp. 18–21, http://www.whitehouse.gov/infocus/iraq/iraq_national_strategy_2 1130.pdf.

20. Thomas A. Mar "Insurgency in a Time of Terrorism," *Journal of Counterterrorism & Homeland Security*, Vol. 11, N (Spring 2005), pp. 46–53.

in part for political reasons at home. The American people naturally prefer that others fight and die in their stead, particularly when the conflict so obviously involves a third country's vital interests.[21] Equally important, allies should be better able to carry out most aspects of counterinsurgency. Their forces speak the language and know the culture, so they are better able to gather intelligence and avoid actions that gratuitously offend the population.[22] Even the best-behaved foreigners may generate a nationalistic backlash among local citizens who feel little sympathy for the insurgents. By most accounts, the U.S. military has tried to respect Afghanistan's culture and empower local officials there. But resistance has grown since the 2001 invasion, and the United States' welcome has worn thin in parts of the country.[23] Finally, perhaps the greatest factor affecting the insurgents' success or failure is the response of the regime: a clumsy or foolish response can be the insurgents' greatest source of recruits.[24]

Allies, however, have their own distinct interests and approaches to counterinsurgency and counterterrorism, as they do with all serious security issues: a point well developed in the scholarship on international relations. Historically, major powers have differed from their allies in such basic questions as, What is the overall level of risk? Who is the primary enemy? How much should different allies contribute? And what is the best means to fight the insurgents?[25] Many of these differences hold true for counterinsurgency as well. Like those of the United States, the ally's interests also include defeating the insurgents: but here the commonality often ends. As discussed below, allied security ser-

21. Stephen T. Hosmer, *Constraints on U.S. Strategy in Third World Conflicts* (New York: Crane Russak and Company, 1987), p. 128.
22. U.S. Army, "Counterinsurgency Operations," sec. 1-10.
23. Ahmed Rashid, "Afghanistan: On the Brink," *New York Review of Books*, June 22, 2006, http://www.nybooks.com/articles/19098. For a discussion on the nationalistic backlash that outside occupiers face, see David Edelstein, "Occupational Hazards: Why Military Occupations Succeed or Fail," *International Security*, Vol. 29, No. 1 (Summer 2004), pp. 49–91; and Bard E. O'Neill, *Insurgency and Terrorism: Inside Modern Revolutionary Warfare* (Dulles, Va.: Brassey's, 1990), p. 137.
24. O'Neill, *Insurgency and Terrorism*, p. 125. Some experts argue that this has happened already in Uzbekistan. See "Prepared Statement of Martha Brill Olcott," reprinted in "Central Asia: Terrorism, Religious Extremism, and Regional Instability," Hearing before the Subcommittee on the Middle East and Central Asia of the House Committee on International Relations, 108th Cong., 1st sess., October 29, 2003, p. 57.
25. The literature on alliances among states is vast. Leading works include Mancur Olson and Richard Zeckhauser, "An Economic Theory of Alliances," *Review of Economics and Statistics*, Vol. 48, No. 3 (August 1966), pp. 266–279; Thomas J. Christensen and Jack Snyder, "Chain Gangs and Passed Bucks: Predicting Alliance Patterns in Multipolarity," *International Organization*, Vol. 44, No. 2 (Spring 1990), pp. 137–168; Glenn H. Snyder, *Alliance Politics* (Ithaca, N.Y.: Cornell University Press, 1997); and Stephen M. Walt, *The Origins of Alliances* (Ithaca, N.Y.: Cornell University Press, 1987).

vices also seek (er goals—for example, propping up an authoritarian regime or maintaining ıvored ethnic group in power—or otherwise have ambitions and problems t undermine the effectiveness of counterinsurgency campaigns. In such cumstances, the ally may not act as the United States wants (e.g., refusing (nocratic reforms) or may act in a counterproductive way (e.g., engaging atrocities against rival ethnic groups) because it perceives such measures service its other interests, even at the cost of counterinsurgency. Thus, wl many of the allies' problems involve incompetence and ineffectiveness, th are not a product of ignorance or chance. Rather, they stem from the very r ıre of allied regimes and societies. Indeed, allies that suffer from these stru ral problems and have ineffective militaries are more likely to experience ir ırgencies.

The basic prc em of divergent interests inherent in most alliances is compounded by d nmas similar to a principal-agent problem in which the United States c not rely on its allies to serve its interests faithfully.[26] For counterinsurger more than other forms of warfare, the United States relies heavily on othe to act on its behalf. A classic principal-agent problem occurs when informati asymmetries make it hard for an employer to monitor the action of an em ıyee, allowing the employee to act in a way that meets his or her needs, not t se of the employer. The United States, like other principals, cannot control agents completely. Allies are sovereign states, and as such enjoy at least d ure independence. As a superpower, the United States has considerable in ence. But as noted below, many of the issues linked to coun-

26. The similarity i from exact: foreign governments are not "employees" of the United States, no matter how dep ent they are on U.S. aid or financial support. Nor are the governments created bodies such as European Commission, which other scholars have pointed to as an example of an agent tl at times acts contrary to the interests of its principals. Mark Pollack, "Delegation, Agenc nd Agenda Setting in the European Community," *International Organization*, Vol. 51, No. 1 (Wint 997), p. 108. Nevertheless, the problems are similar, making the comparison worthwhile. As Jos Stiglitz contends, "The employer cannot travel on the road with his salesman to monitor pr ly the effort he puts into his salesmanship. In each of these situations, the agent's . . . action a s the principal." Stiglitz, "Principal and Agent" (ii), in Josh Eatwell, Murray Milgate, and Peter wman, eds., *New York Palgrave Dictionary of Economics*, Vol. 3 (London: Macmillan, 1989), 57. For other important works on the principal-agent problem, see David. E.M. Sappington, entives in Principal-Agent Relationships," *Journal of Economic Perspectives*, Vol. 5, No. 2 (Sprir 991), pp. 45–66. See also Kenneth Arrow, "The Economics of Agency," in John W. Pratt and hard J. Zeckhauser, eds., *Principals and Agents: The Structure of Business* (Boston: Harvard ness School Press, 1985), pp. 37–51. Principals can try to monitor their agents through a va y of measures, such as threatening to cut budgets or impose other sanctions and providing ince es to follow the principals' desires, but these in turn are costly and often imperfect. Pollack, elegation, Agency, and Agenda Setting in the European Community," pp. 116–129. See als oderick Kiewiet and Matthew D. McCubbins, *The Logic of Delegation: Congressional Parties an Appropriation Process* (Chicago: University of Chicago Press, 1991), p. 27.

terinsurgency involve a regime's very hold on power, a concern that at best limits outside leverage that is exercised in the form of aid or threats of sanctions.[27]

Information disparities compound this problem further. U.S. forces are not present in every village or neighborhood where insurgents are fought, and indeed the United States often does not have a robust official presence in most of an ally's major cities. Moreover, the security services that fight the insurgency are also the ones that gather much of the relevant information. They may inadvertently filter the information according to their own biases and deliberately distort the information to reinforce their views (e.g., that the rival ethnic group's village was a hotbed of al-Qaida-linked unrest). Evaluating the ally's true efforts is difficult for reasons that go beyond the information disparity and involve the inherent complexity of the problem. Many of the key issues involved—for example, the pace of democratic reform, the level of professionalism in a military, and the level of success in wooing local support—are exceptionally difficult to measure.

Counterinsurgency Ideals and Realities

Counterinsurgency is difficult for even the best militaries. It requires not only remarkable military skill but also a deft political touch. The soldier on patrol must be a fighter, a policeman, an intelligence officer, a diplomat, and an aid worker. Not surprisingly, even well-trained, well-led, and well-funded militaries such as those of the United States, Britain, and Israel have foundered when facing insurgent movements.

COIN problems only multiply if the government in question seeks to avoid extreme brutality, which is typically a U.S. goal. Iraq under Saddam Hussein, and the Algerian government in the 1990s, both defeated insurgencies, but they did so in part by widespread slaughter. Embracing such a brutal regime has tremendous normative problems for the United States. Even if these are put aside, the problem of being tarred with an ally's brush grows tremendously as a result.

The problems for many militaries confronting insurgents linked to al-Qaida fall into two categories. First, at the tactical and organizational levels, they are often not prepared for counterinsurgency operations. Second, as a political en-

27. Daniel Byman and Matthew Waxman, *The Dynamics of Coercion: American Foreign Policy and the Limits of Military Might* (New York: Cambridge University Press, 2002), pp. 37–45.

tity the military :quently contributes to popular anger or other problems that aid the insurge ' cause.[28]

TACTICAL AND (;ANIZATIONAL CONCERNS

The characterist of an ideal COIN military at the tactical and organizational levels are vast,[2] ut several of the most important include a high level of initiative, excellen ıtelligence, integration across units and services, leadership, motivated sold , and learning and creativity. The reality for many militaries involved in fig ıg al-Qaida-linked insurgencies, however, is often far from the ideal.[30]

INITIATIVE. (ınterinsurgency fighting rarely involves a set-piece battle, which outgunn and outmanned insurgents typically shun. Soldiers try to flush out hidd insurgents and defeat them through aggressive patrolling and ambushes. do this successfully, COIN forces must also operate out of garrison and at ghttime. Part of their job is to convince the population that they will be pro ted; insurgents will exploit the absence of COIN forces to intimidate locals d sow fear.[31] Fighting occurs either because the insurgents choose to enga ır ideally when government forces leave them no choice. In both cases, pla ıg is difficult: the terrain can vary, the number of forces involved is hard predict, and so on. Much of the effort is done at the small-unit level, as la r units are far easier for insurgents to avoid.

Many devel ıg world militaries, however, are garrison militaries that

28. For a general o iew of insurgency and counterinsurgency issues that pays particular attention to the problem llies, see D. Michael Shafer, *Deadly Paradigms: The Failure of U.S. Counterinsurgency Policy* (Pr ton, N.J.: Princeton University Press, 1988). Other excellent works are Blaufarb, *The Coun ısurgency Era;* George K. Tanham and Dennis J. Duncanson, "Some Dilemmas of Counter ırgency," *Foreign Affairs*, Vol. 48, No. 2 (January 1970), pp. 113–122; William E. Odom, *On Inter War: American and Soviet Approaches to Third World Clients and Insurgents* (Durham, N.C.: Du Jniversity Press, 1992); Harry Eckstein, ed., *Internal War: Problems and Approaches* (New York ee Press, 1964); Nathan Leites and Charles Wolf Jr., *Rebellion and Authority: An Analytic Essay o surgent Conflicts* (Chicago: Markham, 1970); Ian F.W. Beckett, *Modern Insurgencies and Counter rgencies: Guerrillas and Their Opponents since 1750* (New York: Routledge, 2003); Bruce Hoffm Jennifer M. Taw, and David W. Arnold, *Lessons for Contemporary Counterinsurgencies: The Rhod ı Experience* (Santa Monica, Calif.: RAND, 1991); and Marks, "Insurgency in a Time of Terrorisn

29. For one useful see Central Intelligence Agency, "Guide to the Analysis of Insurgency," p. 13.

30. Most of these n aries also suffer similar problems in conventional military operations. The Saudis' lack of initi e in counterinsurgency, for example, is mirrored in their problems in conventional warfare. article focuses on the characteristics useful for effective counterinsurgency, but many of these blems apply to overall military operations.

31. O'Neill, *Insurg and Terrorism*, p. 130; and Central Intelligence Agency, "Guide to the Analysis of Insurgency," 0.

fight, when they do, from 9:00 to 5:00. They often operate poorly as small units, with junior officers and NCOs reluctant to exercise initiative. In Uzbekistan, insurgents "own the night."[32] In Algeria, units often feared to leave their garrison and patrol in dangerous parts of cities where insurgents enjoyed sympathy. The Egyptian and Saudi armed forces historically exercised little initiative, a problem that is more profound farther down the command chain. Even the smallest details had to be spelled out in advance.[33] COIN suffered as a result in all these cases.

INTELLIGENCE. Intelligence is the sina qua non of counterinsurgency. The insurgents' primary advantage is their stealth: if they can be found, they can usually be killed or captured. A corollary is that insurgents' advantage is their superior knowledge of the local population and conditions: denying or minimizing this advantage is therefore vital.[34] To be useful, intelligence must not only be collected but also be analyzed, disseminated, and integrated into the overall strategy.[35]

Many U.S. allies, however, collect, analyze, and disseminate information poorly. Intelligence analysis benefits from superb information sharing and from the proper storage and dissemination of data—general weaknesses in developing societies. Although many allies do a fine job collecting information, they often do not integrate it well and have at best a limited picture of their adversary.[36] The major intelligence agencies in the Philippines frequently do not share information and do not coordinate their activities. Indeed, intelligence money is often paid directly to officials as a form of graft.[37] In Egypt, key information is compartmentalized, and failures are not brought to the attention of senior officers.[38] Often, information is not shared because commanders and units do not trust each other. In the Sikh insurgency, Indian units rarely shared information with local forces because they were perceived as sympathetic to

32. McDermott, "The Armed Forces of the Republic of Uzbekistan, 1990–2002," p. 32.
33. Kenneth M. Pollack, "The Sphinx and the Eagle," 1998, chap. 4.
34. See Fearon and Laitin, "Ethnicity, Insurgency, and Civil War."
35. O'Neill, *Insurgency and Terrorism*, p. 144; and Bruce Hoffman and Jennifer Morrison Taw, *A Strategic Framework for Countering Terrorism and Insurgency* (Santa Monica, Calif.: RAND, 1992), p. 9.
36. For a more complete overview of this problem, see Kenneth M. Pollack, "The Influence of Arab Culture on Arab Military Effectiveness," Ph.D. dissertation, Massachusetts Institute of Technology, 1996, pp. 564–566.
37. Emil P. Jurado, "Need for Coordinated Intelligence Network," *Manila Standard*, February 23, 2005; and Fe.V. Maragay, "Safeguarding the Spy Fund," *Manila Standard*, January 31, 2005.
38. Pollack, "The Sphinx and the Eagle."

(and penetratec y) Sikh insurgents.[39] The International Crisis Group reports that Indonesiar ıtelligence is "marked by blurred lines of authority, interagency rivalry, k of coordination, unnecessary duplication, lack of adequate oversight, and legacy of an authoritarian past."[40]

INTEGRATION ROSS UNITS AND SERVICES. All military operations benefit from synergies, ıd this holds true for counterinsurgency as well. At a most basic level, unit nust work together to ensure proper coverage of a territory and to prevent urgents from slipping between the seams of different units. Also, if unexpe dly heavy resistance is found, units must reinforce their beleaguered comı es, particularly when forces operate as small units.

Information s ring and coordination across services are often exceptionally poor for allies hting insurgencies linked to al-Qaida. In Egypt and Saudi Arabia, comma ers of different services and units frequently do not communicate with eacl ther. In Afghanistan, the United States has worked not only with the Afgha National Army but also with numerous regional warlords, several of whor we little loyalty to the central government.[41] At times a military may have ı ltiple groups within it vying for power. In Algeria, the army has numerous isions based on region and tribe.[42] The division of labor between the polic nd the military is not clear in Indonesia, and the military's own coordinati with regard to counterterrorism and counterinsurgency is poor.[43]

LEADERSHIP ALL LEVELS. Officers must be creative, take the initiative, inspire the soldie vho follow them, and perform other essential military functions. In additic officers doing COIN must play a major role in ensuring the gathering of in igence and reassuring the population—both difficult tasks that go beyond aditional training for conventional military operations. Because much of nterinsurgency is done by small units, having strong NCOs is also vital.

Military lead hip in many of the countries fighting al-Qaida, however,

---

39. C. Christine Fai rban Battle Fields of South Asia: Lessons Learned from Sri Lanka, India, and Pakistan (Santa Monica lif.: RAND, 2004), p. 94.
40. International C Group, "Indonesia: Rethinking Internal Security Strategy," *Asia Report*, No. 90 (December 2004 13.
41. Raymond A. M n, *Afghanistan: Reconstituting a Collapsed State* (Carlisle Barracks, Pa.: U.S. Army War College)5), p. 3.
42. International C Group, "The Algerian Crisis: Not Over Yet," *Africa Report*, No. 24 (October 2000), p. 12.
43. International C Group, "Indonesia: Rethinking Internal Security Strategy," p. 5.

is quite poor. In most Arab militaries, junior officers and NCOs are given little responsibility. In Egypt, for example, colonels have responsibilities similar to those of U.S. captains.[44] In Uzbekistan, officers have often performed poorly when facing insurgents.[45] Afghan army leaders appear better than most of those in this study, but even here the NCOs are not given appropriate responsibility.[46]

MOTIVATED SOLDIERS. Soldiers who believe in their government and their officers are more likely to brave the hazards of COIN warfare. They will confront rather than flee from the enemy and take the necessary initiative to ensure victory.

Many developing world countries facing al-Qaida, however, have poorly motivated soldiers. Afghan recruits often prefer to work for local warlords than for the national government, and many trainees and recent recruits desert their posts. As one Afghan sergeant commented, "Everyone wants to run away."[47] Uzbek soldiers suffer from low morale, and mass desertions are common.[48] In Egypt, many soldiers do not embrace their profession.[49] In India, the emphasis on caste creates problems for cohesion, as soldiers often speak different languages and the caste system creates a hierarchy among them.[50]

TRAINING, LEARNING, AND CREATIVITY. Counterinsurgency requires a high degree of skill and constant refinement. In addition, a successful military must learn from its mistakes and be able to go beyond its standard procedures when confronted with a new situation. Moreover, both successful and unsuccessful insurgencies go through stages, and the mix of conventional and unconventional operations needed to defeat them will vary as a result.[51] COIN is also

---

44. Pollack, "The Sphinx and the Eagle."
45. Farkhad Tolipov and Roger N. McDermott, "Uzbekistan and the U.S.: Partners against Terrorism," *Review of International Affairs*, Vol. 2, No. 4 (Summer 2003), p. 2.
46. Charles DiLeonardo, "Training the Afghan National Army," *Infantry*, Vol. 94, No. 2 (March/April 2005), p. 32.
47. Quoted in Tom Coghlan, "Toughing It Out in the Afghan Army," *BBC News*, June 15, 2005, http://www.news.bbc.co.uk.
48. Ahmed Rashid, "A Long, Hot Summer Ahead," *Far Eastern Economic Review*, April 19, 2001, p. 29.
49. Many Egyptian air force officers, for example, do not enjoy flying. Pollack, "The Sphinx and the Eagle."
50. Stephen Peter Rosen, *Societies and Military Power: India and Its Armies* (Ithaca, N.Y.: Cornell University Press, 1996), p. 243.
51. O'Neill, *Insurgency and Terrorism*, p. 131; and Metz and Millen, *Insurgency and Counterinsurgency in the 21st Century*, p. 25.

more art than s ıce: creativity is vital. Helping this process is the free flow of information an n institutional culture of honest criticism.[52]

Many countr do not emphasize training for a variety of reasons. Most important, trainin till focuses on conventional military operations: the traditional emphasis most militaries. In Uzbekistan, the military was structured from Soviet-era rces intended to fight conventional wars. Although Uzbek leaders have in ıted some reforms, Roger McDermott notes that these are only a "modest ginning" and are focused on a few elite forces.[53] (Indeed, as a sign of how training is, an individual who was picked to lead special forces teams ha not had basic infantry training.)[54] Some of the paramilitary forces involved COIN are expected to be around only temporarily, leaving officials relucta to invest in long-term training.[55] Egypt's military is huge, making it hard do more than rudimentary training for many of the forces. Live-fire exercis or other forms of realistic training are rare.[56]

Many of thes ıilitaries do not learn from their mistakes. The Egyptian military has institu nalized some practices that U.S. trainers see as disastrous, in part because ch ging them would require an embarrassing admission of failure.[57] U.S. train spent years working with the Saudi air force, only to watch it steadily decli In part, this problem occurs because professional military education is w , and the institutions that do exist focus on perpetuating existing doctrine ıer than on seeking to correct mistakes in current operations.

POLITICAL CON NS

In counterinsur ıcy, the military is a political actor as well as a fighting unit. Several other, n e political criteria include proper civil-military integration, a lack of corrupti , a lack of insurgent penetration, and a sense that the army can win over th population.

CIVIL-MILITA INTEGRATION. Defeating an insurgent movement is as much (if not more) a tical effort as a military one. A national approach that incorporates all dim sions of power is essential. If political and military leaders

52. John A. Nagl, *terinsurgency Lessons from Malaya and Vietnam: Learning to Eat Soup with a Knife* (Westport, C Praeger, 2002), pp. 191–226.
53. McDermott, "T Armed Forces of the Republic of Uzbekistan, 1992–2002," p. 30.
54. Tolipov and M rmott, "Uzbekistan and the U.S.," p. 14.
55. Sunil Dasgupta Rise of Paramilitary Forces: Military Reorganization in Developing Societies," Working Dra Washington, D.C.: Brookings, 2005), p. 23.
56. See Pollack, "T phinx and the Eagle."
57. Ibid.

are in harmony, military and political measures to defeat the insurgents are more likely to be as well.[58] The two cannot be done in isolation: the military methods used affect the overall perception of the government, and the perception of the regime influences the ability of the military to operate.

In many of the countries in question, however, civil-military relations are poor. In India, civilian leaders historically saw the military as a vestige of the British imperial mentality and at odds with their nationalistic (and more socialist) vision of the country. In Algeria and Pakistan, military leaders have seized power from civilian officials, while in the Philippines and Indonesia civilian leaders have feared military interference in their control of the country. In Egypt, the government has long been unsure of the reliability of the military to protect the regime: a well-founded perception given that Islamist militants penetrated the military to kill Egyptian President Anwar Sadat in 1981 and that mass riots involving 17,000 conscripts broke out in 1986.[59]

In some countries, the government is divided on issues related to counterinsurgency, making it exceptionally difficult to produce a coherent strategy. The Algerian regime was long split between the "conciliators" and the "eradicators," leading to a policy that was at times incoherent, with olive branches suddenly withdrawn and attempts to intimidate offset by surprising concessions.[60]

HONESTY AND CORRUPTION. The military is more likely to gain the respect of the population if it is not corrupt or otherwise engaged in illicit activities. A lack of corruption sends the message that the military is indeed fighting for the country, not just for the personal interests of a few individuals. This in turn inspires soldiers to fight harder and makes it more difficult for the insurgents to penetrate the armed forces.

Corruption is rampant in many of the countries in question, and the military is no exception. Of the countries surveyed in this article, all were in the lower half of Transparency International's 2005 Corruption Perception Index, with the exceptions of Saudi Arabia and Egypt, which scored in the middle. Indonesia, Pakistan, and Uzbekistan were among the most corrupt countries in the world.[61] Uzbekistan's military leaders often will exempt an individual

58. O'Neill, *Insurgency and Terrorism*, p. 146; and Hoffman and Taw, *A Strategic Framework for Countering Terrorism and Insurgency*, p. v.
59. Lawrence E. Kline, "Egyptian and Algerian Insurgencies: A Comparison," *Small Wars and Insurgencies*, Vol. 9, No. 2 (Autumn 1998), p. 127.
60. Ibid., p. 129.
61. See Transparency International, "The 2005 Transparency International Corruption Perceptions Index," http://www.infoplease.com/ipa/A0781359.html.

from military s ice for the right price.[62] The Abu Sayyaf Group buys weapons and immu y freely from government and military officials—several leading terroris simply walked out of the heavily "secured" national police headquarters i Manila with the aid of local officers.[63] In Egypt and Saudi Arabia, it is ass ed that senior military leaders will skim off the top of military contracts: a ssumption that is duplicated in lesser ways down the chain of command. I lgeria, business rivalries prevent the different military leaders from coope ing.[64] In Indonesia, corruption is rampant in the buying of equipment and er supplies.[65] All of these examples only scratch the surface of the myriad s corruption undermines military effectiveness.

INSURGENT P TRATION. Ensuring that the military remains free from insurgent penetr n is vital. Successful penetration allows the insurgents to avoid regime at npts to arrest or kill insurgent cadre. In addition, it gives the insurgents insi nformation that greatly increases their effectiveness in planning attacks.

Many of the imes fighting al-Qaida have been penetrated by insurgents. In Pakistan and udi Arabia, al-Qaida has made a conscious effort to cultivate military and g rnment officials.[66] U.S. officials working with the Afghan National Army prohibited from sharing intelligence, as they fear it will fall into the hands ex-Taliban.[67] In Algeria, many of the early insurgent successes involved embers of the security forces who collaborated with them, and the regime en hesitated to use the army because it feared that many soldiers would de t.[68]

MILITARY SU RT FROM A POPULATION. Famously, counterinsurgency involves winning "hearts and minds" of the population at large and denying such support t e guerrillas. As the military plans and conducts its operations against in gents, it must also think about how to win over the general population, as of its most important roles is to "serve as the shield for carrying out refor [69] The military needs the active support of the population to

62. McDermott, "T Armed Forces of the Republic of Uzbekistan, 1992–2002," p. 36.
63. Steven Rogers, yond the Abu Sayyaf," *Foreign Affairs*, Vol. 83, No. 1 (January/February 2004), pp. 15–20.
64. International C Group, "The Algerian Crisis," p. 12.
65. International C Group, "Indonesia: Next Steps in Military Reform," *Asia Report*, No. 24 (October 2001), p.
66. Anonymous, *T gh Our Enemies' Eyes*, p. 22.
67. DiLeonardo, " ing the Afghan National Army," p. 38.
68. Michael Willes, *Islamist Challenge in Algeria: A Political History* (New York: New York University Press, 1997) 295; Martinez, *The Algerian Civil War, 1990–1998*, p. 161; and Kline, "Egyptian and Algerian rgencies," p. 129.
69. Marks, "Insurg y in a Time of Terrorism," p. 52.

gain information—a disadvantage, as mere passivity often allows insurgents to operate effectively without being vulnerable to government intelligence efforts.[70] In addition to using the population to collect intelligence, greater popular support gives guerrillas more eager recruits and more money on which to draw. To gain active support, it is helpful if the military is fighting for a system that offers political, economic, and other opportunities to all concerned: something that is often beyond its control. In addition, a military is more likely to win over the population in general if it is seen as fighting for more than just a political or social clique. If the armed forces are viewed as representing all the diverse communities of any state, they are more likely to be seen as trustworthy and not provoke a backlash. Finally, successful COIN is characterized by restraint as well as by violence. Too much destruction can alienate a population rather than reassure it and unwittingly create disincentives to fight for and cooperate with the government.[71]

Such benign characteristics are often lacking among militaries fighting al-Qaida-linked groups, making it harder for them to capture popular support. In India, for example, the army's outlook is more akin to the British imperial army. As a result, it sees itself more as occupier than as part of the local population, with the result that relations are often poor.[72] When suppressing the Punjab insurgency, the Indian forces saw themselves as protecting the local Hindu population from Sikh militants, and as a result it alienated local services that sought to balance Sikh and Hindu concerns.[73] Indonesian soldiers often take sides in local disputes according to whether the soldiers are Muslim or Christian.[74]

If the military lacks popular support, basic counterinsurgency functions such as gathering intelligence and denying information to the insurgents are

70. Christopher M. Ford, "Speak No Evil: Targeting a Population's Neutrality to Defeat an Insurgency," *Parameters*, Vol. 35, No. 2 (Summer 2005), p. 53. T.E. Lawrence noted that the guerrillas needed only a limited amount of active support, but that much of the population must be passive or inactive backers. Beckett, *Modern Insurgencies and Counterinsurgencies*, p. 20. See also Central Intelligence Agency, "Guide to the Analysis of Insurgency," p. 8. For an alternative view, see Chalmers Johnson, "Civilian Loyalties and Guerrilla Conflict," *World Politics*, Vol. 14, No. 4 (July 1962), pp. 646–661.

71. For an assessment of how incentives affect the success of rebellions, see Mark I. Lichback, "What Makes Rational Peasants Revolutionary? Dilemma, Paradox, and Irony in Peasant Collective Action," *World Politics*, Vol. 46 No. 3 (April 1994), pp. 383–418; and Jeffrey Berejikian, "Revolutionary Collective Action and the Agent-Structure Problem," *American Political Science Review*, Vol. 86, No. 3 (September 1992), pp. 647–657.

72. Rosen, *Societies and Military Power*, p. 241.

73. Fair, *Urban Battle Fields of South Asia*, p. 90.

74. International Crisis Group, "Indonesia: Next Steps in Military Reform," p. 4.

more difficult t ılfill. In addition, the lack of popular support facilitates the ability of insur ıts to gain recruits and resources.

Brutality is a ırticular problem. The Algerian military is notorious for its atrocities again ivilians. In Uzbekistan, torture is widespread,[75] and in June 2005, the milit fired on a peaceful political opposition rally. The United States and Uzl istan have dramatically reduced military cooperation because of these p blems. The Indonesian military was linked to numerous human rights ab s in Aceh, Papua, Central Sulawesi, and Maluku.[76] Such actions create s pathy for the guerrillas, particularly when the government's control is weak d people have an option of siding against it with less risk.[77]

As the abov liscussion suggests, most potential U.S. allies against al-Qaida-linked in rgencies do not do well according to these criteria. Indeed, it is no exaggerati to say that several range from poor to abysmal. Tables 1 and 2 provide an ov view of militaries fighting al-Qaida-linked insurgencies, using the above c eria to indicate problems they have.

Structural Ca s of Tactical, Organizational, and Political Problems

A look at the co tries in question indicates that they suffer from several structural weakness illegitimate and repressive regimes, civil-military tensions (particularly w regard to suspicions of a coup), economic backwardness, and social excl on. Even the democracies among the lot suffer from several of these proble . Table 3 displays the extent of the difficulties. These problems, of course, not universal and, as discussed further, the military culture and broader pc cal problems of counterinsurgency vary accordingly.[78]

These structu problems should not be surprising. Although the causes of insurgency can vast, common ones include a lack of popular legitimacy caused by an e ısive government, discrimination, and economic discontent.

75. Jim Nichol, *Uzl tan: Current Developments and U.S. Interests* (Washington, D.C.: Congressional Research Servic ıpdated April 21, 2004), p. 6, Order Code RS21238.
76. Aleksius Jemad Intelligence Agencies Must Be Held to Account," *Jakarta Post*, June 20, 2005.
77. See Leites and f, *Rebellion and Authority*.
78. These structura oblems raise the interesting question of why the insurgencies have not won outright victories. regimes' continued survival stems from several sources. First, the insurgents are often poo led, brutal, and unpopular. Second, they face a much harder collective action problem. Beca of the insurgent groups' smaller size, it is difficult to push uncommitted individuals to acti side with them. Third, not all of the regimes suffer from every problem identified here. Fo , the insurgents' very structure makes eliminating them hard, but at the same time, this mal it difficult for them to mass forces to engage in mid-intensity combat. Thus there is often a stal e or low-level strife, with neither side able to gain a decisive advantage.

Table 1. Allied Militaries and COIN: Tactical and Organizational Characteristics

	Afghanistan	Algeria	Egypt	India	Indonesia	Pakistan	Philippines	Saudi Arabia	Uzbekistan
Poor intelligence					X		X	X	X
Poor integration across units	X	X	X	X*	X		X	X	
Garrison mentality/low level of initiative		X	X	X			X	X	X
Soldiers who do not want to fight	X	X	X				X	X	X
Bad officers		X	X	X			X	X	X
Bad noncommissioned officers	X	X	X				X	X	X
Training, learning, and creativity problems		X	X	X		X	X	X	X

*The Indian army historically did not integrate well across services in its counterinsurgency operations. In recent years, however, the police, military, and paramilitary forces have worked better together. See C. Christine Fair, *Urban Battle Fields of South Asia: Lessons Learned from Sri Lanka, India, and Pakistan* (Santa Monica, Calif.: RAND, 2004), p. 70.

Table 2. Allied Militaries and COIN: Political Characteristics

	Afghanistan	Algeria	Egypt	India	Indonesia	Pakistan	Philippines	Saudi Arabia	Uzbekistan
Poor civil-military integration	X	X		X	X		X	X	
Bad rapport with outside patrons (United States, etc.)		X		X	X	X	X		
Corruption	X	X	X		X	X	X	X	X
Military not fighting for a system that can win over the population	X	X	X	X	X	X	X	X	X
Vulnerable to insurgent penetration	X	X	X		X	X		X	X

Table 3. Structural Problems of Counterinsurgency Allies

Structural Problems	Afghanistan	Algeria	Egypt	India	Indonesia	Pakistan	Philippines	Saudi Arabia	Uzbekistan
Illegitimate regimes		X	X			X			X
Coup suspicions			X	X			X	X	
Economic backwardness	X	X	X	X	X	X	X	X	X
Social exclusion				X	X	X	X	X	X

A weak and dysfunctional government is particularly important, because in such cases even small groups can effectively use violence without being shut down by the government.[79] Indeed, the very shortcomings of the regimes often are major reasons for the existence of an insurgency. Thus, at times the very causes of insurgency also create problems for fighting it.

The structural characteristics produce the distinct interests for the security forces fighting insurgents. Thus, one of the problems common to alliances in general (as well as inherent in a principal-agent relationship)—systematically distinct preferences—is common to U.S. relations with allied security forces. The allies' distinct interests can cause many of the above-listed problems with fighting an insurgency. In addition, the regime often does not make the reforms that would improve its ability to fight the insurgents.

ILLEGITIMATE AND REPRESSIVE REGIMES

Many if not most of the regimes facing al-Qaida-linked insurgencies have a legitimacy problem. Of the countries surveyed, only India, the Philippines, and to a lesser degree Afghanistan and Indonesia qualify as democracies. Freedom House reports that Algeria, Egypt, Pakistan, Saudi Arabia, and Uzbekistan are "not free," and these countries scored sixes and sevens on their scale, with seven being the least free.[80] Being "not free" does not inherently mean a government is illegitimate, but it is suggestive of a problem. Algeria's military government took power so as to overturn elections that Islamists were poised to win peacefully. President Pervez Musharraf of Pakistan also took power in a military coup. The coup had considerable support at the time, but he has subsequently alienated middle-class Pakistanis, while many Islamists view him with suspicion. Uzbekistan is governed by a brutal dictator, and all opposition political activity is banned.[81] Egypt's leader has held power for a quarter century, with only the trapping of democracy. Saudi Arabia is a monarchy that has some legitimacy even though it is "not free," but the regime's corruption and exclusiveness have bred considerable cynicism.[82]

---

79. Fearon and Laitin, "Ethnicity, Insurgency, and Civil War." In such circumstances, the military becomes vital. As Morris Janowitz notes, "The absence of or the failure to develop more effective patterns of political and social control leads military regimes or military-based regimes to rely more heavily on internal police control." Janowitz, *Military Institutions and Coercion in the Developing Nations* (Chicago: University of Chicago Press, 1988), p. 7.

80. Freedom House, "Table of Independent Countries' Comparative Measures of Freedom," *Freedom in the World, 2005,* http://www.freedomhouse.org/uploads/chart33File36.pdf.

81. Jim Nichol, *Uzbekistan,* p. 5.

82. A lack of democracy does not inherently make a regime illegitimate in the eyes of its people. The al-Saud royal family, for example, has long enjoyed legitimacy (though some argue this is fad-

An illegitima ınd repressive regime has several pernicious effects on tactical and organiz onal aspects of counterinsurgency. The flow of information in authoritaria states is limited, particularly if the information may be perceived as cı :al of the regime. In such an environment, information is deliberately cor artmentalized. Nor are mistakes critically examined or even identified. As a sult, the overall quality of intelligence is poor, either because intelligence offi s lack all the necessary information or because many plausible findings (e.ç hat people are rebelling because the regime is brutal and illegitimate) are ppressed because they are unwelcome at senior levels. In Uzbekistan, the gime has resisted intelligence reform that would enhance the information ga d by the military, as it wants to ensure that intelligence is concentrated in e hands of regime loyalists.[83]

Military regi such as those in Algeria and Pakistan face particular problems. In contra o militaries whose senior officers must ultimately report to civilian officials ilitary regimes face less pressure to change their procedures and methods iı sponse to problems.[84]

Militaries th re not accountable to elected leaders and the public in general are less lik to correct mistakes or undertake bureaucratically painful changes. Partic r problems may include poor integration across units and services and a < of creativity when standard procedures fail or when new situations arise. litically, such a military may be more prone to human rights abuses, as it ca over up any problems and not risk broader censure.

Corruption is so a problem, as military figures in power use their positions to enrich thems es at the public's expense, even if it hinders overall military effectiveness. A rrupt military is also a less popular one. Soldiers will not be inspired by the fficers, and the people in general will see the military more as a parasite th as a savior. Uzbekistan's soldiers oppose military service, in part because co ption is widespread, which enables many to buy their way out of serving.[8] Jot surprisingly, officers enriching themselves through their military positio are likely to resist any reforms that increase accountability and oversight (otherwise hinder opportunities for graft.

---

ing) due to its pro n of economic goods, conquest of rivals, and efforts to uphold the kingdom's religious cre tials. For the purposes of this article, Saudi Arabia is coded as a legitimate regime, though it is orderline case. See Mamoun Fandy, *Saudi Arabia and the Politics of Dissent* (New York: Palgra acmillan, 2001); and F. Gregory Gause III, "Be Careful What You Wish For: The Future of U.S.- li Relations," *World Policy Journal*, Vol. 19, No. 1 (Spring 2002), pp. 37–50.

83. McDermott, "T Armed Forces of the Republic of Uzbekistan, 1992–2002," pp. 36–37.

84. Barry R. Posen, *Sources of Military Doctrine: France, Britain, and Germany between the World Wars* (Ithaca, N.Y.: nell, 1984), pp. 53–54, 225–226.

85. McDermott, "T Armed Forces of the Republic of Uzbekistan, 1992–2002," p. 36.

The political problems dwarf the tactical and organizational ones. At the most basic level, the lack of regime legitimacy complicates the ability of the military to portray itself as fighting for a system that its citizens should embrace. The population is less likely to provide intelligence, offer willing recruits, or otherwise support the military; and many soldiers may be sympathetic to the rebels. The regime may rely primarily on repression to stay in power, as it does in Uzbekistan, leading the military to become involved in human rights abuses. In Algeria, this process reached its acme in the mid-1990s, as the military regime there regularly used its forces to commit atrocities. Military leaders may also oppose reforms because they are instruments of the regime and thus they stand to lose power, opportunities for graft, or other benefits. In Algeria, the military feared that an Islamist victory at the polls would lead them to lose their power in the country and their financial influence—a fear that led them to disrupt elections through a coup.[86]

Another difficult issue is that the military is often opposed to reforms that would take the wind out of the insurgency's sails, such as land reform, greater democracy and accountability, or the ending of discriminatory policies. The military leadership may see such reforms as a threat to their political and social position and thus not worth the potential benefits against the insurgents.

The lack of legitimacy also poses a difficulty for cooperation with a foreign power. Close cooperation with a foreign government can inflame nationalism and lead to questions about a government's competence: a particular problem if the government lacks broad support. The widespread unpopularity of the United States in the world today worsens this problem.[87]

SUSPICION OF A COUP

In many developing world countries, the military is viewed as a threat as well as an ally of a regime. As a result, governments go to great lengths to "coup proof" their regimes, emasculating the military in a variety of ways to ensure its political loyalty.[88] Egypt, India, Indonesia, Pakistan, the Philippines, Saudi

86. Willes, *The Islamist Challenge in Algeria*, p. 245.
87. In none of the Arab countries surveyed by the Pew Foundation in July 2005 did a majority have a "favorable" view of the United States, though the poll did show an increase in U.S. popularity from past rock-bottom levels. See Pew Global Attitudes Project, "Islamic Extremism: Common Concern for Muslim and Western Publics," July 14, 2005, http://pewglobal.org/reports/display.php?PageID=811.
88. Risa Brooks, "Civil-Military Relations in the Middle East," in Nora Bensahel and Daniel Byman, eds., *The Future Security Environment in the Middle East* (Santa Monica, Calif.: RAND, 2003), pp. 129–162; and James T. Quinlivan, "Coup-proofing: Its Practice and Consequences in the Middle East," *International Security*, Vol. 24, No. 2 (Fall 1999), pp. 131–165.

Arabia, and Uz istan all have taken steps to control their militaries, even at the cost of thei verall effectiveness.[89]

Coup-proofir hapes a military culture in several negative ways. Most important, the sen officers are chosen primarily for their loyalty to the regime, not for their co etence. In Saudi Arabia, for example, many senior officers are royal famil embers, while others have close ties by marriage and other relationships. A result, many important skills such as leadership, creativity, and knowledge military affairs are in short supply. Indeed, in some militaries charismatic l capable leaders are viewed as a threat rather than as an asset. Finally, go nments also use corruption as a way to placate military leaders.[90]

Coup-proofir lso inhibits the flow of information. The regime discourages leaders from co nunicating with one another, an effective means of preventing antiregime otting but one that also inhibits coordination and learning best practices. ning can also suffer. In Egypt, for example, troops are given little independ e (or ammunition) when doing training, and exercises are unrealistic—in t to prevent a training mission from turning into an attempt to topple the r ne. Without the flow of information, integrating forces becomes much ha r, as does designing or redesigning procedures in a creative way to handle sistent problems.

Poor training nd learning structures can stem from coup-proofing measures (and a po cal system where information is guarded) and have a severe impact on COI ffectiveness. Integration will suffer if units cannot train for it. Without trair g for COIN in particular, integration may prove particularly hard for soldier vho are given standard training for conventional operations to work in sma groups, exercise low-level initiative, be discriminate in their use of firepowe r otherwise carry out tasks that differ from conventional operations. Many icers and NCOs will lack the skills to fight insurgents properly. Without i itutions to disseminate knowledge on the best techniques (and to criticall ppraise what is going wrong), the military will be less likely to adapt new a creative solutions to the problems it encounters.

89. In India, many te parties fear a strong army and oppose a heavy role for it, believing it would be used to ken their autonomy at the local level. At the federal level, however, there was historically bo isdain and suspicion from civilian leaders. Stephen Cohen, *India: Emerging Power* (Washington .: Brookings, 2001), p. 110; and Rosen, *Societies and Military Power,* p. 208. In the Philippines, cor tion and politics both shape promotion. See "Yet Another Coup in the Philippines?" *Jane's For Report,* June 23, 2005.

90. Brooks, "Civil- tary Relations in the Middle East."

ECONOMIC BACKWARDNESS

Many of the countries fighting al-Qaida-linked insurgencies are poor, while others are at best in the middle-income range. Algeria, Egypt, India, Indonesia, Pakistan, the Philippines, Saudi Arabia, and Uzbekistan suffer a range of economic problems, including relatively low per capita gross domestic product, high unemployment, poor infrastructure, and stagnant growth. Again, such backwardness is not surprising: poorer countries are more likely to suffer insurgencies than wealthy ones, and insurgencies themselves are a barrier to economic development.

The impact of a poor economy is relatively straightforward. Corruption, of course, is more tempting when overall wages are low (and, indeed, corruption may be particularly common, as it is often a source of poor economic growth). A poor economy can also limit the military budget of a country, making it difficult to pay recruits well, buy better equipment for the force, and expand the size of the military.[91] Training may also suffer, because a sophisticated training program is expensive and requires more troops, as some must remain actively engaged while others are being trained. In Uzbekistan, the regime cannot afford to modernize its old equipment, making many reform proposals dead on arrival.[92] At times, the army may be huge despite a poor economy, placing particularly heavy strains on the budget. In Egypt, the internal security forces have very low pay and recruiting standards—lower than the regular forces.[93] One observer noted that young Uzbeks joined former Islamic Movement of Uzbekistan's leader Juma Namangani's forces over the government's "because at least he pays them."[94]

Not surprisingly, the quality of personnel may also suffer, as the poor pay and limited resources make other opportunities more attractive.[95] In Egypt, for example, much of the enlisted personnel is illiterate, and few have a technical education.[96] In Uzbekistan, the armed forces had difficulty assimilating U.S. military aid because they lack the technical expertise to maintain and repair the equipment.[97] Perhaps 70 percent of the trainees in the Afghan army are il-

91. For example, much of the Indonesian air force is not operational due to funding shortages. International Crisis Group, "Indonesia: Next Steps in Military Reform," p. 12.
92. McDermott, "The Armed Forces of the Republic of Uzbekistan, 1992–2002," p. 38.
93. Kline, "Egyptian and Algerian Insurgencies," p. 127.
94. Rashid, "A Long, Hot Summer Ahead," p. 29.
95. Of course, if unemployment is high, skilled individuals may seek out the military simply because it offers gainful employment. In Iraq today, many Iraqis appear to be joining the security services for financial reasons despite the great personal risk it involves.
96. Pollack, "The Sphinx and the Eagle."
97. McDermott, "The Armed Forces of the Republic of Uzbekistan, 1992–2002," p. 32.

literate;[98] illiter is also a problem in India, as the emphasis on caste for recruitment mea hat there are not enough literate recruits to fill out some regiments.[99] Pe nnel who are less educated and less motivated are less able to gather and p ess intelligence effectively. The challenge of integration is often particularl ifficult. If the overall quality of personnel is low, both the officer corps ar he NCOs will suffer accordingly as well.

Insurgents a etter able to penetrate the military, both because they can bribe their way o key positions and because overall disaffection in the ranks makes penetrat easier. Training may even be inhibited, as officers are reluctant to have sol rs leave their control because they are skimming off soldiers' pay and suppl quisitions.

Even Saudi A bia—by reputation, a wealthy state—has more than its share of economic pr lems. Despite its oil riches, overall economic development has been limite nd skyrocketing population growth puts serious strains on the country. M over, income distribution is heavily skewed, favoring the royal family an hose connected to it.[100]

SOCIAL EXCLUSI AND DIVISIONS

In many count , power in all its forms is held in the hands of a relatively small group of ple, who in turn exclude or actively inhibit the rise of other groups. In Indi emnants of the caste system have preserved a division between the "wo of the hands" and "work of the minds," while several ethnicities are pa ularly prevalent in the military by tradition. Caste and subcaste often ine regiments and battalions.[101] Even many Hindu-Muslim divisions are re y about caste differences.[102] As a result, individuals are cut off from one an er. Clan and region are also important in Uzbekistan, while in Pakistan the is a bias against the Shiite minority in education and state services.[103] Sau Arabia, of course, is dominated by the al-Saud family, and

98. Mitch Frank, B Bennett, Anthony Davis, and Michael Ware, "Army on a Shoestring," *Time Europe*, August 26, 2, pp. 30–36.
99. Rosen, *Societies Military Power*, p. 209.
100. Alan Richards conomic Reform in the Middle East," in Bensahel and Byman, *The Future Security Environme the Middle East*, pp. 107–117.
101. Rosen, *Societi d Military Power*, pp. 203–209. For a broader look at the persistence of caste attitudes in India, s yron Weiner, *The Child and State in India* (Princeton, N.J.: Princeton University Press, 1990).
102. Cohen, *India*, 14.
103. International s Group, "The State of Sectarianism in Pakistan," *Asia Report*, No. 95 (April 2005), p. i.

many of its security positions are in the hands of particular tribes, particularly individuals from the Najd region.

Such domination has several pernicious effects on the military culture. The officer corps may actively disdain much of the rank-and-file if they are of a different, less-regarded, group. Promotions and rewards may also be skewed with individuals from certain groups receiving a preference, while others have a formal or informal ceiling on their rise. In addition, the quality of personnel may suffer, as certain groups may deem the military to be unwelcoming. Even without hostility, ethnic differences create more mundane problems. In Afghanistan, the problem of coordinating across multiple languages has hurt training. In India, promotion in some units depends on preserving caste ratios: if a particular regiment that is home to one caste has no vacancies for more senior positions, soldiers from that unit will not be promoted.[104] As a result, basic military tasks are more likely to be performed poorly. Initiative will suffer, and a garrison mentality is more likely as officers will not motivate the soldiers. In such a system, one of the hardest military tasks—integration across units and among services—is less likely to be rewarded. More generally, loyalty to the regime or membership in the right group will count for more than creativity and military excellence.

The direct political consequences of exclusion and social divisions relevant to counterinsurgency are also considerable. Politically, the military may be seen as an agent of the ruling clique, not of the nation as a whole. In addition, the military may oppose political and social reforms that disadvantage their members' privileged position.

In some countries, the military may be representative of the majority population but seen as alien by segments linked to the insurgents. The Philippines' military, for example, includes much of the population, but is not seen as representative by the Muslim minority in areas where the Abu Sayyaf Group was active.[105]

Table 4 loosely summarizes the above points. Needless to say, the various structural weaknesses do not necessarily produce the problem in question, but the weakness does make it far more likely the problem will be present.

---

104. Rosen, *Societies and Military Power*, p. 212.

105. The United States has taken steps to offset the dominance of Tajiks in the Afghan military by recruiting more Pashtuns for a range of positions. Joshua Kucera, "Afghanistan Looks to Army Expansion," *Jane's Defence Weekly*, October 13, 2004; and Kenneth Katzman, *Afghanistan: Post-war Governance, Security, and U.S. Policy* (Washington, D.C.: Congressional Research Service, May 19, 2005), p. 30, Order Code RL30588.

Table 4. A Summ of How Structural Problems Create Specific Counterinsurgency Weaknesses

	Illegitimate and Repressive Regimes	Civil-Military Tension	Poor Economies	Social Discrimination
Poor intelligence f s	X	X		
Poor integration a ss units and servic		X		
Leadership probler		X		X
Unmotivated and r- quality soldiers	X		X	X
Lack of training, learning, and creativity	X	X	X	
Civil-military integ on		X		
Corruption	X	X	X	
Insurgent penetrat	X		X	
Lack of support fr the population	X			X
Militaries' oppositi to reform	X			X

Why the Tail gs the Dog

The United Sta has few means of controlling its allies because it has few means to do so Indeed, Washington's very efforts to demonstrate its commitment to son of its allies and to domestic audiences worsen this problem. As Timothy Cr ford contends, a firm alliance can embolden the ally to act contrary to Was gton's interest. Two particular problems stand out. The first is "adverse sele on": the United States attracts allies that are reckless in their policies and cre insurgencies, backing them later as an unintentional reward for their policy stakes. The second is the moral hazard problem: U.S. support enables all to avoid useful political reforms or otherwise stay a foolish course because regime has more resources.[107] When the United States pro-

106. As Mark Poll argues, information that an agent is not following the wishes of the principal is useful only e principal can threaten the agent with sanctions. Pollack, "Delegation, Agency, and Agen etting in the European Community," p. 116.

107. Timothy W. C ford, *Pivotal Deterrence: Third-Party Statecraft and the Pursuit of Peace* (Ithaca, N.Y.: Cornell Unive y Press, 1993), pp. 22–23. See also Douglas MacDonald, *Adventures in Chaos: American Interventi r Reform in the Third World* (Cambridge, Mass.: Harvard University Press, 1992).

claims an ally to be vital in the war on terrorism, and when the ally is indeed fighting insurgents who might later abet an attack on the United States, it is difficult to walk away. As D. Michael Shafer noted with regard to U.S. support for governments during the Cold War, "The more critical the situation, the less leverage the United States can muster."[108]

One way out of the moral hazard is through what Alan Kuperman labels "restricting insurance"—the example he uses is the International Monetary Fund requirement of structural adjustments before bailing out a country.[109] While possible in theory, playing such a role would in practice be politically difficult for the United States. The repeated U.S. declarations that fighting al-Qaida is a "vital interest" (and the linkage of this to the country in question, which is often necessary to get a program under way for political and bureaucratic reasons at home) undermine the ability of the United States to threaten to cut support.[110] Moreover, such declarations provide locals an incentive to exaggerate their insurgents' links to al-Qaida. Immediately after the September 11 attacks, governments around the world began declaring that the local fighters they faced had al-Qaida links as a way of legitimating their struggle in Washington's eyes.[111] Before the recent schism with the United States over the regime's abuses, the government of Uzbekistan has even stressed the dangers to U.S. military personnel as a way of pushing the United States to give more support to the government.[112]

Scale is another problem. As discussed above, solving many of the various military problems requires changing the broader society, economy, and political system: a daunting challenge that requires massive resources to tackle. There will be little U.S. appetite for placing pressure on allies if truly changing their security forces requires transforming them from top to bottom.

Compounding this challenge is that the United States' instrument of change is often the very regime and military forces that are themselves part of the structural problem. The United States cannot by itself foster economic devel-

---

108. D. Michael Shafer, "The Unlearned Lessons of Counterinsurgency," *Political Science Quarterly*, Vol. 103, No. 1 (Spring 1998), p. 64.
109. See Alan J. Kuperman, "Suicidal Rebellions and the Moral Hazard of Humanitarian Intervention," in Timothy W. Crawford and Kuperman, eds., *Gambling on Humanitarian Intervention: Moral Hazard, Rebellion, and Civil War* (New York: Routledge, 2006). The economic analogies, including the International Monetary Fund, appear in ibid., pp. 12–16.
110. Metz and Millen, *Insurgency and Counterinsurgency in the 21st Century*, p. 19.
111. Members of the General Directorate for External Security, interviewed by the author, Paris, France, May 2005.
112. Richard Weitz, "Storm Clouds over Central Asia: Revival of the Islamic Movement of Uzbekistan (IMU)?" *Studies in Conflict & Terrorism*, Vol. 27, No. 6 (November/December 2004), pp. 465–490.

opment in Alge or political reform in Uzbekistan. Such measures require local regimes to ke action. For many local interlocutors, reform is more threatening tha he insurgency: Political reform would throw them out of power; military form might increase the chances of a coup; economic reform would lessen o ortunities for corruption; and social reform would hinder their group's h on power. Not surprisingly, foreign leaders often turn the United States vn when it presses for reform. At times, they may halfheartedly embr reform, going through the motions (and taking U.S. money and resources) it perverting the outcome to ensure the stability of the status quo.

The United S s also suffers from several "moral hazards" as it seeks to exert influence. U support of a government often reduces the necessity for the regime to unde ke the reforms required to gain popular support. U.S. backing comes with degree of legitimacy as well as with financial and other resources. Thus e owered, governments can put off land reform, stop reining in corruption, a avoid other changes that would hurt the insurgent cause.[113] In Uzbekistan, example, the regime used the U.S. embrace to enhance its legitimacy even t cracked down on dissent at home.[114] Ironically, the United States may be t d with the brush of a brutal ally, even if it is urging that ally to reform.[115]

Similarly, U.S upport for a military reduces the military's need to change its leaders and ise its doctrine, organization, and procedures to better fight the insurgency. ange often comes at the point of a knife: if the United States is doing the fig ng for, or even with, locals, they may believe they can carry on with ineffici practices without losing.

Money transf , one of the biggest U.S. levers and in theory one of the key ways that the ited States could influence its allies, are also problematic. Denying the Pa tani security services resources means they are less able to do what the Un d States seeks.[116] Indeed, in the most extreme circumstances, the local milita and regime may not want to completely defeat the insurgents, for finan reasons. Kyrgyz Prime Minister Kurmanbek Bakiev, for example, declared e U.S. military presence in his country to be a "gold mine," a

---

113. Metz and Mill *Insurgency and Counterinsurgency in the 21st Century*, p. 19.
114. "Prepared Sta ent of Fiona Hill," reprinted in "Central Asia: Terrorism, Religious Extremism, and Regional ability."
115. "Prepared Sta ent of Stephen Blank," reprinted in "Central Asia: Terrorism, Religious Extremism, and Regi Instability," p. 53.
116. Pollack identi a similar general problem in principal-agent relationships. Pollack, "Delegation, Agency, an genda Setting in the European Community," p. 117.

comment that suggests just how beneficial such a presence can be to poor areas.[117] Even without U.S. aid, war is often financially beneficial to military leaders. In Algeria, elements of the military wanted to keep the war going with the insurgents indefinitely because of these financial benefits.[118]

Must the United States Go to War with the Allies It Has?

This article has argued that U.S. allies in the struggle against al-Qaida-linked insurgencies are likely to suffer from a range of problems at both the tactical and strategic levels. These problems are not simply the result of poor training or ignorance. Rather, they are structural, growing out of the societal and political characteristics of the regimes and countries in question. Thus, when the United States relies on its allies to fight U.S. enemies, it must recognize not only their limited capabilities but also their fundamentally different interests.

To guard against some of the problems that will inevitably arise, the United States should take several steps. A first is to change the target of intelligence collection. One of the biggest problems the United States faces is that its ally can manipulate U.S. intelligence. It is the ally that gathers the intelligence, and in so doing it can both directly and indirectly shape the views of the United States toward the struggle. The ally can portray insurgents with a local agenda as part of al-Qaida or exaggerate the effectiveness of units receiving U.S. assistance in a bid to increase the size of the overall package. An obvious recommendation is to gather intelligence on the ally itself, particularly with regard to its information collection and dissemination activities. The United States must know what information is being gathered, how well it is being analyzed and disseminated, and what is being passed on to (and, more important, withheld from) the United States.

The United States must also diversify the sources of information instead of relying on the area regimes, which can easily manipulate the information. One way to gather information is to rely on third parties.[119] The international media would be one source of information, as would independent investigative groups such as the International Crisis Group. These bodies can monitor the ally in a credible way, supplementing the overall information available. They also can do so with less risk of a backlash to the overall bilateral relationship than if an ally discovered the United States was spying on its security services.

117. Quoted in Weitz, "Storm Clouds over Central Asia," p. 519.
118. Martinez, *The Algerian Civil War, 1990–1998*, p. 232.
119. See Pollack, "Delegation, Agency, and Agenda Setting in the European Community," p. 111.

In addition t ectifying information asymmetries, the United States must reconsider how xerts leverage over its allies and, if possible, try to minimize the moral haza issue. To increase its chances of success, the United States must recognize at it is not always on the side of the allied government. Rather, Washin n should at times act as a third party, helping fight the insurgency but also manding reforms when possible. Aid and other assistance should be con gent when possible. Given domestic political difficulties, however, such nbleness will be difficult.

Peacetime en gement activities such as training, military education programs, and mi ry-to-military contacts can help change a military culture, but the effects a likely to be limited at best, as they cannot change the fundamental differen in interests. U.S. officials argue that the Georgian military did not interfer the recent process of democratic change in part due to the influence of U. raining and education programs.[120] The United States has made such civi ilitary training a core part of its efforts to engage militaries in the postcom nist world, though the long-term effects are not yet clear. The new persp ives and skills that are learned in these programs, however, often atrophy o re overwhelmed by the powerful cultural, political, and economic forces th created the dysfunctional military culture in the first place. Uzbekistan, for ample, has been a member of the Partnership for Peace since 1994, yet its mi ry culture remains brutal and corrupt.

As a result o ese barriers, realistic expectations are necessary. The United States has no r y solutions for the problem of weak states, which is at the core of many o s allies' weaknesses in counterinsurgency. Diplomatic pressure and peacet e military engagement activities can help improve a government's effort ag st insurgencies, but their track record is likely to be spotty at best. Moreover, ese efforts may take years or even generations to produce significant resu Recognizing the difficulties in this process and the likely limits will help designing programs that are more realistic and have the proper expecta ns.

Implications f Iraq

The United Stat is likely to encounter many of the problems it has faced with other COIN pa ners if it transfers security responsibilities in Iraq to Iraqi forces. Iraq is a hly divided society with a weak economy, both of which are

120. Thom Shanke d C.J. Chivers, "Crackdown in Uzbekistan Reopens Longstanding Debate on U.S. Military Ai *New York Times*, July 13, 2005.

posing the danger of massive civil strife. The Sunni insurgency, though divided, is strong numerically, and in many Shiite parts of Iraq, militias hold sway that are not under the government's control. The regime cannot deliver social services, and crime is rampant. The Iraqi government of Prime Minister Nuri al-Maliki is far from unified, making it likely that military forces will be similarly fractionalized or view the elected leadership with contempt.

No one of these problems is inherently insurmountable, but together they will prove exceptionally troublesome in the years to come. They pose particular problems for the preferred "exit strategy" of both the Bush administration and its Democratic critics: handing over the security of Iraq to the Iraqis. If Iraq follows the experiences of the other countries examined in this article, its security forces will likely be corrupt, brutal, poorly trained, weakly led, unable to coordinate, penetrated by insurgents and militias, and out of step with national political leaders.

Such problems suggest a fundamental flaw with the preferred U.S. strategy of transferring security to Iraqi forces (unless the U.S. goal is to cynically use such a "handoff" as an excuse for cutting and running). Instead, the extreme positions may be the more realistic ones: either staying in the country with large numbers of U.S. forces for many years to defeat the insurgents or abandoning the country to its fate of strife and civil war.

Is Counterinsurgency Worth the Effort?

Americans may legitimately wonder whether the United States should still work with allies that are weak, corrupt, antidemocratic, and brutal. Is it simply better to devote resources to homeland defense and otherwise wage this fight without such unsavory partners? This is particularly true in cases where U.S. partners might still face significant political opposition even if their counterinsurgency capabilities were stronger: the "demand" for reform created by the government's brutality and incompetence is simply too strong.

Americans should keep in mind several counterarguments. First, although U.S. allies range from disappointing to abysmal, the jihadists they fight are typically far worse. The jihadists' ideals and practices are bloody and backward, and the United States can be said to be on the "least worst" side. Second, the area regimes do not want to kill Americans, and the jihadists do. Sheer self-interest dictates recognition of this difference, however distasteful to the allies. Third, the United States can push reform on its allies. As noted above, this is difficult and likely to suffer many problems, but it is not impossible.

These arguments will not hold in every case, however. Washington must be aware that som f its allies' problems may grow despite U.S. help and that this expansion he U.S. role, in turn, can pose a direct danger to U.S. security by raising hosti toward the United States and tarnishing its overall image. In such circum nces, U.S. resources may be better used for improving the United States' nses or increasing its domestic capabilities rather than further expanding ograms to help allies.

NATO's International Security Role in the Terrorist Era

Renée de Nevers

The North Atlantic Treaty Organization's ongoing engagement in missions ranging from Bosnia to Darfur suggests that the alliance has overcome the doubts about its future that arose after the Cold War. The war on terror that followed al-Qaida's attacks on the United States on September 11, 2001, would appear further to reinforce NATO's significance. While unilateral actions by the United States and U.S. co-operation with loose coalitions in Afghanistan and Iraq have garnered the bulk of international attention, experts agree that multilateral cooperation is essential in fighting terrorism. Moreover, several of NATO's current activities, such as its missions in Afghanistan and the Mediterranean, are closely linked to the war on terror, with other NATO missions also contributing to this fight. These activities have led NATO's secretary-general, Jaap de Hoop Scheffer, to declare that "more than ever, NATO is in demand, and NATO is delivering."[1]

This apparent vibrancy, however, may not accurately reflect NATO's true condition. Although its missions have expanded dramatically since the end of the Cold War and alliance members agree on the threat posed by terrorism, NATO's actual role in the multifaceted struggle against terrorists is minor. This could have long-term implications for alliance unity.

This article investigates how the United States has worked with NATO in prosecuting the war on terror. The U.S. government conceives of this struggle broadly, with counterinsurgency and efforts to constrain the spread of weapons of mass destruction (WMD) as essential elements. NATO is the United States' premier alliance, and most of Washington's closest allies are members. But how does NATO contribute to this war on terror? To be sure, NATO is not simply a "tool" of U.S. policy. The war on terror is a U.S. creation, however, and NATO has been forced to adjust to this fact. The United States perceives

Renée de Nevers is Assistant Professor of Public Administration at the Maxwell School at Syracuse University.

The author wishes to thank William Banks, Chantal de Jonge Oudraat, Brian Taylor, Terry Terriff, the participants in the Transatlantic Policy Consortium's Colloquium on Security and Transatlantic Relations, and two anonymous reviewers for their helpful comments on previous drafts of this article.

1. Jaap de Hoop Scheffer, "Speech at the 42nd Munich Conference on Security Policy," Munich, Germany, February 4, 2006, http://www.securityconference.de/.

International Security, Vol. 31, No. 4 (Spring 2007), pp. 34–66

terrorism as th ey national security threat it will face in the coming years. Just as the Uni States is working to transform its strategies in response to this threat, we uld expect it to evaluate key alliances and security relationships with this asure.

I argue that N TO is playing a largely supportive role in U.S. efforts to combat terrorism. T focus of both the European "fight against terrorism" and the U.S. "war on te r" lies elsewhere, leaving NATO's contribution to efforts to quell terrorism newhat tangential. NATO is conducting a defensive mission in the Mediter ean in response to the terrorist threat, and it has adopted strategies rangi from new technology development to consequence management to preven r mitigate terrorist attacks. In Afghanistan the alliance has assumed a fron e role in seeking to deny terrorist groups a foothold there, making this NA 's first de facto combat operation ever. But many of the essential element the fight against terrorism, such as intelligence sharing, occur outside NA . Afghanistan aside, NATO members participate in offensive efforts to respo to terrorism outside NATO through bilateral activities or loose coalitions the willing. There are three main reasons for NATO's limited role: shift alignments and threat perceptions caused by systemic changes, NAT limited military capabilities, and the nature of the fight against terror.

The United S es needs allies in its fight against terrorism, but does it need the alliance?[2] T e sure, the United States values NATO, and indeed has been the driving for behind efforts to expand the alliance by incorporating new members. In ad ion, NATO has become more than simply a military alliance. Glenn Snyder nes "alliances" as "formal associations of states for the use (or nonuse) of tary force, in specified circumstances, against states outside their own men rship."[3] NATO is far more than this. It is commonly de-

2. At the end of t old War, realist scholars predicted the alliance's demise, and during the 1990s, realist and tutionalist scholars sought to explain NATO's longevity. For realist approaches, see John earsheimer, "Back to the Future: Instability in Europe after the Cold War," *International Securi* Vol. 15, No. 1 (Summer 1990), pp. 5–56; and Kenneth N. Waltz, "The Emerging Structur International Politics," *International Security*, Vol. 18, No. 2 (Fall 1993), pp. 44–79. For reali iscussions of NATO's continued utility, see Charles L. Glaser, "Why NATO Is Still Best: Future urity Arrangements for Europe," *International Security*, Vol. 18, No. 1 (Summer 1993), pp. 5– nd Robert J. Art, "Why Western Europe Needs the United States and NATO," *Political Sc e Quarterly*, Vol. 111, No. 1 (Spring 1996), pp. 1–39. For institutionalist approaches, see John uffield, "NATO's Functions after the Cold War," *Political Science Quarterly*, Vol. 109, No. 5 (Wi 1994–95), pp. 763–787; Robert B. McCalla, "NATO's Persistence after the Cold War," *Interna l Organization*, Vol. 50, No. 3 (Summer 1996), pp. 445–475; and Celeste A. Wallander, "Institu al Assets and Adaptability: NATO after the Cold War," *International Organization*, Vol. 54, No. utumn 2000), pp. 705–735.

3. Glenn H. Snyde *lliance Politics* (Ithaca, N.Y.: Cornell University Press, 1997), p. 4.

scribed as a political-military alliance that combines the key political function of guiding members' foreign and security policy and providing a forum for alliance consultation with the operational function of ensuring that members can train and develop the capabilities to cooperate militarily.[4] This dual role helps to explain why NATO has endured.[5] The key issues are whether its members continue to agree on its value and what its core tasks should be, as well as the threat that it confronts. Moreover, if NATO's members do not seek to address their core security threats within the alliance, the alliance's military value to its members is likely to be questioned.

In the next section, I compare U.S. and NATO strategies for confronting terrorism. I then assess NATO's contribution to the U.S. fight against terrorism. The following section examines factors that help to explain why NATO's contribution to the U.S. war on terror has been relatively limited. I look at three elements: systemic changes and their consequences for NATO, alliance capabilities, and the nature of the fight against terrorism. Finally, I discuss the implications of NATO's elusive role in combating terrorism for U.S. policy and for the alliance.

Comparing Strategies for Confronting Terrorism

The U.S. government widely regards NATO as the most important institution that the United States works with, its premier alliance. Not only do government officials point out how much the alliance has done to support U.S. activi-

4. Celeste A. Wallander and Robert O. Keohane propose that NATO has become a security management institution rather than an alliance. See Wallander and Keohane, "Risk, Threat, and Security Institutions," in Helga Haftendorn, Keohane, and Wallander, eds., *Imperfect Unions: Security Institutions over Time and Space* (Oxford: Oxford University Press, 1999), pp. 21–47.

5. Relatively little theoretical research has examined NATO's current situation. Some recent exceptions include evaluations of the alliance's effort to adjust to shifting power relations, and of soft balancing as an alternative to traditional balance of power behavior. See Galia Press-Barnathan, "Managing the Hegemon: NATO under Unipolarity," *Security Studies*, Vol. 15, No. 2 (April–June 2006), pp. 271–309; Seyom Brown, *Multilateral Constraints on the Use of Force: A Reassessment* (Carlisle, Pa.: Strategic Studies Institute, U.S. Army War College, 2006); Robert A. Pape, "Soft Balancing against the United States," *International Security*, Vol. 30, No. 1 (Summer 2005), pp. 7–45; T.V. Paul, "Soft Balancing in the Age of U.S. Primacy," *International Security*, Vol. 30. No. 1 (Summer 2005), pp. 46–71; and Stephen G. Brooks and William C. Wohlforth, "Hard Times for Soft Balancing," *International Security*, Vol. 30, No. 1 (Summer 2005), pp. 72–108. For discussions of alliance persistence and maintenance, see Stephen M. Walt, "Why Alliances Endure or Collapse," *Survival*, Vol. 39, No. 1 (Spring 1997), pp. 156–179; Patricia A. Weitsman, "Intimate Enemies: The Politics of Peacetime Alliances," *Security Studies*, Vol. 7, No. 1 (Autumn 1997), pp. 156–192; and Barry Buzan and Ole Waever, *Regions and Powers: The Structure of International Security* (Cambridge: Cambridge University Press, 2003).

ties against terr sts, but they also note that virtually all of NATO's activities today are shap by the struggle against terrorism.[6]

Terrorism ha merged as a shared alliance concern by the late 1990s. Terrorist attacks ir udi Arabia in 1996 and in Kenya and Tanzania in 1998 led the United Stat o urge NATO to address this threat more seriously. As a result, terrorism s incorporated as a factor contributing to NATO's security challenges in th lliance's 1999 Strategic Concept.[7] It was not, however, a core focus of NATO licy at that time.[8] Terrorism crystallized as a central threat to alliance membe only after the September 11 attacks on the United States. NATO's initial sponse to these attacks was twofold: within twenty-four hours, it invoke rticle 5 of its charter, declaring that the attacks on the United States represent an attack on all alliance members. It followed this in subsequent weeks w agreement on steps to assist the U.S.-led coalition that attacked al-Qaid id the Taliban in Afghanistan in October 2001. These steps included increa ig intelligence cooperation, helping to defend states that were participat ; in the Afghanistan campaign, allowing overflight rights, and deploying val forces in the eastern Mediterranean and NATO airborne warning and c rol system (AWACS) planes to the United States.[9] These actions set the pr dent that the alliance's article 5 commitment could stretch beyond the terr rial defense of member states to include defense against terrorist attacks.[10]

NATO also n ed quickly to develop military guidelines for responding to terrorism. At th November 2002 Prague summit, members endorsed the new Military Conce for Defense against Terrorism as official NATO policy. The political guidar for alliance actions emphasizes that NATO's goal should be to "help deter, ond, disrupt, and protect against terrorist attacks," including by acting again state sponsors of terrorists. In addition, the document iden-

6. U.S. official, int w by author, Brussels, Belgium, June 7, 2006.
7. To be sure, NAT European members have long experience with terrorism. For discussions of European response e Jeremy Shapiro and Bénédicte Suzan, "The French Experience of Counter-terrorism," *Sur* , Vol. 45, No. 1 (Spring 2003), pp. 67–98; and Esther Brimmer, ed., *Transforming Homeland urity: U.S. and European Approaches* (Washington, D.C.: Center for Transatlantic Relati , 2006).
8. NATO, "The Al e's Strategic Concept," NATO summit, Washington, D.C., April 24, 1999, http://www.nato.i ocu/pr/1999/p99-065e.htm.
9. Several alliance mbers also participated in the coalition. NATO, "Briefing: Response to Terrorism," Onlin ibrary, March 2005, http://www.nato.int/docu/briefing/rtt/html_en/rtt01.html.
10. "Transatlantic neland Defense," CTNSP/INSS Special Report (Washington, D.C.: Center for Technology and tional Security Policy, Institute for National Strategic Studies, National Defense University, M 2006), http://www.NDU.edu/inss/press/CTNSP-INSS/spl-rpt.pdf.

tifies four military roles for alliance operations against terrorism: antiterrorism, or defensive measures; consequence management in the event of an attack against a member state; offensive counterterrorism; and military cooperation with nonmilitary forces.[11]

In some ways, U.S. strategies to combat terrorism differ from NATO strategies in the goals they emphasize. The U.S. *National Strategy for Combating Terrorism,* published in September 2006, specifies four short-term policies to address terrorism: preventing terrorist attacks before they occur; denying WMD to rogue states and terrorist groups; denying terrorist groups sanctuary or support from rogue states; and preventing terrorist groups from controlling any nation that they could use as a base of operations.[12] The strategy seeks to ensure that the United States confronts terrorism abroad, not at home. As the U.S. *National Security Strategy (NSS)* of March 2006 notes, "The fight must be taken to the enemy."[13] Moreover, in this rubric, prevention refers to offensive counterterrorism activities. The goal of preventing attacks before they occur is not only to stop a planned attack, but to hunt down and capture or kill terrorists determined to attack the United States. The denial elements of the strategy are largely focused on states that might support terrorists.

NATO's military guidelines are more defensive and reactive than those of the United States. NATO places greater emphasis on reducing vulnerabilities and enhancing capabilities to respond quickly to potential attacks. In contrast, the United States seeks to keep terrorists from striking the homeland or U.S. interests abroad. And, whereas NATO's military guidelines suggest that its forces could play either lead or supportive roles in offensive operations against terrorists, more planning is recommended before NATO-led offensive operations are undertaken, while the recommendations for support missions are more practical. This indicates the alliance's greater comfort and experience with its support role.

The goals of NATO and the United States as outlined in these strategies do overlap in important ways. For example, each recognizes the usefulness of multilateral actions and seeks to prevent attacks before they occur. In addition, NATO's counterterrorism strategy shares with U.S. policy the recognition that

---

11. NATO, International Military Staff, "NATO's Military Concept for Defense against Terrorism," updated April 14, 2005, http://www.nato.int/ims/docu/terrorism.htm.
12. The long-term policy goal is to advance democracy as a means to quell support for terrorism. National Security Council, *The National Strategy for Combating Terrorism* (Washington, D.C.: White House, September 2006), pp. 11–17, http://www.whitehouse.gov/nsc/nsct/2006/.
13. George W. Bush, *The National Security Strategy of the United States of America* (Washington, D.C.: White House, March 2006), p. 8, http://www.whitehouse.gov/nsc/nss/2006/nss2006.pdf.

preventing atta may require offensive action against terrorists or states that support them. NATO's Military Concept for Defense against Terrorism states, "Allied n ons agree that terrorists should not be allowed to base, train, plan, stage, and ecute terrorist actions, and the threat may be severe enough to justify acting ainst these terrorists and those who harbor them."[14]

The overlap withstanding, U.S. strategy documents suggest that NATO's deeply instituti lized, consensus-based model is not the United States' preferred approach r multilateral cooperation in the war on terror. Moreover, NATO appears be less central to U.S. policy and planning. Both the 2002 and 2006 *NSS* docu nts promote the formation of coalitions, both within and outside NATO, to a ress a range of threats.[15] More critically, the 2006 *NSS* makes explicit the U.S reference for a looser form of cooperation, citing as a model the Proliferatio ecurity Initiative (PSI), an activity designed by the George W. Bush admin ration to constrain the spread of WMD-related technology. The 2006 *NSS* es as a goal "[the] establish[ment of] results-oriented partnerships on the odel of the PSI to meet new challenges and opportunities. These partners s emphasize international cooperation, not international bureaucracy. T rely on voluntary adherence rather than binding treaties. They are orient towards action and results rather than legislation or rule-making."[16] The 06 *NSS* also states that "existing international institutions have a role to , but in many cases coalitions of the willing may be able to respond more q kly and creatively, at least in the short term."[17] Similarly, the 2006 *Quadrenn Defense Review* (*QDR*) highlights the distinction between "static alliances rsus dynamic partnerships" and the Pentagon's preference for the latter.[18] ne Pentagon officials insist that the apparent disdain for existing alliances imed not at NATO, but at bodies such as the Organization for American S s, which, for example, has resisted U.S. efforts to revise its charter in an at pt to isolate Venezuela's president, Hugo Chavez, to punish his anti-U.S. sta e. Although NATO's European members are less concerned now that the U d States would use NATO as a "toolbox" than they were immediately after e U.S. invasion of Iraq in 2003,[19] they may not be reassured that the United ates strongly supports the alliance.

14. NATO, "NATO ilitary Concept for Defense against Terrorism."
15. George W. Bus e *National Security Strategy of the United States of America* (Washington, D.C.: White House, Sept er 2002), http://www.whitehouse.gov/nsc/nss.pdf.
16. Bush, *National rity Strategy* (2006), p. 46.
17. Ibid., p. 48.
18. Donald H. Rum ld, *Quadrennial Defense Review Report* (Washington, D.C.: Department of Defense, February 6,), p. vii, http://www.defenselink.mil/qdr/report/Report20060203.pdf.
19. I thank an ano ous reviewer for reinforcing this point.

A central question for the United States and NATO is whether their aims correspond to the nature of the terrorist threat. Both U.S. strategy and NATO's military concept initially focused on a particular type of terrorism: the threat posed by al-Qaida at the time of the September 11 attacks. The threat has evolved since then, partly in response to U.S. and allied efforts to disrupt terrorist groups and their activities. The 2006 *NSS* notes the changed nature of the threat, although the framework of U.S. policy has not changed. For example, whether terrorists need states to support their activities is no longer clear.[20] Not only have individuals proven willing to fund terrorist actions, but increasingly, terrorists operate "virtually," without formal ties, communicating and even training via websites and other electronic media.[21] One result has been the "localization" of threats, as seen in the terrorist attacks in Madrid in 2004 and London in 2005. These attacks were carried out by homegrown terrorists with no clear ties to al-Qaida.

NATO and U.S. strategies thus exhibit both similarities and differences in priorities. The crucial issue is how these strategies affect cooperation between the United States and NATO regarding terrorism.

NATO's Role in the U.S. War on Terror

In this section I assess NATO's contribution to the U.S. war on terror in the following categories: (1) prevention and defense, (2) denial, (3) counterterrorism, and (4) consequence management—all of which are essential to confronting terrorism. These categories incorporate both elements of the U.S. strategy and NATO's political and military efforts to fight terrorism. For each category, I evaluate how NATO's efforts correspond to U.S. goals, as well as to the nature of the terrorist threat.

PREVENTION AND DEFENSE AGAINST TERRORIST ATTACKS

Efforts to prevent and defend against terrorist actions fall into two main areas: intelligence sharing and surveillance to detect preparations for an attack. NATO has engaged in both activities, primarily through Operation Active Endeavor (OAE). It is also exploring new technologies to detect and defend against terrorist attacks, a third preventive activity.

---

20. See, for example, Fareed Zakaria, "Terrorists Don't Need States," *Newsweek*, April 5, 2004, p. 37.

21. See, among others, Ron Suskind, *The One Percent Doctrine: Deep Inside America's Pursuit of Its Enemies since 9/11* (New York: Simon and Schuster, 2006); and Benjamin Wallace-Wells, "Private Jihad: How Rita Katz Got into the Spying Business," *New Yorker*, May 29, 2006, pp. 28–41.

OPERATION A VE ENDEAVOR. OAE is NATO's only article 5 operation, and it was the first s stantive military action the alliance took after the September 11 attacks to ad ess the terrorist threat.[22] This activity corresponds both to Washington's g of preventing terrorist attacks and to NATO's antiterrorism strategy. After ploying in the eastern Mediterranean in October 2001 as a deterrent and veillance measure in support of the U.S. intervention in Afghanistan, O evolved into a broader counterterrorism initiative. It expanded to cov the entire Mediterranean in 2003; and during the U.S. invasion of Ira it escorted ships through the Strait of Gibraltar (at the United States' uest) to alleviate concerns that terrorists might target such ships. OAE has cused on monitoring shipping and the safety of ports and narrow sea-lan A second goal, particularly since 2003, has been to expand participation b on-NATO states, both by countries that are formal NATO partners and by untries participating in NATO's Mediterranean Dialogue, a consultative fo n intended to improve cooperation with countries in the Mediterranean a.[23]

OAE has dev d much attention to expanding its intelligence-sharing activities, includi efforts to develop a network for tracking merchant shipping throughout the diterranean, and improving means to share this intelligence with relevant g rnments. This should help to address not only terrorist concerns but also ance efforts to prevent drug smuggling and the spread of weapons of ma destruction.[24]

OAE has clea ilitary objectives, and NATO has developed valuable experience in mariti surveillance and interdiction through this mission. At the same time, the ssion has had both strategic and political aims. NATO has sought to inclu Russia in OAE, for example, to gain Moscow's agreement to extend the ope ion's activities into the Black Sea. Expansion into the Black Sea has not hap ned, due to objections from both Russia and Turkey to allowing NATO ope ions there, but Russia participated in OAE patrols in the Mediterranean 2006.[25] Efforts to include more Mediterranean countries are

---

22. General James nes, "NATO: From Common Defense to Common Security," Senate Committee on Foreign tions, 109th Cong., 2d sess., February 7, 2006, http://foreign.senate.gov/hearings/2006/hrg 207a.html.
23. NATO, "NATO vates Mediterranean Dialogue to a Genuine Partnership, Launches Istanbul Cooperation Initiat " NATO Update, June 29, 2004, http://www.nato.int/docu/update/2004/06-june/e0629d.htm
24. Robert Cesarett Combating Terrorism in the Mediterranean," *NATO Review*, No. 3 (Autumn 2005), http://www. .int/docu/review/2005/issue3/english/art4.html.
25. Russia was unw ng to agree to this move unless it gained a greater decisionmaking role over the activity, which TO was not willing to accept. Vladimir Socor, "Russians Not Joining NATO Operation Active E avor," *Eurasia Daily Monitor*, Vol. 1, No. 136 (November 30, 2004); Jones,

designed to improve cooperation and, if possible, to share the burden for sustaining the operation with a greater number of countries. This is in keeping with NATO's ongoing efforts to explore expanded partnerships with countries around the globe.[26]

The United States values OAE because it facilitates intelligence sharing and because it is an alliance-wide activity. Still, NATO's efforts do not always go as far as the United States would like. OAE's guidelines allow it to board only ships whose masters and flag states are willing to comply with the boarding, in keeping with international law. In contrast, the United States is willing to act alone if there is confusion about whether ships will comply.[27] This has led to instances in which the United States has boarded ships unilaterally, although based on suspicions raised by OAE's monitoring activities.

OAE is NATO's most prominent defense activity, but the alliance has also undertaken numerous surveillance and patrolling missions to defend against possible terrorist attacks. NATO AWACS aircraft conducted surveillance at more than thirty events ranging from NATO's Istanbul summit in 2004 to the 2006 World Cup in Germany. NATO also deployed its new Multinational Chemical, Biological, Radiological, Nuclear (CBRN) task force to the 2004 Athens Olympics.

INTELLIGENCE. Intelligence is widely viewed as the most important tool in preventing terrorist attacks, and the United States shares intelligence regarding terrorist activities with a broad range of countries.[28] NATO's intelligence contribution to U.S. efforts against terrorism is limited, however, for four reasons. First, most of the military intelligence NATO relies on, which is shared through the NATO Special Committee, is provided by the United States to the alliance. The Multinational Battlefield Information and Exploitation System, for example, is a "near-real-time all-source system" through which the United States feeds information to NATO commands.[29]

Second, the United States and its European allies have diverging views about the role of military intelligence. From the U.S. perspective, military intel-

---

"NATO: From Common Defense to Common Security"; and Igor Torbakov, "Turkey Sides with Moscow against Washington on Black Sea Force," *Eurasia Daily Monitor*, Vol. 3, No. 43 (March 3, 2006), http://www.jamestown.org/.

26. NATO, "NATO Looks to Global Partnerships," NATO Update, April 27, 2006, http://www.nato.int/docu/update/2006/04-april/e0427c.htm.

27. NATO, "Briefing: Response to Terrorism," p. 5.

28. Derek S. Reveron, "Old Allies, New Friends: Intelligence-Sharing in the War on Terror," *Orbis*, Vol. 50, No. 3 (Summer 2006), pp. 453–468.

29. Richard J. Aldrich, "Transatlantic Intelligence and Security Cooperation," *International Affairs*, Vol. 80, No. 4 (July 2004), pp. 731–753.

ligence is an inc ısingly important component on the battlefield. The Department of Defens mphasizes that military intelligence is no longer just a staff function, but ra ːr a war-fighting function that soldiers on the battlefield will be actively eng d in at all times. In addition, as part of its broader interest in network-centri ʼarfare, the Defense Department is pushing to establish a fully "network battlespace," with the goal of "information dominance" in any conflict.[30] N .TO's European members do not place the same degree of emphasis on re time military intelligence.

Third, the ca ilities gap that has presented a chronic problem for NATO is increasing in th ıtelligence area, which suggests growing problems for interoperability. Alr ly in the 1990s, the U.S. military had to maintain "legacy" communication ystems to enable it to operate with other NATO members, and allied forc lepended heavily on U.S. communications and intelligence during the 199 ɔsovo bombing campaign.[31] One reason the United States rejected some E ɔpean offers of military assistance in its intervention in Afghanistan in ɔ1 was the difficulties presented by different levels of technological sophisti ion. The United States spends far more on research and development tha its allies; the Defense Department's budget request for research and d lopment for FY 2007 is $57.9 billion. In contrast, the entire defense budget ır the United Kingdom, NATO's next largest spender, was $50.2 billion in 2006.[32] The United States also has a more robust domestic high-technolog ıdustry than does any of its European allies.

To be sure, a nce members agree on the need for improvements in intelligence capabil ːs and interoperability. NATO adopted an initiative on developing new ıpabilities, particularly in areas such as intelligence and surveillance, in No mber 2002. In addition, some alliance members are working to improve the information warfare capabilities.[33] That better intelligence

30. William G. Boy , "Intelligence Support to Allied and Coalition Operations: Strategic Environment for Coaliti Warfare," Sixteenth Annual NDIA SO/LIC Symposium, Washington, D.C., February 2–4, 2005, ɔ://www.dtic.mil/ndia/2005solic/2005solic.html. On network-centric warfare, see Nancy J. ensten, Gregory Belenky, and Thomas J. Balkin, "Cognitive Readiness in Network-Centric C ations," *Parameters*, Vol. 35, No. 1 (Spring 2005), pp. 94–105; and Paul Murdock, "Principl f War on the Network-Centric Battlefield: Mass and Economy of Force," *Parameters*, Vol. 32, N (Spring 2002), pp. 86–95.

31. David S. Yost, NATO Capabilities Gap and the European Union," *Survival*, Vol. 42, No. 4 (December 2000), p 7–128.

32. NATO Europe nds about $12 billion a year on research and development. See Stephen J. Flanagan, "Sustaini U.S.-European Global Security Cooperation," *Strategic Forum*, No. 217 (September 2005), pp. 1 Steven M. Kosiak, *Analysis of the FY 2007 Defense Budget Request* (Washington, D.C.: Center f Strategic and Budgetary Assessments, April 25, 2006); and International Institute for Strateg Studies, *The Military Balance, 2005–2006* (London: IISS, 2005), p. 107.

33. Aldrich, "Trans ntic Intelligence and Security Cooperation," pp. 745–748.

capabilities continue to be problematic is evident in repeated references to the need for improved intelligence sharing both among national agencies and internationally.[34]

The problem, however, is deeper than merely the need for better intelligence capabilities; NATO's members have developed diverging operational concepts because their military capabilities differ. Differences in their views on the role of information in war fighting are one example of this divergence. The United States approaches the use of force differently than do most European militaries, which means that cooperation on the battlefield could be increasingly difficult.[35] Although joint exercises may highlight these differences, they do not necessarily resolve them.

Fourth, the most vital terrorist-related intelligence information generated in Europe is outside NATO's scope, because it comes from police and domestic intelligence agencies. The bulk of intelligence sharing within Europe, and between the United States and European states, occurs bilaterally or among select groups of states, not in NATO. U.S. intelligence cooperation is closest with the United Kingdom, and its cooperation with members of the UK-USA network is far more intensive than is its intelligence sharing with other NATO countries.[36] The major European mechanism for sharing domestic intelligence is the Berne Group, a club of European intelligence organizations to which the United States does not belong. Three factors hinder greater cooperation in nonmilitary intelligence sharing: the problem of ensuring protection of sources when information is dispersed, differences between the United States and many European allies over appropriate domestic privacy standards, and disagreements over legal constraints on intelligence collection.[37] The turmoil caused by reports of secret CIA detention centers in Europe, and Italy's indictment of several CIA officers for operating illegally on Italian soil when they kidnapped a terrorist suspect, illustrate the differences in views regarding the acquisition and use of intelligence.[38]

34. NATO, "Lessons Learned from Recent Terrorist Attacks: Building National Capabilities and Institutions," Chairman's Report, October 6, 2005, http://www.nato.int/docu/conf/2005/050727/index.html.
35. I thank Terry Terriff for pointing this out.
36. UK-USA was established in 1947. Denmark, Norway, Turkey, and West Germany later joined the network. Reveron, "Old Allies, New Friends," p. 460.
37. Aldrich, "Transatlantic Intelligence and Security Cooperation," pp. 738–740.
38. Dana Priest, "CIA Holds Terror Suspects in Secret Prisons: Debate Is Growing within Agency about Legality and Morality of Overseas System Set Up after 9/11," *Washington Post*, November 2, 2005; and Craig Whitlock, "Prosecutors: Italian Agency Helped CIA Seize Cleric," *Washington Post*, July 6, 2006.

TECHNOLOGY VELOPMENT. NATO's effort to develop counterterrorism technologies re esents the alliance's third defensive activity. The Defense against Terroris (DAT) program was established by the alliance's Conference of National Arr nents Directors after the 2004 Istanbul summit. Its goal is to develop techno ;ies to help prevent terrorist attacks ranging from the use of improvised ex sive devices to rocket attacks against aircraft. Different NATO countrie ıave taken the lead on each of the ten project initiatives.[39]

This effort ha trong U.S. support. As part of the alliance's defense investment program, DAT program reflects Washington's interest in persuading U.S. allies to de te more resources to their military capabilities, and it corresponds to the i easingly high-technology approach to warfare adopted by the U.S. militar ome new defensive technologies, such as mechanisms to detect improvised plosive devices, are currently being developed, but it is too soon to determ whether the program will improve the alliance's ability to prevent terroris tacks. Notably, the United States is using the defense investment program promote allied transformation goals. NATO's new transformation comma , Allied Command Transformation, established after the alliance revised military command structure in 2002, is based in Norfolk, Virginia, near t U.S. Atlantic Fleet's headquarters; and the defense investment program i ed by an American, Marshall Billingslea, who worked in the Pentagon on co erterrorism and special operations before moving to NATO. U.S. efforts to u this co-location to promote NATO's transformation have led to some resentr ıt within the alliance that the United States is "feeding" its views through new headquarters and the defense investment program.[40]

NATO's cont ution to ongoing efforts to prevent terrorist attacks is thus important, but ıany not be central to U.S. policy. While OAE's surveillance activities contri e to tracking potential terrorist movements, the intelligence developed thro h OAE may be more directly relevant to law enforcement than to militar ıissions. To be sure, U.S. officials agree that many NATO members have ɔng intelligence capabilities, and they can provide valuable intelligence tha e United States does not possess. But the most important elements of intel nce gathering in Europe take place outside NATO and are conducted by nestic intelligence organizations. This intelligence is more likely to be sha bilaterally, rather than through NATO. Bilateral intelligence

39. NATO, "Defen gainst Terrorism Program: Countering Terrorism with Technology," Topics, November 14, 2005 tp://www.nato.int/issues/dat/index.html.
40. NATO official, rviewed by author, Brussels, Belgium, June 2006.

sharing among key allies continued despite severe strains in political relations in the months prior to the U.S. invasion of Iraq, as revelations about German intelligence cooperation with the United States to designate military targets and civilian locations just prior to the invasion made clear.[41] Five European states with substantial terrorism concerns developed their own forum for intelligence cooperation in March 2005. In 2006 the alliance established a new intelligence "fusion center" to ensure that needed intelligence can be distributed to troops in the field. It also created the Terrorist Threat Intelligence Unit to provide a forum for joint analysis of nonclassified information. But these are better means to share and interpret information.[42] NATO as such does not generate raw intelligence useful to preventing terrorism. Finally, NATO's effort to develop new defense technologies to protect against terrorist attacks reinforces the U.S. goal of promoting allied defense transformation. Whether the program will contribute to NATO or U.S. defense remains to be seen.

DENIAL: WMD, SANCTUARY, AND STATE CONTROL

Denying terrorists certain weapons and the benefits of state support, ranging from use of a state's territory to outright control over its government, is a central feature of the U.S. strategy against terrorism. Denial is less evident in NATO's strategy; the goal of disrupting terrorist activities comes closest to the U.S. concept. NATO's contribution to this effort varies considerably; it is marginally involved in efforts to deny terrorists WMD, but it plays a significant role in efforts to deny terrorists state support.

DENYING ACCESS TO WMD. Preventing the spread of WMD is a core NATO goal, though preventing terrorist acquisition of these weapons is not. Moreover, NATO's contribution to international efforts to confront the problem of WMD proliferation is complicated by two central questions. First, should denial efforts be primarily multilateral or bilateral? If multilateral, what is NATO's "value added" in seeking to address proliferation problems? Some NATO members have been involved in cooperative threat reduction efforts in Russia and other former Soviet republics. These nonproliferation efforts have been conducted bilaterally or by small groups of states, however, rather than as multilateral NATO initiatives. The United Kingdom, for example, is work-

41. Bob Drogin, "German Spies Aided U.S. Attempt to Kill Hussein in Aerial Attack," *Los Angeles Times*, January 12, 2006.
42. NATO, Allied Command Operations, Supreme Headquarters Allied Powers Europe, "Launch of the Intelligence Fusion Center in Support of NATO," January 17, 2006, http://www.nato.int/shape/news/2006/01/060117a.htm.

ing with Russia n projects ranging from dismantling nuclear submarines to developing sus iable employment for scientists and engineers formerly employed in Sovi WMD programs. Canada, France, and Germany have engaged in efforts develop plutonium disposition methods.[43] And several core NATO countrie -France, Germany, and the United Kingdom—have sought to induce Iran end its nuclear enrichment program since 2004. The group seeking to deal th Iran is generally referred to as the EU-3, and the broader proposals by th e countries and the United States, China, and Russia were presented to Ira n June 2006 by Javier Solana, the European Union's foreign policy chief—n a NATO representative.[44] The only alliance-wide efforts to address WMD roliferation have sought to encourage political dialogue through forums uch as the NATO-Russia Council, established in 2002, and consultations w other NATO partner states such as Ukraine.

Second, what eans are appropriate for preventing terrorists from acquiring WMD? Althou alliance members generally agreed that Iraq did possess WMD capabilit ,[45] this question was at the heart of the bitter 2002–03 debate over invading I . The differences were over the response, and core NATO allies disagreed w the United States about whether preemption was an appropriate counter t raqi efforts to develop WMD. This is not a new debate, but it was sharpened the fight over Iraq policy.[46]

U.S. policy f ors preemption against the potential spread of WMD, as stated in the 2(*NSS*. This reflects Washington's concern that rogue states and terrorists w acquire WMD for use in terrorist attacks. Given alliance differences over m ns, it is not surprising that NATO does not figure centrally in U.S. counterpr eration activities. Moreover, to the degree that it relies on

43. Tony Blair, *The bal Partnership Annual Report, 2005* (London: Department of Trade and Industry, 2005), http: ww.dti.gov.uk/files/file14426.pdf; Robin Niblett, ed., *Test of Will, Tests of Efficacy: Initiative fo Renewed Transatlantic Partnership, 2005 Report* (Washington, D.C.: Center for Strategic and Inter onal Studies, 2005), pp. 25–31; and Matthew Bunn and Anthony Wier, *Securing the Bomb, 20* Cambridge, Mass., and Washington, D.C.: Project on Managing the Atom, Harvard University d Nuclear Threat Initiative, July 2006).

44. Breffni O'Rour 'Iran: Solana Delivers EU Offer on Nuclear Program," Radio Free Europe/ Radio Liberty Nev ne, June 6, 2006, http://www.rferf.org/featuresarticle/2006/06/9ee3bf6e-955d-4ccd-a1b7-a6f 90afae.html.

45. The French go ment supplied the CIA with contrary information from one of Saddam Hussein's cabinet n sters, who was a French spy. According to a former CIA official, however, "He said there wer weapons of mass destruction . . . so we didn't believe him." Drogin, "German Spies Aided U Attempt to Kill Hussein in Aerial Attack."

46. On the ongoing bate over preemption, see Gareth Evans, "When Is It Right to Fight?" *Survival*, Vol. 46, No. eptember 2004), pp. 59–82; and Peter Dombrowski and Rodger A. Payne, "The Emerging Co sus for Preventive War," *Survival*, Vol. 48, No. 2 (June 2006), pp. 115–136.

multilateral efforts to prevent WMD proliferation, the Bush administration has stated its preference for more flexible partnerships, such as the Proliferation Security Initiative.[47] From the U.S. perspective, the PSI has two main advantages: it is a coalition of the willing, involving only those states that share the PSI's goals, and it is results oriented, emphasizing action rather than legislation or rule making.[48] Although many NATO members participate in the PSI, this is not an alliance activity.

The United States demonstrated its preference for informal coalitions to deny WMD to terrorists by agreeing with Russia on July 15, 2006, to establish the Global Initiative to Combat Nuclear Terrorism. Like the PSI, this informal agreement is open to states that share the United States' concern about nuclear terrorism. There is no plan to establish a treaty or institution to formalize this program; its legal authority is based on the International Convention on the Suppression of Acts of Nuclear Terrorism, signed in 2005, as well as on United Nations Security Council resolutions 1373 and 1540, which proscribe terrorist financing and the spread of WMD-related materials.[49] The initiative seeks to set new standards for securing nuclear materials, engaging in law enforcement, and prosecuting terrorist suspects and their supporters. In this, it resembles the requirements of earlier UN resolutions regarding terrorist financing and law enforcement. Several NATO members are likely to participate in this initiative, which had its first meeting in October 2006, but it is not a NATO activity.

Although many of NATO's European members share the United States' concern about the proliferation of WMD and their acquisition by terrorists, this has not translated into cooperation through NATO to actively confront this security problem. Instead, individual states have worked bilaterally or through alliance consultations to address WMD proliferation. The alliance has done better, however, with regard to denying terrorists sanctuary.

DENYING STATE SUPPORT OR SANCTUARY. NATO has contributed substantially to the U.S. goals of denying support or sanctuary from rogue states to

47. Chaim Brown and Christopher F. Chyba, "Proliferation Rings: New Challenges to the Nuclear Nonproliferation Regime," *International Security*, Vol. 29, No. 2 (Fall 2004), pp. 5–49; and Stephen G. Rademaker, "Proliferation Security Initiative: An Early Assessment," hearing before House Committee on International Relations, 109th Cong., 1st sess. (Washington, D.C.: U.S. Government Printing Office, June 9, 2005), http://www.internationalrelations.house.gov/archives/109/21699.pdf.
48. Bush, *National Security Strategy* (2006), p. 46.
49. "Global Initiative to Combat Nuclear Terrorism: Joint Fact Sheet," July 31, 2006, http://en.g8russia.ru/docs/7.html. For the International Convention on the Suppression of Acts of Nuclear Terrorism, see http://www.un.org/sc/ctc/law.shtml.

terrorist groups d ensuring that such groups do not gain control over states. NATO's missio n Afghanistan, the International Security Assistance Force (ISAF), has ass ed control over international military forces throughout the country. NATO rces are also involved in ongoing efforts to train Iraqi security forces.

The U.S. int ention in Afghanistan that began in October 2001 caused some tension w in the alliance. While several NATO states offered to contribute troops to th mission, and NATO declared that the September 11 attacks constituted an cle 5 attack against all alliance members, the United States did not seek N O's participation in the invasion. This reflected President Bush's desire t void having allies dictate how the war would be fought, as well as the pref nce among some in the Pentagon to avoid the headaches of having to gain ied consensus on strategy similar to those that had developed during N 's bombing campaign against Serbia in 1999.[50] Equally important was t question of whether NATO allies could contribute the specialized cap lities needed for the campaign the United States was planning.[51] Noneth ss, a few NATO countries took part in the initial attack against Afghan n—including Denmark, France, Germany, Turkey, and the United Kingdo –and NATO AWACS aircraft patrolled U.S. airspace in the fall of 2001, "ba illing" to ensure that U.S. territory was defended while freeing U.S. forces the invasion.[52]

ISAF was i lly established with UN Security Council authorization under British mand in October 2001, after the United States overthrew Afghanistan's T ban government. NATO assumed control of ISAF in August 2003.[53] Initially F's mission was limited to patrolling Kabul, but since 2004, ISAF has unde ken a four-stage expansion of its mission into the northern and western pr nces of Afghanistan, and later to the south and east. It has also deployed eral provincial reconstruction teams, which are based on a

50. Bob Woodward *sh at War* (New York: Simon and Schuster, 2002), p. 81; Terry Terriff, "Fear and Loathing in N : The Atlantic Alliance after the Crisis over Iraq," *Perspectives on European Politics and Society,* 5, No. 3 (2004), p. 424; and Tomas Valasek, "NATO's New Roles: A Vision from Inside the All e" (Washington, D.C.: CDI Terrorism Project, Center for Defense Information, October 19, 2 , http://www.cdi.org/terrorism/nato-pr.cfm.

51. Indeed, initial ations in Afghanistan were conducted by the CIA, which was able to act more rapidly than Pentagon. See Suskind, *The One Percent Doctrine,* pp. 18–21; Ivo H. Daalder and James M. Lind *America Unbound: The Bush Revolution in Foreign Policy* (Washington, D.C.: Brookings, 2003), 01–102; and Peter van Ham, "Growing Pains," *NATO Review,* No. 3 (Autumn 2005), http:// w.nato.int/docu/review/2005/issue3/english/analysis_pr.html.

52. "Backfilling" is of NATO's support goals in its strategy for confronting terrorism.

53. On NATO's r see "NATO in Afghanistan," last updated December 18, 2006, http://www.nato.int/issu fghanistan/index.html.

model developed by the U.S. military that combines security and reconstruction functions in an effort to help stabilize the countryside.[54] ISAF assumed responsibility for security throughout Afghanistan in October 2006. At that point, it was NATO's largest operation, involving about 31,000 troops, including roughly 12,000 U.S. troops under ISAF command.

ISAF represents a valuable contribution to the U.S. goal of denying terrorists sanctuary or allies, given al-Qaida's close ties with the previous Taliban regime and ongoing efforts to pursue al-Qaida members in the border region between Afghanistan and Pakistan. All twenty-six NATO members participate in ISAF, as do ten non-NATO partner countries.

At the same time, ISAF has suffered from three significant problems. First, since 2003 the alliance has been unable to secure sufficient troop commitments to meet the target force size. When NATO took control of the southern and eastern regions of Afghanistan in August 2006, its 31,000-strong force represented about 85 percent of the troops and equipment that NATO commanders had requested for the mission. Since July 2006, NATO troops have confronted far more intense fighting than expected.[55] The alliance appealed for more troops in September 2006, but only one member country, Poland, offered to send additional troops.[56] At the November 2006 summit meeting in Riga, Latvia, new pledges from member states raised the troop and equipment totals to 90 percent of requirements.[57] ISAF's commander at that time, Lt. Gen. David Richards, said that it can manage with the current troop strength, but additional troops would allow it to conduct major operations more rapidly and with less risk to NATO soldiers.[58]

---

54. While initially designated "provisional," these teams are now called Provincial Reconstruction Teams. Robert Borders, "Provincial Reconstruction Teams in Afghanistan: A Model for Post-conflict Reconstruction and Development," *Journal of Development and Social Transformation,* Vol. 1 (November 2004), pp. 5–12; and CARE, "NGO Concerns Regarding Deployment of U.S. Military Provisional Reconstruction Teams," ACBAR (Agency Coordinating Body for Afghan Relief) Policy Brief, January 15, 2003, http://www.care.org/newsroom/specialreports/afghanistan/a_policypositions.asp.

55. François Heisbourg points out that NATO is trying to stabilize Afghanistan as the Soviet Union sought to do earlier, but the Soviet Union failed, with three times as many troops. "International Perspectives on the Use of Force and Legitimacy," transcript (Washington, D.C.: Brookings, October 11, 2006), p. 32, http://www.brook.edu/comm/events/20061011.pdf.

56. Molly Moore and John Ward Anderson, "NATO Faces Growing Hurdle as Call for Troops Falls Short," *Washington Post,* September 18, 2006.

57. NATO, "NATO Boosts Efforts in Afghanistan," last updated December 8, 2006, http://www.nato.int/docu/comm/2006/0611-riga/index.htm.

58. U.S. Department of Defense, "DoD News Briefing with General Richards from Afghanistan," news transcript, October 17, 2006, http://www.defenselink.mil/transcripts/transcript.aspx?Transcript1D?3757. As part of its normal rotation, Richards was replaced as ISAF commander by

Second, man troops in Afghanistan operate under "national caveats," whereby gover ents place limits on what military activities their troops are allowed to do vhere they are allowed to go in carrying out their missions. These caveats a problematic for two reasons: they hurt operational effectiveness; and allian members do not share risks equally, which can cause friction.[59] German troops can be deployed only near Kabul, for example, and in 2006 Poland r sted sending additional troops to southern Afghanistan, where they are eded the most. Only six NATO members operate without caveats. The prob n is not unique to ISAF; national caveats caused headaches during NATO's eacekeeping mission in Bosnia as well, and they have long been a problem UN peacekeeping missions.[60] Recognition of the operational problems such eats pose has led to a marked decline in their use, but they have made bot multinational cooperation and operations in general more difficult in Afg nistan.[61] Caveats tend to creep back in, moreover, as is evident in repeate fforts to eliminate them. NATO leaders agreed to reduce caveats at the 200 Riga summit, for example, with the result that 26,000 troops of the increase rce of 32,000 had broader freedom to act.[62]

Third, the Af n leadership fears that the United States will abandon it, and it is unsure wha ATO's authority over both the security and counterterrorism mission will me in the long run. Concern has also been raised about whether NATO has the itical will and capabilities to fight a sustained counterinsurgency campaig Since NATO forces assumed responsibility for security in southern Afgha stan, the frequency and intensity of Taliban attacks have increased.[64] This ewed fighting forced the United States to reverse plans to re-

---

U.S. Gen. Dan Mc l on February 4, 2007. Carlotta Gall, "America Takes Over Command of NATO Force as Its sion Grows," *New York Times*, February 5, 2007.

59. Some of the na al caveats, for example, are imposed for technical reasons, such as aircraft that are not prope equipped to conduct nighttime operations. Philip H. Gordon, "Back Up NATO's Afghanist orce," *International Herald Tribune*, January 8, 2006.

60. I thank Chanta Jonge Oudraat for pointing this out.

61. James L. Jones, ague to Istanbul: Ambition versus Reality," presentation at "Global Security: A Broader Co t for the 21st Century," Twenty-first International Workshop on Global Security, Berlin, Germ , May 7–10, 2004, pp. 27–30; and John D. Banusiewicz, "'National Caveats' among Key Topics NATO Meeting," American Forces Press Service, Department of Defense, February 9, 2005, h //www.defenselink.mil/news/Feb2005/n02092005_2005020911.html.

62. NATO, "NATO osts Efforts in Afghanistan."

63. Kristin Archick d Paul Gallis, *NATO and the European Union*, CRS Report for Congress (Washington, D.C.: rary of Congress, April 6, 2004), Order Code RL 32342; and Seth Jones, "Averting Failure i fghanistan," *Survival*, Vol. 48, No. 1 (Spring 2006), pp. 111–128.

64. This was appar y intended to test the will of NATO's member states to sustain their commitment. U.S. De ment of Defense, "DoD News Briefing with General Richards from Afghanistan."

duce its military commitment in Afghanistan and led the British to expand their troop contribution to ISAF.[65] The United States decided in January 2007 to extend the tours of 3,200 troops in Afghanistan, and further troop increases were under consideration.[66] Notably, U.S. forces, ISAF's largest contingent, will continue to conduct the bulk of counterterrorism activities aimed at al-Qaida. The U.S. military also retains 11,000 troops outside ISAF's command to sustain a separate counterinsurgency function in addition to peacekeeping.[67]

NATO has played a far smaller role in Iraq. Whereas the Bush administration sought to frame the March 2003 invasion as part of the war on terror, the alliance remained deeply split and did not formally participate in the invasion. The NATO Council never discussed Iraq, an indication of the depth of discord within the alliance. NATO did offer some support for the U.S.-led operation, however. It contributed to Turkey's defense against possible Iraqi retaliation during the invasion, and it agreed to the Polish government's request for allied support when Poland took over leadership of one sector of the stabilization force in Iraq in May 2003.[68] Fifteen NATO states have contributed forces to the coalition since 2003.[69] And although Germany did not participate in the coalition and strongly opposed the U.S. invasion, it deployed hundreds of chemical and biological weapons–detection troops in Kuwait and Turkey to aid coalition forces in the event of a WMD attack.[70]

In 2004, at U.S. urging, NATO agreed to play a central role in training Iraqi security forces. NATO's training effort has several elements: mentoring of Iraqi military officers by NATO personnel; creation of an officer training facility in Iraq; and training of Iraqi officers in NATO facilities. NATO's target is to train 1,000 officers inside Iraq annually, and 500 outside the state; by September

---

65. Eric Schmitt, "Springtime for Killing in Afghanistan," *New York Times*, May 28, 2006; and "Britain to Send More Troops to Afghanistan," Agence France-Presse, July 10, 2006.
66. Gall, "America Takes Over Command of NATO Force."
67. Amin Tarzi, "Afghanistan: NATO Expansion Demands Common Approach," Radio Free Europe/Radio Liberty, October 6, 2006, http://www.rferl.org/featuresarticle/2006/10/18ba3c2d-cd22-4963-af8d-52ac0963832b.html.
68. Agreement to aid Turkey was reached in spite of French resistance by taking the decision to NATO's military committee, of which France is not a part. On Poland's request, see NATO, "NATO Council Makes Decision on Polish Request," NATO Update, May 22, 2003, http://www.nato.int/docu/update/2003/05-may/e0521b.htm. On NATO debates over aid to Turkey, see NATO, "Consultations on Measures to Protect Turkey," NATO Update, March 6, 2003, http://www.nato.int/docu/update/2003/02-february/e0210a.htm.
69. Some of these troop contributions are quite small. Participating states include Bulgaria, the Czech Republic, Denmark, Estonia, Hungary, Italy, Latvia, Lithuania, the Netherlands, Norway, Poland, Romania, Slovakia, Spain, and the United Kingdom.
70. Daalder and Lindsay, *America Unbound*, p. 190.

2006, NATO ha rained 650 Iraqi officers in European facilities and roughly 2,000 officers o all.[71] NATO has also donated military equipment to Iraq's security forces. nis equipment comes primarily from former Warsaw Pact countries that h e become NATO members, and it is compatible with Iraq's Soviet-supplied ilitary hardware.

NATO's trair g mission has faced significant difficulties, however. First, the need to gai onsensus on all decisions hamstrung efforts to get the mission up and ru ng and greatly slowed the process; residual bitterness over the U.S. decisio to invade Iraq contributed to this problem. Some members objected to the ecedent set by taking on the training mission, which also slowed decisior aking.[72] Second, as in Afghanistan, some troop contributions have operated der national caveats, which has hindered commanders' efforts to coordin NATO's activities. Third, funding for the mission has been a serious probler Countries contributing troops are expected to cover their own costs. NA set up a "trust fund" to pay for the establishment of a defense universit n Iraq, but contributions to the fund have thus far been insufficient. As esult, although the Iraqi government has stressed its preference for in-cour training to help gain popular trust and support for the new security forces, ore officers have been trained outside Iraq.[73]

OFFENSIVE MEA ES: COUNTERTERRORISM

NATO's offensi role in fighting terrorism is limited. Although its Military Concept for De se against Terrorism stresses that NATO must be prepared to take on offen e missions if required, the alliance has operated primarily in support of mer r state efforts to conduct offensive counterterrorist operations. NATO of als point out that this is appropriate given that the alliance's task is to defen s members and support them in the event of attacks, rather than to take th ad in offensive operations.[74]

---

71. Rick Lynch and illip D. Janzen, "NATO Training Mission Iraq: Looking to the Future," *Joint Force Quarterly*, No (1st Quarter 2006), p. 33; IISS, *The Military Balance, 2005–2006*, p. 45; and NATO, "Iraq Gets tional Defense College," September 3, 2006, NATO Update, http://www.nato.int/docu/upc /2006/09-september/e0903a.htm.
72. NATO officials, erviewed by author, Brussels, Belgium, June 8, 2006.
73. Lynch and Jan "NATO Training Mission Iraq," pp. 32–34. The funding problem is not unique to this miss the NATO Response Force has been referred to as a "reverse lottery" because troop-contrib ıg nations must bear all the costs. De Hoop Scheffer, "Speech at the 42nd Munich Conference Security Policy"; and Jones, "NATO: From Common Defense to Common Security."
74. Indeed, some m bers, notably France, continue to insist that NATO's military role should be limited to article 5 rations. NATO officials, interviewed by author.

The only example of NATO assuming a combat role is found in Afghanistan, where ISAF took control over security operations throughout the country in October 2006. Although the security problems on the ground in Afghanistan range from crime and drug trafficking to counterterrorism, ISAF's rules of engagement do not explicitly cover missions other than peacekeeping; ISAF does not have a formal counterterrorist mission.[75] ISAF's limited mandate is due in large measure to member states' nervousness about the prospect of taking on counterterrorism or counterinsurgency responsibilities, as well as concern that acknowledging the potential combat elements of the mission would make it even harder to obtain sufficient troop commitments to ISAF.

NATO's mission in Afghanistan shifted from a primary focus on reconstruction and stability to counterinsurgency when it took responsibility for security in the southern region of the country at the end of July 2006, and it adopted more robust rules of engagement.[76] Since then, British, Canadian, and Dutch forces on the ground have been engaged in counterinsurgency operations. Commanders dropped their earlier vagueness about their activities in Afghanistan and now acknowledge the war-fighting nature of the mission. Lieutenant General Richards of ISAF stated in August 2006 that NATO's goal was "to strike ruthlessly" at Taliban fighters seeking to undermine the Afghan government.[77] Similarly, in parliamentary debates over extending Canada's deployment to Afghanistan in May 2006, members openly acknowledged the combat nature of the mission.[78]

NATO's mission in Afghanistan is of crucial importance to the alliance. NATO troops are engaged in their most militarily challenging mission since the alliance was formed in 1949. NATO leaders regarded the mission as a suc-

---

75. Ali A. Jalali, "The Future of Afghanistan," *Parameters*, Vol. 36, No. 1 (Spring 2006), pp. 4–19.
76. "Oral Statement of General James L. Jones, United States Marine Corps, Supreme Allied Commander, Europe, before the Senate Foreign Relations Committee," 109th Cong., 2d sess., September 21, 2006.
77. Richard Norton-Taylor, "British General Takes Command and Promises Ruthless Strikes on Taliban," *Guardian* (London), August 1, 2006. British forces had killed at least 700 combatants in ongoing battles with Taliban forces in southern Afghanistan by August 2006. It is notoriously difficult, however, to determine the number of Taliban casualties. According to one estimate, 4,000 people died in fighting in 2006, many of whom were believed to be rebels. See "France to Withdraw Special Forces from Afghanistan," Agence France-Presse, December 17, 2006, http://www.france24.com/france24Public/en/news/france/20061217-Afghanistan.html; Thomas Harding, "Paras Claim 700 Taliban Lives," *Telegraph*, July 29, 2006; and "Taleban Death Toll 'Inaccurate,'" *BBC News*, December 10, 2006, http://news.bbc.co.uk/2/hi/south_asia/6166577.stm.
78. Quoted in Stephen Harper, "Canada's Commitment in Afghanistan," 39th Parl., 1st sess., May 17, 2006, http://www.parl.gc.ca/39/1/parlbus/chambus/house/debates/025_2006-05-17/HAN025-E.htm#OOB-1543354.

cess at the end 2006; the alliance has shown the ability to fight and to maintain support fo he mission. But continued success is not guaranteed. Both NATO and U.S :ommanders expressed growing concern in late 2006 that without signifi t advances in reconstruction and development in Afghanistan, the militar effort would ultimately fail. As Lieutenant General Richards noted, "Fightin or its own sake in a counterinsurgency will get us nowhere over time."[79] Th military commanders argued that the international community had failed convince the Afghan people that international involvement would make th lives better in terms of either security or living standards. If it did not do so n, the resurgent Taliban would win their support, or at least acquiescence.[80]

There are als vorrisome hints, however, that some NATO members may be unwilling to ıstain their commitments to ISAF. Not only has the alliance had difficulty nvincing members to send more troops to Afghanistan, but some gove nents were starting to pull out troops at the end of 2006. The French gov nment decided to withdraw 200 special forces troops from the southern re n of Afghanistan in December 2006, for example, although some 1,100 Fren troops would remain near Kabul.[81] The Italian government has faced pres e to set a deadline for withdrawal of its 1,800 troops in ISAF.[82] The am valence toward ISAF is partly explained by the fact that even governm that acknowledged the dangers confronting their troops were surprised the strength of the insurgency in Afghanistan; in other participating state ıe failure to prepare their publics for the true nature of the mission damag support for ISAF. Finally, the Afghan mission suffers from the European lic's residual resentment about Iraq, with which it is often associated.[83]

79. U.S. Departme Defense, "DoD News Briefing with General Richards from Afghanistan."
80. Ibid.; and "Ora ıtement of General James L. Jones." On the fragility of the situation in Afghanistan, see also ıett R. Rubin, "Still Ours to Lose: Afghanistan on the Brink," prepared testimony for the Hous ıd Senate Committees on Foreign Relations (Washington, D.C.: Council on Foreign Relations, ember 21, 2006).
81. "France to Pull ops Fighting against Taliban in Afghanistan," *New York Times*, December 18, 2006. In both the N erlands and Canada, parliaments raised serious questions about sending troops to Afghanist both Dutch and Canadian troops are actively engaged in fighting insurgent forces there. "Cana Committed to Afghan Mission, Harper Tells Troops," *CBC News*, March 13, 2006, http://www. ca/world/story/2006/03/13/harper_afghanistan060313.html; and "More Dutch Troops for ghanistan," *BBC News*, February 3, 2006, http://news.bbc.co.uk/2/hi/europe/4673026.str
82. Helene Cooper, ATO Allies Wary of Sending More Troops to Afghanistan," *New York Times*, January 27, 2007.
83. Moore and An on, "NATO Faces Growing Hurdles as Call for Troops Falls Short."

CONSEQUENCE MANAGEMENT

The U.S. strategy for confronting terrorism gives priority to preventing attacks. In contrast, NATO's Military Concept emphasizes consequence management and has two main goals: to respond to an attack once it occurs, and to minimize the effects of an attack that has taken place. At the 2002 Prague summit, the alliance adopted a Civil Emergency Planning Action Plan to improve its ability to respond to attacks involving WMD, and it has developed a range of capabilities to respond to such attacks, including the multinational CBRN Defense Battalion, a deployable analytical laboratory, an event response team, a chemical and biological defense stockpile, and a disease surveillance system.[84] The alliance has also established a center of excellence to further explore defenses against WMD.

NATO has also expanded its disaster relief plans to enhance its terrorism response capabilities. The alliance has conducted several WMD-related exercises, and its Euro-Atlantic Disaster Response Center has assisted in responding to floods, forest fires, and snowfalls in states both within and outside the alliance, as well as to Hurricane Katrina in the United States. NATO also contributed to disaster relief operations after a major earthquake in Pakistan in October 2005. This was considered a significant step because it represented the first time the alliance had offered disaster assistance outside its own geographic area, which could set a precedent for such operations.

Some analysts have argued that NATO should expand its consequence management abilities because this is a logical role for the alliance, and it would encourage NATO members to do more to enhance their militaries' capabilities to respond and coordinate in the event of terrorist attacks or other disasters. There are two obstacles to expanding NATO's role in this area. First, NATO can act only if its members request assistance. For example, NATO was not asked to aid Spain's response to the terrorist bombings in Madrid in 2004, nor did it respond to the 2005 London bombings.[85] Whether other states will turn to NATO in the future is likely to depend on the gravity of the attack and on

---

84. Dagmar de Mora-Figueroa, "NATO's Response to Terrorism," *NATO Review*, No. 3 (Autumn 2005), http://www.nato.int/docu/review/2005/issue3/english/art1.html; Eric R. Terzuolo, "Combating WMD Proliferation," *NATO Review*, No. 3 (Autumn 2005), http://www.nato.int/docu/review/2005/issue3/english/art3.html; and "Boosting NATO's CBRN Capabilities," *NATO Review*, No. 3 (Autumn 2005), http://www.nato.int/docu/review/2005/issue3/english/features1.html.

85. Jean-Yves Haine, "Military Matters: ESDP Transformed?" *NATO Review*, No. 2 (Summer 2005), http://www.nato.int/docu/review/2005/issue2/english/military_pr.html; and NATO, "Press Conference by NATO Secretary-General on the Extraordinary Meeting of the North Atlantic Council," Online Library, July 8, 2005, http://www.nato.int/docu/speech/2005/s050708a.htm.

NATO's ability provide specialized capabilities such as CBRN. Second, European states d gree about whether this function should be carried out by NATO or by th uropean Union. Moreover, although the need for greater cooperation betw NATO and the EU in areas such as emergency response is widely recogni , little progress has been made in this area.

SUMMARY

This examinati of NATO's participation in the U.S. war against terror yields three main ins ts. First, the chronic capabilities gap between the United States and its a is growing, and increasingly may be limiting the alliance's operational coo ation. Second, the gap between what the United States and European state e willing to do militarily is also growing. This reflects their disparate capa ies and the differences in operational planning that follow from them. Thi the United States' commitment to working through the alliance is uncle While NATO's chief military officer stresses the value of NATO's milita nechanisms and political consultation, the U.S. government is often unwill to rely on NATO in campaigns that relate directly to defending the United es. Not only do Pentagon leaders want to avoid the effort of working to bui onsensus within the alliance, but they see it as compromising the mission d the safety of U.S. forces. Moreover, some U.S. government officials note th he Bush administration sees NATO as unreliable, because of the difficulty i aining troop commitments from member states in recent years. This has tered the view expressed by one State Department official, who noted, "W d hoc' our way through coalitions of the willing. That's the future."[86]

NATO's Limi Role in the U.S. War on Terror

Three factors h to explain why NATO's contribution to the U.S. war on terror has been re vely limited: shifting alignments and threat perceptions due to systemic ch es, NATO's chronic and growing capabilities gap, and the war against ter itself.

ALIGNMENTS A THREATS AFTER THE COLD WAR

Two critical ch es in the nature of the international system have influenced NATO's evolut since the collapse of the Soviet Union in 1991. First, the dis-

86. Guy Dinmore, S. Sees Coalitions of the Willing as Best Ally," *Financial Times*, January 4, 2006.

tribution of power in the international system is no longer bipolar. For all its tensions, the international system was relatively stable during the Cold War, with the two superpowers and their allies aligned in opposition. This made core alliance cohesion relatively easy to maintain. NATO's European members were unlikely to defect from the U.S.-led alliance, and the United States was unlikely to abandon Europe, though fears to the contrary emerged periodically. Although scholars continue to debate whether the current international system is unipolar, multipolar, or something else, today U.S. military power dwarfs that of other powers in the international system.

Second, a security community developed among the European powers, Japan, and the United States concurrently with the erosion and eventual collapse of Soviet power. As a result, the option of war between these powers has become virtually unthinkable. This is an equally momentous change in the international system, given that great power war has been a constant in history.[87]

NATO has defied realist predictions that it would not survive in the absence of the threat it was created to defend against: the Soviet Union. But the aforementioned systemic changes have led alliance members to perceive security threats differently. They have also renewed uncertainties about alliance stability and the U.S. commitment to NATO.

The cross-cutting pressures created by changing and sometimes competing interests have made it more difficult to reach consensus on how to deal with security threats confronting NATO.[88] The disappearance of the Soviet threat made intra-alliance differences on issues including trade, the environment, and human rights more salient. NATO's European members also responded to concern about U.S. willingness to act through NATO, and Europe's inability to act collectively without the United States, by expanding efforts to build a viable European security identity that would make it possible for European states to operate independent of the United States.[89]

NATO has always been a political-military alliance, rather than a purely military union. It has had a long-standing goal of cementing its members' shared democratic ideology and values,[90] as evidenced by NATO's expansion in the

87. Robert Jervis, *American Foreign Policy in a New Era* (New York: Routledge, 2005), pp. 11–36. See also Karl W. Deutsch, Sidney A. Burrell, and Robert A. Kann, *Political Community and the North Atlantic Area: International Organization in the Light of Historical Experience* (New York: Greenwood, 1969), pp. 5–8; and Buzan and Waever, *Regions and Powers*, pp. 343–376.
88. Brown, *Multilateral Constraints on the Use of Force*, pp. 19–21.
89. Press-Barnathan, "Managing the Hegemon," pp. 290–301.
90. Thomas Risse-Kappen, "Collective Identity in a Democratic Community: The Case of NATO,"

1990s.[91] In exp ding eastward, NATO accomplished two objectives: it extended the Eur an security community, and it removed the potential threat of unstable cou ries along the borders of member states. This expansion, however, has l to further divergences in threat perception among alliance members. Whil ome of NATO's new members continue to have territorial security concerns e to their proximity to Russia, some long-standing members feel less threat d by "traditional" security concerns. Moreover, European perceptions of gravity of the terrorist threat vary widely. Some states perceive the threat be limited, whereas others view it as significant. Notably, only five states- rance, Germany, Italy, Spain, and the United Kingdom—had legislation deal with terrorism before the September 11 attacks.

NATO's men rs also differ on the means to respond to threats confronting the alliance. Th vas most apparent in the bitter dispute over the 2003 U.S. invasion of Iraq. e dispute illustrated three points of disagreement. First, it reflected differe understandings of the nature of the terrorist threat and how to combat it. Se nd, it exposed deep differences about the appropriate use of force, and in pa cular about the U.S. policy of preventive war. Whereas the United States isted that the urgency of the threat posed by Saddam Hussein's supp d possession of WMD mandated immediate action, several European allie gued that Hussein was contained and could be deterred. Third, the dis te illustrated increasing European concern about U.S. unilateralism a the fear that NATO's European members might be "entrapped" by th alliance commitments to support a reckless military operation.[92] As a resu both France and Germany balked at supporting the United States.[93] Althou the Bush administration sought to repair relations with key European allies d institutions after the 2004 presidential elections, the acrimony caused b his dispute has left a residue of ill will.

The shifting gnments and attitudes toward threats confronting NATO have reduced t United States' willingness to accept alliance constraints.[94]

---

in Peter J. Katzens , ed., *The Culture of National Security: Norms and Identity in World Politics* (New York: Colum University Press, 1996), pp. 357–399.

91. On NATO exp on, see James M. Goldgeier, *Not Whether but When: The U.S. Decision to Enlarge NATO* (Washi n, D.C.: Brookings, 1999); David S. Yost, *NATO Transformed: The Alliance's New Roles in Intern al Security* (Washington, D.C.: United States Institute of Peace Press, 1998); and Jonathan Eyal, ATO's Enlargement: Anatomy of a Decision," *International Affairs*, Vol. 73, No. 4 (October 199 p. 695–719. For a contrary view, see Dan Reiter, "Why NATO Enlargement Does Not Spread D ocracy," *International Security*, Vol. 25, No. 4 (Spring 2001), pp. 41–67.

92. Press-Barnatha Managing the Hegemon," pp. 301–303.

93. Brown, *Multila Constraints on the Use of Force*, p. 19.

94. To be sure, fric s over U.S. unilateralism are not new to the alliance. Similar tensions were evident during Pre nt Bill Clinton's administration, which rejected several attempts to establish

Moreover, the United States' strategic focus has changed, with greater attention being given to the Middle East, Central Asia, and East Asia. This is evident both in the changing base deployments in Europe and the State Department's decision to shift at least 100 diplomatic positions from Europe to other regions, including Africa, South Asia, East Asia, and the Middle East.[95] This move is a logical step and if anything overdue, given the end of the Cold War, but it is telling of shifts in U.S. policy priorities.

Differences in member states' views of the role of military force have probably contributed to U.S. frustration with alliance constraints. National caveats attached to military operations sometimes reflect limited capabilities, but they can also reveal different political goals. U.S. inability to count on allies for military cooperation in Iraq, Afghanistan, and elsewhere has produced great frustration within the Bush administration. This is evident in Secretary of Defense Donald Rumsfeld's comment, "It's kind of like having a basketball team, and they practice and practice and practice for six months. When it comes to game time, one or two say, 'We're not going to play.' Well, that's fair enough. Everyone has a free choice. But you don't have a free choice if you've practiced for all those months."[96]

ALLIANCE CAPABILITIES

From the United States' perspective, the perennial frustration regarding NATO is the difficulty of convincing its European allies to increase defense spending and thus to improve capabilities. During the Cold War, NATO members agreed that defense spending should be roughly 3 percent of a state's gross domestic product; in 2006 the minimum spending level set by the alliance was 2 percent. Yet only six states other than the United States met this threshold.[97] Furthermore, how this money is spent causes concern in Washington. Many states continue to expend the bulk of their resources on manpower, rather than on transforming their forces in ways the United States hopes they will—and to which NATO has agreed. Some, such as Greece and Turkey, still have military forces focused at least in part on each other.

---

international institutions that it believed might undermine U.S. national security, such as the 1997 Ottawa Convention, which banned antipersonnel land mines, and the International Criminal Court.

95. U.S. Department of State, Office of the Spokesman, "Transformational Diplomacy," January 18, 2006, http://www.state.gov/r/pa/prs/ps/2006/59339.htm.

96. Quoted in Banusiewicz, "'National Caveats' among Key Topics at NATO Meeting."

97. Donald H. Rumsfeld, "Speech at the 42nd Munich Conference on Security Policy," February 4, 2006, http://www.securityconference.de.

As NATO ha ıken on new tasks, differences in capabilities have hindered the alliance's o ·ational cooperation. Moreover, willingness to address this gap appears lir ·d; although many European states acknowledge the prob- lem, defense sp ding and military transformation remain low domestic pri- orities in sever tates because they do not see major military threats to their security. Additi ılly, the large number of operations in which NATO is cur- rently engaged eans that many states do not have the manpower and re- sources to devo o transformation given current budgets. Notably, the United States has func operations in both Iraq and Afghanistan through supple- mental budget quests, rather than the annual defense budget. It has also financed some ed contributions, such as the Polish division in Iraq.[98]

U.S. officials ıuld like to see NATO undertake a transformation similar to what the Unite ates is adopting: that is, to develop expeditionary forces and what Defense I ›artment officials call twenty-first century military capabili- ties. The allianc adoption of transformation as one of its goals in 2003 repre- sents a welcom tep in this direction; indeed, NATO's reorganized command structure desig es one of its two new commands the Allied Command Transformation

The United S es and some other alliance members disagree over the kinds of capabilities N TO members should seek to acquire. The *QDR* affirms U.S. support for "eff s to create a NATO stabilization and reconstruction capabil- ity and a Europ n constabulary force" that could build on the EU's existing constabulary fc ·s. It suggests that allied states should aim to "[tailor] na- tional military ıtributions to best employ the unique capabilities and char- acteristics of ea ally, [to achieve] a unified effort greater than the sum of its parts."[100] This i ›lies the development of "niche" capabilities. If the alliance moves in this d ction, it could reinforce the perception that the United States, along with onl ı few alliance members such as the United Kingdom and

98. Office of the Pr Secretary, "Fact Sheet: Request for Additional FY 2004 Funding for the War on Terror," Septem 8, 2003, http://www.whitehouse.gov/news/releases/2003/09/20030908-1.html.
99. "Briefing on N) Military Structure," August 2005, http://www.nato.int/docu/briefing/nms/nms-e.pdf; an ATO, Allied Command Operations, Supreme Headquarters Allied Powers Europe, "New N Command Structure," May 4, 2004, www.nato.int/shape/issues/ncs/ncs_index.htm.
100. Rumsfeld, *Qu nnial Defense Review*, p. 88. On constabulary forces for NATO, see David T. Armitage Jr. and A M. Moisan, "Constabulary Forces and Postconflict Transition: The Euro-Atlantic Dimension *trategic Forum*, No. 218 (November 2005), pp. 1–7; and Hans Binnendijk and Richard L. Kugler, eded—A NATO Stabilization and Reconstruction Force," *Defense Horizons*, No. 45 (September 4), pp. 1–8.

France, has combat-ready troops able to conduct frontline operations, while NATO as a whole is relegated to postconflict operations and "cleanup." The need for such postconflict capabilities is increasingly apparent, notably in both Afghanistan and Iraq. Less clear, however, is whether NATO states are willing to codify this division of labor, and how this would affect alliance unity and decisionmaking.

Yet there is an element of hypocrisy in Washington's annoyance with its NATO allies, because the U.S.-backed expansion of the alliance contributed to the erosion of NATO's military capabilities. The United States was the strongest voice encouraging two rounds of NATO expansion to incorporate Central European states after the Cold War, in 1999 and 2004, and it supported the decision at the Riga summit to consider further enlargement of the alliance as early as 2008. When the second expansion decision was made in 2004, however, it was already apparent that the states that joined NATO in 1999 had failed to meet the goals set for transforming their militaries to accord with NATO standards; and they were not likely to achieve them soon. Moreover, none of the second-round applicants met NATO's military capability standards, and they were far behind the first-round states in their ability to transform their militaries.[101] Lessened alliance capabilities may have been unproblematic to the United States because it did not intend to incorporate alliance forces in its major operations.

THE NATURE OF THE WAR ON TERROR

The final factor explaining NATO's limited role in the war on terror is the very nature of that conflict. Although the Bush administration determined that this is a war, it is not one in which most "battles" are fought by military forces. Different means are required as well. Indeed, this is partly why Europeans tend to refer to the "fight," rather than "war," against terrorism. Combating international terrorism requires cooperation in a wide range of areas among different countries and international organizations. Key elements of the struggle include diplomatic efforts to maintain and strengthen international treaties and norms proscribing terrorism, as well as economic cooperation to find and eliminate sources of terrorist financing. In addition to military activities, security cooperation is needed to ensure that states can share intelligence regarding ter-

---

101. On this point, see in particular Wade Jacoby, "Is the New Europe a Good Substitute for the Old One?" *International Studies Review*, Vol. 8, No. 1 (March 2006), pp. 178–197; and Zoltan Barany, "NATO's Post–Cold War Metamorphosis: From Sixteen to Twenty-six and Counting," *International Studies Review*, Vol. 8, No. 1 (March 2006), pp. 165–178.

rorists and tha w enforcement agencies can work together across borders. U.S. efforts to (ıbat terrorism in these areas involve extensive cooperation with European tes, but this does not occur through NATO. Rather, it occurs either bilaterall r with the EU.

Additionally, e threats facing the United States and its European allies are different. T United States has chosen to combat terrorism as far from its shores as po ole, through military actions in Afghanistan and Iraq; it also emphasizes th le of covert special-operations forces to conduct counter-terrorist missic overseas.[102] In contrast, several European states face a domestic threat ıeir large Muslim minorities create the potential for "home-grown" terroris particularly to the degree that these minorities have not been integrated ıto the broader society. Indeed, the July 2005 bombings in London were c ied out primarily by British citizens. This gives European states a differer et of priorities in fighting terrorism, because the threat they confront is loca ıot distant.[103]

Conclusion

NATO plays a gely supportive role in the war on terror. To the degree that NATO countrie re engaged in key elements of U.S. efforts to combat terror-ism, they do sc ı the basis of bilateral ties or loose coalitions—not through NATO. Operati Active Endeavor provides important support for U.S. mili-tary operations the Middle East. It contributes to the prevention of and de-fense against rorism; it is not, however, a combat operation. The contribution th IATO members make by providing intelligence in the strug-gle against terr ts occurs largely bilaterally, and it is generated primarily by law enforceme gencies, rather than by allied military intelligence capabili-ties. NATO's d ıse investment programs may help to create better defenses against terroris but it is too soon to tell how successful these will be.

Similarly, NA) does not have a direct role in denying terrorists access to WMD. NATO r ntains political dialogues with countries at risk for the theft or sale of weap or WMD-related products, and individual members partici-pate in threat r ction activities. These are not designed to address the prob-lem of terroris ıcquisition, however. The alliance is split on the use of

102. Rumsfeld, *Qu nnial Defense Review*, pp. 23–24; and Jonathan Stevenson, "Demilitarizing the 'War on Terror, *urvival*, Vol. 48, No. 2 (Summer 2006), pp. 37–54.
103. Jeremy Shapi ıd Daniel L. Byman, "Bridging the Transatlantic Counterterrorism Gap," *Washington Quarte* Vol. 29, No. 4 (Autumn 2006), pp. 33–50.

preemption as a means to prevent the spread of WMD to states that might let terrorists obtain weapons of mass destruction, and the United States prefers the PSI and the new Global Initiative to Combat Nuclear Terrorism to NATO as means to prevent the spread of WMD to terrorists.

NATO's ISAF mission in Afghanistan directly contributes to the U.S. goal of denying terrorists sanctuary there. ISAF troops are in essence conducting counterterrorism as well as counterinsurgency operations, and this is NATO's first combat mission since its creation. The lead role in counterterrorism in Afghanistan continues to be played by U.S. special forces, however, not NATO; and U.S. troops are the largest contingent in ISAF. NATO's role in Iraq is even more limited. Many member states have individually contributed troops to the U.S.-led coalition in Iraq, but the alliance's sole contribution to stabilizing the country has been the training of Iraqi military officers.

NATO has begun to develop consequence management capabilities to respond to terrorist attacks, particularly those with WMD. This could give the alliance a valuable support role. The nature of the terrorist threat confronting individual member-states will likely determine whether they take advantage of NATO's support capability.

Three factors explain Washington's circumvention of the alliance in prosecuting the war on terror. First, two critical changes in the international system, U.S. hegemony and the emergence of a security community, particularly among European states, have led NATO's members both to differ among themselves on a broad range of global issues and to perceive security threats differently. They also differ on the appropriate means for responding to perceived threats, as was most evident in the dispute over the U.S. invasion of Iraq. These shifting alignments and attitudes have reduced U.S. willingness to accept alliance constraints.

Second, U.S. military capabilities are greater and more sophisticated than those of its allies, which makes it difficult for even close U.S. allies to coordinate with U.S. forces in frontline military activities. Some U.S. officers point out that one goal of NATO training exercises is to illuminate these differences, as a way to spur allies to improve their capabilities.[104] But NATO's expansion has eroded its military capabilities further. Combined with the increasing use of national caveats, which constrain what individual military forces can do in NATO operations, the alliance's ability to work with the United States in confronting immediate military threats appears limited, at best.

104. U.S. official, interview by author.

Third, the na e of the war on terror itself constrains NATO's contribution to U.S. strategy. q and Afghanistan notwithstanding, terrorism is fought primarily by nonn tary means, such as law enforcement and intelligence gathering. Moreove NATO's members face different threats.

The United es is unlikely to abandon NATO, however. In spite of its rejection of alli e constraints on its own actions, NATO provides a crucial forum in which e United States can discuss foreign and security policy with its key allies to ch common understandings of shared problems. This is particularly vital t ne United States as the EU's Common Foreign and Security Policy begins to alesce and influence the policies of European states. Only in NATO does the nited States have a voice in European security affairs. This helps explain U support for expanding the alliance, and it has sought to make NATO the rum for discussion of a broad range of security problems affecting Europe d North America.

Moreover, Wa ington recognizes that combating international terrorism requires extensive ooperation, both bilateral and multilateral. This is best built on a shared und standing of the problem states confront, and NATO can play an important ro n generating common views regarding terrorism. So long as the United State iews NATO as a valuable forum in which it can convince its European allies at they share the same goals and that they confront the same threat in the wa n terror, it will continue to value the alliance. If threat perceptions within he alliance diverge further, however, this could make it harder to reach greement on common policies. Notably, European states appear to have ffering views of the threats they face; this is not simply a transatlantic di e.

U.S. policy in asingly acknowledges the importance of nonmilitary measures such as p lic diplomacy and the "war of ideas" in combating terrorism.[105] Increasi recognition that the terrorist threat is evolving means that U.S. approaches e likely to move toward greater concurrence with European policies on terro m, which stress intelligence, law enforcement, and quiet engagement with e Muslim world. This would ease some of the frictions in Washington's re ions with its European allies. It would not, however, lead to a greater role fo ATO in confronting terrorism. Rather, it could accelerate the tendency to util mechanisms outside the alliance framework to address this urgent threat.

105. Bush, *National urity Strategy* (2006), p. 9.

NATO's military value as a partner to the United States in the war against terrorism also remains in question. Should the United States confront terrorists militarily in the future, it will likely do so with special operations forces working either alone or with host-government troops. A few alliance members may participate in such operations, but the alliance itself will not. Further, the bulk of the struggle against terrorism requires substantial nonmilitary means. NATO may have a useful diplomatic role to play, both among its members and with regard to key states such as Russia. But many of the critical tasks in this fight are outside the military domain, leaving NATO with little role.

In 2003 NATO Supreme Cmdr. James Jones noted that if the attempt at defense transformation fails, the alliance may lose its military value.[106] Others point to NATO's ISAF mission as the essential test for its survival. Its success or failure in Afghanistan will be a critical indicator of the alliance's ability to address the type of security threats that will emerge in contested regions around the globe. Success would confirm NATO's unity and capability to act "out of area," but a defeat would undermine NATO's claim to a broader global mission. The alliance would continue to provide for the defense of Europe, and the alliance members' shared values may be sufficient to sustain NATO as an organization, assuming its political consultation and dialogue functions continue to thrive. But such a defeat would raise serious questions about NATO's contribution to its members' core security concerns, if these are seen as out of area. If NATO's major member-states do not seek to address their most urgent threats within the alliance framework, its military value could atrophy.

106. Jim Garamone, "Jones Discusses Changing Troop 'Footprint' in Europe," American Forces Press Service, October 10, 2003.

Assess ng the Dangers o Illicit Networks

T Why al-Qaida May Be Less eatening Than Many Think

Mette Eilstrup-Sangiovanni and Calvert Jones

The globalization of transportation, nmunication, and finance has benefited not only licit businesses but als rofessional criminals and terrorists. Arms dealers, drug traffickers, mor launderers, human traffickers, terrorists, and other sundry criminals, enab by new, affordable technologies, are increasingly organizing into sprawling bal networks. As a result, understanding international organized crime an rrorism in terms of networks has become a widely accepted paradigm in th ld of international relations. In this article we seek to clarify that paradigm, be deeper into the consequences of the network structure, and challenge ventional wisdom about network-based threats to states.

A common t e in recent international relations scholarship dealing with organized crim nd terrorism is the great difficulty states face in combating network-based eats. According to a growing literature, the primary confrontation in w l politics is no longer between states but between states and terrorist netwo such as al-Qaida, drug smuggling networks such as those in Colombia and xico, nuclear smuggling networks in places such as North Korea and Paki n, and insurgent networks such as those in Iraq.[1] And states are widely rep l to be losing the battle. The main reason, according to the existing literat is the organizational advantages enjoyed by networked ac-

Mette Eilstrup-Sang nni is Lecturer in International Studies at the Centre of International Studies at the University of Ca lge. She is also Fellow of Sidney Sussex College. Calvert Jones is a doctoral student in the Department o ernational Relations at Yale University.

1. See, for exampl ona B. Adamson, "Globalisation, Transnational Political Mobilisation, and Networks of Viole *Cambridge Review of International Affairs*, Vol. 18, No. 1 (April 2005), pp. 31–49; Jörg Raab and H inton Milward, "Dark Networks as Problems," *Journal of Public Administration Research and Th* , Vol. 13, No. 4 (October 2003), pp. 413–439; Manuel Castells, *The Rise of the Network Society* (C ridge, Mass.: Blackwell, 1996); Mark Duffield, "War as a Network Enterprise: The New Se ty Terrain and Its Implications," *Cultural Values*, Vol. 6, Nos. 1–2 (2002), p. 161; John Arqui nd David Ronfeldt, eds., *Networks and Netwars: The Future of Terror, Crime, and Militancy* (Sant onica, Calif.: RAND, 2001), especially Phil Williams, "Transnational Criminal Networks," pp. 98; Michael Kenney, *From Pablo to Osama: Trafficking and Terrorist Networks, Government Bureau es, and Competitive Adaptation* (University Park: Penn State University Press, 2007); Audrey Kurt ronin, "Behind the Curve: Globalization and International Terrorism," *International Security*, V 7, No. 3 (Winter 2002/03), pp. 30–58; Sheena Chestnut, "Illicit Activity and Proliferation: Nort orean Smuggling Networks," *International Security*, Vol. 32, No. 1 (Summer 2007), pp. 80–111; a Marc Sageman, *Understanding Terror Networks* (Philadelphia: University of Pennsylvania Press 04).

International Security, 33, No. 2 (Fall 2008), pp. 7–44

tors. A fluid structure is said to provide networks with a host of advantages including adaptability, resilience, a capacity for rapid innovation and learning, and wide-scale recruitment. Networked actors are also said to be better at exploiting new modes of collaboration and communication than hierarchically organized state actors. The suggestion that "it takes a network to fight a network" is therefore gaining currency, both among academics[2] and in the wider security community.[3]

We agree that network-based threats pose serious challenges to state security. But, we argue, the prevailing pessimism about the ability of states to combat illicit networks is premature. The advantages claimed for networks vis-à-vis hierarchical organizations in the existing literature are often not well characterized or substantiated. Although they tend to enjoy flexibility and adaptability, networks have important—and often overlooked—structural disadvantages that limit their effectiveness. Given the high premium on battling networked threats, it is surprising that these disadvantages have not received more attention from international relations scholars.

To fill this lacuna, we combine theoretical and empirical evidence to illuminate some important network weaknesses. A caveat is in order. We are neither terrorism experts nor criminologists. Our engagement with the phenomenon of "dark networks" is motivated primarily by dissatisfaction with the growing international relations literature, where the term "network" is often used metaphorically and is not clearly defined or expounded.[4] Little systematic use has been made by this literature of theoretical approaches to networks developed in other social sciences, and too little effort has been made to build on findings from extant studies on terrorism, insurgency, and organized crime. As a result, we argue, strategic thinking about how networks can be combated lacks both imagination and historical grounding.

The article begins with a brief discussion of the term "network" in the social sciences. We first offer a review of the current literature on networks. Next we highlight some limitations that raise doubts about whether networks, in gen-

2. See, for example, Arquilla and Ronfeldt, *Networks and Netwars;* Richard M. Rothenberg, "From Whole Cloth: Making Up the Terrorist Network," *Connections*, Vol. 24, No. 3 (2002), pp. 36–42; and Anne-Marie Slaughter, *A New World Order* (Princeton, N.J.: Princeton University Press, 2004).
3. For an analysis of the influence of this idea on U.S. intelligence reform, see Calvert Jones, "Intelligence Reform: The Logic of Information Sharing," *Intelligence and National Security*, Vol. 22, No. 3 (Summer 2007), pp. 384–401.
4. The term "dark networks" was coined by Arquilla and Ronfelt in *Networks and Netwars.*

eral, and cland ne networks, in particular, are as effective as postulated in
their ability to llenge states.[5] In general, we argue, international relations
scholars have b too quick to draw parallels to the world of the firm where
networked org zation has proven well adapted to the fast-moving global
marketplace. T have consequently overlooked issues of community and
trust, as well a roblems of distance, coordination, and security, which may
pose serious or izational difficulties for illicit networks.

The second s ion presents historical evidence on the life cycle and operational effectiver of networks. Despite a near consensus in the existing literature about the eriority of networks to other forms of social organization,
only limited his ical and comparative research justifies the claim.[6] To remedy
this weakness, draw from a wider body of research on the dynamics of participation in ur rground movements, the life cycle of terrorism and insurgency, and vul abilities in organized crime to unearth potential sources of
network debilit on in greater theoretical and historical depth. In the third
section, we use se findings as a springboard for analyzing a contemporary,
highly potent n vorked organization: al-Qaida. Although there is much we
do not know al t this network, the evidence in the public domain suggests
al-Qaida is subj to many of the same weaknesses that have beset clandestine
networks in th ast. We conclude by exploring the theoretical and practical
implications of r findings.

Understandin Networks

The term "netw k" has been among the most widely used by social scientists
in the last four ades. Economists, organizational theorists, sociologists, and
anthropologists ve long applied the concept to analyze social and economic
systems in whi ctors are linked through enduring formal and informal rela-

5. We are intereste ly in the organizational advantages that may or may not flow from the network form. We do ddress potential advantages stemming from the psychological profiles, belief systems, or oth ttributes of illicit actors.

6. In international tions, sophisticated single case studies of networks abound, but broad com-
parative work is ra nd often exploratory. See, for example, Arquilla and Ronfelt, *Networks and*
Netwars. Exception Michael Kenney, *From Pablo to Osama*, who explores the comparative adap-
tive abilities of dru afficking and terrorist networks against centralized law enforcement, and
Audrey Kurth Cro who compares al-Qaida to earlier terrorist networks. See Cronin, "How al-
Qaida Ends: The ne and Demise of Terrorist Groups," *International Security*, Vol. 31, No. 1
(Summer 2006), pp 48.

tions. More recently, political scientists have adopted the network concept to analyze the organization of nonstate actors at both the domestic and transnational level,[7] to study new forms of public administration linking governments and nongovernmental actors,[8] or to map the international structure.[9] In security studies, scholars increasingly emphasize the role of networks in insurgency, terrorism, and organized crime.[10]

Much research on networks originates in sociology and organizational theory, and its genesis in these fields is central to understanding why networks, in international relations, are thought to be so effective. Economic sociologists have typically invoked the network concept to analyze the shift away from the classical model of a vertically integrated firm, which relies on top-down management, set bureaucratic routines, and centralized investment to minimize transaction costs.[11] This model has been challenged by new forms of horizontal coordination. Many firms now collaborate with competitors, subcontractors, and research institutions through formal and informal networks.

Broadly speaking, the literature finds that a networked structure enables flexible, on-demand production models that are far better adapted to the shortened product life cycles and accelerating technological changes that typify today's globalized economy than hierarchically organized production.[12] As we show below, international relations scholarship has largely imported this logic, without significant revision, in its conception of transnational networks as effective actors. Yet, this logic may be misleading, at least with regard to illi-

7. Margaret E. Keck and Kathryn Sikkink, *Activists beyond Borders: Advocacy Networks in International Politics* (Ithaca, N.Y.: Cornell University Press, 1998).
8. Bernd Marin and Renate Mayntz, eds., *Policy Networks: Empirical Evidence and Theoretical Considerations* (Boulder, Colo.: Westview, 1991); James N. Rosenau and Ernst-Otto Czempiel, eds., *Governance without Government: Order and Change in World Politics* (Cambridge: Cambridge University Press, 1992); and Fritz W. Scharpf, "Coordination in Hierarchies and Networks," in Scharpf, ed., *Games in Hierarchies and Networks: Analytical and Empirical Approaches to the Study of Governance Institutions* (Boulder, Colo.: Westview, 1993), pp. 125–165.
9. Emilie M. Hafner-Burton and Alexander H. Montgomery, "Power Positions: International Organizations, Social Networks, and Conflict," *Journal of Conflict Resolution*, Vol. 50, No. 1 (February 2006), pp. 3–27.
10. See, for example, Raab and Milward, "Dark Networks as Problems"; Arquilla and Ronfeldt, *Networks and Netwars;* Kenney, *From Pablo to Osama;* Cronin, "Behind the Curve"; Chestnut, "Illicit Activity and Proliferation"; and Sageman, *Understanding Terror Networks.*
11. Ronald H. Coase, "The Nature of the Firm," *Economica*, Vol. 4, No. 16 (November 1937), pp. 386–405; and Oliver E. Williamson, *Markets and Hierarchies: Analysis and Antitrust Implications: A Study in the Economics of Internal Organization* (New York: Free Press, 1975).
12. See, for example, Michael J. Piore and Charles F. Sabel, *The Second Industrial Divide: Possibilities for Prosperity* (New York: Basic Books, 1984); and Laurel Smith-Doerr and Walter W. Powell, "Networks and Economic Life," in Neil J. Smelser and Richard Swedberg, eds., *Handbook of Economic Sociology*, 2d ed. (Princeton, N.J.: Princeton University Press, 2005), p. 384.

cit networks. C ıdestine organizations—whether terrorist groups, guerrilla movements, or ug-smuggling enterprises—face a unique set of constraints that distinguisl ıem from their legal commercial counterparts, and their effectiveness can be reduced to models of economic efficiency. As a result, many advantag claimed for illicit networks in their confrontation with states must be tempe .

DEFINING NETW KS

Despite growin scholarly attention to the network mode of organization, significant amb ıity remains about what constitutes a network. A formal definition descr s a network as "a specific set of relations making up an interconnected ch ı or system for a defined set of entities that forms a structure."[13] This is a ose definition, designating nothing more than a set of linked elements (or "n es"). It could refer to a system of computers as well as individuals and cou embrace both market and hierarchical structures. In international relations, wever, most follow Walter Powell in conceiving of networks as a distinct for of organization, separate from both hierarchies and markets, which link acto working toward common goals.[14] From this perspective, a network can be efined as "any collection of actors ($N > 2$) that pursue repeated, enduri exchange relations with one another and at the same time lack a legitimat rganizational authority to arbitrate and resolve disputes that may arise durin he exchange."[15] In contrast to markets, exchange relations in networks are e uring; in contrast to hierarchies, networks lack top-down command and horitative dispute settlement.[16]

Networks co in many shapes and forms, but all are united by a family of structural prop ies that, taken together, support assumptions about their

13. Grahame F. Th son, *Between Hierarchies and Markets: The Logic and Limits of Network Forms of Organization* (New k: Oxford University Press, 2003), p. 54.

14. Walter W. Pow "Neither Market nor Hierarchy: Network Forms of Organization," *Research in Organizational B ior,* Vol. 12 (1990), pp. 295–336.

15. Joel M. Podoln d Karen L. Page, "Network Forms of Organization," *Annual Review of Sociology,* Vol. 24, No. ugust 1998), pp. 58–59.

16. Two broad app hes to network analysis can be distinguished. Social network analysis seeks to reveal how relati ties among individuals affect social outcomes. See Mark Granovetter, "The Strength of Weak T *American Journal of Sociology,* Vol. 78, No. 6 (May 1973), pp. 1360–1380. Organizational netwo ınalysis (ONA) focuses on the organizational level of analysis, examining how networked gr make decisions, pool resources, and engage in collective action. See Smith-Doerr and Powell, tworks and Economic Life," p. 369. Viewing networks as a form of governance, as we do, f s an ONA approach because it assumes the existence of common goals, values, or other co erations sustaining collective action. Networks, on this approach, are seen not merely as sets nked individuals but as self-conscious collective actors in world politics.

efficacy. First, whereas traditional hierarchies are based on top-down management, networks are flat and decentralized with decisionmaking and action dispersed among multiple actors exhibiting a high degree of local autonomy.[17] Although hierarchy in a traditional sense is absent from the network, the boundaries between networks and hierarchies are not always clear-cut. The existence of relatively few nodes with a large number of connections to other nodes ("hubs") may introduce an element of hierarchy into the otherwise flat network structure. What distinguishes networks from hierarchies is the capacity of lower-level units to have relationships with multiple higher-level centers as well as lateral links with units at the same organizational level.[18] Networks are never managed by a single (central) authority.

Second, unlike hierarchies, which can rely on authoritative rules and legal arbitration to govern relations, networks are self-enforcing governance structures disciplined primarily by reputation and expectations of reciprocity. As a result, networks tend to require higher levels of trust than other organizational forms.[19]

Third, unlike the impersonal, rule-guided relations that characterize interactions in hierarchies, networks tend to be based on direct personal contacts. As a result, they are often composed of members with similar professional backgrounds, interests, goals, and values. Relations and connections within networks tend to be informal and loosely structured. Finally, the lack of central authority and rule-guided interaction implies that decisionmaking and coordination in networks tend to be based on consensus and mutual adjustment rather than administrative fiat. (For a summary of differences between hierarchies and networks, see table 1.)

Beyond these core characteristics, networks differ in structure, size, and goals. Some networks are "open" insofar as they place no restrictions on membership; others are confined to small numbers of like-minded individuals. Some networks are dense, with a large number of connections between individual cells; others are more sparsely linked. Structurally, networks can be di-

---

17. Renate Mayntz, "Organizational Forms of Terrorism: Hierarchy, Network, or a Type Sui Generis?" MPIfG Discussion Paper, No. 04/4 (Cologne, Germany: Max-Planck-Institut für Gesellschaftsforschung, 2004); and Thompson, *Between Hierarchies and Markets*, pp. 22–24.
18. On hierarchy in networks, see Chris Ansell, "The Networked Polity: Regional Development in Western Europe," *Governance*, Vol. 13, No. 3 (July 2000), pp. 303–333, at p. 306; Albert Lászió Barabási, *Linked: The New Science of Networks: How Everything Is Connected to Everything Else and What It Means for Science, Business, and Everyday Life* (Cambridge, Mass.: Perseus, 2002); and Ranjay Gulati, Diana A. Dialdin, and Lihua Wang, "Organizational Networks," in Joel A.C. Baum, ed., *The Blackwell Companion to Organizations* (Oxford: Blackwell, 2002), pp. 281–303, at p. 289.
19. Powell, "Neither Market nor Hierarchy," pp. 301–304; Thompson, *Between Hierarchies and Markets*, p. 43; and Podolny and Page, "Network Forms of Organization," pp. 60–65.

Table 1. Characte cs of Networks and Hierarchies		
	Networks	Hierarchies
Structure	Decentralized/horizontal	Centralized/vertical
Membership	Homogeneous	Diverse, professional
Unit relations	Trust-based, informal	Rule-based, formal
Decision mode	(Qualified) majority voting or top-down command	Consensus

vided into three pes: the chain network where people, goods, or information move along a li of separated contacts and where end-to-end communication must travel thr h intermediate nodes; the "hub-and-spoke" (or "wheel network") where a rs are tied to a central (but not hierarchical) node, and must go through that de to communicate with each other; and the all-channel network where ev body is connected to everybody else.[20] Terrorist and criminal networks te to take the form of either chain or wheel networks, whereas all-channel net rks are commonly associated with the internet world or some social mo nents.

ADVANTAGES O ETWORKS

Much effort has ne into illuminating the benefits of networked cooperation. But the potent drawbacks have received far less attention. This section reviews some o e most common organizational advantages claimed for networks vis-à-vis erarchical state authorities in the existing literature.

EFFICIENT CO UNICATION AND INFORMATION PROCESSING. A key advantage claimed fo ne network is efficiency of communication and information processing. In ditional hierarchies, such as state bureaucracies, information typically p es through a centralized processing unit, increasing the risk of congestion a delay. It may be difficult to transmit information on the local characteristics problems and potential solutions to central decisionmakers. By contrast, th ecentralized yet tightly interconnected nature of networks means commun ation can flow unhindered from one part of the network to another, enablin ctors to acquire, process, and act on local information faster than in centrali l organizations.[21]

20. Arquilla and R ld, *Networks and Netwars*, pp. 7–8.
21. Scharpf, "Coor tion in Hierarchies and Networks," p. 135; Powell, "Neither Market nor Hierarchy," p. 325; an ayne E. Baker and Robert R. Faulkner, "The Social Organization of Conspir-

Information not only flows more freely in networks; it is also thought to be of higher quality. According to Powell, "The most useful information is rarely that which flows down the formal chain of command. . . , rather, it is that which is obtained from someone whom you have dealt with in the past and found to be reliable."[22] Because cooperation is based on trust and reciprocity rather than on impersonal transactions, networks encourage people to share and collectively interpret information rather than merely pass it on, thereby creating new interpretations and connections.[23] As a result, networks are often thought to be more innovative than hierarchies.

SCALABILITY. A second advantage of networks is "scalability," that is, the ability to grow by adding sideways links to new individuals or groups. In principle, a loose organizational structure allows networks to expand freely, integrating new nodes as necessary. If new requirements or problems arise, networks can adapt by adding new links to groups with relevant expertise.[24] A networked structure also facilitates recruitment. Due to their dispersed, transnational structure, networks can tap into wider sets of resources such as diaspora populations, and local autonomy allows networks to tailor their message and activities to different communities, thereby increasing their support base.[25] Scalability is also enhanced by advances in information and communication technologies. As information flows and transfers of funds become quicker, cheaper, and more secure, the construction of complicated networked organizations over long distances becomes more feasible. A large literature documents how transnational, networked actors use the internet to raise funds, coordinate activities, and recruit new members.[26] The upshot, according

---

acy: Illegal Networks in the Heavy Electrical Equipment Industry," *American Sociological Review*, Vol. 58, No. 6 (December 1993), pp. 837–860, at p. 844.

22. Powell, "Neither Market nor Hierarchy," p. 304; and Keck and Sikkink, *Activists beyond Borders*, pp. 18–22.

23. Podolny and Page, "Network Forms of Organization," p. 62.

24. Smith-Doerr and Powell, "Networks and Economic Life," p. 384; Mayntz, "Organizational Forms of Terrorism," p. 12; and Podolny and Page, "Network Forms of Organization," p. 66.

25. Bert Klandermans, Hanspeter Kriese, and Sidney Tarrow, eds., *From Structure to Action: Comparing Social Movement Research across Cultures* (Greenwich, Conn.: JAI Press, 1988); and David A. Snow, E. Burke Rochford Jr., Steven K. Worden, and Robert D. Benford, "Frame Alignment Processes, Micromobilization, and Movement Participation," *American Sociological Review*, Vol. 51, No. 4 (August 1986), pp. 464–481.

26. See, for example, Michele Zanini and Sean J.A. Edwards, "The Networking of Terror in the Information Age," in Arquilla and Ronfeldt, *Networks and Netwars*, pp. 29–60; Dorothy E. Denning, "Activism, Hacktivism, and Cyberterrorism: The Internet as a Tool for Influencing Foreign Policy," in Arquilla and Ronfeldt, *Networks and Netwars*, pp. 239–288; and Gabriel Weimann, "www.terror.net: How Modern Terrorism Uses the Internet," Special Report, No. 116 (Washington, D.C.: United States Institute of Peace Press, March 2004).

to the existing rature, is that networks can expand their scope and boost their ranks wit reat speed and at low cost.

ADAPTABILIT third advantage claimed for networks is adaptability to environmental ch ;es. Compared to hierarchies, network boundaries are more easily redefinal and can adjust more rapidly to situational exigencies. As discussed, netw ks can "scale" to meet new requirements or needs. Similarly, loose coupling nodes prevents locking in of ineffective relationships. If a particular orga ational link is not providing the expected payoffs, it can be terminated at r ively low cost and replaced with alternative links.[27] A relative lack of phy l infrastructure also enables networks to relocate operations from one geog hic area to another in response to changing constraints. This provides a ar benefit for illicit groups that can migrate quickly from areas where the ks from law enforcement are high. For example, Michael Kenney descrit how Colombian drug networks respond to police crackdowns by routi y moving their drug plantings and processing labs and creating fresh tran rtation routes, thereby escaping capture.[28]

RESILIENCE. earch on networks emphasizes their robustness and resistance to infilt on and fragmentation. The personal nature of network relationships— n based on ties of kinship, loyalty, and trust—means that networks are n e resistant than more impersonal organizational forms to temptations of ice and exit.[29] Structural characteristics such as "loose coupling" and "re ndant design" also reduce systemwide vulnerability. Loose coupling (i.e., n imal interaction and dependency among nodes) means that state authoritie nnot use a compromised unit to roll up an entire network, as they might h a vertically integrated adversary.[30] Redundancy (i.e., the existence of a l e number of structurally equivalent nodes) means that, unlike a hierarchi organization that can be disconnected or debilitated if a top node fails, a lar number of nodes can be removed without causing a network to fragment. If node fails, bypass links can be established around it, allowing business t ntinue as usual.[31] Such resilience is particularly useful to criminal actors t must evade detection and capture. The literature on drug trafficking doc ents how, to protect themselves from police, trafficking en-

27. Thompson, *Bet* *Hierarchies and Markets*, p. 144.
28. Kenney, *From I* *to Osama*.
29. Thompson, *Bet* *Hierarchies and Markets*, p. 43.
30. Mayntz, "Orga tional Forms of Terrorism," p. 14.
31. Duncan J. Wat *ix Degrees: The Science of a Connected Age* (London: William Heinemann, 2003), pp. 285–286.

terprises often compartmentalize their participants into separate groups and limit communication among them.[32] Also, many criminal networks allegedly build redundancy into their active groups and leadership to prevent law enforcers from immobilizing the entire network by dismantling a single node.[33]

LEARNING CAPACITY. The existing literature highlights the advantages of networks over hierarchies when it comes to facilitating learning and innovation.[34] By promoting rapid transfers of information, it is said, networks allow participants to learn quickly about new events, opportunities, and threats. Networks also encourage learning through experimentation. In hierarchies, top-down command and heavy initial investments in dedicated machinery and routine tend to lock people into particular ways of working and discourage experimentation.[35] By contrast, a flat decisionmaking structure allows ideas and methods to be tested more readily, without having to wait for approval from above, thereby allowing wider sets of lessons to be learned.

Critical Questions and Historical Evidence

In current international relations literature, the advantages claimed for networks vis-à-vis hierarchies are typically assumed to apply to all networked actors, whether they are transnational advocacy groups, human rights coalitions, or criminal syndicates.[36] Terrorists and criminals—due to their constantly changing environments and their dependence on covertness—are believed to profit exceptionally from the network form. The 9/11 commission describes terrorist networks as agile, fast moving, and elusive, difficult for hierarchical states to combat.[37] Others depict such networks as "nimble, flexible, and adap-

---

32. Kenney, *From Pablo to Osama.*
33. Gerben Bruinsma and Wim Bernasco, "Criminal Groups and Transnational Illegal Markets: A More Detailed Examination of the Basis of Social Network Theory," *Crime, Law, and Social Change,* Vol. 41 (2004), pp. 79–84; Kenney, *From Pablo to Osama;* and Russell D. Howard and Reid L. Sawyer, eds., *Terrorism and Counterterrorism: Understanding the New Security Environment* (Guilford, Conn.: McGraw-Hill, 2004).
34. See, for example, Keck and Sikkink, *Activists beyond Borders;* Kenney, *From Pablo to Osama;* Powell, "Neither Market nor Hierarchy"; and Podolny and Page, "Network Forms of Organization," p. 63.
35. See, for example, Bonnie H. Erikson, "Secret Societies and Social Structure," *Social Forces,* Vol. 60, No. 1 (September 1981), pp. 188–210; and Kenney, *From Pablo to Osama,* p. 7.
36. See, for example, Arquilla and Ronfeldt, *Networks and Netwars;* and Keck and Sikkink, *Activists beyond Borders.*
37. *The 9/11 Commission Report: Final Report of the National Commission on Terrorist Attacks upon the United States* (New York: W.W. Norton, 2004), pp. 87, 399.

tive,"[38] as "liab o change . . . structure according to circumstances,"[39] and as "large, fluid, m le, and incredibly resilient."[40] These somber assessments appear to be partl indicated by the recent experiences of leading states in their confrontation n network-based adversaries. Iraq's fractured, unrelenting insurgency, the tressing evolution of media-savvy al-Qaida, and the apparently futile war ainst Colombian drug lords all suggest a world in which illicit networks a both formidable and adaptive.

Most clandes e networks, however, are not as agile and resilient as they are made out to . In this section we seek to show why many illicit networks may be prone t nefficiencies and short life cycles. Our analysis expands the existing literatu in two main ways. First, although a great deal of scholarly effort has sough uncover and explain the advantages of networks, potential weaknesses and onstraints have received far less attention. As Miles Kahler notes, successfu etworks are relatively easy to spot; failed ones much less so. Failures are sel n revealed or evaluated, either with regard to the formation of networks or ir ability to achieve their stated goals. As a result, researchers may be ove timating the capacity of networks for collective action, and indeed the over strength of the network form.[41] Also problematic is that researchers rarely aluate networks explicitly against their organizational alternatives.[42] How networks in international relations compare to other forms of governance? re they, for example, superior or poorer at coping with change, stress, failure?

A second lim ion of the current literature is the insistence on treating contemporary net ked threats as "new"—witness the emphasis on so-called new terrorism. e notion that contemporary criminal actors are fundamen-

38. Bruce Hoffman l Qaeda, Trends in Terrorism, and Future Potentialities: An Assessment" (Santa Monica, Cal RAND, 2003), p. 12.
39. Rohan Gunarat *Inside Al Qaeda: Global Network of Terror* (New York: Columbia University Press, 2002), p. 79.
40. Peter Clarke, c in *Economist*, "Waiting for al-Qaeda's Next Bomb," May 3, 2007.
41. Miles Kahler, " ective Action and Clandestine Networks: The Case of Al-Qaeda," in Kahler, ed., *Networked Pol Agency, Power, and Governance* (Ithaca, N.Y.: Cornell University Press, forthcoming).
42. See Smith-Doe d Powell, "Networks and Economic Life." Sociologists in the social movement tradition hav plored the comparative utility of a centralized bureaucratic model versus a decentralized, info approach, but international relations scholars do not typically draw from this work. See, for mple, John D. McCarthy and Mayer N. Zald, "Resource Mobilization and Social Movements: Partial Theory," *American Journal of Sociology*, Vol. 82, No. 6 (May 1977), pp. 1212–1241.

tally different from those in the past makes comparative data difficult to find because it suggests history is obsolete.[43] Yet extant studies of terrorism, insurgency, and organized crime are far from obsolete when it comes to understanding today's networked threats. Opposition to the state has often taken a networked approach, as illustrated by the decentralized Greek resistance to the Ottomans in the early nineteenth century, the Muslim Brotherhood's loosely organized, dispersed resistance to the Egyptian state, and the sprawling international anarchist movement in the late nineteenth century. In the Middle East, informal, loosely structured networks of religion and political activism, sustained as much by personal ties as abstract ideas and common purpose, have a long history.[44] Existing research on these and similar entities provides a wealth of data about the strengths and weaknesses of networks.

Below we draw from these data to illuminate potential weaknesses of the network form. The analysis is guided by (and limited to) the question of what the distinct structural characteristics of networks—that is, limited central control, local autonomy, and informal, flexible interaction based on direct, personal relations—imply for the effectiveness and life cycle of an illicit actor. We do not address potential advantages or disadvantages stemming from other factors, such as the psychological profile or belief systems of criminal actors. Each subsection highlights an area of potential weakness of a networked structure and gives both theoretical and empirical reasons to support the claim, using highly prominent examples of networked cooperation in the history of terrorism, insurgency, and organized crime.[45] As such, they should be the most likely to confirm the advantages of network theory. Although we focus spe-

---

43. According to Ian O. Lesser, "The new tendency to organize in networks renders much previous analysis of terrorism based on established groups obsolete." See Lesser, "Introduction," in Lesser, Bruce Hoffman, John Arquilla, David Ronfeldt, and Michele Zanini, *Countering the New Terrorism* (Santa Monica, Calif.: RAND, 1999), pp. 1–6, at p. 2.

44. See Guilain P. Denoeux, *Urban Unrest in the Middle East: A Comparative Study of Informal Networks in Egypt, Iran, and Lebanon* (Albany: State University of New York Press, 1993).

45. The cases from which we draw are not chosen randomly to be broadly representative of the universe of illicit networks. Rather we have focused on prominent networks, which, due to the relative success of their activities, have captured significant media and scholarly attention. These cases should be most likely to confirm the theoretical advantages of a networked structure and thus represent hard cases from our viewpoint. We realize there are key differences in the operational procedures and constraints facing drug smugglers, terrorists, and revolutionaries. Still, we find, along with others (e.g., Matthew Brzezinski, "Re-engineering the Drug Business," *New York Times Magazine*, June 23, 2002, p. 48; and Kenney, *From Pablo to Osama*), that there are important structural commonalities in the way these types of groups organize, which justify a comparative analysis.

cifically on illic ctors, we suggest these weaknesses may apply to networks more generally.

INFORMATION L ITATIONS AND COMMUNICATION FAILURE

The existing lit ture portrays networks as highly efficient information providers. Yet, netv ks may not always be superior organizational structures for gathering, shar , and processing information. First, decentralization implies that searching f information in networks may be difficult and cumbersome. In principle, a tral directory renders the problem of finding information trivial, even in rge, dispersed network. But central directories are expensive to establish and aintain, and may be impracticable in illicit networks due to security concer 6 Decentralized or "distributed" systems, on the other hand, tend to be less icient information providers.[47] Because such systems lack a central director o catalogue information, searches effectively involve each node querying ghboring nodes, which query other neighboring nodes until the information found (or the search is abandoned). As a result, each unit of information ten to be associated with higher transaction costs than in a centralized system

Compartmen ization of nodes, necessary for security reasons, may also present a barri o effective information sharing in illicit networks. As discussed, crimin nd terrorist networks often seek to minimize potentially destabilizing co cts between cells. To shield them from complicity, members are kept minin y informed about the activities of others, thereby making communication fficult. Dark networks may also find it hard to source reliable informatio rom outsiders. According to the literature, a key advantage of the network ts structural access to wider, more diverse sources of information. Yet, so ogical research on underground participation shows that illicit actors are o n isolated from wider social communities.[48] Loyalty tends to

46. Secrecy makes rmation sharing difficult for any type of organization, including hierarchical ones such as, f xample, the Central Intelligence Agency, but a decentralized networked structure compoun hese difficulties due to the absence of reliable means for authenticating information and for rolling who gains access to sensitive data.

47. Duncan Watts s the example of a purely distributed peer-to-peer internet network called Gnutella. Because i ks, by design, a central directory, searches in a purely decentralized system such as Gnutella ar ten far less efficient than a Napster-like network, where queries go to a central high-capacity s er. See Watts, *Six Degrees*, pp. 157–158.

48. Martha Crensh "Decisions to Use Terrorism: Psychological Constraints on Instrumental Reasoning," in Do lla Della Porta, ed., *Social Movements and Violence: Participation in Underground Organization* reenwich, Conn.: JAI Press, 1992), pp. 29–42; Donatella Della Porta, "On In-

run deeper when members are cut off from countervailing influences. Hence, terrorist and insurgent leaders often limit contact with the outside world, thereby restricting the in-flow of information to the network.

History provides numerous examples of networks that fail in their missions due to inefficient communication and information sharing or because isolation and secrecy undermine their ability to identify and react to critical changes in their environment. Problems of information sharing are implicated in the demise of the Quebec Liberation Front (known by the French acronym FLQ).[49] Although it portrayed itself, and was portrayed in the media, as a centralized, monolithic organization, the FLQ was a loosely organized network of militants, clustered around various charismatic personalities. No central leadership controlled FLQ "cells"—these were groups of friends and family sharing the ideal of an independent Quebec. Ronald Crelinsten's account of the 1970 October crisis emphasizes obstacles to effective communication and information sharing as a result of this decentralization. The crisis erupted when two friendly but physically separated cells failed to communicate their strategies to each other. The Liberation cell decided to kidnap a British diplomat. The Chenier cell, apparently not well informed about the strategy, carried out a separate kidnapping of Pierre Laporte, the Quebec labor minister. When the Liberation cell—taken by surprise by the Laporte kidnapping—announced publicly the FLQ would release both hostages if two of its demands were met, the Chenier cell insisted separately that all demands must be met or Laporte would be killed. Failures of communication and coordination deepened as the network was driven farther underground, until in late 1970 Laporte was killed and popular support for the network lost. What is striking about this example is that the FLQ cells were not initially feuding. Rather, as Crelinsten suggests, the loose network structure and lack of central authority made reliable communication and information sharing difficult, with the result that cooperation broke down. One might object that similar communication failures are less likely in the electronic age, where the internet, cell phones, and videoconferencing enable real-time communication across distances. But as we explain

dividual Motivations in Underground Political Organizations," in Della Porta, ed., *Social Movements and Violence*, pp. 3–28; and Donatella Della Porta, "Left-wing Terrorism in Italy," in Martha Crenshaw, ed., *Terrorism in Context* (University Park: Penn State University Press, 1995), pp. 105–159.

49. Ronald D. Crelinsten, "The Internal Dynamics of the FLQ during the October Crisis of 1970," in David C. Rapoport, ed., *Inside Terrorist Organizations* (New York: Columbia University Press, 1988), pp. 59–89.

below, modern ıformation technologies do not solve all the problems of communication ·tween geographically dispersed actors lacking central command, and poli monitoring of phones and internet sites often makes reliance on such techno ies perilous.

POOR DECISION KING AND EXCESSIVE RISK-TAKING

A second probl in networks involves strategic decisionmaking. In the theoretical literatur networks assume an almost organic ability to respond flexibly to the e ronment, weighing the options and adjusting their composition and operat procedures as needs change. Yet, real-world networks are not likely to be smart. First, decisionmaking is unlikely to be as fast or as coherent as the lit ture suggests. In a network, as in a hierarchy, complex decisions have to made regarding resource allocation, tactics, whether and when to use vic ce, what social and political levers to manipulate, and so on. Because these isions will not flow from centralized leadership, decisionmaking is likel be a complicated, protracted process as all members try to have a say—or their own way.[50] Decisions also may not be respected as readily due to t lack of an authoritative stamp. As a result, resources may be used poorly, co adictory tactics selected, and activities carried out that serve parochial short m interests rather than the larger mission.

Second, strat may be virtually nonexistent, or at least rudimentary, without experience ntral leadership. Local autonomy means operations can go forward withou valuation, coordination, and a sober assessment of the overall benefits and sks. Likewise, the absence of central direction implies that important tasks ay be left unassigned or efforts duplicated, causing operational costs to al. Strategic processes may be further undermined by selfcensorship. Alt igh the literature highlights deliberation and free exchange of ideas as ke dvantages of networks, in reality, the norms of collective decisionmaking ithin cells and strong group loyalty—combined with fear of negative sancti , even purging, if one does not go along with the majority—often lead mem rs to keep off the agenda issues that are threatening to consensus building Free exchange of ideas is therefore not likely to be the norm in illicit networ and deliberation and rational decisionmaking may suffer as a result.

50. Powell, "Neith larket nor Hierarchy," p. 318.
51. Gordon H. Mc nick, "Terrorist Decision Making," *Annual Review of Political Science*, Vol. 6 (June 2003), p. 498.

Illicit networks are also prone to excessive risk taking. Sociologists find that decision processes within highly insulated underground organizations are prone to "groupthink," and various forms of delusion, including a sense of invulnerability, which encourage extreme risk taking.[52] Risk taking may also be induced by the pressure to reciprocate. Networks, like other organizations, thrive on results: terrorists must engage in violent attacks to maintain visibility; drug smugglers need to shift their goods lest they lose supplies and clients. Pressure to reciprocate, combined with the high reputation costs associated with failure, can induce recklessness, forcing members to choose a course of action before they are ready. Research on a Montreal criminal network reveals how a networked structure may induce risk taking.[53] This network was subjected to intense police surveillance and disruption over a two-year period. Shipments were routinely seized, but the network itself was allowed to survive so law enforcement could gather enough intelligence to bring it down fully. The effects of stress on the network are revealing. When seizures took place, traffickers tended to blame each other and worry about their own reputations instead of trying to learn how to avoid future seizures.[54] According to conversation logs, those involved with failed shipments grew increasingly reckless in their attempts to compensate for losses and get back into the network's good graces. Rather than seek to interpret their failures and revise their strategy, participants seem to have been so frazzled by their failures and dread of what might happen to them as a result that they were moved to irrational behavior. Although the threat of punishment might have the same effect in a hierarchical structure, it is likely that more formal patterns of cooperation, which give members a sense that their place in an organization is relatively stable and secure, rather than based precariously on informal reciprocity, might prevent similar recklessness.

RESTRICTIONS ON SCOPE AND STRUCTURAL ADAPTABILITY

As we have shown, networks are often depicted as highly elastic entities that combine, recombine, and expand to adapt to transformations in their environment. Yet, both common sense and empirical evidence suggest there are limits

---

52. A wide literature in sociology finds that decisionmaking by consensus induces risk-taking behavior, particularly in underground organizations. See, for example, Michael A. Wallach and Nathan Kogan, "The Roles of Information, Discussion, and Consensus in Group Risk Taking," *Journal of Experimental Social Psychology*, Vol. 1, No. 1 (1965), pp. 1–19, at p. 1. For an overview of this literature, see McCormick, "Terrorist Decision Making."
53. Carlo Morselli and Katia Petit, "Law-Enforcement Disruption of a Drug Importation Network," *Global Crime*, Vol. 8, No. 2 (May 2007), pp. 109–130.
54. Ibid.

to the scalabilit nd structural adaptability of most networks. There are several reasons w networks, and illicit networks in particular, may find it difficult to scal s discussed, because illicit networks cannot depend on hierarchy or the le system to resolve disputes, they are crucially dependent on interpersonal tr . The high premium on trust both limits the feasible size of networks and r icts recruitment. It is well known, for example, that it is easier to generate st and generalize expectations of reciprocity in small collectivities when th social distance" between actors is short, and chains of action are not extend 5 This favors small networks. It is also easier to generate trust when acto are homogeneous in outlook, life style, and culture. As a result, recruitme o illicit networks mostly proceeds through preexisting networks of perso relationships, typically ones that rest on kinship or previous bonding experi es.[56] For example, contemporary drug trafficking largely occurs within et ally homogeneous groups, where kinship generates trust and reciprocity nong criminals reluctant to transact with people they have not known for g periods.[57] Gerben Bruinsma and Wim Bernasco's analysis of Turkish hero trafficking suggests the entire trade chains from production in Turkey to s in Europe are based on close family relationships.[58] In Donatella Della rta's sample of Italian Red Brigades, 70 percent of recruits had at least on iend involved already,[59] and in Marc Sageman's sample of mujahideen, at ast 75 percent had preexisting bonds of family or friendship.[60] These re itment practices restrict the scope of illicit networks, casting doubt on rapid pansion.

55. Thompson, *Bet* *Hierarchies and Markets*, p. 45.

56. Raab and Milw "Dark Networks as Problems"; Erikson, "Secret Societies and Social Structure," p. 195; and K lermans, Kriese, and Tarrow, *From Structure to Action*. The constraint set by preexisting social n orks on recruitment varies across criminal activities. For lower-risk activities, such as trade tolen cars or some drug-trafficking activities, significant migration movements have stimul the growth of extensive cross-border networks held together by shared ethnicity. See, for e ple, John McFarlane, "Transnational Crime as a Security Issue," in Carolina G. Hernadez and R. Pattugalan, eds., *Transnational Crime and Regional Security in the Asia Pacific* (Manila: Ins e for Strategic and Development Studies, 1999), p. 53. But, in general, the more dangerous an sky the activity, the more networks rely on strong personal ties. Thus, Martha Crenshaw find t marijuana users are willing to share information or drugs with a wider range of people t the more endangered and hence more cautious users of heroin. See Crenshaw, "An Or zational Approach to the Analysis of Political Terrorism," *Orbis*, Vol. 39, No. 2 (Fall 1985), pp. 4 489. On this logic, terrorists are likely to be among the most cautious in whom they trust.

57. Brzezinski, "Re gineering the Drug Business"; Kenney, *From Pablo to Osama*, p. 28; and Raab and Milward, "Da etworks as Problems," p. 8.

58. Bruinsma and asco, "Criminal Groups and Transnational Illegal Markets," p. 87.

59. Della Porta, "L ving Terrorism in Italy," p. 139.

60. Sageman, *Und* *nding Terror Networks*, pp. 111–113. Justin Magouirk, Scott Atran, and Marc

Networks grow not only by recruiting new members but also by linking sideways to other networked groups. Evidence suggests, however, that networks that seek to scale in this way often end up splintering as a result of differences of ideologies, goals, and strategies. The splintering of the network of Egyptian militants who assassinated President Anwar al-Sadat highlights the tendency toward fragmentation when networks attempt to grow by linking to other, like-minded groups.[61] The network of Islamic militants that assassinated Sadat in October 1981 was a loose coalition of autonomous groups that had decided the previous year to coordinate their activities. Although they shared the goal of establishing an Islamic state, these various groups held different views on how to achieve that goal, some favoring a violent coup and others focusing on a broad popular uprising. When presented with the opportunity to strike Sadat, local leaders disagreed widely on the desirability of such a strategy. This lack of unity, in turn, led to poor planning and preparation. To avoid dissent and possible leakage, many local leaders were informed of the plot very late—in some cases only hours before it unfolded. As a result, they were caught by surprise and ill prepared for the wave of arrests that followed. The insurrection that followed the assassination was crushed in a matter of days, and more than 300 members of the network were arrested and put on trial. Once the network was hit, it quickly fragmented, as it broke into rival groups.

The Egyptian militants are far from a unique example. There are numerous instances of networks that fracture when they attempt to scale. The original Palestinian Liberation Front (PLF), which was founded by Ahmad Jibril in 1959, merged with other nationalist militant groups in 1967 to form the Popular Front for the Liberation of Palestine (PFLP). In 1977 the PLF splintered from the PFLP due to internal conflict, and in 1983 and 1985 the organization split again into pro-Palestine Liberation Organization (PLO), pro-Syrian, and pro-Libyan factions, each of which claimed to represent the mother-organization.[62] The much-publicized split within the ranks of Jemaah Islamiyah (JI) in 1999–2000 occurred after new links between senior JI operatives and al-Qaida took the organization in a more militant direction, causing rifts among its leader-

---

Sageman document the prevalence of kin relationships within Jemaah Islamiyah in "Connecting Terrorist Networks," *Studies in Conflict and Terrorism*, Vol. 31, No. 1 (January 2008), pp. 1–16.

61. See Sageman, *Understanding Terror Networks*, pp. 30–33. For a more detailed account, see David Sagiv, *Fundamentalism and Intellectuals in Egypt, 1973–1993* (New York: Routledge, 1995), pp. 54–61; and Steven Brooke, "Jihadist Strategic Debates before 9/11," *Studies in Conflict and Terrorism*, Vol. 31, No. 3 (June 2008), pp. 201–226.

62. "In the Spotlight: The Palestinian Liberation Front (PLF)," Center for Defense Information, updated November 14, 2002, http://www.cdi.org/terrorism/plf.cfm.

ship.[63] Aum Sh kyo, the cult known for the deadly sarin gas attack in Tokyo in 1995, experie d rapid growth in the late 1990s counting as many as 40,000 members aroun he world. However, unity suffered as a result. Around 2000, a leadership co st broke out between the founder, Shoko Asahara, and challenger Fumihir yu, who sought to distance himself from the violent teachings of Asahar nd in 2007 the organization split in two. Today the cult's membership st ls at about 1,500.[64]

That some ne orks disintegrate when seeking to expand does not suggest that all network ind it difficult to scale. Research suggests, however, that networks that gro too large often find it difficult to sustain unity of purpose, and that their ctiveness declines as a result. The main reason is the difficulty in coord ting behavior and nourishing agreement among large, diverse groups la ng central leadership. The Basque nationalist group ETA and the PLO both vide examples of networks that have struggled to sustain unity as they g v. The demise of the international anarchist movement also highlights the ficulty of sustaining community and commitment in dispersed network structures. By the early twentieth century, scattered in Europe and the ited States, the anarchists were exposed to a variety of countervailing luences, drawing them away from their commitment to transnational a chism.[65] Historically, many nonstate organizations that have expanded abro have found their base of popular support weakened as a result.[66] A netwo d structure that thrives on local empowerment often struggles to project nified image of itself to the world. With various centers of power claiming speak for the network, its legitimacy and very identity can easily be calle to question. The decentralized Algerian insurgency in the early 1990s is a iking example.[67] The Islamic Salvation Front (known by the French acrony S), the Islamist party banned by the Algerian regime after it won parliamen y elections in 1991, had exiled leaders in both the United

63. See Magouirk, an, and Sageman, "Connecting Terrorist Networks"; and Elena Pavlova, "From a Counter-S ty to a Counter-State Movement: Jemaah Islamiyah According to PUPJI," *Studies in Conflict a Terrorism*, Vol. 30, No. 9 (September 2007), pp. 777–800.
64. Holly Fletcher, m Shinrikyo (Japan, Cultists, Aum Supreme Truth)," Council on Foreign Relations, Backgro r, updated May 18, 2008, http://www.cfr.org/publication/9238/.
65. Martin A. Mill The Intellectual Origins of Modern Terrorism in Europe," in Crenshaw, *Terrorism in Context*, p 7–62.
66. See David C. R port, "The International World as Some Terrorists Have Seen It: A Look at a Century of Memoi in Rapoport, *Inside Terrorist Organizations*, pp. 32–58.
67. Martin Stone, *gony of Algeria* (New York: Columbia University Press, 1997); and Michael Willis, *The Islamist llenge in Algeria: A Political History* (Washington Square: New York University Press, 1997).

States and Germany. Concerned with building international support, these leaders were eager not to espouse violence for fear it would endanger the status of the FIS as a legitimate political party. But the FIS also had leaders in Algeria who refused to reject violence. Conflicting communiqués often emerged from various centers of power, and, as a result, it was unclear who represented the FIS and broader Islamist insurgency. No one had firm control over all the armed groups, and the violence of some ended up tainting the broader political movement, undermining popular support.[68] A similar schism appears to affect Gama'a al-Islamiyya (Islamic Group, or IG) today. IG, an international terrorist network seeking to create an Islamic state in Egypt and implicated in the 1993 World Trade Center bombing, split into violent and nonviolent factions after announcing a cease-fire in 1997. Since then, the network has continued to grow more divided as exiled leaders abroad have advocated the use of mass violence while members of the group's leadership in Egypt reject it.[69]

Not only scalability but also structural adaptability is likely to be limited in many networks. Indeed, networks ties may be "stickier" than the image of "loose coupling" suggests; contrary to conventional network wisdom, networks could be more resistant to change than bureaucratic ties. To be sure, a lack of physical infrastructure and an absence of bureaucracy ensure some flexibility. But consider that much of the flexibility claimed for networks stems from loosely coupled or "weak links," which can be easily redrawn and remodeled. In economics weak ties are seen as a boon because they give rise to more diverse sources of information, fresh perspectives on problems, and new collaboration opportunities. Most clandestine networks, however, are built on strong ties based on kinship and previous bonding experience. Adding or severing links may be difficult, and physical movement and relocation not so easy, when personal relationships are involved. Because networked cooperation builds on expectations of reciprocity, strong reputation constraints on breaking network ties may also limit flexibility.[70] Consequently, not only the ability of networks to grow but also their ability to adapt through restructuring themselves may be far more modest than the literature recognizes.

68. Willis, *The Islamist Challenge in Algeria*, p. 315.
69. U.S. Department of State, Office of the Coordinator for Counterterrorism, "Chapter 6: Terrorist Organizations," in *Country Reports on Terrorism*, April 30, 2008, http://www.state.gov/s/ct/rls/crt/2007/103714.htm.
70. Podolny and Page, "Networks Forms of Organization," pp. 61–62.

COLLECTIVE-AC N PROBLEMS DUE TO COORDINATION

As suggested, n vorks face a variety of collective-action problems. A frequent source of colle e-action failure is internal conflict. In-fighting commonly afflicts clandes e groups, whether modeled hierarchically or not,[71] but networks, with ir lack of centralized control, are especially susceptible to internal strife. L autonomy, though advantageous in some respects, easily nourishes the g vth of competing centers of power with independent bases of legitimacy, lo ty, and material support. Challengers are more willing to assert themselves entral leadership is weak. In networks, moreover, rules and regulations abo the use of tactics, allocation of resources, and so on are not formally establ d. As a result, competing centers of power may fight over such issues mo readily, and without the aid of formal arbitration.

The PLO vivi illustrates how tensions can go unresolved in informal networks, regardl of close social linkages. This loose federation of nationalist groups historic suffered from acute infighting, as autonomous segments vied for control onsor states such as Egypt, Syria, and the conservative Gulf monarchies de ned internal strife by funding rival groups, but they were only partly to b e for Palestinian fractiousness.[72] As David Schiller suggests, structural featu typical of networks—the absence of central authority, the unchecked aut my of rival groups, and the inability to arbitrate quarrels through formal chanisms—made the PLO excessively vulnerable to outside manipulation a internal strife. ETA, which began as a diffuse, heterogeneous moveme with limited central control, provides another example of network fractio ness.[73] In the 1960s, aiming for a broad-based insurgency against Preside Francisco Franco, it was open to people of widely different political and so backgrounds, some supporting Basque independence, others unification h the French Basque territories, still others self-rule within

71. See McCormic errorist Decision Making."
72. David Schiller, Battlegroup Divided: The Palestinian Fedayeen," in Rapoport, *Inside Terrorist Organizations*, p)–108.
73. For this examp ee Cyrus Ernesto Zirakzadeh, "From Revolutionary Dreams to Organizational Fragmentati Disputes over Violence within ETA and Sendero Luminoso," *Terrorism and Political Violence*, V 4, No. 1 (Winter 2002), pp. 66–92. Not only terrorist groups but also other networked actors prone to disunity. Research on U.S. street gangs suggests that loosely configured gangs, ng clear roles, a corporate structure, and central control, cannot effectively control the behavi their members. A study of warring gangs in St. Louis, Missouri, revealed that gang homicid ere more likely to take place within gangs than between them, mainly because of their lack ntral control and discipline. See Scott H. Decker and David Curry, "Gangs, Gang Homicides, Gang Loyalty: Organized Crimes or Disorganized Criminals," *Journal of Criminal Justice*, Vo , No. 4 (July–August 2002), pp. 343–352.

Spain. Differences over the acceptability of violent tactics triggered serious internal friction, and splinter groups multiplied over the generations, with little in common except the franchise label "ETA."

Although fractiousness is certainly not uncommon in terrorist groups, a networked structure appears to nourish it. The Shining Path in Peru, one of the most cohesive, enduring insurgent organizations in the twentieth century, provides a helpful contrast. Research on the group's high degree of social cohesion and effectiveness suggests it was closely tied to its hierarchical structure, centered on the powerful leadership of Abimael Guzmán.[74] Jemaah Islamiyah is another case in point. JI under the leadership of Abdullah Sungkar was a highly centralized organization with a top-down chain of command and clearly defined objectives. Sungkar ruled JI with an iron hand and did not allow any rival centers of power to arise within the organization. After Sungkar's death in 1999, JI split into fractious groups as a militant minority under the leadership of Hambali broke with the moderate majority and carried out a series of terrorist attacks in Southeast Asia from 2000 to 2005. The nominal leadership of Sungkar's second in command, Abu Bakar Ba'asyir, has been largely unsuccessful in stemming fractiousness within what is now a much more loosely structured network.[75]

Distance coordination poses another obstacle to collective action. The network literature tends to assume away problems of distance. The internet and other communications technologies are thought to enable seamless cooperation among geographically dispersed actors. Yet, research on computer-supported collaborative work finds that such technologies do not solve all the problems of distance cooperation, and may generate new difficulties.[76] People

74. Gordon H. McCormick, "The Shining Path and Peruvian Terrorism," in Rapoport, ed., *Inside Terrorist Organizations*, pp. 109–128. Zirakzadeh, too, comes to this conclusion in his explicit comparison of the ETA with the hierarchical Shining Path; hierarchy helped prevent fragmentation of the Peruvian group. Zirakzadeh, "From Revolutionary Dreams to Organizational Fragmentation."
75. See Magouirk, Atran, and Sageman, "Connecting Terrorist Networks"; and Pavlova, "From a Counter-Society to a Counter-State Movement."
76. On the problems of distance collaboration, especially conflict, misunderstanding, and trust, see Pamela J. Hinds and Diane E. Bailey, "Out of Sight, Out of Sync: Understanding Conflict in Distributed Teams," *Organization Science*, Vol. 14, No. 6 (November–December 2003), pp. 615–632; Gary M. Olson and Judith S. Olson, "Distance Matters," *Human-Computer Interaction*, Vol. 15, Nos. 2–3 (September 2000), pp. 139–178; Catherine Durnell Cramton, "The Mutual Knowledge Problem and Its Consequences for Dispersed Collaboration," *Organization Science*, Vol. 12, No. 3 (May–June 2001), pp. 346–371; Pamela J. Hinds and Mark Mortensen, "Understanding Conflict in Geographically Distributed Teams: The Moderating Effects of Shared Identity, Shared Context, and Spontaneous Communication," *Organization Science*, Vol. 16, No. 3 (May–June 2005), pp. 290–307; Sirkka L. Jarvenpaa and Dorothy E. Leidner, "Communication and Trust in Global Virtual Teams," *Organization Science*, Vol. 10, No. 6 (June 1999), pp. 791–815; and Patricia Wallace, *The Internet in the*

easily misinter] t and misunderstand one another when they must rely on
voice transmiss ıs, email, and instant messaging. Without face-to-face interaction, people en fail to identify and correct for misjudgments.[77] Consequently, conflict re more likely to erupt in geographically dispersed teams, as
opposed to colc ted ones. This research also casts doubt on the ability of dispersed network o establish and preserve social cohesion. Face-to-face interaction is cruci n building a social-support structure for communication.
People separate y significant distances often lack the contextual information
to make sense c ehavior, and as a result tend to be less cohesive and trusting
than their face- face counterparts. The absence of a headquarters, though
considered an vantage for security, may also undercut social cohesion in
networks. A ce al base where recruits live, train, or plan activities together
can be essentia r building the trust that sustains collective action. Loyalty
and commitme nay be less easy to instill in networks that are transnational,
dispersed, and iant on temporary, makeshift bases.

Germany's e rience with terrorism in the 1970s highlights these difficulties. Research c ıparing left- and right-wing groups suggests the dispersed,
networked stru ıre of right-wing groups severely reduced their cohesion.[78]
The far more ı fied and successful left-wing terrorists tended to organize
hierarchically, h professional management and clear divisions of labor.
They were conc trated geographically in universities, where they could establish central l lership, trust, and camaraderie through regular, face-to-face
meetings. Und nterrogation, they rarely betrayed their comrades. By contrast, the right- ıg networks were decentralized, scattered about the country,
and involveme was often temporary. They were routinely infiltrated and
their members ested; those captured frequently betrayed their associates.

SECURITY BREAC S

Research on illi networks emphasizes their resistance to infiltration and dis-
mantlement. Yc despite practices of "loose coupling" and "redundant design," which n e networks less vulnerable to leadership interdiction and

Workplace: How Ne *chnology Is Transforming Work* (Cambridge: Cambridge University Press, 2004).

77. Cooperation th elies on distance technologies is also hampered by the difficulty of sharing communication aic or example, in face-to-face meetings, a map is easily shared and partici-pants can use gestu to communicate movements or locations. This efficient "war room" style of coordination, easil ranged for colocated teams, is far more difficult for dispersed team mem-bers using commu tions technologies.

78. See Frieldhelm dhardt, "Left-wing and Right-wing Terrorism Groups: A Comparison for the German Case," Della Porta, *Social Movements and Violence*, pp. 215–235.

random arrests, networks are not necessarily more secure than hierarchical organizations. In fact, once networks are hit, they may unravel spontaneously as participants begin to blame one another, as suggested by the demise of the Montreal drug-trafficking network or the Egyptian assassins.[79] More generally, the absence of central authority, while protecting networks by leaving no obvious locus for attack, can seriously jeopardize security. Dispersed authority makes it difficult to monitor activities and screen new recruits. Rules for safe conduct are not defined and enforced centrally but often evolve locally in an impromptu, precarious way, which may undermine security.

Security breaches are easily observed in the experiences of underground networks. According to research on the Italian underground in the 1970, those militant left-wing organizations that experimented with a decentralized approach were highly vulnerable.[80] They typically engaged local leaders *(squadre),* who were relatively autonomous in their activities. Although local autonomy boosted grassroots recruitment, it was also risky. Because of their operational freedom, *squadre* were able to recruit whole groups of supporters without having to wait for background checks and approval from above. Internal security was fragile, and infiltration by the state rampant. Many groups, in fact, evolved in the direction of greater centralization precisely because of the risks associated with a networked strategy. The Red Brigades, for instance, instilled more hierarchy in their organization and stricter controls over the process of recruitment.

Communication practices among international drug traffickers also highlight the security liabilities of a decentralized approach. Research suggests that, although unofficial guidelines among drug traffickers discourage the use of cell phones and encourage coded language, coordination among actors on the street is often so demanding that agents communicate in an excessively simple, transparent manner that risks security.[81] As a former trafficker explained: "International dope smugglers have to make thousands of phone calls. There are many who say they never use the phone because it's too insecure. They are either lying or not doing any business." Referring to the use of coded language, he continued: "Any attempt at sophisticated coding quickly leads to disastrous misunderstandings. I have never heard or made a dope-

79. Of course, not all networks unravel easily, as the debate about torture demonstrates. Resilience in the face of opposition, however, often has more to do with the extreme loyalty of a few individuals than with a networked structure per se.
80. Della Porta, "Left-wing Terrorism in Italy."
81. Morselli and Petit, "Law-Enforcement Disruption of a Drug Importation Network."

smuggling call ich isn't obviously just that."[82] Such practices may explain why communic ons among drug traffickers, as well as terrorists, are habitually intercepted security services.

LEARNING DISA ITIES

Learning is cru l for illicit actors. To stay afloat in a hostile environment, criminals must rn to identify and circumvent rapidly shifting countermeasures, avoid pa mistakes, and recover from missteps. In the existing literature, networks cast as highly efficient learners.[83] As with much of the logic on networked ctiveness, however, the theoretical learning advantages of networks fit a al, economic context better than the world of illicit actors. One reason net rks are said to be good learners is that they facilitate rapid information flo which allow actors to find out about new opportunities and threats. As we ve shown, however, information does not necessarily flow freely in netwo , especially illicit ones. Loose coupling, combined with pressure to separat e network from its social base for security reasons, tends to reduce social e eddedness and network connectivity, thereby making information sharing ficult. And, as Michael Kenney shows with respect to drug-trafficking netw ks, compartmentalization means individual cells often absorb only those sons they have learned directly rather than benefit from the experience of o rs.[84]

Another alle learning advantage of the network—its superior ability to produce "on-th b expertise"—is also doubtful. Because networks build on personal relatio hips, they are said to be better than hierarchies at transmitting "tacit kno dge"—that is, knowledge that cannot be explicitly codified but is associate vith learning-by-doing and hands-on techniques.[85] Yet, bureaucrats learn the job too, and personal, mentored relationships also exist in hierarchies. ch like their networked adversaries, agents in counterterrorism and drug la enforcement learn when they operate in the field, and much like their netw d adversaries, they can leverage social networks of friends,

82. Quoted in ibid 17, of copy available online from the Social Science Research Network, http://ssrn.com/ab ct?944829.

83. See, for exampl owell, "Neither Market nor Hierarchy"; and Thompson, *Between Hierarchies and Markets*. On t arning abilities of illicit networks, see especially Kenney, *From Pablo to Osama*.

84. See Kenney, *Fr ablo to Osama*, p. 115. Many network scholars recognize that compartmentalization and secre may present impediments to learning, but they still insist that networks are better learners tha reaucracies. See, for example, ibid., p. 7.

85. Thompson, *Bet Hierarchies and Markets*, pp. 121–123; and Kenney, *From Pablo to Osama*.

colleagues, and informers to learn about changing conditions on the ground. But agents have the added advantage of better access to formal training. Most agents receive training in a variety of fields, including investigation, surveillance, intelligence analysis, and undercover operations and technology, and many pursue advanced education.[86] The same amount of routinized knowledge is difficult to transmit in dispersed clandestine networks. The network literature tends to downplay the importance of formal instruction and skill transfer. Informal contacts facilitated by communications technologies are often considered sufficient to transmit skills among networked actors. For example, the literature is rife with examples of how terrorist manuals and bomb recipes can be downloaded freely from the internet. Yet, internet manuals and recipes (on bomb building and other tactics) are often too imprecise to be of practical use.[87] To learn how to use advanced weapons and tactics, already knowledgeable students must be taught by experts. It is no coincidence that some of the most successful militant organizations have relied on central training camps to teach their associates basic skills. Fatah, the PLO, Hezbollah, and the Taliban all built training camps where militants took courses on intelligence gathering, bombing, the organization of cells, and so on.[88] Such centralized learning camps, however, have proven a security liability in an age where these networks have been ferociously targeted by states.

A third barrier to learning in networks is lack of organizational memory. Organizations learn by distilling lessons and storing them in ways that are accessible to others, despite the turnover of personnel and passage of time.[89] To be sure, criminal enterprises can record knowledge, relying on manuals, notebooks, and computers.[90] Yet, there are limits to what can be written down or saved to a computer without compromising security. Informal organizational memories, dependent on error-prone human recollection, are unlikely to be as reliable as formal ones. Organizational memory may end up fragmented and

86. Michael Kenney, in *From Pablo to Osama*, p. 81, details the comprehensive training of "narcs" (narcotics police) but does not believe that this gives them any crucial advantage in the field.
87. See David E. Smith, "The Training of Terrorist Organizations," CSC Report, *Global Security .org*, 1995, http://globalsecurity.org/military/library/report/1995/SDE.htm; and Javier Jordan, Fernando M. Manas, and Nicola Horsburgh, "Strengths and Weaknesses of Grassroot Jihadist Networks: The Madrid Bombings," *Studies in Conflict and Terrorism*, Vol. 31, No. 1 (January 2008), pp. 17–39.
88. For an overview of illicit training camps, see Gunaratna, *Inside Al Qaeda*, pp. 93–101.
89. Barbara Levitt and James G. March, "Organizational Learning," *Annual Review of Sociology*, Vol. 14 (1988), pp. 319–338.
90. On these practices, see Kenney, *From Pablo to Osama*, p. 56.

fallacious, beca › no central authority is responsible for consolidating and
vetting it. Thus, tworked actors may not be able to translate lessons learned
into solid impr ments in organizational practice.[91]

History sugg s illicit networks are far from nimble learners. As we have
shown, in the M treal drug network, police seizures did not prompt any sustained attempts learn and adapt. Traffickers instead struggled ever more
recklessly to ge hings back on the road to sustain their reputation, and the
network collap . The persistent inability in the late nineteenth century of
the anarchists t arn from past mistakes is another example. Research on the
German anarch s, in particular, highlights security liabilities and learning
difficulties flow from a networked structure. The German anarchists were
an informal gr , largely autonomous within a broader transnational structure.[92] No one s responsible for establishing and enforcing security procedures. As a ult, by the early 1880s, the Berlin police had thoroughly
infiltrated their nks and curtailed their activities. In response, individual
anarchists atte ted to institute changes that would enhance security. A
London-based rchist, Viktor Dave, proposed creating a small commission
of known, trust anarchists that would be responsible for smuggling *Freiheit,*
their banned jo al, to its subscribers on the continent. The smuggling process had previo y been informal and unregulated, leading to frequent arrests
of couriers. Riv eaders on the continent, however, felt that reliance on a central distribution nter in London would heighten vulnerability. As no one was
in overall charg no central decision was made, and the police continued to
infiltrate the gr and arrest anarchists. Although they recognized the pitfalls
of their practice he anarchists could not transcend their networked structure
to institute cha s that would make them more secure.

Perils of Netw king: The Case of al-Qaida

So far we have cused on limitations of the network form using theoretical
and mainly his ical evidence. But are clandestine actors in the twenty-first
century more s isticated users of the network form? In this section we con-

91. Michael Kenne cuments this problem with respect to drug-trafficking networks. Kenney,
From Pablo to Osam . 115.
92. On the anarchis nd their structure, see Andrew R. Carlson, *Anarchism in Germany,* Vol. 1: *The
Early Movement* (M hen, N.J.: Scarecrow, 1972), especially pp. 334–376; and James Joll, *The Anarchists* (London: Eyr d Spottiswoode, 1964).

sider a contemporary networked threat: al-Qaida.[93] Al-Qaida is a particularly good case in which to probe the presence of network weaknesses. Received wisdom about al-Qaida emphasizes classic advantages of a networked structure, including adaptability, resilience, and rapid learning.[94] In its evolution so far, al-Qaida has proved both adaptable and robust. From an essentially "visible" organization, running training camps and occupying territory in Afghanistan, al-Qaida has transformed itself into a global jihad movement increasingly consisting of associate groups and ad hoc cells all over the world.[95] Despite losing its base in Afghanistan, al-Qaida has not lost its ability to mount terrorist attacks. The attacks against the Ghriba synagogue in Tunisia in April 2002 provided the first signs of the movement's resiliency. These incidents were followed by attacks in Pakistan (May 2002); Kuwait, Yemen, and Indonesia (October 2002); Kenya (November 2002); Turkey (November 2003); Madrid (March 2004); London (July 2005); Jordan (November 2005); and Algeria (December 2007). Add to this a series of spectacular plots that have been foiled only by a concentrated international effort by police and intelligence services.

Yet, like its predecessors, the al-Qaida network reveals familiar weaknesses. In this section we highlight three points that cast doubt on the strength of al-Qaida as a networked actor. First, al-Qaida carried out its most successful missions when it was relatively hierarchically structured. The al-Qaida that perpetrated the September 11, 2001, attacks was not really organized as a network. Indeed, many of al-Qaida's traditional strengths seem to build on a hierarchical structure, which has been increasingly difficult to sustain as the organization has come under stress. Second, as the organization fans out into a more loosely structured network, it appears to be losing unity, cohesion, and collective-action capacity. To regain capacity for large-scale attacks, al-Qaida may have to recentralize at least some of its core activities; yet this will make it more vulnerable to attack. Third, although the al-Qaida network has perpetrated some spectacular terrorist attacks, many more plots have been foiled.[96]

93. Much has been written and said about al-Qaida, and we do not pretend to be experts. What we have to say is all based on publicly available information.
94. See, for example, Gunaratna, *Inside Al Qaeda;* David Benjamin and Steven Simon, *The Age of Sacred Terror: Radical Islam's War against America* (New York: Random House, 2003); Jason Burke, *Al-Qaeda: Casting a Shadow of Terror* (London: I.B. Tauris, 2003); and Sageman, *Understanding Terror Networks.*
95. Cronin, "How al-Qaida Ends."
96. A statement in November 2006 by Eliza Manningham-Buller, then director-general of the British Security Service, indicated that authorities were aware of nearly thirty plots, many with links to al-Qaida in Pakistan. See Bruce Hoffman, "The Myth of Grass-Roots Terrorism: Why Osama bin Laden Still Matters," *Foreign Affairs,* Vol. 87, No. 3 (May/June 2008), pp. 133–138.

That a majority plots by the world's allegedly best-led and best-trained terrorist organizat are foiled is perhaps of scant comfort to police chiefs and frightened publ , but it does throw doubt on the network as a superior organizational form

HIERARCHY AS TO SUCCESS

What is most re aling, perhaps, is the evidence that al-Qaida's most successful operations t place when the organization possessed a hierarchical structure. In the 19 al-Qaida had a significant degree of hierarchy and formal organization in top tier, though lower levels remained more loosely structured. Organiza nally, the core of al-Qaida (central staff) was a tight hierarchy with Osama n Laden at the top, supported by a *shura majlis* (consultative council). This le ership oversaw a tidy organization of committees with well-defined positio and responsibilities.[97] When defined to include its regional affiliates, al-Qai assumed a more networked form with regional hubs acting as subcontracto who maintained substantial autonomy.[98] But although some operations wer arried out with local autonomy and limited hierarchical management, s essful ones typically received close supervision from above. Indeed, the top r closely managed the 1998 bombings of U.S. embassies in East Africa and e September 11 attacks. Moreover, al-Qaida until 2001 was not stateless; it d Afghanistan under the Taliban as a base to centrally plan and coordinate rrorist operations around the world. Despite conventional wisdom about efficacy of dispersed networks, it appears therefore that many of al-Qai traditional strengths may have built on hierarchy and centralized trainin nd coordination.

NETWORKED VU ERABILITIES

The loss of Afg istan as a base in 2001 scattered al-Qaida, forcing it to adapt by becoming m decentralized and networked. Although observers disagree on the extent to hich al-Qaida's core is still operationally intact, most experts agree that al-Qa today operates less like a top-down structure and more like a loose umbrell roup, offering inspiration and legitimacy to radical Islamists from varying b grounds but not necessarily providing much strategic or tactical support.[99] many the transformation of al-Qaida from a fairly central-

97. The second tie nsisted of a military committee, a finance and business committee, a religious committee, a media and publicity committee. See Gunaratna, *Inside Al Qaeda*, p. 77.
98. Kahler, "Collec Action and Clandestine Networks."
99. Some observers ch as Marc Sageman, argue that al-Qaida has ceased to exist as either an or-

ized hierarchical organization into a more diffuse transnational network has made it a more formidable enemy, better capable of scaling and of avoiding detection. But decentralization and segmentation have also exposed al-Qaida to the gamut of organizational dilemmas associated with a networked structure.

A major problem flowing from a looser networked structure is poorer security. Before the destruction of al-Qaida's logistical infrastructure, the consultative council considered and approved all major operations.[100] Members or associate groups would typically submit proposals to the council, which would select a small number for further development and assist with seed money, training, and tactical support. After al-Qaida was forced to decentralize into smaller operational units, affiliated groups started to act on their own initiative without centralized clearance for attacks and with limited links to the network. The Bali cell, which conducted the 2002 bombings, consisted of around twelve activists that apparently came together of their own initiative, chose their own target, and executed the attack independently.[101] The Madrid train bombings in 2004 were carried out by a local cell of Moroccan immigrants, which was inspired but not directed by al-Qaida.[102] The 2005 London bombings too were carried out autonomously.[103]

As one might expect, enhanced autonomy has led to security problems. Like

---

ganizational or an operational entity; others, such as Bruce Hoffman, insist that "the centre holds." They point to recent intelligence analyses by U.S. and British security services that suggest al-Qaida still exercises top-down planning and command and control capabilities from its new position along the Afghani-Pakistani border. See Hoffman, "The Myth of Grass-Roots Terrorism"; and National Intelligence Council, "National Intelligence Estimate," July 2007. We agree that al-Qaida has not been operationally "neutralized." Pursuit by U.S. and coalition forces has, however, forced it to grow much more dispersed and decentralized.

100. See Peter L. Bergen, *The Osama bin Laden I Know: An Oral History of Al Qaeda's Leader* (New York: Free Press, 2006).

101. The Bali bombing was implemented by a fringe within JI with no input from the majority of the organization, including high-level leadership. See Burke, *Al-Qaeda*, pp. 265–266; Magouirk, Atran, and Sageman, "Connecting Terrorist Networks"; and Pavlova, "From a Counter-Society to a Counter-State Movement."

102. See Jordan, Manas, and Horsburgh, "Strengths and Weaknesses of Grassroot Jihadist Networks"; Loren Vidino, "The Hofstad Group: The New Face of Terrorist Networks in Europe," *Studies in Conflict and Terrorism*, Vol. 30, No. 7 (July 2007), pp. 579–592; and Aidan Kirby, "The London Bombers as 'Self-Starters': A Case Study in Indigenous Radicalization and the Emergence of Autonomous Cliques," *Studies in Conflict and Terrorism*, Vol. 30, No. 5 (May 2007), pp. 415–428.

103. The group responsible for the London bombings appears to have received some support from al-Qaida's network in Pakistan, but the group was not formally linked to al-Qaida and had limited links to the network. See Vidino, "The Hofstad Group"; and Kirby, "The London Bombers as 'Self-Starters.'"

the London boı ers in 2005, newcomers seek guidance, legitimacy, and tactical support froı he network, where they can get it, but are not afraid to act independently. lying on informal connections and rules of conduct and operating in the a ence of institutionalized training or recruitment, many are strikingly naïve out security.[104] Some of the most prominent cells in Europe and North Aı ica, including those in Montreal, London, and Milan, were closely m tored by the police before being uncovered. Recent plots in Britain involve militants under easy surveillance for months and even years.[105] The g p that orchestrated the Madrid bombings also provides a good example c mateurism in autonomous groups. Only one of the group's members had sed through training camps or had experience in terrorist campaigns.[106] T group's lack of professionalism meant it committed grave mistakes, whicl ventually led to its downfall. For example, the bombs the group's membe used were of poor quality, and three of the thirteen bombs did not explod One of these unexploded bombs provided information that led to arrests ju days after the bombings.[107] The group's efforts to secure logistical support so put it in danger. Unlike the September 11 suicide pilots who maintaine few ties with other individuals in the United States, the Madrid group eded to be in close contact with its social environment to gather logistica upport. Lacking secure links to the al-Qaida network, the group's efforts recruit members and acquire arms through local mosques brought them iı contact with a Moroccan police informant, who was posing as an imam, a several police informants on drug matters who almost thwarted the pl [108] This is far from an unusual case. In 2006 seven men in Miami reportedly anning attacks against the Chicago Sears Tower sought to work with som e they thought was an al-Qaida member who turned out to be an FBI infor nt.[109] Lacking formal avenues of access, these militants did not have a secu way of connecting with the greater al-Qaida community. As

104. For evidence c curity naïveté, see Olivier Roy, *Globalized Islam: The Search for a New Ummah* (London: Hurst, 20

105. See, for examp ohn Ward Anderson and Karen DeYoung, "Plot to Bomb U.S.-bound Jets Is Foiled," *Washington st*, April 11, 2006; and David Stringer, "London Subway Attackers Linked to Al-Qaida, Collude th Other Terror Cells," Canadian Press Newswire, April 30, 2007.

106. See Jordan, M as, and Horsburgh, "Strengths and Weaknesses of Grassroot Jihadist Networks."

107. Ibid.

108. Ibid.

109. Jerry Seper, "M ni Terrorism Suspects Planned 'War' against U.S.," *Washington Times*, June 29, 2006.

these examples show, informal links established by dispersed militants are often precarious.[110] The more the al-Qaida network attempts to expand through "weak links," the less secure it may become.

The lack of centralized sanctioning of missions is also proving perilous. To network enthusiasts, al-Qaida's increasingly diffuse structure encourages expansion and innovation through local experimentation. Yet, increased local initiative is a mixed blessing. Take the example of Zuhair Hilal Mohammed al-Tubaiti, who was arrested for planning an operation against U.S. naval vessels in the Strait of Gibraltar. Upon his arrest, he told the Moroccan authorities that al-Qaida had originally rejected him for a martyrdom mission. Reduced hierarchical control following the loss of the Afghan base empowered him to experiment on his own instead of waiting for approval from above.[111] Although he acted alone, his failure harmed the wider organization via his betrayal of sensitive information.

Al-Qaida has also displayed weaknesses in coordination and strategic planning.[112] The 1999 millennial plot against the Los Angeles airport fell apart when the plotters were identified and arrested, one by one, until Ahmed Ressam was left to carry it out on his own. Inexperienced and acting without reliable organizational support, he was easily caught as he tried to enter the United States with a car full of explosives. In 2000 the overloaded boat of explosives targeting the USS *The Sullivans* in the port of Aden actually began sinking before it could do any damage. The locally planned attack against U.S. naval vessels in the Strait of Gibraltar in 2002 appears to have crumbled as a result of communication failures.[113] If the London car bomb plot and Glasgow airport attack discovered in June 2007 are related to al-Qaida, these too reveal poor planning. Even the September 11 attacks show signs of strategic planning failure. Although it demonstrated al-Qaida's ability to hit its "far enemy" at

110. A case in point is Ishtiaque Parker, a student whom Ramzi Yousef, one of the conspirators in the 1993 World Trade Center bombing, attempted to recruit. Yousef wanted to use Parker to transport explosives but their connection was weak. Parker eventually betrayed information leading to Yousef's arrest in 1995. See Bill Keller, "Self-portrait of Informer: An Innocent," *New York Times*, February 21, 1995; and Sageman, *Understanding Terror Networks*, p. 109.

111. Francina Bester, "New Trends in Contemporary International and Transnational Terrorism," University of Pretoria, 2007.

112. For these examples, see Alan Cowell, "Police Find Two Car Bombs in Central London," *International Herald Tribune*, June 29, 2007; Elaine Sciolino, "Casablanca Bombers Were Probably Lost," *International Herald Tribune*, May 20, 2003; and Sageman, *Understanding Terror Networks*, pp. 45–56, 99–103.

113. See Bester, "New Trends in Contemporary International and Transnational Terrorism."

home, Septemb 11 turned out to be a disaster for al-Qaida because it led to the destruction its extensive hierarchical infrastructure in Afghanistan.[114] This outcome d not appear to have been anticipated. As Kahler notes, what is striking abou ne planning for September 11 is the apparent absence of efforts to compre d or undermine the likely U.S. response: apart from escaping Afghanista the leadership does not appear to have made substantial efforts to dispe key assets such as their training camps. This and other strategic failures m be the result of a highly secretive organization that thrives on limited soci mbeddeness and whose members are therefore cut off from wider sources nformation.[115] With increased decentralization, such problems are likely worsen.

Learning too s proven feeble in an increasingly diffuse al-Qaida network. In particular, th ss of Afghanistan as a central headquarters for professional training has m e learning a more improvised and unreliable affair. The Casablanca bo ers, for instance, were trained haphazardly on weekend camping trips, l their homemade explosives were erratic, with only one resulting in mas asualties.[116] Improvised learning is also likely to reduce accountability.[1 n the camps, al-Qaida had the opportunity to evaluate trainees, choosing o the best for formal participation in operations. With less hierarchical over ht, members are now left to evaluate their own capacities and learn from eir own mistakes. Rohan Gunaratna refers to al-Qaida as a "learning orga tion," noting that when bin Laden discovered his satellite phone convers ns were being monitored, he used this knowledge to mislead and evad alition forces targeting him at Tora Bora in 2001.[118] Yet al-Qaida at large l still not learned the lesson. Its informal networked militants continue using sily monitored phones. In 2004 London authorities tapped more than 100 one lines during their operation against the militants planning the infam fertilizer bomb attack.[119] Perhaps bin Laden is learning, but the broader ne rk appears less advanced.

The main be it of increased decentralization and segmentation is that it

114. Bergen, *The O* *bin Laden I Know.*
115. According to es Kahler, al-Qaida's relatively closed network simply did not provide it with useful inform n about the motivations and likely actions of its principal adversary, the United States. See ler, "Collective Action and Clandestine Networks."
116. Sageman, *Und anding Terror Networks.*
117. Bester, "New ds in Contemporary International and Transnational Terrorism."
118. Gunaratna, *In Al Qaeda*, p. 107.
119. Stringer, "Lon Subway Attackers Linked to al-Qaida."

has enabled al-Qaida to scale by building informal links to regional hubs.[120] But although many see al-Qaida's increased reliance on informal connections to other groups as an indicator of increasing strength, it can equally be interpreted as a weakness.[121] Indeed, there are signs that growing inclusiveness is leading to a more disjointed and disunited movement. The al-Qaida network has involved ambitious upstarts such as Abu Musab al-Zarqawi, more traditional organizations such as Egyptian Islamic Jihad, regionally focused groups such as Jemaah Islamiyah, ragtag insurgents in Iraq, converts such as John Walker Lindh and Richard Reid, and "home-grown" militants living in Europe, often with little connection to the Middle East. As Richard Matthew and George Shambaugh note, it would be a grave mistake to assume that all the members of al-Qaida share an understanding of goals and strategy.[122] Problems of disunity could be seen already in the 1990s. Fawaz Gerges, for example, argues that the inner group was "riven by ethnic, regional, and ideological rivalries."[123] Such problems intensified in the late 1990s. After 1998, when bin Laden called for abandoning the struggle against the "near enemy" in favor of global jihad against the United States, al-Qaida lost many members who hesitated to take on the United States.[124] As the network fans out, new rifts are emerging. Challenging the West means different things to different cells that are often engaged in local power struggles. The increasing autonomy of leaders within the network has also fueled acute internal conflicts, limiting expansion and collective action. For example, when Ayman al-Zawahiri brought his Egyptian Islamic Jihad organization into the fold of al-Qaida, several of his top lieutenants opposed the merger and left.[125]

---

120. A sample of groups that are allegedly connected to al-Qaida includes the Moro Islamic Liberation Front (Philippines), Jemaah Islamiyah (Southeast Asia), Egyptian Islamic Jihad, al-Ansar Mujahidin (Chechnya), al-Gama'a al-Islamiyya (Egypt), the Abu Sayyaf Group (Philippines), Hezbollah (Lebanon), the Islamic Movement of Uzbekistan, the Salafist Group for Call and Combat (Algeria), and Harakat ul-Mujahidin (Pakistan). See Daniel Byman, "Al-Qaeda as an Adversary: Do We Understand Our Enemy?" *World Politics*, Vol. 56, No. 1 (October 2003), pp. 139–163, at p. 258; and Cronin, "How al-Qaida Ends," p. 33.
121. See Cronin, "How al-Qaida Ends," pp. 33–34.
122. Richard Matthew and George Shambaugh, "The Limits of Terrorism: A Network Perspective," *International Studies Review*, Vol. 7, No. 4 (December 2005), pp. 617–627.
123. Fawaz A. Gerges, *The Far Enemy: Why Jihad Went Global* (Cambridge: Cambridge University Press, 2005), p. 19, quoted in Kahler, "Collective Action and Clandestine Networks."
124. Sageman, *Understanding Terror Networks*, pp. 45–47; Burke, *Al-Qaeda*, p. 150; and Brooke, "Jihadist Strategic Debates before 9/11."
125. Roy, *Globalized Islam*, p. 73.

AN ADAPTIVE N VORK OF A CENTRALIZED ORGANIZATION IN DECLINE?

The above disc sion suggests a network plagued by internal conflict and coordination pı lems. The diverse, dispersed community that makes up al-Qaida is likely grow increasingly fragile as the memories of Afghanistan fade. Al-Qaida arly has relied on the common experiences of the mujahideen in Afghan ın and the Afghan training camps as a main source of identification and int ation.[126] After the loss of the camps, militants from around the world can longer meet face-to-face in a central location, where they might forge str social ties, unity of purpose, and a clear sense of belonging. Contrary to th xpectation of organizational network theory, the loss of a stable central b may reduce al-Qaida's ability to scale by attracting new recruits.[127]

Forcing al-Q a to adopt a more networked structure may have done a lot to reduce th errorist threat. Perhaps the best indication of the network's increased fragi is the changing nature of its operations. Al-Qaida continues to inspire v ent actions around the world. Yet, following September 11, al-Qaida has d onstrated little ability to plan and execute complex attacks. Since 2001, ter ist actions linked to jihadist groups have nearly all been aimed at soft (n governmental) targets, and all appear to have been initiated by local groups th scant involvement by the al-Qaida leadership.[128] Indeed, Gerges notes, a)aida may have been reduced to "desperate local affiliates and cells," and hat remains of the core is "an ideological label, a state of mind, and a m lizational outreach program to incite attacks worldwide."[129] If al-Qaida as a ınd name or ideology succeeds in inspiring widespread violence, then this clearly a dangerous trend, but it is not one that can be attributed to the stre th of the network itself.

Conclusion

The prevailing ture painted by mass media, public officials, and academics concerned with ıternational terrorist organizations and other criminal net-

---

126. Raab and Mil d, "Dark Networks as Problems," p. 20.
127. See Kahler, "C ctive Action and Clandestine Networks." The reconfiguration of al-Qaida along the Pakistan rder may provide a new "base" but is likely to be a poor match for the Afghan safe haven.
128. Sageman, *Unc ınding Terror Networks*, pp. 52–55.
129. Gerges, *The Enemy*, p. 40, quoted in Kahler, "Collective Action and Clandestine Networks."

works is that of a mounting danger, relentlessly on the increase around the world with governments severely hampered in their ability to combat it. But is this view justified? Theoretical arguments for why we should expect networks to be so formidable are unpersuasive, and a brief review of networks in their historical confrontations with states raises doubts about their effectiveness as actors.

To be sure, networks have many potential advantages, including flexibility, scalability, and resilience. Yet, networks cannot enjoy all these advantages at once. The network structure, though making it easier to survive, makes it far harder to engage in concerted action. Efficiency of information and communication, and hence ability to learn, often comes at the expense of covertness and security. Expansion through recruitment based on informal weak ties may enhance a network's potential impact, but it can also reduce trust and security, trigger internal strife, and intensify collective-action problems. As we have shown, a more centralized structure may often be better at dealing with complex tasks. In the end, several of the challenges facing transnational criminal organizations, including distance collaboration, collective action, learning, training, and security, are best tackled by more centralized hierarchical structures. Yet, if diffuse, clandestine, network-based groups seek to increase their organizational capacity through centralization, they will tend to generate new structural vulnerabilities that make them easier to target and neutralize.[130]

Knowing one's adversary, understanding how he is organized and what advantage this provides, is key to developing sound responses to security challenges. Many of today's transnational threats are said to be so dangerous precisely because they are evolving into diffuse networks. There is veritable nostalgia for the days of the highly centralized mafia and hierarchical drug cartels. To keep up with today's criminal networks, it is suggested, law enforcement must itself adopt a more networked structure. But this recommendation rests on uncertain logic and evidence. The very fact that problems such as drug trafficking and terrorism persist, despite law enforcement's efforts to combat them, does not imply that networks are superior to the bureaucracies pursuing them. Disadvantages claimed for hierarchies are often based on bad management and are not inherent to form. As we have demonstrated, from an organizational viewpoint, law enforcement agencies enjoy several advantages over clandestine networks, such as centralized information processing, moni-

130. Matthew and Shambaugh, "The Limits of Terrorism."

toring of activi , formal training, and reliable organizational memory. All this, combined h a significant force advantage, implies that states can inflict costs on illicit works with a greater efficiency, and for longer periods of time, than illici etworks can with regard to states.

Illicit networ re themselves subject to several weaknesses that may be relatively easy for v enforcement to exploit. Generally, networks may be destabilized by (1) r icing the flow of communication and information through the network; (hampering decisionmaking and consensus formation; and (3) intensifying llective-action problems and security vulnerabilities.[131] As we have shown cursory look at the historical evidence suggests these sorts of failures occu pontaneously in many illicit networks when they come under stress. Law nforcement can precipitate them by targeting networks repeatedly, forcin actors to change their practices abruptly, or sowing doubt and mistrust th ugh infiltration and manipulation of information. Counterterrorism offici may be able to take advantage of organizational splits within terrorist ups by appealing to more moderate members. Indeed, such splits can be en raged. According to reports from prominent dissidents, the internal power ruggle that ripped the Abu Nidal Organization (ANO) in 1989 and led t e execution of more than 150 of its members and 22 of its leaders was ins ated by PLO agents who persuaded some members that the random violen perpetrated by ANO harmed the Palestinian cause.[132]

Terrorism an rganized crime are complicated, eclectic phenomena that have multiple ses and require multifaceted responses. In this article we have sought on o draw attention to, and to question, structural features that are claimed to lvantage networked criminals vis-à-vis law enforcement. Again, we are arguing that illicit networks pose no significant threat to state security. B f they are formidable enemies, it is probably not due to their networked stru re so much as other factors, such as the personal attributes of their membe r their sheer depth in numbers. The argument that a hierarchical structure es not per se disadvantage state actors should not lead to complacency al t the way illicit networks are combated, and there is much room for impro nent in the way counterterrorism and drug law enforcement are practiced. A tates have widely realized, we need better international re-

131. See Kathleen M arley, Ju-Sung Lee, and David Krackhardt, "Destabilizing Networks," *Connections*, Vol. 24, N (Winter 2001), pp. 79–92.
132. Youssef M. Ibr m, "Arabs Say Deadly Power Struggle Has Split Abu Nidal Terror Group," *New York Times*, N nber 12, 1989.

sponses to transnational threats, along with smoother intelligence sharing and interagency cooperation. Red tape can also be profitably reduced. Yet, bureaucracy may still be better than its alternatives. Despite the current mood of skepticism about traditional, inflexible bureaucracies, centrally instituted changes do reduce inefficiencies. In a network, inefficient practices and red tape may be bypassed more easily by autonomous local players, but the resulting ad hoc solutions may prove counterproductive. Although law enforcement agencies may still have far to go, there is nothing inherent in the network form that makes it impossible for hierarchical state structures to combat networked adversaries.

Part IV:
The Future of Terrorism

How al-Qaida Ends

The Decline and Demise of Terrorist Groups

Audrey Kurth Cronin

The war on terrorism might be perpetual, but the war on al-Qaida will end. Although the al-Qaida network is in many ways distinct from its terrorist predecessors, especially in its protean ability to transform itself from a physical to a virtual organization, it is not completely without precedent. And the challenges of devising an effective response over the long term to a well-established international group are by no means unique. Al-Qaida shares elements of continuity and discontinuity with other terrorist groups, and lessons to be learned from the successes and failures of past and present counterterrorist responses may be applicable to this case. Current research focuses on al-Qaida and its associates, with few serious attempts to analyze them within a broader historical and political context. Yet this context sheds light on crucial assumptions and unanswered questions in the campaign against al-Qaida. What do scholars know about how terrorist movements end? What has worked in previous campaigns? Which of those lessons are relevant to understanding how, and under what circumstances, al-Qaida will end?

Radical Islamists will pose a threat to the United States and its interests for a long time to come. But there is a difference between sporadic and local acts of terrorism by religious extremists and the coordinated growth of al-Qaida, with its signature of meticulous planning, mass casualties, and global reach. A central assumption of early U.S. planning was that the elimination of al-Qaida would bring the war on terrorism (or the global struggle against violent extremism) to an end. Yet al-Qaida itself is a moving target, with experts arguing that it has changed structure and form numerous times. As a result, the strategy to counter this group is composed of tactics such as targeting its leader, Osama bin Laden, and his top lieutenants and denying the organization the ability, finances, and territory to regroup. Similar approaches have been employed against other terrorist organizations, with sharply varied outcomes.

Audrey Kurth Cronin is Director of Studies of the Changing Character of War Program at Oxford University. She is also on the university's international relations faculty.

The author is indebted to Robert Art, David Auerswald, John Collins, Patrick Cronin, Timothy Hoyt, Joel Peters, Harvey Rishikof, Adam Roberts, Karen Wilhelm, and former colleagues and students at the U.S. National War College. The detailed comments of an anonymous reviewer were invaluable, and the Leverhulme Trust provided much-appreciated financial support.

International Security, Vol. 31, No. 1 (Summer 2006), pp. 7–48

Careful analysis comparable situations can shed light on what is required to close out an ep dominated by al-Qaida terrorism.

Terrorism stu s are often event driven, spurred by attacks and the need to analyze and res nd more effectively to a specific threat.[1] As a result, the bulk of traditional r arch on terrorism has been descriptive analysis focused on one group, deta ng its organization, structure, tactics, leadership, and so on. True to this pat n, since the terrorist attacks of September 11, 2001, there has been an outpou g of research (bad and good) on al-Qaida, but little attention to analyzing it oss functional lines within a wider body of knowledge and research on ter ist groups. To the extent that broader crosscutting research has been done, weight of it rests on questions of the causes of this threat, as well as the uably narrow matters of the weapons and methods being used or likely t e used. This agenda reflects the strengths of the established international se rity and defense community, where there is far more expertise, for examp on nuclear weapons and proliferation than on the Arabic-speaking netw s that might use them, on operational methods such as suicide attacks th on the operatives who employ them, and on the causes of wars than on h they end. Yet just as war termination may be more vital in its implications the international system than how wars begin, the question of how the al-Q la movement ends may be vital to understanding the strategic implications r the United States, its allies, and the shape of the new era.

The question how terrorist groups decline is insufficiently studied, and the available re rch is virtually untapped. Yet it has a raft of implications for the challenges ed by al-Qaida and its associates, as well as for the counterterrorist policie f the United States and its allies, many of which reflect little awareness or s tiny of the assumptions upon which they rest. For example, national leader cus on the capture or death of bin Laden as a central objective in the cam gn against al-Qaida.[2] Past experience with the decapitation of terrorist gro , however, is not seriously examined for insights into this case. Some ana s concentrate on the root causes of terrorism and urge policies that will sh local public support away from al-Qaida, suggesting a long-term approach ard the movement's gradual decline. Experience from cases where populati s have become unwilling to support other causes is little

1. On this point, se ederick Schulze, "Breaking the Cycle: Empirical Research and Postgraduate Studies on Terrorism in Andrew Silke, ed., *Research on Terrorism: Trends, Achievements, and Failures* (London: Frank Ca 2004), pp. 161–185.
2. See, for example IA Chief Has 'Excellent Idea' Where bin Laden Is," June 22, 2005, http://www.cnn.com/200 S/06/20/goss.bin.laden/index.html.

tapped, and resulting changes in the behavior of terrorist organizations separated from their constituencies are hardly known. In other cases, the use of force or other repressive measures against terrorist groups has been successful. Yet the conditions under which that approach has succeeded or failed have not been examined for parallels with al-Qaida. Most observers assume that negotiations would never lead to the end of al-Qaida because it has nonnegotiable, apocalyptic demands. But experience with other terrorist groups that had open-ended or evolving demands is little scrutinized. In short, the substantial history of how terrorism declines and ceases has not been analyzed for its potential relevance to al-Qaida.

The argument here is that past experience with the decline of terrorist organizations is vital in dealing with the current threat, and that the United States and its allies must tap into that experience to avoid prior mistakes and to effect al-Qaida's demise. The article proceeds in four sections. The first provides a brief review of previous research on how terrorism declines or ends; the second is an examination of the endings of other relevant terrorist organizations, with an eye toward determining what has worked in previous campaigns and why; the third offers an analysis of al-Qaida's unique characteristics to determine where comparisons with other groups are appropriate and where they are not; and the fourth addresses how what came before has implications for U.S. and allied policy toward al-Qaida today.

Previous Research on How Terrorism Ends

The study of terrorism is often narrowly conceived and full of gaps; it is not surprising, therefore, that the question of how the phenomenon ends is understudied. The vast majority of contemporary research on terrorism has been conducted by scholars who are relatively new to the subject and unaware of the body of work that has gone before: in the 1990s, for example, 83 percent of the articles published in the major journals of terrorism research were produced by individuals writing on the subject for the first time.[3] Thus far they have made little effort to build on past conclusions, with only halting and disappointing progress in understanding the phenomenon outside its present political context.[4] Not unrelated, a crippling aspect of much of the research on

3. Andrew Silke, "The Road Less Travelled: Recent Trends in Terrorism Research," in Silke, *Research on Terrorism*, p. 191.
4. Andrew Silke, "An Introduction to Terrorism Research," in Silke, *Research on Terrorism*, pp. 1–29.

terrorism is its n applied nature; analysts willing to examine more than one group or broac noncontemporary, conceptual questions are rare.[5] This is somewhat und andable, given that different groups undertake terrorist acts for different re ns, and it is safer to specialize; efforts to accelerate the demise of al-Qaid however, require more lateral thinking. The thinness of terrorism studies y be giving way to more sustained substantive research in the post–Septe r 11 world, though it is too early to say whether current attention will pe t and mature.

Nonetheless, ious research conducted thus far has produced several overlapping themes d approaches in three areas: the relationship between how a terrorist group gins and ends; the search for predictable cycles or phases of terrorist activit nd the comparison of historical counterterrorism cases.

LINKS BETWEEN GINNINGS AND ENDINGS

Hypotheses ab how terrorist groups end are frequently connected to the broader body o ypotheses about what causes terrorism.[6] The assumption is that the origins terrorism persist throughout the life of terrorist organizations and shed ght on sources of their eventual demise. But this is often an oversimplifi ion. Given the close ties between terrorism analysis and government su ort, when the perception of imminent attacks subsides, support for sol research declines. Work on a declining or defunct terrorist group is theref typically sparser than is the tackling of its origins and evolution. With such glaring imbalance in the available research, great care must be taken in ge alizing about beginnings and endings of specific terrorist groups.

Recognition he interplay of internal and external forces in the evolution of terrorism is o crucial. In any given case, the evolution from political awareness to th ormation (usually) of a terrorist group to the carrying out of a terrorist attac a complex process. Some steps in this process may be acci-

---

5. Silke, *Research o rrorism*, pp. 208–209.
6. Martha Crensha "How Terrorism Declines," *Terrorism and Political Violence*, Vol. 3, No. 1 (Spring 1991), p. 7 d Jeffrey Ian Ross and Ted Robert Gurr, "Why Terrorism Subsides: A Comparative Study of da and the United States," *Comparative Politics*, Vol. 21, No. 4 (July 1989), pp. 407–408. Exam of articles on the drivers of terrorism include Michael Mousseau, "Market Civilization and It ash with Terror," *International Security*, Vol. 27, No. 3 (Winter 2002/03), pp. 5–29; and Aud Kurth Cronin, "Behind the Curve: Globalization and International Terrorism," *International rity*, Vol. 27, No. 3 (Winter 2002/03), pp. 30–58. See also Charles Knight and Melissa Murphy, a Michael Mousseau, "Correspondence: The Sources of Terrorism," *International Security*, Vol. No. 2 (Fall 2003), pp. 192–198.

dental or opportunistic.[7] Likewise, the process by which a terrorist group declines may be as much determined by innate factors as by external policies or actors.[8] A group may make a bad decision, engage in a counterproductive strategy, or simply implode. It may also have an innate compulsion to act—for example, it may be driven to engage in terrorist attacks to maintain support, to shore up its organizational integrity, or even to foster its continued existence.[9]

Studies of the causes of terrorism frequently begin with analyses of the role of individual operatives or their leaders. These include examinations of the psychologies of individual terrorists,[10] "profiles" of terrorists (and future terrorists) and their organizations,[11] assessments of the conditions that encourage or enable individuals to resort to terrorism,[12] and studies of the distinctive characteristics of terrorist leaders and their followers.[13] The relationship be-

7. For more on this argument, especially as it relates to the causes of terrorism, see Audrey Kurth Cronin, "Sources of Contemporary Terrorism," in Cronin and James M. Ludes, eds., *Attacking Terrorism: Elements of a Grand Strategy* (Washington, D.C.: Georgetown University Press, 2004), pp. 19–45, especially p. 22.

8. See United States Institute of Peace, "How Terrorism Ends," Special Report, No. 48 (Washington, D.C.: United States Institute of Peace, May 25, 1999), especially the overview section written by Martha Crenshaw, pp. 2–4.

9. For example, Bruce Hoffman compares al-Qaida to the archetypal shark that must continue swimming to survive. See, for example, Ann Scott Tyson, "Al-Qaeda Broken, but Dangerous," *Christian Science Monitor,* June 24, 2002. See also Martha Crenshaw, "Decisions to Use Terrorism: Psychological Constraints on Instrumental Reasoning," *International Social Movements Research,* Vol. 4 (1992), pp. 29–42.

10. Among numerous sources on these subjects, see Martha Crenshaw, "The Psychology of Terrorism: An Agenda for the Twenty-first Century," *Political Psychology,* Vol. 21, No. 2 (June 2000), pp. 405–420; Martha Crenshaw, "The Logic of Terrorism," in Walter Reich, ed., *Origins of Terrorism: Psychologies, Ideologies, Theologies, States of Mind,* 2d ed. (Washington, D.C.: Woodrow Wilson Center Press, 1998), pp. 7–24; and Jerrold Post, "Terrorist Psycho-Logic," in Reich, *Origins of Terrorism,* pp. 25–40.

11. This approach is well established in criminology and intelligence analysis. See, for example, Irene Jung Fiala, "Anything New? The Racial Profiling of Terrorists," *Criminal Justice Studies,* Vol. 16, No. 1 (March 2003), pp. 53–58; Rex A. Hudson, *Who Becomes a Terrorist and Why? The 1999 Government Report on Profiling Terrorists* (Guilford, Conn.: Lyons, 2002); and Paul R. Pillar, "Counterterrorism after al-Qaeda," *Washington Quarterly,* Vol. 27, No. 3 (Summer 2004), p. 105. As Pillar points out, the Transportation Security Administration already uses profiling to screen airline passengers. Ibid.

12. See, for example, Alan Krueger and Jitka Maleckova, "Education, Poverty, Political Violence, and Terrorism: Is There a Causal Connection?" Working Paper, No. 9074 (Cambridge, Mass.: National Bureau of Economic Research, July 2002), p. 2; Alan Richards, *Socio-economic Roots of Radicalism? Towards Explaining the Appeal of Islamic Radicals* (Carlisle, Pa.: Strategic Studies Institute, Army War College, July 2003); Daniel Pipes, "God and Mammon: Does Poverty Cause Militant Islam?" *National Interest,* No. 66 (Winter 2001/2002), pp. 14–21; and Gary T. Dempsey, "Old Folly in a New Disguise: Nation Building to Combat Terrorism," Policy Analysis Series, No. 429 (Washington, D.C.: Cato Institute, March 21, 2002).

13. See, for example, Leonard Weinberg and William Lee Eubank, "Leaders and Followers in Italian Terrorist Groups," *Terrorism and Political Violence,* Vol. 1, No. 2 (April 1989), pp. 156–176.

tween the moti ions and characteristics of individual operatives, on the one hand, and the ı ıns to end their violent attacks, on the other, is implied but not always obv ıs.

Another app ch especially favored among terrorism experts is analyzing the organizatio dynamics of the group. Important late-twentieth-century research conclud hat terrorism is essentially a group activity: by understanding the dynami of the group, including its shared ideological commitment and group ide y, analysts can isolate the means of ending its terrorist attacks.[14] The foc is thus on the dynamics of relationships between members as a way of gai g insight into the vulnerability of the group's hierarchy, the weaknesses of organizational structure, the group's ideology and worldview, and so or vhich in turn potentially sheds light on how a group might unravel. Such ı arch analyzes the behavior of the terrorist group from the perspective of t needs of the organization itself, an approach that was particularly influenti in studying the behavior of leftist and ethnonationalist/separatist grou of the 1970s and 1980s.[15]

Many analys however, question the relevance of this well-established approach in an er f decentralized, nonhierarchical cell structures that are able to exploit infor ion technology and the tools of globalization.[16] The internet is emerging as t critical new dimension of twenty-first-century global terrorism, with webs and electronic bulletin boards spreading ideological messages, perpetua g terrorist networks, providing links between operatives in cyberspace, anc ıaring violent images to demonstrate ruthlessness and incite followers to ac ı.[17] Likewise, a growing emphasis on individual initiative, the presence of ssion-driven organizations operating with an understanding

14. For an organiz ıal analysis of terrorist groups, see David C. Rapoport, ed., *Inside Terrorist Organizations*, 2d e ondon: Frank Cass, 2001).
15. Martha Crensh "Theories of Terrorism: Instrumental and Organizational Approaches," in Rapoport, *Inside Te ist Organizations*, pp. 19–27.
16. See, for examp ın O. Lesser, Bruce Hoffman, John Arguilla, David Ronfeldt, and Michele Zanini, *Countering lew Terrorism* (Santa Monica, Calif.: RAND, 1999); John Arquilla and David F. Ronfeldt, eds., *N orks and Netwars: The Future of Terror, Crime, and Militancy* (Santa Monica, Calif.: RAND, 200 ınd Ray Takeyh and Nikolas Gvosdev, "Do Terrorist Networks Need a Home?" *Washingto uarterly*, Vol. 25, No. 3 (Summer 2002), pp. 97–108; and Matthew Levitt, "Untangling the T Web: Identifying and Counteracting the Phenomenon of Crossover between Terrorist Gr ," *SAIS Review*, Vol. 24, No. 1 (Winter–Spring 2004), pp. 33–48.
17. Steve Coll and ın B. Glasser, "Terrorists Turn to the Web as Base of Operations," *Washington Post*, August 7, 5; Craig Whitlock, "Briton Used Internet as His Bully Pulpit," *Washington Post*, August 8, 200 nd Susan B. Glasser, and Steve Coll, "The Web as Weapon: Zarqawi Intertwines Acts on Gr d in Iraq with Propaganda Campaign on the Internet," *Washington Post*, August 9, 2005.

of the commander's intent, and a lack of traditional logistical trails all have implications for analyzing how terrorist groups end. Cells that operate independently are much more difficult to eliminate and can even gain a kind of immortality. Mission-driven groups are designed to be self-perpetuating and may not fit traditional organizational models of how terrorism ends.

The nature of the grievance that drives a terrorist organization has some bearing on the speed and likelihood of its decline.[18] On average, modern terrorist groups do not exist for long. According to David Rapoport, 90 percent of terrorist organizations have a life span of less than one year; and of those that make it to a year, more than half disappear within a decade.[19] Whether an organization supports a left-wing, right-wing, or ethnonationlist/separatist cause appears to matter in determining its life span. Of these three, terrorist groups motivated by ethnonationalist/separatist causes have had the longest average life span; their greater average longevity seems to result, at least in part, from support among the local populace of the same ethnicity for the group's political or territorial objectives.[20] It is too soon to compile reliable data on the average life span of contemporary terrorist groups motivated by religion (or at least groups that appeal to religious concepts as a mobilizing force); however, the remarkable staying power of early religious terrorist groups such as the Hindu Thugs, in existence for at least 600 years, would seem to indicate the inherent staying power of sacred or spiritually based motivations.[21]

Finally, because of the degree to which terrorism research has been subsidized by governments and biased by later policy imperatives, the role of

18. United States Institute of Peace, "How Terrorism Ends," p. 1.
19. David C. Rapoport, "Terrorism," in Mary Hawkesworth and Maurice Kogan, eds., *Routledge Encyclopedia of Government and Politics*, Vol. 2 (London: Routledge, 1992), p. 1067. This claim admittedly needs to be updated. A good study of the life span of terrorist organizations, including those that gained purchase in the 1990s, is still waiting to be written.
20. In discussing the longevity of terrorist groups, Martha Crenshaw notes only three significant groups with ethnonationalist ideologies that ceased to exist within ten years of their formation. One of these, the National Organization of Cypriot Fighters (Ethniki Organosis Kyprion Agoniston, or EOKA), disbanded because its goal—the liberation of Cyprus—was achieved. By contrast, a majority of the terrorist groups that she lists as having existed for ten years or longer have recognizable ethnonationalist ideologies, including the Irish Republican Army (in its many forms), Sikh separatist groups, Basque Homeland and Freedom (Euskadi Ta Askatasuna, or ETA), various Palestinian nationalist groups, and the Corsican National Liberation Front. See Crenshaw, "How Terrorism Declines," pp. 69–87.
21. David C. Rapoport, "Fear and Trembling: Terrorism in Three Religious Traditions," *American Political Science Review*, Vol. 78, No. 3 (September 1984), pp. 658–677. Rapoport asserts that before the nineteenth century, religion was the only acceptable cause for terrorism, providing a transcendent purpose that rose above the treacherous and petty political concerns of man.

counterterrorisı s often overemphasized. With easier access to government data, researcheı end naturally to stress state behavior. The degree to which terrorist group ·volve independent of government action can be under-appreciated. Th ·esult is a strong bias toward tying the decline of such groups to specific gove nent policies, especially after the fact, even though the relationship betwe cause and effect may be unclear.[22]

CYCLES, STAGES, AVES, AND PHASES

Some researche argue that terrorist attacks conform to a temporal pattern that provides ir ;ht into increases and decreases in numbers of attacks. Thus another approa to understanding the life span of a terrorist movement is to search for iden ıble cycles.

Walter Ender nd Todd Sandler assert that long-term analysis of terrorism trends during t late twentieth century indicates that transnational terrorist attacks run in c es, with peaks approximately every two years. Enders and Sandler's cycle e tracked across terrorist groups worldwide, shedding light on the likeliho of an attack coming from someone somewhere; indeed, before September they correctly predicted enhanced danger of a high-casualty terrorist attack. t like strategic intelligence that provided general but not tactical warning o e September 11 attacks, Enders and Sandler's findings were of limited use predicting where the attack would occur, by which group, and by what m s.[23] The apparent existence of global statistical patterns is interesting, but it ovides no insight into the decline of specific terrorist groups. In his attempt ıse mathematical analysis to determine risk assessment for al-Qaida attack onathan Farley likewise concluded that while the connections between c can be quantitatively modeled, assumptions about how individual cells rate may be wrong.[24] The usefulness of statistical models based on a larg ıumber of assumptions to determine a specific group's decline is limited.

22. Crenshaw, "Ho Terrorism Declines," p. 73.

23. Walter Enders Todd Sandler, "Transnational Terrorism, 1968–2000: Thresholds, Persistence, and Forecast Southern Economic Journal, Vol. 71, No. 3 (January 2004), pp. 467–482; Todd Sandler, Walter En , and Harvey E. Lapan, "Economic Analysis Can Help Fight International Terrorism," *Challen* anuary/February 1991, pp. 10–17; and Walter Enders and Todd Sandler, "Is Transnational Terr n Becoming More Threatening? A Time-Series Investigation," *Journal of Conflict Resolution,* 44, No. 3 (June 2000), pp. 307–332.

24. Jonathan Dav Farley, "Breaking Al-Qaida Cells: A Mathematical Analysis of Counterterrorism rations (A Guide for Risk Assessment and Decision Making)," *Studies in Conflict and Terroris* Vol. 26, No. 6 (November/December 2003), pp. 399–411. See also Bernard Harris, "Mathemat Methods in Combatting Terrorism," *Risk Analysis,* Vol. 24, No. 4 (August 2004), pp. 985–988.

Other experts have focused on the existence of developmental stages through which all terrorist groups evolve, especially psychological stages of growing alienation or moral disengagement for groups, individuals, or both.[25] Leonard Weinberg and Louise Richardson have explored the applicability of a conflict theory framework—including stages of emergence, escalation, and de-escalation—to the life cycles of terrorist groups. They conclude that the framework is useful in examining terrorist groups originating or operating in Western Europe in the late twentieth century, but urge more research in this area to determine whether it is applicable to other places and periods.[26]

Still other analysts suggest that specific types of groups may possess their own developmental stages. Ehud Sprinzak, for example, argued that right-wing groups exhibit a unique cyclical pattern. Driven by grievances specific to their particular group, members direct their hostility against "enemy" segments of the population defined by who they are—with regard to race, religion, sexual preference, ethnicity, and so on—not by what they do. To the extent that the government then defends the target population, the former also becomes a "legitimate" target. But the cycle of violence reflects underlying factors that may continue to exist, and that can experience periods of flare-up and remission, depending on the degree to which the government is able to bring campaigns of violence under control.[27]

Other researchers study the evolution of terrorist groups as types of social movements and are intellectual descendants of Ted Robert Gurr.[28] The more highly developed literature on social movements posits, for example, that terrorism may appear at the end of a cycle of the rise and fall of movements of mass protest.[29] Social movements may just as easily be drawn toward more

25. For example, referring to the case study of the Weathermen, Ehud Sprinzak argues that left-wing groups evolve through three stages: crisis of confidence, conflict of legitimacy, and crisis of legitimacy. See Sprinzak, "The Psychopolitical Formation of Extreme Left Terrorism in a Democracy: The Case of the Weatherman," in Reich, *Origins of Terrorism*, pp. 65–85. For another argument about the psychological phases for terrorist groups, see Albert Bandura, "Mechanisms of Moral Disengagement," in Reich, *Origins of Terrorism*, pp. 161–191.

26. Leonard Weinberg and Louise Richardson, "Conflict Theory and the Trajectory of Terrorist Campaigns in Western Europe," in Silke, *Research on Terrorism*, pp. 138–160.

27. Ehud Sprinzak, "Right-Wing Terrorism in Comparative Perspective: The Case of Split Delegitimization," in Tore Bjorgo, ed., *Terrorism from the Extreme Right* (London: Frank Cass, 1995), pp. 17–43.

28. Ted Robert Gurr, *Why Men Rebel* (Princeton, N.J.: Princeton University Press, 1970). There is a rich literature from the 1960s and 1970s on political violence, of which terrorism is arguably a subset. Gurr defines political violence as "all collective attacks within a political community against the political regime, its actor—including competing political groups as well as incumbents—or its policies." Ibid., pp. 3–4.

29. Crenshaw, "How Terrorism Declines," p. 82. See also John O. Voll, "Bin Laden and the New Age of Global Terrorism," *Middle East Policy*, Vol. 8, No. 4 (December 2001), pp. 1–5; and Quintan

positive means, owever. Understanding the pattern of mobilization may be important for d ecting the origins of an established group but may not be as revealing of its ely end. On the whole, research on social movements gives more insight int he origins of terrorist groups than it does into their decline.

Finally, Rapo rt posits another broad hypothesis on the life cycles of terrorist groups. He a ues that over the course of modern history, waves of international terrorist tivity last about a generation (approximately forty years). These waves ar haracterized by expansion and contraction and have an international cha ter, with similar activities in several countries driven by a common ideolo . Two factors are critical to Rapoport's waves: (1) a transformation in comn ication or transportation patterns, and (2) a new doctrine or culture. Yet alth gh a wave is composed of terrorist organizations and their activities, the tv need not exist concurrently. Rapoport argues that because most individua rganizations have short life spans, they often disappear before the overar ng wave loses force. The current wave of jihadist terrorism may be differe however, because unlike earlier waves of the modern era, this one is driv by a religious (not a secular) cause. Rapoport is therefore reluctant to predi its end.[30]

COMPARATIVE C NTERTERRORISM CASES

Cyclical hypot es are notoriously difficult to formulate and difficult to prove; they can quire so much generalization and qualification that their relevance to speci groups becomes remote. As with many international security questions, alternative approach has been to assemble volumes of comparative ca studies that draw parallel lessons about terrorist organizations, including w they declined and ended or were defeated.[31] These, too,

Wiktorowicz, "Fran g Jihad: Intra-movement Framing Contests and al-Qaida's Struggle for Sacred Authority," *In ational Review of Social History,* Vol. 49, Supp. 12 (December 2004), pp. 159–177.

30. David C. Rapo , "The Four Waves of Modern Terrorism," in Cronin and Ludes, *Attacking Terrorism,* pp. 46–7 nd David C. Rapoport, "The Fourth Wave: September 11 in the History of Terrorism," *Curren story,* December 2001, pp. 419–424.

31. The best of th is Martha Crenshaw's edited book *Terrorism in Context* (University Park: Pennsylvania State versity Press, 1995), because it examines both the evolution of terrorist organizations and th unterterrorist techniques used against them. It explains terrorism as part of broader processes olitical and social change. Reflecting its own historical context, however, there is a strong bia ward left-wing and ethnonationalist/separatist groups. In the wake of September 11, Yonah ander produced an edited volume of comparative case studies, *Combating Terrorism: Strategies Ten Countries* (Ann Arbor: University of Michigan Press, 2002), which emphasizes countert ist techniques used mainly against European groups. Another promising study is Robert J. and Louise Richardson, *Democracy and Terrorism: Lessons from the Past* (Washington, D.C.: ited States Institute of Peace, forthcoming).

present a host of challenges. First, terrorism studies often look primarily at the attributes of a particular group or at the counterterrorist policies of a state. Rarely are both equally well considered. Because of the heavy state interest in combating terrorism, the emphasis is understandably on a comparison of counterterrorist techniques used by states over the life span of each group, with policy implications for current challenges. Second, with their focus on a relatively narrow functional question, comparative terrorism cases can fall victim to superficiality: regional experts can be reluctant to cede ground to strategic studies experts whom they consider interlopers in their geographic/linguistic/cultural ambit. For this reason, many comparative studies are published as edited collections of articles by regional experts, but these in turn can fail to control relevant variables and to coalesce on a central theme. Third, access to data is a big problem: conducting primary research on contemporary terrorist groups is difficult because making contact with operatives or their targets can be dangerous for both the researchers and their contacts. In addition, governments may restrict access to relevant written sources.[32] Fourth, because of the political nature of terrorism, researchers operate at the intersections of sensitive ideas; maintaining objectivity in studying behavior that is deliberately designed to shock can prove challenging. Finally, studying this phenomenon over a range of terrorist groups in different cultural, historical, and political contexts requires generalization and risks the introduction of distortions when making comparisons.[33] The best case studies are usually completed years after a group has ceased to exist; as a result, their applicability to current challenges is limited. For any given group, it is vital to identify characteristics that distinguish it from its predecessors and those that do not.

How Other Terrorist Groups Have Ended

There are at least seven broad explanations for, or critical elements in, the decline and ending of terrorist groups in the modern era: (1) capture or killing of the leader, (2) failure to transition to the next generation, (3) achievement of the group's aims, (4) transition to a legitimate political process, (5) undermin-

32. Crenshaw, "How Terrorism Declines," p. 70.
33. Crenshaw, "Thoughts on Relating Terrorism to Historical Contexts," in Crenshaw, *Terrorism in Context*, pp. 3–24. One interesting comparative study of terrorist groups in two countries, Canada and the United States, concluded that four factors led to terrorism's decline: preemption, deterrence, burnout, and backlash. Its applicability was limited by the small number of cases, however. Jeffrey Ian Ross and Ted Robert Gurr, "Why Terrorism Subsides: A Comparative Study of Canada and the United States," *Comparative Politics*, Vol. 21, No. 4 (July 1989), pp. 405–426.

ing of popular pport, (6) repression, and (7) transition from terrorism to other forms of \ lence. The relevant factors can be both internal and external: terrorist groups nplode for reasons that may or may not be related to measures taken aga st them. Nor are they necessarily separate and distinct. Indeed individua ase studies of terrorist groups often reveal that more than one dynamic w responsible for their decline. The typical focus on government counterte rist measures slights the capabilities and dynamics of the group itself anc frequently misguided; even among groups that decline in response to cou rterrorist campaigns, the picture remains complex.[34] Counterterrorist tech ques are often best used in combination, and methods can overlap: freque y more than one technique has been employed to respond to a given group a lifferent times. The goal here is to focus on the historical experience of pre\ us groups and study the commonalities, in both the internal and external va bles, so as to determine aspects of the processes of terrorist decline that are levant to al-Qaida. Although listing these seven key factors separately is ad ttedly artificial, they are analyzed consecutively for the sake of argument an convenience (see Table 1).

CAPTURE OR KIL NG OF THE LEADER

The effects of c turing or killing a terrorist leader have varied greatly depending on va les such as the structure of the organization, whether the leader created a ılt of personality, and the presence of a viable successor. Regardless of whe r the removal of a leader results in the demise of the terrorist group, the ent normally provides critical insight into the depth and nature of the gı p's popular support and usually represents a turning point. Recent example f groups that were either destroyed or deeply wounded by the capture of charismatic leader include Peru's Shining Path (Sendero Luminoso), the urdistan Workers' Party (PKK), the Real Irish Republican Army (RIRA), a Japan's Aum Shinrikyo. The U.S. government designates all four as "foreigı rrorist organizations."[35]

---

34. Crenshaw argu hat the decline of terrorism results from the interplay of three factors: the government's resp , the choices of the terrorist group, and the organization's resources. See Crenshaw, "How T rism Declines," p. 80. In another article, she further explores the internal and external factors inting to how government strategies such as deterrence, enhanced defense, and negotiations in ct with terrorist group success, organizational breakdown, dwindling support, and new alter ives for terrorist organizations. See United States Institute of Peace, "How Terrorism Ends," p –5.

35. See the annual . Department of State *Country Reports on Terrorism* (which, beginning in 2004, replaced *Patt of Global Terrorism*) at http://www.state.gov/s/ct/rls/crt. In 2003 the PKK was renamed Kong Gel, which continues to be a designated group.

Table 1. How Terrorist Groups Decline and End

Key Factors[a]	Notable Historical Examples[b]
Capture/Kill leader(s)	Shining Path Kurdistan Workers' Party Real Irish Republican Army Aum Shinrikyo
Unsuccessful generational transition	Red Brigades Second of June Movement Weather Underground Baader-Meinhof group (Red Army Faction) The Order Aryan Resistance Army
Achievement of the cause	Irgun/Stern Gang African National Congress
Transition to a legitimate political process/negotiations	Provisional Irish Republican Army Palestinian Liberation Organization Liberation Tigers of Tamil Eelam[c] Moro Islamic Liberation Front
Loss of popular support	Real Irish Republican Army Basque Homeland and Freedom (ETA) Shining Path
Repression	People's Will Shining Path Kurdistan Workers' Party
Transition out of terrorism:	
toward criminality	Abu Sayyaf Revolutionary Armed Forces of Colombia
toward full insurgency	Khmer Rouge Guatemalan Labor Party/Guatemalan National Revolutionary Unit Communist Party of Nepal-Maoists Kashmiri separatist groups (e.g., Lashkar-e-Toiba and Hizbul Mujahideen) Armed Islamic Group (Algeria)

[a] The factors listed here are not mutually exclusive and can be found in combination.
[b] These are illustrative examples, not a comprehensive list.
[c] This peace process is threatened by renewed violence as this article goes to press.

Shining Path's former leader, Manuel Rubén Abimael Guzmán Reynoso (aka Guzmán), was a highly charismatic philosophy professor who built a powerful Marxist movement through a brutal campaign of executing peasant leaders in Peru's rural areas during the 1980s and early 1990s. Somewhat ironically, Shining Path, which was founded in the late 1960s, began to engage in violence just after the government undertook extensive land reform and restored democracy to t country; the earliest attacks involved the burning of rural ballot boxes in 1980 presidential election.[36] Increased popular access to a university edu on helped Guzmán radicalize a growing cadre of impressionable young llowers. He consolidated his power in part by expelling or executing disse rs, resulting in unquestioned obedience but also a highly individualistic lea rship. By the early 1990s, Shining Path had pushed Peru into a state of near a rchy. Guzmán's capture on September 12, 1992, however, including images the former leader behind bars recanting and asking his followers to lay d n their arms, dealt the group a crushing blow.[37]

The Kurdista Vorkers' Party, an ethnonationalist/separatist group founded in 1974 and ded ted to the establishment of a Kurdish state, also suffered the capture of its c rismatic leader, Abdullah Ocalan.[38] Beginning in 1984, the group launche violent campaign against the Turkish government that claimed as ma as 35,000 lives. Ocalan was apprehended in early 1999 in Kenya (appare as a result of a tip from U.S. intelligence) and returned to Turkey, where urt sentenced him to death.[39] On the day of sentencing, riots and demor ations broke out among Kurdish populations throughout Europe. Ocalan hose sentence was later commuted to life imprisonment, advised his follow to refrain from violence.[40] Renamed the Kurdistan Freedom and Democracy ongress (KADEK) and then Kongra-Gel, the group remains on the U.S. terr t list; however, it has subsequently engaged mainly in political activities o ehalf of the Kurds.[41]

---

36. Audrey Kurth nin, Huda Aden, Adam Frost, and Benjamin Jones, *Foreign Terrorist Organizations*, CRS Repor Congress (Washington, D.C.: Congressional Research Service, February 6, 2004), pp. 103–105, ler Code RL32223.

37. Guzmán was s nced to life in prison in 1992, but the trial was later ruled unconstitutional; he is scheduled to etried (for a second time). His successor, Oscar Ramírez Duran, also known as Feliciano, contin to direct the movement after Guzmán's capture; but as mentioned earlier, the group's membe p sharply plummeted. The State Department has estimated its strength at between 400 and 5 embers, down from as many as 10,000 in the late 1980s and early 1990s. See U.S. Department o ate, *Patterns of Global Terrorism, 2003,* April 2004, http://www.state.gov/documents/organi n/31912.pdf. Duran was likewise captured in July 1999. Some analysts worry that the grou ay resurge, with notable attacks in 2002 and 2003. See Cronin et al., *Foreign Terrorist Organizati* p. 103. Although possible, resurgence on a large scale is unlikely: the capture of Guzmá vas clearly a watershed. See also Art and Richardson, *Democracy and Counterterrorism*.

38. For an explana of the meaning of this term and other main typologies of terrorism, see Cronin, "Behind th urve," pp. 39–42.

39. "U.S. Welcome alan Capture," Agence France-Presse, February 16, 1999. Ocalan's sentence was later commute life in prison.

40. "Turkey Lifts C n Death Sentence," *BBC News*, October 3, 2002, http://news.bbc.co.uk/2/hi/europe/229667 .

41. Cronin et al., *F n Terrorist Organizations*, pp. 53–55.

The Real Irish Republican Army is a splinter group of the Provisional Irish Republican Army that split off in 1997 after refusing to participate in the peace process. It conducted a series of attacks in 1998, including the notorious Omagh bombing, which killed 29 people (including 9 children) and injured more than 200. The Northern Irish community reacted with such outrage that the group declared a cease-fire and claimed that its killing of civilians was inadvertent. In 2000 the RIRA resumed attacks in London and Northern Ireland, focusing exclusively on government and military targets. In March 2001 authorities arrested the group's leader, Michael McKevitt. From an Irish prison, he and forty other imprisoned members declared that further armed resistance was futile and that the RIRA was "at an end." The group currently has between 100 and 200 active members and continues to carry out attacks; nevertheless, its activities have significantly declined since McKevitt's arrest.[42]

Aum Shinrikyo (now known as "Aleph") is essentially a religious cult founded in 1987 by Shoko Asahara, a half-blind Japanese mystic. Asahara claimed that the world was approaching the apocalypse and used an eclectic blend of Tibetan Buddhist, Hindu, Taoist, and Christian thought to attract an international following, primarily in Japan but also in Australia, Germany, Russia, Sri Lanka, Taiwan, and the United States. Asahara declared that the United States would soon initiate Armageddon by starting World War III against Japan and called on the group's members to take extraordinary measures in preparation for the attack. The notable aspects of this group are its international reach and its use of so-called weapons of mass destruction, particularly anthrax and sarin gas. In March 1995, members of Aum Shinrikyo released sarin gas in the Tokyo subway, resulting in the deaths of 12 people and injuries to another 5,000. Asahara was arrested in May 1995 and sentenced to death in February 2004. The group has shrunk from approximately 45,000 members worldwide in 1995 to fewer than 1,000, many of whom live in Russia.[43]

These are just a few of the contemporary cases where the capture or killing of the leader of a terrorist organization proved to be an important element in the organization's decline. Other examples include the arrest of leaders in groups as diverse as France's Direct Action (Action Directe); El Salvador's

42. Ibid., pp. 88–89; and U.S. Department of State, *Patterns of Global Terrorism, 2003.*
43. Cronin et al., *Foreign Terrorist Organizations*, pp. 17–19; and U.S. Department of State, *Patterns of Global Terrorism, 2003.* According to the State Department, in July 2001 a small group of Aum members was arrested in Russia before it could follow through with its plan to set off bombs near the Imperial Palace in Tokyo, free Asahara, and smuggle him into Russia.

People's Libera n Forces (Fuerzas Populares de Liberación); and the U.S. group known a ne Covenant, the Sword, and the Arm of the Lord.[44] From a counterterrorisı erspective, the killing of a terrorist leader may backfire by creating increas publicity for the group's cause and perhaps making the leader a martyı ho will attract new members to the organization (or even subsequent org izations). Che Guevera is the most famous example of this phenomenon.[45] iere is some reason to believe that arresting a leader is more effective in dan ing a group than is killing or assassinating him.[46] But even a humiliating arr can backfire if the incarcerated leader continues to communicate with his roup. Sheikh Omar Abd al-Rahman (the so-called Blind Sheikh), convic l of conspiracy in the 1993 bombing of the World Trade Center, is a not e example.[47] In other cases, imprisoned leaders may prompt further violenc y group members trying to free them (e.g., the Baader-Meinhof group id, again, al-Rahman).[48] Thus, if a leader is captured and jailed, undermi ig his credibility and cutting off inflammatory communications are critica demoralizing his following.

44. Direct Action's r principal leaders, Joelle Aubron, Georges Cipriani, Nathalie Menigon, and Jean-Marc Rouillan ere arrested in February 1987, followed shortly thereafter by Max Frerot, effectively dismantliı he leadership of the group and putting an end to its activities. Members of the People's Libera Forces killed their own deputy leader when she appeared to be interested in negotiating witl ie Salvadoran government; the leader of the group, Salvador Cayetano Carpio, committed ide shortly thereafter, resulting in the disintegration of the group and essentially its absorpt into a larger organization, the Farabundo Martí National Liberation Front. After a four-day sie of their compound in April 1985, eight leaders of the Covenant, the Sword, and the Arm of the d were arrested and imprisoned, effectively ending the group. The Chilean group Manuel Rod ez Patriotic Front Dissidents essentially ceased to exist because of the arrest of its key leaders iı 1990s. The latter reached a peace agreement with the Salvadoran government in 1991. See tl MIPT Terrorism Knowledge Base, a database of domestic and international terrorist organizati at http://www.tkb.org.

45. Che Guevara w aptured and killed by the Bolivian army in October 1967 and subsequently became a legendaı igure who inspired leftist and separatist groups in Latin America and throughout the woı Leila Ali Khaled of the Popular Front for the Liberation of Palestine carried the book *My Friend* with her when she hijacked TWA flight 840 in August 1969. In the United States, the Weather also organized massive protests on the second anniversary of Che's death. Harvey Kushner, *E lopedia of Terrorism* (Thousand Oaks, Calif.: Sage, 2003), pp. 155–156, 372, 406.

46. I am grateful t ia Bloom for sharing this observation.

47. Sheikh Omar is e leader of the Egyptian al-Gama al-Islamiya, which is closely tied with Egyptian Islamic Jil Although imprisoned for life in the United States, he has continued to call on his followers to age in violence, especially against Jews. He was also convicted for plotting to bomb the Hollan id Lincoln Tunnels and the United Nations building and to assassinate Senator Alphonse D'A to and UN Secretary General Boutros Boutros-Ghali. See, for example, Anonymous, *Throu Our Enemies' Eyes: Osama bin Laden, Radical Islam, and the Future of America* (Washington, D.C.: ssey's 2002), p. 274.

48. Members of the ader-Meinhof group engaged in violence during numerous attempts to free their imprisoned c ades, for example. The Blind Sheikh has also prompted violence aimed at his release. Ibid.

INABILITY TO PASS THE CAUSE ON TO THE NEXT GENERATION

The concept of the failure to transition to the next generation is closely related to theories that posit that terrorist violence is associated with the rise and fall of generations, but here it is applied to individual case studies. As mentioned above, the nature of the group's ideology seems to have relevance to the cross-generational staying power of that group. The left-wing/anarchistic groups of the 1970s, for example, were notorious for their inability to articulate a clear vision of their goals that could be handed down to successors after the first generation of radical leaders departed or were eliminated.[49] The Red Brigades, the Second of June Movement, the Japanese Red Army, the Weather Underground Organization/Weathermen, the Symbionese Liberation Army, and the Baader-Meinhof group are all examples of extremely dangerous, violent groups in which a leftist/anarchist ideology became bankrupt, leaving no possibility to transition to a second generation.[50]

Right-wing groups, which draw their inspiration from fascist or racist concepts, can also have difficulty persisting over generations, though, as Martha Crenshaw observes, this may reflect the challenges of tracking them over time rather than their actual disintegration.[51] Examples include the numerous neo Nazi groups in the United States and elsewhere.[52] Still, the racist causes of many of these groups can persist long after the disappearance of the group itself; their movement underground,[53] or their reemergence under a different name or structure, is common.[54] Extensive examinations by academic experts and the Federal Bureau of Investigation of right-wing groups in the United States during the 1990s, especially after the 1995 Oklahoma City bombing, revealed their tendency to operate according to a common modus operandi, ideology, or intent; this includes the so-called leaderless resistance, which involves individual operatives or small cells functioning independently in

49. For an explanation of the major types of terrorist organizations, see Cronin, "Behind the Curve," pp. 39–42.

50. The Red Army Faction, a successor of the Baader-Meinhof group, arguably continued for some years and transitioned to what it called its "third generation," with claims of attacks in the name of the RAF during the 1980s and early 1990s. The degree to which it truly was the same group is debatable. In any case, the dissolution of the Soviet Union severely undermined its ideology. See entry in MIPT Terrorism Knowledge Base.

51. Crenshaw, "How Terrorism Declines," p. 78. On right-wing groups, see Cronin, "Behind the Curve," pp. 39–42.

52. These include the Christian Patriots, the Aryan Nations, the Ku Klux Klan, and The Order (a short-lived faction of Aryan Nations) in the United States, as well as the Anti-Zionist Movement in Italy and the National Warriors of South Africa.

53. In the United States, the Ku Klux Klan is a notable example.

54. Some groups, such as The Order (active between 1982 and 1984), have been idolized by their admirers and continue to exercise influence.

pursuit of an ur rstood purpose.[55] Such organizational decentralization complicates conclus ns about beginnings and endings of right-wing groups, but it may also milita against truly effective generational transition. Furthermore, to support their ctivities, some right-wing groups engage in criminal behavior such as the bing of banks and armored cars, racketeering, and counterfeiting, which, the United States, has provided evidence trails for federal authorities and ndermined group longevity.

The internal cess that occurs during the transition from first- to second-generation terr st leaders is very sensitive. Failure to pass the legacy to a new generation a common historical explanation for a terrorist group's decline or end.

ACHIEVEMENT (THE CAUSE

Some terrorist (anizations cease to exist once they have fulfilled their original objective. T) examples are the Irgun Zvai Leumi (National Military Organization, a known either by its Hebrew acronym ETZEL or simply as Irgun), founded 1931 to protect Jews with force and to advance the cause of an independent wish state, and the African National Congress (ANC). As head of the Irgu Menachem Begin, who would later become prime minister of Israel, order he 1946 bombing of the King David Hotel, headquarters of British rule in estine. The attack killed 92 people and hastened Britain's withdrawal. Irg disbanded with the creation of the state of Israel, when its members transi ned to participation in the new government. The ANC was created in 1912 d turned to terrorist tactics in the 1960s. Its attacks were met with an extreme violent campaign of right-wing counterstrikes as the apartheid regime be n to wane.[56] ANC leader Nelson Mandela, imprisoned for terrorist acts fro 1964 to 1990, was elected South Africa's first president following the end apartheid.[57] The last ANC attack occurred in 1989, and the organization be ne a legal political actor in 1990, having achieved its objective of ending t apartheid regime.

Walter Laque divides terrorist groups that attained their objectives into

---

55. The concept of derless existence" apparently originated with Col. Ulius Louis Amoss, who wrote an essay wit is as the title in 1962. It was later popularized by Louis R. Beam Jr., Aryan Nations leader and mer Texas Ku Klux Klan Grand Dragon leader. See Beam, "Leaderless Resistance," *The Sediti st*, No. 12 (February 1992).
56. During much o is period, the African National Congress was labeled a terrorist organization by the U.S. De tment of Defense but not by the U.S. State Department.
57. The South-Wes frican People's Organization underwent a similar transition: from orchestrating bombings ir nks, stores, schools, and service stations to governing Namibia.

three categories: (1) those with narrow, clearly defined aims that were realistically attainable; (2) those with powerful outside protectors; and (3) those facing imperial powers that were no longer willing or able to hold on to their colonies or protectorates.[58] In the context of twenty-first-century terrorism, additional categories are possible. Although it happens in a minority of cases, using terrorism to achieve an aim does sometimes succeed; to recognize this reality is not to condone the tactic and may even be a prerequisite to effectively countering it.

NEGOTIATIONS TOWARD A LEGITIMATE POLITICAL PROCESS

The opening of negotiations can be a catalyst for the decline or end of terrorist groups, potentially engendering a range of effects. Groups have transitioned to political legitimacy and away from terrorist behavior after the formal opening of a political process. Examples include the Provisional Irish Republican Army, whose participation in the multiparty talks with the British and Irish governments was crucial to the 1998 Good Friday agreement; the Palestine Liberation Organization (PLO), which entered a peace process with Israel during the 1990s; and the Liberation Tigers of Tamil Eelam (LTTE, or Tamil Tigers), which began talks with the Sri Lankan government, brokered by the Norwegian government, in 2002.[59] But the typical scenario for a terrorist group's decline is usually much more complicated than simply the pursuit or achievement of a negotiated agreement.

Despite the successful negotiated outcomes that can result between the major parties, a common effect of political processes is the splintering of groups into factions that support the negotiations (or their outcome) and those that do not. For example, the IRA splintered into the Real Irish Republican Army;[60] and the Popular Front for the Liberation of Palestine (PFLP), Democratic Front for the Liberation of Palestine, and PFLP–General Command (GC) split with the PLO over the Israeli-Palestinian peace process. From a counterterrorist perspective, dividing groups can be a purpose of the negotiations process, as it isolates and potentially strangles the most radical factions. But such splinter-

---

58. For example, among those that had outside protectors, Laqueur includes the Palestinian Arab groups and the Croatian Ustasha. For those facing imperial powers not able to hold on to colonies, he includes the IRA (Britain and Ireland after World War I), the Irgun (Britain and the Palestine Mandate after World War II), and the EOKA (Britain and Cyprus, also after World War II). Walter Laqueur, *Terrorism* (London: Weidenfeld and Nicolson, 1977), p. 118.

59. The talks have stopped and started several times, and at this writing are threatened by renewed violence; however, it looks as if they will result in limited Tamil autonomy.

60. Other splinter groups include the Continuity IRA and the Irish National Liberation Army.

ing can also oc on the "status quo" (or, usually, pro-government) side, as happened in S h Africa (with the Afrikaner white power group Farmers' Force, or Boern) and in Northern Ireland (with the Ulster Volunteer Force). Governments c ront huge difficulties when negotiating with organizations against which t are still fighting in either a counterterrorism campaign or a traditional war The most extreme case of counterproductive splintering of status quo fact s is Colombia, where the signing of the peace accords between the Colo ian government and the Popular Liberation Army (Ejército Popular de Lib ción, or EPL) in 1984 resulted in the formation of right-wing paramilitary gr ps that disagreed with the granting of political status to the EPL. Before lon leftist groups, paramilitary units, and the Colombian army stepped up the attacks, unraveling the peace, increasing the violence, and further fraction g the political actors. Worse, splinter groups are often more violent than th nother" organization, responding to the imperative to demonstrate their e ence and signal their dissent. Splinter groups can be seen as engaging in a "layer" of terrorism with respect to the original group or their own gove nent. This can also be the case, for example, when groups enter elections an ake on a governing role. In such situations, the long-term goal (a viable p ical outcome) and the short-term goal (the reduction in violence) may be dds.[62]

A wide rang f variables can determine the broader outcome of negotiations to end te ism, including the nature of the organization of the group (with hierarchi groups having an advantage over groups that cannot control their members' tions), the nature of the leadership of the group (where groups with st g leaders have an advantage over those that are decentralized), and the re of public support for the cause (where groups with ambivalent constit cies may be more likely to compromise). There must also be negotiable aims hich are more likely to exist with territorially based groups than with those at follow left-wing, right-wing, or religious/spiritualist ideologies. Determ ng the degree to which opening a political dialogue with a terrorist group likely avenue for the decline of the group and a reduction in violence is a hly differentiated calculation.

Negotiations, wever, need not be a formalized process and need not occur

61. For a discussio this problem, see Fred Charles Ilké, *Every War Must End*, 2d ed. (New York: Columbia Universi ress, 2005), pp. 84–105.
62. Negotiations, h ver, complicate a terrorist organization's efforts to perpetuate its own absolutist perspective i tifying the use of terrorist violence. See Adrian Guelke, *The Age of Terrorism and the Internationa litical System* (London: I.B. Tauris, 1998), pp. 162–181.

only with the leadership of a group. Arguably, a form of negotiation with a terrorist organization, or more precisely with its members, is the offer of amnesty to those willing to stop engaging in violence and come forth with information about their fellow operatives. The classic case of a successful amnesty is the Italian government's 1979 and 1982 repentance legislation and the Red Brigades.[63] In another case, the government of Alberto Fujimori in Peru offered amnesty to members of Shining Path, both after Guzmán's capture and during the waning days of the group. As Robert Art and Louise Richardson point out in their comparative study of state counterterrorism policies, an amnesty may be most successful when an organization is facing defeat and its members have an incentive to seek a way out of what they see as a losing cause.[64]

DIMINISHMENT OF POPULAR SUPPORT

Terrorist groups are strategic actors that usually deliberate about their targets and calculate the effects of attacks on their constituent populations. Miscalculations, however, can undermine a group's cause, resulting in plummeting popular support and even its demise. Terrorist groups generally cannot survive without either active or passive support from a surrounding population. Examples of active support include hiding members, raising money, and, especially, joining the organization. Passive support, as the term implies, is more diffuse and includes actions such as ignoring obvious signs of terrorist group activity, declining to cooperate with police investigations, sending money to organizations that act as fronts for the group, and expressing support for the group's objectives.

Popular support for a terrorist group can dissipate for a number of reasons. First, people who are not especially interested in its political aims may fear government counteraction. Apathy is a powerful force; all else being equal, most people naturally prefer to carry on their daily lives without the threat of being targeted by counterterrorism laws, regulations, sanctions, and raids. Sometimes even highly radicalized populations can pull back active or passive

63. Franco Ferracuti, "Ideology and Repentance: Terrorism in Italy," in Reich, *Origins of Terrorism*, pp. 59–64; and Leonard Weinberg, "Italy and the Red Brigades," in Art and Richardson, *Democracy and Counterterrorism*.

64. Other examples cited by Art and Richardson include amnesties or other incentives given to members of the ETA, the Shining Path, the FALN, the IRA, and the Tamil Tigers, with degrees of success related to whether members of a group perceived it as likely to prevail. See "Conclusion," in Art and Richardson, *Democracy and Counterterrorism*.

support for a gı p, especially if the government engages in strong repressive measures and ›ple simply become exhausted. The apparent loss of local popular suppoı or Chechen terrorist groups is a good example.

Second, the g ernment may offer supporters of a terrorist group a better alternative. Refoı movements, increased spending, and creation of jobs in underserved ar are all tactics that can undermine the sources of terrorist violence. They caı lso result, however, in increased instability and a heightened sense of oppor ıity—situations that in the past have led to more terrorist acts. Evidence ggests that the extent to which societal conditions lead to a sense of "indigı ion" or frustrated ambition among certain segments of society during a pe ›d of transition might be a crucial factor for the decision to turn to terroris iolence. Sometimes terrorist attacks are seen as an effort to nudge the flow history further in one's direction.[65]

Third, popul ›ns can become uninterested in the ideology or objectives of a terrorist grou events can evolve independently such that the group's aims become outdat or irrelevant. A sense of historical ripeness or opportunity may have been t. Examples include many of the Marxist groups inspired by communist ide gy and supported by the Soviet Union. This is arguably a major reason w the nature of international terrorism has evolved beyond primary relianc ›n state sponsorship toward a broader range of criminal or entrepreneurial ·havior.

Fourth, a ter ist group's attacks can cause revulsion among its actual or potential publi onstituency.[66] This is a historically common strategic error and can cause t group to implode. Independent of the counterterrorist activity of a governn ıt, a terrorist group may choose a target that a wide range of its constituents ›nsider illegitimate. This occurred, for example, with the Omagh bombir Despite hasty subsequent statements by RIRA leaders that they did not int d to kill innocent civilians, the group never recovered in the eyes of the con unity.[67] Other examples of strategic miscalculation abound.

65. Peter A. Lupsh Explanation of Political Violence: Some Psychological Theories versus Indignation," *Politics Society*, Vol. 2, No. 1 (Fall 1971), pp. 89–104; and Luigi Bonanate, "Some Unanticipated Conse ıces of Terrorism," *Journal of Peace Research*, Vol. 16, No. 3 (May 1979), pp. 197–211.

66. Terrorist operaı s, albeit shocking and tragic, at least as often increase the level of public support for the cau ınd indeed are designed to do so. Examples include the PLO, the Internal Macedonian Revol ›nary Organization, the IRA, and nineteenth-century Russian terrorist groups. See Laqueı *errorism.*

67. See Sean Boyne he Real IRA: After Omagh, What Now?" *Jane's Intelligence Review*, October 1998, http://www.j s.com/regional_news/europe/news/jir/jir980824_1_n.shtml.

In February 1970 the PFLP-GC sabotaged a Swissair plane en route to Tel Aviv, resulting in the deaths of all 47 passengers, 15 of whom were Israelis. The PFLP-GC at first took responsibility but then tried unsuccessfully to retract its claim when popular revulsion began to surface.[68] Similarly, there has been revulsion among the Basque population in Spain to attacks by the separatist group Basque Fatherland and Liberty (Euzkadi Ta Askatasuna, or ETA), which some observers credit with the declining popularity of the group.[69] Public revulsion was a factor in the undermining of support for Sikh separatism in India, a movement directed at establishing an independent state of Khalistan that killed tens of thousands between 1981 and 1995 and was responsible for the assassination of Indian Prime Minister Indira Gandhi on October 31, 1984.[70]

Popular revulsion against terrorist attacks can have immediate effects. Arguably the most well developed and broadly based conduit for resource collection in the world is the connection between the Tamil Tigers and the dispersed Tamil diaspora. The LTTE's desire to avoid the "terrorist organization" label in the post–September 11 world and shore up its base of popular support was an element in the group's December 2001 decision to pursue a negotiated solution.[71] Likewise, a state-sponsored terrorist group can lose support when the state decides that it is no longer interested in using terrorism, responds to pressure from other states, has more important competing goals, or loses the ability to continue its support.[72] Libya's expulsion of the Palestinian terrorist Abu Nidal and cutting off of support to Palestinian groups such as the Palestine Islamic Jihad and the PFLP-GC are notable examples.

---

68. MIPT database incident profile, http://64.233.167.104/search?q?cache:vBXLiW4gwekJ:www.tkb.org/Incident.jsp%3FincID%3D372+popular+revulsion+terrorist+group&hl=en. The PFLP-GC has ties with Syria and Libya and may have had a role in the bombing of Pan Am 103 over Lockerbie, Scotland. See Cronin et al., *Foreign Terrorist Organizations,* pp. 80–82; and Kenneth Katzman, *The PLO and Its Factions,* CRS Report for Congress (Washington, D.C.: Congressional Research Service, June 10, 2002), Order Code RS21235. The state sponsorship of this group from the 1980s may have reduced its dependency on a local constituency.

69. See, for example, Goldie Shabad and Francisco José Llera Ramo, "Political Violence in a Democratic State: Basque Terrorism in Spain," in Crenshaw, *Terrorism in Context,* pp. 410–469, especially pp. 455–462.

70. Mark Juergensmeyer, *Terror in the Mind of God: The Global Rise of Religious Violence* (Berkeley: University of California Press, 2000), pp. 84–101. See also C. Christine Fair, "Diaspora Involvement in Insurgencies: Insights from the Khalistan and Tamil Eelam Movements," *Nationalism and Ethnic Politics,* Vol. 11, No. 1 (Spring 2005), pp. 125–156.

71. Fair, "Diaspora Involvement in Insurgencies."

72. For more on state sponsorship, see Daniel Byman, *Deadly Connections: States That Sponsor Terrorism* (Cambridge: Cambridge University Press, 2005).

MILITARY FORC[illegible]ND THE REPRESSION OF TERRORIST GROUPS

The use of milit[illegible] force has hastened the decline or ended a number of terrorist groups, incl[illegible]ing the late-nineteenth-century Russian group Narodnaya Volya, Shining [illegible]h, and the Kurdistan Workers' Party. From the state's perspective, milita[illegible] force offers a readily available means that is under its control. Although [illegible]rorism is indeed arguably a form of war, terrorists use asymmetrical v[illegible]ence, by definition, because they are unable or unwilling to meet a status qu[illegible]government on the battlefield. Shifting the violence to a form that is familiar [illegible]d probably advantageous for the state is an understandable response. In so[illegible] circumstances, it is also successful. Historically, military force has taken [illegible]o forms: intervention, when the threat is located mainly beyond the bord[illegible] of the target state (as with Israel's 1982 involvement in Lebanon); or re[illegible]ssion, when the threat is considered mainly a domestic one (as with the PK[illegible] More typically, the state will use some combination of the two (as in Colo[illegible]ia).[73]

The effects of[illegible] use of repressive military force in some cases may prove to be temporary o[illegible]ounterproductive; in other cases, it may result in the export of the problem [illegible] another country. The classic contemporary case is the Russian counterter[illegible]ism campaign in Chechnya.[74] Russian involvement in the second Chechen[illegible]ar appears to have produced a transition in the Chechen resistance, with [illegible]e terrorist attacks in the rest of Russia, greater reliance on suicide bomber[illegible]nd the growing influence of militant Islamic fighters. To the extent that the [illegible]chens originally engaged in a classic insurgency rather than in terrorism, th[illegible] have since 2002 altered their tactics toward increasing attacks on Russia[illegible]ivilians. The strong repressive response by the Russian government has ap[illegible]rently facilitated the spread of the conflict to neighboring areas, includin[illegible]gushetia and Dagestan. And there seems to be no end in sight, given the[illegible]creasing radicalization and identification of some Chechen factions with th[illegible]l-Qaida movement.[75]

---

73. On interventio[illegible]e Adam Roberts, "The 'War on Terror' in Historical Perspective," *Survival*, Vol. 47, No. 2 (Sum[illegible]r 2005), pp. 115–121.

74. For recent wor[illegible] this subject, see Mark Kramer, "The Perils of Counterinsurgency: Russia's War in Chechnya,"[illegible]*ernational Security*, Vol. 29, No. 3 (Winter 2004/05), pp. 5–63; and Mark Kramer, "Guerrilla[illegible]arfare, Counterinsurgency, and Terrorism in the North Caucasus: The Military Dimensio[illegible] the Russian-Chechen Conflict," *Europe-Asia Studies*, Vol. 57, No. 2 (March 2005), pp. 209–290.

75. The Internatio[illegible]nstitute for Strategic Studies (IISS) claims that Russian forces suffered 4,749 casualties between [illegible]gust 2002 and August 2003, the highest figure since the second Chechen conflict began in 1[illegible] International Institute for Strategic Studies, *The Military Balance, 2003/2004* (London: IISS, 2003[illegible]). 86–87. For more on the Chechen case, see Audrey Kurth Cronin, "Russia and Chechnya," in [illegible] and Richardson, *Democracy and Counterterrorism*.

Democracies or liberal governments face particular difficulties in repressing terrorist groups. Because military or police action requires a target, the use of force against operatives works best in situations where members of the organization can be separated from the general population. This essentially forces "profiling" or some method of distinguishing members from nonmembers—always a sensitive issue, particularly when the only available means of discrimination relate to how members are defined (race, age, religion, nationality, etc.) rather than to what they do (or are planning to do). Excellent intelligence is essential for the latter (especially in advance of an attack), but even in the best of situations, it is typically scarce. Repressive measures also carry high resource and opportunity costs. Long-term repressive measures against suspected operatives may challenge civil liberties and human rights, undermine domestic support, polarize political parties, and strain the fabric of the state itself, further undercutting the state's ability to respond effectively to future terrorist attacks.

TRANSITION TO ANOTHER MODUS OPERANDI

In some cases, groups can move from the use of terrorism toward either criminal behavior or more classic conventional warfare. The transition to criminal behavior implies a shift away from a primary emphasis on collecting resources as a means of pursuing political ends toward acquiring material goods and profit that become ends in themselves. Groups that have undertaken such transitions in recent years include Abu Sayyaf in the Philippines and arguably all of the major so-called narco-terrorist groups in Colombia.[76] Beginning in 2000, Abu Sayyaf shifted its focus from bombings and targeted executions to the taking of foreign hostages and their exchange for millions of dollars in ransom.[77] The Revolutionary Armed Forces of Colombia uses a variety of mechanisms to raise funds—including kidnapping for ransom, extortion, and especially drug trafficking—running operations that yield as much as $1 billion annually.[78]

Terrorist groups can also escalate to insurgency or even conventional war, especially if they enjoy state support. Notable examples include the Kashmiri separatist groups, the Khmer Rouge, and the Communist Party of Nepal–

76. These would include the Revolutionary Armed Forces of Colombia, the National Liberation Army, and the United Self-Defense Forces of Colombia.
77. See Larry Niksch, *Abu Sayyaf: Target of Philippine-U.S. Antiterrorism Cooperation*, CRS Report for Congress (Washington, D.C.: Congressional Research Service, updated April 8, 2003), Order Code RL31265; and Cronin et al., *Foreign Terrorist Organizations*, pp. 4–7.
78. Cronin et al., *Foreign Terrorist Organizations*, p. 92.

Maoists. Transi ns in and out of insurgency are especially common among ethnonationalis eparatist groups, whose connection to a particular territory and grounding an ethnic population provide a natural base; in these situations, the evolu n involves changes in size or type of operations (do they operate as a milit unit and attack mainly other military targets?) and whether or not the orga ation holds territory (even temporarily). Terrorism and insurgency are n he same, but they are related. Very weak, territorially based movements ma se terrorist attacks and transition to insurgency when they gain strength, e cially when their enemy is a state government (as was the case for most ups in the twentieth century). One example is Algeria's Armed Islamic oup, which massacred tens of thousands of civilians in the civil war that f wed the Islamic Salvation Front's victory in the 1991 parliamentary electio The key in understanding the relationship between the two tactics is to anal e the group's motivation, its attraction to a particular constituency, its stren , and the degree to which its goals are associated with control of a piece erritory. Transitions to full-blown conventional war, on the other hand, can cur when the group is able to control the behavior of a state according to its n interests, or even when an act of terrorism has completely unintended con quences.[79]

Is al-Qaida U ue among Terrorist Organizations?

Four characteri s distinguish al-Qaida from its predecessors in either nature or degree: its fl organization, recruitment methods, funding, and means of communication

FLUID ORGANIZ ON

The al-Qaida of ptember 2001 no longer exists. As a result of the war on terrorism, it has e ved into an increasingly diffuse network of affiliated groups, driven by the ldview that al-Qaida represents. In deciding in 1996 to be, essentially, a " ble" organization, running training camps and occupying territory in Af nistan, al-Qaida may have made an important tactical error; this, in par xplains the immediate success of the U.S.-led coalition's war

79. As Adam Robe notes, the outbreak of World War I is a principal example: the Bosnian-Serb student who killed hduke Franz Ferdinand in July 1914 had no intention of setting off an international cataclysm. Ratko Parezanin, *Mlada Bosna I prvi svetski rat* [Young Bosnia and the First World War] (Muni skra, 1974), cited in Roberts, "The 'War on Terror' in Historical Perspective," p. 107 n. 15.

in Afghanistan.[80] Since then, it has begun to resemble more closely a "global jihad movement," increasingly consisting of web-directed and cyber-linked groups and ad hoc cells.[81] In its evolution, al-Qaida has demonstrated an unusual resilience and international reach. It has become, in the words of Porter Goss, "only one facet of the threat from a broader Sunni jihadist movement."[82] No previous terrorist organization has exhibited the complexity, agility, and global reach of al-Qaida, with its fluid operational style based increasingly on a common mission statement and objectives, rather than on standard operating procedures and an organizational structure.[83]

Al-Qaida has been the focal point of a hybrid terrorist coalition for some time, with ties to inspired freelancers and other terrorist organizations both old and new.[84] Some observers argue that considering al-Qaida an organization is misleading; rather it is more like a nebula of independent entities (including loosely associated individuals) that share an ideology and cooperate with each other.[85] The original umbrella group, the International Islamic Front for Jihad against Jews and Crusaders, formed in 1998, included not only al-Qaida but also groups from Algeria, Bangladesh, Egypt, and Pakistan. A sampling of groups that are connected in some way includes the Moro Islamic Liberation Front (Philippines), Jemaah Islamiyah (Southeast Asia), Egyptian Islamic Jihad (which merged with al-Qaida in 2001), al-Ansar Mujahidin (Chechnya), al-Gama'a al-Islamiyya (primarily Egypt, but has a worldwide presence), Abu Sayyaf (Philippines), the Islamic Movement of Uzbekistan, the Salafist Group for Call and Combat (Algeria), and Harakat ul-Mujahidin (Pakistan/Kashmir). Some experts see al-Qaida's increased reliance on connections to other groups as a sign of weakness; others see it as a worrisome indicator of growing strength, especially with groups that formerly focused on local

80. Rapoport, "The Four Waves of Modern Terrorism," p. 66.
81. Coll and Glasser, "Terrorists Turn to the Web as Base of Operations."
82. Porter J. Goss, director of central intelligence, testimony before the Senate Select Committee on Intelligence, "Global Intelligence Challenges, 2005: Meeting Long-Term Challenges with a Long-Term Strategy," 109th Cong., 2d sess., February 16, 2005, http://www.cia.gov/cia/public_affairs/speeches/2004/Goss_testimony_02162005.html.
83. Possible exceptions include the international anarchist movement, which was confined to Russia, Europe, and the United States.
84. David Johnston, Don Van Natta Jr., and Judith Miller, "Qaida's New Links Increase Threats from Far-Flung Sites," *New York Times*, June 16, 2002. Many commentators have pointed out that al-Qaida is translated as "the base," "the foundation," or even "the method." It was not intended at its founding to be a single structure.
85. Xavier Raufer, "Al-Qaeda: A Different Diagnosis," *Studies in Conflict and Terrorism*, Vol. 26, No. 6 (November/December 2003), pp. 391–398.

issues and now isplay evidence of convergence on al-Qaida's Salafist, anti-U.S., anti-West enda.[86]

The nature, s , structure, and reach of the coalition have long been subject to debate. Des e claims of some Western experts, no one knows how many members -Qaida has currently or had in the past. U.S. intelligence sources place tl number of individuals who underwent training in camps in Afghanistan fro 1996 through the fall of 2001 at between 10,000 and 20,000;[87] the figure is ine t, in part, because of disagreement over the total number of such camps an because not all attendees became members.[88] The International Institute Strategic Studies in 2004 estimated that 2,000 al-Qaida operatives had been ptured or killed and that a pool of 18,000 potential al-Qaida operatives rem ed.[89] These numbers can be misleading, however: it would be a mistake to ink of al-Qaida as a conventional force, because even a few trained fighters n mobilize many willing foot soldiers as martyrs.

METHODS OF RE UITMENT

The staying pov r of al-Qaida is at least in part related to the way the group has perpetuate self; in many senses, al-Qaida is closer to a social movement than a terrorist roup.[90] Involvement in the movement has come not from pressure by sen al-Qaida members but mainly from local volunteers competing to win a hance to train or participate in some fashion.[91] The process seems to be mo matter of "joining" than being recruited,[92] and thus the tra-

86. For an early an is of the arguments of both sides, see Audrey Kurth Cronin, *Al-Qaeda after the Iraq Conflict*, CR port for Congress (Washington, D.C.: Congressional Research Service, May 23, 2003), Order Co RS21529.
87. Central Intellig Agency, "Afghanistan: An Incubator for International Terrorism," CTC 01-40004, March 27, 20 and Central Intelligence Agency, "Al-Qa'ida Still Well Positioned to Recruit Terrorists," July 1, 2 , p. 1, both cited in *Final Report of the National Commission on Terrorist Attacks upon the United Sta* New York: W.W. Norton, 2004), p. 67 n. 78.
88. Anonymous, *T gh Our Enemies' Eyes*, especially pp. 126, 130–131; Marc Sageman, *Understanding Terror Netw s* (Philadelphia: University of Pennsylvania Press, 2004), especially p. 121; and David Johnson d Don Van Natta Jr., "U.S. Officials See Signs of a Revived al-Qaida," *New York Times*, May 17 03.
89. International In ute for Strategic Studies, *Strategic Survey, 2003/4* (London: Routledge, 2005), p. 6.
90. See also "The W dwide Threat, 2004: Challenges in a Changing Global Context," testimony of Director of Cent ntelligence George J. Tenet before the Senate Select Committee on Intelligence, 108th Cong., sess., February 24, 2004, http://www.cia.gov/cia/public_affairs/speeches/2004/dci_speech_0 2004.html.
91. According to S man's analysis, operatives have gathered in regional clusters, which he labels "the central sta f al-Qaida," "the Southeast Asian cluster," "the Maghreb cluster," and "the core Arab cluster." eman, *Understanding Terror Networks*.
92. Ibid.; and Jeffre ozzens, "Islamist Groups Develop New Recruiting Strategies," *Jane's Intelligence Review*, Febru 1, 2005.

ditional organizational approach to analyzing this group is misguided. But the draw of al-Qaida should also not be overstated: in the evolving pattern of associations, attraction to the mission or ideology seems to have been a necessary but not sufficient condition. Exposure to an ideology is not enough, as reflected in the general failure of al-Qaida to recruit members in Afghanistan and Sudan, where its headquarters were once located.[93] As psychiatrist Marc Sageman illustrates, social bonds, not ideology, apparently play a more important role in al-Qaida's patterns of global organization.[94]

Sageman's study of established links among identified al-Qaida operatives indicates that they joined the organization mainly because of ties of kinship and friendship, facilitated by what he calls a "bridging person" or entry point, perpetuated in a series of local clusters in the Maghreb and Southeast Asia, for example. In recent years, operatives have been connected to al-Qaida and its agenda in an even more informal way, having apparently not gone to camps or had much formal training: examples include those engaged in the London bombings of July 7 and 21, 2005, the Istanbul attacks of November 15 and 20, 2003, and the Casablanca attacks of May 16, 2003.[95] This loose connectedness is not an accident: bin Laden describes al Qaida as "the vanguard of the Muslim nation" and does not claim to exercise command and control over his followers.[96] Although many groups boast of a connection to al-Qaida's ideology, there are often no logistical trails and thus no links for traditional intelligence methods to examine.[97] This explains, for example, the tremendous difficulty in establishing connections between a radical mosque, bombers, bomb makers, supporters, and al-Qaida in advance of an attack (not to mention after an attack).

Another concern has been the parallel development of Salafist networks apparently drawing European Muslims into combat against Western forces in Iraq. The European Union's counterterrorism coordinator, Gijs de Vries, for example, has cautioned that these battle-hardened veterans of the Iraq conflict

93. Sageman, *Understanding Terrorist Networks*, p. 119. Sageman's book analyzes the patterns of growth of cells involved in past attacks, including vigorous refutation of the thesis that exposure to ideology alone explains the growth of al-Qaida.
94. Ibid., p. 178.
95. Jack Kalpakian, "Building the Human Bomb: The Case of the 16 May 2003 Attacks in Casablanca," *Studies in Conflict and Terrorism*, Vol. 28, No. 2 (March–April 2005), pp. 113–127.
96. Al Jazeera TV, September 10, 2003, cited in Michael Scheuer, "Coalition Warfare: How al-Qaeda Uses the World Islamic Front against Crusaders and Jews, Part I," *Terrorism Focus*, Vol. 2, No. 7, March 31, 2005, http://www.jamestown.org/terrorism/news/article.php?articleid=2369530.
97. Paul Pillar, "Counterterrorism after al-Qaida," *Washington Quarterly*, Vol. 27, No. 3 (Summer 2004), pp. 101–113.

will return to a :k Western targets in Europe. The Ansar al-Islam plot to attack the 2004 N 'O summit in Turkey was, according to Turkish sources, developed in part ' operatives who had fought in Iraq.[98] A proportion of those recently drawn the al-Qaida movement joined after receiving a Salafist message dissemina l over the internet. Such direct messages normally do not pass through th raditional process of vetting by an imam. European counterterrorism offici thus worry about members of an alienated diaspora—sometimes seco - and third-generation immigrants—who may be vulnerable to the message cause they are not thoroughly trained in fundamental concepts of Islam, alienated from their parents, and feel isolated in the communities in wh ı they find themselves. The impulse to join the movement arises from a de e to belong to a group in a context where the operative is excluded from, re lsed by, or incapable of successful integration into a Western community.[99]

Thus, with al aida, the twentieth-century focus on structure and function is neither timel) or sufficient. Tracing the command and control relationships in such a dram cally changing movement is enormously difficult,[100] which makes compari ıs with earlier, more traditional terrorist groups harder but by no means in ›ssible; one detects parallels, for example, between al-Qaida and the global orist movements that developed in the late nineteenth century, including archist and social revolutionary groups.[101]

MEANS OF SUPP r

Financial supp of al-Qaida has ranged from money channeled through charitable orga ations to grants given to local terrorist groups that present promising plan r attacks that serve al-Qaida's general goals.[102] The majority of its operation ave relied at most on a small amount of seed money provided by the (anization, supplemented by operatives engaged in petty crime and frau 3 Indeed, beginning in 2003, many terrorism experts agreed that al-Qaida (ld best be described as a franchise organization with a

---

98. Cozzens, "Islar Groups Develop New Recruiting Strategies."
99. Sageman, *Unde nding Terrorist Networks*, especially p. 92.
100. On this point, Bruce Hoffman, "The Changing Face of al-Qaida and the Global War on Terrorism," *Studies Conflict and Terrorism*, Vol. 27, No. 6 (December 2004), p. 556.
101. On this subjec e Laqueur, *Terrorism*, especially pp. 3–20; and James Joll, *The Second International, 1889–1914* (l on: Weidenfeld and Nicolson, 1955).
102. Bruce Hoffma The Leadership Secrets of Osama bin Laden: The Terrorist as CEO," *Atlantic Monthly*, April 200 ›. 26–27.
103. Sageman, *Und anding Terrorist Networks*, pp. 50–51.

marketable "brand."[104] Relatively little money is required for most al-Qaida-associated attacks. As the International Institute for Strategic Studies points out, the 2002 Bali bombing cost less than $35,000, the 2000 USS *Cole* operation about $50,000, and the September 11 attacks less than $500,000.[105]

Another element of support has been the many autonomous businesses owned or controlled by al-Qaida; at one point, bin Laden was reputed to own or control approximately eighty companies around the world. Many of these legitimately continue to earn a profit, providing a self-sustaining source for the movement. International counterterrorism efforts to control al-Qaida financing have reaped at least $147 million in frozen assets.[106] Still, cutting the financial lifeline of an agile and low-cost movement that has reportedly amassed billions of dollars and needs few resources to carry out attacks remains a formidable undertaking.

Choking off funds destined for al-Qaida through regulatory oversight confronts numerous challenges. Formal banking channels are not necessary for many transfers, which instead can occur through informal channels known as "alternative remittance systems," "informal value transfer systems," "parallel banking," or "underground banking." Examples include the much-discussed *hawala* or *hundi* transfer networks and the Black Market Peso Exchange that operate through family ties or unofficial reciprocal arrangements.[107] Value can be stored in commodities such as diamonds and gold that are moved through areas with partial or problematical state sovereignty. Al-Qaida has also used charities to raise and move funds, with a relatively small proportion of gifts being siphoned off for illegitimate purposes, often without the knowledge of donors.[108] Yet efforts to cut off charitable flows to impoverished areas may

104. See Douglas Farah and Peter Finn, "Terrorism, Inc.: Al-Qaida Franchises Brand of Violence to Groups across World," *Washington Post*, November 21, 2003; Daniel Benjamin, "Are the Sparks Catching?" *Washington Post*, November 23, 2003; and Sebastian Rotella and Richard C. Paddock, "Experts See Major Shift in al-Qaida's Strategy," *Los Angeles Times*, November 19, 2003.
105. International Institute for Strategic Studies, *Strategic Survey, 2003/4*, p. 8.
106. "U.S.: Terror Funding Stymied," *CBS News*, January 11, 2005, http://www.cbsnews.com/stories/2005/01/11/terror/main666168.shtml.
107. These are methods of transferring value anonymously, without electronic traceability or paper trails. See Rensselaer Lee, *Terrorist Financing: The U.S. and International Response*, CRS Report for Congress (Washington, D.C.: Congressional Research Service, December 6, 2002), pp. 11–13, Order Code RL31658.
108. For information on informal financing mechanisms and U.S. efforts to control them, see testimony of Assistant Secretary Juan Carlos Zarate for Terrorist Financing and Financial Crimes, U.S. Department of the Treasury, before the House Financial Services Committee's Subcommittee on Oversight and Investigations, 109th Cong., 2d sess., February 16, 2005, http://www.ustreas.gov/press/releases/js2256.htm.

harm many ger nely needy recipients and could result in heightened resentment, which in rn may generate additional political support for the movement.[109] Al-Qa 's fiscal autonomy makes the network more autonomous than its late-tw ieth-century state-sponsored predecessors.

MEANS OF COM NICATION

The al-Qaida m ement has successfully used the tools of globalization to enable it to com nicate with multiple audiences, including potential new members, new ruits, active supporters, passive sympathizers, neutral observers, enem overnments, and potential victims. These tools include mobile phones xt messaging, instant messaging, and especially websites, email, blogs, a chat rooms, which can be used for administrative tasks, fund-raising, r rch, and logistical coordination of attacks.[110] Although al-Qaida is not th ly terrorist group to exploit these means, it is especially adept at doing so

A crucial fac ator for the perpetuation of the movement is the use of websites both t onvey messages, *fatwas,* claims of attacks, and warnings to the American p lic, as well as to educate future participants, embed instructions to operati , and rally sympathizers to the cause. The internet is an important factor building and perpetuating the image of al-Qaida and in maintaining th rganization's reputation. It provides easy access to the media, which facil es al-Qaida's psychological warfare against the West. Indoctrinating and hing new recruits is facilitated by the internet, notably through the di mination of al-Qaida's widely publicized training manual (nicknamed "T Encyclopedia of Jihad") that explains how to organize and run a cell, as w as carry out attacks.[111] Websites and chat rooms are used to offer practical ice and facilitate the fraternal bonds that are crucial to al-

109. For more on il l and legal globalized networks of financing, see *Terrorist Financing,* Report of an Independent Force Sponsored by the Council on Foreign Relations (New York: Council on Foreign Relatior ress, October 2002); *Update on the Global Campaign against Terrorist Financing,* Second Report of a dependent Task Force on Terrorist Financing Sponsored by the Council on Foreign Relations w York: Council on Foreign Relations Press, June 15, 2004); Loretta Napoleoni, *Modern ad: Tracing the Dollars behind the Terror Networks* (London: Pluto, 2003); Douglas Farah, *Bl from Stones: The Secret Financial Network of Terror* (New York: Broadway Books, 2004); and mas J. Biersteker and Sue E. Eckert, eds., *Countering the Financing of Global Terrorism* (London: tledge, forthcoming).

110. For more on t phenomenon, see Cronin, "Behind the Curve," pp. 30–58.

111. For an analysi current terrorist use of the internet, see Gabriel Weimann, "www.terror.net: How Modern Terr n Uses the Internet," Special Report, No. 116 (Washington, D.C.: United States Institute of e, March 2004).

Qaida. In a sense, members of the movement no longer need to join an organization at all, for the individual can participate with the stroke of a few keys. The debate over the size, structure, and membership of al-Qaida may be a quaint relic of the twentieth century, displaced by the leveling effects of twenty-first-century technology.

The new means of communication also offer practical advantages. Members of al-Qaida use the web as a vast source of research and data mining to scope out future attack sites or develop new weapons technology at a low cost and a high level of sophistication. On January 15, 2003, for example, U.S. Secretary of Defense Donald Rumsfeld quoted an al-Qaida training manual retrieved by American troops in Afghanistan that advised trainees that at least 80 percent of the information needed about the enemy could be collected from open, legal sources.[112]

Earlier Terrorist Groups, al-Qaida, and U.S. Policy Implications

Al-Qaida's fluid organization, methods of recruitment, funding, and means of communication distinguish it as an advancement in twenty-first-century terrorist groups. Al-Qaida is a product of the times. Yet it also echoes historical predecessors, expanding on such factors as the international links and ideological drive of nineteenth-century anarchists, the open-ended aims of Aum Shinrikyo, the brilliance in public communications of the early PLO, and the taste for mass casualty attacks of twentieth-century Sikh separatists or Hezbollah. Al-Qaida is an amalgam of old and new, reflecting twenty-first-century advances in means or matters of degree rather than true originality; still, most analysts miss the connections with its predecessors and are blinded by its solipsistic rhetoric. That is a mistake. The pressing challenge is to determine which lessons from the decline of earlier terrorist groups are relevant to al-Qaida and which are not.

First, past experience with terrorism indicates that al-Qaida will not end if Osama bin Laden is killed. There are many other reasons to pursue him, including bringing him to justice, removing his leadership and expertise, and increasing esprit de corps on the Western side (whose credibility is sapped because of bin Laden's enduring elusiveness). The argument that his demise will end al-Qaida is tinged with emotion, not dispassionate analysis. Organi-

112. Ibid., p. 7.

zations that ha een crippled by the killing of their leader have been hierarchically structu l, reflecting to some degree a cult of personality, and have lacked a viable cessor. Al-Qaida meets neither of these criteria: it has a mutable structure th a strong, even increasing, emphasis on individual cells and local initia e. It is not the first organization to operate in this way; and the demise of s ilar terrorist groups required much more than the death of one person.[113] like the PKK and Shining Path, al-Qaida is not driven by a cult of persona ; despite his astonishing popularity, bin Laden has deliberately avoided a wing the movement to revolve around his own persona, preferring instead keep his personal habits private, to talk of the insignificance of his own fate, d to project the image of a humble man eager to die for his beliefs. As for iable replacement, bin Laden has often spoken openly of a succession plan nd that plan has to a large degree already taken effect. Furthermore, his c ure or killing would produce its own countervailing negative consequen , including (most likely) the creation of a powerful martyr. On balance, th removal of bin Laden would have important potential benefits, but to ieve that it would kill al-Qaida is to be ahistorical and naive. That al-Qaida i lready dead.

Second, altho h there was a time when the failure to transition to a new generation mig ave been a viable finale for al-Qaida, that time is long past. Al-Qaida has tr sitioned to a second, third, and arguably fourth generation. The reason rela especially to the second distinctive element of al-Qaida: its method of recru nent or, more accurately, its attraction of radicalized followers (both indivi als and groups), many of whom in turn are connected to existing local net rks. Al-Qaida's spread has been compared to a virus or a bacterium, disp ing its contagion to disparate sites.[114] Although this is a seductive analog is also misleading: the perpetuation of al-Qaida is a sentient process involvi well-considered marketing strategies and deliberate tactical decisions, not a ndless "disease" process; thinking of it as a "disease" shores up the unfortun American tendency to avoid analyzing the mentality of the enemy. Al-Qaid s operating with a long-term strategy and is certainly not following the le wing groups of the 1970s in their failure to articulate a coherent ideological ion or the peripatetic right-wing groups of the twentieth

113. Comparable c ased "immortal" terrorist networks have included the social revolutionary and anarchist mov nts of the late nineteenth and early twentieth centuries. I am indebted to Timothy Hoyt for t observation.

114. See, for exam Corine Hegland, "Global Jihad," *National Journal*, May 8, 2004, pp. 1396–1402.

century. It has transitioned beyond its original structure and now represents a multigenerational threat with staying power comparable to the enthonationalist groups of the twentieth century. Likewise, arguments about whether al-Qaida is best described primarily as an ideology or by its opposition to foreign occupation of Muslim lands are specious: al-Qaida's adherents use both rationales to spread their links. The movement is opportunistic. The challenge for the United States and its allies is to move beyond rigid mind-sets and paradigms, do more in-depth analysis, and be more nimble and strategic in response to al-Qaida's fluid agenda.

The third and fourth models of a terrorist organization's end—achievement of the group's cause and transition toward a political role, negotiations, or amnesty—also bear little relevance to al-Qaida today. It is hard to conceive of al-Qaida fully achieving its aims, in part because those aims have evolved over time, variably including achievement of a pan-Islamic caliphate, the overthrow of non-Islamic regimes, and the expulsion of all infidels from Muslim countries, not to mention support for the Palestinian cause and the killing of Americans and other so-called infidels. Historically, terrorist groups that have achieved their ends have done so by articulating clear, limited objectives. Al-Qaida's goals, at least as articulated over recent years, could not be achieved without overturning an international political and economic system characterized by globalization and predominant U.S. power. As the historical record indicates, negotiations or a transition to a legitimate political process requires feasible terms and a sense of stalemate in the struggle. Also, members of terrorist groups seeking negotiations often have an incentive to find a way out of what they consider a losing cause. None of this describes bin Laden's al-Qaida.

This points to another issue. As al-Qaida has become a hybrid or "virtual organization," rather than a coherent hierarchical organization, swallowing its propaganda and treating it as a unified whole is a mistake. It is possible that bin Laden and his lieutenants have attempted to cobble together such disparate entities (or those entities have opportunistically attached themselves to al-Qaida) that they have stretched beyond the point at which their interests can be represented in this movement. Some of the local groups that have recently claimed an association with al-Qaida have in the past borne more resemblance to ethnonationalist/separatist groups such as the PLO, the IRA, and the LTTE. Examples include local affiliates in Indonesia, Morocco, Tunisia, and Turkey. This is not to argue that these groups' aims are rightful or that their tactics are legitimate. Rather, because of its obsession with the notion of a monolithic al-

Qaida, the Uni States is glossing over both the extensive local variation within terrorist oups and their different goals; these groups have important points of diver ice with al-Qaida's agenda, and the United States does no one any favors failing to seriously analyze and exploit those local differences (except p iaps al-Qaida).

The U.S. obje ve must be to enlarge the movement's internal inconsistencies and differe s. Al-Qaida's aims have become so sweeping that one might wonder whethe hey genuinely carry within them the achievement of specific local grievance There is more hope of ending such groups through traditional methods hey are dealt with using traditional tools, even including, on a case-by-case is, concessions or negotiations with specific local elements that may have gotiable or justifiable terms (albeit pursued through an illegitimate tactic). e key is to emphasize the differences with al-Qaida's agenda and to drive a w ge between the movement and its recent adherents. The historical record o her terrorist groups indicates that it is a mistake to treat al-Qaida as a mon th, to lionize it as if it is an unprecedented phenomenon with all elements ec lly committed to its aims, for that eliminates a range of proven counter rorist tools and techniques for ending it. It is also a mistake to nurture al-Q a's rallying point, a hatred of Americans and a resentment of U.S. policies specially in Iraq and between Israel and the Palestinians), thereby conven tly facilitating the glossing over of differences within.

Fifth, reduci popular support, both active and passive, is an effective means of haste g the demise of some terrorist groups. This technique has received much at tion among critics of George W. Bush and his administration's policies, ny of whom argue that concentrating on the "roots" of terrorism is a n ssary alternative to the current policy of emphasizing military force. This superficial argument, however, as it can be countered that a "roots" approa s precisely at the heart of current U.S. policy: the promotion of democracy n be seen as an idealistic effort to provide an alternative to populations in Muslim world, frustrated by corrupt governance, discrimination, unempl ment, and stagnation. But the participants in this debate are missing the poi [115] The problem is timing: democratization is a decades-long approach to a s t-term and immediate problem whose solution must also be

115. As Jonathan M ten demonstrates, democratization is a long-standing goal of U.S. foreign policy; with respec terrorism, however, both the "vindicationists" and the "exemplarists" are missing the point. M ten, "The Roots of the Bush Doctrine: Power, Nationalism, and Democracy Promotion in U.S. S tegy," *International Security*, Vol. 29, No. 4 (Spring 2005), pp. 112–156.

measured in months, not just years. The efforts being undertaken are unlikely to have a rapid enough effect to counter the anger, frustration, and sense of humiliation that characterize passive supporters. As for those who actively sustain the movement through terrorist acts, it is obviously a discouraging development that many recent operatives have lived in, or even been natives of, democratic countries—the March 2004 train attacks in Madrid and 2005 bombings in London being notable examples.[116]

The history of terrorism provides little comfort to those who believe that democratization is a good method to reduce active and passive support for terrorist attacks. There is no evidence that democratization correlates with a reduction in terrorism; in fact, available historical data suggest the opposite. Democratization was arguably the cause of much of the terrorism of the twentieth century. Moreover, democracy in the absence of strong political institutions and civil society could very well bring about radical Islamist governments over which the West would have little influence. There are much worse things than terrorism, and it might continue to be treated as a regrettable but necessary accompaniment to change were it not for two potentially serious developments in the twenty-first century: (1) the use of increasingly destructive weapons that push terrorist attacks well beyond the "nuisance" level, and (2) the growing likelihood that terrorism will lead to future systemic war. In any case, the long-term, idealistic, and otherwise admirable policy of democratization, viewed as "Americanization" in many parts of the world, does not represent a sufficiently targeted response to undercutting popular support for al-Qaida.

There are two vulnerabilities, however, where cutting the links between al-Qaida and its supporters hold promise: its means of funding and its means of communication. Efforts to cut off funding through traditional avenues have had some results. But not nearly enough attention is being paid to twenty-first-century communications, especially al-Qaida's presence on the internet. The time has come to recognize that the stateless, anarchical realm of cyberspace requires better tools for monitoring, countermeasures, and, potentially, even control. Previous leaps in cross-border communication such as the telegraph, radio, and telephone engendered counteracting developments in

116. Nor will withdrawal from occupation in Iraq and Palestine, for example, solve this problem: al-Qaida-associated suicide attacks in Egypt, Morocco, Saudi Arabia, and Turkey belie that argument. See Robert A. Pape, *Dying to Win: The Strategic Logic of Suicide Terrorism* (New York: Random House, 2005).

code breaking, ›nitoring, interception, and wiretapping. This may seem a heretical sugge ›n for liberal states, especially for a state founded on the right of free sp(h; however, the international community will inevitably be driven to take (ntermeasures in response to future attacks. It is time to devote more reso es to addressing this problem now. Western analysts have been misguide(ı focusing on the potential use of the internet for so-called cyberterrorism :., its use in carrying out attacks); the internet is far more dangerous as a ›l to shore up and perpetuate the al-Qaida movement's constituency.[117] Pr(·nting or interdicting al-Qaida's ability to disseminate its message and d: / adherents into its orbit is crucial. Countering its messages in serious ways ot through the outdated and stilted vehicles of government websites and of ıal statements but through sophisticated alternative sites and images attracti\ :o a new generation, is an urgent priority.

As for the oı ›nent's marketing strategy, al-Qaida and its associates have made serious ı ıtakes of timing, choice of targets, and technique; yet the United States a: its allies have done very little to capitalize on them. In particular, the Unit States tends to act as if al-Qaida is essentially a static enemy that will react t :s actions, but then fails to react effectively and strategically to the moveme s missteps. The Bali attacks, the May 2003 attacks in Saudi Arabia, the Ma d attacks, the July 2005 London attacks—all were immediately and delib(tely trumpeted by al-Qaida associates. Where was the coordinated counte: :rorist multimedia response? There is nothing so effective at engendering pı ic revulsion as images of murdered and maimed victims, many of whom ·semble family members of would-be recruits, lying on the ground as the r ılt of a terrorist act. Outrage is appropriate. Currently, however, those ima ; are dominated by would-be family members in Iraq, the Palestinian terr ries, Abu Ghraib, and Guantanamo Bay. The West is completely outflanl l on the airwaves, and its countermeasures are virtually nonexistent on · internet. But as the RIRA, PFLP-GC, and ETA cases demonstrate, the al-Q: ı movement can undermine itself, if it is given help. A large part of this "w. is arguably being fought not on a battlefield but in cyberspace. The time- ›nored technique of undermining active and passive support for a terrorist ɛ up through in-depth analysis, agile responses to missteps,

117. On the broad(ignificance of using the internet as a means of mobilization, see Audrey Kurth Cronin, "Cyl mobilization: The New *Levée en Masse*," *Parameters*, Vol. 36, No. 2 (Summer 2006), pp. 77–87.

carefully targeted messages, and cutting-edge technological solutions is a top priority.

This is a crucial moment of opportunity. Polls indicate that many of al-Qaida's potential constituents have been deeply repulsed by recent attacks. According to the Pew Global Attitudes Project, publics in many predominantly Muslim states increasingly see Islamic extremism as a threat to their own countries, express less support for terrorism, have less confidence in bin Laden, and reflect a declining belief in the usefulness of suicide attacks.[118] In these respects, there is a growing range of commonality in the attitudes of Muslim and non-Muslim publics; yet the United States focuses on itself and does little to nurture cooperation. American public diplomacy is the wrong concept. This is not about the United States and its ideals, values, culture, and image abroad: this is about tapping into a growing international norm against killing innocent civilians—whether, for example, on vacation or on their way to work or school—many of whom are deeply religious and many of whom also happen to be Muslims. If the United States and its allies fail to grasp this concept, to work with local cultures and local people to build on common goals and increase their alienation from this movement, then they will have missed a long-established and promising technique for ending a terrorist group such as al-Qaida.

There is little to say about the sixth factor, the use of military repression, in ending al-Qaida. Even though the U.S. military has made important progress in tracking down and killing senior operatives, the movement's ability to evolve has demonstrated the limits of such action, especially when poorly coordinated with other comparatively underfunded approaches and engaged in by a democracy. Although apparently effective, the Turkish government's repression of the PKK and the Peruvian government's suppression of Shining Path, for example, yield few desirable parallels for the current counterterrorist campaign.

Transitioning out of terrorism and toward either criminality or full insurgency is the final, worrisome historical precedent for al-Qaida. In a sense, the network is already doing both. Efforts to cut off funding through the formal banking system have ironically heightened the incentive and necessity to en-

118. See "Islamic Extremism: Common Concern for Muslim and Western Publics, Support for Terror Wanes among Muslim Publics," July 14, 2005, http://pewglobal.org/reports/display.php?ReportID=248.

gage in illicit a vities, especially narcotics trafficking. With the increasing amount of popp seed production in Afghanistan, al-Qaida has a natural pipeline to riches. T process is well under way. As for al-Qaida becoming a full insurgency, son nalysts believe this has already occurred.[119] Certainly to the extent that Abu usab al-Zarqawi and his associates in Iraq truly represent an arm of the mov nent (i.e., al-Qaida in Iraq), that transition is likewise well along. The allia e negotiated between bin Laden and al-Zarqawi is another example of an ective strategic and public relations move for both parties, giving new life the al-Qaida movement at a time when its leaders are clearly on the run and oviding legitimacy and fresh recruits for the insurgency in Iraq. As many nmentators have observed, Iraq is an ideal focal point and training ground r this putative global insurgency. The glimmer of hope in this scenario, h ever, is that the foreigners associated with al-Qaida are not tied to the territ of Iraq in the same way the local population is, and the tensions that will se between those who want a future for the nascent Iraqi state and those ho want a proving ground for a largely alien ideology and virtual organiza n are likely to increase—especially as the victims of the civil war now unfol g there continue increasingly to be Iraqi civilians. The counter to al-Zarqaw al-Qaida in Iraq, as it is for other areas of the world with local al-Qaida af ates, is to tap into the long-standing and deep association between people nd their territory and to exploit the inevitable resentment toward foreign te rist agendas, while scrupulously ensuring that the United States is not pe ived to be part of those agendas.

If the United ates continues to treat al-Qaida as if it were utterly unprecedented, as if the ecades-long experience with fighting modern terrorism were totally irrelevar hen it will continue to make predictable and avoidable mistakes in respon g to this threat. It will also miss important strategic opportunities. That exp ence points particularly toward dividing new local affiliates from al-Qaida understanding and exploiting their differences with the movement, rat than treating the movement as a monolith. It is also crucial to more effecti break the political and logistical connections between the movement and supporters, reinvigorating time-honored counterterrorism tactics targeted l-Qaida's unique characteristics, including the perpetuation of its message, funding, and its communications. Al-Qaida continues to exploit what is es tially a civil war within the Muslim world, attracting alien-

119. Among them lichael Scheuer, author of Anonymous, *Imperial Hubris*.

ated Muslims around the globe to its rage-filled movement. Al-Qaida will end when the West removes itself from the heart of this fight, shores up international norms against terrorism, undermines al-Qaida's ties with its followers, and begins to exploit the movement's abundant missteps.

Conclusion

Major powers regularly relearn a seminal lesson of strategic planning, which is that embarking on a long war or campaign without both a grounding in previous experience and a realistic projection of an end state is folly. This is just as true in response to terrorism as it is with more conventional forms of political violence. Terrorism is an illegitimate tactic that by its very nature is purposefully and ruthlessly employed.[120] At the heart of a terrorist's plan is seizing and maintaining the initiative. Policymakers who have no concept of a feasible outcome are unlikely to formulate clear steps to reach it, especially once they are compelled by the inexorable action/reaction, offense/defense dynamic that all too often drives terrorism and counterterrorism. Although history does not repeat itself, ignoring history is the surest way for a state to be manipulated by the tactic of terrorism.

At the highest levels, U.S. counterterrorism policy has been formulated organically and instinctively, in reaction to external stimuli or on the basis of unexamined assumptions, with a strong bias toward U.S. exceptionalism. Sound counterterrorism policy should be based on the full range of historical lessons learned about which policies have worked, and under which conditions, to hasten terrorism's decline and demise. Treating al-Qaida as if it were sui generis is a mistake. As I have argued here, while there are unique aspects to this threat, there are also connections with earlier threats. Speaking of an unprecedented "jihadist" threat, while arguably resonating in a U.S. domestic context, only perpetuates the image and perverse romanticism of the al-Qaida movement abroad, making its ideology more attractive to potential recruits. Such an approach also further undermines any inclination by the United States to review and understand the relationship between historical instances of terrorism and the contemporary plotting of a strategy for accelerating al-Qaida's demise. In short, formulating U.S. counterterrorism strategy as if no other state has ever faced an analogous threat is a serious blunder.

---

120. I have dealt at length with the question of the definition of terrorism elsewhere and will not rehash those arguments here. See, for example Cronin, "Behind the Curve," pp. 32–33.

Comparative speaking, the United States has not had a great deal of experience with terr sm on its territory. In this respect, its response to the shock of al-Qaida's attac is understandable. But the time for a learning curve is past. Intellectually, it lways much easier to over- or underreact to terrorist attacks than it is to tak e initiative and think through the scenarios for how a terrorist group, and ounterterrorist effort, will wind down. Short-term reactive thinking is mis ded for two reasons: the extraordinary and expensive effort to end terroris vill be self-perpetuating, and the inept identification of U.S. aims will ensur hat the application of means is unfocused and ill informed by past experie . Failing to think through al-Qaida's termination, and how U.S. policy eith dvances or precludes it, is an error not only for the Bush administration, cr ized by some for allegedly wanting an excuse to hype a permanent threat, t also for any administration of either political party that succeeds or rep es it.

Terrorism, li war, never ends; however, individual terrorist campaigns and the groups at wage them always do. A vague U.S. declaration of a war on terrorism h rought with it a vague concept of the closing stages of al-Qaida rather t a compelling road map for how it will be reduced to the level of a mino reat. The only outcome that is inevitable in the current U.S. policy is that m arily focused efforts will end, because of wasteful or counterproductive e rt and eventual exhaustion. The threat is real and undeniable, but conti ng an ahistorical approach to effecting al-Qaida's end is a recipe for failu the further alienation of allies, and the squandering of U.S. power.

International Security
The Robert and Renée Belfer Center for
Science and International Affairs
John F. Kennedy School of Government
Harvard University

All of the articles in this reader were previously published in **International Security,** a quarterly journal sponsored and edited by the Robert and Renée Belfer Center for Science and International Affairs at Harvard University's John F. Kennedy School of Government, and published by MIT Press Journals. To receive journal subscription information or to find out more about other readers in our series, please contact MIT Press Journals at 238 Main Street, suite 500, Cambridge, MA 02142, or on the web at http://www.mitpress.mit.edu.

Printed in the Unitec ates
by Baker & Taylor Pu sher Services